# ARISING FROM BONDAGE

For
Nannie (the first 'feminist' I ever met)
and
Nana (the loneliest man I ever met)
My nameless sisters – who did not survive
My parents and family
and
my son
Ronnie

# ARISING FROM BONDAGE

## A History of the
## Indo-Caribbean People

Ron Ramdin

NEW YORK UNIVERSITY PRESS
Washington Square, New York

First published in the U.S.A. in 2000 by
NEW YORK UNIVERSITY PRESS
Washington Square
New York, NY 10003

First United Kingdom publication in 2000 by
I.B.Tauris & Co Ltd

CIP data available from the Library of Congress
ISBN 0-8147-7548-9



Printed and bound in Great Britain from camera-ready copy supplied by the author
by CPD Ltd, Ebbw Vale

# CONTENTS

# PREFACE

This book is an attempt to fill a major gap in Caribbean historiography: the first comprehensive narrative which puts into historical perspective the struggles of the Indo-Caribbean people, a study based not only on official reports and papers, but also on unpublished material from disparate British, Indian and Caribbean sources.

Since they first arrived in British Guiana in May 1838 as cheap, disposable labour to replace the emancipated African slaves, the East Indians (as the Indian indentured immigrants were called) have contributed significantly in almost every sphere of life in the former British, French, Dutch and Spanish colonial territories. Yet, by the beginning of the 1970s, scholarship in the relatively neglected field of Indo-Caribbean history, tended to focus largley on the former British colonies, and even so there had been a paucity of material. Since then, however, interest in Indo-Caribbean history and culture has grown, as manifested in academic papers presented at a number of symposia on East Indians in the Caribbean, including those held abroad in 1988 at the University of Warwick in England and at the University of York in Canada, to mark the 150th anniversary of the arrival of the Indians in the region.

But in spite of the many theses, papers, monographs and articles (each emphasizing a specific aspect or aspects of the Indo-Caribbean experience) their limitations have highlighted the importance of a synthesis of the general and the particular, an alignment of the 'truffle' hunter's view with that of the 'parachutist'. Apart from limited introductory background, until the 1970s, very little serious attention has been given to the evolution of Indian emigration to the Caribbean in relation to the geographical areas and the complexities of the cultures and castes from which the Indians came, a theme which, due to the constraint of space, could not be further elaborated upon in this book, as the author had intended. Nevertheless, of special significance are the voices of the recruits themselves that are interwoven in this opening chapter and elsewhere. The second crucial chapter examines the debilitating effects of the indentureship system, the indentured labourers' responses (essentially their resistance) and the ensuing prolonged opposition and campaign which, headed by Mohandas K. Gandhi, among others, eventually led to abolition of the system in 1917.

Chapter three focuses upon the post-indenture period of challenge, including the Indians' concerns and responses to integration and consolidation. No longer under the charge of plantation employers, colonial administrators and the strict legal controls that had circumscribed their movements, the Indians faced the tough challenge of being a 'free' people in direct competition for scarce resources, with other better-favoured economic, religious, cultural and political groups in societies that had hitherto abused and treated them as aliens. As it was, hard experience had taught the Indians that effective religious and cultural organisations were vital in maintaining their sense of identity, *vis-à-vis* the impositions of the larger societies.

Finally, in the most recent phase of their history, the East Indians had set about establishing their identity. As the succeeding generations of East Indians became (and indeed are becoming) more 'Caribbean' people and less 'Indian', historically, they have gradually gained in strength and confidence becoming, less hide-bound to tradition and in some ways, better organised, so that today over one hundred and sixty years after their arrival (according to one authority, they are a force to be reckoned with: an estimated one million people of Indian descent live in the English-speaking Caribbean *alone*, forming a clear majority of the population in Guyana and is close to becoming, if not already, the majority of the population in Trinidad and Tobago) they constitute the backbone of the economies of Guyana, yet (especially in before the long-awaited voting system was re-established in Guyana) they were denied their share of political power. A consequence of discrimination against East Indians in some parts of the Caribbean, in education and employment has resulted in the emigration and exile of thousands to North America and Europe. But after the first 'free and fair' General Elections in Guyana for nearly three decades there was renewed hope among sections of the people that a new-style Jagan-led Government will indeed guide the country along the road to recovery, and win back, at least, some of the confidence of those thousands of Indo-Guyanese who had fled abroad.

ARISING FROM BONDAGE is an epic story of the extraordinary perseverance and courage of an enterprising people, whose contribution to Caribbean societies has been (and is) enormously important, even though it has been little understood and much undervalued. It is hoped that this book, with its invaluable bibliography will not only help students interested in the rich mosaic of cultures in the Caribbean, but will also attract general readers and bring us closer to a more informed view and better understanding of the people and problems of the Caribbean. Given that there is an estimated ten million persons of South Asian descent living outside South Asia (the bulk of whom are Indians – and their descendants – who constitute the Indian diaspora), it is hoped that this work will complement existing and potential studies of Indian populations in other parts of the world, thus retrieving it from relative obscurity. It needs to be said that for too long, the unrelenting struggle of the East Indians have been seen in certain circles, as a footnote to Caribbean studies, a view which it is hoped this timely book will help to correct. If it is true that, until recently, Indians in the Caribbean have been ignored and therefore 'written out' of history, then it would be appropriate to assert that the time has come to 'write them in'.

As I said in my 'Open Letter to a Close Relative' on the OCCASION OF THE 150th Anniversary of the arrival of the East Indians in Trinidad, which was not only published in Canada and reached a massive readership through *The Hindu* newspaper in India, but was also broadcast on Trinidad Radio on Arrival Day, 30 May

1995, and on the BBC (both on Radio 4 and the World Service) to a huge international audience in Britain, South Asia and the Caribbean:

> I share your anticipation of this year's celebratory events, but their significance cannot be taken for granted. I know you will seek, in your meticulous, critical way, a more profound understanding of your identity than you have been allowed at school and college, institutions cited by so many in recent years, as breeding grounds of dissatisfaction and low self-esteem. These have brought a sense of demoralization among Indo-Trinidadian youth and questioning which often leads back to the past.*

Indo-Caribbean history and culture must be retrieved from the margins and placed at the centre as an integral part of discourse on Caribbean historiography, a direction in which there has been continuing movement, notably the 1995 Conference on 'Challenge and Change: The Indian Diaspora in Its Historical and Contemporary Contexts' which was held during this Anniversary year at the University of the West Indies, Trinidad. In the ongoing process of research, this was yet another historic opportunity for scholars from all over the world to direct their attention to neglected and emergent issues. Against the background of rapid global changes, the events in Trinidad had attracted further attention to, and interest in, the Indian diaspora (a Centre for the Study of the Indian Diaspora was recently established in India) and Indo-Caribbean studies, in particular, which deserves it.

Researching and writing ARISING FROM BONDAGE has been a great challenge, an expensive and painstaking process of learning, a humbling and deeply rewarding experience that has taken me back, as it were, to my roots. Now after many years, and at the end of this work, I reflect upon countless journeys (both physical and intellectual) and contacts made, while others were renewed. I am especially indebted to Wendy Greenbury for a series of brilliant and time-consuming design work and to John Henderson for his timely computing expertise. My special thanks also to John Crabb for referring me to Dr Lester Crook, whose wide knowledge had brought immediate recognition of the merits of this book; and to Rey Bowen, Annette Bush, Selwyn Cudjoe, Dave French, Mick Maher, Timothy Thomas and Steve Tribe. Last, but not least, I am deeply thankful to my son Ronnie.

* *Indo Caribbean Review*, vol. 2, no. 1 (Toronto: 1995) pp. 67–72; *The Hindu*, (Sunday magazine), Bombay, India, 28 May 1995; *The Dalit Voice*, Bangalore, India: vol. 14, no. 15, 16–20 June 1995, pp. 20–22.

The natives [are] ignorant of the place they agree to go to, or the length of the voyage they are undertaking.

(Statement from Recruiting Firm Messrs. Gillanders, Arbuthnot and Company.)

I see seven sea
white black green brown
all kind a sea
roughest is Atlantic...
we di want to go back India
but which part e go go back
which ship ...

(Fazal, indentured labourer, *The Still Cry*)

A monstrous, rotten system, rooted upon slavery, grown in its stale soil, emulating its worst abuses and only the more dangerous because it presents itself under false colours.

(Chief Justice Beaumont, *The New Slavery*)

There is an ignorance of the Indian community not only from without, but also from within. Indians here (in Trinidad and the Caribbean) know little of the many things that have made them. ... I think we have to consider the culture from which we have come. ... We forget; we have no idea of our past; it is part of the trouble.

(V.S Naipaul, 'Introduction',
*East Indians in the Caribbean: Colonialism and the Struggle for Identity*)

# CHAPTER ONE

# FROM SLAVERY TO EAST INDIAN INDENTURESHIP

Slavery dates back to antiquity and has assumed different forms as an ongoing institution of coercive labour. Philosophers including Aristotle have made clear pronouncements justifying bondage, and Roman law helped to establish the legal foundations of the system, which has been invoked from time to time, to legitimize it in Europe and elsewhere. But although our knowledge of other slave systems historically is relatively limited, it is nevertheless clear that in terms of its scale and severity (and the stain of racism that has marked it), slavery in the West Indies and the southern States of America stands apart.[1] And while men have for about two thousand years thought of sin as a kind of slavery, with time and a growing though ambivalent acceptance of the fact that the slave was also a human being, Christian abolitionists in the eighteenth and nineteenth centuries began to think of slavery as a sin. But by then the precedents of this 'peculiar' institution had already been firmly established and would thereafter be zealously implemented and developed to serve the interests of those whose commercial ambitions sought wider horizons at the beginning of the modern age of capitalism.

The expansion of trade among European maritime nations, the imagined wealth of the East in general, and of India in par ticular, had long preoccupied enterprising Europeans until access by a sea route to the latter became a real prospect towards the end of the fifteenth century. Prior to 1415, with the Portuguese arrival and conquest of certain parts of the West African Coast, little was known of the East and by 1418, having reached as far as the Congo, Portuguese navigators speculated that by rounding the Cape of Good Hope, they could get to India. Earlier, those who had harboured hopes of an overland route were disappointed that such a passage to India was not only blocked by the Crusades, but also by heavy tolls imposed by the States of Venice and Genoa.[2] However, given the fact that the bounds of scientific and technological knowledge were also expanding, it was thought to be no longer unrealistic that the the East could be reached by travelling westward.

Of central importance during this period of economic expansion was the acquisition of material possessions, especially in the form of land and gold. Politically, as the nation states emerged, Europeans looked abroad to strengthen their Old World economies through exploitation of the resources of unknown lands. As one historian put it, 'economic considerations reinforced the political, the scientific and the religious urge to discover a new world'.[3] Discovering such a world was being slowly realised through contact with West Africa and its inhabitants. Indeed the great ambition of the Genoese-born explorer, Christopher Columbus was the conquest of new lands and wealth for the Spanish Crown and to achieve this end, he displayed a determination, daring, courage and rapacity that was to open up the Americas and change the course of European, Asian and African history.

The trade in African slaves across the Atlantic Ocean, it must be pointed out, was preceded by a trade in European domestic servants. This trade, however, in terms of numbers and the horrors of the traffic, was unlike the African slave trade, which first became a direct trade from Africa to the West Indies in 1518. Much earlier, before the introduction of white indentured servants and African slaves, the indigenous Carib and Arawak Indians whom Columbus had found in the West Indies were subjected, not only to forced labour in the mines and plantations, but also to conversion to Christianity in line with the explorers' objectives. The Indians proved to be unsuitable for this slave labour system (they were the first to revolt and mount strong resistance against oppression in the Caribbean) and were defended by Bartholome de Las Casas, the Spanish priest, who ironically not only defended Spanish colonialism, but had also, at least initially, accepted the argument that African labour was far superior for this kind of work.[4]

The introduction of the sugar cane plant to the West Indies by Columbus on his second voyage across the Atlantic would, in time, lead to an unprecedented demand for cheap labour to facilitate sugar production. As the African slave population in the West Indies gradually increased, it was clear that unlike the treatment received by white servants and domestic slaves, the African captives were subjected to a 'new brand of cruelty', while being abducted in Africa, during their voyage on the slave ships and notably as slaves on the plantations. Furthermore, unlike other forms of labour control, Africans were condemned to their servile status for life. Their loss of freedom and the insatiable demands of slavery, not surprisingly, brought resistance and revolt with notable rebellions before the middle of the sixteenth century in Hispaniola (1522), Santa Martha (1529), Panama (1531) and Puerto Rico (1537). In spite of the enlistment of special forces to contain African slaves, the uprisings moved forward relentlessly.[5] But of course, the oppressed had ultimately to confront their oppressors, including none other than the reigning Spanish monarchs who mapped out the slaves' destinies by issuing Asientos that would, in time, lead to an increase the slave population in the New World and upon which the imperial economy would become crucially dependant.

The growing prosperity of the Spanish economy was enviously looked upon by other European nations, notably the British, Dutch and French; an imperialist rivalry already evident before Columbus undertook his historic voyage, but now clearly underpinned by power politics, as these powers vied for commercial hegemony. Although the Spanish monopoly of the African Slave Trade was reasonably secure (by 1540 several thousand Africans were shipped directly from Africa across the Atlantic), French, Dutch and English encroachments were becoming more frequent and alarming. Though the English traders' interest in the Guinea Coast was still based largely on gold, pepper and ivory, it was John Hawkins's slaving adventures about this time that come to notice, and with his eye on the West Indies, he decided to break the pattern of British trade and compete with the Spaniards for slave cargoes. Of the three profits made from this evolving three-sided trade, the largest did not come from the sale of slaves to planters, but from demand in Europe for slave-grown products, such as sugar (the result of Columbus's foresight in transporting the sugar cane plant to the West Indies) which accrued great wealth to many investors.

European enterprise and slavery during the seventeenth and eighteenth centuries, and also the greater part of the nineteenth century, were closely connected, helping not only the spectacular rise of British, French and Spanish ports such as Bristol, Liverpool, Nantes, Bordeaux and Seville,[6] but also the manufacturing centres at the heart of the British Industrial Revolution.[7]

The aggression with which Europeans competed for Africans as property, at first, baffled the Africans as the slave trade gradually evolved into a vibrant commercial connection between Europe, Africa and the Americas. Over a period of time, the dehumanising aspects of the trade, the increase of the mortality rate, the superior arms of Europeans and complicity of African chiefs, merchants and middlemen, would alter the early European-African trading relationship, characterised by an approximation of equality and self-respect.

By the turn of the eighteenth century, the Dutch were superseded by the British who having acquired the Asiento in 1713, now controlled the trade to the Spanish colonies, though this had become an insignificant part of the entire trade. The British, however, were joined by the French and Dutch who also supplied their colonies with slaves. But 1713 marked a clear departure in the trade in that the value of slaves had increased, and according to one account, an estimated 15,000 mainly in the following years, were transported on British ships, treble the amount stipulated in their contract with Spain.[8]

If during the eighteenth century there was unanimity among the leading Western European maritime nations that the African Slave Trade was an integral part of the international economic system (Malachi Prostlethwayt viewed British trade as 'a magnificent superstructure of … commerce and naval power on an African foundation'), by the end of the century, many Evangelical Christians sought to end the trade. 'Never, never will we desist', William Wilberforce (the foremost Parliamentary spokesman to abolish the trade) said in Parliament, 'till we have wiped away this scandal from the Christian name', and freed England from the burden of guilt of this bloody traffic which had existed for so long, a disgrace and dishonour to the country.[9]

Doubts as to the rightness of enslaving the African and of the slave trade, was evident as early as the seventeenth century. American Quakers were among the first to launch organised protest, through the Society of Friends. Anthony Benezet, a member of this Society, born in France of Huguenot parents, had lived in England before his parents emigrated to Pennsylvania. His books[10] on Africa had a profound effect on many readers in England, such as John Wesley (who used material from them for his sermons) and the indefatigable Thomas Clarkson. Benezet's devoted work in the cause of African freedom was continued through Clarkson who in collaboration (as a collector of evidence) with Wilberforce (the eloquent politician) and other English reformers engaged in winning support for their argument, felt that the African Slave Trade and slavery were morally wrong. They founded the Society for the Abolition of the Slave Trade and began their Parliamentary campaign, but although Wilberforce as spokesman for th Society made stirring speeches in Parliament, it was not enough to overturn the powerful vested slave owners' interests strongly represented in the seats of Government.

The Slave Trade had undoubtedly created many guilty consciences among Europeans, but to allay some of their guilt, it was argued that Europeans had tried to shift the weight of responsibility for this trade on to the Africans. But, of course, the evidence confirms that it was European capitalism which had set slavery and the African Slave Trade in motion.[11]

By the turn of the nineteenth century, changes in the British political climate had brought in a new ministry and new hope among abolitionists. And when the Emancipation Act was eventually passed by Parliament, it was still a long way from relieving the cruelties and distress of Africa and Africans, as Britain launched a new campaign to stem the Slave Trade engaged in by other countries.

So in spite of the new law of 1807, the contraband trade had persisted. The invention of the cotton-gin in 1793, encouraged cotton growing in the southern States of America and enormously increased the carrying capacity of the Slave Trade by the time of the British Abolition Act. Between 1804 and 1807, two hundred and two slavers had landed in Charleston with 39,075 slaves, and in 1807, while the traffic was still legal, 95 slave ships crowded the harbour. Although the American Government made the trade illegal in 1808, after 1812, there was an increase in this trade to Georgia and Louisiana.[12]

The end of the illegal slave trade brought further forward the case for abolition of slavery. By the mid-nineteenth century, both the British and French had abolished slavery in their colonial possessions (essentially because it had become an uneconomic system) and with the passage of time, the difficulties of abolishing the trade in the United States was still a live issue.

Despite the slave owners' attempts to justify enlarging the Slave Trade and slavery, there was continued opposition, not least from the slaves themselves. The deep division over the slave question and President Lincoln's desire to save the union of the United States, led to Civil War. The President was clear about his position:

> My paramount object in this struggle is to save the Union. ... If I could save the Union without freeing any slave, I would do it, and if I could save it by freeing all the slaves, I would do it, and if I could save it by freeing some and leaving others alone, I would also do that ... I have stated my purpose according to my views of official duty and I intend no modification of my off-expressed personal wish that all men everywhere could be free.[13]

Subsequently by 1867 no more slavers were captured along the African coast by the British Squadron, which was withdrawn. The Courts which had tried those involved were no longer necessary and although a few shiploads of slaves had been delivered to Cuba and Brazil in the 1880s, in effect, the Atlantic Slave Trade had ended.

# THE EVOLVING LABOUR PROBLEM

After the African Slave Trade was abolished in 1807, Britain, though still involved,[14] nevertheless faced the problem of how best to acquire a continuous supply of 'free' but low-cost and easily controlled labour for the West Indian plantations. To this end, British policy-makers turned their minds. For their part, West Indian planters who had reaped such fabulous profits from slave-grown sugar, especially in the eighteenth century, had already begun to complain long before the Slave Trade was abolished, claiming that in the first two decades of the nineteenth century there were few sugar estates that had remained with the same owner.[15]

Slavery in the West Indies and in the Americas during this period was, of course, directly dependent upon the Slave Trade and with the diminished supply of slaves in the British West Indian territories, the planters predictably, projected their distress, using the strongest possible means. Time and again, they appealed to the British Government in which they still had many influential friends and allies. But even in this forum of last resort, there had been a change in attitude towards the slaves on the British plantations.

Instead of proceeding towards abolition of slavery, however, the British Parliament began to reassess the degrading nature of the slave system and ameliorative arguments and measures were put forward to make slavery more acceptable to the abolitionists, both within and outside Parliament. The slaves, of course, had no say: they were expected to wait for a dispensation from above as their masters' interests remained paramount. But when unilateral action was indeed taken by Britain, it was not enough to end the contraband slave trade – there were at least four other systems of slavery to contend with in the West Indies: the Spanish, French, Dutch and Danish.[16]

In 1823 the reformers still led by Wilberforce in Parliament founded the Anti-Slavery Society for the 'mitigation and gradual abolition of slavery' which presented its first anti-slavery motion in Parliament in March that year. Wilberforce had passed on the mantle of leadership to Thomas Fowell Buxton, the son of an Essex landowner. Like Wilberforce, Buxton was an Evangelical and humanitarian who moved the famous motion condemning the state of slavery as repugnant to the principles of the British Constitution[17] and of the Christian religion, an institution that ought to be gradually abolished with due consideration given to the well-being of the parties concerned.

Although Buxton was surprised that he was so unpopular,[18] the effects of an Order in Council for the mitigation of slavery introduced in Trinidad and Tobago was considered to be satisfactory, and James Stephen's purposeful speech to free the slaves was reflected in a new drive when Brougham proposed immediate Emancipation, at a time when France was on the eve of the 'July Revolution' which was a stimulus for Parliamentary reform in Britain.[19]

The passage of the first Reform Bill in June 1832, both relieved and delighted Buxton whose concern now was to work towards a Government bill for Emancipation in the new Parliament, which was still undecided on the issue. Meanwhile, behind the scene of Government, an important appointment at the Colonial Office was James Stephen, son and namesake of Wilberforce's brother-in-law. His knowledge and experience made him one of the most influential Government officials, playing the key role at the Colonial Office to the extent that he was later called 'King Stephen' and 'Mr. Over-Secretary Stephen' among other sobriquets.[20] He wasted no time while working on the Bill and eventually, the British Parliament not only gave the planters £20 million compensation, but also provided for an intervening period of Apprenticeship which began in 1833, another form of labour control to assist the planters in the transition from slavery to the employment of free labour, a regime which did not apply to Antigua and Bermuda. The planters grudgingly accepted the Apprenticeship system (a temporary phase of semi-slavery which was strongly resisted by ex-slaves) having had for so long, captive labour at their command. Generally, these employers were unwilling to establish a new relationship with free labour on the estates. And in 1835 Buxton had moved in Parliament that a Select Committee be appointed to inquire into the planters' compliance with the conditions under which the £20 million was granted; and on the return of the Anti-Slavery Society investigators Lloyd, Scoble, Sturge and Harvey from the West Indies in May 1837, a pamphlet concerning the apprentices was published to good effect. With the introduction and passage of the Bill abolishing Apprenticeship, West Indian Governors directly responsible to the Colonial

Office were empowered to take charge of the administration of prisons, thus giving James Stephen enormous latitude to implement his Utilitarian ideas. But by the time that Apprenticeship had ended in 1838, plans were already being considered for instituting East Indian indentureship, a new form of labour control and, as some feared, a new form of slavery, as a substitute.

As early as 1810, a British Parliamentary committee was appointed to consider the practicality and expediency of supplying West Indian colonies with free labour from the East, a consideration that was part of the Government's wider design of emigration within the British Empire, shunting labour here, there and, it seemed, everywhere.

In the nineteenth century the Colonial Land and Emigration Commission was established to supervise emigration within the British Empire. During the period of British Colonial policy known as 'Centralisation' (1783–1837), if the attitude of Britain towards her colonies was one of apathy, there was also the preoccupation between 1783–1815 with a war, through which as one writer noted 'almost unconsciously a new Empire was acquired'. In these years, the House of Commons was little concerned with colonial affairs, and legislation, left largely as the responsibility of the Colonial Secretary which was thereafter delegated to James Stephen, who was described as being 'very distrustful of democratic institutions'.[21]

In Britain, a combination of factors would force a change in the relationship between Britain and her overseas possessions. For one thing, the industrial progress made in England after 1815 had brought about serious social problems, as the fear of overpopulation and the failure of crops deepened the concern of many who viewed the colonies as offering at least the potential of some relief. The motive for attempting this new approach to emigration, however, was primarily economic. Taken together, it was the spectres of overpopulation, unemployment, poverty and famine (the social and economic fall-out from the Industrial Revolution and land enclosures) that were the push factors. The pull factors, on the other hand, were essentially an abundance of land and the opportunity of a new start in life.

As it was, Stephen had all the up-to-date information on Colonization at his command and definite ideas for improving the emigration system and the settlement of Crown Lands in the colonies. Although there were already in existence two organisations, Stephen had planned the establishment of one body. Thereafter, the CLEC came into existence in January 1840 with Messrs Elliot, Torrens and Villiers as Commissioners. For E.G. Wakefield and the Reformers of 1830, this practical step by the Government was seen as a triumph.

The Colonial Land and Emigration Commissioners, during the period 1840 to 1872 supervised all the general emigration from Britain. And while the Commission existed (from 1840 to 1878) hundreds of thousands of Britons had emigrated: the outflow was predictably greater at some periods than others, an emigration that was conducted mainly to South Australia, New South Wales, Victoria, Queensland, Van Dieman's Land (Tasmania), Western Australia, New Zealand, Cape of Good Hope, Natal, the Falkland Islands and Vancouver. From 1840 to 1872, the total British emigration to the North American colonies was 956,748; United States 4,487,497; Australia and New Zealand 958,077 and All other places 175,736.[22]

The need for white labour in the form of white settlers to open these lands was imperative. There had been a continuous shift in focus from the older British West Indian colonies to the vast, untapped natural resources of the new colonies, though significantly, there was no question of non-White emigration to these lands. Before its abolition, however, the Colonial Land and Emigration Commission was involved in a new phase of mass emigration, supervising (at least during the crucial years when the indentureship system was firmly established) the movement, apart from those who went to Mauritius, African, Chinese and East Indian emigrants further afield to the West Indies.

The failure of African sources of free labour (liberated Africans rescued from illegal slavers by the British navy and emigration of free Africans from Sierra Leone) forced the West Indian planters to look elsewhere for their labour supply. When East Indian emigration to Mauritius was re-opened in 1843, the West India Committee sought permission to introduce Chinese 'coolies' on contract from the Straits Settlements and predictably argued that there was a great need for labour in the West Indian colonies.[23] The first shipment of these labourers was made in 1845 from Amoy to Bourbon,[24] but after a temporary setback, it was restarted in 1846–49. The turning point in Chinese labour emigration, however, came in 1859 when a regulated system of Chinese emigration under contract to the Caribbean was set up and lasted until 1861 with the establishment of sub-Agencies at Swatow and Amoy.

Emigration from Canton in the 1859–60 season was encouraging. Six ships carried 1,973 Chinese labourers, 80 per cent of whom were males. The health of these labourers was good and another 10 ships, chartered for the next season, left with 3,496 Chinese. But the high mortality incurred and the general ill feelings towards the Chinese mandarins did not instill confidence in the trade, which had started to decline almost immediately, even though there were grounds for optimism, as during 1861–62, when eight ships sailed to the Caribbean, one to Trinidad and the other seven to British Guiana with a total number of 3,057 Chinese labourers.

The high cost of improving this traffic brought the two main importing colonies, British Guiana and Trinidad and Tobago, together. They agreed to import 2,000 Chinese labourers a year for the three succeeding seasons (1,250 to British Guiana and 750 to Trinidad and Tobago); and after British Guiana had received 1,766, Trinidad and Tobago 612 and Honduras 480 in 1864–65, the number dwindled to 796 and 611 for British Guiana and Trinidad and Tobago, before this emigration came to an abrupt end.

By the close of 1872, the West Indian Colonies had received 16,222 persons from China. But this Chinese labour experiment, in spite of being to some degree successful as a temporary economic measure, failed to bring about permanent social value because it claimed to be neither initiated nor pursued in the interests of Colonization.[25]

The long journey across the Pacific Ocean to California and Peru, and over the Indian and Atlantic Oceans to the West Indies (the 'middle passage' of the Chinese coolies) was fraught with difficulties and danger. To begin with, fraudulent methods were used to recruit the labourers, and on the voyages a shortage of food and water combined with ill-treatment inflicted by some ships' captains and crew members, tended to result in riot and death. In addition to this, during the early 1850s, the average mortality on these Chinese emigrant ships was described as high, and in spite of the Earl of Malmesbury's request to improve conditions on ships,[26] the voyages of the Chinese labourers continued in much the same manner, the scene of many reported horrors and forgotten sufferings.[27]

On arrival in the West Indies, Chinese labourers quickly realised the harshness of the terms of their labour contracts, and it has been argued that if the East Indian indentured labour system in British Guiana's 'free' society was open to grave criticism, in Cuba, where slavery was not yet abolished, it was subject to intolerable abuses.[28]

# EAST INDIAN* EMIGRATION

Prior to large-scale emigration from India, labour had taken various forms including slavery which, as an institution in India, dates back to the distant past. Although the Greek traveller Megasthenes stated in the Fourth century B.C that he saw no evidence of slavery in India, Kautilya's famous work, the ARTHASASTRA and Asoka's accounts refer to the slaves in ancient India. It seemed that people were drawn into slavery because of indebtedness or because they were captives of war, and although it has been suggested that slavery in ancient India does not appear to have assumed the magnitude and cruelty that characterised it in Europe, surely it would be difficult to judge this because of the paucity of information available on Indian slavery of that period. Nevertheless slavery had existed since time immemorial under Hindu rule and during the Moghul period, it had become a more cruel system, which remained in existence long after British rule was established. It is clear, however, that Indian slavery differed from West Indian slavery in that the West Indies was supplied with slaves from Africa, whereas in spite, of slaves being imported into India from the East African Coast,[29] Madagascar, the Persian Gulf, Aden, Java and other British territories, the vast majority of the Indian slaves were from the indigenous population.

Writing on the 'Abolition of slavery in India and Egypt', H.B.E. Frere claimed that comparing information 'district by district with the very important estimates of the total population fifty years ago, the lowest estimate I have been able to form of the total slave population of British India, in 1841, is between 8 and 9 million. The slaves set free in the British colonies on 1st August 1834, were estimated at between 800,000 and one million, and the slaves in North and South America, in 1860, were estimated at 4 million ... So that the number of human beings whose liberties and fortunes, as slaves and owners of slaves, were at stake when the Emancipation of the slaves was contemplated in British India, far exceeded the number of the same classes in all the slave-holding colonies and dominions of Great Britain and America put together.' Furthermore, it should be remembered that in 1840 British India did not extend from the Karokoram Range to Cape Comorin, and from Persia (Iran) and Afghanistan to China and Siam. At this time, Sind, the Punjab, Travancore, Nepal and Burma were not part of the British administration. As it was, the East India Company's territories consisted essentially of the Presidencies of Bengal, Bombay and Madras, within which 8 million slaves were contained. Slavery was so extensive in India that in both the non-British territories and the British Protected States, there was an estimated 16 million (or more) slaves.[30] This was the tragic and deplorable state of affairs that persisted in British India, long after freedom came to African slaves in the West Indies.

In fact, it was only as as recent as 1843, ten years after legislation in the form of the Emancipation Bill had passed through Parliament to end slavery in the British Caribbean colonies, that an Act was passed for the abolition of slavery in India. The British authorities were therefore fully conversant with the historical background and contemporary conditions that had created an enormous pool of cheap labour in India.

In 1834, many planters in the West Indies were predictably concerned that with the end of the period of Apprenticeship four years later, and the final abolition of slavery, the plantation labour supply would be seriously depleted. Their immediate task was to find a new source of disposable labour. It was important, however, that this labour should be separated from the former slave population, which were no longer bound to, but free to leave, the plantations. For a while, at least, the planters' fears were justified, as the end of Apprenticeship brought a marked shortage of labour in Trinidad and Tobago and British Guiana (the newer colonies) and in Jamaica (an older colony). There was also the scarcity of labour in a few of the smaller colonies. The paramountcy of maintaining sugar production (at least to at its acceptable pre-Emancipation level) dictated that those African labourers who had left the plantations should be replaced, temporarily, while the search continued to find the desired labour force. To compound their difficulties, the idea that free African labour would now demand high wages (given the high premiums placed on labour scarcity) was to be avoided, at all costs, by the planters. Thus, it was maintained that the importation of workers to fill the labour vacuum on the plantations would provide a solution to the labour shortage in the Caribbean. Against this background of producing sugar without slaves, the planters and Colonial governments, acting together devised various labour schemes to rescue the sugar industry from impending ruin and they lobbied for direct Imperial assistance to meet the cost of immigration.

The growing pressure to prohibit importation of Chinese indentured labour, brought renewed cries for Indian labour. Why was it necessary to establish such a system in the West Indies? Conditions on the islands were such that friends of the West Indian planters in Liverpool expressed their views to Lord John Russell in a statement admitting the productive powers of the British colonies in the West Indies could not, under existing circumstances, be maintained by the existing labouring population. Consequently, they demanded that attention should be directed to an alternative and viable source of labour. 'We have said nothing of millions of miser-able human beings in Hindoostan', they concluded, 'who have irresistable claims upon the composition of the people of this country and who would receive as wages, for one day's labour in British Guiana, fully more than they receive as wages for a whole year in India. In behalf of these perishing outcasts, who are a quiet, sober and industrious, as well as an obedient race, we earnestly implore the kind interposition of the British Parliament'.[31]

The planter's statement reiterating the labour problem and offering a solution to it brought into focus the subject of East Indian emigration to the West Indies. Later when this immigration was firmly established, the planters'demand and the availability of a supply of cheap labour in India was irrefutable, providing a strong case for immigration.

It is perhaps logical at this point, to ask: how did the millions of 'miserable human beings' in India came to be the 'perishing outcasts' whom the West Indian planters confidently looked to as their best hope of labour exploitation?

In part, at least, these Indians, it was claimed, had reached their state as a result of British economic policies in India, such as the land revenue policies of the late eighteenth and early nineteenth centuries, which resulted in the unemployment of millions of Indians. The introduction of the land revenue system (known as the Zemindari System) in Bengal (1793), Madras (1820) and in Northern India in 1822 brought dramatic changes to the old village community system, depriving thousands of peasants of a livelihood and forcing them to seek employment away from their villages. Hitherto the British intervention, the social and economic organisation of these self-sufficient villages were based on long-standing traditions,[32] governing such economic relations as labour in the villages according to the caste and skills of individual labourers. The dismantling of this archaic system, was perceived to be advantageous to the British, who had hoped to bring Indians into the ambit of the modern international trading system.

Revenue collection under the Zemindari system, essentially involved the big farmers and revenue collectors, who were granted the ownership of land in their areas. Through this complicity of Indians with their British rulers, the new system was established, bringing unprecedented financial reward. The last great Muslim landlord and ruler of Bengal, for example, collected land revenue amounting to £818,000 in 1764–65 and within thirty years British income had risen to £3,235,259.[33]

In the areas of Bombay and Madras, and later in the North East and North West, a different kind of land revenue system was applied. Under, the systems called Royatwari and Mahalwari, peasants, though entitled to the land, were ultimately bound to make payments to the Government. So the new land revenue systems not only changed the village communities, but also destroyed communal land ownership. In effect, the Zemindari system made the landlord master of the village, while the Royatwari system cut through the heart of village communities by introducing separate arrangements between cultivators and the Government.[34]

Commercial agriculture led to a shift in emphasis from crop cultivation for family consumption to production of jute, peanuts, sugar cane and tobacco for market sale and, as a consequence, small farmers unable to pay their debts became landless labourers. This disadvantage to the Indian economy, however, had a beneficial effect in England, where the raw materials produced in India made a significant contribution to the Industrial Revolution.

The Indian economy also suffered from an unfair tariff system, which helped Britain to maintain a growing advantage.[35] As a consequence, manufacturing industry in India was drastically reduced, bringing unemployment to millions of Indian artisans. Commenting on the Indian cotton weavers in 1834 (at the time when African slavery was abolished) Lord William Bentinck, Governor-General of India, wrote that the 'misery hardly finds a parallel in the history of commerce. The bones of cotton weavers are bleaching on the plains of India'.[36]

As further economic in-roads were made in India and free trade enjoyed its heyday, British imperial policy remained unchanged; if anything, the imbalance of trade between the two countries became more marked. It was, in effect, one way 'free' trade, which created an even greater reservoir of labour, amounting to millions of miserable human beings.

In Trinidad, as early as 1814, William Burnley, a prominent planter felt that the large-scale introduction of free labour from India would improve the prospects of the Colony. He argued for a change in the composition of the population, welcoming an infusion of a 'new race' of men healthy and free, 'with habits and science ready formed' to stand as a separate group from the existing population on arrival. This was the essential requirement.[37] To Burnley, East Indian labour was the answer. That same year, his proposition received the support of Trinidad's chief administrator, Governor Woodford, who urged the Colonial Office to introduce Indian workers to demonstrate the advantages and/or disadvantages of the debate in England on the question of free-labour versus slave-labour. About this time, Jamaican planters had also become interested in Indian labourers,[38] and thereafter, the arguments in favour of importing free labour from India continued for several years.

With African labour no longer available, the Mauritius planters had, by the early 1830s, already turned their attention to India. Among planters there was a strong determination to attract trusting Indians, whom they had expected to labour diligently for little gain, and somehow through this business-like approach to Indian immigration, they were able to win the support of Indian Government officials. To this end, the visit of a Bengal official to Mauritius was revealing. Conditions were deplorable, and on 29 July 1839 he wrote that it was not unduly reproachful to the slave owner to say that he had despotic habits, which he has to change entirely when he comes in control of free men.[39] If there was hope that the planters' attitude, rooted in slavery, would indeed change with time, writing eighteen months later, the same Bengal official was even less hopeful. The policy of the planters, he argued, had consistently been to weed out any tendency to allow more freedom of action to the Indian.[40]

By then it was clear that there was a real possibility of instituting a new system of slavery that would incorporate many repressive features of the former slave system. With this inheritance of slavery, and ignorant of what awaited them (a lack of information that was fully exploited by those who bound them to questionable indentured contracts), the Indian emigrants undertook an extremely hazardous journey to the plantations, which would mould their destiny, a bondage based on the fact that slavery had produced not only a system but also 'an attitude of mind, in which the products determined everything, not the people'.[41] Thus the 'foreign aid' of Indian immigration loomed large in an attempt to rescue the sugar industry in many of the British, French and Dutch territories in the Caribbean.[42]

Unlike the African slave trade which was an international trade, the East Indian indentured labour traffic was essentially a British monopoly. Although the planters had tried immigrant labour from various parts of Europe, including Ireland, Scotland and the Portuguese Atlantic islands, such as Madeira (and from the populous smaller West Indian islands) these schemes of imported labour failed to produce the desired results.

In British Guiana, the planters seemed to be particularly uncertain that they would be able to attract enough free labourers to work on their plantations. John Gladstone, father of the English statesman, who owned Vreeden Hoop and Vreedestein estates wrote to a firm in Calcutta, Messrs. Gillanders, Arbuthnot and Company on 4 January 1836 enquiring about the possibility of obtaining Indian immigrants for his estates in British Guiana. The reply was encouraging. The firm informed Gladstone that they did not forsee any insurmountable difficulties in supplying immigrants to British Guiana and that the Indians would be unaware of their destinations or the 'length of the voyage they are undertaking'.[43]

After receiving the support of Sir Cam Hobhouse, President of the Board of Control of the East India Company in March 1837, Gladstone won Glenelg's support in getting an Order in Council passed on 12 July 1837, which provided for five-year contracts for indentured emigrants.[44]

Much was expected of the Indians who first arrived in British Guiana on 5 May 1838, ironically following in the wake of Columbus, three hundred and forty-six years after he had set sail from the small port of Palos in Spain in the hope of meeting people from India when he made his initial landfall in the New World. This was the background of expectation at the beginning of East Indian immigration to the Caribbean which, having become well-known to speculators, both in the Caribbean and in Britain, aroused abolitionists to examine the labourers' condition and, in a relatively short time, assert that the system of immigration was indeed a new slave trade.

Soon, the euphoric optimism of the planters that immigration would work suffered an unforeseen (though not entirely unpredictable) setback. While the 'Gladstone experiment' was believed to be unsuccessful by Lord John Russell, the vigilant Anti-Slavery Society focused attention on the high sickness and mortality rates[45] of Indian emigration with special reference to Mauritius since 1834. Apart from contending with the moral elevation of the former slaves, now the Society had also to deal with abuses endemic in the importation of Indians and the system of indenture. After due consideration, as a result of Anti-Slavery Society pressure, the Colonial Office decided to stop further Indian immigration to the Caribbean because it was unconvinced that good treatment could be guaranteed during the long voyage.

By the time that Indian emigration was again declared open in 1844[46] (from this time on and throughout the period of indentureship, the inclusion of Indian women among the recruits was seen as significant, because the ongoing paucity of women was likely to lead to grave social problems), many of the first Indians who had arrived in British Guiana in 1838 were preparing to return to India with 'substantial savings', a feature of the indentureship experience which would be repeatedly used by planters and Government officials to support the continuation of Indian emigration. Predictably, the cessation of this Indian outflow to the West Indian colonies resulted in even more persistent demands for labourers, which reached sympathetic ears.[47] Responding in 1844, Lord Stanley, Secretary of State for the Colonies, despite misgivings, allowed a resumption of the traffic in Indian labour.

During this phase of Indian emigration administered by the Government, the emigrants were promised return passages to India after five years;[48] and so in accord with the planters' representations in 1845, two shiploads of Indians arrived in British Guiana,[49] two others went to Trinidad and Tobago and Jamaica[50] respectively, with the promise of large numbers to follow.

In 1846, it seemed that at least in principle, the immigration policy was working fairly well. But this was a problematic year as the economic crisis in the Caribbean, precipitated by abolition of the Imperial preferential sugar duties of 1846, threatened the continuation of what was considered to be both regular and dependable Indian immigration, because of its high costs.[51] Furthermore, there was a marked increase in the number of Indian labourers who deserted the estates.[52] But in spite of the planters' agitation (and the Whig Government's abandonment of the moral arguments against slave-grown sugar) the Sugar Duties Act was implemented in 1846, and the planters were successful in persuading the Colonial Office and British officials that most West Indian problems could be solved by less costly, but more immigration.[53]

That commercial trinity, sugar, prices and profit had again become topical. While the 1847 sugar crop in the West Indies was an improvement on that of 1846, there was a sharp fall in price because of competing slave-grown sugar from Cuba and Brazil.[54] The ensuing financial difficulties in the West Indies made it more problematic to meet the cost of immigration and, as a consequence, Trinidad and Tobago was unable to raise its immigration loan and Jamaica was forced by finanacial constraints to abandon the scheme.[55]

By 1848, colonial financial resources were still inadequate to fund large-scale immigration.[56] In London, the West Indian Interest, ever conscious of maintaining profits, was quick to respond, pressing for a necessary infusion of imperial support in order to reduce production costs.[57] But the planters best efforts were not enough in 1848 to sustain the flow as a second 'experiment' in Indian immigration was halted because of financial difficulties.

The framers of emigration legislation and the interested parties persisted in pressing their claims for a resumption. It was in fact not until 1851, through the finances of the Guaranteed Loan, that mass Indian immigration was fully resumed, particularly to British Guiana and Trinidad and Tobago. Jamaica did not engage in the scheme, foregoing her part of the loan until 1852.[58] By 1851 there was cause for some optimism among the ruling planter class, as West Indian decline had been generally stemmed and increasingly, it became clear that Indian immigration meant more to British Guiana and Trinidad and Tobago than to Jamaica, basically because British Guiana and Trinidad and Tobago were relatively under-populated new sugar producing colonies, better equipped with more modern techniques. The introduction of plough and harrow in Jamaica in the 1840s proved to be labour-saving devices, but although Indian immigration was not a pressing concern, Jamaican planters felt more labour was required.[59]

Given its relative success, more Caribbean planters were encouraged by the promise of immigration. In the 1850s, the Windward Islands were allowed to recruit small numbers of Indian labourers on the usual terms. Grenada was permitted to do so in 1856, St. Lucia in 1858 and St. Vincent in 1861. Requests from other colonies, though infrequent, lasted until the 1880s.[60] The total number of indentured

Indians imported into the various British West Indian territories down to termination of the system in 1917 were as follows: British Guiana – 238,909; Trinidad and
Tobago – 143,939; Jamaica – 36,412; Grenada – 3,200; St.Vincent – 2,472; St.Lucia
4,354.[61] Thus, Indian immigration, intially adopted as an experiment, a temporary
measure to stem the decline of the sugar industry, became a regular source of cheap
labour.

The *laissez faire* approach was now a thing of the past, it was claimed. In fact, the
dangers endemic in private recruitment, for example, the safety and welfare of the
immigrants, were allegedly eliminated because the system was placed on a new
footing being wholly operated by the Government. And although financial considerations in the colonies now posed no serious problems, nevertheless, the planters
persisted in keeping a tight hold over the migrants. But in their zeal for continued,
total control, abuses and malpractices which engendered deep resentment among
the aggrieved indentured labourers, remained contentious issues throughout the
period of indentured immigration. If the British experience was instructive, French
and Dutch observers as potential exploiters were neither lacking in interest nor
commitment.

In 1848 the impending Emancipation of slaves in the French West Indian is-
lands also engendered the need for Indian, Chinese and African immigrant labour.
When production on the estates fell that year, the planters, aware of emigration to
British colonies and the French colony of Reunion, demanded as alternatives to
European labour which had failed to respond, the importation of Indians, Chinese
and Africans.[62] What followed was the passage of an immigration law in 1852, which
made provision for the welfare and recruitment of labour from Europe, Africa and
Asia; and plans were set in motion by the Compagnie Generale Transatlantique to
supply between 2,000 – 3,000 Indians annually. Two years later, the whole operation was controlled by an Immigration Committee, an example adopted by
Martinique in 1861 as more elaborate and efficient immigration laws followed in
1855 and 1859.

Various considerations were put forward to meet the demand. And after persuading the French to abstain from recruiting African labour in 1861, the British allowed the French, through a Convention of that year, to recruit labour in British
India on the same basis as the British colonies, with the proviso that return passages should be offered at the end of five, instead of ten years. Consequently, the
recruitment of labour by the French in Africa was finally abandoned.

As in the earlier British case, Indian immigration provided the solution for the
French labour problem. In spite of the limited supply from the French Indian
territories of Pondicherry and Chandernagore, more than 9,500 Indians were introduced to Martinique, about 1,000 to Guadeloupe and 1,750 to French Guiana
between 1853 and 1871. India proved a fertile recruiting ground: between 1853 and
the end of the Anglo-French agreement in 1885, approximately 25,509 Indians had

arrived in Martinique and 45,000 in Guadeloupe, coming mainly through the ports of Calcutta and Pondicherry, while an estimated 9,200 went to French Guiana.[63]

Ever mindful of its imperial responsibility, under the terms of the 1861 Convention, the British authorities monitored the conditions of the Indian emigrants who, still protected by the British, laboured in the French West Indies, even though each French colony had its own immigration administrators for this purpose. The British Government had the right to scrutinize the Indians' condition and were alarmed in the 1870s by the serious abuses of the system in the French colonies, especially the failure to provide adequate facilities to effect return passages due to time-expired emigrants. Over the years, the British Government became increasingly concerned about the Indians' welfare, stopping emigration to French Guiana in 1876 and eventually terminating the Anglo-French agreement in 1885.

In the Dutch Colony of Surinam, Indian immigration also proved attractive in the 1850s, a time of labour scarcity. When slavery was abolished in 1863, a period of transition covering ten years (similar to the British Apprenticeship system which lasted for four years) was introduced. This did not, however, prevent many ex-slaves from leaving the estates and, with a fall in sugar production (as was the case in the British West Indies) the Dutch planters feared that their labour shortage would bring ruin.

For its part, however, Britain was willing to allow recruitment in London only for a Government-controlled scheme. And so in 1870, the Dutch Government agreed to a Convention with Britain along the lines of the Anglo-French Convention of 1861, thus drawing Surinam within the British pattern of recruitment of Indian labour. By the time this Convention became operative in 1872, India had clearly emerged as the southern Caribbean's primary supplier of plantation labour.

The first Indians to arrive in Surinam did not fulfill the planters high expectations and it seemed that the careless selection of emigrants resulted in sickness and mortality, and a general demoralization. Two years later, the situation had improved, paving the way for more immigrants, and between 1873 and 1916, when indentured immigration ended, 34,304 Indians were introduced to Surinam. In the 1880s the Dutch sought labour in their own East Indian colonies on the grounds that, in the long run, the importation of Dutch subjects was preferable and better than the British. Thereafter, the annual importation of Javanese lasted until 1931 (except for 1911, 1915–16 and 1921); and according to one estimate, a total of 32,976 Javanese were introduced of whom 7,684 returned to Java as stipulated in their contracts.[64] By now the full implications of Indian immigration[65] was clear. 'Throughout the Caribbean, with the sole exception of Cuba', as one historian wrote, 'it was the Indian immigrants who were most numerous, and most important. It was Indian immigration which determined the general characteristics of the whole system of contract of indentured labour'.[66]

# RECRUITMENT

It is important to remember that Indian emigration during the period (1838–1917) with which we are concerned was 'not the movement of free people for bettering their conditions', but rather the export of 'indentured' workers demanded by planters to satisfy their alleged dire need for plantation labour in the post-slavery period. What remained abundantly clear and of primary interest, however, were the persistent planters' demands. To fulfill their needs, it was necessary to plan an effective strategy to attract labour, a strategy in which deceit, fraud, coercion and kidnapping[67] were endemic.

In other words, colonial planters' pressure had forced the British authorities to devise a system of recruitment. In the early years of emigration, planters were supplied with labourers by firms in Calcutta which, in turn, hired local agents (known as arkatis in northern India and maistries in southern India) to procure such labour. That these agents were paid on the basis of the number recruited was incentive enough to lead to abuse of the system and in time, even though officials argued that there was less abuse, the system of recruitment remained essentially the same.

Who were the arkatis? For the duration of Indian indentured emigration, it was the recruiter at the sharp end, essentially the arkatis, who kept the system of recruitment in operation. They included shopkeepers, peons, domestic servants, labourers and sometimes emigrants. Always on the move, from agency to agency, they roamed the Indian countryside and towns, an ubiquitous presence during the years of indentureship, and from evidence given to the Sanderson Committee the recruiting staff were said to be drawn generally from 'very low class' men who often tried to entice married women away from their husbands. But this Committee did not conduct its investigation until the indentureship system was nearing its end, and could not therefore give us a more accurate picture of the workings of the system for the previous sixty-five years or so. On the face of the Committee's evidence then, few men, allegedly only men of 'bad character' (and therefore of low caste!) were employed as recruiters for the Caribbean colonies.[68] These unscrupulous recruiters, men and women, under the direction of British Agents, in securing plantation labour, particularly during the 1830s and 1840s, misled country-folk with false prospects, trickery which was so deeply ingrained that it has remained in the East Indians' collective memory for generations and given full expression thus:

> 'Oh recruiter, your heart is deceitful,
> Your speech is full of lies!
> Tender may be your voice, articulate and seemingly logical,
> But it is all used to defame and destroy
> The good names of people'.[69]

Above the arkatis, in the hierarchy of the Calcutta recruiting firms, were the duffadars described by the *Bengal Hurkaru* as the 'grand decoy' of Indian labourers and the 'mainspring of the system'. With money, passes and badges issued by the Calcutta firms, the cunning duffadars, accompanied by their subordinates, invaded Chota Nagpur and other areas where the unsuspecting, impoverished people, the 'Hill Coolies' became their main targets. Against a background of poverty, starvation and various forms of oppression, which overshadowed their hapless existence, the prospect of a better life was used to coerce these Indians into the agents' entrapment.

The victims of the recruiters' trickery were herded together at a well-guarded place in Calcutta, reminiscent of a similar operation involving African captives held in the barracoons on the West African coast. In terms of the psychological approach used by the recruiters, an important stage in their recruitment drive had been achieved in that their captives were now entirely at their mercy.

Under constant guard in Calcutta (and forbidden from seeing anyone) the confused Indians were largely ignorant of the contracts to which they were bound. Timid and ignorant,[70] but hopeful, recruits were further intimidated by the police before boarding the waiting ships. If as a natural reaction, some of the recruits felt deeply concerned at this stage, perhaps the doubts in the minds of many of them dissipated as regimentation and exploitation of their wretchedness (a portent of things to come) became clear at the Immigration Depot. The minimal advances of money paid to the prospective labourers were now taken away, as they were issued with a 'red cap, a blanket and one or two brass utensils', before embarking for their unknown destinations. Mindful of their own unscrupulousness and ultimately to protect themselves, the officials gave a semblance of responsibility to the proceedings. We are told, according to one account, that the Magistrate would ask the labourers perhaps the most important question: whether or not they had voluntarily reached agreement with the agents, and only when the Magistrate was satisfied by such an agreement, it was pointed out, that the labourers were allowed to embark. But by then it was all a formality.

If deception was, in general, the normal approach of the arkatis in procuring labourers, another form of recruitment at least during the early years, was kidnapping, a practice prevalent in relation to Mauritius, for example, before legislation was introduced in 1837. Apart from kidnapping, 'surreptitious shipment' was practised to the extent that in October 1836 it was found that an estimated two-thirds of the labourers, who had boarded the *Sophia* had no police pass! And in the case of the *David Malcolm* 200 'unauthorised labourers' were found aboard. In effect, the officials were conveniently working the system to suit the emigration agents' purposes.[71]

When legitimate attempts failed, the recruiters resorted to foul means to ensnare their victims. In the rush to fill the immigrant ships (indeed the same intent was evident among Europeans in filling the African slavers) with hands for the impatient planters, law enforcers turned a blind eye to the recruiters' misdemeanours. But, in time, malpractices accumulated and it is therefore not surprising that since it had started, the system of recruitment had deteriorated alarmingly.

Fierce competition between 'coolie depots' in the 1850s resulted in bribery between recruiters. Caught in this struggle, the labourers were rendered incapable of action to alleviate their distress. But by the 1860s, there was more tinkering with the system of recruitment involving agents representing the relevant West Indian colonies. In practice, the agents recruiting their own staff, provided them with circulars printed in Bengali and English (describing the products of the different colonies, climate, soil, rates of wages) and the name of the colony to which they were bound, was engraved in the above languages on badges and brass plates.[72]

What remained unaltered, however, was the fact that deception was still used by the sub-agents to mislead the Indians who were not told that their labour was required in countries only reached after a long voyage. Thus Calcutta was the last sight of land for many months for the indentured emigrants *en route* to their destinations. Their dilemma was compounded by the fact that after leaving their homes 'under a wrong impression' and having incurred the liability of receiving money in advance, they felt committed and submitted with grave misgivings.[73]

Among the earliest attempts to stop abuses to the system of recruitment was legislation passed in 1837,[74] which apart from laying down specific conditions in the Agreement Form, left the illiterate labourers defenceless against the recruiters who found various ways of getting round the law. Calling for a ban on the emigration of Hill coolies, Lord Brougham drew attention to the fact that these poor and ignorant creatures were 'smuggled away under the idea that Mauritius, to which they are going, is a village belonging to the East India Company'.[75]

The abuses of recruitment and transportation of the emigrants had deteriorated further before positive action was taken in 1839, when the Government suspended the indentured traffic and set up a Commission to look into the whole question of indentured immigration. But the colonial planters were able to get more labourers when Indian immigration was resumed in 1844. Included in the 'new methods' of recruitment and shipment, was the stipulation that private companies would no longer be allowed to recruit labourers, that emigration agents representing the various colonies should be appointed in Calcutta, Madras and Bombay; and that ships transporting emigrants should have the necessary licence.

Arkatis continued to participate in the recruitment process, receiving payment in accordance with the number of people delivered to the Depot at the port of embarkation. Although there was no fixed rate, by mid-century, it was 'generally two rupees for a man, six rupees for a man and wife, half the above rate for children from 10 to 16 years of age, and a quarter for those below ten years'.[76]

As it was, the reformed system of recruiting labourers from the country districts by paid local agents failed to stop the abuses. To its credit, the press remained vigilant reporting an overwhelming number of charges against recruiters. The *Bengal Hurkaru* stated that during a five to six week period there was evidence of labourers 'inveigled under false pretences from the interior; of their illegal detention in Calcutta and even of an attempt to force them on the public wharf to embark against their will'.[77] And George Thompson, the British radical leader, in a letter to the editor of the same newspaper commented on the 'forcible detention' of the labourers.

While the system of recruitment had changed little, its pattern was variable, recruiters having less trouble in some parts of the country than in others, where they feared being assaulted. Against this background of protest and change then, by the mid-1860s legislation was passed to monitor fraud or misrepresentation and checks were imposed to minimise malpractices by recruiters.[78]

In spite of the fact that many intending labourers were wiser when they arrived in Calcutta to face the proper authorities, there were many more who found the city and the whole process bewildering. Indeed it was only when they had arrived on the colonial plantations that they fully realised how cruelly they had been deceived. But for them it was too late. 'Challaying sugar', the job many of them were told they were being recruited to perform, was not the same as physically demanding indentured plantation work. If at the beginning, immigration officials did little to redress these wrongs, thirty three years later the recruitment procedure was still more or less defective, as was borne out by the case of Mohamed Sheriff who gave evidence to the Commission of Inquiry of 1871 into emigration, while he was on the high seas aboard the *Medea* bound for British Guiana. Sheriff gives us a rare first-hand account of how he was recruited:

> I was a gentleman's servant in Bombay (Colonel Adams of the 13th Native Infantry). I went to Lucknow where I was buying flowers for the table in the bazaar and I was there met by a peon, who asked me if I wanted service. I said 'yes'. He then asked me if I could boil sugar. I said 'yes'. He told me then there was plenty of work for me if I would take it – boiling sugar and other work, if I liked it; that I should have to go to Demerara, and I should get ten annas to two rupees a day, and nineteen dollars present.
>
> So I went with him to Calcutta and was approved in the office, stayed there five days and then embarked. Some of the people were allowed to take their lotas with them, but all the others had everything taken away by the peons when they embarked, and were served with government clothing. I got no extract from the register. Nine men came from Lucknow with me; they were not all cultivators – some barbers, coachmen, porters, and other followings. I have not received 19 dollars and do not expect it.[79]

If the system of recruitment remained questionable, it was also clear that the demoralisation of the indentured Indians began well before they actually boarded the ships for the Caribbean on a very long and dangerous journey, during which fear and uncertainty weighed heavily upon them with every passing moment, often for at least three months.

During the 1870s and 1890s recruitment of labourers became more extensive, covering most of the country. While payment to the Head recruiter was a contractual arrangement, the price for each labourer varied with the rail journey to Calcutta. The Trinidad and Tobago and Guiana agencies, for example, paid rates of 18 rupees and 26 rupees for men and women respectively, especially in areas such as Baksar, which incurred these higher rates because of its great distance from Calcutta. Nevertheless, payment was only made for labourers who had actually boarded the ships.

Labourers rejected on medical grounds were of no value to the recruiter and should a labourer escape from the depot or die, only half the rate was paid. Head recruiters from some agencies received bonuses of 50 rupees for each group of 250 labourers. The smaller agencies, however, supplying Surinam and the French colonies paid higher rates, essentially because the smaller scale of business required a higher profit to attract recruiters. And even though the rate paid to the head recruiter varied, generally (given the scarcity of women) more was paid for a recruited woman than a man.[80]

At this stage we should consider a well-known argument in the 'recruitment' debate. In his article 'The Meek Hindu: The Recruitment of Indian Indentured Labourers for Service Overseas, 1874–1916', P.C. Emmer offered his interpretation of the system of recruitment, arguing in essence, that the indentured Indians were fully informed about their destinations and therefore made rational choices to emigrate. Thus, they were not coerced. But although the 'meek Hindu' was a 'ready substitution' for the African slave, the indentured emigrants were not only Hindus but also Muslims who formed an integral part of this emigrant flow, a distinction which Emmer does not make. The process of recruitment, according to Emmer, was one of the aspects of indentured emigration which differed from the Slave Trade. And it should be added that in spite of its shortcomings, the indenture system was not the African Slave Trade.

Nevertheless, Emmer begins his analysis of the recrutment process from 1860, twenty-two years before which the Anti-Slavery Movement in Britain had expressed their concern of the alleged press-ganging of illiterate Hill Coolies into becoming indentured labourers, without fully informing them of the distance they must travel to their overseas destinations and their obligations once they had arrived at their place of labour, at least for the duration of their indentureships. In these early years, both the BENGAL HURKARU and the BRITISH EMANCIPATOR expressed their concern over stories of kidnapping, fraud and fears of a 'new' system of slavery. Indeed soon after the first shipment of indentured 'coolies' had arrived in British Guiana, reports of their ill-treatment and the deaths of many led to an official investigation and soon after in 1839, the scheme was disbanded. Interestingly, because of bad diet and inadequate screening of the Indians' medical condition and fitness for such long voyages, the highest rates of mortality for the whole period of Indian indentured emigration aboard ships bound for the Caribbean had already occurred in the 1850s, a tragedy with which Emmer was not concerned. No doubt in these early years of teething problems when the tragedies and misdemeanors were perhaps most acute and prevalent, lessons from which the emigration agents and the Indian and colonial governments concerned had learned much. For the later period he had chosen, Emmer does identify a number of the system's deficiencies and the changes that were suggested for its improvement.

He noted that the recruiting agencies were not against changes that would improve the system of recruitment and indeed their representatives had met occasionally to consider complaints received and to discuss common problems. They were, it seemed, especially concerned with the charge of fraud and deception, and in seeking ways to get a better 'class of recruiter', they were agreed that their 'ideal' recruiter would be a returned emigrant, who would be able to give potential recruits the benefit of their overseas experience. And because of the paucity of women emigrants, ex-indentured women were regarded as especially invaluable in recruiting more female labourers.

Moreover, for the period under review (1860–1916) Emmer was of the opinion that there was not 'a single indication' that any of the recruiting agencies were interested in kidnapping, fraud and deception 'as a regular practice' (which implies its occasional occurrence!) because as L.F.S. Lutchman put it, both the recruiter and sub-agent faced 'a financial loss' when a fraudulently recruited emigrant changed his or her mind. Such financial losses, however, should not obscure the imperfection of the system of recruitment in relation to which many of those directly involved had to make difficult, but important voluntary choices, while for others circumstances dictated their emigration. Some Indians, for example, would not have survived had they remained in Calcutta, while a large number of women took the opportunity of emigration to free themselves from abandonment, poverty and the strictures of Indian society.

Ultimately, the many attempts to improve the system of recruitment failed to harmonize nineteenth century European optimism in relation to the Indian emigrants making a rational decision about a better life and the deeply entrenched 'emotional aversion' which Indians had towards overseas travel, a disjuncture which was transcended only by gnawing hunger and intractable family problems.

Emmer also touches on the intending emigrants perception of the future. Major Wiersma, a well placed observer of the Dutch East Indies informs us that the recruiters did their best to convince potential emigrants, emphasizing in particular the much higher wages they would receive overseas, compared with wage levels in India. And, of course, there was the added incentives of guaranteed rations, free housing, medical care and, on completion of their contracts, a free return passage to India. The recruiters were also forthcoming about the colonies to which the recruits were bound. But, they remained silent about the long, boring and dangerous voyages, of the small sea-going vessels at the mercy of the vast oceans, a difficult decision for many Hindus. Often with-holding such information proved to be foolhardy, for after learning the truth at the Calcutta Depot, not surprisingly, many intending emigrants absconded. For them, it was a lucky escape, which was, in retrospect, regarded as better late than never. But for those who were already in transit, there was nothing they could do that was negative.

Even though Indians had come to know about the material advantages of emigration, while the system lasted, fraud, deception and misunderstandings remained endemic. But while such blemishes were often referred to by opponents of the system of recruitment, it was the cultural and religious changes arising from leaving India that constituted the 'main theme' when the campaign for abolition came into being.

The opportunistic recruiting agencies persisted in maintaining that the 'term expired' indentured labourers, who returned to India were the 'best advocates' of Indian emigration overseas. And, as a result, later on, re-indentured returned Indians were used to promote the idea that the free return passage was more an opportunity which Indians took to see relatives and friends rather than a right which they exercised, but there was no question of them staying on in India! While some 'return coolies' had in deed re-indentured, there was a tendency for the agencies to exaggerate their importance.

While there were differences of opinion as to whether or not the emigration of indentured labourers meant a 'net loss' to the Indian population, it was argued that this was beneficial given that India was an over-populated country, where the masses were subjected not only to a low level of subsistence, but also to periodic famine. The fact that as many as two-thirds of the Indians who had been indentured while the system lasted, was seen as evidence that, on balance, they were better-off and therefore preferred to stay in the colonies where they had been indentured, hence the 'benevolent neutrality' of the Indian Government in allowing (through a continuation of the system) whatever benefits might accrue to indentured recruits. Such positive effects as there were, however, should not obscure the fact that this *laissez faire* approach by the Indian Government gave the employers of indentured labour (in the tea, jute and sugar industries) enough latitude to optimise their labour intake. So it was that hitherto the end of the nineteenth century, the reasons for not continuing recruitment were not enough to halt the system.

But the First World War and its consequences had dramatic effects on the British Empire and, in particular, the British Indian Government found that it needed the support of Indians and therefore it could not forestall the insistent pressures arising from the Indians, whose spokesmen were nationalists. The end of the system in 1916, according to Emmer, was 'mainly caused' by Indian nationalists, who were largely middle class and had no direct experience of overseas emigration. To support his thesis, he cited only one reference, which occurred as late as 1915, where indentured labourers were themselves opposed to the continuation of the system. But it must be said that what eluded Emmer was not so much the Indians' opposition to going overseas, but necessarily their retrospective assessment of the manner in which they were recruited, the very process which Emmer argues thoroughly,[81] but says nothing of how the harsh experience of indentureship was so consistently challenged by the indentureds, especially in the form of strikes and riots, while the system lasted in British Guiana and Trinidad. This persistent and instinctive opposition, often occurring soon after indentured labourers began their indentures, had serious implications on the system, indeed on the very process of recruitment, especially the recruiters economy with the truth or silence on the duration of voyages and details of the severity of the manual work and the social, religious and cultural consequences of living in such an alien environment, to which Emmer attaches little or no value, as though the one had little to do with the other!

Let us look now at the Indian recruits, where they came from, and their experience before embarkation and during the voyage from India to the Caribbean.

# THE RECRUITS

Before industrialization in modern India, over 80 per cent of the population worked on the land while the rest worked on hereditary or hierarchic occupations as craftsmen, priests, soldiers and officials. In India's rural economy, among the mass of landless labourers, some sought new land while others joined the drift to the large cities, where they offered their labour for hire. Earlier, by the mid-sixteenth century, this reserve of urban labour attracted many employers who paid the going rate of wages, and although this was relatively low (between Rs.2–3 a month in south India for work in warehouses and wharves) in the minds of European employers, keen to exploit the situation, the image of the 'dumb, patient endurance' of the Indian 'coolie' was indelibly etched.[82]

At this stage, it is perhaps necessary, given its origin, to define the word 'coolie'. The terms 'Koli' or 'Coolie' were not necessarily identical. According to Charles Lockyer, writing in 1711, the 'better sort' of people who travelled in Palankeens, 'carry'd by six or eight cooleys', were hired for three pence a day.[83] Towards the end of the eighteenth century, however, instead of being the term connected with any group or race, it referred to those at the 'lower end' of the labour market.

Later, between 1753 and 1759, Indian 'cooley' labour was employed by the East India Company in lower Burma and significantly, even though these Indians laboured long distances away from home, they tended to return to their families after a relatively short period. But increasingly, as Indians travelled overseas, 'forced banishment' frustrated their return home and, by the end of the eighteenth century, a 'modified form' of the slave trade to Malaya had emerged.

Of course slavery in eighteenth century India was an established practice[84] and thereafter, there was an extension of the internal forms of slavery as labour was exported to produce sugar in the Mascarenes.[85] Surprisingly, however, emigration from India in the nineteenth century proceeded in spite of the objection to 'crossing the black water' among Hindus, who regarded sea journeys as polluting because of the problem of obtaining 'pure water'.[86]

In comparison with the high castes, Indians destined for the sugar plantations, at least initially, were recruited mainly from the lower castes, such as the semi-aboriginal people, the Dhangars who (regarded as a group outside the caste system) were not constrained by dietary rules. The Dhangars from Chota Nagpur (the 'Hill Coolies' as they were referred to) lived in the hilly areas, near the densely populated Bihar and Bengal provinces. Their first contact with the British administration in India was in the early nineteenth century in the indigo industry in Bihar. The European planters were more willing to use Dhangars than Biharis in the labour-intensive process of indigo manufacture and soon malpractices and abuse of the labourers were such that sensitive reformers in Calcutta, honouring their sense of public responsibility, inquired into the matter.[87]

Not surprisingly, the planters retained their Dhangars who proved to be among the best workers. It is significant that after their engagement in seasonal agricultural employment, the Dhangars, like other Indian labourers, usually returned home. But unlike the people from the Ganges plain, who left their families at home, the planters were able to persuade the Dhangars to move with their families. And so these hill people, despised by Hindus, of necessity descended from the hills and made their way into Calcutta in search of employment. The deep-seated nature of their plight was reflected in the fact that during the 1840s and 1850s, among those recruited under the indentureship system, an estimated two-fifths to a half of the emigrants to Mauritius and the Caribbean were Dhangars. Although their numbers declined from the 1850s, during the decade, on the long voyage to the Caribbean, the death rate among them was 'considerably worse' when compared with recruits from the plains. While the reason advanced for this was obscure, many factors could have contributed, for example the loneliness of the sea voyage and the realisation that they could do nothing to turn back, may have induced psychological disorders causing depression, leading to suicide and unexplained deaths, which puzzled European doctors.

British capitalists, especially during those early years of emigration, had little real concern for the welfare of cheap disposable labour, and by all accounts, there was a lack of mutual respect in the relations between the exploiters and the exploited so that after exhausting the supply of Dhangars, the emigration agents and their recruiters looked for other labourers in the cities of Calcutta, Madras and Bombay. Apart from the mass of country people in search of work as 'burden-carriers' (in other words 'coolies'), the unemployed included cooks, footmen, washermen, grooms, coachmen, entertainers and prostitutes. Clearly not all the immigrants were agricultural labourers, and even though their suitability for manual work was checked by the Emigration Agent, in order to fill the ships (undue delay was costly), many musicians and barbers, for example, were shipped abroad.[88]

If the search for Indian labourers was, at times, indiscriminate, it was also unrelenting, growing ever extensive. Until about 1870, Calcutta was the most important port through which organised emigration was conducted, and much further away, beyond Benares and Bihar, the North West area was scoured by the recruiters. The new victims were the destitute, but relatively dependable and hard-working Biharis, who had earlier resisted the excessive exploitation of the indigo employers. According to officials of the emigration traffic, these Hindus, who spoke Bhojpuri, accepted recruitment in 'the spirit of adventure' and, in time, officials would come to romanticize this acceptance. 'As fond as an Irishman is of a stick', wrote G.A.Grierson, 'the long-boned stalwart Bhojpuri with his staff in hand is a familiar object striding over fields far from his home. Thousands of them have emigrated to British colonies and have returned rich men'.[89]

Both economically and socially, as people from the lower-end of the social structure in India, the low-caste, landless people bore the brunt of landlordism in the Bengal Presidency, especially in Benares Province and Bihar. Indeed, labouring under conditions of semi-slavery in Bihar, the poor were forced to sell the services of themselves and, in many cases, of their children far into the future simply to meet immediate needs. Amidst this state of desperation, the recruiters' promises of a rosy indentured future abroad, understandably, seemed a viable alternative. The economic circumstances overwhelmingly favoured the Emigration Agents for if the promise of wages at the rate of Rs.5 a month appeared generous in 1838, the cheapness of labour in Calcutta was such that the best labourers could be employed for only 'two pice' a day. (A pice was one-twelfth part of an anna the equivalent of about one-sixth of 1d.)[90]

Impoverishment (though marginally relative) was all-pervasive cutting across caste and religion. It was found that among the early emigrants to the West Indies, there was much difficulty in accurately identifying their caste and religion, as was the case with those aboard the *Hesperus*, which arrived in British Guiana in 1838. Although all the emigrants were described as 'mahometans', their names, in almost all cases, were Hindu. Clearly a push factor for many of the early emigrants, regardless of the divisive nature of Indian society, was famine, notably during the 1840s in upper India. Initially they migrated to Bihar from where they were 'persuaded' to board the ships at Calcutta. This movement of Indians overseas had extended westward to include recruits from Delhi; and among the districts of the North Indian plains providing recruits for the Emigration Agent in 1857 were Benares, Azamgarh, Gorakhpur and Jaunpur in North-Western provinces, and Ghazipur, Muza, Harpur, Champaran, Shahabad, Patna and Gaya in Bihar, along with Hazaribagh and Chota Nagpur.[91]

The recruits from southern India came mainly from the populous Tamil areas, where landless labourers barely eked out a living. The majority of these recruits (many of whom were Untouchables) came from Tanjore, Trichinopoly, South Arcot and from Vizagapatam, Ganjam and Rajamundy. Others taken from the Malabar

Coast were bound for Ceylon (now Sri Lanka) and Mauritius, rather than the West Indies. Many Madrasis, according to the Emigration Agent at Madras, were unwilling to be recruited for the Caribbean colonies because it was found, even as early as 1857, that there was prejudice towards South Indian emigrants; a prejudice deriving partly from the 'Untouchables' allegedly disgusting eating habits and work-shyness.

In comparison with Madras, more satisfactory information was collected about the social and caste composition of the emigrants from Calcutta, showing an emigration of 2,521 of high castes; 4,974 of agricultural castes; 1,537 artisans; 5,309 of low castes and 2,910 Muslims.[92]

Hitherto, even though a cross-section of castes were to be found among the emigrants, the receiving colonies were dissatisfied with the low caste, undesirable Indians who were being exported overseas. Even after three decades of emigration, the view that the recruits were from the 'lowest caste' of each Presidency, remained unaltered, and in spite of evidence to the contrary, criminality among low-caste recruits was exaggerated, thus stigmatizing the entire group.

By the 1880s the social background of emigrants became clearer. Among the areas of recruitment during this period were the North-Western Provinces and Oudh, while a few came from the Punjab; and from Rajasthan, among those who emigrated were Rajputs and Pathans. In fact, the supply of emigrants from northern India (mainly from Benares and its environs) was maintained for the rest of the period of indentureship.[93] As the area of recruitment widened, a steady traffic was maintained to the Caribbean, and by 1908 it was found that about 90 per cent of the migrants had come from the poorer districts of the United Provinces, including such areas as Basti, Fyzabad and Gonda. Three years later, the Immigration Agent for Trinidad at Calcutta, complained of the unsuitability of the recruits (mainly people exposed to famine, flood and semi-starvation) and lamented exclusion of the Dhangars (their most favoured victims) from recruitment. While at this time emigration from northern India was in its closing stages, southern India provided the mass of emigrants for two more decades. As it was, both the emigrants and those who remained in the villages were affected by the experience of indentured emigration.

# PERSONAL ACCOUNTS

Five Indians, Fazal, Moolian, Maharani, Bharath and Sankar, who left their homes and villages in India within the last decade of the indentureship system, tell us how they were recruited.

Fazal came from a small village (he does not say where exactly, though we know he came from northern India) of about 2,000 people, where 'all is grass house'. He was a labourer, working his own land (planting rice, for example) in a Muslim village. He makes the point that although there were Hindu businesses about, they were on 'one side', separate from the Muslims. Both groups tended not to live in 'one place'.

He had no brother, but had left four sisters, who were all married with children, behind in India. He had no doubt as to what motivated him to leave his village. 'I come to wuk for money', he said, 'an go back'. He had some experience working on a ship which had docked at Calcutta. But, he says, a 'Muslim fellar' fooled him into emigrating to Trinidad. The recruiter told him that he had a lot of money and asked Fazal how much he was earning each month. Three rupees, Fazal said. The recruiter chided his stupidity and spoke of earning as much as 25 cents a day overseas.

Fazal remained in Calcutta (where he had stayed while working on the ship) never to return to his village. Having decided to emigrate, he was accommodated at the Immigration Depot, where he said there was no fear among the Indians. It was after all some 72 years since this traffic had begun. Yet what the Indians were told in India was not the reality in the Caribbean. Fazal spoke of the barracks where the Indians were closeted for about three months, with nothing to do. There his diet consisted of roti, rice, biscuits and sugar. At this late stage of Indian emigration, he was of the view that those who were with him were 'glad' to come to Trinidad. The idea of 'challaying' (sifting) sugar in this new land was attractive even to women; or was their decision to volunteer for this work, an act of desperation to change their unsatisfactory lives. So once more, Fazal boarded a ship, except that this time it was not going to 'Dakka', and there were hundreds of other people, including 'plenty oman', some of them with children, though he was not sure whether or not they were married. (Many years later, in Trinidad, he still held the view that 'Everybody glad to come dis country'.)[94]

Moolian had left his father, two brothers and two sisters (both married) in India. His mother was dead. His father sent him to a school, where there were no books to read, but he recalled making marks on the sand. He may not have had many memorable lessons, but he never forgot a beating he received from one of his teachers, which was endorsed by another thrashing from his schoolmaster. The result was a swollen hand and the end of his schooldays.

Moolian's concerned father put the options open to his son – minding animals, buffalo, goats or cows. In fact, this was the work he did until the time he left India. He was in no doubt that there were no poor people, and that there was no hunger among the people from his part of the country. There was also a lot of work, planting ground-nuts, peas and rice and selling pumpkins to the towns people. But in spite of all this, he needed to leave the village and was therefore open to offers. Then one day he overheard a conversation between two men, one telling the other about a nice place, with nice food and money. For Moolian, the teenager, this was most tempting. So after the 'big massa' in the town spoke to him, he was offered $40 'to come away', by 'some smart fellar'.

At the Immigration Depot, details of Moolian's departure was recorded. He was told what questions he would be asked by the 'inspector'. For example, why you going to Trinidad? His response ought to have been that he had the permission of his mother and father to go to Trinidad, work there and return with money. But, Moolian said, he was fooled into coming to the island. So there he was, closeted with other Indians at the Depot, where business was good. The shop, he recalled, sold a variety of things, including channa; and he spoke of the doctor's visit to inspect him in all his nakedness. Imagine how unusual this must have been for him! Overall, he says of the days he spent at the Depot that there was very little to do, except to cook and eat. He could not forget, however, that bachelor men and women were accommodated in separate barracks, until three ships appeared.[95]

Relating her story, Maharani said that before leaving India, she had been married. But when her husband died, she lived with her in-laws. One day while she was boiling some milk for the family, a cat approached with the intention of drinking the milk. She aimed a blow at the cat and milk was spilled on the floor. Previously, her brothers in-law had been beating her, and she was particularly concerned that lately she had been 'getting too much lix'. She could not face another beating for the milk incident and decided to run away without telling anyone except her 'ole modder-in-law'. And so, one day while her husband's brother was eating, she quietly slipped out of the house forever.

To quench her thirst, she made her way to a well where a 'one foot fellar' was sitting. This man asked her to follow him and she did so. He was kind to her, offering her much-needed food. Soon after they arrived at the recruiting area, where there was a large crowd. The man said that she could earn 25 cents challaying sugar ('cheenee challay') on an island. This was an attractive proposition and she was encouraged by the number of people there. She said, she soon found herself on board when the ship arrived at Calcutta, and from where she stood, she could see the crowd of people outside urging her 'not to go, not to go'. Like her, the other Indians in the ship were also watching the people, who kept saying 'jahaj (ship) dey far … not to go, dey shaking hand so, not to go'. But by then it was too late. Maharani recalled that moment:

> 'e done gone
> everybody de inside dey (the ship)
> everybody
> nobody cyan come out from dey again'.[96]

Bharath was among twenty young men who travelled together to Trinidad 'to make money'. They were all able-bodied and ready for work. Bharath tells of his escape from his family, one night when with all his clothes tied in a bundle, he left the household of ten, while his father slept. 'No modder fadder, nobody no know' is how he described his quiet departure. He remembers arriving at a 'long long house' full of rice (dhan) and millet (jundri). Among the people in search of work at that place, there was no trouble; and at that time, no one had told Bharath about 'Chinedad' where he would do White people's work. The story circulated, however, that those who were engaged for this 'white people's work' in Trinidad, would not be required to work on Saturday and Sunday. But it was only years later, that Bharath realised that the man who had told him so in India, had fooled him. 'De fellar meet me', and offered to pay 25 cents for the work expected of him. But, it seemed, that Bharath was not told how long he would have to labour for that 25 cents.

He found himself in the midst of a constant stream of people coming in from Hyderabad, Poona, Gorakpur and Goa, representing the various castes and groups of workers, including Brahmin, Chamar, Khattik, Bhangi, Dhanak, Ahir, Challani, Vaise, Kurmi, Kanaiya and Dhobi. All these people did the work appropriate to their castes, while they waited for further instructions. When he eventually signed his contract, Bharath said that neither was his destination known, nor was there any hint that he might never see his village again. At this time during the years of indentureship, about 1910, there was no automatic return passage; and with hindsight, Bharath related the full impact of that moment of innocence in the village, before he was taken to the Calcutta Depot: 'e no come back, e no come back', he would never see his mother and father again, he says, for he was bound for the kala pani, to cross the seven seas.

At some stage, however, the recruiter had to deliver the truth and while he was still at the village stage of his journey, Bharath tells us next that 'e say, all you cyan come back hyar'. Various propositions of indentureship were put to Bharath. If indentured for five years, 'ha to pay six dollars, ha to pay, ha to wuk', and if indentured for ten years, 'ha to pay three dollar'; and if accompanied by a small child, the payment was sixty cents.

The promise of a house, land, clothes, a fork to work with and accommodation in a barrack-room was offered as inducement for him to go to the Caribbean. He then made a train journey, which he said lasted 'seven day, night and day', before reaching the Calcutta Depot. Overcrowding here was evident, and the atmosphere was stifling. 'All a dem near', Bharath said, meaning the various castes. Unlike the openness of the village from which he had come, the Depot seemed like a high-security prison. Fortified by bars and patrolled by watchmen, the 'Depot dey high high, nuh jump', he said.[97]

In India, Sankar knew the reality of being poor without land or a house, having no job and borrowing and repaying debts. He did many odd jobs: fetching water from a well, watering his family's garden and ploughing the fields with the aid of a bull, usually in September before the planting season started in October.

Sankar's mother died while he was still a young child, and he was taught by his step-mother, who brought him up, to do 'garden wuk'. Tragedy struck again, when he was seven years old. His father died and his step-mother found another man.

His sister married a rich man who, after losing his money, left her. The boy felt insecure and unhappy with his step-mother, who said hurtful things to him. He had reached an important juncture in his young life, yet he was forced, by circumstances, to harbour serious thoughts. He began to think of leaving home, of moving to the town. He confided in a friend, whom he hoped would join him, promising to pay his travel expenses, when the job he was doing in the country was no longer available. Sankar and his friend discussed the matter and soon his last day in the village came. He stole some money, and after dinner that night, he said his final farewell to his neighbour. 'I sit down in de yard', he said, 'an I say, bhai you seeing me, I seeing you' and so he began his last conversation, while still at home. 'Whe you going?' his friend asked, still unclear about Sankar's direction.

'I no know whe I going, but I going', Sankar said.

Referring to Sankar's step-mother and step-father, the friend and neighbour said hopefully, 'When dem dead, two ah dem, you holding everything'. But at that moment, such an inheritance had no part to play in Sankar's life. 'I eh want dat, I eh want dat', he repeated himself. 'Me heart brek already wha me step-mother tell me'.

Sankar then recalled that on one occasion, when he fell down a well and was fortunate enough to just hurt a toe, his step-mother, through no fault of her own, was not around.

But when she did hear of the accident, she said if she was there at the time, she would have belted him. He did not answer her, but he could never forgive or forget her attitude or what she said next. He recalled her hurtful words: 'She know she chile, she en know nex man chile', she said, 'she eh make me, so she eh have no feeling for me'.

This was the build-up to Sankar's decision to leave his village, one night in 1912. He arrived at 'fore dey morning' at the station at Kanpur city, and was immediately approached by an Arkati. There, he was asked if he was looking for work. 'Yes, I going to look for wuk', Sankar said.

'I ha plenty wuk, … and I eh getting enough people', the Arkati said, leading him towards a house where they sat down. After about ten minutes, a doctor arrived and inspected him, especially his hands, to be sure that they were capable of hard manual labour.

Sankar then said that he and other emigrants were taken to a bigger house. There was no dahl and 'no takarie', but he recalled being given sweetie, which was insubstantial. Here, of necessity, he made his own roti, until the moment came when he was brought before the White man, who asked him his name and, in turn, the names of his village, his father and the location of the Post Office. The friend from his village, who had accompanied him thus far, said he wanted to go back home. So at 8.00 p.m one night he was taken to a railway station and put on train that was homeward bound. If Sankar had missed his 'partner', the Arkati and other immigration officials had missed him even more for, as Sankar said, for 'every head' that was brought into Benares city, money was to be made.

A full shipload of Indians was the target. But, as Sankar observed, when the 'White man from de boat' came among the Indians, he wanted to know 'who going wid dey good mind, or who going by compelling power, he eh want to compel nobody'. If there was anybody for the White man to compel, it was the book-keeper, 'de one wha dey in de office'. The ship's officer leaves only after the finally tally is reached and the names of those not embarking are deleted. But this was not the end of the story behind filling the ships. Once the White man from the boat is gone, Sankar informs us with characteristic repetition, of the skulduggery of the officer at the Depot who, he said, 'Go hot oil and trow on you, dey go hot oil an trow on you, dey go make you fraid, dey go hunch you', so that the prospective emigrant would say 'I going'! At that stage, Sankar had no doubt that the Depot officers 'go compel you, put you in de flower garden' and he stressed 'dey go hunch you'. For him, the evidence of compelling Indians to emigrate was strong. Keeping the emigrants at the Depot and feeding and clothing them was a form of blackmail. 'I minding you so long', was the White man's reminder to those who dithered about going. The White man's argument to reluctant emigrants was that they should have expressed their doubts before. Psychologically then, the officials pushed the Indians to the limit, initially using their skills in the form of fine tuning, but when this failed to achieve the desired results, they inevitably resorted to sledge-hammer tactics: 'you have to come, you have to come'.

Sankar gives us a sense of the mood of at least some of the emigrants, in those last days at the Calcutta Depot where, he said, they ate goat meat, roti and dahl, and bathed. Even now with little chance of escape, they were under the watchful eye, the effective control of the authorities. Unlike their first contact with the recruiter at Kanpur and Benares, here at the waters edge of the great city of Calcutta (to lift their spirits, as the hours of the day dragged-on) they engaged each other in light-hearted wrestling, playing various games and doing physical exercises. Some women played a game of tug-of-war and Sankar mentions women with small children, though he did not know if they had run away from their parents or father-in-law's houses. 'I eh know how dey come', he said, but there they were!

The vessel that would transport Sankar and his fellow indentured Indians remain-ed at the Depot for five days. He scrutinised the various ships alongside, including one that was 'wukking wid de wind', a sail ship (the form of transportation used during the earlier years of indentureship, before steamships were employed), which, dependent on the wind, either moved at a steady pace, swiftly or was becalmed for long periods. Once Sankar was on the ship, he realised that people were not the only cargo: there were goats and sheep and hundreds of bags of flour. [98] Soon the journey would begin. How long would it last? Sankar had not the faintest idea.

Commenting on Indian emigration as an 'escape to opportunity', Tinker wrote that it was a view 'seriously held' by a few well informed and sympathetic British and Indian observers, although this did not reflect the grim experience of the majority of the bonded Indian immigrants during the period 1830 to 1920.[99]

Before they left India to embark on the journey overseas, whether for five years or a lifetime some emigrants seemed to have cared little, while others showed more than mere interest, though it is clear that their understanding were, at most, vague of the life and events that would unfold before them. The Indians generally referred to their destinations as 'Tapu', which they were misleadingly assured was a place near Calcutta; and according to one account, among south Indians, British Guiana (or Demerara) was known as Damra, Damraila or Doomra and Trinidad was called Chinedad or Chinitat.[100]

The distance between India and the Caribbean colonies was a major factor in determining whether or not those who emigrated would return to their homes. Given the argument by a Consular Agent at Karikal in 1875 that native Indians were not 'naturally inclined' to leave their villages, whenever they did so it was with the intention of returning and there was little doubt that if the West Indian colonies and Mauritius were 'as near the fields whence the emigrants are drawn as are the Central Provinces and British Burma' it was more than likely that few who emigrated would have remained as permanent settlers. Thus 'push' rather than 'pull' factors took precedence: the need of desperate people seeking relief from an intolerable situation.[101]

Finally after their recruitment, the day came for them to leave their villages and cities. As people with few, if any, possessions, these indentured recruits made their way to the coast and it was not unusual, certainly in the early days of immigration, for these destitute people to walk very long distances, even 'hundreds of miles', on the first leg of a journey fraught with uncertainty. But their commitment reflected the fact that there was more to gain and little to lose by the ordeal of travelling from the districts surrounding Benares and Patna, which lasted between thirty to forty days. When they eventually arrived at the post, those who suffered most were the footsore women and children. Their delicate health, at this stage of their sojourn to the Caribbean was, to say the least, disturbing. It was perhaps a blessing of sorts that they had no conception of how far their destinations were and how long they would be travelling on the high seas before they got there. Even as they made their way in this bedraggled state, rival recruiters were up to their tricks, taking every opportunity to capitalize on the physical and psychological disadvantages of emigrants. Walking was not the only means of getting to the ports of embarkation. With the advent of the railways, such journeys were quicker and less painful, even though the carriages were packed 'ten in a third-class compartment'.[102] In this public place, the prospective indentured labourers were objects of curiosity, if not ridicule, and it is not surprising that ordinary passengers were prone to discourage them from going overseas.

The Emigration Depot[103] was, in a real sense, the next stage in the process of becoming an indentured labourer. To deal with the human cargo being prepared for shipment, there were, in the 1880s, a number of emigration agencies at Calcutta and separate depots. The British Guiana or (Demerara) Depot situated in Garden Reach 'contained a number of barracks, with bungalows for the staff'. This separation in housing between management (in the bungalows) and the labourers (in barracks), a portent of things to come would indeed be replicated on the colonial plantations.

The immigration process had its own drawbacks and despite the urgent business of clearing the port, as quickly as possible in order to avoid incurring further costs, it was not unusual for indentured labourers to await embarkation for three months. Sailing schedules (given weather conditions at sea) became increasingly important especially on the long voyages to the Caribbean which, before the introduction of steamships, were undertaken in the summer and autumn to British Guiana and Trinidad and Tobago, and in the winter to Jamaica.[104]

The manager of the Depot was the Emigration Agent whose residence was necessarily within the compound where the procedure usually followed when a group of new emigrants arrived was to first bathe themselves and wear the new clothing provided; and while their dirty clothing was being washed, they went through a medical inspection, before being allowed to embark. Many felt reassured by engaging in 'depot marriages' before the moment of embarkation. This bond no doubt fortified them for what was obviously a stern test ahead, their 'last act of individual choice'. For those who got married there was much to be gained from such a relationship, especially the man who, it was argued, benefited from the advantage of having someone to attend to him in a society that was alien and potentially hostile. 'But there was also advantage to women in securing a protector', Tinker wrote, 'and in establishing some sort of recognised position in a social order which held no place for an adult single woman'.[105]

Why did single women take the opportunity of a new life abroad? The scarcity of Indian women on the Caribbean plantations was a persistent problem that had been evident since the inception of the indentureship system. In fact, when emigration to the Caribbean was resumed in 1845, it was stipulated that more female emigrants should be included[106] and as the system evolved, the quotas were raised from 35 women to every 100 men in 1857, to 50 women to every 100 men in 1860, which was extremely difficult to achieve. This target was realistically lowered to a ratio of 25 women to 100 men when Indian emigrants began entering the French West Indies.[107]

Given this background and the fact that few families were willing to leave their homes, included among those women who emigrated were young widows (especially Brahmin widows and others forbidden to remarry), married and/or single women who had broken relationships or had left home, or had lost caste, and those who were either practising or faced with the prospect of prostitution. In addition, the ravages of famine provided a powerful incentive, particularly to women of high caste to emigrate rather than face starvation.[108] One thing was clear: the majority of these Indian women (both high and low caste) who had emigrated to the Caribbean were not simply the victims of circumstances, but more importantly (when they were not kidnapped), they must be seen as having made conscious, courageous decisions to emigrate across the tabooed and dreaded kala pani (dark water).

The transition from the old traditional ways to a new life posed tough challenges, testing to the limit, the stamina and strength of character of the indentured Indians generally. Indeed, from those last moments at the Depot, these emigrants were caught up in the process of deculturisation, almost dehumanization, which was imposed upon them. The warm clothing, reminiscent of the garb of Indian convicts, issued to emigrants, were indispensable in anticipation of climatic changes that occurred on voyages to the Caribbean. Another significant part of the process, which had also started with congregation of the Indians at the Emigration Depot, was that of bringing together individuals of varying castes, dialects and religions. And there also began a homogenizing process, a mingling that would work irrevocably towards less strict caste divisions among the Indians in the colonies. While they were at the port of embarktion, a latter-day folk poet described what many of them had to come to terms with.

> When we reached Calcutta, our miseries increased.
> We were stripped of all our beautiful clothes,
> Rosary beads and sacred threads.
> Bengali rags decorated us now.
> The Sadhu's hair was shaved,
> And Sadhu, Dom, Chamar, and Bhangi
> All were thrown together in a room.[109]

And once they fully realised that they had, through their indentured contracts, signed away their freedom for a few years, at least, (and the real possibility that they may never see their homeland again) their lament, while still at the Depot, was encapsulated in a couplet:

> 'What sins have we committed, oh Lord,
> That thou hast given us these miseries'.[110]

While there was a great deal of soul-searching among the huddled groups, the necessity of an Interpreter was yet another aspect of the emigrants' stay at the Depot that would be replicated later on the plantations. But language was not the most pressing problem now. Soon, however, this phase of the indentured Indians' journey would end and the great sub-continent, Mother India, would recede in the distance, as the small ships, fragile against the elements of nature, glided into the overpowering vastness and terror of the open seas.

# CROSSING THE KALA PANI: MORTALITY

In comparison with others who made difficult sea voyages, the European emigrants to North America took about four to five weeks at sea (reduced to 14 days or less with the coming of steam ships); the African slaves 'middle passage' lasted from three to four months. For the Indian emigrants who made the crossing during the 1870s, the estimated time it took to complete the voyage from Calcutta to Jamaica was 26 weeks, and from Bombay or Madras to Jamaica it was 25 weeks. Return voyages to India were also time-consuming, the longest on the *Bayard* lasting 188 days in 1882–83 and in 1885 the *Foyle* arrived in Calcutta from Jamaica after 174 days. Journey times were reduced 'almost by half' with the introduction of steamships.[111]

Disease was not absent at the Emigration Depot in India. Cholera and typhoid played havoc among the frightened emigrants who were contained in overcrowded spaces. And even though they were supposed to have been subjected to a medical examination, Indians affected by cholera somehow found themselves aboard the ships.

How did the Protector of Immigrants at Calcutta (in whose care and custody the welfare and rights of the Indians were entrusted) cope with emigrants on the eve of their hazardous voyages? It was argued that the Protector was subjected to insistent pressure to ensure the continuation of emigration, instead of alleviating the obvious distress of the emigrants. This should not surprise us, for he was employed to advance vested interests and not to expose questionable practices.

Physically (and no doubt psychologically) the emigrants gradually assumed a changed appearance, and on the day of their departure from the Depot, the Protector witnessed their embarkation, as each emigrant 'with a pass and a "tin ticket" (an identification disc) hung around the neck or strapped to the arm', took their last glimpse of India and disappeared into the ship. As far as the officials were concerned, the sooner the immigrants were packed aboard, the better. Bewildered by all that they had experienced at the Depot, they usually were then led to their ship sometime between 4.00 a.m and 5.00 a.m. Although this was a routine, uneventful operation, the occasion when things went wrong left indelible impressions as was the case with the *Clarendon* in March 1861, when the Protector was censured by his superiors in London.[112]

The embarkation procedure was clearly defective, especially because it was not unusual for one or two days to elapse between the medical examination and embarkation. For those so inclined, the chances of substituting of the infirm for healthy emigrants during this interval were great. In fact, this was a period when the Protector's office did not supervise the emigrants. Abuse of this kind was most evident on board the *Tyburnia* which harboured 82 emigrants without passes and 81 certified medically unfit. The defects at the Calcutta depot had devastating consequences at sea, particularly during the 1856 -7 season. Among those who spoke out was the

Captain of the *Merchantman*, (which had the highest mortality for this season –
30 per cent of the 385 emigrants died during the voyage to British Guiana) who
believed that the greatest evil of emigration to the Caribbean was 'the want of
selection at Calcutta, so long as a man can go on board the quality is nothing'.[113]

Overseeing the emigration of Indians, the Colonial Office in conjunction with
the Government of India and the Colonial Government worked together. The
first set of revised regulations to the traffic came off the press in 1845, much too
late for many Indians who, prior to this date, had made the journey to the Caribbean braving the cold weather of the Cape of Good Hope without adequate clothing. With successive disasters at sea, stricter rules were introduced,[114] so that during
the last third of the nineteenth century the rules governing the 'coolie ships' were
tightened and effectively enforced, we are told.

Many of the ships in the earlier period of Indian emigration were built in Indian
shipyards, some were small such as the *Whitby*, 350 tons, and the *Ganges*, 839 tons,
(1861), but by the 1880s larger ships were introduced. Steamers were first used in
the East Indian indentured traffic to the Caribbean in 1872, when the *Enmore*
arrived in British Guiana with 517 emigrants after a significant reduction in voyage
time which lasted 49 days. The main shipping firms competing for this traffic to
the Caribbean were James Nourse and Sandbach, Tinne and Company, who also
operated as planters and merchants in British Guiana.[115]

During the voyage, the Surgeon Superintendent (or Surgeon, as he was sometimes referred to) played a central role; indeed much depended upon his expertise
and direction, and while many of them served to the best of their ability (and were
highly competent), in the 1850s there was serious concern for the welfare of the
emigrants. In 1856 the Governor of British Guiana expressed his concern over the
possibility of quarrels between the Surgeon and officers of the ships in connection
with their allowance of alcohol. In fact, given the Protector's view that generally
doctors could not be trusted, mortality on ships bound for the Caribbean were
unusually high between 1856 and 1860. Yet while suitable doctors with a knowledge of the emigrants' languages was a dire need, Indian doctors were regarded as
being not 'professionally qualified'. And while efforts were made to maintain certain standards, the Medical Inspector of emigrants at Calcutta stated that only in
exceptional cases did professionals of 'first class talent and education' join the immigration service.[116] With time, however, the quality of many 'Coolie' ships' doctors improved markedly; and in a few cases, competence extended to acts of hero-
ism, in spite of a generally depressing trend.

Understandably, the Indian emigrants who crossed the 'dark waters' had grounds
for fear. Sailing conditions, by no means ideal, tended to be variable, unpredictable
and while some journeys were tedious, others were a haunting nightmare for when
the emigrants were not devastated by the weather at sea, cholera took its toll. In
1883 of the 451 emigrants who had arrived in Surinam on the *Sheila*, 49 had died of
cholera.[117] Apart from disease aboard ships, the emigrants also suffered from home-

sickness. Sickness and death then, were constant dangers to the emigrants. Not-withstanding shipwrecks, the *Salsette*[118] in 1858 with many Dhangars aboard suf-fered the highest mortality. Of the 323 emigrants on this ship bound for Trinidad, 124 had died by the time the ship had docked at Port of Spain. From the Journal of the ship's Captain we get a clear picture of the full horror of this tragedy as it unfolded during the voyage which began on 17 March. On that first day when the ship left Calcutta, several Indians, separated from their families, were already sick. Were they sick before their medical inspection at the Depot? Or did they become mysteriously ill with fright at the moment of embarkation? We know that a sick old woman, though rejected on coming aboard was allowed to stay, because eighteen men were unwilling to make the journey without her. She died of cholera on the second day of the voyage.

The next day several Indians (referred to as 'Coolies' – then common usage – by Captain Edolphus Swinton) were sick; two days later a six-year old girl died of dysentery in her mother's arms and on the 24th an old woman died of diarrhoea. The composition of this shipload of Indians gradually emerged. Ten days into the voyage, Captain Swinton recorded that a four-year old orphan girl had died in a state of advanced emaciation. 'She was in this state when put on board', he wrote, 'with an aunt only ten years old, to take care of her'. The Captain proceeded, at this early stage of the journey, to say more of the plight of the Indians under his charge:

'An old woman brought a baby two years old, quite dead from starvation, having taken no food and having lost its father and mother before embarkation. Sent for the little girl two years old, before mentioned, and from her history it appears that her brother and sister died at the Depot before embarkation, and the infant was sent with her. Three children, from six to ten years old, were sent on board without parents. Saw a little boy dying on deck; a most dreadfully emaciated creature; won't eat'.

Captain Swinton noted that a little boy had died the day before and that an infant whose mother was sick and unable to nourish it died. He stressed the great need for preserved milk for the sad, howling emigrants who were dying for want of it;[119] and in the next few days infants, children, men and women of all ages were either dead or dying mainly because the food was not suited to them – dried fish was urgently needed for adults and milk for the children.

Mrs. Swinton, who undertook the journey with her husband, pitied the poor Indians, acting as a nurse, especially to the children and women. As the days passed, the growing number of deaths revealed the tragedy of the unfitness of many emig-rants and, in many cases, the break-up of families. Intimidation was indeed used to fill the immigrant ships. Following the death of a twenty-eight year old man, Capt-ain Swinton interrogated an old man and his sons, who admitted that they had been rejected by the doctor, but they were warned by the Sirdar at the Depot that if they did not get on board, he would beat them.

There seemed to be no age limit to those who boarded the *Salsette*. A seventy-five year old man, for example, who refused to eat for a few days died and the death of a number of infants was quite surprising. It is significant that the myth of the passive Indian woman was debunked judging by those, young and old, who were on the ship. In a desperate attempt to end her misery (on this sad and lonely ship of sickness, death and little or no hope), one woman suffered head injuries while trying to jump overboard; others in their own way hastened death. Mortality among the Indians increased each day, but what stands out is the number of infants and young children who were victims. The unfolding tragedy was left for posterity in six consecutive entries for April by Captain Swinton, who dutifully recorded:

| | |
|---|---|
| 3rd. | An infant died, who lost its mother. A coolie fell and cut his eye. |
| 4th. | An infant died, and a girl of twelve years old; also a fine lad of sixteen, gasping. Another girl died, ten years old. Two children died, three years old, and a little girl aged seven years, who lost her parents on board and has been lingering ten days. |
| 7th. | A little girl, five years old died with marks on the throat and back, and foot bruised (supposed murdered). Flogged father and mother; the father known to be of a desperately bad character in his own country. An old woman fifty years old died; the doctor said she had been rejected. Was allowed to come because many others would not come without her |
| 8th. | A girl three years old, died. |
| 9th. | Boy fifteen died; this completes the family of father and two sons, rejected at the depot for spleen enlargement. |
| 10th. | A little blind girl died, and now its mother is all but gone.[120] |

By the 16th April twenty-nine adults had died and many were sick, but amidst all this Captain Swinton noted that the 'Coolies were all merry'. As the days passed and more Indians died, it became clear that there was a reluctance among the Indians to report their illnesses. A boy six years old, who was dying, was brought up from the hold to see the doctor only at the last moments before he expired; and a young woman who had fallen down the fore-hatch and hurt her spine, kept the injury to herself. It was the ship's mate, a witness to the accident, who informed the doctor; and there were instances where Indians died through fear, many of them pining after entering the ship, unsure of their destinations. For those families who had decided to emigrate, sickness and death, either at the Depot or on the voyage, brought separation and inconsolable sorrow, leaving those who survived in a state of shock to the extent that some mothers, according to Captain Swinton, neglected their children.

The death toll had reached seventy by 3 May, and faced with this dreadful mortality, Captain Swinton noted that one should not wonder at this because the Indians were so badly neglected at the Depot, thus allowing many diseased people to enter his ship. He was of the general opinion that the Indians needed male and female nurses, who should be well-paid for their services. It had become quite clear to Captain Swinton that the food issue was crucial to the well-being of the Indians. He argued that 12 ounces of rice, without dhal was not enough (given the physically weak, emaciated state of many Indians) even though his wife did all she could, feeding the sick mutton broth and the infants' sago. A few days after the last member of the splenetic family had died, Captain Swinton felt helpless in the face of the rising mortality without any means of checking it. 'A great reformation is required in the system of Cooley emigration', he wrote.

Diarrhoea and dysentery had severe and fatal effects on the Indians, and so concerned was the doctor when a man died of dysentery that he was dissected and found to have had diseased tubes. On 8 June, as the last member of another family died, the death toll had reached 111 including 81 adults. Captain Swinton, it seemed, was more puzzled now than he had been since the voyage began. 'How very suddenly these people go off from apparent medium health to general debility', he observed, 'though kept up with port wine and soup'.[121]

Repeatedly on this voyage, the character of the Indian women was tested. The woman who had hurt her spine died a few days after the accident, but the pride and courage she had shown was also evident among others who hid their illnesses.

Overall, amidst the tragedies of this voyage, resilience, courage and determination were not lacking among the indentured labourers. Less than two weeks before landing at Port of Spain, and in spite of the alarming mortality, for three consecutive days, Captain Swinton noted that the Indians were in high spirits and, as he put it, they were 'very musical', performing their 'native games and war-dances'. Four days before the *Salsette's* arrival at Trinidad Captain Swinton reckoned up the number of Indians still alive and found only 108 men, 61 women and 80 children under ten years of age, two infants and two interpreters left of the 324 who had embarked at Calcutta. He feared another three would die before they reached the island. In fact, two more children died, and at the end of the voyage only 182 adults had landed alive. It is remarkable that this great loss of life was not due to an epidemic (which could so easily have devastated all aboard the ship) but to isolated cases of cholera, diarrhoea, dysentery, fear and accident, and perhaps more profoundly, to a general psychological debility. The Captain's request for an investigation into the high number of deaths was granted.

Captain Swinton did not live to see publication of his Journal, but his widow who had ensured its publication, added her observations on Coolie emigration. She first pointed out that the Captain of the ship transporting Indians to the West Indies had no voice, either in their selection or in the choice of the doctor, or in anything connected with their emigration. Of the 324 Indians who had boarded the *Salsette* at Calcutta, significantly, Mrs. Swinton did not believe that five at most knew their destination or what would be their occupation. The Indians were entrapped and many of them were clearly incapable of the work they were asked to perform. The need for changes in food on the ship, was stressed: different foods were necessary and more should be given in three meals a day, rather than two. She felt there was an urgent need for well-selected female nurses, particularly to attend to sick Indian women, who even in their apparently demoralized state would not 'take remedies from a man'. But in spite of all of Mrs. Swinton's undoubted acts of kindness and interest in the sufferings of the 'Coolies' (which seemed to be of secondary importance), her primary concern with the mortality rate was directly related to the financial loss of the shipowners! 'I think it is most unjust and illiberal to the owners of any Coolie ship', she wrote, 'to be paid only for such as are landed alive, particularly when put on board in such a diseased state by the emigration office in Calcutta'.[122]

Indeed the pecuniary interest of the *Salsette's* owners were at risk in that every dead Indian emigrant incurred a loss of £13 so that the deaths represented a total loss of £1,500 of the charter money. Ironically, before the *Salsette* had sailed, Captain Swinton was reminded by his agent in Calcutta that the Government would only pay him for the number of 'Coolies' landed alive![123]

Apart from the *Salsette*, the *Delharree,* also on a voyage to Trinidad from Calcutta, had a high death rate of over 8 per cent of the immigrants on board; and the *Souvenance,* a French ship with 376 emigrants from Pondicherry, bound for Martinique, mysteriously disappeared. In 1871, however, 167 bodies of Indians and wreckage were found along the shores of Natal.[124]

The mid-1850s were the 'most disastrous' years coinciding with the increase in annual migration to the Caribbean. If the early years of shipping indentured labour to the colonies revealed the lack of concern for the emigrants leaving India, as the system evolved, the Emigration authorities became aware of the need for stricter regulations relating to the safety and well-being of the Indians involved in this traffic. In fact, by the 1956–57 season, the mortality rate was 'beyond precedent'. According to one account, of the 4,094 emigrants who had left Calcutta on 12 ships, 707 or 17 per cent died. Mortality among infants was highest 53. 76 percent, followed by children at 30.09 per cent.

By comparison with the previous years 1850–56, the average mortality rate was only 3.7 per cent or 20 per cent of the succeeding 1856–57 period. Further, for the latter period, compared with the emigrant ships leaving the port of Madras, the deaths occurring on the Calcutta ships were seventeen times greater.[125] Among those most affected during the early phase of emigration were the 'Hill Coolies'. The death rate among these people declined, in part, because there was a greater demand for their labour by tea planters. By the 1864–65 season, however, the mortality rate of ships bound for Guyana was again appalling – 30.01 per cent compared with 3.03 per cent for the Trinidad voyages. The reason advanced for this marked difference was the fact that the British Guiana Depot was on the bank of the polluted Hooghly (Hughli) River, while the Trinidad Depot was about half a mile away.

Further comparisons can be made concerning the disparity in mortality levels on Calcutta and Madras emigrant ships, given the higher mortality rate of the former compared with the latter – 13.18 per cent on the former compared with 1.23 per cent on the latter, during 1856–1860.

Emigration officials have tried to explain the dissimilarity by arguing that the emigrants borne on the Calcutta ships were exposed to the unhealthy climate in and around the Hooghly River and the Sand Heads, while the location of Madras was less of a health risk; that the north Indians were a more land-bound people, lacking physical stamina for the tedious, dangerous sea voyage; and that the broody Bengali tended to suffer from fear and helplessness and could do little to avert the modification or loss of his traditional way of life.

By contrast, it was argued that the Madrasis were better equipped to cope with the sea voyage because they lived in villages not far from the sea; that they were more inclined to migrate for employment than the Bengali; that they needed less 'seasoning' for the voyage than the north Indians; and that there was less acquiescence to conditions at the Immigration Depot among the Madrasis than among the Indians from the north. Furthermore, embarkation procedures were different at the two ports: it seemed there was closer supervision in the provision of pure (distilled) water and qualified Surgeons at Madras and a longer period of detention at the Depot, which helped to detect persons affected with disease before they embarked, although this did not imply a total lack of concern at Calcutta. There were also general differences in attitude between the Bengalis and Madrasis aboard ship. The former was prone to be apathetic, staying below deck, while the latter stayed on deck as long as possible, being active, engaging in singing and 'merry-making'. Another noticeable difference between the two groups of emigrants was the superior physique of the Madrasi.[126]

By 1861–62, although the average mortality rates remained high, they were lower than during the previous decade, essentially because of the greater concern to prevent the spread of Asiatic cholera (which raged at the Calcutta Depot and during the Calcutta-Caribbean voyages) and other forms of sickness through the use of distilled water and the employment of qualified surgeons from the Australian service.

Against this scenario of death and disease, though the potential remained high, only on one occasion had there been any evidence of shipboard revolt among the emigrants. This happened a few years after the Indian Mutiny when about 30 sepoys (Indian soldiers), perhaps trying to escape persecution had managed to get past the emigration Depot administrators and made an abortive attempt to mutiny aboard the *Clasmerden* on her voyage to British Guiana.

Like the African slaves before them, the Indians either committed suicide or resisted conditions on the ship as best they could in their frightened and unhappy state. The biscuit diet full of weevils, not only unfit for human consumption, but also inadequate to sustain life on the rough seas, contributed to the emaciated, skeletal and dying emigrants. The high mortality, over ten times that on Government ships sailing to Australia, spurred the Colonial Office bureaucracy into action which, unfortunately, came too late for many Indians. Characteristically, thoughout these crucial years of drama, horror and disease, death and shipwreck, as one writer observed, the Indian emigrants survived preserving that 'stoical acceptance of fate which is the strength of the Indian poor'.[127]

# VOYAGERS' VOICES

In the last years of emigration, to get a better idea of the Indians' view of the voyage to the Caribbean, let us return to the personal accounts of Fazal, Moolian, Maharani, Bharath and Sankar.

On the voyage Fazal said the ship stopped at Natal (South Africa), for coal and water; and at British Guiana for a couple of hours, before coming to Trinidad. And for the first time (not knowing he would meet such people again in the island to which he was bound), while he was in Natal, he saw Africans. But more demanding of his attention on this journey was the overwhelming power of the oceans. He was particularly impressed by the colours of the sea (white, black, green and brown), the roughest being the journey up the Atlantic from the Cape of Good Hope, the ship tossing from side to side, as the emigrants sought cover from the spray.

Although he said that there was no fear among the Indians at the Calcutta Depot (almost certainly an exaggeration), Fazal talked about some of them resorting to prayer on the ship. He himself did not pray, but he said that the Christians were 'making noise like hell', which he did not consider as prayer. 'La ella ellallah Mohammed rassul ellall', was far more like the prayer he understood and respected. Bawling was not praying, and as the voyage neared its end, he became preoccupied with Mother earth as his God, the one and only God.[128]

Moolian was a little carefree boy when his voyage began, and after the ship had travelled for several days, it stopped for coal at South Africa, where he also first saw Africans. He was struck by their darkness and the fact that they carried baskets of coal. He seemed more impressed by the 'so big' ship he was in, and remembered drinking tea in the morning and climbing up on deck, where he felt the strong winds and saw the vastness of the moody silvery sea. At the sound of a bell at midday, the emigrants were steadied by a rope wound around them, which they held on to steadfastly to enable them to move along the swaying ship, otherwise they would have fallen.

The noise on the ship was particularly disturbing, Moolian said, mimicking the sound 'doong, doong, doong'. On Sunday mornings, he had a bath, changed his clothes and ate goat meat and channa. And here too, at all times, bachelor men and the women were separated from each other and monitored by the watchful gaze of the White men. On this voyage, as in many others, the regimen of separation from their homeland, their family and friends was too much for many indentured Indians, regardless of the circumstances of their departure. Moolian believed that for every ship making the journey to Trinidad, one life had to be sacrificed, and the vessel he was in was not exempted. Suicide was not uncommon: he recalls one man taking his life by jumping overboard.[129]

Maharani remembered five girls ('gyuls') on the ship, who were unaccompanied, as they milled about among the emigrants. Was Maharani encouraged by the presence of other women? She did not say. On the voyage, unlike many of the Indians, she did not vomit because 'me no eating all kinda ting'. Rice and dahl, she accepted, but refused fish and meat. And by contrast with the depressing voyage of the *Salsette* some fifty years before, in these last years of Indian emigration to the Caribbean, Maharani gives us this impression of the mood of the emigrants aboard ship:

> everybody beating drum an dancing in de boat
> dem gi dem drum an ting
> dem eh bringing no trouble
> dem bringing happy
> nobody to study notting
> das why dem bringing happy.

Such seeming merriment as there was, she said, was interrupted 'when submarine coming'. Then the lights were put out, the singing stopped and everyone was silent. One of the surprises on her journey to Trinidad was seeing a 'kirwal' (African) for the first time at Natal, where the ship had stopped. 'I never know dat nation', she said, 'I never see da kind people'. Another aspect of the journey which stood out in Maharani's memory, was the sleeping arrangements for the emigrants. As she put it: 'one one side man, one one side oman'.[130]

In 1910, after all the immigration procedures and his final thoughts of leaving his father and mother, his village and India, and with no idea of where he was going, Bharath finally boarded his ship, which was bound for Trinidad. He too, spoke of the separate sleeping arrangements for single and married men and women, during the voyage on a ship with sails. The sea was rough and clothes were changed when it was cold /or wet, or both. Food on the 'boat', as he described the ship, did not bother him and he recalled eating 'peynoose', made from cow's milk.

Further into the voyage, Bharath recalled a badly-behaved Indian being disciplined, having his foot tied to the ship (flogging was not unusual) and an incident involving an Indian woman who had to go to Jamaica, while her Indian admirer had no choice but to get off at Trinidad. The man wanted to marry the woman, and because this would not have been possible, given their different destinations, the man cut-off her nose. Bharath felt that the emigration of Indian women to Trinidad was a positive move, and he was right in that it would have helped to even-out the provocative imbalance in the ratio of Indian women to Indian men on the Caribbean plantations. But then he added 'De oman go make cheren, go make country rich', adopting a position (though it is unlikely that this was his intention) that could have been misconstrued as being not dissimilar to the Colonial officials who, even at that stage of Indian emigration, were determined to keep the system of indentureship alive. And for all those Indians, who came with him, and those who had preceded or followed him, he had an all-embracing warmth and highly-charged emotional relationship, a feeling of brotherhood. As he says: 'everybody coming, any ship coming, me, all a dem, I go an meet e an cry bhaiya (brother) wha country you come from'.[131]

On the ship in which Sankar came, many of the indentured emigrants had signed for 'B.G.' (British Guiana), while others were contracted for 'Chinedad' (Trinidad). He said when he entered the 'boat', he was given a tin disc with a number on it, attached to a piece of string and put around his neck, his garland of goodbye to India and to freedom, as he had known it. Every emigrant, man, woman and child had one, with different numbers inscribed for 'B.G' and Trinidad. With their identification badges in place, they were then counted and separated accordingly. Did they have a choice? Maybe not, for this was the Immigration officials' prerogative. And even if they did have a choice, with no prior knowledge, they would have been none the wiser in their selection of either place.

Sankar reiterated what we already know about the sleeping arrangements aboard ship for men and women and also spoke about the hospital which not only had a doctor, but also a nurse, the latter so desperately needed on the *Salsette*'s voyage 52 years earlier. Sankar confirms the kind of amusements that engaged the emigrants attention. On deck, he said, they engaged in card-games, played music and sang. But even these pleasant distractions were inadequate in the face of each day, when he said you go upon deck and 'sit down watching the sea, watching the sea all de time'.

Giddiness was the most disturbing aspect of Sankar's voyage. He felt he was going to die. He could not eat, and if he vomited, there was nothing to 'trow up'. All he could do was to 'lie down one side'. His life, he felt, was ebbing away.

Occasionally, he would ask the doctor for a biscuit. Eventually, overcome by hunger, he was forced to eat something and after drinking a mixture of sugar and water, he would lay down. When he was not feeling giddy, he would go on deck and because he was not interested in card-playing, he sat 'watching the water', he said, repeating himself, as he had done several times before, 'watching the water'.

Sankar felt strongly about those Indians who committed suicide during the journey. If they wanted to kill themselves, he said,'dey nuh have to make everybody see'. One jump is all it took and 'dey gone'. At that stage, it was no good worrying about the fact that they could not go back.

Discipline on the ship was strict, and Sankar remembered one Indian being severely beaten and tied, and made to stand all day and night without food. He did not say much more than that a 'oman' was involved. The partition, which separated the men and women, it seemed was not enough of a deterrent for determined individuals.

Not long after leaving India, Sankar said the 'White man' pointed out 'Lanka' (Ceylon, now Sri Lanka) a 'lil white' speck on the ocean. At that moment, he could not comprehend where he was in the vast expanse of the sea that stretched out before him; and yet it is possible that the sight of land so near to India, may have renewed the hope that his voyage would be short. But this was not to be. Day and night, for two and a half months, 'only water, only water', is all he could see, and after two and a half months, the ship reached British Guiana, discharging those indentured Indians assigned there, before proceeding to Trinidad.[132]

So it was that these five Indians, with hundreds of thousands of their bonded compatriots who had gone before them, came to form not only an integral part of the expanding and ever-changing Indian diaspora, but also an important focus of demographic charge, struggle and development, which followed Emancipation of the African slaves in the Caribbean.

# EUROPEAN PERCEPTIONS AND ATTITUDES TOWARDS AFRICANS

As mentioned above, when Europeans first made trading contact with Africans their attitude was more or less, one of respect for Africans as allies and partners. But with the passage of time and superior technological knowledge, the divisions of the coastal states in West Africa were exploited by competing European nations for African captives, and the degradation and death which attended the African slave trade across the Atlantic Ocean brought a change for the worse.[133]

Misunderstandings based on fear and ignorance, and nurtured by greed, grew rapidly between Europeans and Africans. By the eighteenth century, most Europeans were convinced (or had convinced themselves) that Africans generally were barbarous people who practised cannibalism. Anti-Slavery agitations, however, had forced Europeans to reconsider their view of Africans and increasingly two opposing views evolved. As Davidson wrote 'the traditional tending to hold that Africa had ever possessed cultures that were worthy of respect or even of serious investigation (and the) scientific, tending to argue the reverse.'

Although abolition of the Slave Trade added a greater sense of inquiry about Africans, it was not long before the 'scramble for Africa' reversed whatever progressive trend there might have been towards a better understanding and respect for African peoples, their religion and cultures. So deeply ingrained were their attitudes that by the turn of the twentieth century, European opinion of Africans were essentially racist.[134]

European perceptions and expressed opinions, on the other hand, were no less condescending. During the course of their long presence in India, the British remained aloof, harbouring ambivalent, and at times, racist and benevolent attitudes in an attempt to justify their rule. Of course, their conquest of India was not for the benefit of the Indians, as indeed it was for the British, who saw themselves as the superior race. Commenting on the comparison made of British rule in India and the Romans in Greece, in terms of the ability to confer peace, order, law and justice upon the conquered peoples, it was argued that both Imperial governments were convinced that they had every right to dominate their subjects and therefore conceived their 'civilizing mission in messianic terms'. In this sense, it was pointed out that although the examples of cultural tolerance and humility were few and far between, among the administrators of both conquering nations, there was nevertheless a consensus of opinion that the Roman and the Briton had come dangerously close to acquiring a divine right to rule.[135]

But whatever similarities there might have been between the Roman and British Empires, they were fundamentally dissimilar in this respect: at the outset, 'a sense of guilt and the desire for atonement' remained an insistent element throughout British rule in India in spite of a disposition 'for fanfare and pride in grandeur' that ended with Curzon. 'What better for men burdened by moral doubts', it was stressed, 'than to disavow considerations of narrow self-justification, self-interest or shallow grandeur to invoke the utilitarian creed as an answerable justification?'[136]

In the early years of British penetration of the Subcontinent (prior to the Crown's assumption of full responsibility from the East India Company) it was not by accident, but by design that a 'gifted and eccentric ruling class' took full responsibility for the government of India. Unlike their contact with Africa, the British handed down to the alien Asiatics 'the spirit of the Renaissance ... the Reformation and the Enlightenment'. Although the British had fully exploited divisions among the African coastal states, needing new horizons, they persisted in their civilizing mission in India, as if by divine right, of dealing with the alien Hindu by effectively destroying the menace of 'Oriental despotism', an insistent irritant. In their attempts to do so, the British became the 'chief landlord ... an improving proprietor on an enormous scale'. Whatever divisions there had been in India (and there were, and still are, an enormous variety) the imposition of these, at times, contradictory British standards would have a countervailing and unifying effect that would, in time and in turn, help Indian nationalists to free India from alien rule.

It was felt among the alien rulers that the Indians needed to be guided, to save them from themselves. In short, the government of India should be left in the hands of a handful of Englishmen. Several theories have been advanced towards the government of India and in the 'state of muddle', four approaches emerged:

Burkean trusteeship, Platonic guardianship, Benthamite utilitarianism and Evangelicalism.

These doctrines were useful for Imperial administration, as well as apologetics;[137] and at various times, these approaches were adopted by the British ruling elite in India. They could all become legitimate theories if they were underscored by a divine right. But, as Seeley pointed out, the British could not easily astonish the Hindu.

If there were contradictions in Burkean trusteeship, platonic guardianship and Benthamite utilitarianism, what was necessary for the British to justify their rule in India was the integration of a providential element. This, to some extent, was provided by Evangelicalism and the Evangelicals (men of action and emotion, who avoided theological subtleties and speculations) especially Wilberforce, who stirred the British conscience in its attitude to colonials. The Evangelicals, however, had no doubt that British rule in India was a divine dispensation.[138]

Even though the interaction between the four doctrines was disjointed and lacking in stability, what united them was the view disseminated primarily by the Evangelicals, that India was corrupt and hopeless and did not particularly mind tyranny. Moreover, the four doctrines had been applied in various ways, at various times and were abused.

Apart from the many phases through which the four doctrines had been during British rule in India, the diverse personalities of the various rulers and the disharmony between the doctrines, much attention was focused on the nature of the system that was installed and finally abandoned; a 'centralized, enlightened despotism', which even though it became 'an elaborate, autocratic bureaucracy' was essentially a despotism founded on the view that the British had to do what the Indians could not do for themselves.

Within the system, utilitarianism compensated for the absence of communication between the British ruling elite and the subordinate classes, but was unable to cope with the social and cultural problems of the country. In effect, the system was maintained by divide and rule, unable to satisfy its objectives and obligations equally to the British people as well as the Indians. As it was, what the system was unable to provide for the people of India was, in part, contributed by the moral code and personalities of the proud and exclusive caste of men who administered it.

Historically, at different times, the four main doctrines were challenged by Indian nationalists, including Ram Mohun Roy, Ranade, Gokhale and Gandhi. Before Gandhi it was common for nationalists to attack the system rather than appeal to the individual. Gandhi's unique contribution encompassed many methods. Appealing to the British conscience, he criticised British Imperial political theory and expressed a lack of confidence in the system.[139] In short, he challenged the assumptions underlying trusteeship, guardianship, utilitarianism and evangelicalism, stressing that British Imperialists were victims of a bad system, therefore it was the system that should be destroyed rather than the individual, and he attacked the utilitarian rather than the moral principles of British Imperialism.

Underlying the triumphs and failures of the political theories of British rule in India was the fact that the system was indeed a despotism administered by aliens whose downfall came by the application of their doctrines.

Of the four doctrines, Iyer argued that apart from other aspects of their appeal, they could also be employed to justify authoritarian regimes and enlightened benevolent despotisms. 'More generally and more plausibly', he wrote, 'an imperialist could claim that he can protect the negative liberties of his subjects better than they could do by themselves or through representatives of their own race and nationality'.[140]

Such deeply held Imperial notions over the centuries, have affected European attitudes and perceptions of both Africans and Indians, so much so that the stereotype became the norm, wherever these people were to be found. Referring to African and Indian emigrants in the nineteenth century, it is instructive to consider what Lord Harris, Governor of Trinidad and Tobago said: 'The only independence which they would desire is idleness, according to their different tastes in the enjoyment of it; and the higher motives which actuate the European labourer … that to be independent in circumstances, whatever his station raises a man in the moral scale amongst his race; and that his ability to perform his duties as a citizen, and, we may add, as Christians, is increased by it. These, and such motives as these, are unknown to the fatalist worshippers of Mahomet and Brahma, and the savages who go by the names of liberated Africans'.[141]

Such perceptions and attitudes were to be found at the very core of the frontiers of British Imperialism overseas; and it was against this background that the indentured emigrants left the strictures of their various communities deeply rooted in ancient Indian tradition, hopeful (and no doubt fearful), but nonetheless ignorant of the open prison that was the Caribbean plantations, which they were about to enter.

# CHAPTER TWO

# INDENTURESHIP, FREE INDIANS AND ABOLITION OF THE 'SYSTEM' (1838–1920)

## THE INDENTURESHIP EXPERIENCE
## BRITISH GUIANA

Compared with other Caribbean countries receiving Indian indentured emigrants, in terms of physical size, British Guiana, located at the northern end of South America is much larger than the islands of Jamaica and Trinidad and Tobago. But although it covers an area of approximately 83,000 square miles, only a narrow area of land along the coast (between thirty and forty miles at its widest point), covering an estimated 1,750 square miles had been under continuous occupation and cultivation. One of the constant problems in this water-logged area of land is persistent flooding both from the invading waters of the sea and heavy rains.[1]

For the European colonizers, it was therefore crucial to keep the cultivated land properly drained. The Dutch experience and their development of a technology of land reclamation has helped to make agricultural production in this coastal area viable. In the aftermath of slavery, the free labourers were engaged by planters to fulfil work schedules before they received payment for their nine-hour working day. These 'schedules' were comprised of two major tasks: first the physically demanding job of digging canals and 'throwing back six-foot parapets from above – 72 feet in nine hours'.[2]

The effect of persistent flood and drought on the lives of working people generally were, at times, catastrophic and predictably sea defence, drainage and irrigation were problems that preoccupied not only the capitalist planters, but also those upon whom they depended most – the land-bound labourers and small peasant farmers. So it was that the various waves of incoming Indian indentured workers were all confronted with the obvious and pressing ecological preconditions of life and labour.

In terms of ecological conditions, British Guiana was markedly different from Trinidad and Tobago. After Emancipation, the estimated 70,000 slaves did not have the option of occupying either unclaimed hilly land or 'subsistence plots'. They were confronted with the stark fact that the bulk of the best land for cultivation was to be found on the strip of coastal land, bounded by the Essequibo and Corentyne rivers. This area was further demarcated to the South by forest; and given that deeper towards the interior, the soil was largely unsuitable for cultivation, those intrepid pioneers who had left the coastal plain found their progress checked by the forbidding reaches of dense forest which constituted 84 per cent of the area of British.[3]

Even though free from the restrictions of slavery, the former slaves were now faced, on the one hand by the sea, and on the other, by the forests of the interior. For many there was no option but to stay on the flat land along the coast which was 'relatively underpopulated'. But having been freed from the trammels of estate labour, as in Trinidad and Tobago, the former slaves in British Guiana had no inclination to return to the estates to labour under the prevailing conditions. 'The emancipated slaves were willing to work after 1838, but positively not as wage earners', Williams argued. 'This aspiration to peasant proprietorship was clearly more easy of attainment in British Guiana, with its open spaces, than in Barbados, where all land was appropriated'.[4]

Unlike Jamaica, however, British Guiana and Trinidad were relatively underpopulated plantation economies by 1838 when slavery was abolished in the British Caribbean. Both colonies also had large areas of unreclaimed land that could be brought into sugar cultivation and food production, which further encouraged the ever-present desire among ex-slaves for full independence from their masters, through the acquisition of land. At the time, the planters in British Guiana and Trinidad and Tobago were economically better placed to win financial support that would enable them to pay for the desired Indian indentured labour, so that the current level of sugar production could, at least, be maintained.

Soon after abolition in British Guiana, lands along the coast became available with the abandonment of a few plantations; some were purchased either by absentee speculators or by groups of former slaves, who pooled their resources.[5] Williams has noted that emancipated slaves were able to buy plantations from a price range of £2,000 to £16,000; and Farley cites their accumulation of capital by selling foodstuffs and savings from Apprenticeship savings, which they used to purchase land, shared out as lots among them.

The freedom of movement afforded by the former slaves' purchases of lands and squatting, led to their occupation of an increasing area along the coast, resulting in 'peasant freehold and village development'.[6] So that by the time that the first Indians were imported into British Guiana, the freed slaves had already embarked upon a determined effort to establish themselves on the available lands around the sugar estates.

## First Arrivals

Aboard the *Whitby* and *Hesperus* (the first 'coolie' ships that sailed to the Caribbean colonies), the majority of the first Indian immigrants to arrive in British Guiana were the Dhangars[7] from the Chota Nagpur area of northern India. These people were identified as 'Coolies', a term that had (as mentioned earlier) by the eighteenth century been used to describe manual workers at the bottom rungs of the labour market, such as the porter and labouring classes.[8] The presence and allocation[9] of these bewildered, illiterate, impoverished people to various Guianese sugar plantations was evidence of the success achieved through private recruitment by John Gladstone (father of the English politician), Messrs. Davidson, Barclay and Company, Andrew Colville and Messrs. John and Henry Moss, all plantation owners.[10] The Indians who had arrived on 5 May 1838 on the *Whitby* were the concern of Davidson, Barclay and Company, and Andrew Colville, who owned the Highbury, Waterloo, Berbice and Belle Vue estates. Fortunately, of the 249 immigrants who had left India in January 1838, only five had died. Those considered to be fit and well were dispatched in various directions: 117 including three women and six children were allocated to Highbury; forty-seven to Waterloo and Berbice, and eighty, including two women, to Belle Vue. By the time that the Indians on the *Hesperus* had landed in Georgetown, sometime between 8–10 May 1838, thirteen of its 165 immigrants had died. John Gladstone, who owned two of the three estates to which the immigrants were bound, was among the main beneficiaries during this early period of East Indian immigration.[11]

This experiment in acquiring Indian labourers, however, was fraught with danger and difficulties. Overnight, it was not to be expected that the planters, who had profited enormously from slavery, would change their basic approach (in terms of attitude and practice) towards the labour at their command. Before Lord John Russell's prescient warning in February 1840 (concerning the transfer of labourers from British India to British Guiana) that such a movement of people was likely to lead to a dreadful loss of life, on the one hand, and on the other, to a new system of slavery, the portents were there for the abuse and maltreatment of the Indians who were entering the plantations. By all accounts (except, of course, the planters and their supporters' version), the 'first batches' of indentured immigrants who had landed in 1838, served a rigorous term of hard labour. If slave labour was in deed a hard act to follow, this was precisely the kind of work scenario within which the indentured Indians were expected to give (under the watchful eyes of their employers – the former slave-owners) a virtuoso economic performance. And to compound their problems, their introduction to the various territories were bitterly opposed, not only by the Black (African) and coloured middle classes, but more importantly by working class Blacks and the black peasantry that had emerged. The Indians were, in the main, derided by Blacks for their strange dress habits and religion, and the fact that as cheap indentured labour, they had a depressing effect on the bargaining value of 'free' Black labour. Thus, they appeared to many as strangers; an unwelcome reminder not only of the Blacks' slave past, but more immediately and threateningly as competitors.

## Violence and Death

Fortunately the atrocities of the African Slave Trade was still fresh in the minds of those who forcefully and publicly opposed it, and were now vigilant during the 'illegal' slave trade and similar actions taken to coerce colonial labour. To this end, in 1837 Thomas Fowell Buxton had set up his Aborigines Protection Society and two years later, the British and Foreign Anti-Slavery Society was established.

Generally, the decade of the 1830s was a time of real concern by a group of people from the British and Indian communities on social and political issues in India. These reformers, based in Calcutta, published the influential *Friend of India*, through which their ideas were expressed on education, law reform, freedom of the press, local self-government and religious toleration. The revelation of Thomas Boaz, a member of this group, that 'coolies' were being kidnapped in Calcutta and that Indian labourers were ill-treated in Mauritius, aroused unusual public curiosity and indignation, resulting in the call for a full enquiry. Subsequently, the Government of Bengal, Madras and Bombay were instructed to stop the shipping of emigrants to the West Indies, an action which was also applied to all the other British colonies and Ceylon.[12] Other enquiries were made concerning the exportation of 'Hill Coolies' in 1838, and the Committee formed to do so, amassed a great deal of evidence which, published in 1840, exposed the evils of recruiting indentured labour in India.

Apart from the Calcutta enquiry, the Indian Government encouraged the setting up of a Commission of Enquiry in Mauritius. In the far outpost of British Guiana, however, where the first two shiploads of indentured Indians laboured, all seemed well according to William Bertie Wolseley, acting Agent for Emigrants, who took the view that the coolies had adapted well enough and had suffered no disadvantage by emigrating to the colony. The death toll among them, by his reckoning, was only fifteen,[13] but this report, in the light of evidence gleaned from further inquiry, proved to be false. The British public was first informed of this matter in the *British Emancipator* on 9 January 1839. 'I see the British public has been deceived', its reporter stated, 'with the idea that the coolies are doing 'well'; such is not the fact; the poor friendless creatures are miserably treated, at least I can speak confidently of plantation Belle Vue. On this estate they have made two attempts to escape as they say to go to Calcutta'. The plight of the harrassed Indians, in this strange land, also caught the attention of the British Anti-Slavery Society which sent its Secretary, John Scoble, to British Guiana, where he was provided with an alarming report of abuse of the Indians on the estates.

In these early years, the indentureship experience was especially severe and even fifteen years after its inception, Edward Jenkins, an allegedly impartial British observer, recorded the intolerable conditions that the Indians were subjected to:

> Take a large factory in Manchester, or Birmingham, or Belfast, build a wall round it, shut in its people from all intercourse save at rare intervals, with the outside world, keep them in absolute ignorance, and get all the work you can out of them, treat them not unkindly, leave their social habits and relations to themselves, as matters not concerning you who make the money from their labour, and you would have constituted a little community resembling, in no small degree, a sugar estate village in British Guiana.[14]

There followed the appointment of a Commission of enquiry to look into the serious allegations of gross ill-treatment of the Indians; and although the documentation of first-hand accounts of the Indians' sufferings under the 'system' is sparse, we are nevertheless afforded glimpses of their harsh experience. 'The coolies were locked up in the sick house', Will Clay, foreman of the Vreeden Hoop plantation told the Commission, adding that he 'saw them today after they were flogged; their backs were swollen; they were in the sick house for two days after flogging'. Alexander Barrington, a labourer on the same plantation attested: 'When they run away and are stubborn, they get two or three lickings; they are flogged with cat-o'-nine tails; they were tied with a rope round the post and were licked on the bare back'. Other labourers on the Vreeden Hoop plantation told the same story of severe, bloody floggings with cat-o'-nine tails, and the sick nurse Betsy Ann spoke of the Indians being hospitalized with bruised backs. Of course, the Indians' dread of the plantation, and their desire to escape within the short time that they had been in British Guiana, is not surprising, especially in the light of evidence given by Naran, a labourer on the estate. 'Their hands were tied behind their backs', he said, 'they were beaten with a rope; ten times they lick them; heard them complain to manager Mr. Jacob lick Moduir every day. When licked they put the breast to the post with hands stretched out; some tie hands before, some behind. Coolies run away because they are licked'.[15] Henry Jacob and Charles Scharhib, overseer on the estates, were convicted and charged with maltreatment of the Indians.

In addition to the violence meted out to them, the Indians were beset by much sickness resulting in a high death rate. Of the 396 emigrants who had arrived in May 1838, sixty-four had died by September 1839. Plantations Highbury and Belle Vue had the largest percentage of deaths. The driver's whip and overall violence then and later, though fearsome were integral to the Indians working conditions on the estates. It is no wonder that in their sadder moods, during a life of boredom within the confines of the plantations, the descendants of these exploited people should come to express themselves in song recalling in essence, the indentured experience of fear and insecurity.

> On one side are sitting Pama and Pulma;
> On the other side sits Hulkar.
> Pama said to Pulma, 'Wake up all the Kafris'
> "How much work do you have for them?" asked the boss.
> 'To cut Number 20 field'.
> The Kafris were hardly sleeping when they were awakened.
> They awoke startled, and Pulma reported,
> 'I have shown them their way at 5 AM.,
> To cut the cane in Number 20 field.'
> With cutlasses in their hands the Kafris ate half-boiled
> rice and plaintain.
> Reaching Number 20 they crossed trenches after trenches,
> full of alligators,
> And began to work.
> So the ships and chains began to pour on them.
> What's next, oh Lord?
> Our bread is snatched away too.[16]

## Immigration Ban and Resumption

Although the blame for atrocities committed were attributed to the intractable Indians instead of the planters, the British Government, reluctant to concede that private recruiters would ensure the emigrants' welfare, stopped Indian emigration between 1838 and 1844.

Predictably, the emigration ban was opposed by planters in Mauritius and the Caribbean, but countervailing efforts were made by the Anti-Slavery movement to maintain the embargo. They took their agitation outside Parliament and addressed the public both through meetings and in the press in London and Calcutta. Unfortunately, the force of public opinion which the Movement had, to some extent, won and sustained since the 1820s was lost by the early 1840s. The planters seized the advantage, pressing their claims with greater urgency. In fact, the deterioration of the labour situation in British Guiana, was aggravated as free workers drifted from the estates into peasant proprietorship.[17]

During the suspension of Indian emigration, the planters insisted that more labour was necessary. Consequently, 4,729 labourers from Madeira temporarily filled the gap.[18] But this too was stopped in May 1842. A number of factors contributed to this stoppage. While the wages they received in British Guiana were higher than in Madeira (between 4–6 pence per day in Madeira as compared to 4 shillings per day in Guiana) this worked against them, thereby leading to the failure of this form of immigration. Though willing and eager to adapt to the more strenuous conditions of labour in British Guiana, they became increasingly ill-suited and, in spite of the relatively high wages they received, they put their precarious health at further risk by buying the cheapest food (lacking in nutritious value and which they were unaccustomed to) so that they could save the rest of their money. As a consequence, the Madeirans became too ill to work and the high death rate among them became cause for concern.[19]

A few months later, in December 1842 emigration was permitted from the ports of Calcutta, Madras and Bombay through Act XV which regulated the emigration of native inhabitants of the territories under the government of the East India Company to Mauritius. In 1843, the Colonial Office made representations to the Court of Directors requesting that in view of the serious difficulties facing the sugar industry in British Guiana, and the West Indian colonies generally, the ban on Indian emigration should be lifted as was the case with Mauritius. Lord Ellenborough replied to the Directors on 9 March 1844, pointing out the problems involved in emigration from India to the West Indies. Responding to some of the questions raised, Lord Stanley suggested emigration should be allowed only to British Guiana, Trinidad and Jamaica and proposed that one official should take overall responsibility. Thus, the resumption of Indian emigration to British Guiana in 1844 saw the appointment of Thomas Caird at Calcutta to act as Agent for the three colonies and Captain Wilson, as Agent at Madras.

Through Lord Stanley's intervention in 1844, the British Guiana Court of Directors, were persuaded to increase the number of immigrants from 2,000 to 5,000. Moreover, 5,000 and 2,500 were allocated to Jamaica and Trinidad, respectively.[20] On 26 January 1845, the first emigrant ship the *Lord Hungerford* was allowed to leave the port of Calcutta since the embargo was imposed, with 362 indentured Indians, and so Indian emigration was resumed without further delay.

During this period, Indian emigration never developed on a large scale and three years later, the financial crisis in the sugar colonies, the improper administration of labour recruitment in India and care of the Indians on arrival in the colonies, brought the indentured traffic to an end again in 1848. 'It has become necessary', the Colonial Office informed the Board of Control on 14 February 1848, 'to relinquish the idea of sending any more coolies to them (the West Indian planters) for the present, at least'.[21]

This action was well received by the concerned Calcutta press which published Major Fagan's letter to Lord Harris, Governor of Trinidad, condemning the unrelenting, 'ungrateful and heartless neglect' of the Indians. Harris, in turn, wrote Lord Grey, Secretary of State for the Colonies agreeing with most of the charges and cited a number of reasons for the general failure of Indian emigration. Revealing his own prejudice, however, he resorted to a stereotypical argument against the Indians, namely their habit of wandering and vagrancy.[22] Harris's words carried much weight, and as early as 1845, the wandering habits of the indentured Indian (already confined in his movements by the laws of indenture) was to be even more severely dealt with through the enforcement of proposed vagrancy laws, as contained in the Labour Ordinance of 1846.

When emigration was opened again in 1851, with additional restrictive legislation, emigrants arriving after that date could only lay claim to free return passages after completion of five years 'industrial residence'. About six years later, a change in Government policy further circumscribed the emigrants''liberty', and in an effort to keep them as indentured labourers on the estates between 1851 and 1853, instead of alleviating the strictures placed upon them, the legislature introduced additional inducements for them to renew their indentures. The Des Voeux Commission stated that the effect of the latter legislation had been to keep the immigrant population, as a whole, out of the free labour market and argued that although no man was bound to indenture a second time, the system was so carefully constructed as to exert upon labourers a 'strong inducement to reindenture'.[23]

In effect, the rough justice imposed upon the Indian immigrants resulted in employer rights being zealously protected as immigrants held on to the 'slenderest of protections'.[24] While the Indians resisted their oppressors (either individually or in small groups) at every opportunity, especially at this critical time of their indentured history, two of those colonial administrators (vastly more fortunate than their charges were, and well-placed in the Colonial hierarchy) who campaigned on their behalf were James Crosby and George William Des Voeux.

As a champion of the indentured Indians' cause in British Guiana, Crosby, the Immigration Agent-General opposed both planters and local Government officials. Deeply sympathetic to their vulnerable position, he waged an extraordinary battle in their defence against his chief adversary, Sir Francis Hincks, Governor of British Guiana from 1862 to 1869.

Before Crosby (a graduate of Trinity College, Cambridge and a Barrister-at-Law) went to British Guiana, he had served in various important posts on the island of St.Vincent. The imprecision of the 1864 Ordinance allowed Crosby the latitude to use his own discretion in all matters connected with his duties without reference to the Governor, except in matters of extreme importance.[25] 'I had in effect almost the entire control of the Immigration Department', he stated, 'that is to say, I exercised under all circumstances my own discretion, subject of course to the approbation or disapprobation of the Governor. If a difficulty arose, I consulted him, and if occasionally his acquiescence and authority was necessary under the Act I applied to him; but otherwise I was completely at the head of an important department'.[26] The intervention of officialdom was vital if the wrongs of the Indians were to be redressed, and clearly such matters could not have been more fitting than in this case.

In 1864 relations between Crosby and Governor Hincks had become very difficult because of Crosby's continuing defence of the Indians' grievances which did not meet with the Governor's approval. Thereafter, the relationship between the two men deteriorated, and Crosby's powers were so diminished that he became 'a sort of chief clerk in an office directed in its minutest detail by the governor in person'.[27] Isolated, he nevertheless had to obtain approval from the Governor before prosecution could be brought against an employer on behalf of an emigrant. In spite of this cumbersome procedure, Crosby persisted, thus attracting even more official rebuffs and warnings.[28]

Crosby tried to explain the demerits of the guidelines suggested, but was overruled and the administration of the Indians was placed firmly under the Governor's control. Predictably, Crosby's opposition to this move aroused Governor Hincks's displeasure, and to underline his overall authority, Hincks lodged a number of complaints against Crosby, directing him yet again to submit 'every insignificant paper to the Governor for approval before taking action'.[29]

Unwilling to accept defeat, Crosby ignored Hincks's instructions, with the result that his representation of immigrants' cases were transferred to the police, a change that had the effect of sealing Crosby's fate. Thus the Indians' protector was censured by the Home Government, and while he was forced to accept the Governor's instructions, he did not do so willingly. Following their inquiry, the Des Voeux Commission reported that the Governor's powers were not absolute and that instead of using his powers to defend individual members of the planter class, he should have used his office to protect the Indian emigrants.

Thereafter, not only was Crosby's position fully vindicated, but the Agent-General's status was 'considerably raised' being regarded as an important Civil Service office with a seat in the Court of Policy.[30] Crosby, however, continually seconded as a Puisne (petty) Judge, was prevented from staying in his position as Agent-General. His failure to be more effective in his defence of the Indians can be attributed, in part, to his strong personal convictions, concerning colonial rule, which were opposed to the Governor's and planters' interests, and partly because of the imprecison of the 1864 Ordinance. Crosby died on 30 August 1880. His struggle and contribution won the confidence of the Indians, leaving an indelible impression among them, to the extent that Crosby became synonymous with the designation of his office; and more than fifty years after his death, all those who had succeeded him were known as 'Crosby'.[31] But although the act of mounting a marble likeness of the man may have been an appropriate gesture, it was unnecessary because his name, as one Indo-Caribbean writer noted, had gained a 'permanent place in the memory of all'.[32]

In comparison with Crosby, George William Des Voeux, appointed as Senior Magistrate in the East Coast and Demerara district in 1866 was to have greater success. Even though he had little contact with the Indian immigrants when he was first posted to the Upper Demerara River district, he was sufficiently acquainted with the indenture system to show an extreme dislike for the job of enforcing its 'draconic laws,'[33] perhaps because of his grandfather's maltreatment as a Huguenot immigrant in Ireland. He expressed disfavour with the duties of his appointment, it was not long before he confronted the powerful planters.

He was appalled by the fact that immigrants were arrested for simple breaches of the labour laws, and discharging such immigrants as being in 'illegal custody', he aroused the indignation of several influential managers.[34] On the question of the helpless position of the medical officers in charge of the estate hospitals, Des Voeux wrote that at the time their tenure of office was 'almost entirely dependent on the will, or rather the caprice of the managers of estates. Several of the most upright of them have, at different times, deplored to me their position in this respect; and have shown me that any serious complaint on their part in respect of abuses which they saw going on under their eyes, would only be followed by the loss of their livelihood and the instalment in their practice of less scrupulous practitioners'.[35]

Given their unsatisfactory position, even the most conscientious of the medical officers could only carry out work perfunctorily. In these circumstances, Des Voeux was unsure whether the immigrants' failure to work was the result of illness. Nonetheless, in spite of estate managers' opposition, he was unrepentant for dismissing 'sick' immigrants from work. If anything, he felt he should have resorted to this course of action more often!

Governor Hincks's unfriendly attitude towards Des Voeux was not made any less so when Des Voeux criticised Government policy. Within a few days, he was transferred to the West Demerara district; a move that incurred more than just 'considerable financial loss'. In his new and dreary surroundings, Des Voeux lived alone 'with practically no society' as the planters' hostility towards him mounted. Persistent pressure had made his position so unbearable that he applied for a transfer at a reduced salary[36] and within two months, he was offered the appointment of Administrator of St.Lucia. He left British Guiana in May 1869.

Like Crosby, Des Voeux was not only sympathetic, but acted in his official capacity to alleviate the distress of the indentured Indian immigrants in British Guiana. Although he found the island of St.Lucia to be a relatively less tense and agreeable place, he was deeply touched when informed of the unrest on plantation Leonora in December 1869;[37] and at the risk of jeopardising his career, he was determined to make a final stand on behalf of the Indian immigrants' in British Guiana, in spite of a busy work schedule. Several months later he wrote a long letter to Lord Granville strongly indicting the indentured system. The press in England was stirred and a good deal of interest [38] was aroused, which included the appointment of yet another Commission of Inquiry on 5 August 1870. Before the Commission met, Des Voeux, with time to spare and in a state of failing health (and partly to escape the ill-feeling generated towards him), went on leave to Trinidad where he met Governor Sir Arthur Gordon. Still shaken by a horse-riding accident on this visit, he returned to Georgetown where he found that his unpopularity among the planters was no less serious than before: he was, for example, subjected to much abuse and accommodation in hotels and boarding houses were denied him by proprietors who feared being boycotted'. Such a pariah he had become.

Des Voeux was called to give evidence early in the Commission's proceedings, and given the continuing allegations of abuses of the indentured labour system, the soundness of his evidence to support his claims was, of course, crucial. Realising the difficulty of proving his case, he told the Commission that his letter to the late Secretary of State for the Colonies was written in a great haste, without any notes or statements to guide him at a time when he was busily engaged with public and other duties. His writing was underscored by a strong conviction based on five years' experience in the colony.[39] Years later, after considering the circumstances under which his letter was written, and stating his reasons for its defectiveness, he admitted in his autobiography: 'But as it was, carried away by enthusiasm for the cause and by the sense of urgency, I took no account of personal consequences, forgetting altogether that what was so real and true to my own mind might turn out to be very difficult of proof'.[40]

While he remained unrepentant as to the course of action he had taken concerning the defects of the system, and responding to the commissioners' condemnation, thirty years later, he wrote of the Governor's withdrawal of all the powers of the officer charged with the protection of the immigrants; the lack of confidence among the Indians in the administration of justice in terms of welfare and the weakness of the Executive in enforcing remedies to alleviate an extremely defective system.[41]

Des Voeux, however, received due recognition (albeit indirectly) for his overall contribution in, first of all, recognising and then opposing the deplorable condition of the Indians in British Guiana when, at the end of his employment in St. Lucia, he was appointed Acting Governor of Trinidad, and later, was offered the Governorship of Fiji, where thousands of Indians had been indentured. On his retirement in 1893, he was honoured with a KCMG, a reflection of the sympathy and high regard in which he was held by the Colonial Office, in spite of his unusual administrative approach.

Publication of the Des Voeux Commission Report in 1871, led to certain reforms of the system of indenture.[42] Dr. Comins, who visited British Guiana in 1891, was satisfied with the improvements.[43] He saw the system as a model of 'successful and liberal management' and endorsing this view, were those planters, managers and officials giving evidence before the Sanderson Committee in 1909.[44] The Indians, of course, disagreed. But how did this defective system really affect them?

## Resistance and Revolt

The indentured Indian labourers were held 'captive' by the legal controls which affected every aspect of their lives. Furthermore malnutrition, disease, inadequate and bad housing and persistent indebtedness (closely monitored by narrow-minded estate managers) produced a sense of helplessness that was psychologically devastating to many. Death and misery were endemic in lives that were denuded of much hope beyond mere subsistence and, pushed to the margins of survival, many among these 'stoic' people expressed their feelings in various ways.

Over the years, they mounted strong resistance against their deplorable living and working conditions, and often had no recourse, but to come out in open revolt against their oppressors. Strikes were the ultimate weapons which the Indians used. And although such actions were, at times, 'attended with insubordination and grave acts of violence', as Surgeon Major Comins observed, 'the rate of wages was more often than not the ostensible cause of the strikes and occasionally the complaints as to price of work were found to be well grounded'.[45]

Those at the forefront of the struggle were identified as 'ring- leaders' and 'mischievous persons', names given by the colonial authorities to legitimate spokesmen for the Indians, who it seemed,were always blamed for the 'disturbances'. In fact, many strikes, such as those at the Devonshire Castle, Friends, Lusignan and Rose Hall plantations that led to violence with fatal consequences, had deeper causes.

In 1872 the first of four major confrontations during the period of indenture, took place. Five Indians (Maxidally, Beccaroo, Kaulica, Baldeo and Sukhoo – Guiana's 'forgotten heroes') were killed and seven wounded at Plantation Devonshire Castle, located along the Essequibo coast, when police fired at a crowd, the first time this had happened since State-sponsored East Indian immigration began in 1845. The point at issue in this conflict was the question of wages. It has been argued that the only course open to the labourers was to stop work and seek redress from their employer. In this case a crowd of about 200 to 300 angry labourers, after an unsatisfactory meeting with the Magistrate, made their way to the Overseer's residence where the Magistrate, accompanied by the Police Inspector and 24 policemen ordered the crowd to disperse. They refused. The Magistrate then read the Riot Act, but the crowd did not move on. According to one account, no order was actually given to the police to fire, but soon after the 'accidental explosion' of a rifle, the 'order to fire was inferred' and shooting ensued with fatal results.

The Coroner and the Jury showed little sympathy either for the Indians who died or for their grievances, which were still outstanding. They breathed a sigh of relief that the riot was confined to one estate and justified themselves by stating that were it not for the 'fortunate explosion' of these rifles, the rebellion would have become widespread and 'most disastrous in its consequences'. In the aftermath of the shooting, the planters' newspaper *The Colonist* showed no regard for the Indians who stood up for their rights. As Ruhomon, the Indo-Guianese writer put it 'their almost sadistic violence of tone and temper are reminiscent of the dark age of human history with its flagrant examples of man's inhumanity to man ... revealing the cruel mentality of the ruling class of those far off days in relation to the control and management of the defenceless immigrants'.[46]

In this second tragedy, six Indians were killed and seven were wounded in an incident on Plantation Friends on 7 May 1903. Here again, the inadequate wages paid was the bone of contention between Indian labourers and the Manager of the estate. Predictably, the arrest of several 'ring leaders' incensed the unhappy labourers and while a volley of shots was fired as a 'warning', the crowd that had assembled did not disperse. A second volley found its fatal marks. In the aftermath, a pattern would become increasingly familiar was revealed. While the Magistrate defended the police violence, the defence lawyer for the Indians and the Rev. H.J. Shirley spoke of the rights and liberties of the oppressed.[47]

Plantation Lusignan, on the East Coast of British Guiana was the scene of the next major strike, when Indian labourers in a shovel-gang walked out on 18 September 1912 and encouraged other workers to follow them. The 290 men involved, made their way with their shovels to Government House in Georgetown rather than to the Immigration Department, as was usually the case. Of course, the superior force of the police prevented the labourers' entry into the compound, but undaunted they congregated outside Government House. When the Governor, Sir Walter Egerton, sought an explantation for their assembly, a familiar story unfolded. The labourers explained that they had taken strike action because of their dissatisfaction with the price of 20 cents per rod, which was paid to them for the arduous task of trench digging. This payment was woefully inadequate to support them and their families when the increased cost of basic foods, such as ground provisions and rice, was taken into account. Indeed the depth of feeling among the Indians was reflected in the fact that they had travelled twelve miles to reach Georgetown.

Before this journey, however, the men said they had tried to make their complaint to the estate Manager, but was unable to do so because instead of being in his 'office', he was ensconced in his house. Was he avoiding the problems he should have faced? Among the men was a labourer named Nankoo, who was seriously wounded by a shot fired by the Manager. Shooting Nankoo, it was hoped, would quell the spirit of rebelliousness among the Indians. The Manager was of the view that while in the house, his life and those of others, including two women and two children, were endangered and it was because of this that he fired at the labourers. Krishna, a witness at the inquest had no doubt that Nankoo was indeed shot by the Manager. But the Jury at the Coroner's inquest took a different view: Nankoo had died 'from the effect of a gunshot wound', they ruled, 'the shot being fired by a person or persons unknown, to prevent serious outrage'.

Subsequently, although the Manager was charged with murder, he was acquitted by the Jury. Any other decision would, of course, have contradicted the line of reasoning behind their verdict. To add insult to injury, twenty-four of the alleged Indian trouble-makers were charged with rioting and sixteen of them were later removed from Plantation Lusignan to other estates.[48]

Prior to 13 march 1913, working conditions on the Plantation Rose Hall appeared to be 'normal', but on that day there was unrest among the Indian labourers, who were unwilling to work, on the understanding that it was a holiday endorsed by the Manager.

Custom and practice, it seemed governed worker-management relations on this estate, although at times, only when it suited the Manager. As it was, between two to four days holiday were granted at the close of the grinding season. In fact, during the grinding season of 1912, the indentured labourers had performed their punt-loading tasks to the satisfaction of the manager, who had promised them the four-day holiday, an entitlement which they felt was due to them morally, if not legally, and one that was in addition to what was granted to them under the Immigration Ordinance.

Early that year on 27 January, within a few days of the end of the grinding season, the Manager said he would grant the holidays, provided that the labourers spent that time tidying up the surroundings of their homes. Predictably, this unusual request aroused the Indians' anger, which was aggravated when the Scottish-born Manager changed his mind the next day about granting the holiday, on the grounds that there was some planting to be done. The 'blunt' uncompromising Scotsman ordered the Indians to be present at work, reassuring them with another promise that their holiday will be granted later. At that point, the labourers had had enough; many of them disobeyed the order, and prevented others who were willing to trust the Manager. Two days later, however, they returned to work, but by the end of the week, the Manager, clearly with no regard for the feelings of those under his charge, blundered yet again, by setting in motion proceedings against those who had persuaded others to stay away from work. Receipt of the summons provoked a wave of anger and resentment, and the labourers who, having finally confronted the Manager, asked why only seven of their colleagues were singled out when they had all been absent from work. The stubborn, vindictive Manager refused to accede to the Indians' request of withdrawing the proceedings against the labourers. Having exhausted the possibilities on the estate, the Indians took their case to a higher authority, a Mr. Fairbairn (the 'Chota' Crosby) at New Amsterdam.

Perhaps on the advice of the District Agent, the Manager agreed to grant the aforementioned four days holiday and to withdraw the summons issued against the seven men, on condition that they paid the cost of the proceedings! And when these hard-working labourers (not known for having large cash reserves) requested that payment be made in instalments (the only way they could have made good this outrageous demand), the unpredictable, spiteful Manager turned down the request and proceeded with the charge. On the day of the hearing, an estimated 200 to 300 Indians congregated at the Court House and naturally feelings among them were high, because they felt that their fellow-labourers were wrongfully charged. On the advice of their Counsel, the Indians pleaded guilty. They were ordered to pay costs and were expected to keep the peace for three months. Understandably the Indians' feeling of unrest remained strong for this was yet another instance in support of the fact that the law (and indeed justice) was not on their side.

On 4 March, a number of fresh charges were brought against a few labourers for bad workmanship and wilful deception. In support of their fellow-workers, the Indians attended the hearing of the cases, instead of turning up for work. The acting Manager of the estate was taking no chances, and called in the police in case of trouble. A large crowd had assembled at the Court on the day of the hearing, prior to which the Manager had decided to transfer some Indians to other estates because they were 'ring leaders' in the unrest. Permission was granted to effect this move and the police were instructed to take the necessary action. The victims of the transfer, having won the respect of the colleagues, were of course, reluctant to submit to their impending transfer. During the hearing, the Deputy Manager, the Inspector of Police and the District Immigration Agent agreed that the available police cars should be used to transfer the men. As they tried to persuade the men to go, assuring them that their personal property would be forwarded to them later, one of them, Jangy Khan, who moved to enter the car, was stopped by Ganga. While this was happening, the excited crowd looked threatening, many of them carried sticks. Taking steps to avoid confrontation, the authorities desisted from the transfer. From that day, until 13 March, it was said that the labourers had stopped work, became increasingly aggressive and showed signs of 'getting out of control'.[49]

They were in a defiant mood, determined to prevent the removal of their Jahaji Bhai, their workmates from the estate. It was against this background that on 13 March, a large show of force was positioned at Rose Hall to forestall any lawlessness. Even though the likely outcome of pursuing their 'indiscreet policy' was clear, the insensitive estate authorities applied for warrants so that they could arrest five of the Indians, including Ganga for alleged 'threats of violence'. And so armed with warrants, the police, ignoring the restlessness of the crowd, proceeded to arrest the targeted men. According to one report of the events that followed, given that warrants for the men to be arrested for threatening language coincided with the number of men to be transferred, 'a grave misunderstanding arose which in the din of the excitement and shouting, could not be known to the infuriated mob'.

The fear of violence led to the Riot Act being read. At this moment of danger, Chotey Khan, one of the Indians, spoke to the angry crowd, asking them to stand back. But while this order was being obeyed, the arresting authorities, led by Corporal Ramsay, took Ganga, and almost immediately, the crowd closed in on the Corporal and his men. In the mêlée, Ramsay was thrown into a trench and the order to fire signalled the end of 'several immigrants'.

After this strike, the Commissioner appointed by the Governor to enquire into the cause of the unrest, regretted the problems that arose over the question of holidays, the lackadaisical approach made to get at the truth of allegations made against certain Drivers (Foremen) and bribery concerning the Indian labourers. In conclusion, the Commissioner stated that it would have been wiser to specify, to clearly identify, the Indians to be arrested.[50]

Time and again, during indentureship (and in the post-indentureship violence that occurred at the Ruimveldt and Enmore riots), we see the heavy-handed attitude of the planters and the colonial administration in dealing with the many glaring grievances of the Indians who, in spite of the repeated, tragic consequences, bravely resisted their oppressors, as and when they thought it necessary. This spirit of resistance was epitomized towards the end of the nineteenth century by the indentured courageous labourer Bechu, who testified against the brutalizing effects of the system of indenture before a Royal Commission.

Despite marginal improvements, it is significant that the number of prosecutions on the estates reached its highest 39.2 per cent, during 1907–1908. About a year later, there was a steady decrease, and in 1911 the Sanderson Committee recommended that a determined effort be made to deal with the problem. By 1915 the percentage had decreased about 13 and a year later, after publication of the McNeill and Lal Report, the Secretary of State for the Colonies, instructed that imprisonment for labour offences should cease.[51] Dissatisfaction was such on the Guianese sugar estates that between 1910 and 1917, there were 79 strikes.[52]

As in Trinidad, the hospitals and jails tended to be full, because the sick-indentured Indians who could not work in the field was not allowed to stay in their barracks. One way of coping with, and of easing the unbearable pain so endemic in their legal bondage, was to voice it, to sing it out. Some of their deepest concerns, handed down over generations, have been, for example, encapsulated in this lament:

> It drives one out of his mind,
> British Guiana drives us out of our minds.
> In Rowra there is the court house,
> In Sodi is the police station,
> In Camesma is the prison.
> It drives one crazy,
> It is British Guiana.
> The court house in Wakenham,
> The police station in Parika
> The prison in Georgetown,
> Drive you crazy.[53]

Although several reforms to the Labour Codes were introduced, including recovery of wages due to immigrants' leave and desertion, and prosecution for labour offences, *inter alia*, perhaps one of the more poignant episodes of this period (reflecting in part, both the severity of the system of indenture and the overwhelming desire of some to return to their homeland) was the notion held by a group of estranged Indians that they could indeed reach India by taking an overland route! It is significant that the members of this group who could no longer accept life and labour on the estates and eventually deserted had the same story to tell: that through information they had received 'after a few days journey through the forest they would arrive at a mountain on the other side of which a road was to be found leading to Calcutta'[54]

## Community Development, 1880–1917: Free Indians and Employment

Forty-two years after they first began entering British Guiana, East Indian indentured labourers had become the largest immigrant group resident on the sugar estates, and remained so for the period from 1880–1917.[55] Once they had served their terms of indentureship and became 'free', incentives were offered to them by planters to keep them as labourers on the estates. Many Indians found such offers attractive. Low cost housing, lands for cattle-grazing and rice and provisions' production were opportunities not to be missed. And unlike the planters in Trinidad, in British Guiana free medical facilities were available to estate residents, indentured or unindentured. For the poor Indians, exposed as they were to disease (especially malaria and dysentery) medical attention was clearly an important incentive. But it was argued, the planters had calculated well the benefits that would accrue to them, by using the facilities they offered in a way that would only reward industriousness and keep in check the ever-present fear of labour unrest on the estates.[56]

Free Indian labourers were therefore prone to be less militant than the indentured Indians with whom they had disagreements. This was not surprising for unlike the free Indians, the indentureds had to rely entirely on their depressingly low estate earnings. Far from being a homogenous group, there were other divisions among the Indians, notably differences between the Madrasis and Calcuttans.

Occupationally (and predictably) we find that Indians constituted the overwhelming majority of labourers on the estates, for while those few Afro-Guianese who remained on or near the estates were predominant as artisans (blacksmiths, mechanics, carpenters and engineers *inter alia*), the Indians were pressed within the narrow band of field labour. More fundamentally, however, Indian cultural factors contributed to their continued presence on the estates. Unlike other immigrant groups, the Indians' survival on the estates was dependent upon such factors as keeping their food costs low [57] – a simple diet of curry and rice; being isolated for a long period through the pass system; and the fundamental family bonding (so necessary to the Indians, which encouraged child labour, thereby perpetuating the family tradition of life on the estate) all of which contributed to the kind of work they did, and this, in turn, was reinforced by a further depletion of Afro-Guianese labour on the plantations because of the attractions of gold prospecting.

The withdrawal of Afro-Guianese estate employees meant that the jobs of cane-cutting and trench-digging were necessarily done by Indians and, with time, successfully so. Much later, Indians began to take on jobs as artisans.[58] At the time of the First World War they had already begun to enter the middle to lower levels of estate management, thus the former Creole 'Drivers' became known as 'Sirdars'.

For the majority of Indians, hope was never lost that they would indeed one day escape the confines of the estates for a better life. Already early in the period from 1880 to 1917 evidence of their remarkable thrift and initiative had begun to emerge. They were determined to be independent enough to live and work away from the estates, engaging in their own enterprises.

As it was, the depletion of the Indian estate population was tentative. For many of them, some employment (intermittent though it was) was still necessary as they worked the land which they had acquired in lieu of return passages to India. Like the 'Negro peasantry' before them, the Indians who farmed the land faced the enormous task of coping with the costly problems not only of flooding and consequent drainage, but also of irrigation. Nevertheless, by 1900 most of the Indians who had settled in villages continued to show their willingness to become less dependent on the sugar estates, especially by devoting their labour to independent rice cultivation. The transition was not an easy one. Yet the endemic hardship suffered was generally embraced, until by 1895 a viable rice industry had come into being, giving village Indians the boost they needed. The push-factors aiding this development were first, the sugar depressions (1884–86 and 1894–98) as planters cut-back on their costs (lowering wages and reducing part-time employment); and second, the implementation of a more flexible Crown Lands regulation policy, which came into effect in 1887. The effect of these changes upon the Indians was that they could not now buy land, which they did as and when the opportunity presented itself, and increasingly much of the acreage acquired was turned to rice cultivation.

As a consequence, more and more free Indians left the estates: the number of them resident outside the estates rose from 33,371 in 1881 to 57,649 in 1891, with a further increase to 62,893 by 1911.[59] In effect, the Indians had abdicated from their primary function as a ready surce of labour for the estates, the *raison d'etre* of their presence in the colony. Few who had left anticipated ever returning to the estates, while the business prospects of rice cultivation remained viable. Adding to the growing population of free village Indians was a small number (1,100 in 1914) of Indian immigrants free of indentured contracts, who had arrived with large sums of money and jewellery. Some of them had previously been indentured labourers (not only in British Guiana, but in other territories) and with their knowledge of the Colony, they were able to put their money to good, practical use among their fellow Indian villagers.

Given that they were the last of the immigrant groups to move away from the estates, the Indians confronted an enormous challenge in trying to establish themselves in the economic life of British Guiana. Other ethnic groups had already moved into their particular slots within the socio-economic structure. Occupationally the Afro-Guianese were dominant in the Public Service, while the Portuguese and Chinese monopolised the retail trade.[60] Indians, by comparison, though still dominant as estate labourers, nevertheless looked to a future elsewhere.

Petty shop-keeping was desirable among Indians soon after they began arriving in the Colony, yet as late as 1903, only four Indians were granted 'spirit' shop licences. Significantly, their 'shops' were located in the newly established Indian settlements on the Essequibo Coast, and in the Corentyne and Mahaica, where the Portuguese had yet to penetrate.[61]

Huckstering was another occupation through which the Indians mounted a challenge to the Portuguese monopoly. The Indians' progress was clear, their numbers as licensed Hucksters rising from 830 in 1885 to 1,317 in 1921. Unlicensed Indian Hucksters in remote Indian settlements were not unheard of, and in time, many of them were able to set up small shops.

Employment in the gold industry proved more attractive to Creoles than to Indians. Money-lending, however, though confined to a small group, provided an invaluable economic service to Indians, and with the changes to caste, as it applied to British Guiana, Indians other than the traditional money-lending and business caste were able to aspire to, and indeed become, money-lenders. With time, their activities transcended the bounds of the Indian villages and settlements, as they reached out to provide a service to members of the wider society.[62]

Other occupations to which Indians applied themselves, included maintenance work to canals and polders,[63] the jobs of watchmen, axemen, trench-diggers and weeders; and also as a major part of the workforce engaged in building the Vreeden-Hoop – Parika Railway in 1896.[64]

Already Public Service employment remained problematic, namely the Goverrnment Service and the Police Force, areas that would continue to rankle among the Indians. Again, it must be remembered that they were the last ethnic group to leave the estates and, as such, they compared badly with Creoles in Public Service jobs, occupying the lowest levels, which was due allegedly, in some degree, to their lack of education. In 1912 the Public Service had 596 Indian employees, 448 of whom filled the ranks of porters, messengers, gardners and the like.[65] The discrimination that Indians faced in the Police Force was no less evident. For the duration of the period of indentureship (1838–1917) of the 700 Constables policing the Indians, there were no more than 20 Indians, none of whom ranked higher than Constable.

No wonder then, in view of their low status in Creole society, the Indians were determined to improve their economic standing, especially those who opted for permanent residence in British Guiana. They were conscious of their difference and the treatment meted out to them by the wider society, a difference reflected markedly in aspects of their culture, language, religion and dress, as opposed to the ways of Western culture. The acquisition of wealth was therefore paramount to the relatively poor Indians, who were acutely aware of the gap between themselves and the rest of the population.

In the years 1880 to 1917, there was a clear shift from their humble beginings as indentured labourers to property owners; indeed some were on the way to becoming men of wealth. Characteristerically, they worked diligently wherever land could be found in the remote rural areas, along the banks of the Berbice, Essequibo and Demerara rivers and the Mahaica and Mahaicony creeks, where the threats of flood and droughts were negligible or absent. Thus, the Indians spread their economic activities over a wide area, much of it unattractive, virgin land.[66]

But if land was one form of the Indians' wealth, so too was their investment in gold and jewellery, which to them represented savings, for hitherto, there were no banking services available in the country areas. Gold was melted, re-formed and worn, mainly by women, whose scarcity elevated them to become most desirable in the affections of Indian men, who showered them with gifts. Thus, it was said (though with some exaggeration) that in British Guiana Indian women were 'laden with gold and silver ornaments'. Not surprisingly, for men and women who had arrived with little or nothing more than the rags on their backs, of necessity, it seemed the idea and reality of saving had taken a firm hold upon them generally.

The changes which the caste system had undergone from the moment the Indians had reached the Immigration Depot in India, through the voyages and for the duration of their stay in British Guiana, had made it possible for many Indians to undertake new forms of employment, which was aided by the less restrictive new environment. Both socially and economically there was greater mobility, which empowered the burgeoning new Indian settlements with a zestful ambition. So much so, that in their isolation, they developed their own craft skills, thereby providing services such as carpentry, tailoring and barbering to the demanding community.

Underscoring these economic activities (and indeed generating further confidence) in the villages and settlements was the Indian trait of thrift (the means through which they steadily accumulated capital) and a growing independence from the estates. But this thrift, cruelly misunderstood by some Creoles and Colonial officials, led to an attack on the Indians for hoarding and making money.[67] Of the few who recognised the necessity of the Indians' thriftiness was Governor Swettenham, who commended them, not only for helping themselves, but also, and significantly, British Guiana. The absence of competition from the wider society was a boon for the fast-growing, but self-contained villages and settlements in that it helped them to make speedier economic progress. In the main, Indians lived cheaply (eating low-cost vegetarian food) and dressed simply in their Dhotis and Saris. To their credit, by 1917, they had become 'an important land-owning class', their presence extending across the country from the Corentyne to the Orinoco.[68]

Yet it would be false to give the impression that during this period, British Guiana was good for all Indians. Unfortunately, the successes of Indians in Georgetown and New Amsterdam contrasted sharply with the desperation of a great many Indians in these urban areas. The wages they received for portering and unskilled manual work was woefully inadequate, and so they tended to gather around the marketplace and shopping centres, where porterage was in demand. Many were forced to beg, even as children, as young men and in old age, sleeping rough under trees and on pavements, before succumbing to merciful death. So the Indians' economic gain had its desperate, ugly, obverse side.[69] To those who had foregone the right of the return passage to India (the rising cost of which had first brought about serious consideration among Colonial officials of the formation of Indian settlements) their ownership of land proved invaluable, primarily through the establishment of the rice industry and cattle-farming, and the development of agriculture generally, which formed the backbone of the Indian community.

Indian immigrants had begun to carve a niche for themselves, to stake their claim in British Guiana. With this commitment and as new generations came of age, their earlier bright dreams and visions of India became less precise; a past which, obscured by the more pressing concerns of daily life, assumed an increasingly distorted and unreal, even mythical and yet comforting place in the imagination.

## Relating to Creole Society

In the period 1880 to 1917, however, the Indians as a land-owning class was still isolated and largely unaffected by the 'value system' of the wider society. So how did they relate to Creole society?

For the vast majority of Hindu Indians, who had made the voyage to British Guiana, religion played a key role in their social life. Inescapably, before they left India (as part of their heritage), religion sanctioned caste upon which social status, marriage, eating arrangements and occupation were based. In the main, adherents of the Hindu religion in India tended to accept the 'rigidities' of caste. But unlike other immigrants in British Guiana, the Indians faced a much more severe social and personal dislocation to their lives, almost from the moment they had reached the Emigration Depot. Once they had left their villages and towns, the process of change had begun, forcing them to adapt to circumstances outside their experience and the accepted way of life in India. For example, caste distinctions were necessarily modified first, at the Emigration Depots, on the ships, and thereafter on the plantations in British Guiana. Imposed upon all the Indian indentured immigrants were new arrangements in their relations with each other, at work and in marriage new approaches, which Hindus, especially perceived as a threat to dislocate religion from the central place it held in their social life.

Indeed, crossing the kala pani was a courageous step, because it was contrary to the caste-based Hindu way of life to do so. (Yet, it would seem, that Indians of another age as traders and businessmen have been travelling overseas without mention of suffering a loss of caste!). In this sense, Muslim and Christian Indians suffered less disruption from the voyage.

On the plantations, the planters nevertheless saw all Indians, regardless of religion, essentially as labour units. Caste distinctions had no place within the system of indenture and were therefore further violated, not only in the barrack-rooms, but also at work (in the field gangs) and in the selection of 'Drivers' of foremen. Brahmin attempts to pull rank were often met with rude shocks, until they came to some accommodation with the new pattern of social life being formed. Thus the lower castes gained a new-found sense of freedom, as they embraced hitherto unthinkable opportunities that allowed them the desired occupational mobility that they were denied in India.

But while caste was of lesser significance in British Guiana, among Brahmins (who had gained most from its strictures) it was still of importance, particularly after they re-emerged to dominate Hindu religious and social life by performing the much sought after rituals of birth, marriage and death. This reimposition of a Brahmin structure upon the Hindu community was not lost on the Reverend Bronkhurst, who observed their 'pernicious and powerful influence'[70] over the people. Known as 'Maraj' and 'Coolie Parsons' by Creoles, these Brahmins soon achieved the desired respectable and prominent status of Pundits.

There was also disruption to the hitherto stable Indian family life, which had to adapt to the new circumstances in British Guiana. The core issue in relation to this was the paucity of women, as reflected in the sex ratio of Indian men to women. According to one account in 1880, the ratio was 51 women (including children) to every 100 men; in 1890 it was 56 per 100 men; 64 in 1900; 69 in 1910 and 75 in 1920.[71] This gradual increase (in the number of women recruited) helped, but the social problems it caused remained throughout the period of indentureship. The official view that the women recruited were not 'respectable' (intended to devalue them as docile and passive) was not entirely true, for they were, whatever the push factors, remarkably independent and self-seeking, traits of character that would accrue considerable benefits to their presence in the new colonial environment.[72]

Given their scarcity and proneness or coercion to cohabit with the White estate managers and overseers, and Chinese and Portuguese men, there was increased competititon among Indian men for Indian wives. This was clearly a new scenario to which Indian men had difficulty in coming to terms with. Child marriage, especially among Hindus, once prevalent, began to give way to marriage at an older age, as the sex imbalance was very gradually being redressed. But in spite of this, Indians tended to marry much earlier than other groups. Nevertheless, as workers and marriage partners, Indian women, especially during the period under review (1880–1917) were at a premium, and a very high one. But in terms of their duty to their families, in most cases, they formed the bedrock of the Indian family, exercising their new-found power with a deeply committed sense of responsibility.

And it was just as well that the family unit remained strong, for Indian marriages in British Guiana (as in Trinidad) were not recognised by the Colonial government. As far as the Indians were concerned (both Hindus and Muslims), it was not so much Government recognition, but approval of the Indian community that mattered. They baulked at the registration of their marriages and paid dearly for their perceived recalcitrance, as their children were deemed illegitimate, having been born 'out of wedlock'.[73] The 'illegality' of these unions had grave consequences on the off-springs, as some husbands and wives broke their marital vows.

More and more, the Indians as a social group, had to contend with a number of thorny problems namely, the continuing sex disparity, the 'class' of women recruited, the lack of recognition of their marriages and the serious and drastic alteration to traditional and marital behaviour, which taken together, had tragic results in the form of wife murders. So great was the disruption of the old social order that no one could doubt the passion with which these crimes were committed, and indeed their frequency. In the period 1885 to 1890, for example, according to one account, of 46 murders, 33 were committed by husbands and 'reputed' husbands.[74] And between 1886 and 1890, another aspect of the violence was reflected in 35 wives or 'reputed' wives being cut or wounded by that ever-handy agricultural implement, the cutlass. It is significant that more wife murders were committed on estates, where the sex imbalance was greatest.[75]

The fatal blows to which the 'unfaithful' victim fell, had its own cost to the Indians generally, and were perceived by the wider society as crimes to be identified with Indians. Apart from the violence, the sex disparity also had the effect of further relaxing the caste strictures by bringing into effect the hitherto unlikely event of inter-caste marriages. For those who transgressed the caste lines, it was a point of no return. But, for others, doubts remained. Indian tradition died hard.

Another area of social adjustment for the Indians was their observance of religious festivals, which occurred mainly on the estates, away from the cultural influences of Creole society. One of the most popular of these celebrations was the Muslim Muharram (Hosein or Hosea), during which 'Tadjahs', symbolic of the tombs of the murdered grandsons of the Prophet Muhammad was carried in procession through the streets.[76] So popular had Muharram become that it attracted the support of Hindus and Afro-Guianese. This meeting of the Indians and Afro-Guianese caused much uneasiness among estate officials and Colonial administrators, who were determined to discourage it because of its potential for violence and disaffection, not to mention its political implications. But if by the end of the nineteenth century the Tadjah procession had lost its vitality and social attractiveness, by 1913, it had become even less of an event.[77] For Hindus, however, there were other important celebrations, such as Phagwah (Holi) and Divali, in which to immerse themselves.

The Indians' entry into the plantations added a new element to the racial mix. Separated from the rest of the society, they were further differentiated by the clothes they wore. Their Oriental dress, especially the Dhoti (during the early years) was not acceptable by the more (perhaps hyper-) sensitive conservative Creole elite. Worthy of note is the fact that apart from their Saris, the Indian women were not shy in displaying their wealth by adorning themselves with gold and silver jewellery.

As far as language was concerned, of the languages they had brought with them, the majority of the Indians who were Hindus spoke Hindi, and to a much lesser extent, Bengali, Tamil, Gujarati and Punjabi, *inter alia*. The Muslims, who by 1915, formed about 18 per cent of the Indian immigrants, spoke Hindi and Urdu.

In religion, the Indians were determined to keep their faith, primarily as Hindus and Muslims – the Hindus, in the main, belonging to either the Vaishnavas or Shaivas sects. Later, they faced the challenge of the reformist Arya Samaj, which was in opposition to the caste system and child marriage, but in favour of education for women. The high priority of education was reflected in the establishment of a Hindu College in Georgetown.

As a counterpoise to the Arya Samaj, the Sanatan Dharma Sabha was formed in British Guiana in 1927. Religion, throughout the years of indenture and after remained fundamental, and as soon as the Indians could afford it, they erected Hindu temples and mosques.[78] In turn, these centres of worship, coupled with the Indians' isolation, aided the process of cultural perisistence.

Their settlement in the remote rural areas did not, however, mean that the Indians were unaffected by Creole society. Indeed they were, to the extent that they were consumers of British Guiana's most popular drink, rum, which, with time, gradually replaced the cannabis they smoked. The depressed state in which many of them had arrived, and the hard labour necessarily demanded of them, was tempered by the sense of levity they felt imbibing a stimulant from time to time. The Indians also adopted the practice of wakes, whenever someone died.[79] And rather than cremate their dead (one reason advanced was inadequate facilities) they buried them.[80] Furthermore, recognising that a change of name could make them socially mobile, many Indians (especially those converted to Christianity) adopted English names.[81]

The institution of education could have assisted in bringing about more social interaction, but unfortunately the Indians had to wait for this until the 1920s (the end of the period under review here), when more attention was directed to their urgent needs. The dichotomy between attending to the educational needs in the towns, rather than in the country, where the vast majority of Indians resided, was no consolation for those among the Indians who were most concerned and the employment of child labour by the estates, contributed in no small measure to Indian children's lack of education and under-education.[82] The employment of children under the age of nine, labouring in the mud and rain (and, of course, always under the merciless heat) was 'pitiable'. Yet, estate officials and the colonial authorities were not convinced of the 'physical and moral degeneracy' this might have had on the children, whose lives and that of their families were underscored by insistent poverty, a hand to mouth existence, with no indication of change during their life times. Economic necessity dictated both the exploitative order of the planter and the compliance of the Indian labourer in maintaining the employment of child labour. This marriage between capital and labour would keep generations of Indians in ignorance, for it was the planters' view (and they did everything in their power to enforce it) that an educated Indian would be a liablity, rather than an asset.

Those with Christian leanings, the Colony's established leaders in education, namely the Anglicans and Roman Catholics took some notice of the Indians, but were, on the whole, non-committal. It seemed to these good Christians that the contagion of 'Hindoo heathenism' was to be avoided, if not eradicated. Colonial Governors came, proposed their various educational schemes and went. But the problem remained, the Indians none the wiser for it. Their attitudes to the education system could be said to fall into three main divisions: first, for those intending to return to India, there was obviously no benefit in educating their children and, in particular, in learning English; second, for those who had decided to settle permanently in British Guiana, there seemed to be nothing wrong with the education system as it was. (Here the distinction must be made, as Ramnarine has pointed out, between the children of the India-born parents and those of the Guianese-born parents. The latter were more attuned to the potential benefits of educating their children,[83] and asked for schools to be located in their villages. The economically better-off among the Indians even insisted on regular school attendance[84] from their children. Thus education became a priority among the Luckhoo and Ruhomon families, whose children went on to take positions of leadership in the community. Such families were among those who had become Christian converts). Thirdly, there were those Indians who having decided to settle in British Guiana were nevertheless unwilling to allow their children to attend denominational schools, because they feared conversion to Christianity and the learning of English in preference to their own language or languages. These Indian parents felt that their children should be instructed in both an Indian language and in English. Among the prominent supporters of this request, was the Immigration Agent-General, James Crosby. And although the Arya Samaj Movement had established its own school for the teaching of English and Hindi, officialdom still seemed unconcerned.

But if the Christian denominational schools (the Anglicans and Roman Catholics) displayed benign or studied neglect of the Indians' education, it was the Canadian Missionaries who came to the rescue, with the arrival of the Reverend John Gibson in 1885. In Trinidad, the Canadian Missionaries had already made their own mark among the Indians and, were now in Guiana initiating their course of action by instructing the Indians in both Hindi and English. One of the Canadian

Presbyterians, J.B. Cropper, insisted on education for the Indians, to the extent that soon after his arrival in British Guiana, the first CM School opened its doors to Indian children at St.Helena. Almost two decades later in 1917, there were 28 Primary schools and one Secondary school to meet the needs not only of indians, but also others who wished to attend. Sensitive to the Indians' deepest fears, the Canadian Presbyterians allayed them by teaching in the Indians' language.

Social integration of the Indians within a short time-scale was, of course, not a reasonable expectation. Conversion to Christianity was not a simple matter, especially when one remembers the central role that religion played in the Indians' social life. (And even when, as happened later, many Indians took advantage of the increased prospects of gaining jobs and social mobility, by converting to Christianity and adopting Christian names, in their heart of hearts, they still adhered to their former Indian religious customs and cultural practices such as Tadjah[85] – Muharram – Phagwah and Divali). In spite of their separation, the gap that existed between the Indians and Afro-Guianese was reflected in the unsatisfactory level of race relations; and although conflict between them, during this period, was minimal, their perception of each other was, in a word, uncompromising. In the eyes of the Afro-Guianese, the incoming Indian immigrants had an adverse effect upon them by reducing their labour value. They despised the 'coolie' who could not match their superior physical strength.[86] The Indians for their part, were condescending towards the Afro-Guianese, whom they viewed as being inferior, less civilised.[87] As a late-comer to the plantation, however, the Indian was seen, more often than not, as an unwelcome presence, a person who should 'clear out'. To further devalue them, the Creole attitude was to identify Indians with the peculiar name 'Sammy'. Those who had long been settled in British Guiana resented[88] this name, which was, in time, replaced by the even more disparaging 'Coolie', still in usage today in the late twentieth century.

Tension between the Indians and Afro-Guianese were exacerbated by the estate managers who adopted a divide and rule strategy, using one group against the other, so that the instances where black Drivers ordered around Indian gangs, were fraught with difficulty, ill-feeling and danger. According to Jenkins, the English observer, it was the selfish, bullying and cheating black drivers who were at fault in relations between the two groups on the estates.[89] Violent confrontation and Court cases formed part of the pattern of race relations between the two groups in the nineteenth century. But with the end of indenture in 1917, consequent assimilation of the Indians in Guianese society augured well for the future. No new indentured Indians were arriving (previously a culturally reinforcing factor of 'Indianness') to ensure that acclimatisation and acculturation of those already in the Colony would be interrupted. This stoppage was, however, not in itself enough to effect assimilation of the Indians, for their growing success in establishing both the rice industry and cattle farming, drew them further away from the Afro-Guianese population, a distance which was maintained by the lack of good communications. So by the end of the period 1880 to 1917, the majority of Indians were still very much isolated from the rest of Guianese society.

# TRINIDAD
# GENERAL BACKGROUND

Trinidad, situated at the southernmost part of the chain of West Indian islands, is separated from Venezuela on the mainland of South America, by the Gulf of Paria and the Dragon's and Serpent's Mouths. Bounded to the north by the Caribbean Sea and to the east by the Atlantic Ocean, the island is roughly of a rectangular shape, the most mountainous parts are in the north (the Northern Range), in the centre (the Montserrat Hills) and along the southern coast (the Trinity Hills), which Columbus first sighted as he approached the island.

Tobago is situated some 22 miles north-east of Trinidad and although it has been twinned with Trinidad as one Colony (and later with political Independence in 1962, as one State) it is with Trinidad that we are mainly concerned, for it is to this island that the East Indians had emigrated. (Hereafter, in this section and the rest of the text, Trinidad will be referred to instead of Trinidad and Tobago).

By comparison with Jamaica, Trinidad was a comparatively new island settlement, which was most attractive to planters. 'None of the other islands, I believe,' wrote De Verteuil in the early 1880s, 'offer such advantages as Trinidad in an agricultural point of view. Even its highest summits are not inaccessible to beasts of burden and there the soil is commonly of excellent quality'. Of its estimated area of 1,287,600 acres, about 213,292 were appropriated of which only 53,000 acres were under cultivation. The rest was Crown Land.[90]

By the time of Emancipation, the slave population of Trinidad (one of the later slave colonies) amounted to only 17,439 on the plantations[91] and like Jamaica, with Emancipation, many of the former slaves withdrew from the plantations[92] to occupy the available unreclaimed lands on the periphery of the estates, thus unwittingly making way for the indentured labour that would replace them.

In view of the impending introduction in 1844 of emigrants into Trinidad to increase the sparsely populated plantations, that same year, a House of Commons Committee on the West Indian colonies, expressed the hope that the laws which regulated the relation between employers and labourers would undergo early and careful revision.[93] And as in British Guiana, to prevent the payment of higher wages to free labour, the British Government felt it necessary in order to maintain the level of profits, to consider a new class of labourers who, by virtue of their contracts, would be effectively tied to the land and more specifically, to sugar production.

When the first of the 'fresh' labouring population arrived in Trinidad from Portugal in 1834 and 1839, they found the contract labour system extremely harsh.[94]

Reports of alleged ill-treatment were familiar among the Portuguese labourers within months of their arrival. Their collective disillusionment over working conditions resulted in a petition to the Governor of Trinidad in 1835, requesting that they be transported back to their country. The failure of this tentative Portuguese experiment increased the possibility of East Indian immigration, as a more 'reliable' source of labour.

And so it was finally agreed in 1844 that immigration from India to Trinidad should proceed permitting the entry of 2,500 Indian indentured emigrants from the ports of Calcutta and Madras.[95] While the system lasted, a medical service and policing arrangements were set up to attend to and control the emigrants;[96] and the imposition of higher taxation, led to the Government stepping in to fix the rate of wages, which they did in the interest of the planter, and in the name of the Imperial Government. Not surprisingly (to the incoming emigrants' disadvantage), for its duration, East Indian immigration to Trinidad remained contentious.

Already by this time, Trinidad had an 'ethnic-class structure', which reflected a 'close correspondence of ethnic identity to class and power'. Apart from the ethnic diversity, there was also cultural diversity, characterised by linguistic diversity, evident among the many languages, which the former African slaves had adopted from their French and English creole masters, and that which they had created themselves. Linguistic innovation, arising from the exploitation of plantation labour was remarkable.

In addition to the Africans, there were the French and English groups; and later, the entry of the Chinese, Portuguese and Syrian-Lebanese, which further complicated the island's ethnic group relations. But these groups were no match when compared with the demographic change brought about by the emigration of over 144,000 indentured labourers from India (who brought with them their own 'alien' cultures, languages and religious traditions to enlarge the colony's ethnic composition) in the years from 1845 to 1917.[97] The Indians would have seen and known little of this ethnic diversity, for they would be, over a remarkably long time, effectively contained (a condition endemic in the race, class and power design of their presence), as waves of them landed.

## Arrival and Allocation

The arrival of the *Fatel Rozack* (also spelt *Futtel Rozack*) in Trinidad with 225 Indian emigrants on 30 May 1845, heralded the beginning of Indian immigration to the colony.[98] After the long, unpleasant, boring and dangerous voyage, the Indians disembarked at Five Islands Depot, to face other difficulties that were not of their own making. It seemed that the lessons of Indian immigration to British Guiana were not learnt, namely that adequate administrative measures should have been taken to deal effectively with the Indians and their problems, and more specifically that there was no legislation to regulate relations between employer and employee. In fact, as the Captain of the *Fatel Rozack* was well aware, there was no Government official who had any knowledge of the Indians' character, language and customs.[99] Trinidad was unprepared to receive these strangers and utter chaos ensued with much misery for the emigrants. This, then, was the harsh reality of the Indians' initiation to a labour system in a land which may have promised much, but now seemed, to say the least, hostile. At that moment, the instinct for survival was imperative and although the journey had been a period of shock and dramatic change for many, it was indeed, and unknowing to them, necessarily a preamble and portent of how they might have to adapt (at least socially, given the strictures of their caste background) in coping with their new island environment. And no doubt they were relieved too, not only to be on land again, but also to be freed from the endless speculation their fevered imagination were subjected to from the moment they were recruited.

The 225 Indians were allocated to the Carolina, Diamond, Mount Pleasant, Les Efforts, Perseverance, Reconnaissance, Beausejour, Williamsville and Cedar Hill estates, where some were to make temporary homes, and others to settle permanently.[100] Stipendary Magistrates appointed to the various districts, reported on the Indians, describing them in general as industrious, but noted their dissatisfaction over wages and allowances, [101] especially on the Carolina, Cedar Hill and Mount Pleasant estates. These officials also commented on the Indians' consumption of alcohol, and generally observed that the Sirdars (work gang leaders) were quick to exploit their fellow Indians, tricking and coercing them to pay a percentage of their wages.[102] As a result of abuses to the labourers, Major James Fagan was appointed as first Agent General of Immigrants.[103] Two years later, however, the early promise of industriousness shown by many Indian workers changed as they became largely 'utterly disorganised', seldom remaining long in any one estate, and many of them wandered around the country in a 'wretched condition'.[104] The general malaise affecting this small group of Indian labourers was reflected in the fact that there was a shortage of hospitals to accommodate the sick emigrants. Of course, this should not surprise us, given that even before embarkation at the Calcutta Depot, officers had often displayed callous disregard for the Indians' well-being and, as we already know, notably during these early years, planning for their arrival in Trinidad was never a matter of serious local administrative concern. At the outset then, they were perceived as alien.

## *The Early Years (pre-1870s)*

Against this background of unpreparedness, the opposed parties of employer and labourer (with the employer having, as it were, the whip-hand) necessitated, at least in theory, regulatory guidelines. Thus in 1847 the Legislative Council introduced legislation defining the rights of planters and labourers, and subsequently estates were required to keep records. In these early years, essential details of the framework within which the Indians lived and worked were: that their indentureship would last five years after which they were entitled to free return passages to India; that their working hours were to be specified and medical care provided by their employers; and that they be provided with accommodation and a food allowance per month consisting of rice, dhal or peas, ghee or oil, salt, saltfish, onions and chillies. They also received cooking utensils (a small tin or iron pot) issued annually, and clothing allowances, which included for males, two trousers, a woollen cap, woollen cloth jacket, a felt hat, two check shirts and two blankets each year; each female received two blankets, two strong shifts, two strong petticoats, one wrapper and two handkerchiefs. To meet all the expenses which they would inevitably incur under the indenture system, the monthly wages they received, according to the 1847 Ordinance, were $3.50 to Sirdars; $2.40 to male workers, $1.45 to female workers, and $1.45 to boys under twelve years of age.[105] Here it is important to note (as the employer and colonial authorities had no doubt been fully aware) how precious the value of child labour would be to a poor but large family, constantly in debt. Moreover, this practice had, in the long term, negative implications for the Indians, retarding their growth and development as a social group.

Given the stipulated wages, allowances and taxes, generally the overworked and underpaid Indians faced a stern test of survival. In their defence, the Anti-Slavery Society protested that the regulations under which the Indians were indentured 'gave legislative sanction to a condition very similar to slavery'.[106] Consequently, the Secretary of State disbanded these regulations.[107]

In the circumstances, without the regulations of the disallowed Ordinance, the Indian workers' condition deteriorated; and to compound their difficulties, they were not always paid the full wages due to them. In 1848 it was found that on one estate about forty 'coolies' were admitted to the Port-of-Spain Colonial Hospital 'all in a state of starvation, and more or less of disease', and though every care was taken of them after their arrival, 'scarcely any survived'.[108]

In spite of death, sickness and general deprivation of the Indians, it seemed the planters were not entirely unhappy; indeed they were impressed by the hard-working, contented, 'docile and obedient' disposition of the Indians, whose stoic qualities belied their suffering. In cases where Indians abandoned work on the estates, it is significant that many planters felt this was the result of their 'subjection to ill usage on the particular plantation to which they had been assigned'.[109]

Thus Indian immigration to Trinidad between 1845–48 failed (for which Governor Harris gave his reasons)[110] with the Indians bearing the brunt of suffering and death. While the Governor saw the need for 'some regulations' to ensure better planter-indentured labourer relations, in 1848 the Government of India (aware of the abuse in other colonies) took positive action, terminating all emigration from India. When immigration recommenced in 1851, unlike the unplanned, unprepared approach to the first group of Indians, it was agreed between the Home Office and the Governor of Trinidad to introduce immigration laws, requiring a 'large staff' for their enforcement.

With further refinements to the system of indentureship, in 1854 the Protector of Immigrants, retitled Agent-General of Immigration, was responsible for assigning Indian immigrants to their prospective employers and inspecting estates where the Indians laboured and lived. He was the officer of last resort to whom an indentured labourer could seek redress for grievances. Yet again in 1878, the post renamed as the Agent-General reverted to being called the Protector of Immigrants, a title to which there was, at least, a humanitarian ring, if nothing else. Prior to this change in nomenclature, however, there were other officers of importance in the immigration administrative hierarchy[111] who tried to ensure that the emigrants understood the indenture laws, notably through translations into Hindi and Urdu, the latter derived from Arabic and Persian. With time, the process of arrival and allocation became more regulated, even though there was conjestion at Five Islands Depot, and the sick who suffered mainly from eye complaints, gonorrhoea and venereal disease,[112] were admitted to the Colonial Hospital.

During these years of immigration, after being assigned to their estates, the healthy emigrants, engaged on contracts, either began work at once or were granted two weeks of rest before they began to serve their full term of Industrial Residence.[113] By 1862, the five-year term of indenture had become established.[114]

Although there were efforts to keep married couples and children under the age of fifteen together in their new environment, the Indians were unaware of the stark reality of living and working, in sickness and health, under the existing labour laws, at the time of their arrival, and subsequent legislation,[115] which controlled their every move.

Increasingly, they were attuned by experience to the fact that every aspect of their lives were being encroached upon. 'The regimentation of life at home, in labour and in leisure', wrote one historian, 'undoubtedly had the effect of slowly but surely changing the Indians' way of life'.[116]

Rooms in the barracks (wooden ranges), which housed the emigrants, measuring an estimated ten feet by twelve feet in area, accommodated either two or three single people or a couple with children.[117] Overcrowding was a real and persistent problem which did not allow any privacy. Conditions in these dwellings, even as late as the first decade and a half of the twentieth century, were described thus: 'The partitions between rooms were low, and by standing on a box the occupant of one room could look or climb over the partition into the adjoining room. All noises, conversations and odours passed easily from one room to the other'.[118] Allowing for the fact that the *raison d'etre* of Royal Commissions was to present seemingly balanced (if not optimistic) reports, it would not be outlandish to envisage even worse conditions if one read between the lines.

Apart from the fact that cooking facilities were, to say the least, cramped, among the health hazards, was the appalling lack of latrines. It is not difficult to imagine how primitive conditions were during these early years. Indeed it was not until about 1914 that some facilities were provided on most estates, and before this, the immigrants tended to relieve themselves in the fields and the adjoining open ground near the barracks only because there was no alternative. The provision of latrines, it was hoped, would help to reduce the large number of Indians suffering from ankylostomiasis, a kind of hookworm disease.

The expectation that immigrants would earn enough to buy adequate supplies of food was not always realised. In fact, indebtedness was more or less the norm. Many first-year immigrants with children above the age of ten were issued with rations at a cost of five and a half pence (11 cents). This money was later deducted from the immigrants' pay. The ability to earn a living had been increasingly under threat and had, in fact, deteriorated to the extent that by 1870, the 'rationing period' included second year indentured Indians, who received their rations uncooked.[119]

Bearing in mind the beneficial effects of the two-year period which, it was argued, decreased absenteeism, the Immigration Agent-General felt a rationing system should be generally enforced. But this optimism, masked the system's defects. Many immigrants, especially the few women, found themselves in 'considerable debt' by their second year; and newcomers were allocated the hardest work, so that by the end of their first year they, more often than not, found that their earnings could not pay for their rations. In practice, what was given by the employer with one hand, was taken away by the other, thus perpetuating indebtedness and poverty among the Indians.

Resourceful immigrants, through extraordinary thrift over a period of time, eventually became owners of livestock, including cows, sheep, chickens, goats and pigs,[120] which provided eggs, meat and milk for their needy, under-nourished and, in many cases, large families; and as in British Guiana and Jamaica, the estates perhaps recognising their difficulties, allowed the immigrants to turn their hands tentatively, at first, to planting rice on abandoned land.

Leisure time, so necessary and therefore precious to the immigrants was restricted. Although by 1865 an immigrant would not take more than seven consecutive days off a year, by the turn of the century, it was relatively easier to get leave from the estate. Leisure time, however, allegedly resulted in the development of 'pernicious habits' such as a 'predisposition to intemperance' leading to 'prolific drunkeness'.[121] Clearly, there was also a beneficial side to the consumption of alcohol (not mentioned by the moralising officials) both to the immigrant (who, in many cases, found the restriction and boredom of life on the plantations, at times, almost unbearable,) and also to the owners of shops, many of whom were estate managers, who profited. In addition, these shops served crucially as points of social contact, a central meeting place where the oppressiveness of the estates on the Indians, was to some extent, alleviated by comradeship, a rekindling of the brotherhood of the ship, characterised by an animated airing of shared grievances and the therapeutic value of general conversation, if only briefly.

By the last half of the 1870s, according to one account, the problem of drunkeness among the immigrants had increased, and predictably the Christian missionaries complained loudly. Colonial officials, on the other hand, attributed marital violence to intemperance and the planters were already increasingly concerned that a continuing shortage of Indian women would engender a higher crime rate.

## From Indentured Labourers to Indian Peasantry 1870–1900

While in theory the main objective of Indian indentured immigration was the continued exploitation of the plantation economy, through a large pool of cheap labour on the estates, in practice, there was an equal distribution of the benefits among the estates from this labour force. The sugar interests, for example, politically and economically dominant gained more than the less important cocoa and coconut estates. The conflict between the sugar and cocoa and coconut interests over such matters as medical facilities and the allocation of indentured labourers, persisted. In fact, the cocoa and coconut industries remained deficient of this source of labour; and in 1894, when the employment of Indian indentured labour on the cocoa estates was highest, it was argued that only 741, just 6.9 per cent of the total indentured labour force were employed.[122] On the other hand, from the outset, the sugar estates received the bulk of this labour force, to the extent that with its decline from 10,247 in 1872 to 6,381 in 1900, sugar estates were allotted an estimated 91 per cent of this number.[123]

It is important to note that as the estate Indian immigrant population evolved from the early years of the last three decades of the nineteenth century, it contained not only indentured Indians, but also unindentured (free) resident and non-resident Indians, with ('Negro') Afro-Trinidadian resident and non-resident workers. Indians formed the clear majority of the labour available on the estates, with the 'proportion of unindentured non-resident Indians rising from 11 per cent of the total estate labour force in 1872 to 24 per cent in 1895, while for the same period unindentured estate-resident Indians increased from 19.6 per cent to 24.5 per cent'. By comparison, Afro-Trinidadian estate labour (resident and non-resident) declined from 24.7 per cent to 13 per cent for the same period.[124] Afro-Trinidadian labourers were unwilling to accept both the reduction in wages and the servile and degrading status which they associated with agricultural work. This prejudice towards field work was not just a passing thought, but one that would become deeply ingrained. And it is significant that despite the considerable influx of West Indian Creole labourers into Trinidad, direct competition between Indians and Africans on the estates, was limited.

By contrast, the withdrawal of Afro-Trinidadian labour led to Indian immigrants (indentureds and unindentureds) increasing their hold and in so doing, they became the main source of estate labour between 1872 and 1895. The Indians' importance as an identifiable group in and around the estates could no longer be ignored; and indeed they were not.

Planters, with the labour flexibility at their disposal in 1877, called upon 'free' Indians to supplement their depleted workforce of indentured Indians and Creole labour. Thus recurrent shortages of indentured labour on the estates were filled, and when the number of indentured labourers on the estates rose, the unindentured labourers were released from the estates. This trend, over the years, led to an increase in the unindentured Indian population and a decrease in the number of indentureds.[125] A calculation from one survey showed a proportional increase of unindentured Indian labourers from 30.6 per cent of the total estate labourers in 1872 to 48.5 per cent in 1895, as against a proportional decline of indentured Indians, from 44.7 per cent in 1872 to 38.5 per cent in 1895.[126]

Nevertheless, indentured Indian labour formed the core, the mainstay, on the estates; a labour force composed both of those indentured for the five years of their contract, and those who at the end of this first commitment, reindentured for a year. Then there was the system of bounties designed to keep indentured immigrants, particularly those with experience, on the estates. In effect, the system was introduced by the planters in the hope that those who had completed their five-year contracts would reindenture, the incentive being a bounty of two to three English pounds, valued at between ten to fifteen Trinidad dollars.

Apart from the money offer, what in fact did the Indian indentured immigrants expect to gain? For one thing, the bounty system provided the opportunity of saving some money by foregoing the expense of housing and medical care, which they would have incurred as non-resident estate labour. For many, who felt entrapped, living a hand-to-mouth existence on very mean wages, such an offer (at least, when it was first made) was attractive, which also indicated the sense of desperation the Indians felt in breaking the cycle of poverty. This system, the immigrants found to be acceptable because, at the time, they were required to be resident for another five years in the island, before they could claim eligibility for a return passage to India. As it was, the majority of those Indians who received bounty certificates had been resident in Trinidad for between five to twelve years before they were issued. But attractive as it may have been then, during the thirty years from 1870 to 1900, the bounty system was not a success. In fact, it had begun to decline as early as 1860. Why? Among the chief reasons, one researcher noted, were first, that the premium itself showed a tendency to stay below what it was previously; second, free labourers seemed, on balance, to be better off as labourers; and third, planters took a tougher line by pressing their claims on absence from work, which had the effect of prolonging the completion of such contracts.[127] But why did the gradual decline of the bounty system become 'drastic' in 1885? Because, it was argued, the 'commercial depression' forced upon planters a reduction in costs so that they could no longer offer bounties and perhaps, more fundamentally, there was no longer a shortage of agricultural labour, which cancelled out the need for the inducement to re-indenture.

The question might well be posed: what was an 'adequate' labour force on the Trinidad estates during the last third of the nineteenth century? In a perfect market, this might be determined, it was claimed, by the relationship between wages and labour. Given the theory that wages would fall when there was a large labour force, in practice, the wage rate of indentured labourers was fixed at a low level and, at times, this fell further. Abundant indentured and non-indentured estate labour supply in 1875, 1884–5 and 1895 had indeed tempted planters to reduce wages, and significantly 1884–5 saw a decline in the bounty system, which was made redundant as far as the planters were concerned, because the labour supply was 'adequate'. Also indicative of this was the fact that at the time, sugar cultivation was 'stationary',[128] and with the combined growth of the indentured and unindentured Indians resident on the estates for most of the period from 1880 to 1900, there was still no corresponding increase in the cultivated acreage of sugar cane.[129]

As a consequence, in contrast to the 1860s, planters were now unwilling to accept more indentured Indian immigrants on the estates. Furthermore, the depressed sugar industry meant there was less work, even for resident labourers, some of whom could only be employed for three days of the working week.[130] The result was an ample supply of indentured and unindentured estate labour in the later decades of the nineteenth century under review, a period which saw important changes in the evolution of Indians from their status as transient indentured labourers towards achieving economic independence.

A reduction in the indentured labourers' wages after the 1884 depression encouraged the drift of Indian immigrants from the sugar estates. Despite their departure, they retained links as part-time workers on the estates; a departure which nevertheless emphasized the act that work in the sugar industry was seasonal, and therefore, an indentured labourer could work on land he had acquired (more will be said of this later) when his or her labour was not required on the estate. Economic depression and reduced wages then, pushed 'free' (or time-expired) Indians to withdraw, many of them entirely, from work on the estate; a movement which did not escape the notice of a foreign visitor, D. W. D. Comins, who wrote in the 1890s that the 'free coolies' would never return to the sugar estates.[131] In effect, the number of Indian immigrants working on the sugar estates had dwindled to a few, so much so, that the indentured labourers could not be said to form the main group of the Indian population. According to one source, there was a sharp decline in terms of the percentage of indentured Indians as a proportion of the total Indian population, from 38.7 per cent in 1871 to 20.6 per cent in 1881, and 15.3 per cent in 1891, to just 8.5 per cent in 1901.[132]

It is evident that the Indians' economic interests had shifted away from the sugar estates, where hitherto they were expected to stay, thus justifying the very reason for their presence and survival on the island. Economically then, the Indians had moved from just being estate labourers to becoming peasant proprietors. Their acquisition of land was vital factor in helping them to identify more and more with the colony, to the extent that they resented being referred to as 'immigrants'.[133]

The gradual establishment of an Indian peasantry came about primarily through the land commutation system and through the purchase of Crown lands. It must be borne in mind that this Indian peasantry came into being essentially as a spin-off of indentured immigration. In fact, 1869 was the year when it was possible for adult male Indians who had served their ten-year industrial residence in the colony, to own ten acres of land in lieu of a return passage to India. The intention behind this offer of land in exchange for the Indians' right of a return passage, was to cut the cost of such passages which was proving highly expensive to the colony.[134] There was always the nagging fear (even in the 1870s when the number of land commutations was high) of the possibility that Trinidad would be in financial difficulties should a very large number of immigrants, in a given year, decide to claim return passages. So indentured Indian immigration and the desire for a continuous labour supply on the estates, led to the necessity of allowing land grants, the first of which were at Savonetta and Pointe-a-Pierre, areas that were significantly near enough to the estates to preclude the planters' worry of a labour shortage during the crop season.[135]

In 1880, more than ten years after the land commutation scheme was introduced, 2,643 Indian men and their families had been settled on 19,055 acres. The 'Scheme', an attempt to encourage settlers among the time-expired labourers was, however, not uniform in its application. Ten acres of land was not the only option; five pounds (sterling) and five acres were also on offer to time-expired immigrants. Another variation designed to arouse greater interest (five acres if the immigrant selected the land or ten acres if the selection was made by the Government) came in 1879 when the land commutation Scheme was stopped, having peaked in 1874–75, when 497 land grants were made.[136]

From the beginning, at least one important Government official, Dr. Henry Mitchell, was unsure of the Scheme's success.[137] According to the calculations of one Indo-Trinidadian scholar, the majority of those (especially in the early years) who accepted the offer had, in fact, been in Trinidad for a minimum of fifteen years before receiving their land grants. In the years 1871 to 1879 grants were made to 2,508 male immigrants. The acreage granted to Indian immigrants was 'substantial' enough to lay the foundation of a growing body of Indian peasant land owners. Most of the 19,055 acres granted (both in ten and five acre plots) were in the Western part of the island, particularly in the southern districts. The exception was the Arima Ward where attractive land grants were offered. There was unevenness of distribution in terms of size and location, the largest settlements being located in Montserrat, Lower Caroni, Arima, Oropouche and South Naparima, where proximity to the estates was of course important in filling labour demand as and when the need arose. For example, by 1875, the settlement known as Madras (Lower Caroni) supplied free labour to the Mon Jaloux and St. Helena estates, while Chandernagore in Chaguanas, did the same for the Petersfield and Edinburgh estates, the Montserrat settlements for the Couva group of estates, Barrackpore (South Naparima) for the Wellington and Picton estates, Lengua (Savanna Grande) for the Inverness estate and Fyzabad and Rousillac (Oropouche) for the Otaheite and Aripero estates, respectively. Taken together, these land grants constituted no fewer than 26 settlements established by the Government in an effort to persuade Indian immigrants to forego their return passage claims.[138]

The land grant system was, however, not without its difficulties, one of which was the government's failure to provide adequate roads to and from and through Indian settlements. As a special report of 1875 put it, eleven out of fourteen settlements were 'in need of a road or of its repair and extension'.[139] Also, the Indian settlers had to contend with the payment of a land tax over which there was much misunderstanding and dissatisfaction, thus leading to a large number of defaulters. Apart from these difficulties, the land grant system was underscored by a number of other fundamental problems. First, some of the land acquired by Indian labourers (formerly squatters' plots) not only had, as a result, 'an unpleasant reputation', but were either on or located near swamps; second, because of 'slash and burn' cultivation adopted by the settlers and consequent low yields, the Indians though disenchanted, persevered; third, inadequate drainage; and fourth, the absence of schools, police constables and general government neglect, all tended to discourage the growth of the settlements. Overall, the effect upon the Indians was a lack of confidence in the 'settlements scheme'. As it was, the land commutation scheme (1869 to 1879–80) was never revived. Yet, it had brought considerable gain to many Indian peasants, who strove with great dedication to achieve economic independence.

Aiding the process of owning more land and thereby establishing an Indian peasantry, was the deepening economic problems which the sugar industry faced following the depression of 1884, when there was an increase in demand for Crown land. This increase in demand was such that the Trade and Taxes Commission had identified the availability of Crown land for sale as being one of the factors that tempered the severe effects of the sugar depression upon the labouring population. In fact, during 1885 to 1891 Governor Robinson's policy was designed to help more Indian labourers to acquire Crown land and to encourage 'minor industries' so that the depressing effects of the sugar crisis on the labouring classes would, at least, be minimised, if not counteracted.

In the following decade, the 1890s, the sugar crisis was no less serious and the trend of free Indian labourers demanding Crown land of tilling the plots they already had, continued with greater urgency, for it was upon the land that their survival now ultimately depended. Since 1875 then, the increase in the sale of Crown lands was steady – 54,188 acres being sold in the period 1875–1884; 77,624 acres during 1885 to 1894, and 90,006 acres between 1895 and 1904.[140] Moreover, the effects of the sugar crisis was particularly severe on the 'free' labourers who, unable to find worthwhile work, drifted away from the sugar industry to acquire and settle on their own grants of land.

Now, one might well ask, did these mainly low-paid labourers find the money to buy a plot (or plots) of Crown land? Before the land commutation system came into effect, unindentured Indians approached Indian shopkeepers for loans, the amount of money varying in relation to individual means and requirement. The interest on such loans which ranged from 60 per cent to 120 per cent and was conditional and the borrower was required to purchase all his goods from the shop-keeper. Tied in this way to the money-lender, the poor debtor was at a great disadvantage. Thus, it was often the case that many Indians could not maintain their ownership of land, which accounts for the fact that the village money-lenders and shopkeepers among them, extended their acreage of land-ownership.[141] These unattractive conditions, however, were often the only recourse for the Indian labourers, whose savings were simply not enough to meet the cost of Crown land. Nevertheless many Indians were prepared to risk many years of indebtedness until their land yielded adequate gains. It was the poor Indians' remarkable attitude, their willingness to take a calculated risk, of grasping an opportunity (often against great odds) which had indeed for many led to their departure from India in the first place.

Over the years, the increase in demand for Crown land also brought about other opportunities for borrowers. Alone, the individual Indian labourer had little, but in association with others, he had much to gain. The 'chitty' involving between ten and twenty Indians who clubbed together worked on the basis that on pay-day each person contributed an agreed sum of money which was collected in rotation by each of them.[142] If necessity was the mother of invention, then the 'chitty' was innovative enough for a former Mayor of Port of Spain to describe it as 'the first informal "joint stock companies" in Trinidad'. Of course, the larger the number of people pooling their meagre resources the greater the amount of money each individual could draw. Predictably, the popularity of this method of borrowing money grew among the Indians, to the extent that indentured labourers soon after their arrival became members of these 'societies' and bought land. According to evidence given to the Sanderson Committee a few immigrants became landowners only months after they had started their indentures. But, it seems, that such cases were the exception, rather than the rule.

Apart from those who bought their land outright, there were many more who could only manage to rent land. They were Indian peasants nonetheless, though of different status. In 1875 when the land connutation system had peaked, many settlements including Calcutta settlement and Coolie Town, had Indians who rented land. Of the 3,756 Indians to be found in the fourteen settlements established by

May 1875, 284 were tenants.[143] So for many among the poorest of the Indians, who were unable to raise enough money to become owners of land, renting from other Indians was an attractive alternative. In fact, some village settlements, unlike those which received official sanction (like Peru Village, just outside Port of Spain) constituted, in the main, Indians who were engaged in the rental of small parcels of land on which they reared cows and cultivated vegetable gardens.

While the economic problems persisted in the sugar industry, increasingly 'waste lands' not only within close proximity of the estates, but also 'abandoned' estates came on the market as rentable land in three-acre plots, especially suited to both cane-growing and the cultivation of provisions.[144] Thus the transformation of hitherto vacant land into Indian settlements were becoming more evident. In 1883, for example, one estate became a village, while the abandoned acreage of another was being offered, bit by bit, either for rent or sale; and five years later, Orange Grove estate had established a policy of renting its 'barren canefields'. Still the trend of the growing Indian peasantry continued, comprising of Indians as owners of the lands they cultivated and those who were tenants.

From the mid-1880s to 1900 no fewer than 2,540 Indians brought 37,256 acres of Crown land, even though the average acreage for each Indian buyer fell during this period.[145] (By 1912 the total area of Crown land granted to Indians had increased to 89,222 acres).[146] Nevertheless, the clear trend by 1900 was that a greater number of Indians were buying Crown lands, though in smaller portions.

By the end of the nineteenth century, among the main areas where Crown lands were purchased were Oropouche, Savanna Grande in Chaguanas, Naparima, Tacarigua, Arima, Montserrat and Lower Caroni.[147] A shift in the use of the lands acquired was now clear. More 'ground provisions' were cultivated, thus helping self-sufficiency in local food production. This trend was also to be found in the activities of many indentured Indians who used rented lands to grow corn, rice and ground provisions in their spare time, thereby supplementing their fluctuating, but steadily debased estate earnings. Hitherto and increasingly, as the ravages of depression in the sugar industry spread among the sugar estates, the cultivation of 'kitchen gardens' by the Indians became crucial to their survival.

Although, by and large, they now showed courage and characteristic determination as they laboured on their own lands, the difficulties they encountered were many. For one thing, they were looked upon suspiciously by the estate officials, because they cultivated essential food crops, an activity that was not to be encouraged. Two influential Creoles, R. Johnstone (Warden of Naparima Ward) and L.A.A. De Verteuil (author of a book on Trinidad) took a rather dim view of the Indians' satisfaction with their yields of corn, rice, pigeon-peas and tannias, among other crops. Furthermore, the Indians' unintelligent 'slash and burn' approach as cultivators of the land (a practice which it was said, reduced soil fertility) was cause for official concern, and as a consequence, Indian peasants were required to obtain licences to burn heavily forested land before preparing the ground for planting their food crops. Also, the lack of an efficient road network continued to hamper Indian peasants who urgently needed to get the all-important perishable produce to the market place. When railway transport finally came in 1899 linking such places as Sangre Grande, Basso Caparo, Williamsville and Cunupia, Indian peasants found the charges of getting their produce from the point of production to the consumer, disappointingly prohibitive. Finally, the perceived potential demand of the sugar estates' population for food crops, was not realised. As it was, lack of interest on the part of large landowners led, for example, to an increase in the local price of corn.[148]

In spite of the difficulties from the early years of the last three decades of the nineteenth century, the growing trend in food crops was unmistakeable. Taking precedence was the production of rice, corn and peas followed by plaintains, tannias, cush-cush, sweet potatoes, yams, ochroes, a variety of pumpkins, manioc, breadfruit, a wide range of fruits (including oranges and mangoes) and tomatoes, cucumber and lettuce, *inter alia*.[149] This food harvest, the hard-won products of Indian labourers resident in newly-formed settlements, had achieved the importance of decreasing food imports from St. Vincent, Grenada and Tobago, and it was the hope of one official that maintenance and growth of provision cultivation by the Indian settlements would 'eliminate the scarcity and expensiveness of food'. So as early as the mid-1870s, Indian peasants in places such as the Montserrat area, were clearly at the forefront of those Indian settlements engaged in vital food production. And if at this time these settlements had made San Fernando less dependent upon the Spanish Main for its provisions (thereby 'laying the foundation of the Colony's food supply') by 1882 Indian peasants were said to be gaining ground over their foreign rivals in provision and vegetable production. The primacy of the Indian peasantry in this development was evident. The emergence of rice as the pre-eminent food crop among the Indian peasants, led to the establishment of Trinidad's rice industry. But to begin with, rice cultivation was looked upon by some officials disapprovingly and by others, as devaluing the land. And although it gained in importance, as an essential part of the Indians' food consumption (prior to 1883, the cultivation of rice, even in Caroni was 'negligible') the year 1884 saw its 'extensive expansion' in various parts of Trinidad. As the Indian population rose (especially in the settlements) the potential demand for rice in their diet led to the cultivation of an even greater acreage.[150]

At first, the rice produced found ready buyers among non-indentured Indians, who while still employed on the estates, lived in the settlements; and even though the rice grown locally had gained prestige *vis-a-vis* foreign-grown rice, because of low public demand at the time, the market orientation of the rice crop had yet to be achieved.

Rather than play it safe and limit themselves, Indian peasants were most enterprising, cultivating both 'swamp' and 'upland' rice on lands which they felt were appropriate, contrary to the thinking of non-Indians and the State in whose hands such lands would have remained derelict. The Reverend John Morton was convinced that 'swamp' (wet) rice had pre-eminence over the 'upland' variety grown, in the years of the late nineteenth and early twentieth centuries.[151]

Of course, much depended upon the weather in rice cultivation. Planting was done in June, the start of the 'rainy' season and in October to November, the crop was harvested, a seasonal activity not devoid of 'certain social effects' on the Indians,[152] namely that (apart from the planters' charge that work on this crop, in part, explained the Indians' abstention from estate labour) the time of planting tended to result in Indian children spending less time at school. Because the application of family labour was crucial to the various stages in the cultivation of this crop, with the Government's blessing, Morton was able to change the Easter and Midsummer school vacations in one part of Chaguanas to facilitate the labour of children of school-age whose help, so minimal economically, was nevertheless perceived realistically by their parents, as vital in the face of their pressing, short-term concerns. All the available labour was necessary, at all stages of cultivation, from planting and cutting to threshing and cleaning, in this labour-intensive undertaking.

In the main, rice cultivation was an East Indian preserve, the number of Creoles engaged in this work being very few.[153] The turn of the twentieth century (the years 1904–5), saw rice cultivation occupying an estimated 6,862 acres. If by the beginning of the last quarter of the nineteenth century, the main rice producing areas were Montserrat, Chaguanas, Couva and Lower Caroni, in 1904–1905 the focal point of rice cultivation (reflecting a marked shift) were Tacarigua, Savanna Grande, Oropouche, Manzanilla and Naparima. Five years later in 1910, another remarkable change had taken place. Imports of this staple food fell significantly as the Indian population grew, thus enabling rice production to become 'a permanent and important branch of agriculture' in Trinidad.[154]

Coconuts were also grown in some Indian settlements, though this crop came nowhere near achieving the same success as cacao (commonly referred to as cocoa) the production of which did not interfere with the Indians' interest in cultivating other crops. Apart from its production in newly acquired land, cacao was also cultivated in already established settlements such as Montserrat, Chatham and Coromandel. The Indian peasants had developed their expertise to such a degree that by the mid-1880s, they were regarded as 'remarkably good' cacao planters.

Of greater importance still was the Indian peasants' engagement in cane farming, perceived during the sugar industry's depression as the way out of the crisis. The abandonment of sugar estates in the 1890s was a reflection of this depressing trend. Yet it was in these conditions that cane farming developed, the process of cane cultivation being separated from the manufacture of sugar, while the venture was jointly financed by the manufacturer and the cane farmer.[155]

There were three kinds of cane farmers: the first group used their own land for the cultivation of canes; the second cultivated rented land; and the third group used land owned by the factory.

Considerably more capital was needed by Indian peasants to farm their canes, and given a shortage of capital, they tended to rely upon the sugar manufacturer. In this respect, the peasant who rented was at a greater disadvantage than the peasant landowners. In certain areas such as Barrackpore, towards the end of the nineteenth century, Indian settlers switched from growing rice to cane farming, with some success. The main cane farming district was Savanna Grande, where of the six sugar factories, five were rescued by cane farming, and increasingly cane-farmers were operating independently.

Among the pressing concerns of cane-farmers were transportation of their canes from field to factory, and the price range for their canes. Nevertheless, the Indian peasant farmers persevered and, in time, carved a niche for themselves in the sugar industry. Often they turned what seemed like liabilities into assets (as they had done with other crops) converting abandoned estates into an integral part of cane-farming land. With the establishment of this activity in Naparima and Oropouche, the progress of Indian cane-farmers was obvious. By 1898 it was found that they accounted for 37.8 per cent (2,326) of all cane-farmers, 44 per cent (2,826) in 1900 and 52.9 per cent (6,127) in 1906, when their economic contribution in cane-farming in Trinidad was second to none![156]

During the last thirty years of the nineteenth century there had been a marked change among the Indians in Trinidad, a transformation from their status upon arrival as indentured immigrants to acquiring 'some degree' of economic stability. In effect, their total dependence on the sugar estates as indentured labourers was being transformed into greater economic independence, an achievement made possible by extraordinary thrift and industry. And with their determination to bring ever higher yields to the lands they tilled tirelessly, with ever-growing families to be raised and cared for, the Indians became more rooted in Trinidadian soil. Whether or not a return passage was in the offing, many Indians had already opted for permanent settlement on the island, which they had only vaguely known as 'Chinedad' while still at the Immigration Depot in India.

## Community Development

So much had the immigration become attached to the island that by 1900, as Indian settlers, they had constituted a large section of Trinidad's fundamentally immigrant society.[157] As a group, they accounted for approximately one-third of Trinidad's population, rising from 25 per cent in 1871 to 33.8 per cent in 1901; and significantly by this latter date, Indians born in Trinidad amounted to some 44.8 per cent of the total Indian population. It was clear, therefore, that even though they were the largest among the most recent immigrant groups, it has been noted that the Indian population was 'no more "immigrant"' than the other groups in Trinidad.

The Indians' more recent appearance, however, did little to alter the highly strati-fied and divided society, a stratification defined in terms of race, colour, caste and class. National identity and religious adherence were also divisive issues, as was the case among members of the white upper class within which there was an ongoing struggle for dominance between the Catholic French Creoles and the Protestant English, a struggle characterised by 'deep and bitter divisions' over marriage and religion.[158] While some of these matters were resolved during the nineteenth cen-tury, others persisted, often bringing these two most influential groups (the Eng-lish and the French) into sharp conflict. Of lower status in the nineteenth century were the Portuguese and Indian immigrants who were, to some extent, 'outside the social system'. Moreover, a few immigrant groups, such as the Portuguese main-tained their identities through their religion, social behaviour and national identifi-cation, while the Chinese tended to do likewise. As a whole, there was little doubt about the heterogenous nature of Trinidad society was clear.[159]

For the Indian immigrants in Trinidad, who had been arriving with regularity each year, the continuing French-English conflict during the last thirty years of the nineteenth century was a matter of much unease and was not respected as an ex-ample for their acculturation. With such conflict so deeply embedded in the social fabric, as they became more familiar with conditions in the island, Indians were beginning to find much in their own culture that was invaluable. In view of the inhibitive effects of race, language and religion that were such as not 'to admit any basic change in the Crown Colony system', it was argued that the Government should exercise 'large powers' in order to protect the various classes, as and when conflict arose.

Regardless of the divisive forces in the society, by the 1870s, Indians had man-aged to retain their conspicuous presence, not only in terms of numbers, but more evidently by their physical stature, style (many of them looked more robust than their counterparts in India!), style of dress and language. Not only were they gener-ally of small build, but also when they landed in Trinidad as native Indians, their dhotis (kurtas) and purgree were highly visible.

Indian women were no less so in their saris, orhni, ghungari (a long shirt) and jhula ( a close-fitting top). To Europeans and the Europeanised groups, the Indi-ans' dress style was shockingly new and gross, a difference that could not be ac-commodated in the existing order of things and hence their 'nakedness' was to be rejected as improper. Among those who condemned the Indians' clothes, few had any knowledge of the social import either of the dhoti (which reflected caste sta-tus) or the kurta, which signified the Indians' religious affiliation.[160] Yet, Victorian attitudes prevailed as local newspapers pressed for legislation to civilize the Hindu heathens.

And so it was, that towards the end of 1875, the Emigration Agent at Calcutta in charge of Indians embarking for Trinidad, drew attention to additional items of clothing such as jackets and petticoats for males and females, respectively, clothes designed to make them less 'Indian' and thus more acceptable upon arrival in the colony. As immigrants, the Indians had no choice in the matter, but there were other reasons why they became more amenable to altering their dress. Europeanization of the Indians' dress sense had the effect of engendering interest in the English language (a substitution of their own languages, which they feared) fluency in which the vast majority of adult Indians were incapable, at least, by 1900.

Diet was another important feature of Indian life in the last three decades of the nineteenth century. From the food rations doled out hitherto 1897 to Indian new-comers (who laboured on, or in close proximity to the sugar estate), rice and dhal constituted the basic diet;[161] and this was just as well because of its cheapness. But with the passage of time, and acclimatization to their new country of settlement, there were traces of change, as some Indians integrated ground provisions and meat, thus (at least in theory) going against the grain of their religious adherence to 'food restrictions and the slow erosion of their conventional practices of ritual purity and caste'.[162] John Morton and D.W.D. Comins have commented on the change of attitude among the Indians towards meat such as pork and chicken.[163] More than that another change had been set in train, one that may have seemed unlikely only a generation or so before, as gradually with the approach of 1900, flour took precedence over rice and dhal in the Indians' diet.

Although the above changes in dress, language and diet were not all-pervasive, they were nevertheless indicative of a degree of flexibility on the part of many Indians (especially as 'new kinds of social relationships on estates and villages' came into being) to adapt to their new environment. It is important to note that if most of the indentured Indians had embarked on the immigrant ships as individuals, by the time their tediously long voyages were over, a strong bond of social relationships (jahaji bhai or brotherhood of the ship) had been formed. This 'relationship' outlasted the voyage and acquired a deeper social value with the passage of time; a shipmate bond that became increasingly evident with the implementation of strike action, notably in the last twenty years of the nineteenth century. Nevertheless, such combined action were limited 'to moral support and solidarity', which itself was 'vulnerable to estate demand'. And given the probability that such a 'relationship' was indeed the essence of social relationships formed on the estates, it was argued with justifiable caution, that Indian social cohesion was 'rather fragile and tenuous'.[164]

But around this core jahaji relationship, there were supporting social bonds forged and strengthened through the organisation of regular Sunday 'dinners', which brought together Indians resident on the estates.[165] Before a 'feast' or 'dinner' was held, paid messengers informed the invitees, who were induced to offer rice or money, thereby giving rare material mutual support. Often these gatherings were spread over the weekend and those invited felt duty-bound to be present, coming as many of them did from near and far. On such occasions, Morton observed a fall in school attendance and saw these important social functions simply as Indian amusements.

Undoubtedly there was solidarity among the Indians congregated at such feasts, but there was also division. For example, between those who had been in the island for sometime and the newcomers. Hitherto, geographical location also created tension as between those Indians from Madras and those from Calcutta, fortunately a short-lived division, because in the period 1870 to 1900, few Indians came to Trinidad from Madras. Festive though these 'feasts' were, the division between those who had arrived earlier and the newcomers persisted.

The potential for social cohesiveness of visits made to 'dinners' by Indians resident on estates was, therefore, limited. The very fact that the Indians resided on the estates, placed constraints in the development and maintenance of durable social relationships. For one thing, those who visited each other, making the journey from estate to estate, needed a pass which could only be granted by an estate official; and even when this was allowed, not only was it lacking in written guidelines, it also placed the visitor in the vulnerable position of being arrested as a trespasser, because there was 'no right of way to the barrack of an estate-resident Indian'.[166] So the power and control of planters and managers over the indentured Indians frustrated the forging of stronger social ties among them which, in turn, acted as a brake upon the growth of an Indian community.

What was necessary in fostering the emergence of such a community was a fundamental change in the Indians' circumstances, if they were to be released from the control of the estates. In fact, this change came in the closing decades of the nineteenth century, when there was a dispersal of the Indian population consequent upon the sugar crisis, which led to the growth of settlements removed from the sugar estates.[167] This shift in residence from the estates to villages and settlements, according to one calculation, was reflected in a marked decrease in the number of estate-resident Indians as a proportion of the total Indian population from 67.6 per cent in 1871 to 21.6 per cent in 1901.[168]

By 1901, it was clear too that this movement had resulted in a consequent change which showed that the majority of Indians who had become non-estate residents, opted for the greater privacy and freedom of life in small villages and settlements, instead of conglomerating in the already burgeoning villages and towns.

This new scenario was vital in bringing about the independence required for a 'stable' Indian community. So, it was with this movement away from the estates that the Indians became free to develop their social life; and in the newly-established villages and settlements there seem to have been an improvement in the ratio of women to men and a better distribution of Indians than on the sugar estates[169] which, in turn, prepared the way for social relationships that were healthier and more stable in the villages than on the estates. Unlike the villages and settlements that were relatively free of 'serious social conflict', the sugar estates were often the scene of violent conflict, including wife murders.[170] Overall then, the change in environment facilitated more durable social relations, thereby strenghtening communal bonds among the Indians.

An important aspect of this development was the village shop, a focal meeting point for Indians. Here social relations were initiated and developed; a place where people came not only for economic reasons, but also to hear gossip and news generally. Apart from his role as retailer, the shopkeeper, as we have seen, was also a money-lender and banker. With his influence and social standing, he was able to give advice to those customers who sought it. Various kinds of community action were related to the shop. Shopkeepers were supportive of social and religious ceremonies, through which they drew together important strands of Indian social life.

The consequences of the Indians' acceptance of their new environment were neither predictable nor desirable, from an official standpoint. But as they gradually assimilated Western social habits to suit their estate-work predicament, many became addicted to alcohol and the smoking of ganja. And what a contrast they presented through their use of the former. From teetotal water drinkers in their homeland, some became regular alcohol drinkers on the estates. Why the rise in alcoholism among these 'proverbial abstainers'? The probable cause, according to Dr. H. Mitchell, was the fatiguing nature of the duties that Indians were called upon to perform. In time, being godly and 'good', in the eyes of both the Canadian Presbyterians and the colonial officials who ministered to the Indians, came to mean in practice, the total rejection of alcohol.

While alcoholic beverages were a taste acquired locally, ganja smoking was not. It is more than likely that the Indians had either at least known of it or had themselves been ganja smokers in India. If ganja was non-addictive, and said to engender 'passivity' while being a 'euphoriant', which carried a man 'above his sorrows',[171] then in the prevailing social climate of anti-Indian habits, the allegedly dangerous effects on the Indians' mental health, eventually led to restricting its growth locally[172] and the imposition of a prohibitive duty in the hope that its price would increase. It should be noted that the ganja issue was based on ignorance of the Indians' social habit, and to eliminate its use among them was a crass act negating their social behaviour. But such acts were the order of the day as dictated by the Colonial authorities who seemed more comfortable in enforcing among defenceless Indians a pattern of social behaviour by law.

The last thirty years of the nineteenth century was also a time when Christianity made significant in-roads into the lives of Indians, who increasingly participated in All Saints Day and the Roman Catholic celebration of La Divina Pastora. While Indians tended to observe Christmas Day as a 'social event', those who were converted to Christianity, at this time, were adherents also of the religious aspects of yuletide. Among the Indians' more secular pursuits was that of horse-racing, which seemed to have preoccupied many of the more sports-minded among them, some of whom were remarkably successful.[173]

The expression of Indian social life also took the form of celebration through such festivals as the Durga Puja, the Fire Pass and Hosein (Muharram, Hosea or Hussay). More religious than the Hosein celebration, the Fire Pass, a South Indian festival lasting about a month, was observed especially in Peru Village. This noisy and colourful procession attracted a good deal of public attention in Eurocentric Trinidad, and not surprisingly, much of it was negative. The last years of the nineteenth century saw the Fire Pass come up against yet more obstructions to its observance, an attitude of Trinidad officialdom which becomes more intelligible when one considers that the ceremony was a 'social event' with immense potential for bringing about 'social integration'[174]

On the other hand, the Hosein festival had far greater popular appeal. It is important to note that unlike the Fire Pass with its unindentured adherents, Hosein attracted its celebrants largely from estate-resident Indians. As early as the 1870s, Hosein also began to attract unfavourable responses, and although there were some 'disturbances', they posed no great threat to public order. In 1884, however, the two most popular festivals (Carnival and Hosein) perceived by the authorities as providing a 'political grouping' in the midst of the sugar crisis of that year (with an estimated twelve strikes, arising from hardship suffered by indentured workers), was a real fear among planters who found it expedient to impose control through the regulation of Hosein, thereby forbidding processions. Undeterred, the defiant Indians faced the trigger-happy forces of law and order, which had brought the Hosein procession of 1884 in San Fernando to an unprecedented and bloody end.[175] Frustrated, the Indians fought against prohibition of this festival. But by 1900, there was little participation in what was once an exhilarating and popular celebration. Thus, the action of local officials had the effect not only of further widening the gap, rather than bringing together Trinidad's two main ethnic groups, but also of separating non-estate resident Indians from those who were estate-resident. What followed was a further polarization of the Indians and Afro-Trinidadians. And whatever its religious significance, Hosein in Trinidad had come to symbolize, if only briefly, an evocation of close social relations, enriched by music and display.[176]

There were other festivals which the Indians celebrated in their villages and settlements where about the mid-1890s, there was a 'revival' of Hindu ceremonies in Hindu community. For example, Ramlilah was celebrated at Dow Village, the Mumsah festival at Tacarigua and the Siva Ratri (religious ceremony inspired by Siva) in Tunapuna. These community-based celebrations increasingly underlined the 'social aspects over the religious', a reversal of the traditional Hindu approach, and with time, a more secular approach was adopted. The Siva Ratri and Divali celebrations, for example, were social occasions which attracted a large number of people, who congregated (having left their various villages and settlements) in a show of communal celebration and solidarity.

Indian villages also formed the scenario against which dramatisation of parts of the *Ramayana* were performed, such as the Dhanak Jug and Ramlilah episodes, which drew large crowds, among them Creoles. The effect of this growing interest in communal ceremonies towards the end of the nineteenth century was a greater commitment on the part of Indians from the villages and settlements to community-oriented activity. And not surprisingly, these ceremonies encouraged social intercourse, social solidarity and a clearer identification of Indians by members of the wider society, as a distinctive group removed from the rest of the population. This gradual movement towards the formation of an Indian community in Trinidad had implications on the Indians' social organisation through institutions such as marriage, religion, caste and social control.[177]

## Social Adjustment of the Indians

In effect, the arrival of Indian immigrants in Trinidad added a new and substantial element to the social structure, a group of people with a very different pattern of social organisation. At the time, the overwhelming Britishness of the island was, it seemed, reason enough to be unconcerned with social cohesiveness, thus engendering an attitude from the top of resisting change. So it was that Indian social organization was stifled, especially while the Indians remained bound to the estates. But their withdrawal, to form villages and settlements, afforded them some autonomy, and they capitalised on this new situation by reviving essential social institutions to bring about order and some control over their disrupted and disoriented lives.

The institution of marriage was a dominant aspect of Hindu social life in India in the nineteenth century, the male being pressurized into getting married so that the family line could continue.[178] Among those Indian immigrants who came to Trinidad in the period 1870 to 1900, it was found that the majority were of single status and while the sex ratio of these immigrants fell, they were still high at 220.9 males per 100 females in the years 1870–79, 217.4 between 1880–89 and 194.0 during 1890–99.[179]

The upshot was that female Indian immigrants were at a premium much higher in Trinidad than they were in India, where the unequal male-female relationship was all-pervasive.[180] The heavily-weighted disadvantages they suffered were crucial in pushing many of them to emigrate to the Caribbean, for they had nothing to lose. But little did these female immigrants know of the potential for beneficial change that awaited them in Trinidad, where (as in British Guiana) the shortage of women emphasized their crucial importance in the establishment of an Indian community. If female children were undervalued in India, in Trinidad they were greatly appreciated even though there was an improvement in the male-female imbalance. As one Trinidad official noted in 1888, the men needed women and daughters were 'very valuable property' to their parents.[181]

Among the Indians, certain aspects of tradition died hard, and child marriage was no exception. But this began to disappear with an increase in the female Indian population and in the marriageable age of Indian brides. Overall, as in British Guiana, their relative scarcity and independence added to the attractiveness of many Indian women, the majority of whom were, in the eyes of prospective husbands, invaluable assets. Most of these women, vilified by Colonial officials, nevertheless formed lasting unions, that constituted the foundation upon which Indian communal life in the alien environment of the New World was built.[182]

Prior to their arrival in Trinidad, Indians rarely crossed caste lines in marriage. But their presence in the island (given their relative scarcity) brought a major shift reflected in many inter-caste and inter-religious marriages. Linked to Indian marriages was the problem of 'wife murders', particularly in the period from 1870 to 1900, a time when 87 Indian women were murdered, 65 of them being the victims of their husbands. Yet again one of the causes attributed to this, the 'foulest blot' on East Indian immigration to Trinidad, was the paucity of Indian women. But while the sex imbalance remained a problem, Indian men were reluctant to intermarry with Creole women. Guided by their heritage, they felt bound to a deep sense of group identity, and in order to preserve their traditions, they petitioned for an Ordinance for the registration of Indian marriages. Legality (marriages solemnized by their own pundits and maulvis were not recognised) was important to ensure that any person could bring their marital complaints to Court.[183] And so what should have been a private intra-group matter became an issue of major public concern.

For the Indians, the aim of the petition was not divorce, but the essential need to keep families together. Subsequently, legislation was passed in 1881 to facilitate marriage and divorce among the Indians,[184] a law which related only to the new arrivals of the Hindu and Muslim faiths. The Christians among them were not bound by this legislation, but by the law on marriage and divorce affecting the wider society.

Interestingly, a year after the marriage and divorce legislation was imposed, no naturalized married Indians had applied for registration, thus defeating the purpose of the law, at least during the beginning of the 1880s. By early 1887, apart from the routine registration of new immigrants, there was still no Indian marriage registered and, a year later, there were only four such marraiges. As it was, a significant penalty for those who did not register a marriage conducted according to Hindu or Muslim customs was that the children born to such parents were regarded as 'illegitimate'.

By 1890 the District Registrar recorded that of the 65 marriages involving native Indians, only 12 were conducted in conformity with Hindu and Muslim rites.[185] That year, a change in the Indians' attitude towards the marriage law (especially in Couva and Chaguanas) was apparent in the greater interest shown in the registration of marriages.[186] But in spite of this improvement by the turn of the twentieth century, and while in 1904 the Protector of Immigrants reported that 28 marriages had been registered, he was nevertheless concerned that there were thousands more whose marriages were not registered.

The institution of marriage (even when Indian marriages were registered) did not help mothers, particularly those with young children. The employer's prime objective was to get the best out of his labourers, regardless of their family commitments. The Santa Marta estate in Tamana, for example, 'wished to compel a woman who was still nursing her baby to do her required work and did not wish to help her until the baby was weaned although she had no husband to assist her at the time'.

How did the Indian family maintain its cohesiveness? While the jahaji relationship, to some degree, compensated for the extended family life known in India, there was in Trinidad, a shift away from the traditional patrilocal extended family relations to the nuclear family.

Like marriage, the Indians' religions were outside the ambit of the given norms and were therefore viewed as alien to the wider society. The inclusion of non-Christian Indians on an equal basis was, it seemed, almost unthinkable. Nevertheless, the Indians paid their taxes which contributed to the island's economy, but were not allowed an equal chance to practice their religions. As one writer in the *Trinidad Chronicle* stated, it was beyond the bounds of reason 'to expect a "Christian Assembly" to place "pagan worship" on the same legal and equal footing with the Christian denominations in the allocation of state aid'.[187]

While most of the Indian immigrants (the number of Muslims had fallen from 20.8 per cent in 1879–80 to 13.9 per cent in 1898, and few Christian Indians had emigrated) were of the Hindu religion, life as they had known it was disrupted by the plantation experience. They had to start anew, to adapt to an unaccustomed way of life, so that the absence of Hindu temples in the early years was followed by their increasing appearance in the last decade of the nineteenth century. It was the massacre of the Indians at the Hosein procession in 1884 that spurred on the Indians to erect a temple because they attributed the 'disturbance' on that fatal occasion to their 'neglect of religious duties'.[188]

Hindu worship was, however, conducted largely in the home, where Hindus being 'individual and private' worshipped and performed their pujas. Until the mid-1870s, there were instances of animal sacrifices, and by the 1880s, there was clear evidence of Hindu revivalism with the introduction of the reformist sects, the Kabir Phant, the Seunarine Phant, the Oughir Phant and the Ramanand Phant.[189]

During the years from 1870 to 1900, the perception of the Indians as a homogenous group, had begun to reveal more clearly the distinction between Hindus and Muslims, a cleavage respectfully recognised by both groups in British Guiana. Muslims resisted idol-worship and in Trinidad they showed a sensitivity to their customs and practices, remaining a strongly committed group, which was less prone to Christian conversion than were Hindus.[190]

Of the Christian faiths and their adherents who pondered the 'heathenism' of the non-Christian Indians, two churches were dominant in Trinidad – the Anglicans and the Roman Catholics. At first, the former felt that the 'coolies' were best left alone, while the Catholics employed a strategy which included denying the Indians their images.[191] It was, however, the Presbyterian Church which made the furthest and lasting inroads into the emerging Indian community, during the last thirty years of the nineteenth century.

Another hitherto vital Indian institution, caste, had in the new milieu, undergone radical change. Contrary to Charles Kingsley's belief that most of the Indian immigrants were of low caste and that few were of high caste, Tikasingh found that 'recruitment neither necessarily nor inevitably meant a reversal of caste ranking', and that caste in Trinidad was made 'more complex and controversial' by the regular influx of immigrants which the effect of strengthening Indian traditions among the settlers, thereby making necessary social changes less likely.[192] He identified three aspects of caste: traditional occupation, jati endogamy and jati commensality through which 'profound changes' in caste in Trinidad were effected, thus making it far removed from its Indian counterpart. In fact, from the beginning of the process of immigration (the entire experience prior to boarding the ship at the Emigration Depot and during the voyage) this social institution was under threat as the restraints endemic in Indian social organisation was replaced by a less rigid Western one, which gained in momentum, once the Indians had begun to adapt to their new environment.

European dress styles, mainly among those living in the new towns and villages tended to eliminate the outward features of caste.

Traditional occupational organisation along caste lines was also broken up by the common experience of indentureship. Hitherto, all Indians had been socialized and controlled through as 'ascriptive occupational hieracrhy', but on the plantation a rather different situation existed, one in which a member of a low caste, such as the Chamar, from example, could well be in a commanding Headman's position, thus subordinating Brahmin labourers on the estates.[193]

But towards the end of the nineteenth century, in spite of changes mirrored in occupational flexibility and economic status, the institution of caste was not entirely eliminated. In fact, to some extent the 'ideology of caste' persisted in Trinidad and was maintained by the continuous inflow of Indian immigrants. Overall, however, it was clear that the caste structure had disintegrated and so its traditional hold on the Indians' behaviour had evidently weakened. Nevertheless, some aspects of caste was maintained through 'ideas and beliefs' in it. This juxtaposition of caste maintenance and the breaking up of its traditional structure, resulted in caste being transformed into a kind of social status. In other words, caste affiliation conveyed either social 'approval and prestige', or its opposite, 'disapproval and abuse', so that caste affiliation was a matter of much sensitivity among Indians and this was attested to by Rev. John Morton, who (like the Rev. Bronkhurst in British Guiana) observed instances of the tenacious control and superiority of Brahmins over other Indians.[194]

Nevertheless, by the 1880s the influence of caste, while being kept alive by new-comers, was further weakened by the lack of respect for its obligations by Trini-dad-born Indians. In short, caste was no longer absolutely necessary. The Indians' presence in Trinidad had, irrevocably set in motion, a drift away from the rigidities of the hidebound traditions of society in India. They were more free than ever before. Their individuality and social mobility gathered momentum on the island and, unlike the strictures endemic in their former lives in India, they were now less divided and many made good use of the leverage they had for manoeuvre. Yet, they found themselves being stratified by other factors such as wealth, education and occupation. Shopkeeping, for example, was beginning to emerge as an influ-ential business, especially in the Naparima District. In essence, at this time, it could be said of the Indians that they were a distinct social group. But although they had brought their own institutions of social control with them, at least in their first five to ten years on the estates, they were subjected to the control of the estate authori-ties. To counteract planter interest, they had to achieve a greater degree of coop-eration and unity among themselves, which unfortunately was lacking. Once they had departed from the estates to the villages and settlements, however, they had to rely solely on their own institutions of social control. Apart from 'Dunning' (a passive 'sit-in' method of resistance in obtaining redress for grievances) one of the most important of these institutions from the mid-1880s was the village Council or Panchayat which failed to meet the needs of the Indians in Trinidad, where Courts of law provided an alternative; and increasingly, the Indians found their own institutions of social control being undermined by the institutions of the wider society.[195] The otherness of the Indians as an emergent group deterred them from making progress in Trinidad Creole society. The Indians' separateness emphasized their position as a subordinate group, and as such, they faced many difficulties in adjusting to the dominant social pattern.

In process of adjustment, the Indians were deeply concerned with the provision of social services, or more accurately, the absence of them. The expense of hous-ing the indentured Indians was borne by the estate owner, and we are told that the 'style of estate housing' had given way to the demands of the new form of Indian wage labour. Robert Guppy ( a long-standing Trinidad resident) had no doubt that the 'cottage system' of slave days was replaced by the barrack system of indentured immigration, more a renovation than any real improvement in either living space or comfort. Barrack dwellings first appeared on Palmyra Estate in the Naparima area and with the growing number of indentured Indians on five-year contracts from the 1850s, there was an extension of this kind of accommodation, which had very nearly overtaken the 'cottage system' by the early 1870s. But given the choice, it was claimed that the Indians would have preferred the 'cottage system'![196]

So what did the barrack system look like? One writer has described it as a 'long wooden one-storied range containing several single rooms, separated by wooden partitions, with a low four-foot wide gallery to the front'. (The year 1872 marked the beginning of attempts through which specifications of these dwellings were regulated). Ventilation, the spaciousness of rooms for both single and married immigrants and cooking facilities were monitored as the East Indian immigration system evolved. By the time that D.W.D. Comins had visited Trinidad in 1891, he saw no uniformity in accommodation. He chose to emphasize the few variations, in terms of barrack-roofs and floors, and noted that the Chulha (or cooking area) tended to be in an 'enclosed gallery'. He also observed that the unindentured Indians were, in the main, better housed in at least two of the estates he had visited.[197]

But the defects of this type of housing was soon evident. For one thing, where galvanised-iron roofs were fitted, the rooms became too hot. Other complaints included poor ventilation. Of more significance, however, was the Indians' lack of privacy. They felt exposed in these small rooms, in sharp contrast to the traditional privacy which many of them were accustomed to in India. Given their impoverishment, possessions were few and therefore their rooms tended to be sparsely furnished, and the space they lived in was hardly comfortable.

Off the estates, in the Indian settlements, where the 'free' Indians lived, the housing was said to be about the same as their fellow Indians in the barracks. One feature of such settlements, was the appearance of 'mud huts', not of course made entirely of mud, but with wood and galvanised-iron on the roof; homes that alas proved unsuitable for those who, of necessity, inhabited them; monstrosities which set the alien Indians even further apart from the rest of the population.

How did Creoles relate to the residential arrangements of the Indians? In some estates, as at Petit Morne in 1891, 'double barracks' were the abode for many Indians and Creoles who lived together.[198] Such close proximity between the two groups was not always regarded (by their members and by officials) as either a good or desirable thing. While there was a mixture of Afro-Trinidadians and Indians in Tunapuna in 1881, there was another and more serious development in Port of Spain, for as one Government official put it, the undesirable appearance of 'coolie huts' was certain to disfigure the capital.[199] In San Fernando too, the segregation was unmistakeable; and by the turn of the twentieth century, the pattern of 'residential segregation' continued.

Segregation between Indians and Creoles was also to be found in education. Not only were Indians seen by the Anglican Church as temporary residents on the island, but also as the victims of racial prejudice. The Reverend Morton was surprised to find in 1868 a 'virtual absence' of East Indian children in the local schools.[200] For their part, the Indians themselves contributed to this absence. In addition to their general attitude to education, they could little afford the school fees required.

Moreover, no special educational facilities were provided for them and bearing in mind recent arrivals and the different languages that they spoke, the fact that their settlements were scattered over a wide area, posed the problem of where schools should be sited. Given these circumstances, in 1890 an 'Education Code' was put in place, which provided for 'separate' Indian schools. In time, the relationship between Canadian Mission Schools and the Indians' education would become a close and enduring one.[201]

Considering the small number of Indian children at school and their low attendance, there was the added difficulty of the even lower enrolment of Indian girls, estimated at about two and a half times 'below' that of Indian boys. (More will be said of this later). And while enrolment of Indian girls was markedly lower than that of non-Indian girls, it was also found that of the small number who attended, 'fewer still' went on to complete their Elementary school education. In addition, impassable and inadequate roads (which made the long distances from home to school a real problem), coupled with the Indians' fear of religious indoctrination, and their more immediate interest in economic concerns, were factors that contributed to the absence of Indian children in school.

Beyond all this, a more general reading of the educational system brings to light the fact that among those in authority (namely estate and Government officials), it was thought that Indians should not become too educated. As far as the estate and Government officials were concerned, the idea of educating the Indians was to be approached with caution. It was against this negative attitude that Canadian Missionaries entered the field. Their perseverance brought steady improvement in school attendance, underlined by the fact that they were astute enough to teach Indian children reading lessons both in Hindi and English, in conjunction with other subjects. Though the Canadian Mission schools' educational achievment had been exemplary, it was argued that they had missed a clear chance 'for promoting the social integration' of Indians, especially in view of stark fact that the Indians' education demanded to be addressed and acted upon in a situation of 'social segregation' involving the Government, and the Roman Catholic and Anglican Churches, who were reluctant to educate Indians, but spared no effort in educating the non-Indian masses. In effect, then, the Canadian Mission schools were born out of uncompromising neglect shown by the two most dominant churches, a negative attitude which hindered rather than helped in bridging the gap between the Indians and the wider society. Nevertheless, these schools' modest aims, to begin with, had later to cope with a vibrant expansion, graduating from primary education to the establishment of institutions of higher learning. (More on the Canadian Mission and East Indian education will follow). The stigma and stereotyping of the Indians as an impoverished and parasitic class by the ruling elites of Trinidad's Creole society was not only unfair, but false. So virulent were the attacks upon the Indians as a group, that there were calls for their repatriation.[202]

Also, within the villages and settlements, the Indians faced their own problems of social adjustment, as they struggled to form charitable and philanthropic organisations, a means through they attempted to come to terms with their own sense of self and community. There was, among them, a tendency to look to India, rather than to Trinidad for their 'Indian' identity. Their charitable contributions to Indian famine relief, for example, was but only a starting point in their acceptance of a Trinidadian identity. Once they had begun to do this, locating their position in Creole society became of prime concern; and as they gained in confidence, they engaged more positively in the process of establishing an Indian community.

Relations between Indians and the wider society was always an uneasy one and was no less so in the decades before 1900. How the Indians perceived themselves and identified with their group was crucial to bringing about recognition (not only among themselves, but also from members of Creole society), of being an Indian community.

It should be remembered that the social integration of the Indians in Trinidad was a process in which difficulty arising from inter-group differences as endemic. For one thing, indentureship kept the Indians separate from the Afro-Trinidadians, the other major group in the island, which tended to reinforce stereotypes, particularly at times of conflict. Persistent provocation by Creoles generally, caused further withdrawal from Indians who were prone to avoid and limit their association with Creoles; and at times, it seemed that the society, as a whole, was against them. It was as though they had not come from one of the world's great civilizations, the entire group being treated as pagan 'Hindoos'.[203] There was, however, unanimity on one thing – the *raison d'etre* for their presence in Trinidad: they were valued primarily for the economic contribution that they would make as units of 'steady' and 'docile' labour, which perpetuated Indian immigration, and had, over the years, brought about a large and growing Indian population. This substantial body of Indian labourers posed a threat to the smooth running of the plantations, as was the case in the 1880s, when disgruntled Indians went on a series of strikes. Such actions, in turn, brought the wrath of the ruling Creole elites to bear upon the Indians, who were seen as dangerous 'coolies' and 'Asiatics' to whom no mercy should be shown. (The response to their presence elsewhere in the Empire, for example, in South Africa was little different).

The mere notion of Indian dominance in Trinidad aroused fear and suspicion. The *Port of Spain Gazette* and the *Trinidad Chronicle* led the attack upon the Indians, aided and abetted by colonial officials and the upper classes, who continued their campaign of stereotyping the Indians as a heathen, 'worthless' and 'very filthy set', in short, as a group of 'low social value'.[204]

Resentment of the Indians by the 'respectable' classes over-emphasized the true and constrained position of the Indians, who were attributed with low social status because their foreignness was at variance with the Eurocentric values of the society. As 'Aliens' (in fact, at this time in the 1880s, thousands of Indians had been in the island for several years) they were fair game for the authoritarians. Either through bloody-mindedness and/or plain ignorance of the Indians' heritage, the oppressive elite felt the overwhelming need to teach 'Hindoos' the lessons of 'Civilization'. It seems that the Indians were only 'civilised' when they were compliant labourers. But even their value as labourers was severely criticised as public attention again focused on the Indian immigration. The two-pronged attack on the system was based on the principle of non-interference by the Government (Indian immigration was State-aided) and the vexed issue of political reform. This immigration, it was argued, benefited Indians more than Creole labourers. A more egalitarian approach was necessary as the voices of reform (essentially the Coloured and Black middle classes) of the Crown Colony Government were raised. But far from favouring the Indians, the planters were the main beneficiaries of Indian immigration, especially after the mid-1880s, for rather than being 'impartial' (with few exceptions) no Protector of (Indian) Immigrants was outside the influence and control of the planters. So the much needed protection that poor labourers had expected in the early years, and continued to hope for, was largely unrealized through the individual designated with the appropriate authority, the Protector himself. His position was therefore threatened with growing calls for Constitutional change to stem the flow of Indian indentured labourers.[205] In short, it was felt that the Colony of Trinidad could no longer bear the cost of Indian immigration.

Nevertheless, the steady influx of Indians during the last years of the nineteenth century, adding to the growing, vibrant population which resided in the villages and settlements. The demographic importance of the Indians' presence in Trinidad could not be ignored. In fact, an Indian community, long in the making, had by now become clearly visible, much to the annoyance of the Indians' detractors. The so-called special privileges and protection afforded to the Indians, it was argued, should be disbanded for it had the effect of separating the Indians from the rest of Creole society. If only the Indians would conform, the venom directed at them could, at least, be less insistent and, at most, be less virulent. As it was, their Eastern cultural orientation evoked a violent contrast with the Western value system of Colonial Trinidad society.

But the Indian community was not the homogenous picture that the Creoles had painted. There was much more movement within this community than many officials cared to consider. Not all Indians viewed India as their homeland. For as long as they had been arriving in the Colony, an increasing number were foregoing their return passages, and accepted Trinidad as their home. Blinded by the profit-motive, the planters and Colonial officials were oblivious (or chose to be), of this attitude among the Indian population. The Indians' growing commitment to the island was most pronounced among the Trinidad-born, who became increasingly attached to their villages with each generation. So much had this been the case, that in the last years of the nineteenth century, Indians who had long been 'free' with many years of residence behind them, deeply resented being referred to as 'immigrants'. Paradoxically, their freedom was relative, and they began to question it. The legal requirement, under an Immigration Ordinance of 1897, imposed upon those seeking a passport was clearly discriminatory, and to this the Indians, as free British subjects, quite rightly raised their objection. They claimed equity with their fellow-Trinidadians, and by so doing they became more self-conscious of their race and class position.

Consequently, before the last decade of the nineteenth century, the Indians mounted strong opposition to being referred to as 'Coolies'.[206] 'Indian' and 'East Indian' were preferable. Not surprisingly, the Canadian Missionaries were most sensitive to the offensiveness of the 'coolie', 'Hindoo' and 'heathen' epithets, and wasted little time in changing them to 'East Indian', which was recognised officially, for the first time, in the Protector of Immigrants Report for 1896. East Indians they were, but with an undoubted Western orientation. The name they preferred evoked the depth of their search for an identity that would eventually align and, more and more, keep them rooted with a strong sense of belonging to the local Indian community, a commitment which some non-Indian Creoles were beginning to evaluate, if only to reject it as of little consequence.

More consciously now, Indians showed a tendency to assert aspects of Indian civilization, to take pride in their heritage. They strove for unity and representation, especially on those occasions when they felt they were unjustly treated, and they showed a willingness to integrate certain aspects of Western life into their own ways. Nevertheless such great strides as they had made were not convincing enough, for by 1900, their permanent settlement in Trinidad was still a matter of discussion among officials. But by then, they had already staked their claims on the island. They had made, and continued to make, an important economic contribution in a growing number of occupations, other than as indentured labourers, and with some justification, they claimed to have 'saved the colony'.

What was regarded as an 'Indian opinion' did not, however, come until 1897, when Indians protested against Immigration Ordinance No.12 and asserted their rising confidence and pride as members of a community, by forming the East Indian National Association to represent the Indian community's concerns. They held meetings at Princes Town (attended by Charles Soodeen, David Mahabir, Abdul Aziz and Sheik Meeran, among others), and in San Fernando.[207] The large attendance at these meetings added further credence to the belief among Indians that by combining their efforts they would be better able to protect their community interests. In effect, the Indians had evolved during the last third of the nineteenth century, from being 'transient' indentured labourers, non-persons in limbo, neither belonging to Trinidad nor India, to becoming a large section of the population, comprising responsible members of Indian villages and settlements, locations where they developed essential institutions and social services, through trial and error, thereby realizing a collective identity which, in turn, drew more serious attention and the grudging recognition of them as an identifiable community from some sections of Creole society.

## The Experience of Indenture after 1900

During the early years of indentureship (and in varying degrees throughout the entire period of the system), the Indians fought against disorientation by adapting to their new surroundings and living conditions, experiencing and resisting, at every turn, certain policies and practices that were, more often than not, insensitively administered. The overall effect, as we have seen, was that this placed the traditional Indian caste system under severe pressure. We are told that apart from a determined effort to stop child and bigamous marriages among Indians, many caste rules lapsed and dietary laws became meaningless, as more meat was consumed by a growing Trinidad-born Indian population. So it was that in the post-1900 period, Indian traditional patterns were becoming, less restrictive, reflecting an evolutionary form of domestic life.[208] And there were indications of some official interest in the Indians' education and health.

For all their seeming benevolence then, the Government and planters never averted their gaze from the profitability of their various schemes. Even when the idea of educating the Indians became, to some limited degree, acceptable by a precious few persons, there were strings attached. An educated Indian, it was now argued, became better adjusted to his environment. More specifically, a knowledge of the English language, at least, conferred eligibility for economic gain through non-agricultural higher-status employment (and in the long-run, for the development of the economy), thus facilitating easier assimilation into Trinidad society.[209]

Many Indian immigrants were, however, still reluctant to send their children to English schools, which they felt would lead to religious conversion, and, not everyone among Government officials and planters regarded education for the immigrants as a good thing. In fact, the time allocated by estate managements for education was minimal, because they claimed that educated Indians left the fields for other jobs, especially white-collar employment.[210] Notions of rising above their bonded-labour status was therefore to be discouraged.

So whatever instructions they received, Indian children were, in essence, 'educated to work', and Indians generally (although they had by then been in Trinidad for almost 70 years) were still misunderstood by both the British administrators and the Creole population. In his testimony before the Sanderson Committee, which reported on the Indians in the Caribbean, the Colonial Secretary formed the general impression that when the Indian first arrived in the island, he probably found his new environment and work 'a little irksome, nothing more than say what an English boy sent to an English school for the first time would'. He assures us that everything was made as pleasant as possible for the immigrant, adding confidently (without remotely considering the possibility that he could have been misinformed, or indeed be telling a deliberate lie!) 'I think in a very short time he' (the Indian) would settle down to his work 'very comfortably'.[211]

Official perceptions, though varied, only rarely approximated the truth of the Indians' predicament. Institutional differences, the traumatic process of adjusting to a new way of life, had little bearing on the administrators. In the eyes of some British administrators, the Indian was the beneficiary of the indentured system, progressing, as one sympathetic official put it, from the 'downcast depressed look of the newcomer' to a 'free and independent bearing' which was devoid of either 'servitude or oppression'.[212] Unfortunately, this well-meaning administrator's progressive view of the Indians' was not shared by those who succeeded him.

The Indians found that the health problems that had beset them in the early years, were still formidable, as time wore on. From a production point of view, the good health of the Indian immigrants was of primary concern to the planters and Government officials. In this sense, even the administrators recognised that field-work was physically demanding, and accordingly, laws were enacted to administer health care at a time when the medical facilities were described as being in a 'wretched state', and the mortality rate an on-going problem. Special attention was given to ganja smoking which health officers believed to be peculiar to the Indian sub-continent; a 'vice', brought to Trinidad (and elsewhere in the Caribbean) by the Indians, which allegedly caused more problems.

Even though the creation of an estate health programme was, for many years of central concern, by 1892 it was found that visits to estate hospitals by medical officers had declined to a very low rate.[213] Two years earlier, when D.W.D Comins arrived in Trinidad, he noted the decline of attendance at hospitals by medical officers, a consequence of which he pointed out, was the admission and discharge of patients, without medical authority.[214] Since Comins's visit, this 'evil' remained relatively untended to the extent that the Sanderson Committee opposed estate hospitals and felt improvements in size and equipment in Government hospitals were necessary.[215] Later, in 1915, even McNeill and Lal in their Report recommended that the Government Medical Officer should visit hospitals more often.[216]

Predictably, however, the desire for profits continued to outweigh human concern and the immigrants' health lapsed. In spite of efforts by the Government to ensure proper medical care, evasion of the laws on certain estates, resulted in the Indians languishing in wretchedness. Even the McNeill and Lal Report cited the deficiences and weaknesses in health regulations which should not be allowed to persist. This, they pointed out, was the result of deplorable conditions on the estates. Merely to maintain a modicum of sanitary and health standards in estate hospitals was evading the issue.[217]

Against this background of poor medical care, it is not surprising that the Indians dreaded becoming ill, because it further depressed their economic position.

Placed on the Invalid List following their discharge from the hospital, even though it was the estates' responsibilty to supply them with food, they were acutely aware of the difficulties they would later face in order to meet their food bill, the cost of which was deducted from their wages.[218] This was, to say the least, an unsatisfactory arrangement which often led distraught Indians to prematurely attempt their normal weekly working schedule (often difficult to achieve for many Indians discharged from hospital, because they were only capable of half or quarter of a day's work!) thus incurring a significant shortfall on their normal wages. Taken together, these pressures were likely to, and often did, lead to relapses,[219] and to add to their predicament, even when they were ill, the one crucial need, food, which they urgently expected more of, was almost always in short supply. This was a persistent, common and bitter complaint among the Indians, all the moreso, because for many, it was fatal.

For thousands of Indians, life was not only hard, but also short. Throughout the period of indentured immigration, the problem of estates with high mortality rates, remained of concern to only a few officials, such as the Protector of Immigrants in Trinidad. Although in 1861 the Protector had tried to 'explain away' the high mortality rates, seventeenth years later, the death rates on some estates, were so consistently high as to clearly rule out the possibility of allocating new immigrants to them. By the mid-1870s, according to one account, the estates with high death rates, included Felicity (8.9), Maracas Bay (11.1), Perseverance, Chaguanas (8.2), Woodford Lodge (6.4), St. Clair, Lower Caroni (8.4), and Trafalgar (10.2). The estates with low death rates were Lothians (1.0), Glen Roy and Palmyra (1.5) and Fairfield (1.4).

Mid-way into the last decade of the nineteenth century, the main causes of illness was malaria, followed by dysentery, diarrhoea and anaemia.[220] Five years later, the Bien Venue estate suffered a serious outbreak of malaria,[221] and a cluster of estates in the Couva area, were most affected by a number of diseases.[222] As if there was not sickness enough, ankylostomiasis spread rapidly among the underfed, under-nourished Indians and the alleged unabated smoking of ganja was invoked yet again by officials, who believed it to be the cause insanity![223] Given that British medical officials saw ganja smoking as an important contributory factor to mental disease, and the fact that ganja cultivation was 'considerable', the Surgeon General recommended a tax increase on the land used for its cultivation.

The seemingly growing concern and care shown by officials for the Indian emigrants, arose from two motives: first, bearing in mind that planters had paid for their importation, illness among the immigrants would reduce the return on this labour investment, and second, to ensure that the indentured system remained in existence, the planters became, only to a degree acceptable to them, more sensitive to criticism of the condition and treatment of the Indians.[224]

Gradually as the indentureship system evolved into the twentieth century, its bounds were extended to include more and more virgin lands, so that by about

1915, most of the sugar estates in Trinidad were to be found along the thirty-mile long narrow belt of flat and undulating land between the Caroni Swamp and the Oropouche Lagoon, where the vast majority of Indians had worked and lived since their arrival from India. Undaunted, the irrepressible indentured Indians had their sights firmly set on freedom from the strictures imposed upon them by the succession of rules and regulations that governed every aspect of their lives (especially within the ambit of work which included labour and wages, leave and desertion, their status as 'free' Indians, grievance procedure, the managerial grading structure, employer-labourer relations, the indentureds' grievances and strikes), as they laboured, day in and day out.

The Indian workforce, through the indenture system which had been regularized over the years, was divided by the various types of work they were assigned. Broadly speaking, work done by field hands fell into two categories: Task work and Time work. The prescribed task was not to be of a greater extent than could be performed by the immigrant to whom it was assigned within one working day of seven hours 'without extraordinary exertion'. Although Task work was normally selected by estate managers, novices relied on skilled subordinates to assist in setting the tasks. Generally, it seemed, that both the immigrants and estate managers favoured Task work: for the former, it meant a shorter working day, while the planter benefited from greater productivity for the 6 $^1/_2$ to 7 hours than in a 9 hour day.[225]

More often than not, the canes were burned, an effective means of clearing the roots, the stalk and the ground of any impeding thrash, before the job of cutting began in the early hours of the morning. The cutting of canes (which involved wielding a cutlass with great speed and dexterity) and forking were physically demanding jobs on the sugar estates. During the crop time, the canes were cut, bundled, picked up and carted-off to be weighed at a central point, before being taken to the factory. Among the hardest tasks was 'heading', which involved the Indians carrying the cut canes on their heads to ox-drawn or horse-drawn carts and railway cars, over long distances and often on uneven, muddy ground. Forking and trenching (digging trenches) were also physically demanding work, usually done by Indian males and Afro-Trinidadians. The job of draining offered fewer opportunities for employment, providing jobs usually for skilled men who earned relatively good wages. On the other hand, light work such as weeding and moulding were allocated to weaker male immigrants and to women. (Shovel-gangs formed another category of estate work). Indoor work and miscellaneous outdoor jobs were done by those with certain skills or by those who were unable to undertake tasks demanding steady effort. Other jobs included stock-keepers, carpenters, blacksmiths, grooms and watchmen. Beyond the sugar estates, alternative employment was available in the cocoa estates, where the jobs of picking, and breaking cocoa pods and 'dancing' on the beans, occupied the labourers for half the year.[226]

Any immigrant willing and able to work, but left unemployed on any working day was entitled to his full day's pay. The indentured labourer was required to work every day (except Sundays and authorised holidays) for nine hours during which he was allowed half an hour for eating and resting, after he had been at work for four and a half hours. An indentured labourer who, without reasonable excuse, refused or neglected to amend any work which was not accepted because it had been improperly done, was liable on the first conviction to a maximum penalty of $4.80 (£1) or 14 days imprisonment and on a subsequent conviction, to a maximum penalty of $9.60 (£2) or one month's imprisonment. It was also unlawful to withhold the payment of wages and to pay such wages in kind.[227]

The rate of wages for any description of Task work performed was not to be less than what was ordinarily paid, for the same description of work to the creole or other unindentured labourers working on the same plantation; and the money wage agreed upon for a task was set at not less than the minimum amount of day wages payable for Time work.[228]

On the question of Time work, the immigrant received wages for the prescribed hours each day, on which he had been present at work, at the rate of not less than one shilling and one half-penny (25 cents), if indentured as an able-bodied adult immigrant, and not less than 8 pence (16 cents) if the indentured labourer was other than able-bodied. If, in the opinion of the Government Medical Officer, an indentured immigrant was considered physically incapable of earning the minimum amount, at the ordinary rates of wages, his name was likely to be placed on the 'Invalid List'. Consequently, he received daily rations for work approved by the Protector of Immigrants. If his contribution, as a labourer did not meet the requirements of the Protector, with the approval of the employer, his contract of indenture was cancelled and provision made, if the immigrant so desired, for a return passage to India.

On the other hand, the employer was bound by law to keep a Pay List and labour book in the prescribed form, of all wages paid to the indentured immigrants on his plantation. The overtime arrangements required that an indentured labourer might, by agreement with his employer, work extra time on the field provided that the description of work to be assigned to him during extra time, was expressly stipulated before hand. Extra time was to be paid for by the hour, at a rate not less than that paid for ordinary Time work.

It was, in addition, unlawful for any employer to employ an indentured labourer for more than fifteen hours a day, and no labourer was compelled to work for more than the stipulated nine hours. Any employer found guilty of such offences was fined a sum not exceeding two pounds.

By about 1916, during the last stages before the indenture system was abolished, between 80 and 90 per cent of the work was done by Task.[229] In fact, almost all field work was Task work. The grooms, watchmen, store-keepers, carpenters and blacksmiths were usually paid by the week or fortnight, at wages in excess of ordinary daily rates set for indentured labourers by as much as 50 to 100 per cent. Work in buildings, and outdoor jobs allocated either to steady effort, was paid on a daily basis.

Taken together, Time and Task work were governed by the fact that, subject to the provisions for leave of absence from the plantation, every indentured labourer was expected to be present at the work assigned to him or her for nine hours each day, except Sundays and authorised holidays. No indentured labourer employed in the field, who had been present at the work for forty-five hours (or had earned, if able-bodied, five shillings and two and a half pence wages, or if other than able-bodied, three shillings and four pence over the working week) was compelled to present himself again at work during that week.

The hours of work for all labourers usually commenced between 6.00 and 6.30 a.m. At about 10.30 a.m there was a break for the mid-day meal. Legally, this stoppage was for the duration of half an hour, but in practice, it was extended to last an hour. Soon after 2.00 p.m, Task workers began to leave the field and return to their barracks, leaving behind the slower workers and men working in excess of the standard Task, who finished by 4.00 p.m. Time workers stopped at about 4.30 p.m.

On the cocoa estates, however, it was not unusual for Time workers to be kept on longer and be compensated with 'some form of remuneration in kind'. The managers of the cocoa estates were of the view that the workers 'cheerfully agreed' to this prolongation. This arrangement conflicted with sections 125 and 126 of the Ordinance, which made provision for labourers being employed voluntarily on overtime work, at not less than the ordinary Time rates. Further, the Government of Trinidad was willing to insert a provision requiring that all overtime be paid at a rate of one cent per 12 minutes – a rate substantially higher than that paid for ordinary time.[230]

Payment in kind was therefore an ad hoc estate arrangement, at variance with the legal definition of overtime work and pay. An examination of the sketchy statistical record of wages on the estates was carried out by Messrs. McNeill and Lal, into the daily register of wages for each of the estates visited.

The only official return relating to wages was an annual return, which showed for each estate, the percentage of adult male immigrants whose earnings fell below six pence (12 cents) daily for all days and not merely working days. If 30 per cent of the adult males on an estate earned less than six pence a day, no additional immigrants were allotted to that estate by the Protector of Immigrants in the following year, unless of course, the Governor on inquiry (that is if he was sufficiently interested to enquire) was satisfied with the reason for the deficient earnings.

Of the three estates visited by McNeill and Lal, it was found that more than 30 per cent of the male adults earned less than six pence a day! The incidence of sickness had been exceptional in two of these estates and, in the other, a combination of bad management and sickness contributed to the overall result. This last estate, through the evidence presented of its apparent neglect of its labourers' condition, was warned by the Immigration Department 'to amend its ways speedily'.[231]

In the absence of reliable information as regards average wages, it was nevertheless estimated by McNeill and Lal that earnings on the estates averaged about four shillings and three pence a week for an indentured labourer. Of course, earnings varied from estate to estate. For example, on a few of the better-run estates, earnings were about five shillings while on others, it dropped below four shillings. During the year, all days including those lost by sickness, bad weather, desertion, imprisonment for any offence or attendance in Court, were included. It was estimated that a man of 'ordinary industry and physique' worked on approximately 260 days a year.

Average earnings of women varied widely for two reasons: firstly, because women could not be ordered to work after three years' residence in the colony and, secondly, because the employer seldom used pressure, throughout their five-year term of indenture, to exact work except through the express wishes of their husbands. Consequently, their normal earnings amounted to one-half to two-thirds of the amount earned of an indentured man.

A new recruit or newcomer to the plantation was very much a novice. the practice on most estates was that newcomers should, for a few weeks, be employed as Time workers until they were more efficient.

The majority of the Indian indentured labourers, though drawn from the 'Agriculturalist Class' in India, had little or no experience of working systematically seven hours a day, for five and a half days a week, at work which required 'constant muscular effort'. In the experience of many, the reverse was true: they were used to long hours of casual work as it was found, and performed at a leisurely pace with irregular breaks. The initiation of a newcomer to the plantation system was therefore not easy. It was usual for such a labourer to be paired-off with an old hand, who helped and encouraged him. In return for his efforts, the newly introduced labourer earned from 10 to 15 per cent less than the older hands. This difference in wage reflected also the difference in productivity, which the employer had to impress upon the new recruit. Tied to the land, the carrot of inducement was dangled before the newcomer, although it was generally felt that the field workers disliked being kept on Time work, essentially because Task work was superior in status, in that kind of agriculture-based society. Relegation to Time work, recognised as punishment for sickness or unruliness, even though earnings were not reduced, was a clear warning to a newcomer to the plantation system.[232]

The basic provisions on leave for indentured immigrants were that they should be bound to reside on the estate on which they were under indenture; that an immigrant found on a public highway or on land, or any house other than his employer's could, if he failed to produce a certificate of industrial residence or of exemption from labour or a ticket of leave, be arrested without a warrant and taken to the nearest police station, until arrangements were made for him to appear before a Stipendiary Justice of the Peace; and that every indentured immigrant, who had earned at least five shillings and two and a half pence ($1.25) – Trinidad dollars – wages per week during two consecutive weeks, was entitled to leave of absence of one day and one night from the plantation. Except for 'Special cases', no indentured immigrant was entitled to more than seven days leave at any one time, or more than twenty-six days in one year.

The three main points, summarised, on the problem of desertion were that if an indentured immigrant without leave absented himself from the plantation, the manager could bring a charge against him as a deserter and, consequently, apply to the Magistrate for a warrant – granted free of cost – for his apprehension; that a manager who did not bring forward such a charge within fifteen days after desertion was liable to pay a fine of five pounds and should in addition, pay 'an absolute accumulating fine of one shilling for every such default'; and that every indentured immigrant who deserted should be liable to a penalty of five pounds or to imprisonment, or to both.[233]

The implementation of these basic provisions of the Ordinance of 1899 resulted in an inefficient labouring population on the sugar plantations. Overcrowding in the 'stable-like' estate barracks, malnutrition and bad sanitation were the major factors contributing to over 24,000 cases of sickness in 1911. The hospitals and jails were fully utilised. Between 1909 and 1912, an estimated 7,899 Indian immigrants were prosecuted; desertion and absence from work without lawful excuse accounted for 3,134 of these prosecutions.[234]

Usually, at the end of their five-year contracts of indenture, many Indians became 'free' labourers. As was the case with the African slaves after Emancipation, they did not, however, leave the estates *en masse*, in search of employment in the towns. In control of their labour power for the first time since their arrival, as free labourers, they were in greater demand on the estates, where the majority stayed. Given this pool of free labour, a distinct pattern of employment emerged, which was (to some extent) still the case in the post-1900 period. Both skilled and unskilled jobs were monopolised by Afro-Trinidadians in the towns and also on the estates. The occupational differences (or preferences?) between East Indians and Afro-Trinidadians were evident, even on the sugar estates, the main area of employment for the Indians, where for every five skilled workers engaged as blacksmiths, mechanics, carpenters, engineers and coopers, four were Afro-Trinidadians.

The indentured and free labourers were ordinarily paid the same rate for Task work. However, the free labourer's advantage over the indentured labourer was in his superior skill and, as such, he commanded a higher wage for Time work. The free labourer either because of his superior physique or his advanced experience in pruning cocoa trees was sometimes paid more. The earning power of the free labourer who possessed such physical superiority or skill, was further enhanced by the premium paid for his 'casual' employment for which he received an additional five to fifteen cents.[235] Much of this type of work was done on a daily basis. The difference in earnings posed a problem for the estates: should they pay the same rates for 'casual' as that paid for labour engaged over a much longer period? This was an anomaly not foreseen by the Ordinance.

As regards Task work, there were no differential wage rates in force whether the labourer lived on or off the estate. The *free* Indian labourer, for example, worked for the same Task rate as the *indentured* Indian immigrant, a tendency which favoured employers who were determined to keep wages low. Previously the employers' liability, the burden of such expenses as food, clothing and shelter, now fell on the 'free' labourers, thus keeping them more or less in debt; and like free Afro-Trinidadian labour before them, free Indian labour also saw indentured labour as under-cutting their value on the labour market.

A grievance procedure was set up for indentured labourers on the sugar estates, and there were eight Courts with resident Stipendiary Magistrates. Complaints and requests, in practice, were made both to the local Inspector and to the Protector of Immigrants. This commonsense and practical approach, another loose interpretation of the Ordinance, which strictly referred complaints *only* to the Protector or a Magistrate, highlighted the urgent need for the submission of workers' complaints directly to the local Inspector to be made lawful. Generally, indentured labourers were dissatisfied with the Clerks and Interpreters who listened and noted their cases in the absence of the Inspector or the Protector. They felt strongly that their cases should be placed personally before the Inspector or Protector, especially after a long and tiring journey, 'often, fifteen or twenty miles'.[236] It was not unusual for such journeys to be covered on foot.

Obviously, the inadequate arrangements for grievances did not take into consideration the enormity of the workers' predicament on the estates. To compound the problem, complaints were frequent and even the local Inspector was often unavailable. In fact, there was no fixed day on which the Inspector would be present to receive personal complaints. In principle, the grievance procedure seemed a reasonable development, but the practical arrangements, or the lack of them, were too loose to stem the undoubted and rising discontent among the workers.

Movement of labourers between estates was an important workers' issue. The transfer of an indentured labourer from one estate to another was made only with the consent of the estate *receiving* such a labourer. The right of transfer from one estate to another was accepted as necessary if, for example, relations between the indentured labourer and his employer, Headmen or other employees had deteriorated to a point where 'serious trouble' was likely to occur.[237]

The grading structure of the managerial staff on most estates was composed of a Manager, Deputy Manager, Overseers and Headmen. The Manager had overall control, aided by the Overseers who took charge of a number of gangs of workers. Each 'gang', in turn, was immediately supervised by a Headman.

The hierarchy of managerial grades, however, varied with estates. For example, a Deputy Manager could be employed on a very large estate, while on very small estates no Overseers were needed to bridge the gap between the Manager and Headman. This lowering of the promotion ceiling effectively minimised any promotion opportunities. By and large, Managers and Deputy Managers were drawn from among the Headmen, which showed, as far as it went, that the promotion stream functioned correctly. How fairly, was another matter.

Although managerial responsibility was conveniently delegated, not all Overseers, because of considerable variations in character, temperament and education, were regarded as embryonic managers. The instances had been many where some Overseers had deliberately created trouble expressing through foul language their impatience at disobedience, idleness or neglect, on the part of workers. On the face of it, most Overseers were able to exercise authority with consideration and with the minimum of friction.

The majority of the Headmen were East Indian with coloured Creoles filling the other positions. The Headmen played a pivotal and controversial role, the spin-off of which had a direct bearing on the overall contentment or discontentment of the labourers. The fact that they exacted and supervised all the field work meant that practically all the complaints lodged by workers, to some degree, originated with them. While some Headmen inspired trust and even 'cheerful obedience', others were aggressively authoritative. If this aggressive authority was indeed delegated, then the interpretation put upon it by some headmen was not only wide, but also coercive in trying to control 'perverse labourers'. Some Headmen, for example, were inclined to exact petty personal services outside the labourers' working hours.[238] One gang of labourers complained that one of their Headmen went as far as levying contributions towards the expense of building a mosque! This particular Headman, who had been barred from work within the scope of 'indentured labour' following the 'repeated requests of the whole estate's population', was later reinstated and placed in charge of 'Free labourers' on another estate, thus shifting in this instance, the stigma of malpractice in administration from one group of labourers to another. Clearly, a Headman's job was hazardous, his safety dependent upon the skill and intelligence he brought to bear on a given work situation.

The relationship between the employers would have been regarded as satisfactory were it not for the large number of prosecutions. On the well-managed estates, which were few, and where the number of prosecutions was low, the employer-labourer relationship was described as 'excellent'. In such a situation the employer played the role of a Patriarch in the community. His authority was readily recognised and estate labourers willingly laid their troubles before him. He exercised judgement in disputes between immigrants, was entrusted with the care of personal and family savings and acted as confidential adviser.

However, on the badly managed estates, where the relationship was clinical and business-like to the point of being almost inhuman, there was more suspicion than trust. The relationship between managers of this type and the workers was not cordial, because of what they called 'interference' from the Immigration

Department and its officers. In fact, some managers were reluctant to believe that a Headman's unpopularity among the workers could ever be due to anything but his conscientiousness. As a disciplinarian, ever-ready to please his superiors, who were more often than not of European extraction, he was tended to interpret the rules strictly. For example, after giving a warning or perhaps two, to an errant labourer, he did not hesitate to prosecute. Fortunately, the attitude or indeed the working policy of such employers in dealing with their labourers was tempered by the intervention of the Immigration Department.

In the cases where remonstrance was not effective, the employer was addressed. If this official remonstrance was persistently disregarded, the manager was certified 'not a proper person to have charge of immigrants', and although this extreme measure was rarely necessary, immigrants were indeed removed from one estate on this account.

The grievances of the indentured labourers covered a wide range of matters. For instance, many immigrants were inclined to complain (as they had done earlier) of the dearness of food as compared with Indian prices, but it was found that on those estates where earnings were considered 'good' and where prosecutions were few, this was regarded more as an argument in weighing up the pros and cons of Indian immigration, than as an immediate grievance.

While some managers had a fixed time daily for listening to all complaints, other managers appointed no fixed time and adopted no regular procedure. This irregularity in dealing with workers' complaints was a major defect in the relationship between the manager and the indentured labourers, particularly on the larger estates. On the smaller estates this relationship was more personal and consequently somewhat better.

As regards conditions of employment of Indian immigrant labour, a complaint which generated strong feelings was the labourers' 'liability to imprisonment'. Many labourers felt that although they sometimes required 'reproof or correction' he should not be imprisoned. A man who had been imprisoned was more than likely to bear a grudge against his employer, and in this respect, the liability to imprisonment was oppressive and provocative.

Upon arrival in Trinidad, many indentured labourers underwent a period of bad health and general home-sickness, which affected their capacity to work. These individuals were used to less strenuous work and in view of this, it was felt very desirable, under the circumstances, that in the labourer's first few months 'he should be broken into harness gently and paid for his efforts rather than results'.[239]

On most of the larger estates, managers were suspicious of a few old hands, who were 'restive under any control or discipline'. They were therefore regarded as 'dangerous mentors' to the new recruits. The employment of 'good' Headmen was therefore seen as the best immediate antidote to dissipate the 'imaginary or trivial' grievances of the labourers. Those accused of fomenting disturbances were transferred to other estates, and while conceding that the butt of the 'trouble maker' was the estate Manager, Overseer or Headman, it was usually a very imperfect inquiry which traced the trouble no further. In this connection, McNeill and Lal wrote: 'There is always some tinder for the spark, and while the spark may not be under control the tinder should not have been ready to hand'.[240] No doubt, trouble on the estates was directly attributable, in large measure, to the conditions of restraint and ignorance under which the immigrant laboured and lived.

There was always the undeniable potential of serious trouble which was intermittently expressed in 'informal' work protests for example, through desertion, go-slows and sabotage on the sugar estates. In fact, the combined grievances of their daily working lives found expression at public festivals such as the Muharram (Hosein or Hussay) processions.

At first the new arrivals on the estates posed no problem. But after gaining some work experience, they realized that their rights, though few, were constantly being undermined. On the other hand (and this added to their frustration) they found that most actions taken to redress grievances, resulted in breaches of contract. Thus they were prosecuted almost always in an effort to prevent them from 'evading work'. Consequently, the Indian labourers responded to their oppression, through mass labour resistance in the form of 'strikes' which frequently occurred between July and October, during the wet (rainy) season or immediately after.[241]

Among the few officials who had, prior to the turn of the twentieth century, bothered to inquire into such strikes was Charles Mitchell, who was able to confirm his earlier suspicions that the funadamental cause was the low earnings of the indentured labourers. Moreover, such earnings showed wide fluctuation between the crop and out of crop seasons. In 1891 D.W.D. Comins had found that on one estate 55 men each earned during crop-time an average of 16 cents a day, as compared with 12 cents a day out of season.[242] And five years later, W.H. Coombs calculated that indentured labourers on a large estate earned an average of \$3.67 a week during 20 weeks of crop and \$2.40 a week during 32 weeks out of crop, or 34.6 per cent less in crop time, an 'enormous difference' in seasonal earnings. Around this time, female indentured labourers' earnings (in relation to males) were found to be even lower than they had previously been. It needs but little imagination to comprehend the difficulties these women faced in maintaining their self-respect while bringing up their growing and demanding families.

Although by the early 1870s a few estates permitted their labourers to use a certain acreage to grow provisions, this practice was restricted and short-lived. But regardless of the fact that wage rates of indentured labour were supplemented by housing and medical care, it was argued that in real terms, indentured labourers' 'theoretical earnings were rarely, if ever, attained'.[243] Persistent low earnings, therefore, frustrated indentured labourers' attempts to rise above their poverty, and not surprisingly, they resorted to desperate acts to redress their grievances.

The strike action of these labourers had become of much concern, enough to absorb the attention of other Government officials, who punished the ring leaders and participants. But while such action was repressed, rebellion among the Indians continued. In 1885, no fewer than 21 labourers were convicted for inciting immigrants to strike, and although by the end of the century, committals averaged seven per year, the number in 1889 was unusually high.[244] These strikes were not without violence. The first major action taken was at Cedar Hill in 1882, when an Overseer was attacked by a group of labourers. During 1882–4 there were serious strikes involving police intervention on estates in Naparima, El Socorro and at Laurel Hill. And in 1891, a strike lasting six weeks took place on the Golconda estate.[245] According to one acount, this was caused by 'excessive tasks' and, as a consequence, the size of the tasks was reduced. The immigrants, not satisfied with the concession, asked to be put on 'time work' of 9 hours a day; but discontent still prevailed until finally a few of the ring leaders were sent to estates in Cedros.[246]

Officials were agreed that all the serious trouble on the estates, essentially after 1900, was primarily the work of re-emigrating Indians.[247] Of course, this was only partly true. The real causes of the trouble had much to do with the long-standing grievances of labourers, many of whom, at times, acted 'spontaneously' in an employer-worker relationship, based essentially on confrontation and conflict.

In 1900 a strike over wages broke out on Harmony Hall estate, resulting in sixty-four of the strikers being sentenced to 21 days hard labour. The officials found that the leaders of the strike were 'returned immigrants' and in this case the chief instigator was a 'returned immigrant' from British Guiana. Regardless of the fact that they were returned immigrants, their discontentment was profound. According to one account, after leaving jail, 'the men asked for and received Time work. Although most reported and worked the full 9 hours, they did not work diligently, usually completing only half a task. When paid proportionately to their work, they made angry threats. To quell the unrest the ring leaders were transferred to other estates where they lost status and were thereby rendered harmless'.[248]

Another example of this state of unrest among the Indian workers was the 'last large disturbance' during the period of indentureship, which occurred in February 1914 at the La Reunion estate when 16 immigrants, without passes, abandoned the estates and made their way to Port of Spain to complain against harassment by the management. There was some evidence to support their claim. But although these Indians promised to resume work, they sought the support from other immigrants to strike, and when they broke into the manager's house, they were charged with 'riotous behaviour'.[249]

The many disputes between Overseers and labourers and the Headmen and labourers over Tasks, often ended in violence, and very rarely to their mutual satisfaction. The manifestation of widespread discontent suggested that there was much room for improvement. Nevertheless apart from the contentious issue of the prosecution record of indentured labourers, the relationship between the Manager and workers was, considered to be reasonably good, particularly on the smaller estates, where there was evidence of mutual good-will and 'more intimacy'.

However, sexual relations between members of the managerial staff and female indentured workers were regarded as an absolute disqualification from exercising authority.

Despite the good intentions of exceptional managers, the indentured worker was, in effect, a man or woman who laboured under conditions of 'half-slavery'. And such as it was, every moment of the employer-labourer relationship, which was broken by violence[250] (seemingly unco-ordinated, but with regularity), remained potentially explosive until the system of indenture was abolished.

Almost a decade and a half before the 'system' was terminated, the Indians had already become a remarkable and largely misunderstood presence. And even though many of them wanted to, and had returned to India, many more, an estimated two-thirds, had decided to remain in the island.

## Indentured Voices

Before moving on, let us return to Fazal, Moolian, Maharani, Bharath and Sankar, to hear their accounts, the authentic voices of indentureship as they experienced it in Trinidad, during the last two decades of the system.

### FAZAL

Fazal was overjoyed, after his long voyage, to again feel the earth beneath his feet. He regarded the earth as his 'mother', his God. Once he had cleared the Immigration Depot 'dem white man go an pick up people', he said, dispersing the tired and bewildered Indians, clutching their few possessions, to the various estates. He and nine others, four women and five men, went to Picton estate, where the Indians already 'in harness' had gathered to see and welcome them. Fazal said that the Indians had enquired about his name and that this initiated conversation. He soon realised that they were hungry for fresh news from India.

Soon he was installed in his barrack room, one of six in the wooden structure he was assigned to. Given the traditional close-knit family and village ties they knew in India, what thoughts might these bare, silent spaces have provoked on entry and for the days and weeks to come. Men and women living in separate rooms, shared the premises. Married men, however, lived in 'different barrick'. The close proximity of the rooms, did not allow any privacy to the occupants and Fazal felt it was 'just like living in de bush'. Bad behaviour amongst the Indians was not tolerated. Fighting or running off with another man's wife or daughter, was severely punished by the Indians themselves, sometimes ending in murder.

One can therefore imagine the whole barrack population of bewildered Indian people in an alien sugar estate, seeking from each other friendship, solace and support. Fazal was no exception, but with time, his deep sense of brotherhood and belonging helped in making him an integral part of the Indian community of Picton. Here there was no butcher selling beef, and Friday was set aside by Muslims, as a day of prayer at the mosque. The pundit, on the other hand, adminstered to Hindu needs. He did no work, but was given an estate barrack-room in which he 'could read like hell'. And as customary, the pundit also had the good fortune of receiving from the people, free of charge, goods such as flour, rice, dhal (or dahl) and salt.

Off duty, the indentured Indians were ever-resourceful and creative. At home, the Indians were entertained by songs from each other, or the music played by a group of musicians on sitar, majeera and sarangi, instruments which they had brought from India. According to Fazal, there was no dhantal or organ.

At these times of relaxation, the many Indians who smoked, indulged in ganja, which was priced at 'three cent'. This ganja, brought from India, was preferable to the rum that was sold at forty cents. The ganja was not sold in a shop, but could be bought at someone's house, with a licence (of sixty dollars a year) to do so. Song, food and ganja-smoking, tended to go together; and the effect of this smoking was the desire for sweet-tasting things, that excluded the consumption of meat.

But the pleasures of leisure time, so well taken, were counterbalanced by the insistent demands of indentured work. At times, Fazal said, the labourers had to go to work in the early morning in their 'same wet clothes'; and that in crop-time, it was normal to work also on Sundays. The working days were often long and the discomfiture of clinging 'wet clothes' left in him, an indelible impression. The tasks were hard, as the Indians toiled in all weathers, including the extremes of merciless heat and torrential rain. The physical stamina they needed, was underscored by enormous courage and hope. How else could one explain their forebearance, survival in the face of incredible demands upon their mental and physical strength? The nutritious value of a roti, fried in oil with some salt, that Fazal ate before leaving his room in the morning was not enough to sustain him for long. By midday he was too far away to go home, so with the minimum of effort, his lunch consisting of 'bout two cane' (two lengths of sugar cane, sucked dry), was taken right there on the estate.

Fazal and his fellow labourers found it very difficult to adapt to the conditions of life and work on the estates. Even though the tasks varied, he was paid the same money. So low his spirits had fallen that he said he wanted to go back to India. But this raised serious questions: where in India would he and his compatriots have gone to, and who would have been beneficent enough to give them a ship. He had obviously thought through the idea in the light of his experience as an indentured labourer, and deliberated long and hard over the potential of a return journey, with a chastened sense of realism.[251]

## MOOLIAN

Moolian began his labouring days at Usine Ste. Madeleine, cutting the canes and loading bundles of it on to carts drawn by mules and oxen to the derrick (weighing cranes) where the canes were weighed. Each working day Moolian was engaged in this frantic toing and froing, leaving the formerly dense fields increasingly bare, so that the undulating land can again be clearly seen, as it was before the cane plants had taken root. From the derrick, tons of canes were loaded on to railway carriages and transported to the sugar factory. This process repeated itself, time and again, during crop-time, and for men like Moolian, the tasks set were difficult. When rain fell, the thick mud caused havoc, as man and beast made desperate efforts to get the loads of cane, piled precariously high on the carts, off the fields, over undulating land. To compound his problems, Moolian said that heavy rains meant that his working clothes would, almost certainly not be dry before it was time to get back to work the next day. Morning for the labourers was not daybreak. Often while still tired and drowsy, Moolian remembered being woken up at 1.00 or 2.00 a.m, so that he would not miss the truck that would take him many miles away, which was only part of the journey. After the truck was gone, and in the slowly clearing mist and darkness, he had to walk a long distance from the derrick to the place where his task of cutting and loading canes for that day would actually begin. Understandably, he dreaded the approach of morning and often the vigorous knocking on the door of his barrack-room, demanding that he 'get up'! On one occasion, when a pushy Driver had forced the door open, Moolian said, a few labourers beat the man severely.

And like Fazal, Moolian confirms that sanitary conditions at the barracks left much to be desired. Of course, when things went wrong (and this was the case more often than not for the Indians) freedom from indentured bondage was never far from the labourers' mind. Indeed, going back to India, was always a possibility, and for many a realistic option. Yet, no matter how depressing the conditions (and by 1910, there would have been some relative improvements to the system) there were inducements to keep the Indians on the land, to prevent them from going back. If some wanted to return after five years, by the end of their ten year indentureships, many were not interested. 'Ship no coming, ship no coming', as Moolian said. But why? The reason was simple: the Indian labourer, as it were, was already on the ground, and the Colonial authorities made every effort to deflect his attention from India, and keep him transfixed to the land. This, however, was not enough for Moolian, who at one stage had paid his own passage, but because of sickness he was unable to make the journey. At the time he was married to a 'gyul' (girl) he had known for some time, and his mother-in-law took the 'ship money' (hard-earned savings). Having been denied this money, he felt his chance of his chance of returning was lost forever. But while the flush of disappointment aroused reluctance at first, with time, be became reconciled to life, for what he felt it was worth, on the estate.

The ubiquitous 'White man' astride his horse, with a 'big long whip', surveying the arched backs and rhythmical swings of the cutlass-bearing arm of Indian workers, traversed the fields with his ever-watchful Indian and Black Headmen. Sometimes the 'White man' came in a buggy and scrutinised Moolian's cart. He confessed that he was afraid of this man with the whip (the epitome of insensitive colonial authority) and with good reason, for he had seen enough of the violence on the estates. The act of a Driver kicking an injured Indian labourer, which Moolian had witnessed, was commonplace. And he himself felt threatened on one occasion, but he overcame his fear and anger and managed to carry on.

He reflected on other aspects of his life. He was not married (did he divorce the 'gyul'?) but he said that the first woman he had taken was from Calcutta, a woman who loaded cane during the working week and washed clothes on Sundays. As time wore on, the immediacy of daily toil monopolised his attention. He concentrated on work and related matters of life in Trinidad. He was now working at Caroni, at the very heart of the sugar-belt, boiling sugar; and all that he had seen and done so far, was in fact, a far cry from the 'challaying sugar' he was promised years before in his village. After so many years in the island, he felt a sense of loss, of resignation about recurrent but fleeting thoughts of going back to India. And as if to convince himself finally of his destiny, 'I no go no way again', he said, 'I have to wuk, I have to slave Trinidad'.[252]

## MAHARANI

Maharani was brought to Woodford Lodge estate. She was given 'goods' to cook and if she wanted it, rum was on offer. But why was alcohol offered to a Hindu woman, who may never have indulged in its consumption? Was it perhaps intended to steady her nerves and ease the depressed state she might have been in? Very soon, however, she was handed a hoe and cutlass, agricultural implements she would come to know so well that in time, it would have been difficult to think of life without them. But, so soon after her ordeal of the voyage, she felt incapable of weeding, of doing anything. She cried a great deal and even as she tried to work the tears fell profusely. She cut the canes and carried small bundles to the cart or truck; and weeding and toting were among her regular tasks. She had to do as she was told, and received between 25 to 30 cents for the job of weeding. She was not sure of the going rate, yet she carried on her daily tasks, working, cooking and, of course, eating. Maharani was unmarried and unattached, but in this situation where women were still relatively scarce, the question was: how long could she remain so? She must have been aware, at every turn, of the pressures upon her. Or was she too preoccupied with the as yet fresh thoughts of India. Then one day the question was put to her: Maharani do you want a man? No, she said. Why not? Because I would be going back to India, she reoplied. More pressure was applied. She was told that she had to 'have somebody' in the event of sickness, for example, but in any case she should not remain alone. If sickness came, she said she would look after herself. At this stage in the conversation, the man in question, took hold of her hand and carried her into his room. 'I no want nobody', she pleaded, 'I stop alone'. The man assured her that he liked her, but 'me nuh like!', she retorted. In the struggle that ensued, he took her.

The man with whom Maharani lived had been released from indentured labour after ten years. He was free to go to the nearby village, but Maharani could not, because she was still bound by her indentured contract. The man pleaded with the 'White man', saying that she will come to work each day, if he let her go. In turn, Maharani begged the white manager, who allowed her to go and live in the village, on condition that she returned to work on the estate.

Other pressures took its toll. Maharani was now able to speak a 'lil bit' of English, in spite of the fact that she spoke to few people. Then one Sunday while she was cooking, the man she lived with and her shipmate (another man) began to fight. Her shipmate was killed in the struggle and the police took her man away. Soon after this tragic incident, Maharani said there was plenty of rum-drinking and ganja-smoking. Whether or not she had tasted the rum on her arrival at Woodford Lodge, now she she was ready for a drink. The effect on her was immediate and devastating. She began to roll, experienceing a rising and falling sensation, as she broke into uncontrollable laughter.

Thereafter, she settled down to the boring routine of life on the estate. On Sundays, she did house-work, washed her room, washed clothes, fetched water and bathed herself. We also get an indication of one of the consequences of walking around bare-footed in the unsanitary surroundings of the estate dwellings. She spoke of extracting jiggers from her foot with a pin.

One consolation was that all Maharani's 'jahaji' lived in the barracks, almost the same way as when they first came. She felt an overwhelming sense of warmth and comradeship for her shipmates, especially the older women whom she called mousee (aunt). 'Dem like family self', she said. Her first child, a boy, was born dead, a terrible tragedy (after carrying him for nine months) which caused her grief. She cried as a local carpenter made a box-board coffin for the infant and then buried it. Fortunately, her other children survived, rooting her more firmly where she was. And when she was urged to go to India, she felt her time for that had passed. 'No', she said, 'I studying dem cheren'.[253]

## BHARATH

Once he had arrived on the estate to which he was bound, the coming and going of indentured Indians had been matters of special concern to Bharath. More than likely, the sudden separation from his family and the extraordinary experience on the ship deepened his sense and appreciation of comradeship and community. He went to meet those who embarked from the various ships, to greet them, and to cry 'Bhaiya (brother) wha country (where in India) you come from'. For Bharath, the brotherhood of the ship, was extended to the barracks, where he said, 'everybody living like one'. But this public self could not compensate for a more private satisfaction. It has been a long time, he said, since he had a brother and sister and the only way to make a brother and sister was to get married. Though he had tried for a long time in the same village, marriage eluded him. So he continued his warm relations with those whom he called jahaji and brothers.

Like most Indians, Bharath was proud of his heritage, especially in this hostile land. In fact, he confessed to resorting to fights, if a man talked in English, because he thought the man was 'cussing'. He spoke about Indians who played bad, and said he kept a lathee (stick) and a cutlass to chop attackers, even if it was a White man. Bharath not only had a strong sense of community, but also tells us of presiding over relations between men and women: if a man, already involved with a woman, ran off with another woman, the aggrieved woman should beat him; that members of a higher caste would not take water from a lower caste. These clear views, reflecting traditional Indian life, was particularly evident among the India-born. He said, although the Indians he had known came from Calcutta, some were different, belonging to different castes. Yet, as workers on the estates, they used the same cutlass and the same hoe. Neither was there any caste distinctions in the barracks. He was convinced that making smoking-pipe and smoking ganja, cured sickness, 'no cough, no fever', he said, and that this was a popular past-time, an activity which was, to some degree, supplemented with libations of rum.

He had no doubt that a document entitling him to land and house was stolen by the Government and believed that if you were sick, you either had to go to the hospital or jail. He says also that the estate manager tried, in so far as it was possible, to house people according to their married or bachelor status, whether or not they were fowl and/or beef-eaters, and those of other like-minded habits. He said that some barracks were fully occupied, in some cases with one hundred or two hundred and fifty people. One of the obvious problems at that time, he said, was 'no have oman chinedad'. For a wife, you had to go to India; and Bharath, who had tried for so long in his village, was as aware as anyone else who had tried, of how difficult finding a mate really was.

But some men were more fortunate, being married and with large families, especially those who hade been in Trinidad between ten to twelve years. For them the chances of going back to India had diminished to virtually nothing. As Bharath said of them, 'e can go, e have cheren'. He also relates the story of a lady who said 'son have hyar, me no having nutting India, all e have have chinedad'.

Work, jail, sickness, the hospital and 'lix' (beatings) preoccupied the Indians, who could not stray too far from either their physical surroundings or from what was expected of them. Yet they posed, at every turn, a strong resistence to the system. And for the womanless man, like Bharath, keeping a 'kirwal' (Afro-Trinidadian) woman meant leaving his estate. Attractive as such a union may have been, Bharath settled for other pleasures, especially after work and on Sundays. Reading the *Ramayana*, singing, the clashing of the jhaal (large cymbals) and majeera (small cymbals), the delicious taste of mango, musk-melon, water-melon, cane and corn. More than this, it seemed, he could not have, for so long as he remained an indentured labourer. He said he carried his 'pass' on Saturdays and Sundays and that he came back to work on Monday. On Saturday, he worked half a day and by two o'clock he would take a train (with the full protection of the 'pass' – and what a sense of freedom he must have felt!) to Chowhana and Couva and return home on Sunday evening. He would take a drink only on Saturday and Sunday. These spells of freedom were precious reminders, engendering an ever-greater desire to attain full freedom. Until that moment when the strictures of indenture were removed, he knew he must persevere, that he must continue to learn as much as possible, and to gain in confidence. If there was any fear of authority in him in earlier years, he was no longer afraid of either the 'White man' or the Driver.

Physically, Bharath was strong. He repeatedly spoke of hard work, of draining, forking, planting, cane-cutting, and except for a 'lil fever an ting', he had no liver pain, no 'eye sickness', no hookworm and no sickness generally. How fortunate he was. Few Indians, under indenture, could boast of such good health. Yet he too, was unimpressed by the latrine facilities on the barracks, the over-crowding in some barrack rooms, and the poverty of indentured labourers, who had to work for five years 'in de same clothes', because they could not afford it. Their beds were bare boards and they rested their heads on pillows of cut tapia grass. The flambeau that lit their rooms were fuelled by pitch-oil which, at six cents a measure, was a large part of their income.

Bharath gives us an indication of the terrain of the estate and its isolation from the wider society. He said it was on high, undulating land, with a high wood surrounding a lagoon area. There were few people of African descent near his estate (unlike the experience of many indentured Indians in Jamaica). He says, the 'kirwals' presence varied from estate to estate.

Tension and conflicts on the estates (as shown earlier) and in the barracks were ever-present, as Indians fought and some escaped into the 'high wood'. The lack of money was the core problem. To survive, many had to pool their shillings and cents, so that they could get enough to eat; and through extraordinary thrift some labourers even managed some savings. Bharath spoke of the trust the Indians had in the Chinese shop-keepers, with whom they deposited their savings. Five, six and twelve dollar deposits were not unusual. He said, 'If ah ha million dollar, put it Chinee, if ah ha jewel, gi dem'. Over a long time, they had proved themselves as trustworthy. Indeed, the Chinese were generous to those, especially the sick, who could not pay for certain essential goods.

Regardless of their problems (and there were many), some Indians treated themselves to drinks and dancing, usually at the weekends, before facing yet again, the prospects of work on Monday. But the gaiety of the weekend sometimes led to violence meted out to women. Bharath informs us that 'if oman do wrong', she must be beaten. But even when she did no wrong there was no guarantee that she would not be in danger of a violent attack upon her!

At times of marriage, or during a ceremony for the dead, or if he had prayers in his house, Bharath said no Afro-Trinidadians could attend. And he spoke of the separation of the 'kirwal', who lived on one side of the barracks. Education was, until then, still hard to come by, and Bharath says there were no schools. But he spoke of his shipmates attending the newly established schools at Couva, Chowhana, Petit Bourg and Penal.

He says little about marriage (or was he simply living with someone), but now he spoke of his children (not stating how many) all of whom were born and married in the same estate village. By now he had acquired a small plot of land on which he supplemented his earnings, by planting rice, tomatoes and ochro. The 'kitchen garden' was a necessary adjunct to the low earnings on the estates; and at this time, it seemed that rice-planting was growing in acreage on lands occupied by the Indians.

Even though Bharath's commitment to the land was undoubted, naturally he had recurring thoughts about India and those among his compatriots who were returning. There was a steady trickle of Indians making the journey back, after their five or ten year indentures, and according to Bharath, there was a tendency among the returnees to congregate in the same place in India. He was pragmatic about the freedom to either stay in Trinidad or go back to India. One still had to work, he said, 'any way going, ha to ork'. He had toiled long and hard and had established a close relationship with the land, his shipmates, friends and family. He had accumulated a great deal of experience and a unique perspective. In all, he was able to make a judgement of his adult life on the estate, and now by comparison, India had 'notting'. To support his acceptance of Trinidad, he drew attention to the evidence, 'plenty people going come back, two two time'.

Nevertheless, Bharath acknowledged that life on the estates was no bed of roses. The economic problems and social tensions showed no sign of easing, even though most of the Indians had already been through most or had completed their indentures. Social life, however, tended to lift the spirit. Marriages, more often than not, were big occasions, with music and dance, plenty food for all those who attended, including Afro-Trinidadian guests and others who were invited to share in the feast. Festivals such as Hosein were also well-attended by all. Bharath did not attend Carnival, which he said was for Afro-Trinidadians. And symbolically, indentured labourers reminded themselves of their continuing bondage at the end of crop-time, when they each pooled their hard-earned 25 cents for another celebratory get together.

Over the years, the barrack population had grown, and Bharath spoke of the many children on the estate to which the people were bound and where they lived and died in humble barrack rooms. When death came (for many much too soon) their bodies were interred in the burial ground, which adjoined every estate. The death of a friend or member of the family was a solemn and important occasion for the Indians on the estate. 'Nobody na going wuk', Bharath said, 'o if you going, wuk doneing 9 o'clock, 10 o'clock all people coming'. The ship brotherhood and sisterhood remained very strong, as the dead indentured immigrants and their descendants made the last journey, borne on a bamboo platform and carried on the heads of close relatives and friends to the cemetery. At times like these, after years of wearing threadbare clothes on the estate, the Manager was at last magnanimous, and to his credit no charge was made for the burial cotton which enshrouded the deceased. But this was, according to Bharath, only possible when this man who wielded so much power in life (and now in death) was approached.[254]

## SANKAR

Sankar and his shipmates alighted at the jetty and walked unsteadily inland. Finally he was on firm ground on the island which he had tried to imagine for several months. He travelled to his estate on a train which ran just like the trains in India, except that this one was smaller. From the window of the train, he saw houses and a village, and who knows what thoughts may have crossed his mind, for even at that moment, he was not sure where he was going. At the Robertson estate, which he would, in time, come to know very well, a mule-cart awaited him and his travelling companions, who loaded on their few personal belongings tied in bundles. This was not to be another free ride for Sankar and his fellow-labourers who walked, while the driver of the mule-cart led the way to their final destination, the barracks.

Sankar was accommodated in a room next to four bachelors, who helped each other by gathering firewood and cooking communally. He was given the normal rations of dahl, rice and salt, basic ingredients of the food that would help to sustain him for physically demanding work that would earn him 25 cents a day. Interestingly, he was assigned to work on a cocoa estate. His job was 'bagging cocoa', which he did for three years, and for the next two years of his bonded labour, he tapped rubber from the bleeding rubber trees.

Discipline on this cocoa estate was no less severe than on the sugar estates. Sankar says that anyone who escaped was hounded down by the police, and once caught, the escapee was not only beaten, but also had to pay the estate in labour-time lost during his or her absence from work. In terms of supervision of the work on rubber and cocoa estates, Sankar said there was no Driver or Overseer on the rubber estate, but both line managers were in attendance on the cocoa estate. He spoke of the beating and kicking Indians received on the sugar cane estate, without implying that punishment on his cocoa estate was any better. The work was hard and you had to earn the money to buy your rations. The Saturday work of 'dancing cocoa', involved men, women and children. No labourer was spared from this work, which was conducted in three houses. Here too, malingering was dealt with through violence. If a labourer did not work, he or she was liable to be kicked, and if sick, the labourer had to go to the hospital. Work, work, work was the insistent, demanding, compelling activity that influenced all aspects of the indentured Indians' lives. To say no to work to an Overseer standing at your door, early in the morning, was to invite easily-provoked violence. Sankar underlined the fact that the Overseer and the Manager were united in their oppression. So why did the

Indians not combine in a similar fashion to achieve certain necessary gains? Sankar explains: 'if all a we make one head, dey cyan do nutting, but we not one head'. The divide and rule principle and the fear of violence from the Drivers, Overseers and managers kept the Indians apart. Individual Indians were singled out, victims of violent intimidation. Sankar related one instance when a cocoa estate manager, who repeatedly robbed Indians of the work they had performed, received his come uppance, by being hit with a spade handle. This was not the only Manager to die from cheating the Indians, who may have practised 'passive' resistance, at times, but more often than not, they showed their aggression whenever this was necessary. It struck Sankar that in spite of the many cases of conflict and of breaking the law, 'dey eh lock up nobody', for if they pursued this strategy there would be nobody to work in the fields. While almost all the Drivers were Indian, Sankar identified one 'kirwal' Driver, who could read, but could not write. There were, at least, three other Afro-Trinidadians on the estate, who did draining, the work of a carterman and a groom. Others came and went, but there was not a large 'kirwal' presence. Sankar gives us his view of Afro-Trinidadian-Indian relations on his estate at this time. 'We eh interfering wid dem, we living for weself', as an Indian community, 'talking among ourselves, singing, playing drums, eating and sleeping', said Sankar, 'we Indian self, we eh meddle wid them'. The nature and circumstances of the system of indentureship in Trinidad reinforced this separation of the two groups.

Sankar also said that whistling or singing was not tolerated at work, especially when the 'White man' was around to oversee the work being done and the workers. He fully recognised how precious his off-work hours were and gives us an account of how fond he was of the weekend relaxation and of music, in particular. On Sundays, he would routinely bathe himself, gather fire-wood, often enough for the whole week, and rest, for much too soon Monday morning dawned and he was again back at work.

Musically, he was no drummer, but admitted to being a singer, especially of Bhajans. On Saturday nights, the Chattri (warrior caste) owner of a shop in the barracks would encourage singing until midnight. Indeed Sankar's fondness of bhajan-singing had been known to lead to excess, continuing until 1.00 a.m, and sometimes through to the hours of four, five and six on Sunday morning, when "sleep take me an I sleep". As a Bhajan-singer, it is no wonder that he kept company with many of the Sadhus (Hindu ascetics), who read the *Ramayana*. Over the years, however, these Sadhus, usually older men, died and Sankar was left alone to sing his Bhajans to an audience, including a new generation of Trinidad-born Indians. He spoke of the building of a Hosein (Tadjah or Hosay), for which money, collected from all the Indians on three estates, was used to buy paper and other essentials necessary to build a Tadjah. Alas, he could not sing the `hosay song', but he remained interested and supportive of this essentially Mohammedan festival.

Another aspect of Sankar's Saturdays was that of doing the shopping, such as it was, buying the usual food items – ghee, salt, oil and rum from the 'Chinee' shop.

On this day, he also had a tendency to treat himself to salmon and bread and pepper-sauce (adaptation to local creole food tastes) and have a drink of rum. How did he relate to predominantly Christian Trinidad society at Christmas time? He said that on the Robinson estate at that time of year, Sohari (fried bake) and Tarkarie (cooked vegetables) were given to the Indians, and the cocoa-house was open for all the people from the three estates, an assembly which included 'Indian, Kirwal, everybody eating'.

In his account of life as an indentured labourer, Sankar, at various times, has been sick and hospitalized. And on behalf of his fellow-labourers, he had walked for miles, on one occasion, as leader of a delegation representing a labourer whose release from jail, they requested when they approached the white Manager. These poor labourers had aggregated their few hard-earned shillings, which was offered as payment for the man's release, a man who it was alleged had illegally picked a few ears of corn from the estate. After three months, the Manager released the 'corn thief', much to Sankar's satisfaction. This lesson he learned well, and was determined that it should not be repeated by any other labourer.

Relations between Indian men and women (given the scarcity of the latter) were particularly fraught with dangers, often ending violently. Sankar makes a special point of telling the story of a man who murdered another man, because the woman he was living with was not a home when he returned from work one day, but was found at a Chattri man's house. Sankar also spoke about the presence of women on the estates, and the distance that was expected from bachelor men. 'Everybody have dey wife', he said, and some of the single women who worked tapping rubber could only be approached with some awkwardness, for no one was allowed to 'go an talk any kinda rudeness wid dem'. He then tells us of his personal attitude towards women, particulary married women. He refused an invitation from a man who had invited him to his house so that he could teach him to read and write English, over a three-month period. The reason for this, Sankar said, is 'because e have wife, an I eh have nobody, so my name go sell he, every day, every day I coming, if he dey or nuh dey, an he an all go perhaps swell up, e go get vex, an before dat, I eh take, I eh take'. So he forfeited the chance of learning, of acquiring knowledge, something he had come to believe in. In effect, the principled Sankar proved himself worthy by taking a stand, both for his fellow Indians and for himself. While he accepted Trinidad with a cautious embrace, the loss of family and friends in India rankled and lingered. 'I tell de man write a letter for India, to family, an ley de letter come back, den I could know', he said repeatedly, before saying 'e send three letter, an up to today, I eh get no answer'.[255]

From these rare accounts of the indentureship experience, we get an idea, at a particular juncture in their Caribbean history, of the Indians (especially the India-born) brand and rhythm of speech, adapting English words in a unique way. Before moving on, it should be mentioned here that this broken English pattern of speech, within the English-speaking Caribbean varied, from territory to territory;

and similar differences in the Indians' adaptation of other mother tongues were evident elsewhere in the French, Dutch and Spanish-speaking Caribbean. Succeeding generations of well-educated Indo-Caribbean people, having achieved greater fluency in these European languages would (as students and writers of Indo-Caribbean history and culture) provoke a growing interest in reclaiming, refining and reassessing the linguistic style of their indentured forebears, especially as the Indians became more exposed to the wider society in the post-indentureship period.

# JAMAICA

By the time of Emancipation in the British Caribbean, unlike Trinidad and British Guiana, only Jamaica (with a larger slave population) could claim a plantation economy that was fully developed. The physical features of Jamaica provided the former slaves with two possible areas of settlement, the interior lands, which rose steadily from sea-level towards the mountains reaching 7,402 feet at the eastern end (including large tracts of hilly country), and areas of rich alluvial plains on the southern coast. Jamaica, near to Florida and a larger island with a greater population was about 1,000 miles from Trinidad.

Unlike British Guiana where the indentured Indians were concentrated in a narrow ecological strip along the coast (the sugar-growing areas), in Jamaica, there was a proliferation of sugar plantations;[256] and it has been argued that because of 'severe labour shortages in the 1870s East Indians brought to Jamaica tended to be sent to sugar estates in only a few of the parishes'.[257] One cannot, however, accept the suggestion that there was a comparable concentration of Indians in Jamaica, as there was in British Guiana and Trinidad. In British Guiana, the coastal plain was conducive to Indian settlements within a restricted area of about 100 miles long and between two to eight miles wide[258] (of about 100 miles long and between two to eight miles wide), within which there was a small area where the majority of Indian immigrants lived and worked. In Trinidad, on the other hand, the sugar plantations were located largely along a thirty-mile stretch of land on the western side of the island.

Jamaica also differs sharply from Trinidad and British Guiana in that the number of indentured Indian immigrants were not only fewer, but in addition, the area of their settlement was, at least as large, if not larger than in Trinidad and British Guiana. Among other comparisons that can be made, one researcher concludes that given 'the stage of historical development of the plantation system in the three areas directly influenced the reception of the indentureship scheme' while the production of sugar was rising in Trinidad and British Guiana, in Jamaica the opposite was on the case And though it was economically viable to import greater numbers of indentured labourers into the former colonies, in Jamaica, the 'economic fetters of the past confined the flow of indentured servants and limited the trickle'.[259]

# Housing, Labour and Education

Of the estimated 37,000 East Indians who had landed in Jamaica between 1845 and 1916, to labour on the estates, plantations and 'pens', approximately one-third were women. Here, too, the male-female disparity among the indentured Indians was clear, and having abolished a ratio of 40 women to every 100 men on each 'coolie' ship, the difficulty in recruiting more women remained unresolved, as the Indians generally struggled with the problems endemic in their status and work as indentured labourers.[260]

A summary of the housing of Indian indentured immigrants in Jamaica showed that the dwellings were similar to those in other colonies, and as in Trinidad and British Guiana, the space allotted to immigrants was 50 square feet per adult, or 120 square feet for three single men, or a man, his wife and two children, exclusive of verandah space. The latrines were hopeless, as 'serious defect' on most estates which one report stated 'should be remedied without delay'. Sickness and death from ankylostomiasis made it necessary to insist on the use of latrines among the immigrants.[261]

Comparing the merits and demerits of a central hospital system, official investigators argued that on the whole, they preferred a system whereby estates, or small groups of estates, provided separate hospitals for immigrants. On diseases such as malarial fever and ankylostomiasis, deserving of urgent attention, they pointed out that preventive measures were at least as important as curative treatment.

In Jamaica, as elsewhere in the Caribbean, where the indentured Indians laboured, great concern was expressed over the number of working days lost through sickness in relation to the available medical facilities. It was pointed out that the balance of advantage was generally with the 'separate' hospital system conditions in Jamaica, rather than combining that with the central system.[262] Seriously concerned with lost labour-time incurred by the immigrants, the McNeill and Lal Report recommended that a local committee be appointed to investigate the whole question and report to the Governor, arguing that such a committee would be strengthened by including a medical officer with first-hand experience of the estate hospital system in British Guiana and Trinidad.

Beset by illness, the Indians in Jamaica were also affected by phthisis, a disease which was, in 1912–13 responsible for several deaths 'more than twice the number who died as a result of malarial fever, 50 per cent more than those dying from ankylostomiasis and more than a quarter of the total deaths. It was officially stated that in the case of free immigrants, as in other West Indian colonies, the medical relief arrangements seemed to be 'susceptible of improvement'.[263] McNeill and Lal felt it 'undesirable' that an exclusive day of nine hours should be the time measure in the case of Task work. On the question of wages and labour, they felt that the existing arrangements in British Guiana were 'sound and satisfactory', and noted that the labourer should not be legally bound to work for more than five and a half days or after he had earned five shillings and six-pence in any week except during certain short seasons, when special demands could reasonably be made. Given that in practice, very few labourers achieved a five and a half-day working week in any season, there was concern that 'special inducements' were necessary to attract labourers to make 'unusual exertions'.[264]

Although the tasks in Jamaica were 'carefully and equitably' assigned, indentured immigrants had made successful appeals to the Protector. Commenting on employers, who in an effort to save time, assigned such as would induce labourers to take advantage of the rate, there was no provision in the Ordinances similar to Section 116 of the Trinidad Ordinance or Section 97 of the British Guiana Ordinance, which debarred an employer from requiring from the labourer classed as not able-bodied, the performance of a full task.

While all the Indian immigrants were initially indentured on one-year contracts which were renewable, by 1850 three-year contracts were served until 1862, when it was replaced by five-year contracts. Female workers could not match the higher earnings of male workers, even when 'task work' took precedence over day labour. The theoretically fixed rate of 9d, per day in the 1840s for women workers, was rarely if ever, achieved. By comparison (and even though they were both relatively badly paid) indentured Indian men earned between 7s. 6d, to 10s. per week.[265]

Given that many indentured immigrants were unable to earn enough, daily rations were supplied for three-month periods consisting of 1 1/2 lbs. of rice or wheat flour; 3 ozs of fish or goat's meat; 3 ozs of dhal or peas; and weekly – 6 ozs of coconut oil and 1 1/2 ozs of pepper or 1/4 lb of salt. Non-adults were entitled to half of the adult ration. Of course, the cost of such rations were recoverable by deductions from the immigrant's wages. From 1880 to 1891 the deduction was fixed at 3s. 6d and since 1891 the cost had been fixed at 2s. 6d. The hard times that had befallen the Indians became harder and it was suggested that the 'Demerara morning' ration should also be introduced. This hardship among the indentured Indians in Jamaica was due to the cost of living being 'slightly higher' than in Trinidad, because of the fact that rice (given a lower acreage under cultivation) was more expensive.[266]

Even though the number of indentured labourers in Jamaica (by March 1913 there were 4,152 on 83 estates) was smaller than those in British Guiana and Trinidad, according to one report, justice was administered 'impartially'. At this time, the Indian population was about 2 1/2 per cent of the total population, and this, it was argued, was sufficient reason why some magistrates were not acquainted with Indian customs, thoughts and methods of expression. However, taking note of the Sanderson Committee's findings on the imprisonment of labourers, McNeill and Lal regarded the penal clauses in Jamaica as 'antiquated' and the maximum penalties 'severe', adding that imprisonment should be avoided by 'allowing time for the payment of fines and recovering small periodic instalments for wages'.[267] Changes in the law also affected other aspects of life and labour among the indentured Indians, such as return passages and the marriage law.[268]

Relations between employers and labourers described as 'satisfactory' was followed by the emphatic statement that 'Habitual ill-treatment (of the labourer) is not and could not be practised'. It is difficult to accept McNeill and Lal's view that ill-treatment of the Indians, at the hands of the Overseers and Headmen was occasional. Nonetheless, they recognised that disputes about tasks, though not frequent, occurred often enough to merit notice. 'The somewhat vague definition of task' they stated, 'may account for most of the misunderstandings'. The thinking behind this was to forestall 'organised strikes' among discontented labourers, which to some extent, contradicts their statement above.

The Report also stated that the Indians had 'ample' facilities for lodging complaints, no obstacles were placed in the way of those anxious to meet friends and there were 'no difficulties' in performing marriages (or other ceremonies) or in celebrating religious festivals.

By about 1914 the free Indian population in Jamaica was approximately 16,000. In 1911, according to the Jamaican Census, the total Indian population was 17,380, including those under indenture. While one-half of the total Indian population were employed as agricultural labourers, a few hundred were engaged in farming and market-gardening, and employed in a range of about 50 different manual occupations.

Compared with Trinidad or British Guiana, the Indian population was small and many who had prospered (albeit in small ways, for example, as landowners) – annual incomes of £1,000 was still rare. Nevertheless, the potential for further progress was there, as one account put it, among their successors 'whose energies are not hampered by their parents' defective education and ignorance of English' and who 'will doubtless be more enterprising'.

Thus by 1914 education was of primary importance among Indians. Of the 455 Indian boys and 272 Indian girls attending Primary schools, an estimated one in three boys, and one in five girls attended Primary Schools. Commenting on the Indians' education, the investigators observed:

> A few years ago three special East Indian schools were established under a special vote. Two of these schools were under the management of the Society of Friends and one under that of the Presbyterian Church. The average attendance at the three schools was ninety. The parents are said to be apathetic, but a reason for the generally poor attendance is the absence of Indian teachers … It seems a pity that the painstaking thoroughness of the Canadian Presbyterian Mission in Trinidad cannot be more generally imitated by school managers in localities where Indians are numerous. There is in Jamaica every desire to educate Indian children without interfering with their religious convictions.[269]

While in theory, this respect for the Indians' 'religious convictions' seemed genuine, in practice, this was not the case. In fact, during their indentured lives, Indians were pressurized to conform to the standards of the dominant culture. But generally the legal framework within which the Indians in Jamaica had lived and laboured were, more or less, the same as in British Guiana and Trinidad, being based on the fundamental premise of strict control.

# SURINAM

Surinam, located between British Guiana and French Guiana in South America, and also known as Dutch Guiana, covers an estimated area of 54,300 square miles. The country is bounded to the East by the Marowijne River which separates it from from French Guiana, and to the West by the Corentyne River which passes through British Guiana.

To the South, the southern mountain range marks the boundary with Brazil. Moreover, like the neighbouring Guianas, Surinam's climate is of the tropical rain forest type characterised by high temperatures and heavy rainfall, though with slight variations, spread over each year.

After Columbus's arrival along the British Guiana coast on his third voyage to the New World in 1498, perhaps the earliest description of the area was that of Antonio de Berrio, Governor of Trinidad, who observed that European settlements had not yet been established, although there was some trade especially in tobacco between the Dutch and the aboriginal Indians. Several months later, Sir Walter Raleigh reached the British Guiana coast, and in 1595 published *The Discoverie of the Large and Beautiful Empire of Guiana.* He was followed by another British explorer, Lawrence Keymis, and in spite of earlier attempts at colonization, it was not until 1650 that a permanent European settlement was established in Surinam, through Lord Willoughby.

Exploitation of the country's natural resources necessitated the presence of more people, the exploiters and, of course, the exploited. Thus British and French colonists were joined by African slaves in the evolving plantation economy of Surinam. In the growing competition among European nations for colonial possessions, hostilities between England and the Netherlands between 1665 and 1668, resulted in Surinam becoming a colony of the Netherlands on 1 May 1668. Since then (except for two periods of interruption during the Napoleonic wars 1795–1802 and 1804–1816) the colony remained in Dutch hands.

While this plantation colony continued to develop during the eighteenth century, by the mid-nineteenth century it began to decline for various reasons: abolition of slavery in 1863 had reduced the labour force significantly; transportation through the newly-opened Suez Canal in 1869 allowed European capitalists access to an abundance of labour and land in the Far East; and competition from European and American beet-sugar all competed with Surinam's sugar plantations. These factors forced a change in agricultural production in Surinam, a shift from large plantations to small, individual farms, owned and operated by Javanese, Creoles to a lesser extent, Dutch farmers and East Indians.

## *The Javanese*

The influx of various groups of indentured plantation workers to Surinam left much to be desired. So it came as no surprise when the Dutch Government drew an additional supply of labour from its own colonies. Java, in particular, offered the best prospects, being a densely populated area. This was fortuitous, for it was against this background of population explosion, and subsequent land shortage, towards the end of the nineteenth century, that relief plans were drawn up by the Dutch authorities to encourage the migration of Javanese to their sparsely populated Indonesian islands.

To fulfill the planters' demand for labour in Surinam however, the Dutch Government granted permission to Surinam in 1890 to recruit 100 labourers. Consequently, 94 Javanese emigrants landed in Surinam in 1891: 61 men, 31 women and 2 children, reflecting though less problematically (as in the case of East Indian emigration) the disparity of the male-female ratio, which characterised the shiploads that followed.

As it was, these Javanese workrs performed the tasks so well that the Dutch authorities were encouraged to recruit a second group of 614 emigrants, who were shipped from Java in 1894. This ambitious enterprise, more than six times as large a shipment as the first, was attended by many difficulties familiar with other groups of indentured Asians, such as overcrowding, inadequate general sanitary and other conditions, resulting in 32 deaths during the voyage and the immediate hospitalization, on arrival in Surinam of 85 emigrants, 32 of whom had died. In the wake of a public outcry and an investigation, new regulations relating to general conditions on the plantations were enforced with evident beneficial results. The immigrants who had survived this voyage went on to become productive plantation workers, and so generated greater interest in this source of labour. Over the period from 1890 to 1939, Surinam received a total of 32,956 Javanese labourers.[270] Although 7,684 Javanese had been repatriated, the majority of the immigrants took advantage of these concessions and became a permanent part of the independent farming community in Surinam.

What were the motivations of the Javanese themselves to emigrate? The Java-born informants had more or less, the same general story to tell: their recruitment took place outside the *desa* (village); that the recruiter was a stranger who made his approach while the potential emigrant was alone; that magic was used to effect loss of memory of one's family; and that memory was regained too late. 'It is typical of the Javanese to attempt rationalization of their past mistakes', wrote Malefijt. 'Shame is an important sanction, and since leaving one's family is one of the most shameful acts that a Javanese can commit, blame had to be placed upon an outside agent'.

The Javanese labourers' claim of trickery being used to lure them from their ancestral land, bears an uncanny similarity to the East Indians' reaction in Trinidad,[271] although the Javanese tended to rationalize their acquiescence to the recruiter's trick. While Trinidad-born Indians, reflecting upon the manner in which their forebears were recruited, almost unanimously believe that they were 'damn fools' for allowing themselves to be tricked, the Java-born in Surinam stubbornly adhered to 'an injured innocence', perhaps to maintain certain standards of the Javanese value system, which required the respect of younger people for the older generation. So it was claimed that the 'common feeling of being tricked' was another contributing factor to the 'close internal cohesion of the group', that was drawn together by their common cultural background, language and religion and by a 'common fate'.[272] In fact, they are said to remain aloof from the rest of the population and tend to regard themselves as Javanese or Indonesians, rather than as Surinamese.

## *The East Indians*

As in Trinidad and British Guiana, the Portuguese and Chinese labour experiments proved unsatisfactory and in the search to remedy the manpower shortage, the Dutch Government signed a Treaty with England, giving them access to Indian labour until Britain stopped recruitment of Indian indentured labour for the British colonies.[273]

Before the first ship the *Lalla Rookha* had landed at Paramaribo in Surinam from India on 5 June 1873 (with 279 men, 70 women and 32 boys and 18 girls under the age of ten) a small group of Indians originally from British Guiana, had already settled in Nickerie and Coronie.[274]

It was not long, however, (given the interest in labour following the 'Gladstone experiment' in British Guiana), before the Surinam planters made a more realistic appraisal of the Indian immigrants. 'Not only was the incorporation of these new workers in the organisation of the plantation difficult owing to the ignorance of their customs and language', it was argued, 'but what was worse, they proved to be little suited to the heavy work in the fields'.

As was the case in the British Caribbean territories, the Agent General for Immigration was responsible for the indentured immigrants. His efforts had evidently helped to pacify the immigrants to the extent that in 1875 the Kolonial Verslag reported 'the spirit of recalcitrance and even resistance which was formerly noticed among the coolie immigrants, has entirely disappeared'.[275]

Such experiences did little to promote further immigration. By 1877, however, immigration was reopened and in 1878 an Immigration Fund was established. During the period 1873–1916, an estimated 34,304 immigrants were sent to Surinam in 64 ships. The percentage of women among the Indian emigrants was estimated at less than 50 per cent of the number of men.[276]

The organisational structure of the plantations were as follows: plantation Manager, Overseers, 'basjas' (or Drivers) and the Foreman. The distinction must be made that the Overseers were 'often white men', though there were some Creoles, and down the line, essential contact with the labourers was made through the 'basjas' whose ranks were joined by many Indians. The figure who commanded the full attention of the community was the plantation Manager, whose 'patriarchial position' afforded him 'great autocratic power'.

By 1911 there was approximately 27,000 Indians (including 5,876 under indenture) nearly one-third of the population in the colony. Within the ranks of the free Indian population, probably the largest class were petty landowners, while on the periphery of Paramaribo, a considerable number were cattle-keepers, cart-owners, market gardeners, mechanics and day labourers.

Since they arrived, much progress had been made by the Indians. Unlike British Guiana, it seemed that there were more opportunities to earn higher wages, acquire land and become economically independent. By 1915 the milk supply of Paramaribo was in Indian hands, and they had also taken over from the Afro-Surinamese almost the whole of the land transport business. More than that, the total area of Crown Land held by Indians in 1912 was 12,671 hectares or about 30,000 acres, and many had purchased or leased free-hold land from private owners. The Annual Abstracts of 1897 showed that the landed property of Indians had, in fifteen years, increased at least ten-fold.[277]

Given the need of Indian settlers for security of tenure and exception from indefinite liabilities which exposed them to meddlesome interference of official underlings, by 1915, Indians in small numbers were constantly moving between Surinam and British Guiana. That same year, approximately 2,000 Indians had arrived in Surinam from the British West Indian colonies; and of course, Indians who had originally gone to Surinam, in turn, moved to the British colonies. Thus it was noted that if tasks and wages in Surinam were modelled on those of British Guiana, and if the colonisation policy of Surinam was adopted by British Guiana, 'industrious labourers emigrating to either colony could not fail to prosper'.[278]

The progress of the Indians in Surinam was also reflected in education. By 1914 an estimated 147 Indian boys and 23 girls attended school in Paramaribo and 510 Indian boys and 55 girls attended rural schools. Nevertheless, McNeill and Lal felt that a beginning had been made in teaching Hindustani in schools, with the gratifying result of higher attendance at schools where Hindi was taught, and stated that parents who had not fully decided to settle in the colony naturally regarded Dutch as an even less attractive medium of communication.[279]

In Surinam, as in the British colonies, the Immigration Agent General exercised general supervision and control over the Indians. The problem of communication between the administration and the immigrants remained uncorrected, and it was left to McNeill and Lal who stated that although Indians were not merely wanted as indentured labourers, but a colonists, both the Government of the colony and district officers should recognise that the latter cannot successfully organise settlement work unless they can converse with settlers.

There was no system of testing officers' proficiency in colloquial Hindi. Therefore in the interests both of the labourers under indenture and of the colonisation policy of the Surinam Government, attention was focused on a reasonable knowledge of colloquial Hindi as a necessary requirement among officers holding permanent appointments. McNeill and Lal were pleased that Hindi was being taught in some schools and they were encouraged by one Commissary who talked with school children in both Dutch and Hindi; that many of the higher officers had an excellent knowledge of English; and felt that it could be to everyone's advantage if all district officers possessed the same ability. Although settlers' children learned Dutch and grew up bilingual, and settlers spoke Hindi, it was crucial in relation to the complaints procedure that the officials should be able to understand the complainants language.[280]

The housing accommodation provided for the indentured immigrants in Surinam was about 15 cubic metres and 6 square metres for each adult, in addition to room for cooking. While McNeill and Lal found the dwellings to be in 'good order', the barracks' huts, as they were called, remained inadequate, to say the least.

Among the main diseases which plagued the immigrants were malaria, ankylostomiasis, pneumonia and tuberculosis. While it was admitted that ignorance of the Dutch language rendered reference to the medical reports of the colony impracticable (a lame excuse!) they stated that the annual sickness from all causes varied from 20 to 28 days per head. By comparison, the rate of sickness among Javanese was considerably less from 15 to 18 days. The above investigators recommended the introduction of forms of hospital registers similar to those proposed for the British colonies. With the death-rate of indentured Indians much lower than the general death-rate of the colony, the prospects of gaining the maximum productivity (a prime objective throughout the period of indenture) was particularly encouraging during the last years of the system.

On the crucial question of tasks, hours and wages, the regulations embodied in the Surinam Ordinance closely followed the provisions of the British Guiana Ordinances. The working day, for example, was fixed at seven hours, and the payment for a day's work or a Task was 24 cents. McNeill and Lal agreed that the wages on most of the estates they visited in the colony were low. And, as in other colonies, women's earnings ranged from one-half to two-thirds of the men's earnings. In their long, detailed Report McNeill and Lal (who supported a continuation of the indenture system), preoccupied with the number of working days lost, reckoned up their findings in terms of industrial efficiency. Their concern with the sums of money indentured Indians (after extraordinary sacrifice) either remitted to India or deposited in the Savings Bank, led to the recommendation that while immigration to Surinam continued, the abstract of the annual report furnished yearly to the British Consul at Paramaribo, should be accompanied by returns of 'work and wages'. Ignoring the obvious but astonishing achievement of the Indians' thrift, which resulted in some savings, and the fact that not many earned enough to save, predictably, McNeill and Lal could do no more than identify just two estates where the labourers were 'well paid and well treated'.

The judicial system of Surinam was, of course, Dutch. The British official in yet another detailed breakdown of the administration of justice on matters affecting the immigrants, such as complaints against employers, marriage, the period of indenture, Time and Task work, were satisfied with procedures. 'We received no complaint regarding the manner in which complaints against immigrants were dealt with by the Courts', they stated.[281]

And after spelling out the facilities available for the immigrants to lodge complaints and celebrate marriages and religious ceremonies, McNeill and Lal returned to the fundamental relationship between employers and labourers. Bearing in mind that generally the estates in Surinam were small, only four estates cultivating sugar, necessitated the employment of a large number of immigrants for field and factory work. Admitting that more detailed information about all matters affecting relations between employers and labourers was necessary, the official investigation recommended that the 'real grievance about low earnings be promptly remedied'.[282]

Generally, the pattern of life of the Indians in British Guiana and Trinidad was similar to those in Surinam. One account, informs us that, after his evening meal 'the coolie retires to his couch, or goes to his neighbour's house, there to chew betel and nut or smoke his pipe – "the pipe of peace", the hukka or singa passed from one to the other – and thus lounge the hours away until the time for retiring arrives, which is usually from eight to nine o'clock'.[283] The Indians also made regular contact with friends and other immigrants on the neighbouring plantations.

Social life was of particular interest. The most popular feast days, for example, were Phagwah (Holi) and Muharram. During Phagwa (commemorating 'an event in the life of the great Vishnu worshipper Prahluda') songs were sung and generally there was a feeling of committed devotional activity within the Indian community. The most spectacular of the festivals was Muharram, with its *Tazia* (or Tadjah) procession. So popular had it become that even Creoles participated.

Life within the community was evidently stratified. 'Even though it is hardly possible to speak of difference in status within the group on the grounds of division of labour', Speckman observed, an 'internal and informal social stratification could nevertheless be discerned'. For example, the bold, forceful immigrant gained prestige in his work-group and tended to play a leading role in disagreements, disputes between drivers and work-gangs. Of course, they could also arouse aggressive reaction. Indeed, interpreters were of particular importance. 'I fear the influence of these men is not always exercised for the good', wrote D.W.D. Comins, 'and they are to be profoundly mistrusted'[284]

In their new environment, it is necessary to consider the question of caste, so integral a part of the social system in India. Given the shared experience resulting from crossing the sea, such as close contact, eating the same food and drinking water from the same receptacle, rigid caste distinctions were difficult to maintain. In the process of social organisation, however, after suffering the initial 'confusion and calamity' the Indian immigrants were able to re-group broadly, along the old pattern existing in India. 'The influence and restrictions of caste are much modified and in some cases disappear altogether', wrote Comins, 'though certain traditions and superstitious always remain'.[285]

With the gradual reforming of the caste hierarchy, the Brahmins who retained positions of leadership, worked towards maintaining the traditional structure and values. This meant that the status and prestige of the lower castes, the Dhobis and Chamars remained low in their new environment.[286] In effect, caste as they existed in India, had become virtually redundant.[287]

Nevertheless, in the new social reorganization, the low castes remained in a 'more or less peripheral position'. Thus it was ironic that while the dominant group subjected the Indians to rigid control and separation from the other social groups, even though Indians, in general, laboured under common disabilities, a few of their leaders struggled to maintain traditional divisions through a caste hierarchy.

Given this contradictory pattern, however, while the Indians, as a group, struggled to reorganise their lives in relation to the insistent demands of the plantation structure firmly based on laws of control, throughout the period of indentureship in the Caribbean (in Fiji and elsewhere), the appalling abuses of the system led to continued calls for change and eventual abolition.

## *The Campaign and Abolition of the Indentureship System*

Since the abortive 'Gladstone experiment', questions were raised (as early as the late 1830s) concerning abolition of the indentureship system. The colonial sugar planters' lobby, however, proved decisive in reviving and expanding the system with renewed determination. Though for a long time, between 1840 and 1900, there was 'only questioning' as the system was maintained with 'virtually no modifications',[288] towards the end of the nineteenth century, Indian emigration to the colonies was seriously opposed.

In 1839 concern was expressed in India. The *Friend of India* was moved to comment that safety could only come through 'absolute prohibition'.[289]

But such hopes were dashed in 1842, when the British Government endorsed the continuation of 'regulated' Indian emigration.[290] Unlike their uncompromising opposition to slavery, the abolitionists (notably the wealthy James Cropper and Joseph Sturge, a Birmingham corn merchant) were less demanding in their approach to the 'new system of slavery'.

Among the leading Abolitionists, at this time, was T.F. Buxton, chosen by Wilberforce as his successor to the Parliamentary leadership for the abolition of slavery. The son of a popular Essex landowner and Sheriff of the County, Buxton played a central role in the work of the Anti-Slavery Society, formed in January 1823. But fifteen years later, he was no longer a force in representing the concerns of the Anti-Slavery Society in Parliament, having lost his Weymouth seat at the General Election in 1837.

The attention of the abolitionists was now focused on the Anti-Corn Law League, which campaigned for an end to the monopoly of Tory proprietors and landlords. With this shift in attention, the Anti-Slavery Society, relied on Secretary John Scoble to monitor the system of indenture and take initiatives. But with his reputation damaged, in 1852 he left Britain to live in Canada. In his absence, the Buxtons (Edward and Charles) monitored the 'coolie traffic', but unlike their earlier efforts, now they worked within the established framework 'rather than without'. But hitherto such staunch defenders of the oppressed, they were now reluctant to give fuller support towards ending the system of Indian indentureship? Politically, about this time of increasing mortality among the emigrants, the issue of India and Indians was an extremely sensitive one because of the Indian Uprising (or Mutiny as the British preferred to call it) of 1857. There had been signs of unrest prior to 10 May 1857, when the Uprising broke out in Meerut. The causes were identified as being political, social, religious and military. Dalhousie's policy of annexation was not well received by the Indian Princes, who felt their security and control was threatened by the unemployment and consequent distress and bitterness among the mass of people who were dependent upon them. Incensed by this action, Nana Sahib, one of the affected rulers (and Rani Lakshmi Bai of Jhansi) played a prominent role in organising the Uprising. The latter fought valiantly to the death against her British enemies. The annexations, coupled with the new land tenure system deepened the social unrest among all classes in Oudh, for example. Further, the public criticism of Hindu Mythology by English literary figures such as T.B. Macaulay and Charles Dickens, who fervently wished he was Commander-in-Chief in India, for in such a position he would do his 'utmost to exterminate the (Indian/ Hindu) Race ... to blot it out of mankind and raze it off the face of the earth ... '.[291]

The strong sense of inferiority, which Sepoys (Indian soldiers) were made to feel by the British was even more galling by the fact that they were ordered about by an alien minority, 45,322 British soldiers as opposed to a total of 233,000 Indian soldiers. Amidst rising discontent, then, the Sepoys were pushed to the edge of desperation, when they were ordered to carry Enfield rifles using cartridges greased with pig's fat, an imposition which was contrary to the religious beliefs of Hindus, but also the Muslim soldiers in the Army. As it turned out, the greased cartridge issue, triggered the first shot which started the Indian Uprising.

While the battle raged in Delhi, Cawnpore, Lucknow and Bundelkhand, even though the mutineers scored great successes, the British, with the help of Sikhs, Gurkhas and other Sepoys on duty in South India, regained control of the disturbed areas. On 8 July 1858, Lord Canning, the Governor-General, proclaimed the end of the 'Mutiny', but the extent of the violence and the atrocities committed by both sides, rankled deeply. The aftermath signalled the end of the East India Company's rule in the Subcontinent, the administration of which was transferred to the English Crown, headed by Queen Victoria. It is interesting to note the concluding comments of one well schooled authority in this episode of Indian history: ' ... the British victory over the Mutineers, who represented a very small section of the Indians, was secured with the active as well as, the passive support of the vast majority of Indians who found nothing to enthuse over in the actions and activities of the mutinous sepoys'.[292] So at the stroke of a pen, we are expected to believe that none of the foregoing grievances had ever existed! And perhaps we should not be surprised to find that those who, in theory at least, were committed to defend the ongoing atrocities committed against oppressed colonial peoples (especially the indentured Indian labourers, during this period) were not so keen to do so in practice, after the Indian Uprising.

About this time, far way on the colonial plantations, the high percentage of deaths among indentured Indians had aroused much questioning in Britain. Buxton was reassured by the Secretary of State for the Colonies, Edward Bulwer Lytton that the 1856–7 mortality could in the future be avoided, and explained that the statistics exaggerated the claims. Without dwelling unduly on this issue, he deflected attention to the financial gains made by emigrants, who had returned to India. Others supported the merits of the system. A former Secretary of State for the Colonies, Labouchere thought an inquiry would serve no useful purpose, and Buxton abandoned his opposition. Moreover, a call for a Commission of Inquiry on 'coolie' emigrants by Lord Brougham in July 1859 was rejected on the grounds that it was too late for that session of Parliament and that 'individuals' rather than the law were at fault.[293]

It is significant that opposition in Britain to exploitation of the Indians, albeit at a low level, was still greater than it was, at that time, in India. Active interest in the Indians had not improved by the 1860s, in spite of the joint efforts of the Anti-Slavery Society and Baptist Missionaries to stop the influx of Indian emigrants to Jamaica, because they would undercut wages and were also 'pagans and idolators'.[294] One form of pressure brought to bear on the problem of wrongs committed during transportation of the Indians was press exposure. For instance, the British public was confronted with the news of the Indian emigrants who were drowned after being abandoned aboard the *Eagle Speed*. The tragedy which occurred soon after the disasters of the ALLY, the *Clarence, Golden South* and the *Fusilier*, resulted in a major *Daily Telegraph* article on Indian immigration. The newspaper described the traffic as 'a system almost as detestable as that of the "middle passage" ', adding that instead of earning money `those credulous pagans are feeding the sharks at Table Bay or the Sand Heads'.[295] It also argued for a `searching, unsparing inquiry' into the traffic and its `infamous inhumanities'. But this grand gesture had little effect, for this was a period reflecting the oppressiveness of British Imperial rule which not only crushed the Indian Uprising, but also directed its force, a few years later, to the violent quelling of the Jamaican Morant Bay revolt in 1865, thus neutralizing the humanitarian movement.[296]

Public awareness and sympathy for the Indians were not enough. By the 1870s, according to one account, there was ample evidence to support the fact that the Indians received treatment better suited to 'animals than men'.[297] In British Guiana, as mentioned earlier, growing tension exploded at Plantation Leonora when the Indians who had been on strike confronted armed police. This development had moved George Des Voeux to write his famous Christmas Day letter in 1869, which led to the setting up of the Royal Commission whose report was published in 1871.

Coincident with this Royal Commission's concern was the news from labourers who had returned to India from Natal, of their distressing experiences.[298] Among their complaints were beatings and inadequate payment for work done; allegations that coincided with exposure of the case of 'attempted kidnapping' of women and children and the illegality of immigration to the Straits Settlements. Although there were changes in the regulations, to minimise the malpractices of recruiting in India, the situation resulted in 'a comedy of misunderstanding'.[299] While there was much 'uneasiness' about the wrongs revealed in the system, there was an absence of firm intention by Whitehall and the Indian Government to tackle the causes. Meanwhile, yet more damaging evidence of flogging was forthcoming, followed by another protest from the Government of India, concerning Natal.

Admirable as their humanitarian approach, men like Campbell and A.O. Hume were faced with the daunting 'complacency and indifference' of British politicians. A Royal Commission, not unlike the Des Voeux Commission, investigated the situation in Mauritius between 1872–73, and when its report was published in April 1875, it was 'longer, more thorough and supported by a greater account of historical evidence, than its British Guiana counterpart'. In short, the report condemned 'almost everything and everybody' in Mauritius. The Commissioners' urged 'complete reform' of the Immigration Office and the need for Hindi-speaking officials.[300] The reports on British Guiana and Mauritius rekindled the interest of the Anti-Slavery Society and Victor Schoelcher (a French Creole from Martinique, and the leading figure in French West Indian abolition), visited London for talks with the Society.[301]

Indian emigration was put in further doubt by the high mortality during the voyage of the first shipload of Indians to Surinam. If the system of indenture in Surinam and the French island colonies were at fault, conditions in Cayenne (French Guiana) were worse. Between 1856 and 1867, 4,017 Indians were brought to Cayenne, and a further 2,534 in 1872. This increase did little to suppress deep concern[302] over the deplorable conditions under which the Indians laboured. Regardless of strong protests, the system remained intact. In 1876, however, a move was made by the Indian Government to stop emigration to Cayenne.

By the end of the 1870s, indentured emigration had already peaked[303] and during this decade, two experiments in the system of indenture were conducted in Burma and Ceylon (Sri Lanka).[304] As in 1861,[305] the Indians' deplorable condition in the island of Grenada was brought to the authorities' notice.[306] So appalling was the 'inhuman treatment' meted out to the Indians there, that on one estate a fine of £50 was imposed on the Manager and the workers' indentures were cancelled, while on another estate, the Indians' physical appearance had deteriorated to the point of arousing great concern. However, such was the importance of the indentured system to the planters that although the main estate owners discharged some managers in order to win back administrative confidence,[307] indentured emigration to Jamaica was reopened in 1878 before it was again stopped in 1885.

While the Anti-Slavery Society was against emigration, Indian labourers continued to be imported into the French islands of Martinique and Guadeloupe. The Government of India took no positive steps to stop indentured emigration or the system of indenture, adopting what seemed like a neutral position.[308]

After the importation of Indian indentured labourers to Jamaica had restarted in 1891, a year later, Major Comins was commissioned to visit the Caribbean and report upon the Indians' condition in Jamaica, Trinidad, British Guiana and some of the smaller islands, Surinam, Cayenne and the French islands Martinique and Guadeloupe.[309] The flow of emigrants from India, by no means uniform, posed 'insoluble problems'. After they had stopped emigration to Reunion and Cayenne, and procrastinated on the question of providing labour for Guadeloupe and Martinique, the British officials concerned found there was little they could do to help the Indians indentured in the French colonies.[310]

While there was a substantial body of official evidence of 'horror stories' accumulated both in India and in the British Foreign Office, during 1880–82, nevertheless an estimated 6,424 indentured Indians were introduced to Guadeloupe; and in the French, as in the British colonies, intermittent concern about ending Indian emigration and the system of indentureship brought no change.

Attention on overseas Indian activity was again focused on South Africa, for it was there, in Natal, that the leadership of the Indian community would provoke a new wave of protest that would strengthen the campaign to bring an end to emigration and indentureship. In 1894, the British-trained young Indian lawyer, Mohandas K. Gandhi, the 'secretary and scribe' of the Indian community recognised the Indians' inferior position and acted. Official responses came from various quarters, including the highest levels, but opinion was divided. Addressing the heads of Government of the white self-governing colonies in 1897 on the question of 'Alien Immigration' the imperialist Joseph Chamberlain, favoured controlled entry of the Indians. Counteracting this position was Lord Curzon who, as Viceroy of India, stressed the welfare of the 'lesser breeds'. And on the question of the abolition of return passages, although Curzon stood in opposition, his intervention, at this stage, did little to alleviate the pressing problem. It was, in fact, Lord

Landsdowne (a former Viceroy of India) who in 1899 publicly stated his disgust over the treatment of the Indians in South Africa, a gesture which aroused hope among the Natal Indians.[311]

By the turn of the twentieth century Gandhi's persistence, and the concern of Lords Curzon and Hardinge, were prominent in opposing further Indian indentured emigration and the system of indenture, as a whole. Indeed, Gandhi would later help to make the question of ending the system a political issue in India. In his condemnation, Curzon said the evidence against indenture was 'overwhelming' and found it difficult to comprehend a defence of the system which harboured such problems. Politically conscious Indians could not ignore this lead taken by the Viceroy.

One of the evils of the indenture system, which came to the foreground with added force, at this time, was the wide gap between the number of male and female immigrants and the moral consequences arising therefrom. Aware of the need for change in South Africa, Curzon was frank, stating that he would adopt a 'very stiff attitude', since public opinion in India would be 'justly indignant' if any concessions were made to Natal Government officials, without dealing with well-known 'notorious wrongs'.[312] In this spirit, he continued his efforts to redress the wrongs done to the Indians in South Africa, until he resigned in August 1905. (His successor, Lord Minto, was considered to be less concerned about the defects of the indentureship system).

Meanwhile, in South Africa, Gandhi was joined by H.S.L. Polak, and amidst growing interest in India of the 'darker side' of Indian indentureship, the Congress leader, Dadabhai Naoroji, the first elected Indian member of the British Parliament, questioned the unacceptable number of suicides among indentured Indians, and so too did M. Bhownagree, another Indian-born M.P. The essentially Indian agitation against the system was embodied in an Indian National Congress resolution passed in 1905, protesting against the status of Indians in South Africa and pressing the British and Indian Governments to stop the export of indentured labour.[313] This pressure, however, was much too mild to shake the smug complacency in London and Simla.

In additon to those who opposed the system, there was also pressure (though of a different kind) from the colonies to end the system. The white working class in the major cities in Australia, New Zealand and Canada, feared that wage rates and the standard of living would be depressed if Indian labour was introduced. The question of colour was imperative. And in South Africa, the white population was alerted to the 'Asiatic Danger', which was feared meant the movement of Asia's surplus population to the various colonies and Dominions would compete with the British population for economic opportunities in the lands of the Empire. This was the central problem, simply because it was clear that even though the East Indian workers in South Africa were at a great disadvantage, they had managed to make some self-improvements, while making their essential contribution as labourers. The value of such labour was recognised in relaton to the prosperity that they had brought to the West Indian colonies of British Guiana and Trinidad. In Natal, too, it was the East Indians' production of cheap fruit and vegetables that became the envy of the Transvaal.[314] Given the undoubted economic importance of the East Indians, the demand for their labour was greater than the supply. Therein lay the danger and British policy-makers were warned to be careful. The Indians who had come into Natal, had not only increased in number, but what was even more alarming was the implications after their contracts had ended. Unlike Chinese labourers, they became free, but were not satisfied with their status as labourer. They had other ambitions. The white population, however, had become seriously concerned about the Asian population explosion. Since they first arrived on 16 November 1860 in Natal, their numbers had increased enough to cause great concern, which augured badly for the continuation of Indian emigration to South Africa in particular, where Indian economic progress resulted in Vigilance Associations' 'Black Lists' of Asians who had dealings with white property owners who had let property to Indian traders.

Given the foregoing concerns, the danger of large-scale Asiatic immigration was great; indeed, this kind of immigration was described as a 'serious menace to the prosperity of a White Man's country'.[315] What was the remedy? An appeal was made to the Home Government for its sympathy and assistance in maintaining a united policy of settlement in all the great colonies (mainly the White Dominions, the West Indies was already beyond the pale) of the Empire. Emigration of Asians (essentially Indians) to these lands clearly had to be stopped. 'To encourage the Asian at the expense of the Englishman', it was contended, 'is a policy which can only end in the loss of the colonial Empire'.[316]

## Gandhi's Leadership

Though for different reasons, the alarmists in South Africa now pressed for an end to the system, while Gandhi warned that continuation of the system could only lead to persistence of 'some trouble or other in connection with Asiatics'.[317] In fact, hostility towards Indian settlement in South Africa was such that a bill to end Indian indentured emigration was put forward in 1908, but was withdrawn after a Commission of Inquiry. It is significant that about this time, Gandhi had initiated his 'civil disobedience' campaign in opposition to the Black Act. Under his leadership, a series of meetings were held and Indians were instructed to desist from registering under the Act. To emphasize his point, Gandhi dressed like his fellow-indentured Indians 'to make it more in keeping with that of the indentured labourers'.[318] This identification with his Indian brothers went further when he led a number of Indians to jail for breaking the law.

Meanwhile, as the Sanderson Committee was being set up, in India public opinion became more 'fully conscious' of the oppression of Indians in South Africa, and as Gandhi's activities received growing support, in Mauritius, Manilal Doctor (like Gandhi, a Gujarati barrister) stirred protest against the system of indenture.[319] Putting the struggle in the Indian diaspora in perspective, one historian wrote: 'In South Africa, the indentured Indians were on the march; in Mauritius they were moved to sporadic protest; but in the Caribbean the only political movement was that of Creole Blacks. In Trinidad, the Working Men's Association claimed the membership of a thousand; they were opposed to further Indian immigration as a threat to wages and living standards. Similarly, British Guiana had its Peoples Association, a black organisation which protested against taxation levied to promote immigration'.[320] This widespread resentment and resistance to the system of indenture was followed by the deliberations of the Sanderson Committee, the composition of which, and the evidence presented to it by witnesses, proved most interesting.[321]

By the time the Sanderson Committee had reported, opposition to the system had reached a heightened stage in India. Introducing a resolution to the Indian Legislative Council in 1910, G.K.Gokhale stated that 'no single question of our time has evoked more bitter feelings throughout India'; a statement which received the full support of all the Council's Indian members.[322] From this moment on, there was a steady weakening of interest in continuing Indian emigration to the colonies.

As though sensing victory, the oppressed Indians in South Africa heeded Gandhi's call to join in his *satyagraha* (passive resistance) campaign. Confrontation between Indians and the South African authorities led to deportations and strong and bitter public feelings in India. Writing to Lord Sanderson in May 1912, Lord Hardinge, Viceroy of India stated that the Colonial Office 'should realise the seriousness of the feeling in India ... the demand in India is for the total abolition of the system and for nothing but abolition'.[323] This issue remained of central importance. 'I had always heard rumours of the sufferings and degradations of indentured Indians in plantations in our colonies', he recalled later in his life, 'and I deputed McNeill [sic] ... to undertake a Mission of Inquiry into the position of indentured Indians in the British colonies. His report confirmed my apprehensions and I never ceased to press the Home Government to give me a definite assurance that this form of servitude or even slavery should be abolished'.[324]

While it was hoped that the evidence collected by investigators McNeill and Lal (who visited Fiji, British Guiana, Trinidad, Jamaica and Surinam), would lead to either restriction or abolition of indentureship, to the disappointment of many, their report, in general, recommended that the system be maintained. By now the *satyagraha* campaign which Gandhi had pursued relentlessly, now achieved massive proportions as Indian labourers and others left their workplaces and homes and marched with Gandhi.

An estimated 2,000 Indians were arrested, and Gandhi was imprisoned for nine months. This news sent shock waves throughout India and Whitehall. The Indians in South Africa and public opinion in India could not now be pacified with mere reforms of the system of indenture and its full implications. Lord Hardinge rejected any 'pacificatory attitude' and he became emotionally embroiled having read reports of violence against the passive resistance of those who protested. If this was an extraordinary response from the Viceroy, there was more to come that could be politically damaging and possibly end his career. Whether or not it was preconceived for political effect, Hardinge made an unexpected speech in Madras, where many Natal Indians had recently returned. Instead of admonishing the Indians for breaking the law in South Africa, Hardinge said they had violated the laws intentionally, knowing well the penalties involved. 'In all this', he added, 'they have the sympathies of India – deep and burning – and not only of India but for those like myself', who sympathised with the Indian people.[325]

Following this unusual and dramatic development, Gandhi felt he had done enough in South Africa and was preparing to return to India. Before he left Cape Town, he wrote that the only 'real and effective remedy' was to end the system of indenture.[326] As Gandhi, the emergent political leader headed home, much interest was focused in India, where the McNeill and Lal Report was receiving attention from officials. While there was much speculation among Indians as to the conclusions of the Report, the intervention of the First World War pushed the issue in the background.[327]

By the end of 1915, at the foreground of Indian politics, was the system of indenture; and earlier in the year, India had become much more concerned than hitherto with the emigration question. In launching his political ambitions, Gandhi sought to remedy the unacceptable helotry of Indian labour overseas, as he familiarised himself with Indian politics, after his long absence.

Additionally, crucial support came from C.F. Andrews, who in his own personal way tried to reveal the ugly workings of the system. His alliance with Gandhi in South Africa had served him well, and after calling on Hardinge to take action, in June 1915, he stated that he was more than ever certain that the McNeill and Lal investigation lacked depth. He wrote:

> What shocked me most of all, I think, was the way in which the coolies were talked of. It was always like so many cattle. … And when this attitude is taken by the educated the grossest evils among the coolies scarcely raise a blush of shame. It was the cold-blooded way in which Dr. Booth talked that startled me more than the facts he told, yet he was a very good and kind man. It is the system which makes this attitude. Conditions which make men and women herd and breed like cattle were not even noticed as evil.[328]

Already disturbed by the wrongs of the system, Hardinge responded quickly by reiterating his dislike of indentured labour. He hoped that McNeill's Report would have supported his view, but instead it had only made it 'more difficult to press it'.[329] Nevertheless, he urged 'strongly upon His Majesty's Government the total abolition of the system of indentured labour in the four remaining British colonies and Surinam, thereby removing a racial stigma that India deeply resents and which reflects upon His Majesty's Government and the Government of India in the sanction granted by them to a system of forced labour entailing much misery and degradation and differing but little from a form of slavery'. The position of the Government of India (in spite of all the projected favourable arguments for continuation of the indentured labour system in the McNeill and Lal Report) was clear: the system must be ended! To this effect, Hardinge and his Indian officials sent a dispatch to the British Government, an act through which Hardinge was able to bring in closer harmony, his own personal feelings on this question of indenture with the political mood in India. The period of questioning the system had been interminably long and Gandhi had become impatient, calling for abolition within a year. Relentlessly attacking the system, he maintained the momentum through his speeches and writings, which gained ever larger audiences.

Predictably, with the McNeill and Lal Report recommendations ready for implementation, Whitehall was unhappy with the political mood in India. But now there was no turning back. The year 1916 saw further developments towards abolition. In February, Andrews and W.W. Pearson published *Indian Labour in Fiji: An Independent Inquiry*. This indictment of the system of indenture, revealed an appalling degradation of the indentured Indians.

Between January and February 1917 (as a number of organisations protested to abolish indentureship) Gandhi was most active, making several speeches calling for an early end to the system. The accumulated effect of years of opposition was getting through, and a 'worried' Government of India sent a cable to the India Office explaining the situation and asking that they be allowed 'to stop recruiting forthwith'.[330] But before the cable was sent, recruitment had already ceased; and although in 1917 the system of indenture had, in theory, ended, many Indians were still bound by indentured contracts. Eventually, the close of 1919 saw the final termination of all outstanding indentures in British Guiana and by 1920, all indentured Indians were effectively free. The abolition of indentureship begged comparison with the abolition of slavery. Put simply, abolition brought to an end the captivity of Africans whose enslavement lasted a lifetime, while the abolition of indentureship ended the East Indians' bondage usually after a decade at most, except in the cases of repeated reindentures. But coming so soon after African slavery, East Indian indentureship (in marked contrast to white indentured labour which preceded African slavery) was not without some of the worst excesses of an oppressive attitude of mind so endemic among the former slave masters who took charge of the Indians. Both systems of labour control had, in varying degrees, subjected defenceless human beings to intolerable hardship and indignities. Humanitarian and economic considerations[331] had no doubt been integral elements in bringing the system of indenture to its conclusion, *but not* (as was the case with the African slaves) *without the insistent resistance and revolt of the Indians themselves.*[332] (Author's emphasis)

# Returning to India

In the wake of abolition, and indeed for as long as the system of indenture lasted, many Indians from the Caribbean (some with relatively large sums of money, some impoverished) made their way back, often after many years in the Caribbean, to their beloved India. For thousands of these courageous and resourceful people, the chance of returning home was not to be missed.

Those who had laboured in Surinam were no less eager to return than their fellow-Indians from other parts of the Indian diaspora. Since the commencement of emigration to Surinam in 1873, up to 1912, 31,203 immigrants were introduced and 8,823 were repatriated. Four years later, an estimated 12,000 had returned to India. The reasons why immigrants decided to return varied. But there was little doubt that apart from the introduction in 1895 of the payment of a premium linked to commutation of the claim of a free passage, immigrants who were either born in the Colony or who had arrived in childhood, seldom wished to return. Many, we are told, stayed on account of their children, and in some cases, inter-caste marriages rendered the parties unwilling to return. Moreover, if the head of a family commuted his claim, the others tended to remain with him, and commutation by a near relative or even a close friend, resolved some immigrants' uncertainty and induced many of them to stay. Of those who made the journey back to India, a considerable number went because a free passage was available, and not because they had decided to abandon the colony to reside permanently in India. By 1915, an estimated one in three had decided to return.[333]

As far as the Trinidad experience was concerned, while some returned to India on completion of their five-year indentureship, by about 1850, the payment of a bounty was enough to attract others who re-indentured themselves for another five years. Although at first, the Secretary of State had refused to authorise this money in lieu of a return passage,[334] aware of the essential merits of this payment, in 1851, he wrote to the Governor of Trinidad (where the Legislative Council had already approved a resolution to pay every 'able-bodied Cooly of good character' $50 bonus) to express his agreement with the 'Coolies' remaining in the colony.[335]

The Ordinance which provided for the payment of the above bonus was amended so that the reindentured immigrant was paid ten dollars for each year during the second term of industrial residence.[336] Even though the bounty payment fluctuated generally, it tended to follow a downward trend. Interestingly, there was also a tendency for the number of those accepting the bounty and reindentureship to fall.[337] Those who chose to stay remained free labourers to whom higher wages were paid, and significantly, they were not bound by a labour contract.[338]

Since the first group of Indians had arrived in the Caribbean in 1838 (given unconditional free return passages) the idea of returning to India remained a realistic proposition among them. In spite of Governor Harris's reservation[339] (he felt that the Indians should be advised to stay in the island) the guarantee of a free return passage[340] to India had been by 1853 subjected to change. Thereafter those Indians wishing to return to India were discouraged by the enactment of legislation prohibiting them from leaving Trinidad without a passport, hitherto granted free of charge at the end of the five-year period of indentureship. And so, the saga of the free return passages' issue was effectively ended.

There was also the question of Trinidad-born children of indentured immigrants who were ineligible for free return passages. Payments were made for the return passages of children, as was the case of returnees on the *Strand* in 1854.[341] To redress this grievance, the Colonial Office stepped-in, informing the Governor that the colony must meet the expenses of repaying the immigrants, whose savings were used for the passages of their Trinidad-born children.[342]

Amidst growing restrictions upon the Indians who desired to return, paradoxically the Government of India opposed the schemes to detain them in Trinidad. At this time, the Government saw it as beneficial to India for returnees to spend their hard-earned savings in India, and for other Indians in need of employment to emigrate.[343] The Indian Government also argued that abolition of the return passages was counter-productive in that Indians would be reluctant to emigrate. Of course, the official line was put forward that the return and remittance of indentured immigrants had important implications in helping to widen horizons and creating the pre-conditions for capitalist modernization in India. As it happened, for its duration, the indentureship proved to be not only a disorienting experience, but also one of relative alienation.

What then was it like for those who eventually made the return journey? While there were similarities with the outward voyage (for example, in terms of food, medical and clothing requirements) there were also marked differences in the immigrants' mental and physical condition. The sense of uncertainty which underscored the physical debility and mental depression of many immigrants was, upon departure from the Colony, replaced by a sense of optimism among the returnees, who were 'physically vigorous and mentally uplifted'. According to one account, repatriation of the Indians was conducted as follows:

'Before embarkation the immigrants were sent by barge to Five Islands Cooly Depot, there to await departure. At the Depot all necessary documents were prepared, remittances to India checked and return passage money paid. A roll book was made up of all immigrants with a special list of paupers and invalids. The invalids received special care during the voyage. The Medical Inspector examined the immigrants and the crew of the returnship. The stores and medical supplies were checked to see that they were as listed in the specifications of the charter. The amount of money deposited in the ship's treasury was certified. Finally, the Calcutta Emigration Agent was notified of the expected arrival time of the ship'.[344]

For those who had arrived in Trinidad in 1845, however, repatriation was less straightforward. One of the difficulties, at this time, was obtaining a ship to transport a smaller group back to India than was expected.[345] Time-tabling (the arrival of ships and the embarkation of Indians at Port of Spain) posed additional difficulties. Over the years, Indians who had hoped to return to India, were kept anxiously waiting for months. They had become so disappointed in 1851 that Governor Harris urged prompt arrival of the ship in question, to avoid a 'serious disturbance'.[346] Interestingly, in these early years, although the price of the return passage was £20, through extraordinary thrift, Indians were able to save a 'considerable amount' of money during their five years in Trinidad.[347]

The significance and implications of returning to India with this capital was not lost on the British Government which, when emigration reopened in 1852, informed the Government of Trinidad that if return passages were not insured the Indian Government would view the promotion of emigration unsympathetically.[348] Earlier in 1849, of the 3,700 Indians in Trinidad, 'most' wanted to return to India, [349] and it was especially unfortunate that given the paucity of women in the Trinidad Indian population, there were more women than children among the returnees.[350]

While the 1850s and 1860s saw a decline in the number of Indians wishing to return to India, it was in the mid-nineteenth century that the largest number of returnees with savings left Trinidad.[351] In 1865, five hundred and fourteen Indians embarked on the *British Trinidad* with a total savings of £12,401.3s. 7d. Four years later, an Indian known as Heerah had transmitted $6,000 to India and an extra $4,000 which he took with him. This success story, a remarkable feat of self-denial (though not rare among the Indians) was made possible because Heerah, after serving his indentureship, lived in Mission Village, Savannah Grande where, for a decade, he was both shop-keeper and money-lender to the Indian community.[352]

For the early immigrants at least, the uncertainty that accompanied them from the Immigration Depot in India (and during their voyages, to the stark realisation of life on the plantations) was replaced by hopeful anticipation which accompanied their return. Over the years, many Indians had put down root in their new environments, never to see India again. But among those who returned to India, few were able to make the necessary readjustment after having adapted reasonably well to the new attitudes and lifestyle in the Caribbean. Comparison with the Motherland was unavoidable. Some who had returned with money bought land and settled down without much difficulty. But, many who had been away for long periods were virtually forgotten in their native villages. The shock of return was not anticipated. Nevertheless, the majority, despite the problems they faced, chose to stay in India. But for others the story was different. Upon arrival at the Calcutta Depot, they went no further, having made a remarkably quick decision to return to Trinidad.[353] The irony of this much anticipated home-coming was that their only hope, as they saw it now, was to embrace the only option, which was to travel back to the sugar plantations where they had suffered untold abuse and ill-treatment, thus bringing a 'strange end to a strange story'.[354] In fact, for them the shock of return to their homeland and its ancient traditions brought sharply into focus serious re-assessment of a new beginning of positively coming to terms with new standards to which they had already been exposed; indeed to incorporate in their disrupted lives, a fresh vision of the future, thus incorporating their new world view. And so the dream of a better life in India, gave way to the reality of permanent settlement in the Caribbean.

For those Indians who did not try to return to India (a multiplicity of reasons have been advanced for this, as attested to by Fazal, Moolian, Maharani, Bharath and Sankar), but had resigned themselves to life in the Caribbean, it was also the start of a new phase of struggle, as they adjusted to their new environment. Yet, at this time, and on various occasions ever since, for all India-born Indians, India would remain an ever-present past that continued to sustain them. And even though indentureship as a system of bondage, had been legally abolished, the Indians, for so long disabled by low wages and indebtedness, poor health, bad housing and little education, (having managed through their traditional communal wisdom to transcend the derision directed at them and establish a sense of themselves as a worthy ethnic group), now faced the herculean task of rising to meet the enormous economic, social and political challenges that awaited them as a 'free' people still essentially bound to the land.

So by the turn of the twentieth century, the Indians' marginality in British Guiana and Trinidad, was evident in the quality and extent of their responses and involvement in public life. Having been excluded from the raging debates concerning their emigration and subsequent presence, they expressed their autonomous opposition to colonialism within the estates, by relying upon their own devices. Beyond their contact with the Immigration Department, their links with the established larger society were, to say the least, insignificant, though their economic contributions were clearly crucial to the colony's well-being.

The visiting British MP, Joseph Pointer was struck by the conditions prevailing among indentured workers, whom he found to be living under a system 'justly entitled to the epithet slavery'. The common difficulties of the Afro-Trinidadian and East Indian labourer were enough to incorporate them into the same workers' organisation, namely, the Trinidad Working Men's Association, which operated along trade union lines. The proof of their common bondage in wage-slavery was to become apparent a few years later in the 1919 strikes.[355] Yet the mass of Indian workers remained marginal to the representations of the TWA. It was against this background, that the Indians had to come to terms with the colonial society they had adopted and hoped to be recognised as a part of, after 1917.

Whatever tensions there were within the Indian and African sections of the British Guiana and Trinidad working populations at the end of the period of indentureship and Indian immigration, there was a need for some form of Afro-Indian solidarity to counteract the depredations of colonialism. But as relative newcomers, the Indians needed more time to adjust to their new homes. In both

British Guiana and Trinidad (unlike other area of the Caribbean with smaller Indian populations), occupationally and residentially, the vast majority of Indians *vis-à-vis* the other racial groupings, lived in self-contained communities, strangers to each other's lifestyles and history. The Indians were, by 1920 and later, a 'tribe apart', impervious to Creolization from below, and Anglicization from above. Within the relatively cocooned Indian village communities, however, certain basic processes had already been set in motion, as Indians continued to incorporate new social differentiations and new place loyalties,[356] an accumulation which would become powerfully evident in the post-indenture years.

# CHAPTER THREE

# EAST INDIANS
# AND COLONIAL
# CARIBBEAN SOCIETY

When Indian emigration to the Caribbean was resumed in 1845, the colonial social structure, at least in the British Caribbean, had been essentially as it was during slavery: at the top, the dominant white ruling elite; at the bottom, the black working masses; and between them, a Black and Coloured middle class, which had emerged to claim its share of political power.

With the end of slavery, repression and racism were integral to the pattern of continued colonial exploitation. Race, class, colour and culture, basic to the colonial structure, played their part in policy-making and it is significant that the dominant European culture which was adopted by the Black and Coloured middle classes had, by the nineteenth century, become synonymous with 'civilisation'. What could have brought about this Eurocentric approach to the Caribbean colonies? It was, as one writer has argued, not that the colonial ruling class wished to be cruel towards the 'subject races', but rather (as noted earlier) that they wished to exploit the labour at their command and impose 'an idealized paternalistic control over them'.[1]

Attempts by working people to gain their independence from the plantation owners (their former masters) through peasant proprietorship, were closely monitored and checked by the colonial authorities. Indeed, so high were the stakes that the ruling elite was determined to keep control, even at the risk of provoking revolt.

In effect, emancipation, as far as the ex-slaves in Jamaica were concerned, had yet to be realised, and the prospects for self improvement, as free labourers, were not encouraging. The British Colonial Office and the Colonial Government imposed strict rules over the island until the Morant Bay rebellion revealed the folly of the European mentality in the West Indies, which was strikingly like that of Whites in the Cape Colony. 'Above all', wrote Macmillan, 'their attitude to the Coloured people – the dignity and assurance to some genial kindliness with bursts of sudden, almost brutal self-assertion – is born of many generations of being fetched and carried for by hosts of slaves, and of exercising unquestioned authority over them'.[2]

As a consequence of this response to colonial oppression, the system of Crown Colony Government was imposed in the British Caribbean with the intention of easing tension between the various groups. But this system was no panacea for the deep-seated ills of Colonial society; and for those administrators who were inclined to oppose and expose the repressive system under which the masses laboured, the full force at the command of the ruling class was brought to bear upon them. Thus, Governors and other officials, with few exceptions, tended to blend-in with the designs of the Colonial regime.[3] Among those who had been criticised for their public opposition to colonial administration were George Des Voeux and James Crosby in British Guiana;* Henry and Charles Mitchell, Protector of Immigrants, and more recently, in the late 1930s, Governor Fletcher in Trinidad.

Although the Colonial Office knew of the maladministration of Crown Colony Government in its far-flung Empire, there was little it could do to prevent the growth of European racist attitudes. This convenient approach to justify and intensify colonial economic exploitation was, of course, part of a wider pattern reflected in the metropolitan ruling class attitude towards their own British working class people, the 'swinish multitude',[4] whose impoverished condition in the nineteenth century, it was argued, was perhaps 'just as harrowing' as that of the labourers in the West Indies.[5]

In Trinidad, formerly a possession of the Spanish Crown, unlike British Guiana and Jamaica, the local Spanish elite and French planters, who had emigrated from the French islands of Guadeloupe and Martinique, Dominica, St. Lucia, St.Vincent and Grenada from 1783, felt ill at ease with the growing influence of British rulers who had wrested imperial control. In spite of the intra-White ruling group tensions, there was a clear understanding that their political, economic and cultural control could only be assured through maintenance of the plantation economy which structured social relations within the wider framework of the Imperial–Colonial relationship, as it existed in the nineteenth century.

The introduction of the British Sugar Duties Act in 1846, however, added to the testing troubles of the post-Emancipation planter-free-labour relationship of paying relatively high wages. The lack of control of this labour, and the labourer's bargaining advantage was a point which sugar planters consistently made. In the British colonies, cheap, reliable and, significantly, controllable indentured immigrant labour from the Indian subcontinent was potentially the solution to the problem, as was argued earlier.

Thus began that identification of the Indians in the Caribbean with sugar plantations, an association which other groups such as the dominant Whites, the Black and Coloured middle classes and the former slaves and their descendants resented. In terms of culture, the Indians were markedly different from the European oriented Caribbean Creole culture. In the eyes of European Christians, as mentioned above, the Indians were 'heathen' and 'coolies' (even those born locally were not 'creoles'), who engaged in 'barbaric' customs and practices. Moreover, their

*British Guiana gained its Independence and was renamed Guyana during the period covered by this chapter. The reader should therefore note that hereafter both British Guiana and Guyana will be used where appropriate in the text.

perceived immoral conduct did not help to bring them closer to the main body of self-righteous European culture. At the outset, then, the culturally 'inferior' Indians had to be isolated from the rest of society, and gradually as they became economically integrated, it was hoped, they would also become 'Westernized' or 'Europeanised'. Until their assimilation was achieved, the Indian indentured immigrants and their descendants would remain outside the pale of West Indian society. In the case of Trinidad, this was particularly evident. 'Those who ventured into the towns as decrepit beggars or able-bodied jobbers', wrote one historian, 'did so at the risk of harassment and physical abuse'.[6]

Nonetheless after 1917, the Indians had settled in what became the Indian diaspora, albeit uneasily, beside the African diaspora in the Caribbean. By 1921, out of a total population of 297,691 in British Guiana, there were 124,938 of Indian origin. The Indian community constituted a sex ratio of 69,130 males to 55,808 females. In Trinidad, the Indians were also becoming Trinidadians and less 'immigrants'. From a total population of 365,913 in 1921 there were 122,117 of which 37,341 were India-born, while 84,776 were Trinidad-born.[7] British Guiana and Trinidad, with the largest East Indian populations in the Caribbean, had settled communities with a sense of permanency. Their links with the Indian sub-continent, for example, through the Arya Samaj Society, engendered in many a deep pride in being Indian, which was still abundantly evident towards the close of the period of indenture.

Two years after cessation of Indian emigration, the Combined Court of British Guiana was still insisting on the value of new emigrants and alternative emigration schemes to maintain the colony's industries. To this end, the Court requested that the Governor should make arrangements to send to the United Kingdom a multiracial deputation from the colony to present their case to the British Government. Consequently the first Nunan-Luckhoo Deputation arrived in England in 1919 and conferred with officials at the Colonial Office and leading Indians. On the recommendations of Lord Sinha, Under-Secretary of State for India, five members of the Deputation (including Dr W.Hewley Wharton, Mr. Prabhu Sawh and Dr J.A. Luckhoo, who represented the Indian community) travelled on to India in October 1919 to negotiate conditions, under which intending emigrants from India may be recruited, and the terms of their residence in British Guiana.[8]

Following representations made by the Nunan-Luckhoo Deputation and the recommendations of the Pillai-Tivary Report, with no agreement on an emigration policy after abolition of the system, the Government of India sent Kunwar Maharaj Singh to investigate the situation first in Mauritius and later in British Guiana, where, Singh reported on the Indians' condition and prospects for the Nunan-Luckhoo scheme. Although he felt that the prospects for Indian emigration was good, he was unsure of the success of the land settlement scheme. Accordingly, when in March 1926 emigration to British Guiana was re-opened, few Indians were willing to take the risks, even though Singh had stated that, on the whole, Indians in British Guiana enjoyed a 'somewhat higher standard of living and is certainly more independent that his confrere in India'.[9]

In spite of their presence in the Caribbean for eighty years, by the early 1920s, the Indians were not simply an identifiable group, but one towards which certain attitudes were clearly in evidence. 'The Blacks on the West Indian plantations were known as chattel slaves', Tinker wrote, 'the dictionary defines a chattel as a "moveable possession", and such an ascription is also appropriate to the condition of the coolies, the successors to the chattel slaves'. He added that with the legal termination of slavery, bondage on the tropical plantations persisted and with the 'formal termination of indenture and of other kinds of servitude, there came no end to the unequal situation of the Indians ... For slavery is both a system and an attitude of mind. Both the system and the attitude are with us still'.[10]

Given the 'economic threat'[11] of lowering wages, posed at the beginning of Indian emigration, over the years, some hostility (at times strong and bitter resentment) did develop between Creoles and the Indians, and by 1917, it was claimed that the difficulties arising from group hostility in a multiracial society were 'decidedly present'.[12] In fact, the Indian immigrants were not entirely accepted by those who were supposed to be their friends and protectors. Even the Anti-Slavery Society did once comment on the undesirable ways of 'idolatrous Hindoos' and James Stephen himself had also been suspicious of them on religious grounds.[13]

In some Caribbean colonies, the East Indians were much less of an identifiable group. In 1921 out of a total population of 858,118 in Jamaica, there were only 18,610 Indians; an estimated 7,000 were born in India. The India-born in the smaller islands, as listed in the census returns, show that in 1921 the number of such Indians in St.Kitts was 23; Grenada 181; St.Vincent 60; and St.Lucia 328.[14] Between 1873 and 1916, when immigration to Surinam ended, 34,304 Indians had entered the country.[15] Altogether, between 1853 and termination of the agreement with Britain in 1885, no more than 25,509 Indians had landed in Martinique and some 45,000 in Guadeloupe, embarking mostly from the ports of Calcutta and Pondicherry, while about 9,200 went to French Guiana.[16]

Inevitably, within these Indian populations, there were tensions between those who, understandably, clung tenaciously to their Indian roots and the less conservative local-born Indians; a sense of unease that was maintained through cultural persistence (a unifying force) as the Indian communities and their leaders (or, at times, lack of leaders) evolved to meet the challenges before them.

The settlement of large populations of former indentured Indians overseas was, to say the least, an unplanned eventuality, one that was forced upon the Colonial authorities. In fact, the history of the Indian indentureship shows how *ad hoc* arrangements were. For the post-indenture years, these Indians were 'differentially affected by the various social, political and economic developments' of the countries where they settled. Commenting on the 'process of consolidation and incorporation' of Indians abroad, three uncomplementary directions into which they were pressed were noted: first, 'upon their free settlement in colonial countries, Indians wished to be treated as equals, although there usually existed in each society a pre-established system of social stratification; second, through residing in foreign lands, Indians wished to remain part of the social and cultural body of India; and third, overseas Indians sought in many ways to become fully incorporated into the economic and political structures of their adopted societies; yet they wished simulataneously to remain communities acting for their own social, cultural and religious interests'.[17]

Bearing in mind, the varying size of these populations in the different Caribbean countries, let us briefly consider more immediately some of the economic and later, cultural aspects of some of the main Indian communities' development in relation to the wider society. First: to what extent have East Indians developed economically? How much have they contributed? And how much have they gained?

## ECONOMIC CONTRIBUTION: GUYANA

Since their arrival in the Caribbean, the Indians and agriculture have become synonymous. In British Guiana, they are still to be found predominantly in the rural areas. They have participated fully in the land settlement schemes, rescued the sugar industry from decline, brought into being a vigorous rice industry and, in recent times, have proven to be the main food producers.

In the sugar industry which had remained 'King' in Guyana, the Indians followed their predecessors, the African slaves, occupying the same barracks and labouring hard and long, with an outpouring, at various times, of blood, sweat and tears on the sugar plantations. Demonstrating their dissatisfaction with ongoing deplorably low wages, bad housing and working conditions, among other grievances, they protested through strikes and violent confrontations, notably, at Devonshire Castle in 1872 and, by the turn of the twentieth century, in 1903 at the Plantation Friend in on the East Bank in Berbice. Other disturbances (or riots) occurred in 1913 at Rose Hall, in 1924 at Ruimveldt, in 1939 at Leonora and in 1948 at Enmore.[18] Realising that unity is strength, over the years, they have, through trial and error, learned to combine, as trade union members, more and more effectively. So much so, that the threat they posed aroused fear among their insensitive employers.

After the 1948 tragedy at Enmore, which claimed the lives of several workers, the Venn Commission found that apart from low wages, pressing matters included the employment of child labour and the 'general resentment of women to be employed in certain types of work', and disturbingly it was observed that by the time East Indian field workers had reached fifty years of age, they had already passed their best working days, and at fifty-five years of age were 'quite unfit for arduous work'.[19] After making several recommendations, the Commission commented that there could be no peace on the sugar estates 'until this depressing legacy from former days is removed'.[20] In addition, it was felt that while sugar workers were better housed (in fact, dense population resulted in over-crowding in their new accommodation) and enjoyed modern amenities, their wages still lagged behind the rising cost of living. These basic problems were further compounded by unemployment and under-employment, which inevitably led to industrial unrest.

The sugar workers' desperation had, it seemed, hit a new low. In fact better working conditions had been a persistent demand of these workers, who were exploited in different ways both by local and international investors. It was argued, for example, that foreign capital had reaped profits from the sugar industry to the detriment of sugar workers; that in 1975, while an estimated $15 million was made, wages were increased by only 5 per cent; that the Social Sugar Levy accruing about $135 million in 1974 was expected to yield profits of $250 million in 1975; and that sugar workers had not only subsidized the price of sugar in Guyana, but by comparison with workers in the bauxite industry, sugar workers received only half of their wages.[21]

From its early beginnings during the period of slavery, the rice industry in British Guiana had gradually developed into a thriving concern by the East Indians. Initially, as a food, it was, of necessity, grown in small plots of land by the Indians to supplement their low earnings. With time, however, and the increased demand generated both locally and throughout the Caribbean, the industry moved apace. Between 1898 and the period 1916–1920, the acreage under rice cultivation increased from 8,500 yielding 5,200 tons to approximately 58,397 acres producing 35,239 tons.[22] The end of indentureship acted as a 'catalyst' to rice production with the value of the rice produced, increasing from $1,080,644 in 1916 to $9.1 million in 1957 and $21 million in 1964. Since 1964, given increases in production cost, buying price and fluctuations in the acreage cultivated and harvested by 1871, the value of the rice industry was estimated at $200 million.[23]

Although rice production was a 'viable enterprise' it was undoubtedly a hard-won achievement. More often than not, when the Indians moved from the sugar plantations to the villages and river bank areas, the land they found were unsuitable for rice cultivation, lacking 'adequate drainage and irrigation'.[24] As in Jamaica, the best lands (in terms of soil fertility, drainage and irrigation) owned and controlled by foreign capital, were allocated to sugar production. Consequently, those Indians engaged in rice cultivation were faced with risky ventures. Fortunately, with Government assistance, many rice farmers were able to improve the prospects of increased production.

But both the rice and sugar industries had been politically controversial. Given that rapid strides were made in the rice industry, through implementation of the People's Progressive Party's agricultural policy (which included an increase in the guaranteed price for rice) it was claimed by opposing politicians and groups, that Indians were the main beneficiaries of the Government's policy. However, when the PPP was replaced by a new Government in 1964, the Indians, in turn, complained that a reduction of guaranteed rice price discriminated against them.

Furthermore, the Indians maintained that the sugar belt 'provided the usual area of both political and racial discrimination'.[25] Nevertheless, in spite of more recent Burnham Government policies designed, as they alleged, to check their progress, Indians in Guyana have dominated the agricultural sector of the economy.

Rice and politics became inseparable. According to one account, the industry became economically viable after 1953 when the PPP Government instituted land settlement schemes, providing 1,500 rice farmers with land. As it was, much racial and political debate was centred on the Government Scheme and land development projects. Allegations were made that the PPP Government was 'partial to projects accruing benefits primarily to Indians', thus neglecting the Afro-Guyanese and other ethnic groups.[26] Arguments against this kind of 'racial analysis' involving external factors were put forward,[27] bearing in mind that in the Black Bush Polder area, for example, approximately 90 per cent of the population were East Indians. But although applications for land were invited from other ethnic groups, few applied and, as a consequence, the majority of those who received land under the Scheme were said to be East Indians. Other reasons advanced as to why Afro-Guyanese and East Indians from certain areas refrained from applying for land under the new Scheme were the 'inadequacy of social and welfare services', and related shortcomings in transportation, education and medical services. So, it was the 'primitive' living conditions that proved unattractive to Afro-Guyanese wage earners, who either migrated to Georgetown, the capital, or sought employment in the bauxite mining towns in Demerara and Berbice; and secondly, that Afro-Guyanese people decided against the land development schemes because of the 'low' productivity and income accruing to work on the land. For the Indians, however, their proven expertise in rice-growing and their remarkable accumulation of capital were decisive factors.[28]

Given its description as a 'political substance', by about 1975, the Guyanese Government's policy was, as one writer noted, to 'take rice out of politics and politics out of rice', thus lessening the problems of instability and exploitation in the industry. Ten years earlier, it was argued that the depression in the rice industry began with organisational changes in the Rice Marketing Board, and following these changes, Indian rice farmers felt alienated from the controlling body of the industry.[29] Consequently, there had been various attempts to rehabilitate this vital industry.

Occupationally, while the mass of Indians were concentrated at various levels in the sugar and rice industries (in 1931 about 70 per cent were engaged in agriculture), a 'significant proportion' were to be found in other occupations. The 1931 population census showed that in the Public Service out of 2,982 employees, there were 241 Indians;[30] and that 16 per cent of the country's professionals were East Indians, accounting for one-third of all merchants and shop-keepers. In fact, by the mid-1970s they had made considerable progress not only as traders in rural districts, but also as strong competitors in business largerly conducted by the Chinese and Portuguese; and by the turn of the twentieth century, the Indians had made marked advances in virtually all aspects of economic activity. They were, however, acutely aware that higher education and financial independence were vital to further economic advancement.

After three decades, by 1960, the Indians had made remarkable progress. They formed 48 per cent of the total population, while the next largest group, the Afro-Guyanese, accounted for 33 per cent, and 46 per cent of the total male working population as compared with Afro-Guyanese males, who constituted 34 per cent. Afro-Guyanese women, however, outnumbered Indian women in the working population. There were 11,438 Afro-Guyanese paid workers compared with 6,093 Indian women. The figures for Indian and Afro-Guyanese male paid workers were 34,785 and 32,942 respectively. However, according to one computation, only 60 per cent of Indian males were paid workers, while Afro-Guyanese accounted for 76 per cent.[31] There was therefore a predominance of wage-earning activity among the Afro-Guyanese compared with the Indians. And, apart from agriculture, Indian male workers were 'equitably distributed' when compared with the other groups in the population.[32]

Among Indians in the agricultural sector, a new class of entrepreneurs and workers emerged, many of whom needing greater challenges migrated to the urban centres with their accumulated capital. The 1960s marked the beginning of a continuous drift, especially among the educated, an influx into the towns which was not without its inter-group problems. Indians have repeatedly complained of discrimination against them in Government employment, citing the Civil Service and teaching professions as areas where they were denied entry.[33] Such barriers forced them into other economic activity. But while competing for white-collar jobs in urban centres, they also experienced difficulties. Moreover Indian participation in the management and decision-making process in the Public Sector of the economy revealed a serious racial imbalance with the minority Afro-Guyanese group in the dominant positions.[34]

Having invested the original capital accumulated on new lands and agriculture in rural areas, there were no more incentives for enterprising Indians, except to migrate to the urban centres. The push factors of the countryside, together with the pull factors[35] of the towns, encouraged many Indian capitalists and workers (especially the educated) to leave their rural environs for expansion and development in other communities.

The urbanization of East Indians was not a development which the Afro-Guyanese, as older residents, welcomed and consequently, there was intense competition between the two groups for urban-based occupations. This seemed understandable, given the Afro-Guyanese fear of the 'expansion characteristics' of Indians and their alleged exploitation of Afro-Guyanese workers. (Incidentally-and this point is often overlooked – not all urban Indians were professionals and employers. Like their fellow Afro-Guyanese, many were and still are, very poor, ekeing out a bare existence in the city's slums).

Nevertheless, the competition for white-collar jobs became one of the main battlegrounds between the two main competing groups. Even though they were reasonably secure as Government employees, the Afro-Guyanese did not take the perceived Indian threat lightly, for the Indians regarded themselves as part and parcel of Guyanese society. But, not sirprisingly, this fear of the Indians was, to some extent, justified, given their dogged determination and insistent rise from bondage and isolation during the period of indentureship. According to the Wynn Parry Commission which investigated the 1962 disturbances, it was through habits of 'hard work and thrift' that the Indians elevated themselves above the status of manual labourers and, to some degree, gained entry into the professions of law, medicine, commerce and the Civil Service.

One writer has stressed the changing positions of the various ethnic groups as being more relevant to occupational status, rather than urbanization of these groups, arguing that the former was especially susceptible to 'anxieties and jealousies' and that given Georgetown's function as an administrative and commercial centre, the professions and the public service were the principal sources of 'high status' employment.[36]

Whatever the Indians did in the rural parts of the country seemed legitimate, but their presence in the urban areas posed an 'economic threat' of which they were sharply reminded. Cheddi Jagan knew well the reason for this discrimination. 'It was only when Indians began to ... compete at the middle class level for jobs and positions of prestige', he pointed out, that 'the conflict began clearly indicating the economic basis of racism'.[37]

But in spite of this gloomy history (and while many Indians continued to leave the country, according to one considered view, there was a 'wind of change' on the horizon, based essentially on the Peoples National Congress Government's philosophy of socialism.[38] Evidently, the majority of Indo-Guyanese,* given a whole range of economic and social grievances, were less optimistic during the years of the Burnham-Hoyte regimes than they seemed to have been with the recent change of Government that had again made Dr Cheddi Jagan, the Head of State.

When the PPP-Civic Government took office in 1992, it inherited a large foreign debt amounting to $US 2 billion, high unemployment, social services in disrepair, a weak infrastructure and a Structural Adjustment Programme that was diametrically opposed to the policies of the new Government. Unlike the previous government, the PPP-Civic emphasized that sustainable economic growth cannot be achieved without human and social development. Thus with the agreement of the World Bank and the International Monetary Fund, an Economic Recovery Programme was drafted with the purpose of balancing economic growth with social equity and human resources development. Signs of progress had already been identified. For example, in 1993, the eight per cent of the Budget allocated to the

---

* In recent years following the Afro-prefix identifying people of African descent from the Caribbean (or elsewhere), East Indians in the region had also come to adopt the general designation Indo-Caribbean and, more particularly, Indo-Guyanese, Indo-Trinidadian, etc.

development of social and human resources had increased to 14 per cent in 1994. And although the huge foreign debt remains an uncomfortable reality, the economy had, it was claimed, continued to grow at a 'phenomenal rate', with the Gross Domestic Product (GDP), growing from 8.3 per cent in 1987 to 9.6 per cent by the end of June 1994.

Interestingly, the PPP-Civic Government saw economic growth as not only dependent on foreign investment, but also on a combination of investments that would crucially include the people's participation in all aspects of economic, social and cultural developement. Working in favour of the new Government is the mood of optimism among a large section of the Guyanese people, both at home and overseas. And it is fortuitous that this sense of home, seemed to be well-founded. The traditional staple industries sugar and rice, surprised many as new markets were found abroad. Conseqiently, sugar production increased by 20 per cent during the first half of 1994, while rice production increased by 23 per cent in 1993, reaching an unprecedented 90 per cent in the first half of 1994. Against these successes, however, bauxite production fell because of a decline in demand on the world market. But, for the first half, of 1994, there was a dramatic increase in gold production, with the Omai Gold Mines achieving a 79 per cent increase.

President Jagan had no doubt that Guyana was in a position 'to grow rapidly'. He had taken his message abroad, addressing thousands of Guyanese expatriates, inviting them to help in rebuilding Guyana. He knew only too well the price the country and its people had paid, over three decades, which saw an escalation of the second migration of East Indians (the first being the inward flow under indenture), an outflow from the country, mainly to North America and Europe. Economic growth and human rights are, by any standards, worthy goals. Achieving them, however, would indeed take much time and effort. But Dr Jagan was convinced that the lessons learnt in Guyana can become a 'model' for developing Third World countries. [39] As it was, time was not on the side of this highly unusual President, who until his death recently was still engaged in honouring the pledge he had made in 1948, of dedicating his life to the cause of the Guyanese people.

## TRINIDAD

For the Indians in Trinidad too, generally, the increasingly unsatisfactory economic outlook, in the recent past, had led to questioning. Historically, many of the post-indenture economic activities and the progress made by the Indians had their roots in the period of indentureship. Towards the end of the nineteenth century, as the Indians became more settled as a community, instead of being simply a group of transient indentured labourers, their growing attachment to their new environment generated greater self-belief and drive,[40] which resulted in 'upward economic mobility'. During this period, they constituted the 'largest section' of the labour force[41] and with more young male than female immigrants, there was the potential for years of productive labour.

As a migrant group entering the island in large numbers, the Indians aroused the anger of the host population, particularly during periods of economic depression, as in the 1880s and 1890s, when competition for employment led to decreased earnings. By the turn of the twentieth century this 'competition' was waged between the two main groups, Afro-Trinidadians and East Indians, creating a tension and hostility which further widened the gap between them; a separation reflected in the type of work these groups did and where they lived.[42]

Not surprisingly, therefore, until the 1920s, the Indians were largely engaged in agriculture, the main sector in the economy. Their role in the production of sugar and cocoa was crucial as far as exports, land cultivated and the size of the workforce, were concerned. According to one account 62 per cent of the Trinidad population engaged in agriculture in 1891 were Indians. By 1921, approximately 60 per cent were said to be so employed. While the Indians' impact was greatest in the sugar industry, they also contributed substantially in the cocoa and coconut industries.

Undoubtedly, Indian immigration affected wages and the conditions of labour. Indians were employed in agricultural work at lower rates of pay than workers in other occupations.[43] Apart from the wage differentials endemic in agricultural employment, such work was generally regarded as being of low status, and the effect of 'worsening conditions' during the twentieth century resulted in Afro-Trinidadian workers withdrawing more and more from field-work to undertake factory work. Although prior to the 1920s an estimated two-fifths of the agricultural sector's labour force (still the most important in the economy) were non-Indian labourers, most of whom were engaged in the cocoa industry, the sectoral shift had nevertheless been marked. The creation of alternative employment in the developing mineral industries and clerical opportunities, attracted much of this labour, with the result that the agricultural sector became the main employer of Indian labour. This identificaton of Indians with agriculture had 'lasting effects', even though many Indians had moved away from the estates.

Placed in this economic position (and faced with a declining sugar industry) Indians turned to the production of cocoa, rice and food crops (their survival depended upon such produce), which were cultivated on plots of land they had acquired. In 1916, they owned 97,962 acres of Crown Lands. By the end of 1917, in addition to the rented and leased lands, it was estimated that more than one-fifth of all the land owned and cultivated was under Indian ownership, a 'new economic development',[44] which contributed significantly towards bringing hitherto unused land into cultivation.

Against this background, throughout the 1920s and thereafter, the group differences in occupation and residence, were emphasized. Indians were to be found largely in the rural sector, while Afro-Trinidadians became more concentrated in the urban areas.[45] With the continuing decline of sugar and the boom and bust of cocoa production, oil increasingly became important in the economy. The hunger marches and wartime hardships which the Indians endured were beginning to show signs of becoming less severe at the end of the Second World War, when Trinidad's total acreage under food cultivation was two and a half times what it was in 1939. But this ray of hope was little consolation for as one of the country's economists observed, the people of Trinidad and Tobago unhesitatingly returned to the questionable pattern of 'consuming' what we 'do not produce and producing' what they did not consume.[46]

While oil and sugar were the foremost products in the economy in the 1950s, as the 1960s approached, agriculture generally, and the sugar industry in particular, suffered further set backs in production, at a time when the Dr Eric Williams's People's National Movement Government had embarked on a number of Five-Year Plans. But in the short term, little had changed for poor working class Indians. In fact, a well-known study published in 1953 found that after the war, status and occupation were still based on racially ascriptive colour-class stratification, which showed no signs of changing because of economic stagnation. There was no change in the status quo in the 1960s. If anything, the gap between the rich and well-off (including middle class Christian Indians) and the poor did little to diffuse rising ethnic tensions,[47] which peaked in the early 1970s, with the rise and revolt of the militant Black Power Movement.

As ethnic tensions became more severe, this Movement served to emphasize the dichotomy between the Government-favoured urban, industrial-based Afro-Trinidadians and the Indian workers who, despite their difficulties, continued to manage a steady, but diminished output in the neglected rural areas. Thus the Indians played (and continue to play) a vital economic role in the agricultural sector. But one has to be cautious about the conclusions that might be drawn from this contribution. According to Dookheran, although Indians have made significant strides, they remained essentially an 'economically depressed' group. Commenting on the rate of Indian economic participation, he drew two inferences from the 1960 data examined: first that the 'rate of participation in active and paid economic activity is lower for the East Indian community than it is for the Negro community' and second, 'on average, each worker in the Indian group has four dependents compared to 2.8 for the Negro group'. In his opinion, this not only effectively reduced per capita income, but also emphasized dependence of the average income wage earner on his employment. Thus 'the higher growth rate of the Indian population coupled with lower level of participation in active economic life already suggest a smaller share of the national wage bill (for example in relation to) share of population and a lower per capita income. This situation is even further aggravated by an examination of the income levels of both groups'.[48] He went on to paint a depressing picture of the income level of Indian wage earners and concluded by underlining the Indians' predicament.[49] (Since then, another researcher has found that the Indian 'community' had, to some extent, benefited from the economic changes that had occurred in the 1970s and 1980s.)[50]

More particularly, enterprising Indians have always been an integral part of their communities. Historically, on their entry into Trinidad, the vast majority of the Indians found themselves doing the least desirable jobs and were culturally alien, stuck at the lowest levels of society with few opportunities for social mobility. Such societal constraints as there were, hampered the Indians' progress, notably during the years of indenture and led to attempts, by many, to 'break the bonds of indentureship' by using the land and money received in lieu of their return passage to India to start a family business, usually as shopkeepers.

Initially, these Indo-Trinidadian entrepreneurs tended to fund their small businesses through family savings. But as they grew into larger enterprises, the have resorted to the Commercial Banks for loans. These entrepreneurs, however, were the exception, rather than the rule, for the majority of Indo-Trinidadian businesses were of small family concerns. and in spite of the growth in this business sector in recent years, the economic recession had had a greater impact upon the small businesses than on the larger ones, some 48 per cent of the former going out of business, compared with only 8 per cent in the latter. Commenting on the conomic progress that they had made as owners of enterprises in the wider society, one writer in a recent study of Indo-Trinidadians in business, published in 1993 stated that 'less than 25 per cent of the businesses in Trinidad were owned by Indo-Trinidadians'. Against this background, Government bureaucracy was cited as a major constraint to entrepreneurship by 54.5 per cent of the larger Indo-Trinidadian entrepreneurs and by 22.3 per cent of those who were in the 'smaller' category. But although none of the larger entrepreneurs said they were discriminated against as Indo-Trinidadian business people, 9.5 per cent of the smaller entrepreneurs identified racism as a 'major constraint' to entrepreneurship.

In terms of asset size and growth in income, Ramsaran noted that the majority of Indo-Trinidadians in business experienced some growth, moreso those with larger enterprises; and in general, Indian businesses had 'done well', about 79.3 per cent of the larger and 77.3 per cent of the smaller entrepreneurs had no doubt that, over the years, their standard of living had improved. In these bisinesses, family influence played a big part, being 'the single most important reason' for Indo-Trinidadians, especially Hindus and Muslims, as opposed to their Christian counterparts in the wider society, who were better educated. In this phase of their development (given the constraints) 'business' took precedence over education, the latter becoming increasingly more important to succeeding generations. The family is also important in that such undertakings tend to draw their labour requirements from the family and the extended family. But with the reduction in Indo-Trinidadian family size, this pattern of labour input may well change in the future.

Nonetheless in the above-mentioned study, it was found that 'All entrepreneurs (barring one) who were the subjects of this exercise have sought to improve the quality of life for themselves, but especially for their children', thus ensuring continuity of a family tradition. 'The growth of the the Indo-Trinidadian business sector, on the whole', Ramsaran concludes, 'can be seen as an attempt by a group of people to improve their standard of living in a society that initially gave them few opportunities to do so. What may once have been a forced situation due to lack of opportunities, may now have become a social trait synonymous with a particular ethnic group'.[51]

Bearing in mind that oil had, for many years, been an alternative to the plantation economy, the decline of agriculture in Trinidad, already evident in the 1950s, had become even more depressing by the 1970s. This was due to a number of factors, primarily the fact that the Williams's PNM Government never favoured agriculture. Put simply, in place of sugar, he preferred to 'produce iron and steel'.

While some middle class Indians benefited considerably, through their business dealings in the 1970s, the vast majority of Indians, including farmers and agricultural workers, resented the Government's outrageous neglect of their needs in and around the sugar estates. They had, for long, been deeply immersed in sugar production, through the good years and the bad. The decline of sugar has predictably done nothing to improve their welfare, to ease the enormous problems endemic in their autonomous acts of survival. Yet, money was no problem, as Williams and his well-oiled supporters boasted. Consequently, as agriculture (dominated by hard-working Indians in food and sugar cane production) declined in the 1970s, oil assumed unrivalled precedence in the economy, accounting for over 40 per cent of the Gross Domestic Product in the early 1980s and 80 per cent of all export earnings.[52]

But although the years 1973–1982 had brought profound socio-economic change, the primary beneficiary of the massive wealth which poured into the island was the PNM Government, which was allowed 'to undertake large-scale industrialization efforts as well as to bolster its patronage and the working class African community – through selective spending'. The portion of the prosperity accruing to rural Indians through 'secondary' means' served crucially to deepen their sense of ethnic identity.[53] Their desperate economic struggle (compounded later by the recession which followed the 'boom') was pointedly observed by Kelvin Singh thus:

> They abound in the petty retail and huckstering business, selling oysters, sweet-meats, coconuts and garden produce; they are to be seen in the swamps, poorly drained, living for years in makeshift cottages with their wives and children, growing rice and other food crops; they are to be seen on the thin strips of arid land near the sugar plantations and highway trying to eke out a living from the hard-yielding soil. Traditional cow-keepers, they have hardly benefited from state-aided farms; traditional rice-growers, they have received no state encouragement, though the country periodically suffers from a shortage of rice.[54]

This economically depressed position has led Indians to hold certain strong, well-founded beliefs and opinions concerning their position in society. They feel that their economic contribution (both historical and contemporary) is not recognised. Although many Indians possess educational qualifications (and in spite of the suggestion of change that has been beneficial to them) expectations of Civil Service employment was a contentious issue. So, it was argued that the 'contradiction between their valuable role in the colony's development and the disadvantaged position in which they find themselves, provoked a deep sense of insecurity and anxiety in the Indian mind with respect to their future role and position in the society'.[55]

## JAMAICA

The ever-resourceful East Indians in Jamaica were also able to apply themselves to cane-farming and rice cultivation, especially in the parish of Westmoreland. The acreage under cultivation, in this area, rose from 53 acres in 1919 to 1,200 in 1943. To make economic sense of their lives, whenever possible, the Indians relied heavily on the cultivation of sugar cane and rice. In terms of the use of labour between these crops, the Indians 'sold their labour outright' in the cultivation of sugar cane, while in rice-growing they utilized their own labour.[56]

When rice cultivation (an integral part of the Indians' livelihood) was abandoned because the morass lands they had rented were withdrawn, most families in the affected villages put forward the case that there had been a 'steady decline' in their well-being, to the extent that there was among the villagers, 'an air of depression and hopelessness'.[57]

With this shift in land use, the Indians, given their two-fold economic activities as peasants and wage earners, were forced into being part of a rural proletariat by the mid-1960s. The rice they had hitherto grown, primarily for their own consumption and for sale, now had to be imported from Guyana, because of the lower cost of production, as Government officials claimed. But, at the village level of economics, such an argument was 'meaningless' countered one researcher who wrote:

> On the contrary ... almost any price the Indians ... have to pay for rice is far more costly than if they grew it themselves ... That rice from Guyana can be marketed more cheaply than Island-grown rice is of little matter to the Indian villagers. What matters is that they must pay cash for every store-bought bag of rice. When families had rice lands their rice came from their own labour which cost them nothing. With the rice lands withdrawn, that same potentially productive labour lies idle.

Thus the Indians remained under-employed, waiting for croptime.[58] But not all Indians in Jamaica, even during the last years of indenture, were content with rural life. While 94.4 per cent of the total Indian population lived in rural villages in 1911,[59] by 1914–15 many unskilled workers, having completed their indentures, made their way to the towns in search of employment. About eighteen years later, the Indian population in Kingston and St.Andrew were 1,279 and 2,769 respectively.[60]

Apart from such non-agricultural occupations as shop-keeping, craftsmanship and a range of activities in the jewellery trade,[61] the urban Indians also applied their agricultural know-how to the cultivation and sale of vegetables and flowers. But, in spite of market gardening being one of their most economically viable activity, the Indians in Kingston were adversely affected by high land rents and water rates, a discriminatory Kingston and St. Andrew Corporate Law, Slum Clearance activities and much-dreaded unemployment.[62]

In the 1940s many desperately poor Indians who sought employment under the Relief Work Scheme were discriminated against.[63] And with the exception of a few professionals (for example, shop-keepers, landlords and jewellers) as urban dwellers, the poor Indians whose housing could be likened to the deplorable barracks on sugar estates during indentureship, formed an economically depressed community.[64]

Taken together then, wherever the Indians sought economic betterment to alleviate their distress, they more often than not, found themselves placed at a disadvantage. Fortunately for them and the Jamaican economy, they remained undeterred in the pursuit of their necessary goals.

## SURINAM

In Surinam, after the period of indentureship, the Indians were largely engaged in peasant production. British experience had taught Dutch Imperialists an invaluable lesson, dictated by common sense. And so like the Indians particularly in Guyana and Trinidad, the East Indians in Surinam were also granted parcels of land as an inducement to stay in the Colony, instead of returning to British India. Challenged by the acquisition of such property, the Indians were not merely enterprising, but pioneering, bringing into cultivation forest and swamp land. Several years before indentureship was finally abolished in Surinam, the Indians had established a strong position as land-holders. In 1903, some 1,972 Indians held a total area of 14,182 acres of public land varying from 'free use', 'leasing' or in property; and eight years later, 4,250 Indians were in control of 30,448 acres of land.

While some Indian peasants relied on self-subsistance, others sold some of their produce to the market. In the environs of Paramaribo, Indians cultivated vegetables and horticultural products, and they supplied meat and milk demanded in the city. Beyond these districts, rice was produced for the peasant household and for export. Handicrafts occupied only a few. In Paramaribo itself, however, many Indians were to be found as cart-drivers, tailors, small traders and shop-keepers.

In the years after indentureship, the process of stratification (already in the pre-1916 period there were differences between contract labourers and free immigrants) accelerated. 'The peasantry was not one big homogenous mass', it was pointed out. 'There were ... different categories of Indian peasants'. The poor subsisted beside the upwardly mobile. And among the rice cultivators in Nickerie and Saramacca, Hira noted, 'there was a small layer of rich peasants owning rice hulling works (some 133 of them in 1939) and tractors'. They were also involved as middlemen buying the produce of many small peasants, and in the Commewijne, by the 1920s some middlemen were owners of cars, while in Paramaribo, along with the flow of free Indian immigrants from British Guiana (in 1921 they accounted for eight per cent of the total number of Indian migrants), Indians achieved higher social status in the city, through trade. By 1925, over 30 per cent of the houses in the city belonged to these Indians. Shop-keepers and traders in Paramaribo formed a select but rich elite, which maintained its hegemony through the sons (daughters were home-bound!) of such families whose acquisition of Western education assured them of well-placed positions in society.

Significantly the period 1916 to 1940 saw the rise of the Indian petty bourgeoisie. Given the paucity of data for 1940 to 1980, in the words of one account, the Indians' economic position was 'characterised by the dispersion over all sectors of the economy', namely the Civil Service, mining, manufacture, trade and banking, property ownership and the professions, even though by 1964, a 'large group' still worked in agriculture. The dichotomy between the few rich and the mass of poor Indians was clear and the difference between the sexes was marked. Although the number of Indian females had increased by 1939, they faced much hardship in fulfilling their crucial role as mothers. 'They were not only taking part in production', it was argued, 'but the household work was augmented by the absence of the system on the plantation whereby others could look after the younger ones'.[65]

Generally, it was observed that although there were some tensions, relations between Indians and Creoles in Surinam were good.

## GUADELOUPE[*]

In Guadeloupe also the East Indians worked essentially in agriculture and the cattle-breeding sectors of the economy. In fact, several decades after the abolition of indentureship, by the mid-1970s an estimated 60 per cent of the Indian population still worked in the primary sector and were therefore more concentrated in rural areas, rather than the towns. A few educated Indians, however, had been employed in banks, insurance companies, as small-scale retailers (posing no threat to the large urban-based companies), but unlike the Indian merchants and traders in Port of Spain, Trinidad, those in Guadeloupe were 'backward'. Overall, however, given their agriculture-oriented activities, they had rescued the country from 'total disaster' since Emancipation, through their exemplary thrift and hard work. But significantly, their contact with the tertiary sector of the economy, as Singaravelou argued, is 'a token of economic integration', viewed by Creoles as perhaps a 'new threat'.[66]

It must be pointed out that not all the Indians who went to the Caribbean, were indentured labourers. Many Indians, especially after the system was abolished, ar-

*For more detailed information on the East Indians' economic contribution in Guadeloupe (and in Martinique, where fewer of them had settled) see Singaravelou's works as listed in the *Bibliography*.

rived as businessmen, who seized the golden opportunity of making a fortune by capitalising on what must have been to them a 'captive' market. The truly great success stories,[67] however, concerns those Indians who had through extraordinary thrift, courage and determination rose to become rich and successful, thus appearing as role models for the less fortunate, exploited majority, whose *raison d'etre* for leaving India was indeed to have money and a better life. It was from this economic foundation that East Indians, in their quest for improvement, were able to engage in, and develop their all-important cultural activities.

Nevertheless, taken as a whole, the West Indies in the post-war years, notably the late 1950s and in the 1960s, remained economically depressed as a result of the uneven development of world capitalism. In particular, British (also United States and Canadian) capital demanded cheap Black and East Indian labour, as the economic boom assisted some among the lower working classes to achieve upward occupational mobility and social status. Against this background, the problems of unemployment, underscored by racism (particularly in Guyana and Trinidad) helped little. Thus, Indo-Caribbean women joined the outflow of immigrants, accompanying, in some cases, their husbands, while thousands of other younger women went away to be trained as nurses or to study. Alas, for those men and women who had left the Caribbean, their initial ambitions were, in many cases, never realised and, of necessity, their attentions were shifted to other occupations and they became settlers in their adopted country.

As the years wore on and the economic situation worsened in the Caribbean (notably in Guyana and Trinidad), the exodus of Indo-Caribbean people increased markedly. In their countries of adoption (apart from being immigrant and foreign) they were further marginalised by institutionalized racism which did not (until very recently, and only to a very limited degree) recognise the East Indians' presence in the Caribbean and, as a consequence, they remained relatively unknown, buried beneath other more numerous popular and general ethnic categories, like 'Indians' or 'Pakistanis'.

Economically then, Guyana, Trinidad and Jamaica were further impoverished by their loss of essential labour and skills that migrated to the receiving countries of the industrialized, developed world.[68]

# CULTURAL INTEGRATION?

## *The Plural Society in the Caribbean*

Referring to colonies in the Far East, John Sydenham Furnivall observed that the combined social structure of dissimilar racial and cultural groups was not of their making, but imposed upon them by the Colonial power and 'by force of economic circumstances'.[69] This observation is not only historically correct, but also shows that in a social system where the cleavages are marked, the sense of community

between the different elements will be minimal, thus reflecting the essential structure of the plural society.[70]

The slave societies in the West Indies (among the oldest colonised by Europeans) are good examples of the plural society as described by Furnivall. Enterprising Europeans decimated the defenceless Carib and Arawak Indians and while
seeking a more suitable source of plantation labour, they initiated and developed
African slavery in the New World and keen competition among leading European
nations for colonial possessions. The European colonies in the Caribbean were
similar in that they were all ruled by force in an attempt to establish a unified
system, incorporating the unbridgeable differences between masters and slaves.
Michael Garfield Smith has noted that pluralism 'explicitly enjoins a holistic view
of societies and their cultures as units having historical continuity'.

Historically, according to Alfred Mayer, the concept of culture first appeared in
Germany and Russia as a 'typical ideological expression of the rise of backward
societies against the encroachments of the West on their traditional culture',[71] and
many academic definitions of culture have been advanced.[72]

In their march towards freedom, colonial peoples have made important, though
variable connections between their culture and nationalism. But cultural unity is
not the only means through which they have sought to attain their nationalistic
goals. In fact, at various times they have invoked the ideologies of race and communism.[73] The ideology of culture, however, has been invaluable to nationalist
movements; and while cultural distinctiveness has undoubted value among West
Indians, the problem of cultural identity, though 'unusually acute' poses the question: Is there a West Indian (or Caribbean) culture?

## Ethnic and Cultural Pluralism

Prior to Independence, the British Caribbean included Jamaica, the Leeward Islands (St. Kitts, Nevis, Antigua, Montserrat and the British Virgin Islands), the
Windward Islands, St. Vincent, St. Lucia, Dominica, Grenada, Barbados, Trinidad
and Tobago, British Honduras in Central America and Guyana (British Guiana) in
South America.

The islands are more or less over-populated, while British Guiana and British
Honduras contain large areas of unsettled land. Agriculture is the mainstay of the
economy of all these territories, even though industrialisation had been steadily
making inroads in Jamaica and Trinidad. Put simply, in spite of continuous foreign
capital injection over many years, these essentially monocultural economies are
still poor and underdeveloped.

Significantly, these societies are all multiracial, containing immigrants (the two
mainland territories also have elements of indigenous Indians) from Europe, Africa, China, India, the Middle East and elsewhere. The African-European associations arising from slave society have resulted in the presence of a large culturally

and biologically mixed group. Thus, a Coloured grouping was added to the Black–White social structure dominant in the British Caribbean. While there are racial and cultural cleavages within the Black-White structure, 'miscegenation, acculturation and assimilation have established a single continuum in racial, cultural and social terms'.[74] The introduction of East Indians meant a new and significant group became part of this social structure, especially in British Guiana, Trinidad and Tobago and Jamaica, thus adding a new dimension to the process oc creolization. In this context, how can 'creole' be defined? Bearing in mind the particular country, 'creole' refers to race, colour, national origin, class, ethnicity, language and religion, 'or some combination of these' and given its 'marvellous elasticity', Allahar and Varadarajan have identified creolization as being best thought of as 'the product of cultural mixing',[75] which had its genesis from the inception of colonial plantations and their evolution to the present day, incorporating first conquest, then slavery and indentureship, the basis of the political and economic systems that had entrapped and brought in close proximity the indigenous Caribs and Arawaks, Amerindians, Africans, East Indians, Chinese, Javanese and various groups of Europeans in inter-group relations that would, over the centuries, be highly unpredictable. The 'cultural forms' that evolved from these relations could not be applied to the Caribbean as a whole, but rather as existing in each separate country in the region.

From the beginning the Indians were set apart from the wider society, a deliberate policy of the Colonial Government and plantocracy. The geographical containment of the Indians on the estates and control of their movements, ensured their separateness; and of course, this exclusion from the rest of society helped the Indians to practice their religions and generally maintain their culture. In Jamaica and Grenada, where there was less land and fewer Indians than in Trinidad and British Guiana, the incoming emigrants lived and worked closely with the rest of the labouring population, and with time, not only became acculturated, but through inter-marriage, they were assimilated to a considerable extent. In British Guiana and Trinidad, the historical and ecological conditions were more conducive to a retention of Indian culture.[76]

The separateness of the East Indians is reflected in the fact that while persons of African, European or mixed Afro-European ancestry are called 'Creoles'(natives of the Caribbean), persons of East Indian descent were, and still are, referred to, more often than not derogatorily, as 'coolies' or 'Indians'. 'It is impossible to interpret the historical association between Africans and Europeans in the West Indies as an instance of symbiosis', wrote Smith, 'but between West Indians of African or mixed stock and those of Indian ancestry, competition rather than symbiosis has hitherto prevailed'.

Cultural plurality is said to exist where two or more different cultural traditions are part of the population of a given society. The societies in which cultural plurality is to be found are called plural societies. But given their cultural and social constitution, plural societies are units only in a political sense, because each has a single government. Apart from government and law, the institutional differences relating to cultural plurality are marriage, family, education, property, religion, economic institutions, language and folklore. While the differences in each of these institutions reflect the essential condition of cultural plurality within the Afro-European Caribbean community, the cultural difference is clearly much greater between the East Indians and Afro-White Creole section.[77]

'In the hsitory of the British Caribbean', as one writer put it, 'drastic attempts to solve this riddle of integration' have been made, at least on three occasions'. In 1838 the abolition of slavery 'freed a race, but failed to create a society', in 1865 Crown Colony rule in Jamaica was seen as the 'only alternative' to a collapse of the social structure'; and since 1945 the Crown Colony system had been replaced by responsible government based on adult suffrage and operating through ministerial systems. Political parties and trade unions are now recognised institutions and have flourished under the new regime. At the same time (with the exception of what was then British Guiana, British Honduras and the Virgin Islands) the idea of British Caribbean Federation had been actively publicised.[78]

To what extent has East Indians as an economically depressed group been integrated culturally? For generations, East Indian cultural heritage in the Caribbean had been transmitted with varying degrees of emphasis and success, and although European-Creole culture had been imposed upon the East Indians by Governments, Christian missionaries and the churches they led also feared the Indians' 'heathenism'.[79] The Indians' cultural persistence, especially in the nineteenth century, posed a threat to those who wanted total dominance over the increasingly closely-knit Indian communities in the Caribbean, particularly in British Guiana, Trinidad and Surinam.

In their efforts to win Indian converts to Christianity, in 1868 the Scottish Presbyterian Church, which constituted the main thrust in the Westernisation of the East Indians, began its mission of bringing the Christian faith to the Caribbean to save the barbarian races from their wicked ways and idolatrous religions. According to K.J. Grant, the mission spread from Trinidad to Grenada in 1884, to St. Lucia and British Guiana in 1885, and the indentured Indians in Jamaica were visited by East Indian 'pastors' who helped the Presbyterian Church missionaries.[80]

Various methods were used by the missionaries in their campaign of conversion among the Indians. Given their self-appointed role as the protectors of the morals and 'well-being of mankind', the missionaries' moral fervour,[81] it seemed, was legitimized and strengthened by the force of British industrial power. The Scotsmen John Morton and K.J. Grant, who had migrated to Canada, shared a belief in 'Canada's mission to Christianize the world'[82] and after visiting India in 1854, Morton decided to go further, making his way to Trinidad in 1868. Both men were particularly concerned with the heathen Indians.

The focus of the missionaries' activity was the conversion of the Indians from their religions to Christianity. Among the methods used to achieve this conversion of faith in India and the Caribbean were meetings conducted in Hindi which included bhajan-singing and the publication of books and articles in various languages. Interestingly, female missionaries worked with the 'more promising' of the Indian women converts and medical missionaries (absent in the Caribbean) also contributed to the conversion process. An important link between India and the Caribbean was the 'exchange of native helpers and Canadian missionaries'.[83]

Reinforcing these 'methods', the Christian missionaries enjoyed the support of the British commercial and planter interests. In India, missionary activity was intertwined with the unity and strength of the British Empire, and in the Caribbean there was close co-operation with the planters and Government.[84] In Trinidad, for example, Governor Arthur Gordon was, to say the least, on friendly terms with the missionaries.

Thus, with powerful friends and allies and imperial backing,the Presbyterians moved forward by interpreting Hindu words and practices, and integrating them in their Christian messages, churches and organisations. Moreover, 'Hindi Bibles' were sent to the Caribbean by missionaries in India.[85] A few years later, the investment had increased and the scope of such literature had widened as the agents of Christianity maintained their essential interest in winning Indian converts in the Caribbean.[86] Apart from the visit of the Rev. W. J. Jameson from India to Trinidad in 1906 (followed by others), in 1929 C.F. Andrews visited local Presbyterians and spoke to the Indians,[87] and Sadhu Sunder Singh's arrival in 1932 was also an occasion which aroused great expectations. More recently, in the late 1960s, the Rev. Motilal was engaged for several months, ever-hopeful that he would maximize the number of converts among the East Indians in British Guiana, Trinidad and Surinam.

Predictably, 'doctrinal matters' became a battleground on which the Presbyterians fought against the Indians' religions. John Morton used the words 'loathsome', 'wicked, wild and unkept' and 'not worthy of respect' to describe Hindu Gods, Hindu women and Hindu temples, respectively.[88] K. J. Grant also assailed the Indians' religions, linking their non-Christianity to the devil and deplored the committing of wife murder. In so doing, he clouded the issue of wife murders among the Indians, which needed to be clarified. As one historian argued the main cause of Indian murders was 'infidelity' among Indian women (a situation that was heartily encouraged by the perennial problem of their scarcity), a 'major social problem' in the Caribbean during the years of indentureship. A year before the system had ended, the Indians' predicament was recognised by the Rev. J. T. Taylor.

But Grant had also conveniently ignored an important contributory factor to Indian violence, namely that Hindu and Muslim marriages were illegal. (They did not become legal until 1936 and 1945 respectively). In effect, Indian children (both Hindus and Muslims) were labelled 'illegitimate' and 'with their mothers' possessed no inheritance rights and so disputed successions were often resolved in a violent manner'. Furthermore, Presbyterianism not only required Indians to deny their religions, but also to study, as a subject, the 'False Religions', namely Hinduism, Buddhism and Mohammedanism.[89]

But regardless of the various approaches used by these missionaries, there was a low rate of conversion among the Indians in the Caribbean. In British Guiana, after about three decades of missionary activity, by 1927, from a total Indian population of 127,017 only an estimated 500 Indians were won over. (As it was, the spread of Hinduism and Islam in Asia, seriously disrupted Christian missionary work in India and the Caribbean). In Trinidad also, there were few converts[90] and interestingly, by the turn of the twentieth century, Muslims were particularly reluctant to join the Presbyterian Church.[91] The Hindus, for their part, instead of waging an offensive against the aggressive Christians, time and again, simply wanted to be allowed to worship in their own way. Another reason advanced for the Indians' lack of interest in Christianity was the persistent belief of the White race that the native peoples were 'inferior'. Religious imperialism was therefore to be resisted mightily by the subject races.

The Presbyterians' work in the education of the East Indians in the Caribbean is worthy of special mention. Indeed, given the East Indians respect for, and the importance they attach to education, the missionaries were pressed both in Trinidad and British Guiana to establish schools and colleges, such as Naparima College in San Fernando.[92] In fact, the Canadian Mission Schools in the rural districts were of central importance. Taken together, by the 1930s, these educational efforts by the Presbyterians were reflected in the fact that East Indians had become professionals, participants in commerce and were among those concerned with bringing about political change.

But education was 'only peripheral' to missionary activity, as far as Presbyterians were concerned. Although Grant and Morton did not agree on this matter, the education derived from Canadian missionaries was of great value to the increasingly Westernized Indian in the Caribbean.[93] Educating the Indians was viewed as secondary, not only for economic but also for religious reasons.[94] Nevertheless, the Indians would not be denied. Many of them, though sceptical of religious indoctrination, recognised the value of education in the new and changing environment. It was therefore not surprising that by 1946 there was a significant rise in the number of Indian pupils attending Secondary schools.

Overall, one of the main aspects of the Canadian missionaries' work in British Guiana, Grenada, St.Lucia and Trinidad is the point alluded to above: that it was the Indian model of Presbyterian activity was implemented in the Caribbean.[95] Commenting on the 'nature of the responses' of the Indian population, Samaroo cited three types of responses: first a determination to resist conversion; second, acceptance of Presbyterianism, but not full church membership; and third those 'Trained to believe that to be a good Christian one had to be a good Anglo-Saxon (who attempted to deride their East Indian heritage in a way that surprised even the Canadians whom they imitated'. This last small conspicuous group was to be found not only in India, but also in Trinidad and British Guiana.[96] They constituted a hard-core of indigenous Indian Presbyterians who had replaced the missionaries from abroad; men and women devoutly engaged in managing church affairs in Trinidad, Grenada and British Guiana.[97]

# GUYANA

Commenting on the Indians in British Guiana, Hill stated that the majority of the immigrants were from the following castes: Ahirs (cow-minders), Kahars (carriers), Chamars (dealers in skins), Kewats (cultivators and boatmen), Lodhs (cultivators), Jats (cultivators), and Mallahs (boatmen). In addition, it was estimated that Muslims ('Mussulmen') amounted to about 20 percent of a shipload.[98]

Although it has been noted that because the immigrants were brought together aboard ship and on the plantations, where they acted in a communal, brotherly (*jahaji*) manner, thus creating a 'homogenous' culture, it seems 'more probable', as one account informs us, that the immigrants 'originated in certain specific areas and formed specific castes, and that they maintained their cultural identity to a far greater extent than is generally believed'. Yet there is some truth in Weatherly's conciliatory view that the Indians in British Guiana and Trinidad 'although derived from diverse geographical and social environments in India have sufficient degree of solidarity to be treated, as in local practice they are treated, as a unit since their reaction to Western influences are essentially alike'.[99]

In British Guiana, Christian missionary enterprise was not lacking. 'We feel this mission among the tribes of India', stated Rev. H.V.P. Bronkhurst 'to be as necessary as it is important and while much gratified and encouraged by past successes, we are impressed with the greatness of our responsibility'.[100] But in spite of the attempts of the Wesleyan Missionary Society (established in British Guiana in 1814) the Anglican East Indian Mission, the Canadian East Indian Mission, the Lutheran East Indian Mission and the Roman Catholic Church, by 1938, the whole Christian missionary project was not as successful as it was expected to be.

The editor of the *British Guiana Mission Journal* commented that future missionaries to the East Indians 'will need to learn one or two different branches of the Indian language and presumably to acquire and maintain complete sympathy with their mentality. That will involve long and careful training and other difficulties which have in the past proved insurmountable. But the task, let us hope, is not impossible'.[101]

Be that as it may, there was a 'sufficient degree of solidarity' among the various castes to strengthen and develop their own social movements *vis-à-vis* the wider society. Following abolition of the indenture system in 1917, the impact of the Christian missionaries, the influence of Western institutions and gradual educational progress had brought about an intellectual awakening among the Indians, arousing renewed speculation beyond the bounds of agricultural labour. And as they made contact with the other racial groups comprising the other free citizens of British Guiana, they found it not only desirable, but also necessary to seek fuller and closer association among themselves.

## EAST INDIAN ASSOCIATIONS

Although Indians had some freedom of movement and association within and between plantations and villages, organisation for the purpose of their moral, social and intellectual improvement was not forthcoming until around 1892, when Thomas Flood, Verasammy Mudliar, James Wharton (solicitor) and W. H. Wharton formed the East Indian Institute, to bring about a better social relationship among educated Indians in the city. Unfortunately, the Institute declined after forwarding an address of congratulation to Queen Victoria on the occasion of her Diamond Jubilee, leaving a strong need which was emphasized in a lecture entitled 'India: The Progress of her People at Home and Abroad and How Those in British Guiana May Improve Themselves' by Joseph Ruhomon, founder of the British Guiana East Indian Association (New Amsterdam).

Ruhomon showed a rare zeal for the well-being of his fellow Indians and pursued the idea of an organisation that would benefit Indians. In 1916 he called together a group of prominent citizens with a view to forming an association for the moral, social and intellectual development of Indians; an idea which attracted Mr. E. A. Luckhoo who chaired the meeting at which it was decided to call the proposed society The British Guiana East Indian Association. At this important meeting, Ruhomon outlined the aims and objects of the Association, which covered a wide range of activities.[102]

To carry out its work successfully, the Association needed to transcend the bounds of the small County of Berbice. In 1919, the year of the Amritsar Massacre in India, Madhoo Lall Bhose, 'an ardent Bengali patriot and nationalist', called a meeting a his home in Georgetown and it was agreed to convene another meeting at St. Andrew's Hall. The Chairman of the meeting, J. A. Luckhoo, called for unity and co-operation among the Indians of British Guiana in helping the Association in its efforts to bring about desirable reforms that would affect many aspects of Indian communal life. Thus the Georgetown (BGEI) Association came into being with Wharton and Flood as Honorary Presidents and Luckhoo as its first President, a post which he held until 1923, when the membership stood at about one hundred.

Thereafter, the Berbice Association functioned as a branch and the inaugural meeting of the BGEIA was held in the Town Hall, Georgetown on 24 April 1919, in the presence of the Governor of the Colony, Sir Wilfred Collet and Dr Wharton acting as Chairman. On this historic occasion, Luckhoo gave an address entitled: 'The East Indians in British Guiana; From Their Advent to the Colony to the Present Time; Being a Survey of the Economic, Educational and Political Aspects'. After Luckhoo spoke, the Governor said that he 'did not believe in professional agitators who did no good, but a body like the Association could do a great deal for the East Indians, *in a quiet way*' (author's emphasis). Surely the good Governor was not intending to separate the leadership from the rank and file. But for those among the black intelligentsia (and radical Indians) with any reservations, he had this to say: 'It is impossible for the Government to deal with a vast mass of Indians in the colony, if it had to deal with each separately. There must be some kind of body with which the Government could work'.[103]

And so blessed with official recognition from no lesser person than the chief Administrator, the Association proceeded with its work of representation, and almost immediately began to deal with a Scheme of Colonization, involving Indians from India to supplement and eventually fill the labour shortage, consequent upon the abolition of indenture. Three years later, when the Wood Commission arrived in British Guiana, the Association prepared a memorandum concerning the welfare of the Indians. Among the issues put to the Commissioners were the penal clauses of the Immigration Ordinance; hours of labour; the rice industry; the education of East Indian children; East Indian cooks and nurses in public institutions; East Indian employees in public offices; East Indian paupers; East Indian marriage and divorce laws; East Indian voters; the political constitution; drainage and irrigation; imperial loans, hinterland development and Colonization.[104]

About this time, another organisation, the Indian National Congress appeared on the political scene. Rivalry between the two organisations it was thought could do no harm to the Indian community, as a whole. Reconciliation between the two bodies was the only way forward, and at the special meeting held on 2 April 1922 it was resolved that both organisations would operate as the British Guiana East Indian Association.

In 1928 the Rev. C. F. Andrews, an outstanding friend of India, who had known Gandhi well in South Africa, arrived in British Guiana on a good-will mission and was given a 'rousing reception' by the Association at a public meeting held at the Town Hall on 20 May. Andrews came with the full support of the Indian National Congress and the Citizens Association of Bombay, and brought the blessings not only of Mahatma Gandhi, but also of the great Indian poet Rabindranath Tagore. To the Guianese Indians, the value of such links with India was incalculable, engendering among them a deep sense of pride and belonging to the land and culture of their forefathers. The Association took the opportunity of discussing and presenting a memorandum, which again raised the question of the Indians' welfare.

Apart from some financial problems and certain organisational difficulties, by June 1936, the Association was able after three attempts, to launch its organ *Indian Opinion*, express its concern on unemployment among the Indians, and the educational difficulties East Indian children faced in the country districts. Over the years prior to 1940, a number of important contributions from high-ranking officials, towards keeping the Association's work alive and vibrant, men who all helped to boost confidence and give added spiritual strength to the Association.[105]

In 1938 C.R. Jacob was returned as President of the Association and the future augured well. Indeed this was the Centenary year of the arrival of East Indians in the Colony. 'In the history of Empire migration', the Governor said, 'centenaries do not mark the completion of a movement, they are milestones on the road to fulfillment of its ultimate destiny'. It is significant that although one hundred years of their presence in the colony was marked with pomp and circumstance, here and there, the vast majority of the Indians were at work on 5 May 1938 'with only a vague sense of appreciation of the importance of the day which brought to a close an unforgettable chapter in the history of the Indian community and ushered in the dawn of a new era.[106]

Hitherto the centenary year, however, a great deal of difficult organisational groundwork had been done in promoting East Indian interest through a number of other important social organisations, including the Susamachar East Indian Young Men's Society, the Balak Sahaita Mandalee, the Hindu Society, the Arya Samaj, the British Guiana Dramatic Society, the Corentyne Literary and Debating Society and the East Indian Cricket Club.

In line with a suggestion made by Rev. Bronkhurst, the Rev. Yates approached a few young Indians, including Peter Ruhomon, with a view to forming the East Indian Young Men's Society. At its inaugural meeting held at Bourda, Cecil Clementi (later Sir) who was then administering the Colony, gave the first address to the Society entitled: 'The Kinship Between Indian and British Races'. Yates obviously saw the need for training a cadre of Indian youths, who would act as mediators and agents to help in bridging the gap between East Indians and the wider 'creole' society. Also in attendance at this meeting, was the Rev. E. Donald Jones of the Methodist Society, who chaired the meeting. He made it clear, according to one account, that 'the Society would not be limited to any particular denomination, but would have for its objects, the development of the intellectual, moral and social side of the Indian community and all Indians, irrespective of creed or caste, would be eligible therein, for membership'.[107] Thereafter, at periodic intervals, the addresses given to the membership focused on the cultural and intellectual aspects of life. These talks became a major feature of the Society's activities which, as Yates saw it, helped to establish better relations between the Indians in Georgetown. In this work and in the affairs of the Society generally, Yates played a central role until his retirement from his missionary calling. It was to his credit that those who followed him proved to be worthy successors, such as the Rev. J. R. Hudson who had spent many years doing missionary work in India. Hudson immersed himself in the Society's activities, was optimistic of its responsibility in creating 'a healthy public opinion on the great moral issues', and praised Yates for his part in helping to bring about 'some solidarity' in the Indian community.

The early death of Hudson inaugurated the leadership of another man of the cloth, Rev. H.H. Chick, another missionary with experience in India. Chick is said to have introduced a 'virile atmosphere' into the Society's activities. Indeed in 1934 the Society was engaged in discussions of problems relating to the welfare of British Guiana's Indians and, as a public relations exercise, at a meeting held at the East Indian Cricket Club, the value of the Society to the general public was clearly emphasized as an integral part of its agenda. After outlining the organisation's history, its aims and objects, Chick spoke on the theme 'Whither Indians', during which he called upon young Indians to forge a new philosophy of life in British Guiana.

The next speaker, J.I. Ramphal, involved in educational work, addressed 'The Educational Needs of Our community' and Francis Kawall, a local philanthropist, spoke on 'The Education of girls'. The importance of education to the Indians could not be over-emphasized, they knew how difficult it was to acquire it. Chick had recognised the merits of recording the Society's progress and stressed the necessity of an authentic history of the East Indians in British Guiana, which he regarded as a task to be undertaken by the Society. At the close of his term of office, Chick looked back on the Society's work and the prestige it had gained, and said that it was the task of the membership to take the lead intellectually, morally and socially to effect improvement of the Indian people in British Guiana. Thereafter, the Society's prestige was maintained, as it pursued a programme of social work that included helping poor children.

When the Balak Sahaita Mandalee, also known as the Child Welfare Society, was formed in June 1936, Mrs. J. B. Singh was its first President. This organisation came into being in order to meet the extensive relief work arising from the considerable poverty that existed in the Indian community. The Mandalee faced the daunting task of tackling a backlog of problems, reflecting residual elements of the Indians' indentured past. It was necessary to spread educational propaganda among Indian mothers as to the care of children, and encouragement was given to them to attend the clinics available in the city, where free advice was on offer in accordance with their needs.

It was found, however, that housing accommodation left much to be desired and that there was a shortage of better food and clothing among school children. In order to satisfy the growing demands on their limited financial resources, the BSM launched occasional appeals to the public and engaged in fund-raising activities such as garden parties and concerts, not only to maintain its work, but also for its extension in the city and country districts. In an attempt to help Indian mothers who were stuck in their 'old fashioned ways', BSM members attended lectures on mothercraft, and visits to the country areas were undertaken from time to time. On the whole, it was stated that the organisation's grand ideal was 'Better mothers, better children, better home life and a better Indian community'.[108]

Since it was founded in 1922, the Hindu Society had been remarkably successful in achieving its aims and objectives concerning religious, social and educational work, so much so that by 1938 it had 'abundantly justified the anticipations of its founders, and its triple objects of providing temple, school and dharamsala'.

Ramsaroop Maraj, who played a central role, laid the cornerstone of the Society's temple in the presence of D.B.K. Pillai and Pandit V. N. Tivary, the principal members of the Indian delegation which visited British Guiana. In 1923, the temple was opened for public worship, and a few years later, the cornerstone of the Hindu school was laid by another visiting Indian, Kunwar Maharaj Singh. The school was formally opened three years later by the Governor Sir Cecil Hunter Rodwell. Another cornerstone, that of the Dharamsala, was laid by R. Maharaj in February 1928 and on 14 July it was opened by the Rev. C. F. Andrews, who had for them become, a 'friend of the country'.

Known also as home for the poor, the Dharamsala was funded by voluntary subscriptions from the general public; and although this sanctuary was intended primarily for Indians, we are told that in practice, no poor applicant, regardless of race, was turned away. Here there was accommodation for as many as 250 persons, who were provided with one free meal each day and free lodging; an extraordinary example of a voluntary charitable institution during these early post-indenture years.

Education was, for the Society, a primary concern. The Hindi school, located not far from the temple, offered tuition in Hindi, Urdu and English; and not surprisingly the general success of the school impressed the colonial Government to the extent that a maintenance grant was given to ensure continued educational work.

The prime mover of the Society, the 'soul of the movement', was Ramsaroop Maharaj whose personal qualities, sincerity, humility and vision, were fortuitous in arousing the wide support so necessary, at that time, in advancing the Society's work. No lesser person than Governor Denham attested to Maharaj's contribution when he visited the Dharamsala in 1930. This symbol of Colonial authority not only commended Maharaj for his foresight in combining religion with charity, through which he had established a Colony-wide reputation, but also for his dedication and his 'desire to help all races'. The Governor underlined how impressed he was by promising the Society further financial assistance when the Colony's economic position improved.

The indefatigable Maharaj, clearly a man with a mission, was dissatisfied with the limited focus of the Society's activities and moved towards inclusion of those Indians who lived in areas far beyond the city. Fortunately, through a Government concession of land, he was able to build a Dharamsala for the poor on the southern bank of the Canje Creek, near the town of New Amsterdam in Berbice.

This long-established organisation has had many branches scattered across the country, and having functioned well, it had become necessary to consolidate its gains. So in 1937 the various branches came together to form the American Aryan League, which was inaugurated by India-born Professor Bhaskaranand who was President. Membership of the Arya Samaj did not discriminate on the grounds of race, sex or colour, and here again we see a post-indenture organisation, at least in theory, adopting an openess towards the wider society, without losing sight of its cultural base.

Registered under the Friendly Societies Ordinance, the Arya Samaj's objects were 'to organise and control Vedic mission and Vedic studies in the New World'; to win the cooperation of other nationalities, with the aim of for ming a 'common brotherhood', as embodied in the principles of the AS; to promote education through the teaching of Sanscrit and Hindi in schools and colleges; to eliminate religious intolerance and religious prosecution; to exalt religion 'from mere belief to logical philosophy'; to offer protection to 'orphans, widows and disabled people'; to further its work through publications such as books and magazines; to institute a Vedic studies library; to establish guidelines for the followers of the Vedic faith; and finally, to formulate a means through which people in general, could be reformed in order to 'remove all social and moral evils'.[109]

Altogether, the above reflected the deep concerns of the majority of Indians. For one thing, given the disabilities that were placed upon the Indians during indentureship to discourage any ambitions for education, the Arya Samaj, acutely aware of its importance, built the Guiana Oriental College so that it could fulfil its third objective.

The British Guiana Dramatic Society was created following the success of the plays *Savitri*, staged in 1929 by Mrs. J.B. Singh, and *The Maharani of Arakhan* which, in 1936 was jointly directed by Mrs. Singh and the India-born S.N. Ghose. These dramatic successes aroused the latent creative energies of Indians who felt that such talents could be developed for the benefit of the community. Consequently, the BGDS came into being with a view 'to assist the cultural advance of its members through music and drama'. The scope of the Society's activities was broad, including lectures, mock trials and the teaching of Hindi.

A monthly bulletin was issued and between the production of plays and dances, variety entertainment and social evenings helped to maintain interest and involvement. It is significant, as in previously mentioned organisations, that the BGDS was 'not necessarily Indian in its outlook', incorporating scenes from English dramatic works.

In addition to this organisation, the Corentyne Literary and Debating Society was formed in 1937 with B. Yisu Das as its first President and to its credit, the Society provided a much needed forum for Indians to give expression to their social and intellectual concerns.[110]

The English game of cricket was one form of colonial activity which had the potential of bringing together all social classes. The sport attracted many Indians, who played hard and well, all in all, a pleasant way of spending leisure hours that were very restricted during indentureship. But even then, enough interest had developed, and not surprisingly, the East Indian Cricket Club was formed about 1914. A year later, the Club was able to play matches on its own ground, leased for five years by a local cricket enthusiast J.A. Veerasawmy. The opening of this playing field was graced by the presence of the Governor, Sir Walter Egerton, in December 1915. After serving such a good purpose for many years, to the relief of the Club, the ground was finally acquired. But soon it was found that a larger pavilion was needed to accommodate the growing membership, and that in order to qualify for entry into the Parker Cup competition, a larger ground was needed. Soon, through the intervention of Kunwar Maharaj Singh, the Club was able to move to a larger site. Even though it was a 'veritable swamp', the Indians' hard work and determination made it the 'ideal' cricket ground, which was opened in April 1928 by Governor Rodwell. On this occasion, the first ball bowled by H.B. Gajraj was hit for a boundary by the Governor, and thereafter, as a sports organisation, the EICC (a regular and successful competitor in the Garnett Cup matches since 1916), evolved to spread friendly rivalry and goodwill beyond the bounds of the cricket field.

Overall, the work of the foregoing organisations in promoting Indian culture in British Guiana has been noteworthy. Just over two decades into the twentieth century, one of the most fearless and outstanding Indians in the colony, Peter Ruhomon, recorded their progress in *Timehri*, in 1921. 'A quarter of a century has gone by', he wrote, 'and I do not see that the situation has improved to an extent reasonably proportionate to this length of time. The progress that should have been made has yet to be made. The race has been languidly marking time, more or less'. The sad truth, he felt was that the average creole East Indian neither showed interest in high aspirations, nor was he 'stirred and enthused by great ideals'.

But seventeen years later in 1938, which marked the 100th anniversary of the East Indians' arrival in British Guiana, Peter Ruhomon (brother of Joseph), was able to state, in a centenary address to the Susamachar East Indian Young Men's Society, that on the whole, they had a 'record that in all circumstances of their case, redounds distinctly to their credit'.[111]

Given their cultural heritage, from the moment the Indians had landed, they began, as soon as they could, to build their own organisational structures to incorporate acceptable elements of their new environment. In doing so they displayed tenacity, imagination, ingenuity, courage and skill, which were crucial to their survival, and indeed in the darkest hours of their history, religious beliefs and practices, have shed much light and given them succour.

## *Religious Activities*

The Indian immigrants brought with them strong religious customs and beliefs, which were an integral part of their lives. But in British Guiana (as in Trinidad, and elsewhere in the Caribbean and Indian diaspora), certain adjustments had to be made. Bronkhurst observed:

> In this country, we do not see the streets and estates crowded with temples of all
> descriptions; we do not see parties of Brahmins and others in procession with

drums and music celebrating some particular holiday; we do not meet with troops of yogis or penitents and religious mendicants on the roads, journeying to some sacred river to wash away their sins by bathing in it; we do not see in this colony the Hindu going to Gaya to perform the obsequies of his ancestors. ... Although we do not witness these things yet their religion exercises prodigious influence over the people.[112]

The same could be said of the much smaller Muslim community in that one could not see devout Muslims in conspicuous crowds heading for a local Mecca. In fact, it seemed to be in keeping with the followers of these faiths among the Indians that they should be recognised, despite their relatively small number in British Guiana, compared with India. If religion was crucial to the Indians in India, it was no less so for the Indians in British Guiana, at least in the years immmediately after abolition of the indenture system. Through religion, life made sense; a lived experience that was increasingly becoming an acceptable way of life. It is therefore not surprising that after two Hindu temples (there was no mention of mosques), were discovered by the Royal Commission of 1870, twenty years later, when Major Comins visited British Guiana, he found twenty-nine 'Mahometan' mosques and thirty-three Hindu temples, on various estates and villages, which led him to question whether the 'large increases' indicated was due to a 'revival' of religious zeal among the immigrants, or the influence of 'their Brahmins or priests whose status and power are necessarily increased by the existence of temples in which they can officiate'.[113]

By the end of indentureship, the places of worship among the Indians had increased to forty-three temples and forty-six mosques. Virtually every plantation had its temple and/or mosque. Since then, the establishment of these places of worship had helped immeasureably to consolidate the religious faiths through the instruction and training of each generation

Many overseas Hindu communities are characterised by changes in caste, devotional orientation and, as a consequence, the emergence of new forms of socio-religious practice. Hinduism's revered BHAKTI MARGA (path of loving devotion) is the source from which the main features of the BHAKTI tradition developed in Hindu communities abroad. Elements of this tradition have a long history of many centuries in North and South India.[114]

Quite distinct from the family and caste-based forms of worship which 'characterize village Hinduism in India', Vertovec states, 'in BHAKTI-centred Hindusim the importance of communal feeling often finds expression in congregational activity. Recitation of the *Ramayana* by laymen, expositions of the *Bhagavata Purana* by pundits, and the group-singing of BHAJANS (hymns of praise) are foremost examples of BHAKTI-congregationalism. BHAKTI-centred Hinduism, then, is a religious orientation ideally suited for overseas Indians'.[115] Although it would not be possible here to give a full account of the immensely complex system of laws, customs and practices that constitute Hinduism, it is nevertheless necessary to attempt an outline of the system that had, and still governs, the lives of the Indians of this religious persuasion.

Hinduism, like other religions, seemed to have evolved from ancient beliefs rooted in the Vedas and Hindu scriptures. One learned definition of Hinduism informs us that it is

> a unique religion. It is APAURESHEYA, that is to say, not founded by any particular human being and it is also SANATANA, that is to say, eternal. It insists on no creed to be believed by its adherents. It believes in one supreme being who rules the creation, but does not exclude from its fold those who believe in many gods and goddesses as well as those who hold that God does not exist. It holds that the Supreme being is formless, yet it recognises the worship of images. It believes in the existence of the soul and that the soul transmigrates from birth to birth which is caused by the KARMA or action of a being. It believes that MOKSHA or MUKTI, that is to say, freedom from rebirth and from all the sorrows that human flesh and blood is heir to, can be secured by both JNANA (knowledge) and good KARMA and that MOKSHA means merging of an individual soul into the Supreme soul (PARAMATMA). It holds that sacrifices (JAJANA) are efficacious in propitiating the divine beings, but considers these as inferior to knowledge and devotion. It is bold enough to declare that man is God (SOHAM) but at the same time it recognises the duality between man and his creator to whom devotion can be rendered. Its outward symbol is adherence to the caste system and to recognition of the Vedas as the sacred scriptures, though modern Hinduism differs much from the ancient Vedic religion'.[116]

It is historically inaccurate to assume that Hinduism is not a proselytizing religion, for there is much evidence (both epigraphic and literary) which informs us that Greeks, Sakas, Gurjaras and Hunas, invaders of, and settlers in India, were among those who adopted Hinduism. More recently, the Ahoms who first arrived in India at the turn of the thirteenth century and established themselves in Assam, were also converts to Hinduism. Moreover, it is historically incorrect to take the view that Hinduism was confined to India. In fact, it had spread well before the coming of Islam to places as far west as Madagascar and eastward to the Malay Peninsula, Java, Sumatra, Champa and Cambodia, where Indian colonists carried their rule, their religion, philosophy, sacred language, Sanskrit, and their arts and architecture, the legacy of which can still be found in monuments that have survived in Cambodia and Java.

Hinduism is a religion with many sects, the main ones being the Saivas (worshippers of Siva), the Saktas (worshippers of Sakti) and Vaishnavas (worshippers of Vishnu), all of whom came under the authority of the Vedas. The philosophy of Hinduism can be found in the UPANISHADS of which the BHAGAVAD GITA is a symposium that is developed in detail in the SADADARSHANA or Six Systems of philosophy. Within the great epics, the RAMAYANA and the MAHABHARATA are contained religious and social ideas and ideals greatly revered by Hindus.

Another much respected and important aspect of Hinduism is its spirit of toleration, accommodating religious dissent to a degree which, it is contended, makes it more tolerant of other religious persuasions such as Roman Catholicism, Protestantism and Islam, faiths whose relations with each other is marked by antipathy and, at times, by violent confrontation. And while the proliferation of temples (housing Hindu gods and goddesses) can give a sense of devoted adherence and popularity throughout India, such places are not necessary, because the Hindu form of worship is essentially individualistic, though congregational worship is also accepted practice. Followers of Hinduism have indeed found it attractive because they believe it allows them a great deal of freedom in the content, form and place of worship and prayer.

The fundamental principles of Hinduism lead us back some three thousand years to the Vedas, the four books of which (the RIG VEDA, YAJUR VEDA, SAMA VEDA and ATHARVA VEDA) encompasses Divine Knowledge. The RIG VEDA concerns ritual, worship and first causes; the YAJUR VEDA concerns ceremonies relating to sacrifices and instructions on religious services, castes, feasts, purification, gifts, building of temples, ceremonies at birth, marriage and death; the SAMA VEDA contains odes and hymns exalting the Supreme Being and lesser deities; and the ATHARVA VEDA, containing mystical verses or incantations (mantras) relates to a system of mystical theology and metaphysics. For a Hindu, all true religion stems from the VEDAS. There are, however, other subsequent writings called the BRAHAMANAS that are instructive in the use of the Vedic texts. The UPANISHADS linked to the BRAHAMANAS help to give a full explanation pointing to the vagueness of the older writings relating to the great questions of the universe.

The VEDAS is particularly invaluable to human thought, and as Professor Max Muller put it, Vedic literature:

> opens … a chamber in the education of the human race to which we can find no parallel anywhere else', incorporating the 'historical growth of … language and thought … of the first intelligible development of religion and mythology … the first foundation of Science, Astronomy, Metronomy, Grammar and Etymology, … the first instructions of philosophical thoughts, … the first attempts at regulating family life, village life and state life as founded on religious ceremonials, traditions and contract.[117]

Apart from the corpus of work relating to the VEDAS, in essence, Hinduism is also interpreted as a theory consisting 'of one impersonal reality, and the unreal, phenomenal world which undergoes cyclical changes; transmigration and karma; the explanation of the world; release from transmigration and reunion with one Reality'.[118]

Another writer informs us that there are certain pre-conditions in order to be a Hindu.

Thus a person:

> ... must be born into one of the four castes or the Hindu social groups; must conform to the usages of the group into which he is born in regard to marriage, food, occupation, residence and the observance of certain domestic ceremonies; must observe certain ceremonies in relation to ancestor worship, such as funeral ceremonies and SRADDHA or memorial ceremonies; worship of the gods, consisting of daily prayers and sacrifices; daily worship of the household gods and the worship of the Temple.[119]

Against this background, in British Guiana, according to Bronkhurst, an estimated one-third of the Hindus from the Bengal Presidency and some from the Madras Presidency belonged to the Vaishnava sect, the others were of the Shiva sect. Followers of the Vaishnava sect, as mentioned earlier, worshipped Vishnu (the second person of the Hindu Triad or Trimurti), while the Saiva worship Siva, the third person of the Triad.

Another form of worship, known as the 'Kali mai puja' has been popular in British Guiana. But what does it entail? One authority explains it thus:

> If Siva is the great God (Mahadeva) of the Hindu Pantheon, to whom adoration is due from all indiscriminately, Vishnu is certainly its most popular deity. He is the god selected by the greater number of individuals as their saviour, protector and friend; who rescues them from all the powers of evil, interests himself in their welfare and finally admits them to his heaven (Vaikantha). Vishnu is worshipped especially in his incarnation as Rama or Krishna. Siva is better known and worshipped under the names of Durga and Kali, with which is associated a ghastly ritual, animals must be slain to appease her lust for blood; and men and women make offerings who desire boons or to avert her wrath.[120]

The most revered divinities of the Hindu Pantheon are Brahma the Creator, married to Sarasvati the Goddess of learning; Vishnu, the Preserver (married to Lakshmi, the goddess of wealth also called Sri; and Siva, the Destroyer, married to Umai the daughter of Himalaya, also called Pirvati, Durga, Kali, Bhavani.

The Puranas and Tantras are the modern and sectarian phases of Hinduism. 'The sole objects of worship in the Puranas', wrote Wilson, 'are Vishnu and Siva, the former representing the principle of free grace, and the latter the principle of human merit. Vaishnavas ... take as their special bible the Vishnu Purana with its extravagant praises of Vishnu. The Saivas take the Bhagwat Purana as their bible and from it preach salvation by works and faith in durga. These two sects represent almost all the present religious thoughts and life of popular Hinduism and they reveal it in a condition of decay'.[121]

Whether or not Hinduism was previously in a 'condition of decay' in British Guiana, there were by the 1930s two bodies representing divergent views, namely the Sanatan Dharm Maha Sabha, promoting orthodox Hinduism, and the Arya Samaj, preaching the 'pure and unadulterated' religion as directed by the VEDAS.

The leading light of the Arya Samaj, Swami Dayanand who appeared in the latter part of the nineteenth century is said to have drawn attention to the ancient truths of the VEDAS, exposing the weaknesses and inconsistencies of orthodox Hinduism. Dayanand denounced Brahminical orthodoxy and rallied his followers under the banner 'Back to the Vedas'. Moreover, the Arya Samaj has formulated its own official creed, proclaiming God's primary place in the quest for knowledge; that the VEDAS are the books of true knowledge, which followers of the Arya Samaj must foster; that one should make the distinction between truth and untruth, and act to promote the former; that central to the believer's life is doing good in order to improve the physical, spiritual and social conditions of mankind; that love and justice should prevail; that ignorance should be fought against; that one should be aware of the goodness of others; and finally that one should act to promote the general well-being of society.[122] Although the 'Satyarth Prakash' promotion of the Swami's teachings has been criticised as being morally and ethically crude, in an effort to promote its teachings locally, a number of Arya Samaj missionaries visited British Guiana.

The Sanatan Dharm Maha Sabha, on the other hand, was formed as a protest organisation to counteract Swami Dayanand's radical teachings, and to promote its own brand of Hindu orthodoxy. From the Punjab, Pandit Din Dyal Sarma declared that the Sanatan Dharma or eternal religion promised unusual Dharma for all mankind. And in accordance with its beliefs, the Sanatan Dharma's five objects were:

> To promote Hindu religious education, in accordance with the Sanatan Dharm; to diffuse knowledge of the Vedas, Puranas and other Hindu Shastras and, in the light of such knowledge, to introduce useful reforms into Hindu life and society; to enrich Sanskrit and Hindu literature; to introduce useful reforms into Hindu religious and charitable institutions, according to the Shastras; to establish and extend the Sabhas; to found and maintain Hindu colleges, schools, libraries and publishing institutions.[123]

Against this historical background, in 1927 the British Guiana Sanatan Dharma Sabha was formed to maintain and propagate the principles of orthodox Hinduism. And with time, the organisation's interest in social and educational work resulted in many branches being formed iin various parts of the country.

Followers of the Islamic faith were also among the thousands of indentured Indians who came to the Caribbean, and like their Hindu fellow-labourers, they too brought with them their religious customs and practices. The following is a summary of the essential features of Islam:

> It affirms the unity of God. It tolerates no priesthood and upholds no monasticism but emphasizes the direct responsibility of man and his Maker and applies the principles of morals to every phase of man's life and relationships. It places reason above obscurantism and mysticism and regulates all social life. No less than the

unity of fatherhood of God, it abolishes the false barriers of race and caste and tribe and preaches the brotherhood of man, as a necessary corollary.[124]

Another learned definition informs us:

> From its very beginnings Islam was a religion of action rather than of belief. The first half of the Islamic profession of faith, 'There is no god, and Muhammad is the messenger of God,' posed no problem for Muhammad's pagan contemporaries in Arabia, and even less for the adherents of the revealed religions in the surrounding territories when, having been conquered by the Arabs, they came to adopt the religion of the ruling class. And the acknowledgement that Muhammad was the messenger of God amounted for all practical purposes to unquestioning obedience to the Prophet; this is why the *Koran* is full of injunctions to 'obey God and His messenger', who is the exclusive transmitter of God's commands. For the same reason, Islamic religious law and not Islamic theology has always been at the centre of Islamic religious learning, and even the great al-Ghazali, that champion of mystical piety in Islam, while putting religious law firmly in its place as a science of this world and not of the world to come, nevertheless continued to regard it as a religious and not a secular science ... Islam is not merely a religion in the western meaning of the term, but a form of society, albeit an ideal one, an ideal which has surivived the disappearance of 'medieval' Islamic society in the greater part of the world of Islam.[125]

## EARLY MUSLIM ORGANISATIONS

The *Koran* is the book containing the sacred scriptures (consisting of the revelations delivered orally by Muhammad and collected after hsi death), upon which the followers of Islam place their faith. The call of the Muezzin, heard down the ages in mosques, proclaim to unbelievers that there is but one God Allah and Muhammad is his Prophet.

By 1938 in British Guiana there were over fifty mosques, located all over the country. Such places of worship had not always been easy to come by. Indeed, it was only through sheer determination and sacrifice that the various mosques were erected. Taking pride of place, at the time, was the triple silver-domed Queenstown mosque, the central mover of which was Gool Mohammed Khan, its first Imam. The philanthropic India-born Khan, a businessman (one of many Indians who went to the Caribbean solely for this purpose), recognising the dire need of the local Indians for a physical and symbolic place of worship, bought two lots of land for $500 upon which construction began, and in 1897 the mosque was completed at a total cost of $12,000 towards which the devoted members of the Muslim community made generous contributions. In 1899, before Mr. Khan left British Guiana, the mosque was administered by a Board of Trustees and, after being closed for a while, the mosque was reopened in 1935.

The Islamic Faith was maintained and furthered in British Guiana by a number of organisations. The Islamic Association of British Guiana was formed to disseminate knowledge and thereby to advance the interests of the local Muslim community. The Association's official organ was the Nur-e-Islam (Light of Islam).

The Sad'r Anjuman-e-Islam was founded by Moulana Sayed Shamshuddin Nizamuddin Alhoseini Quaderi, a Bombay-based Muslim missionary, who came to British Guiana in 1937. According to Ruhomon, Quaderi is 'the 35th direct descendant of the Holy Prophet through Hazrat Imam Zainul Abideen'. The aims and objects of the organisation, apart from being faithful and loyal to King George V1 and his representatives, were: 'To live peacefully and encourage peaceful living among the various peoples in the community; to seek at all times the rights of the Muslim community; to safeguard the interests of the Sumaat-al-Jamaat (Hanafi or orthodox teachings of Islam) School of Thought; to guard the education of Muslims and; to arrange for the proper burial of Muslim paupers'.[126]

A number of Maulvies (priests) were attached to the Anjuna to administer the Islamic Laws in accordance with the Hanafi School of Thought. A library was also organised and classes were held for the teaching of Urdu and Arabic to members. The importance of continuing this essential work was reflected in the fact that Mr. S.A. Sattaur, President of the Association was assigned the task of compiling 'A Life History of the Holy Prophet Muhammad', a work that was subsequently published in British Guiana.

Apart from the various Muslim celebrations such as Eid-el-Fitr and Ramadan, among others, the celebration of Muharram has remained controversial. Since indentured days, Indians, especially Muslims, have indulged in the Muharram festival. Over forty years ago, an historical description of this question in British Guiana was recorded by an Indo-Guianese writer who outlined the background of Muharram being 'held in memory of the Imam Hussein,[127] grandson of the Caliphate and consequently betrayed and slain … The Tazia (or Tadjah),[128] a distinguishing mark of the celebration, is designed to represent a tomb of the martyred hero and carried before the procession, as was done by his devoted disciple, Mukhtar, in rebellion against the ruling Caliph and as an act of vengeance for the death of Hussein'.

The celebration essentially involving the Shia sect, this celebration was regarded as idolatrous, and as a consequence, the participants had been joined by Hindus and Creoles in what has evolved into a general fete, during which alcohol was freely consumed, thus enlivening the participants who were often involved in disorderly and violent behaviour. Predictably, many Muslims see this spectacle as bringing shame and dishonour to their religion; a stigma which they felt could only hinder their social progress. In fact, this is precisely what happened with the introduction of Ordinance 16 in 1869 to control the activities of the Muharram celebration.[129]

Among Indians the birth of a child, especially if it was a boy (the prized child of Indian families) was an occasion for rejoicing with the observance of certain ceremonies in accordance with their religious customs. 'Hindus consulted the

Pundit', we are informed, 'to ascertain the planetary conjunction at the time of birth, with a view to discovering the good or bad forces that are likely to play upon, or influence the life of the child and determine its future, as well as fix upon a suitable name for good luck'.[130]

Both Hindus and Muslims shave the child's head. Hindus do this when the child reaches the age of three, but for both Hindus and Muslims, once the shaving process is over, other religious rites follow, for example, circumcision in the case of Muslim boys.

In British Guiana (as in Trinidad), Hindu and Muslim marriages were, and are, performed by their own priests. For Indians generally a wedding is an important event, a time of rejoicing when much money is spent, the larger the sum, the richer the families of the contracting parties. Among Hindus, in particular, a wedding ceremony involves many stages. A Hindu girl is said to have reached a marriageable age any time between the ages of twelve and sixteen, when her parents took the initiative to find a suitable husband. Once such a partner is found, the parents and relatives of the girl and a Pundit gather at the bridegroom's home, where his PATRA (or almanac) is consulted to ensure compatibility of the parties, in accordance with their planetary conjunctions.

Once it was agreed that the marriage should go ahead, the date is named and again this is guided by astrological considerations. The wedding itself is preceded by the ceremony of TILAK, when a dowry is given. Succeeding this is the ceremony of cleansing performed at the homes of the intended bride and bridegroom, a couple of days or so before the marriage.

On the wedding day, the bridegroom leaves for his bride's home dressed in his marriage head wear (maur) and robe (jama) accompanied by relatives and friends and his brother, his siballa (bestman). In the meantime, there is an air of expectation at the bride's home, where on arrival of the bridegroom at the front of the house, the DWAR PUJA welcome ceremony is conducted. The bridegroom is then taken to an appropriate place about the house, where his entourage is entertained. During this welcome ceremony, water, flour and rice is passed around the bridegroom's head; then comes the ceremony of JANWAS, which entails guiding the bridegroom to a convenient room to spend the night. At this stage, he is approached by the bride's father, accompanied by a priest and the menfolk (friends and relatives) with food for the bridegroom and those with him. The priest's chants extols the bridegroom's qualities and the honour conferred on the bride's parents by the union of the families. After her preparation to meet the bridegroom (bathing and getting dressed) the bride makes her way to the wedding tent where TAGPAT and DAL (garland and strings) are thrown around her neck and presents offered. She then returns to the house, while the bridegroom takes his place in the wedding tent.

Prior to the wedding ceremony, passages are read from the NAURETAN BIBAH PADATI and the bride, covered with a veil, returns to the tent and takes her place to the right side of the groom. Their marriage ceremony then begins with the giving away of the bride by her father, and the offer of presents to the bridegroom. Relatives and friends then pay their respects to the persons being married, offering gifts, including brass receptacles, money, land and cattle during the ceremony called PAO PUJA. The bride and bridegroom make religious offerings to the deities, followed by the LAWA (or BHAARA), a ritual in which both parties go around the sacred fire at the centre of the tent seven times, with the bride leading, during the first four rounds, while the bridegroom does so for the last three. This is followed by other rituals, including the SENDURA DAN, the seven promises and finally, the ASIRVAD, when the couple is blessed by the priest, thus completing the wedding ceremony.[131]

After the wedding ceremony, the invited guests sometimes numbering over a hundred (depending on the economic circumstances of the contracting parties) are offered food, usually consisting of rice, dhall, roti, channa, curried vegetables, and anchar, which is placed on clean strips of banana leaves. More often than not, this part of the wedding evolves into a lavish feast.

On the morning of the next day the bridegroom, prior to eating khichari (green split peas and rice) receives presents. He then makes his way to a particular room in the house of the bride's parents to meet the bride, where the ceremony of GANTH BANDHAN (tying of the sacred knot) is performed, and after PARCHAN (the passing of rice, flour, and water around the bridegroom's head) is observed, the BIDA (departure of the couple) takes place, bringing to a close an event in which meaning and symbolism were endemic.

But the marriage had yet to be consummated. At the bridegroom's home, the couple is again welcomed by the PARCHAN ceremony, before proceeding to the apartment (specially prepared for them) where the sacred knot is untied. At this stage, female relatives present gifts to the bride as customary, for the privilege of seeing her. The bride's stay is short-lived, perhaps for a day or two, before going back to her parents' home. Indeed it is only when she returns to her husband, is the marriage consummated.

Throughout indentureship and for the four decades or more since its abolition, Hindu weddings had remained more or less, the same, and have been regarded by Hindus as a solemn and sacred affair, which does not permit divorce, especially among the higher castes. Indeed the strictures of the marriage contract was such that in ancient India widows tended to commit SATI, (burning themselves on their husband's funeral pyre) rather than re-marry; a custom which fortunately is no longer the practice in modern India.

Over the years, much has been said about the 'Bamboo' weddings among Indians in the Caribbean. As it occurred in his time, Ruhomon puts the Guyanese experience in perspective:

> This inept and vulgar designation is based on the fact that in India a large tent is considered necessary and unavoidable to accommodate the large number of guests

invited and where the bamboo is indigenous and readily available, this difficulty is easily surmounted. When brilliantly lighted and decorated, a bamboo tent, constructed for such a purpose, presents a very pleasing and artistic appearance.[132]

In British Guiana, as in Trinidad, Hindu weddings have incorporated many activities which have become highlights. The 'cooking night' for example, when the food for a large number of guests is prepared, is also the occasion for a display of live Indian music, song and dance. Many Indian orchestras, often accompanied by costumed dancers have, over the years, appeared to delight audiences on such important occasions. Indian instruments such as the harmonium, tabla, and dhantal are essential components of these musical groups, augmented and complemented at times by more modern instruments and musical arrangements, as Indian music is fused with other styles. Popular Indian songs are performed by top local singers and Indian dancers, men and women, appropriately dressed, add a touch of unrivalled excitement at some weddings. Recorded music is a regular feature of these weddings, and on the wedding day, music is played during the procession and at the homes of those getting married, virtually non-stop.

Commenting on kinship in British Guiana, Jayawardena and Smith stated:

> we have already stressed the shallowness of the kinship system and this is matched by the relatively narrow range of kinship recognition. Little attention is paid to kin further removed than descendants of one's parents' siblings or quasi-siblings. There are no prohibition on intermarriage with anyone further removed than first cousin, and even first cousins occasionally marry despite objections that they are 'too close'. No distinction is made in this respect between parallel and cross cousins. There are a number of social relationships which are not properly a part of of the kinship system. ... We have already noted the tendency for children who live together in the same house to call each other brother and sister.

The investigators found that this kinship applied equally to Hindus and Muslims, that both use the same terms, and in conclusion that their analysis of the Indian family structure was one 'in which the nuclear family is the key unit; early marriage is the norm; paternal authority is respected; and ideally young married couples should live in the household of the husband's parents. We have tried to show the extent to which actual relations between family members and kinsfolk conform to and deviate from the structural norms'.[133]

As at birth and the various stages of life, a ceremony at death is also provided among Hindus. First the body is prepared for burial by being washed and the face is shaved, before being enshrouded and placed in a coffin. Prayers are said usually at the home of the deceased by a Pundit, as family and friends pay their last respects. Leading the mourners, in the case of the death of the father of a family, is the eldest son, who with the assistance of the Pundit, administers the last rites at the cemetery. After a brief ceremony, with the head facing northwards, the body is interred.

Three days later, the 'Dudh Mukhi' is performed: food which the deceased had in life been fond of is placed at some distance away from the house where, it is believed, the spirit of the dead person will return to consume it. Deep mourning is observed for ten days, a time when relatives refrain from using salt in their food; and on the tenth day, a ceremony is conducted by a special priest who accompanies grieving relatives. The eldest son's head is shaved and, on their return home after the ceremony, the mourners eat food prepared with salt, which was forbidden during the ten-day period of mourning.[134] The final service is held with a dinner for the priest, relatives and a few poor people. And in line with religious custom, this function is graced by the presence of thirteen Brahmins who receive gifts!

In British Guiana, Muslims* attend to, observe certain ceremonies and bury their dead in more or less the same way, as they did (and still do) in Trinidad. (For details see the relevant section below on Trinidad).

Among the most successful of the Christian missionaries who brought their religion to the East Indian indentured labourers in British Guiana were the Canadian Presbyterians who went there in 1885. The Scottish Presbyterians, Anglicans and Methodists have tried and failed. But it was the Canadian Presbyterians (with their experience among the indentured Indians in Trinidad) through pioneering representative Rev. John Gibson, who established schools and churches initially on the West Coast of the Demerara River.[135] The Rev. James Basnett Cropper succeeded Rev. Gibson, who died of yellow fever in 1888. Although there was an eight-year gap between the succession, Cropper's dedication, education and experience were crucial to the next stage of this mission.

Historically, and perhaps of necessity, paternalism played an important part in the work of the Canadian Presbyterians. The three men who headed this work, James Basnett Cropper, Gibson Fisher and James Scrimgeour were responsible for Demerara, Essequibo and Berbice, respectively. They ruled as they saw fit, until the mid-1930s when death, other appointment and old age brought change.

Although the Presbyterian church had many East Indian catechists within their ranks, in effect, 'all the decision making power and financial control' were in the the hands of the Canadian missionaries.[136] The collusion of the white planters was necessary in financing the well thought through missionary schemes (including land and buildings) which, in turn, bred obligation and dependence on the part of the Canadians. On the other hand, the planters, not feeling bound by any moral obligations, employed Indian children to work on the estates also on Sundays, thereby not only depriving them of education, but also of family worship and, as one researcher found, these planters did nothing to minimise the use of alcohol which became one of the country's 'major social problems'. In effect, then, this white planter-missionary relationship, though not perhaps initially intentional, became endemic in the oppression of the Indians.

For better or worse, evangelism and education were intertwined. Things had to change and many estate proprietors saw the value of 'educating', at least, some of

* The paucity of material on the Muslims' rites of passage demands fuller attention from researchers.

the Indians. And so by 1916, the desired help came to the Canadian Mission. But why did this assistance come at this time, rather than earlier? Dunn put forward three reasons for this: 'First, times were prosperous and money was available. Second, the proprietors knew that after 1917 no more East Indians would be allowed into British Guiana under the old indenture system which was not much better than slavery. To keep the Indians from returning to India or even from leaving the estates, they tried to improve conditions in the estates and saw the Canadian Mission as the agency through which they could promote peace and order among the people'.[137] Of course, the Canadian Mission whole-heartedly approved of this.

After Cropper, Fisher and Scrimgeour had departed, by the late 1930s, a new Canadian Mission leadership became necessary, and local East Indians moved into positions as ministers and elders of the Presbyterian Church. In this process, many had travelled to Canada for training. By 1945 this movement towards local leadership was consolidated, although some Canadian missionaries still held high positions, influencing and controlling policy decisions. Inevitably, it seemed, the Indians came to reject this continued missionary domination; a struggle which could be seen in direct relation to the rise of the indigenous People's Progressive Party to power in 1953.

The result of these struggles was the advent of a new generation of East Indian church leaders to play an important role in the next three decades. In effect, the Guyanese took over from the Canadian missionaries, the last having arrived in 1967, to finalize local autonomy. When he eventually left in 1970, Guyana had indeed become fully independent. And although the Guyana Presbyterian Church and the Presbytery of Guyana, seeking Christian brotherhood came together with the All African Congregationalist Union in the umbrella organisation the Reformed Church Council, racism reared its ugly head to deny any meaningful co-operation. However, in its relationship with the East Indians in Guyana, the Canadian Presbyterian Church has played its part in the process of acculturation.

For many Indians, seeking personal advancement, the evolution of this 'process' was much too slow. It is clear that the Indians were regarded by Europeans and Creoles in Guyana (who were largely Christian), as heathen, essentially because of their religions. In fact, Hinduism and Islam were little understood by those who denigrated them. Upholders of Christianity in Guyana like the Rev. Bronkhurst and Archdeacon Josa, misrepresented the Indians and reduced them and their beliefs and practices to a 'series of stereotypes'. Thus Hindu gods became 'idols', Indians were 'very lascivious and committed awful crimes', Hindu priests were impostors who preached falsehoods, and the Indians' religious beliefs in the great Ganges River was seen as 'superstitious'. Furthermore, the Indians were denounced as 'ignorant idolators' and 'sensual' migrants, Bisnauth noted. 'The men were stereotypes as blood-thirsty wife-killers and the women as dissolute wantons'. And even the Courts of Law, the last refuge of many who sought justice to wrongs done to them, were prone to regard Indians, as a race, as 'habitual liars'.

Commenting on these stereotypes, Bisnauth argues that the point is not 'to justify or vilify the larger society for perceiving' the Indian immigrant in this way. Nonetheless, he took the view that 'as long as the immigrants were so seen, the chances
of their becoming assimilated in the larger society were considerably reduced'.
Against this background of the Indians' marginal position in Guianese society,
Bisnauth found that the 'conversion of Hindus and Muslims to Christianity and
the employment of educated Indians in fields other than in the cane brake', helped
considerably to undermine the stereotypes such as the ignorant idolator' and 'coolie'.
'The insistence of the Mission', he added, on 'sound family life, the importance
that the Church placed on womanhood and the training and employment of women
did much to bring "Indian" institutions into closer conformity to the ideals of the
"greater tradition". These factors, in turn, helped the process of cultural and social
assimilation of East Indians into the larger Guianese society'. In this sense, the
Mission Church's role was significant. But beyond this, it also had an impact (though
not consciously) on Guyana's political life,[138] imparting Western-style education to
many future Indo-Guyanese political leaders.

The Canadian Presbyterian Church was therefore an agency for change among
the Indians, upon whom it left an indelible impression, a lasting legacy of which
Dunn wrote:

> Able, well-trained East Indians from the Guyana Presbyterian Church have gone
> to all parts of the world and have contributed significantly to their new home-
> lands. Many Guyanese East Indians who live in Canada, for example, can trace
> their roots to the schools and churches of the Canadian Mission. When the Guy-
> ana Presbyterian Church celebrated its centennial in 1985, it paid tribute to its
> Canadian past, and rejoiced in the fraternal visit so many Canadian friends paid to
> them in that special year. But the Church also rejoiced in its unique place in Guy-
> ana, as the Christian ecclesiastical and social structure through which East Indians
> can express their faith and their hopes[139]

In recent years (particularly during the period of the Burnham-Hoyte regimes)
strong arguments have been put forward against the de-emphasis of East Indian
culture in Guyana (especially the Hindu festivals of Phagwah and Divali) and the
Indian section of society, as a whole. It was claimed that if culture should reflect
Guyanese society in all its complexity, Indian (Muslim and Hindu) cultural heritage
should not be devalued or ignored in the schools and media. Bearing in mind that
there is still much ignorance in the Caribbean about festivals, it is perhaps appropriate here to elaborate a little on the autumnal festival of Divali (or Deepavali).
This great festival of lights was observed by the early groups of Indian emigrants
who came to the Caribbean. The Diya is described as a wick dipped in wax or oil,
and vali is the ring or wreath. Together, they form the word Divali, meaning the
'wreath of light' or the 'feast of lamps'.

Light has been a significant phenomenon in all ancient religions, and the ancient
Hindu scriptures is no exception. Allegorical references in Vedic literature refer to

the inner significance of light and the UPANISHADS also mentioned its meaning. The lights of Divali are said to have a dual significance: first, as an outward sign of jubilation and welcome commemorating the homecoming of Shri Ramchandra to Ayodha and his coronation after fourteen years of trial and tribulation some three thousand years ago; and second, as a means of dispelling the powers of darkness and evil lurking around scenes of grandeur.[140]

This annual festival of light is dedicated to the triumph of goodness over evil. Many legends are attributed to the origin of the Divali festival (the most popular among Hindus in the Caribbean) is said to be the home-coming of Rama, hero of the *Ramayana* and an incarnation of the God Vishnu. The act of cleaning and illuminating dark recesses is emphasized in the preparation of this festival. Hindu homes are white-washed, decorated, replastered and marked with a swastika in chalk and coloured powder; and metal vessels and ornaments are thoroughly cleaned and rearranged.

Writing in 1891, Mohandas Gandhi (later to become a 'leading light') regarded Divali as a 'beautiful contrast' to the Phagwah (Holi) festival; an occasion when, for both rich and poor Hindus, happiness and a sense of joy is expressed amidst thousands of glittering lights. It is evident from such festivals that in spite of their daily struggles, the Hindus are imbued with optimism. The Diyas symbolize the 'unfailing faith in the unusual love and brotherhood', wrote Jha, as this annual festival 'reminds the Indians that good ultimately triumphs over evil, light over darkness and knowledge over ignorance'.[141]

If this festival seems like another example of the stereotypical Indian trait of passive and meditative philosophy, one must not be misled. By contrast, Indians have also used other forms of artistic expression to evoke their struggles, most significantly (not just through religious music), but through poems, chants and protest songs. Many of these songs, deal with the recruitment of indentured labour, the long sea voyage to Guyana, the experience of indentureship on the estates, history and politics, and the decline of Indian consciousness and moral values in Guyana. Unlike the earlier protest songs, which were sung in Bhojpuri, the later ones were sung in 'creolized Hindi', reflecting the process of adaptation to the new environment. The songs were usually accompanied by such instruments as the tabla drum, harmonium, saranji and cymbals. The music, specially of the later songs, though essentially Indian in form, incorporated African and Western influences.

The name 'coolie', deeply resented by the Indians, is an epithet with which they came to Guyana. 'Why should we be called coolies, we who were born in the clans and families of seers and saints?' they sang. Other songs relate to the variety of tasks performed by the Indians and the conditions under which they laboured; songs that were translated into action in the form of strikes and riots from 1872 onwards. An assembly of workers (a combination inspired by the jahiji spirit SPIRIT, a brotherhood of labourers) at Port Mourant in 1939 was immortalised in the words of a song:

Listen to the astonishing event of 1939;
Come and see the rally at Port Mourant.
All the people entered the hall for the rally
And began to play instruments.
After the music they ate,
And then a fire, two fires, five fires were shot.
Poor Mr. Singh fell down shot dead,
Shot dead by planters.
Police came to take statements,
But for what?[142]

Other themes which the Indians' folk songs drew attention to were the break-down of Indian values and traditional behaviour, reverence for their own religious beliefs, Gandhi's struggle in South Africa and the achievement of Indian independence. After this political milestone in India's history was achieved, during the years from 1927 to 1953 the Indians looked forward to the possibility of winning Guyana's independence, and in so doing, they became increasingly politically-conscious, proclaiming and saluting through folk songs their revered leader Cheddi Jagan: 'He went to jail for us poor; Jagan is the man of the poor', they sang; and he was considered to be the great provider for the people. After Guyana's independence, however, there were in the folk-songs a noticeable decline in reliance upon India for cultural and political inspiration. Indian films and music were much more than just mere entertainment. The sounds of the unique instruments evocative of sadness or happiness and positive images of India, fortified the Indians in their struggle. But instead of India, Guyana now became the 'Motherland', even though the growing sense of alienation among the Indians has had the effect of invoking the ingrained value of (and renewed interest in) Indian culture, language and traditions.

And while the Burham and Hoyte Governments reigned supreme, it was acknowledged that a wide range of activities at the cultural level, were indeed taking place in Guyana. But the fact that Indian festivals had become national holidays, did not lessen the serious concern among Indians that the Afro-Guyanese sub-culture was being 'lopsidedly encouraged'. The focus on Creolization, as one writer noted at the time (despite Government gestures) was therefore misplaced, projecting a misleading image of East Indians in Guyanese society.[143] Since then, Dr Jagan had again become his country's political leader and much was expected of him and the PPP-Civic Government in the promotion of *all* cultures that seek expression in contemporary Guyana.

'Creole culture is born of struggle', wrote Allahar and Varadarajan. 'It is a culture of resistance which gives birth to itself. For in resisting it traces the contours of the new culture, which of necessity, must reflect the resistance, the capitulation, the hybrid progeny that is "creole"'. Such resistance, however, is 'not always successful or complete' for among the Indo-Guyanese (and other Indo-Caribbean people) many had, over the last century and a half, been creolized, while others still fear erosion of their Indian way of life by the pressure of dominant Western creole culture. And one can understand this fear among those Indo-Guyanese, notably in Georgetown, the Essequibo Coast and Berbice), who are emotionally attached to Indian music, especially in the form of celebrated singers such as Lata Mangeshkar, Mohammed Rafi, Kishoor Kumar and Mukesh, among others.

Yet the fact remains that Indo-Caribbean people are deeply influenced by, and rooted in their countries of birth. Their ancestral Indian home is a remembered past, increasingly fragmented and obscured by time to a point where, for many, it is a memory that is now non-existent, as opposed to their 'real' Caribbean 'home'. And as Allahar and Varadarajan stated, Indians in the Caribbean can no longer afford to over-emphasize the untenable position of their 'otherness and alienation'. Put simply, their future lies not in India, but in the Caribbean. Indeed, ever since their arrival, they have been engaged in a process of reciprocity with the indigenous Creole culture, a cultural exchange that has been irrevocably at work, reshaping their cultural identities. In fact, today in Guyana, 'without recognising it', the creolized Indians, in the main those among the younger generations, are more and more gravitating towards the 'national norm in their country, which is neither purely Indo nor Afro',[144] thus underlining their Indo-Guyanese identity.

# TRINIDAD

## *Post-indenture Settlement and Consolidation*

Given that on average only an estimated one in five immigrants returned to India from Trinidad with substantial savings.[145] The vast majority decided to stay in the Colony. For them there was no going back. They had come through years of unimaginably new and common experiences, which had the effect (despite of their differences) of bonding them ever closer together.

And, as it was, this constituted a vital prerequisite for settlement. 'As a rule a locality is selected, surveyed … and a settlement is thus formed of Indian immigrants only', de Verteuil wrote, 'and an Indian name is given to the settlement'. Such a coming together had a knock-on effect, encouraging immigrants 'to form small communities, speaking the same language, and having the same habits and ways'.[146]

In the post-indentureship period, then, the process of settlement persisted with the steady growth of Indian villages which formed the basis of Indian communal life in Trinidad, as the population increased. This 'free' population was not homogenous. In fact, we are afforded some idea of the background relating to the various cultural groups that emigrated to the island.

While the majority of immigrants came from the Bihar and Uttar Pradesh areas of Northern India, the element of caste (notwithstanding its modifications in the new circumstances of the Caribbean) as far as the official records were concerned, reflected a tendency to play down the differences which resulted, by 'grouping and classifying' individuals regardless of the different regions from which they came.[147]

In addition to influx of emigrants from Eastern India, from 1845 onwards, Hindus and Muslims were also recruited from the Central Ganges Plains, Banaras in Northern India, and from the Tamil and Telugu regions in South India.[148] One researcher has noted that the areas from which the Trinidad immigrants came, included Bengal, Orissa, Oudh, the North West Provinces, Bombay, Madras and the Punjab. As far as cultural groups are concerned, allowing for some variation, they can be separated into the following regions: Bengal, Southern India, Western India, the Central Provinces and Northern India.[149]

The predominantly Muslim population of East Bengal (now part of Pakistan) is an area from which a large group of immigrants came to Trinidad. Their common Bengali culture explains, to a large extent, the comparatively peaceful relations between the Hindus and Muslims in Trinidad, and although the majority of the Bengalis were farmers, literature, art and commerce were also highly developed among them.

The emigrants from Southern India were called Madrasis, regardless of the fact that they came from several ethnic groups and were probably recruited along the southern part of the peninsular. The peoples of Southern India have been roughly divided into three groups from the Andhra area, Tamilnad and Kerala. The first group, from the East coast, spoke Telugu; the second spoke the Tamil language; while the third group came from the Malabar Coast, which included the state of Mysore, Cochin and Trevancore. The Telugu-speaking peoples, as stated in one account, formed probably the most numerous single caste in the south of India, and were largely engaged as cultivators, farmers and landowners.[150]

Among the other groups were the Tamil people, 'harder headed' and said to be of a more practical turn of mind than the Telugu speakers, the Brahmins had a flair for mathematics and physics, while among the lower classes could be found the 'criminal' tribes – cattle thieves. Other notable Tamil castes cited were the Kammala or Panchal, who comprised the goldsmiths, braziers, carpenters, stone masons and blacksmiths; the Chetti whose members were bankers, brokers, shop-keepers, money lenders and traders; and finally, the Kuruba, who were sheep-herders and weavers.

The Kerala people constituted a diverse group. Differing little from the Telugu and Tamil peoples, the Kerala Brahmins, we are told, show great affinity to the Benga. While the Todas of the Nilgiri Hills bear certain similarities (for example, their 'unique physique, their dark complexion and their occupation with the buffalo') with many Trinidad Indians, it was unlikely that these people were recruited because of their reluctance to leave their environment'.[151]

An important group of immigrants came to Trinidad from Western India. Parsis (who had originally emigrated from Persia) well known as merchants and traders, became established businessmen in Trinidad, having emigrated not as plantation workers, but as traders.[152] This class of Indians was essentially engaged in trade with India.

In contrast to the Parsi, is the numerous and humble Koli caste from which it is more than likely that a large group of the Indian immigrants were drawn. Unlike the Parsis, they have been described as dark-skinned with coarse features and worked on the land. (It was with this caste, as mentioned earlier, that the word 'coolie' was derived.) Above the Koli in status were the Kunbi, regarded as 'typical' peasants of Western India, who contributed to the rank and file of the fighting Marathas, from whose ranks were the many Kshatriyas to which some Indians in Trinidad claimed to belong.

The people of the Central Provinces of India showed marked cultural differences from those of the West. Among these peoples were the Baiga, Gond and the Chamars. The Chamars were said to be of a different physical type from the the Gonds, and also differed from their 'caste comrades' in other regions in that they were not leather workers, but agricultural labourers.

The peoples of Upper and Northern India lived in the Punjab and the Province of Bihar and Oudh. Buddhism had established itself in these Northern Provinces, where Brahmins were strongly represented and among whom there were many practising lawyers, land-agents, clerks and cooks. The next caste down the hierarchy, were the Bhat and the cultivating caste of Bihar and Oudh known as the Kurmi. On the same elevation, were the cattle-rearing Ahirs, many of whom went to Trinidad. Among the lower castes were the Bhar (cultivators), the Kalwar (distillers of spirit from molasses), the Parsi who taps the toddy palm for liquor, the Dhobi (washerfolk), the Bhangi (sweepers), the Khatik (butchers), the Chamar (workers in leather) and the scavenging castes, the Bhangi and Dom. In the last decade of Indian indentured immigration to Trinidad, many 'tribals' were among the emigrants. It seemed there was little recruitment from Rajasthan and the Punjab. Of the three major groups to be found in the Punjab, few Sikhs had emigrated to Trinidad.

Taken together then, although the majority of the Indian emigrants to the Caribbean came from the lower rungs of the social structure, there was adequate representation of the higher castes which helped 'to preserve to an appreciable extent a facsimile of the total Indian culture'.[153] But among the main difficulties in effecting any 'simple re-establishment of Indian traditions was the remarkable heterogeneity of the migrant population', wrote Vertovec. Given that in the early years of indentured immigration to Trinidad, Indians had embarked from Calcutta and Madras, he argues that then (as today), 'some of the most fundamental differences in Indian society and culture existed between North and South ... The fact of a common port of embarkation ... by no means meant that migrants shared common social or cultural traditions. Such significant variations in geographic, economic, social and cultural backgrounds must have presented enormous hurdles for migrants thrust together in the constrained contexts of estates overseas. The quandary of trying to communicate and arrive at consensus social forms was exacerbated by the continuous arrival of migrants from different regions of North India'. Nevertheless, in the entirely new scenario of the Colony, the diverse Indian population gradually created a widely accepted 'style of life, system of social relationships and set of cultural institutions'.[154]

The machinations of the planters and Government to undermine and devalue the Indians' culture had the effect of the Indians rallying-round the villages, thus strengthening their communities and village social life. In a real sense, as owners of land in these villages, they had indeed established a more secure grounding. The composition of these villages was revealing, reflecting, in the main, separate cultural groups, rather than a mixture. The names of villages and towns, for example, inform us of the areas in India from which at least the majority of the original inhabitants came, including Fyzabad, Calcutta and Barrackpore; and there were no doubts as to the identity of the inhabitants of 'Coolie Town'

Situated near the plantations (and isolated from the rest of the Colony's population) the Indian villagers, in terms of language, dress and religion, tried to re-establish their traditional life style, to live much as they would have done in India, even though the new circumstances militated against any faithful replication. The establishment of a cohesive settled community, provided the basis for a social structure, along traditional lines, as the village elders came to prominence. Although the Brahmins and Sadhus assumed the positions of authority, which they were denied on the plantations, the caste system as they had known it, could not be resurrected essentially because there were not enough adherents. In practice then, caste in Trinidad was dead, but it would remain an 'ideal' of Indian culture to be passed down the generations.

With the consolidation of Indian settlements through cane-farming, from 1882 there was a greater sense of stability in the Indian village communities, which provided a cultural hinterland for the waves of newcomers during the period of indentureship, and increasingly, in the later years of the system, as the villages became more populous and structured, the indentured labourers were afforded the opportunity of making contact with their particular cultural group. In turn, newcomers provided a renewal of the villagers' cultural links with India. And despite the Presbyterian missionaries' success in drawing young Indians away from their parents' culture, they had failed to satisfy 'all the needs which were previously taken care of by Indian institutions'.[155]

## Language, Education and Culture

Removed from their Indian homeland, the immigrants were generally confronted with a double-foreignness: a foreignness of place and language. Commenting on language as a guide to 'social reality', Edward Sapir wrote 'Human beings do not live in the objective world alone, nor alone in the world of social activity as ordinarily understood, but are very much at the mercy of the particular language which has become a medium of expression for their society'.[156]

From the moment they first made contact with the recruiter, the problem of language necessitated an Interpreter. Although the indentured labourers in Trinidad spoke a whole range of native languages, including Punjabi, Bengali, Tamil, Gujarati, Telugu, Hindi, Urdu, Oriya, Nepali and their accompanying dialects (including Vanga, Radha, Varendra, Raj Bangshi, Magahi, Maithili, Shadri, Awadhi, Bhojpuri, Eastern and Western Hindi, Bangaru, Ajmeri and Tondai Nadu), English was the dominant language, officially recognised in colonial Trinidad. Indeed linguistic differentiation was among the earliest and most formidable problems that Indian immigrants had to overcome; a 'characteristic feature' among the first arrivals, who spoke a 'Babel of … tongues'. Imagine the sheer frustrations during those early years of estrangement when their needs were perhaps greatest, and the desire to give expression to a multiplicity of thoughts was a matter of urgent concern. In effect, the powerless 'Coolies' of low status in Trinidadian society, were for many years, also voiceless in terms of communicating through a language that both they and their oppressors understood, but in which they were much less fluent.

Regardless of the problems they encountered, the indentured Indians were, however, not entirely mute for by about the 1880s, they began to complain in writing of the treatment meted out to them as labourers, and in 1893, a poem 'The Cooly Man Has Come to Stay' appeared in D.W.D. Comins's 'Note on Emigration from India to British Guiana', though it may not have been written by an Indian. By the end of the 1930s, Trinidad had evidently become 'home' to the Indians, as increasingly India receded in the background, a faded but very precious memory. Gradually English words appeared to constitute part of the Indians' vocabulary. And so out of the crucible of the indentureship experience, yet another act of creation (in addition to earlier patterns of Indian plantation speech) was given form (in the evolutionary chain of linguistic expression, arising from ever-changing circumstances) in a new odd-sounding, but effective plantation language through Indian immigrants and their descendants gave expression to deep-seated longings. As one indentured labourer put it:

> I tell de man
> write a letter for India …
> e send three letter
> an up to today
> I eh get no answer.[157]

The isolation of the Indians on the estates and their sense of separation had ensnared them in a 'linguistic cocoon' which has fortunately been retrieved for posterity by the Indo-Trinidadian writer, Noor Kumar Mahabir:

> We eh interfering with dem (the Africans)
> we living for weself
> We talking between weself
> we singing
> playing drum an eating
> sleeping
> eating together
> we Indian self
> we eh meddle wid dem'.[158]

The Indians' separation from the wider society was bound to promote ethnic identity and, given the paucity of material relating to the Indians' adaptive language as it developed over the years, Mahabir, the great-grandson of one of these immigrants has achieved the rare distinction of bringing together in his book *The Still Cry*, personal accounts of the indentureship experience, through the words of a new language pronounced by five Indians. Few Caribbean writers, notably the novelists, have bothered to catch the essence of the evolving language of the Indians. Mahabir has rightly identified novelist Sam Selvon, as the first to write realistically about the indentured labourers' speech rhythms. He quoted Selvon's *A Brighter Sun* published in 1952: 'You gettam house which side Barataria, gettam land, cow well. You go live dat side. Haveam plenty boy chile – girl chile no good, only bring trouble on yuh head. Yuh live dat side, plantam garden, live good', and pointed out the yawning gap in Indo-Caribbean literature and history. Many would agree with him that a great deal of work needs to be done in the folk genres; narratives, kheesas (tales), songs, religious chants, proverbs and aphorisms, much of which are not unconnected with what he had recorded. His *Still Cry* then, is an important contribution, though only a beginning, in the task of retrieving the Indians' use and inventiveness of language spoken 'in a rhythm based on the chants of the Indian religious scriptures ... the source of all fables and folklore'.[159]

Given that like Afro-Trinidadians, the East Indians of necessity had to create new linguistic forms to give expression to the various aspects of their lives, and their language 'began to signify the manner in which they encountered and transformed their social reality and, in turn, the way in which they articulated that reality inescapably determined the manner in which they arrived at their sense of their people-hood and consciousness'.[160]

Although it is difficult to say when the many languages of the Indians began to coalesce into 'one common language', once Indian immigration had ceased in 1917, the need for a generally accepted language and national solidarity had become much greater. Despite the planters' divisive tactics, the Indians had indeed, not long after their introduction to the estates, begun to give expression to a common language known as 'plantation Hindustani'.[161] 'While a pidgin English sufficed for important transactions with plantation staff', wrote Vertovec, 'the Indians developed a shared language among themselves which facilitated communication irrespective of regional or caste origins'. And so the Hindi dialect of Eastern Bihar, Bhojpuri, became the Indian lingua franca in Trinidad. Furthermore, in the process of language change and cultural blending among the immigrants, given the disintegration of the caste system 'as part of the trend towards common linguistic forms', Vertovec argues that 'caste dialects were dropped' and that 'speech indicators conveying higher-lower caste status, were eliminated in favour of inter-caste forms'.[162] Since that time, Indians in Trinidad had, through relatively freer movement, continued to consolidate the gains they had made, always impressing upon their children the importance of language, namely the more orthodox Hindi and Urdu.

If teaching the language posed difficulties, in the post-indenture years, there was the added problem of the lack of incentive among Indian youth to learn the traditional languages. For one thing, even though there was oral communication in Hindi and Urdu among the Indians, particularly in the rural areas, there was little written material. All around them, at every turn, the Indians who were dedicated to promoting their own languages, could hear the dominant accented sounds of the English language. The lack of texts in their Indian languages was disappointing to Indian youths, who desired and should have had a lot more of this kind of material available. By the time they had been through several 'standards' at school, they knew that to make their way through life, hopefully up the social scale, time spent on the English language would indeed be worthwhile. Even if they were proficient in Hindi and Urdu, to what purpose could it be put when in the shops, in businesses and in the wider society generally, these languages were useless and could, at times, have a negative effect and arouse aggressive feelings among those unable to understand the language, such as Afro-Trinidadians and others, who 'became irritated when Indians speak Hindi among themselves in a mixed group'.[163] Nevertheless by the late 1950s, many young Indians in the rural parts of Central and South Trinidad spoke Hindi and/or Urdu, mainly to communicate with older Indians and their parents. Among themselves, however, the medium of communication was the English language, which was used, more often than not, and there was good reason and every opportunity to do so. Therein lay the weakness in maintaining the Hindi and Urdu languages among the Indians in Trinidad.

There was then, a strong generational conflict, considerable resistance from younger people towards Hindi and Urdu, and a strong pressure from the older Hindu and Muslim leaders to make the language they used functional; a last-ditch attempt that marks a watershed in the transition towards further acculturation. Hindi-Urdu was crucial to preserving Indian traditions, as far as the older, more traditionalist Hindu and Muslim leaders were concerned. It was the key to all the sacred literature, the meaning of which is devalued, if not lost, when translated into English. If all the religious leaders knew the traditional languages, the majority of followers in the Indian community lagged far behind. This was very much the case, for during the performance of many ceremonies the Hindu Pundit and the Muslim

Imam felt bound (and increasingly so) to summarize in English, all that was said in the traditional language.

Indian movies, however, has had the effect of reviving interest in spoken Hindi-Urdu, despite the considerable degree of language change. The language, as spoken on the sound tracks of these films, had the effect of giving added confidence to those who still knew or spoke the language fluently, and encouraged those who were less conversant. As a consequence, at movie houses, there was much explaining of the dialogue between mothers and children. The feeling that they did not speak Hindi as well as those Indians in the movies, added a sense of inferiority among local Indians. Psychologically, although this was the wrong attitude to adopt, it was understandable. 'The social position of the speakers evidently influences the feeling toward the language', Niehoff wrote. 'Consequently, the attitude toward Hindi might have been shaped largely by the social status of Indians which has been low during most of their residence in Trinidad. That is because their status was low, their customs and language were also considered inferior'.[164] But with the spread of education and the changing perceptions of new generations, English has continued to be integrated, to be absorbed into what can be termed the Indo-Creole language, which today is spoken widely within the various East Indian communities. If the 'heritage (including language of course) of a people is not something one puts up for display' as Cudjoe argues, 'but something one takes and integrates into one's present to create a meaningful future', then the Indians in Trinidad and Tobago can take pride in their achievement.

## EDUCATION

Since it was reported in 1945 that at least 60 per cent of the Indians in Trinidad were illiterate in any language,[165] it seemed that some thirteen years later, much had changed, though it was still doubtful that the Indians were the least educated group. This lack of education was due primarily (as we saw earlier) to the plantation owners' reluctance to provide an education for the field labourers (though some of them, in turn, were reluctant to send their children to school), but also to the fact that because the immigrants came from a predominantly poor educational background, the incentive among them, certainly during the early years of indentureship, to gain an education, was not great. Their main concern, during this phase, was economic stability of some sort, and to this end their children complemented their parents' labour both at work and at home. This home help and the tradition of early marriage also hindered Indian children from school attendance.

An important aspect of the East Indians' education, relates to the arrival of Rev. John Morton, the Canadian Presbyterian Minister, who while on a visit to Trinidad for health reasons, in 1867, became interested in the East Indians he had met and was particularly concerned that no attempt was being made to instruct them in the teachings of Christianity or to educate them. The impression that Morton had formed was so strong that he returned a year later to begin his mission among the Indians.

From the outset, Canadian missionary activity (as mentioned earlier) was based on the twin principle of evangelization and education. Our immediate concern, however, is the latter. Morton may not have had any qualms about the task he faced, but by 1868, he was rewarded for his hard work and determination with the opening of the first Primary school at Iere Village, not far from Princes Town in south Trinidad. If this was an encouraging start for the pioneering missionary, twenty-six years later, he was able to count fifty-two Primary schools, and by 1942 this was increased to sixty-eight.

Earlier, however, in 1870 Rev. Kenneth Grant who had come to the island to work with Morton, did much to establish training at college level for Indians. Twenty-four years later, his endeavours brought success with the inauguration of Naparima Teacher's College in San Fernando; and by 1942 the Canadian Mission had six colleges to its credit.[166]

Overall, the work of the Canadian Mission had a pronounced effect on the Indians, whatever religion they adhered to. If during the early years, the missionaries were intent on getting the Indians into the churches, they had also succeeded, to a marked extent, in attracting them into schools and colleges. The fact that Hindi and English were used as the means of communication from the beginning, gave the Canadian Missionary enterprise a good chance of success, because of the flexibility endemic in Hinduism, and also because of the many disadvantages Indians suffered. Since the first Indian was engaged as a teacher in 1869 (only months after Morton's return), as more Indians trained as teachers and clerics, the Mission's aims and objectives were fulfilled. Soon these educators and/or religious indoctrinators were scouring the remotest corners of the countryside in search of new converts. The fact that Indians were now recruiting people like themselves (at least in appearance) made the thought of Christianity and education less intimidating. 'Sure, they wanted to make Christians of them' (Hindus and Muslims) said one Muslim, 'but isn't it better to be a respected and educated man even though a Christian than an ignorant Hindu or Muslim?' With this attitude towards the persistent work of the Canadian Mission, the Christian Indians, at least educationally, benefited enormously.

If the foregoing was advantageous to the Christian Indians, what were the disadvantages of the Canadian Mission schools to Indians who remained Hindus and Muslims? For one thing, Christian Indian children were clearly favoured over non-Christian Indians at these schools, a disheartening problem for parents. And so in an attempt to bridge the disparity, Hindus and Muslims gave Christian names to their children, to ease their alienation in the CM school system which, while concentrating on Christian religious instruction, ignored the children's Indian heritage. This was, as many Hindu and Muslim leaders saw it, a serious defect of the CM schools and they had, as a consequence, in small ways ventured to provide

instruction (more in private rather than publicly) in the religious and cultural heritage of India. But many such attempts, though admirable, too often lacked co-
ordination. The Indians struggled on alone until 1931 when a recommendation
was made by the Education Commission to set up schools run by Indian organisations with Government assistance. Since the first such school was erected in Curepe
by the Arya Samaj in 1940, many more have been built by various Hindu and Muslim organisations throughout Trinidad.[167]

By 1960 it was said that much controversy had been aroused as a result of the
dramatic rise of the Maha Sabha school system, within and outside the Indian
community. It is to the credit of the MS that they were able to build 33 schools in
just over ten years, between 1938 and 1959. The leading light in this educational
campaign was Bhadase Maraj, also head of the People's Democratic Party, a man
who had channelled a great deal of energy towards increasing consciousness of the
Hindu religious heritage. Denominational schools were seen by Maraj as an important means of promoting the cause of the Indians.[168]

What was the Government's role in the construction of these schools? In line
with its provision, a school could be constructed if the need for it was demonstrated to the Government's satisfaction; and if one-third of the funding could be
met, the other two-thirds of the cost was supplied by the Government. But although the school was to be administered by the denomination, significantly this
could only be done under Government supervision. Culturally, this was potentially
disastrous for those who were deeply concerned with promoting the cause of the
Indians in the face of the dominant culture, for it was contended that the Government curriculum had to be followed and that children had to prepare themselves
for the Government examinations.

Moreover, as a school registered by the Government, there was the need to
prepare children of the non-Christian denominations to enter the Christian-
dominated school system. To meet the one-third costs, donations were made from
a wide cross-section of the Indian community and more often than not, wealthy
Indians made large donations. Self-help, they had learned, was the best policy and
in fact at times when the Government was financially unable to, or unwilling to
meet the costs of a particular school, the local people with the support of the Maha
Sabha were able to eventually build the school. Among the generous donations
towards education made by Hindus was the land on which some schools were
erected.

Despite the laudable construction programme, there was much criticism of the
school buildings, most of them being 'large one-room structures with concrete
floors and walls, and with galvanized iron roofs ... Various temporary partitions
were used inside to partially separate the classes, though in general, the effect was
that of a one-room country school house'. Such structures often accommodated
from 300 to 400 children and in comparison with the Primary schools (in south
Trinidad) the Maha Sabha schools were 'temporary looking'.[169]

On the other hand, about this time, the late 1950s, two Arya Samaj schools, one at Avocat in the South, the other at Curepe in the North, were more solid structures and not surprisingly by contrast with the cost of Maha Sabha schools (approximately $16,000) the Arya Samaj school at Avocat had cost $29,000. Beyond the expense (and significant as these achievements were) the Hindu schools had to contend with the fact that both the Government and Canadian Mission schools were regarded as more 'permanent' than the Maha Sabha schools.

Notwithstanding the criticism, the growth of the Hindu and Muslim schools around this period, mirrored the 'changed attitude of the Indians towards education, and the development of strong independent organisations and leaders within the Indian community'.[170] Underscoring their desire for education was the economic strength of the Indians who had patiently built a solid base, enough to alleviate the overcrowding and neglect of rival schools.

Separated for over one hundred years from the wider society, the Indian community had become by the 1950s more self-conscious of the need to preserve its heritage through its schools. Many Indians were alarmed, having observed the combined effects of education and religion, among the many children attending Canadian Mission schools, who were converted to Christianity. This had to be stopped and replaced by schools teaching the Indian religions of Hinduism and Islam. It was therefore no coincidence that Hindu Maha Sabha schools were erected on temple grounds, at any rate within close proximity of each other. But how much latitude did these denominational schools have to promote their cultural heritage? According to Niehoff:

> All recognised schools, that is those supported by the state, have a rigid curriculum which gives very little leeway for optional subjects. Examinations for the students are prepared by the State. There are 45 minutes each day, however, which can be used for religious instruction, and it is this period that the Hindu and Muslim schools attempt to teach their own religion and language – Hindi in the Hindu schools and Urdu in the Muslim schools. Urdu is basically the same language as Hindi but the writing system uses an Arabic-derived alphabet, while Hindi uses the Devanagri alphabet which is ultimately derived from Sanskrit. The consequence of this difference is that although the spoken language is practically identical, the two writing systems are completely different. ... Most of the Indian children in the lagoon area [Oropouche], and probably in the other rural areas of Trinidad, can already speak Hindi-Urdu, so the training concentrates on teaching them to read and write in this language. It was estimated by one headmaster of the Hindu school in the lagoon area that 80 per cent of his students could speak Hindi.[171]

Among the difficulties Trinidad children were faced with in learning to read and write Hindi and Urdu was the fact that many of their teachers had imperfect knowledge of the languages and in some cases, none at all. And to compound the problem, the low pay that primary school teachers received was not attractive to well-qualified teachers. Qualified teachers were the vital link in transmitting and maintaining cultural continuity and because there were so few of them, the Indian community was faced with a dilemma. Part-time student teachers were not the answer. In fact, in the face of this crisis, the Maha Sabha were perhaps unfairly criticised for their 'excessive use' of student teachers. Another crucial qualification for the teachers in these circumstances was their ideally-suited Indian background. But falling short of this, a narrower view was taken for it was felt that one's religious background was indeed essential in choosing those who should teach, an approach which the Hindu and Muslims schools had already taken. The best example of this to which the Hindu and Muslims could point, were the CM schools which trained many of their teachers from among the Christian Indians. The Hindu and Muslim schools were further disadvantaged in having fewer qualified teachers of their particular religious persuasion.

But the resilience of the Indians guided them towards a revivial of interest in speaking their languages. By the early 1960s Pundits became teachers and instruction, for two or three nights a week, focused on the written language. Despite the growth in Hindi-Urdu and Indian cultural matters generally, Christian Indians showed little or no desire to learn the languages of their forebears. Nonetheless, at the forefront of those organisations fostering this revival were the Hindu and Muslim denominational schools for whom there was every justification, because of a younger generation of children were utterly unfamiliar with these languages.

## THE PRIMARY EDUCATION OF INDIAN WOMEN AND INDIAN CULTURE IN SECONDARY SCHOOLS

For a number of reasons East Indian women in Trinidad had been denied receiving a primary education, while the opposite was largely true of Indian men. According to one study there was a very slow change in the proportion of boys and girls attending Primary school from 1900 to 1956. On the evidence of school registers, prior to the First World War, the ratio was 44 girls to every 56 boys, but by 1950 there was a marginal increase of 48 girls to every 52 boys.

If generally the schooling of girls was stopped earlier than boys, the problem was of particular significance to East Indians. The reasons for 'under-attendance' and the 'interrupted attendance' of girls were largely cultural. It was found that the average Hindu or Muslim girl was 'betrothed while barely an adolescent and thus entered into a relationship which dominated and set the pattern of her life. If by the ages of twelve or thirteen one was married, then the skills which school imparted were regarded as unnecessary. Thus, the habit of early marriages rendered the formal education of girls a very low priority, a problem compounded by the fact that Indian men 'shared the general male view that the female mind was incapable of learning non-domestic skills'.[172]

Taking into consideration the fact that the traditional values of Hindu culture were at variance with encouraging secular education among Indian women, the passage of time and the circumstances 'slowly eroded the cultural values' which debarred them a Primary school education; so much so that by the 1950s, the earlier disproportion had given way to the attendance of Indian girls in Primary schools in 'relatively the same proportion as other groups'.[173]

Given that the 'culture of a people is their total shared way of life which comprises their modes of feeling, thinking and acting expressed in their religion, language, law, art and custom as well as in material products such as houses, food, clothes and tools',[174] it is the frame within which a socio-historical being is defined and through which others derive their perceptions and images of a person.

The colonial administrators' perceptions and racist attitudes of some Indians had the effect of drawing them together more tightly as a group, engendering a determination to preserve their cultural traditions against their oppressors. It is no wonder then that the Indians viewed Christianity as a threat, particularly when it was linked (as was then the case with the Canadian Mission Schools) with education.

From the moment of their arrival, many were subjected to 'education', the casualties of displaced persons whose cultural traditions were obscured by more immediate and appropriate instruction. From 1867 the Presbyterian Canadian Mission launched their campaign of conversion of the Hindus to Christianity by translating hymns into Hindi. This was a telling cross-cultural link, an important inroad in getting the English language across as a medium of communication. Aiding and abetting this process were the insistent demands that the methods and practices of the CM schools made upon the young East Indian minds at their disposal. Recognising the positive gains to be made through education, many Indians embraced Christianity as a means to an end. But before it was too late, many leaders of the Indian community, keen to maintain and strengthen their Indian cultural heritage, decided that the best way forward was to win the legal right to administer their own schools. Having won this Government concession (the Muslims in 1949 and the Sanatanists in 1952) by 1976, both these representative groups of East Indians had been adminstering six Secondary schools, three each.

If education is an integral part of personal development, how had the secondary school system in Trinidad's multi-cultural society dealt in recent years with students from the East Indian community? And if self-awareness and self-esteem are directly related to academic performance then the concept and image that Indian children have of themselves, and the image that others have of them[175] are crucial. Underscoring this, however, is the curriculum which in satisfying students' potential, should fundamentally relate to their needs for it is the key to orienting students either positively or negatively. As Anand noted 'a curriculum with which the child feels no affinity attacks his self-esteem ... it persuades the child that his interests and aspirations are of no account (since they seem to be ignored or brushed aside) and it tells him, quite brutally that his powers are valueless in dealing with its demands. This double rejection annihilates the prospects of getting anywhere and motivation falls to zero'.[176]

The Trinidad and Tobago Government, in spite of its policy (the Draft Plan for educational development 1968–1983) of developing a multi-racial society, in practice failed to do anything about bringing to the attention of the nation's students, the existence and relevance of Indian culture. Gajraj has argued that the Plan, instead of promoting the works of great musicians and the world's various cultures, fell far short in practice: while students' attention was directed to Chopin and Beethoven and the local steelpan, traps and recorder, there was no mention of outstanding Indian musical artists like Ravi Shankar and Mungal Patessar. And incredible as it may seem, it was stated that some students had never seen essential Indian musical instruments such as the sitar, harmonium or dhantal. This ongoing negation of Indian culture is seen as preparing the Indian for a subservient role. For those who face a 'crisis of identity,' the school system (especially the Government-run sector) is a long way from offering any real hope. And given the absence of a Government policy for the promotion of Indian culture in schools, it was argued that a number of Principals did not recognise it as something they could either initiate or campaign for in the school. It comes as no surprise then that Indian students were debased, feeling 'culturally inferior' and entrapped in a system described as a 'vicious circle of alienation, frustration and self-rejection (which) circumscribes the educational'.[177]

What could the Indian-controlled schools do to redress this racist imbalance? There were four Secondary schools under the control of the Sanatan Dharma Maha Sabha, the Sanatanist Hindus. Although the General Secretary of this organisation Sat Maharaj had stated that their policy was 'to propagate the religion and the culture full stop! through Hindu religious instruction, compulsory celebration of Hindu festivals, Hindi classes, Indian cultural activities, supplies of text and literature on Hinduism', it was found that of all the students attending Maha Sabha schools, only fifteen students wrote Hindi at the 1984 GCE O Level examinations. Gajraj claimed that the SDMS was more concerned with Hinduism, instead of Indian culture as a whole.

On the other hand, while the Anjuman Sunaat-al-Jamaat Association (ASJA) in line with its policy and practice were successful in promoting Islam in its Secondary schools, it was found that the Association's contribution to cultural life was minimal being, as the SDMS, more preoccupied with religion than with culture.[178]

Teachers, so crucial to the educational process, had been prone to conform to 'unfavourable stereotypes' which assist much in forming 'the attitudes of blacks and whites towards Indians'. Thus the point was made in 1984 that 'the problem of culturally deficient educators attempting to teach culturally different children' had become significant in Trinidad, resulting in 'far-reaching negative effects on teacher-pupil relationships, pupil self-esteem, motivation and achievement'. Indeed a teacher of Indian background who takes a negative approach to his Indian cultural heritage tends to transmit this to his or her students who see them as role models to be imitated, thus perpetuating the 'vicious process of deculturisation'.[179]

In certain areas, however, educational establishments offered some hope, as at a few Secondary schools. Sansrkitic Sangam run by Pandit Ashram Maharaj, where volunteer teachers were committed to inter-school cultural activities, including dance, music and debates, engendered positive feeling among students about their cultural heritage, which is vitally important to adolescents.

There was also good reason for optimism considering the increase in Indian cultural activities in some Secondary schools largely due to committed teachers. But overall Indian culture remains to be integrated in Secondary school life. And given that a derided culture 'burdens its bearers with shame and grief', the 'disrespect and mockery' that had for so long attended displays of Indian culture is, to say the least, an intimidating experience for adolescent Indians, which compounds their difficulties.

Derision also leads to alienation which is 'particularly high among rural Indian students', Gajraj argues with conviction. 'The child is derided (for bringing a lunch of aloo and roti and dahi and for wearing coconut oil in the hair) by schoolmates. … No derision is directed at the student who wears the long matted locks of the Rastafarian cult – he is admired for "carrying on his culture"'.[180]

The historical stain of the Indian stereotype that has marked the society is still prominent and any evidence of 'Indianness' looms as a threat. More generally, it is lamentable that until recently so little has been done to bring out the hidden, unforgiveable omission of the East Indians' presence in the Caribbean in history texts for schools. Apart from the author's recent publication *World in View – West Indies*,[181] educational resources at this level relating to the Indians remain, more or less, a footnote, their history and culture in need of 'official' recognition is now, however, being actively reclaimed and placed increasingly at the centre of discourse on Caribbean historiography, where it belongs.

## *The Indian Family*

Given that kinship relations is the first allegiance of the East Indian, the joint family has been, and to a large extent still is of paramount importance to East Indian life in Trinidad.[182]

Traditionally, this type of family constituted several married couples and their children inhabiting the same house, the men being all blood relatives.[183] Vital assets such as money and property are commonly held, and the family funds are usually managed by the eldest male. Other major family functions include religious rites, the selection of spouses for family members (a crucial matter considering that marriage is seen first as a relationship between the families concerned, and secondly as a relationship between the persons engaged) and the control of marriage arrangements by senior members of the family. The inter-relationship between caste and family is best seen in the institution of marriage for although the selection of a marital partner is circumscribed, it is underscored by the rule that the family member should not marry outside his or her caste.

While there is similarity with the extended family elsewhere in the world, the inter-relationship between the extended family in India and its caste system is unique. Both institutions were transplanted into the alien environment of the Caribbean, in this case Trinidad. Concubinage and non-legal unions ('living under one roof ... without the formal religious, civil or social ceremony')[184] as practised by the Afro-Trinidadian family differed from the extended family. From the early days of their arrival in the island, there was the insistent, and seemingly overbearing presence of the Afro-Trinidadian population that has challenged the extended family. But prior to this challenge, traditional family ties had already begun to loosen during the process of immigration, which recruited individuals and sometimes whole families. In addition, during this early period (and relatively throughout the years of the indenture system) there was the problem of the ratio of women to men recruited.[185] As field workers, men were superior to women, as far as the planters were concerned, regardless of the social and moral difficulties that this disproportion created everywhere that Indians were sent as workers in the nineteenth century.[186] The shortage of Indian women did not lead, with few exceptions, to Indian males marrying Afro-Trinidadian women. Instead they competed with each other for the available Indian women. This scarcity had the effect of increasing the demand for Indian women who enjoyed a degree of independence greater than they had in India. Although as wives, they held their families in high esteem and were fond mothers, it was claimed that they were lacking in fidelity towards their husbands.[187] Surely such women were more the exception rather than the rule! East Indian women clearly enjoyed much leverage. 'When the last immigrant ship came in', as a Brahmin widow is said to have informed Morton, 'I took a man. If he does not treat me well I shall send him off at once'.[188] This is particularly interesting because of all the castes, Brahmins were the most vigilant in preventing widows from re-marrying. In other reported cases, a woman deserted her husband because he wanted to have a second wife in the home, a practice that would have been unacceptable in India.[189]

The shortage of Indian women resulted in violence committed by jealous lovers and husbands, creating a stereotype of the East Indian man, which gained in infamy through men like Froude who stated that the 'coolies' reputation with the police was bad and significantly while the 'Negroes' use their tongue in argument, the Indian commit murder, and given the scarcity of Indian women, without hesitation.[190] Thus the stereotype is reinforced ascribing to the Indian husband a 'frantically jealous disposition' which, at the time, accounted for sixty per cent of the colony's murders.[191]

Historically the Indian family has suffered other disadvantages, for example, in the conduct of their marriages, which were unrecognised by the Government until they became legal in 1936 for Muslim marriages performed by the Imam, and in 1946 for Hindu marriages performed by the Hindu Pundit.[192] As a consequence, all Indian marriages previously performed under Hindu and Muslim rites were registered as legal. But because these marriages were unrecognised for so long (except to members of the Indian community) unregistered marriages were referred to as 'under the bamboo'. The effect of the illegality of these unions was that the 'wife' was not entitled to widow's benefit and had no legal right in the event of her husband's desertion and to crown it all, her family's disabilities were further compounded by the fact that her children were 'illegitimate'.

The great disadvantages that the Indians have endured over the years in Trinidad had not markedly diminished their distinctiveness, their 'Indianness' vis-a-vis other ethnic groups. If anything, compared with caste, the extended family had by the late 1950s, in essence, retained much of its traditional structure. Indian marriages have been, and are, essential to this family structure for it is through this institution that a newcomer is introduced into the 'circle of kinship', an ever-widening circle that must maintain its unity, thus the betrothed is carefully chosen.

If marriages prior to 1940 were 'arranged', twenty years later, they were described as being of 'free choice'. 'The actual difference consists solely of the fact that, today, both boy and girl are introduced to each other before the marriage and each has the right to veto the proposed match', wrote Klass over thirty years ago. 'Otherwise in the old days, the two fathers usually initiate the proceedings, and handle all arrangements'.[193]

By and large most Indian marriages in Trinidad were (and in many cases still are), arranged by parents or family elders. Normally (especially prior to 1940) there was little contact between unmarried Indian youths, and girls did not go out on dates or to dances. A girl seen talking to a man in a public place was regarded as 'suspect'. And in line with tradition, once a potential partner is found, the parents arrange a meeting between the boy and girl. If both parties are pleased with each other, then with the parents agreement arrangements for the marriage proceed. At this stage of selection, parents employ much diplomacy to effect their choice. As soon as an agreement is reached, a new phase in relations between the partners ensue, with the boy gaining access to see the girl several times before the wedding. On the other hand, there are many cases where the young women either never saw their husbands until the day of the marriage or only very briefly.

In exceptional cases, young men who are attracted to a girl or woman seen at a public place, can approach her parents to arrange a marriage; and in cases where a young man's father is dead, he initiates arrangements with the parents of a partner of his choice. Marriages were and still are, arranged by the Agwa method, which involves the payment of money to a person to find an appropriate partner. This practice (like many others) has, however, in recent times, become far less important.

Unlike Hindu and Muslim marriages, in the approach to Christian marriage among Indians, the couple involved is given more latitude in selecting their partner. But like Hindu and Muslim marriages, parents arranges most Christian marriages, the boy being allowed to make calls on his intended partner before reaching a decision. The idea of dating between unmarried children among rural Christians is also rarely practised.

In Trinidad, the legal age of marriage among the Indians, though low, differs between Hindus and Muslims. For Muslim males the legal age is sixteen and for females twelve, while for Hindu males it is eighteen and for females fourteen. The commitment to marry known as the Gona ceremony, is now very rare in Trinidad. This entails the betrothal of children (even as young as five years old) but who only live together when they become much older.

As in Guyana, horoscopes figure prominently among Hindus who are about to be married, both in terms of compatibility and the wedding date. This planetary work, conducted by the Pundits can, at times, be of lesser importance than the temperaments of the couple concerned, for when there is compatibility in this sense, the same could be applied to horoscopic orientation. While the Hindu marriage period as stipulated in the *jotis*, the book of horoscopes, stretches from January to April and during June, this is not strictly adhered to and people marry whenever they choose. Normally, the day of marriage is Sunday.

In Hindu marriage arrangements, the dowry which is agreed by the parents, plays an important part. Of the many occasions on which a boy is given money, the Chekhai (the engagement) and the Tilak (the dowry itself) are most significant. The amount given varies with the income of the families concerned, ranging from a few dollars to houses, cars and shops. Though effective, a high dowry is not always successful in wooing a reluctant young man. Unlike the Hindus, dowries are not given to Muslims. Instead, the bride usually receives the Mahaar, a sum of money to spend as she pleases. In Trinidad, as in Guyana, for both Hindus and Muslims, observance of the marriage rite is one of the most important socio-religious events. Niehoff observed that 'a series of rituals' which begins on Friday night and lasts until Sunday evening, a time when men play a major part in cooking the large quantity of food required. If the cooking is important, there is much visiting during these days up to and including the wedding ceremony on Sunday. Home-bound Indian women find that weddings provide the opportunities (and are indeed occasions) for making social contact. They are deeply interested in all that goes on at these occasions, including the alleged heavy drinking. Not all women, however, are as strict as one Pundit, who towards the end of the 1950s, was quoted as saying that although Hindu marriage 'is a beautiful ceremony ... nowadays it is a mess'. It disturbed him that people made 'a fete out of it, drinking rum, smoking and generally having a good time'.[194]

Even though there is less 'open' drinking, as a social occasion, Muslim marriages are similar to Hindu marriages. But while eating procedure and the calls made by guests are roughly the same, the bride remains hidden 'in a closed room' accompanied by women only, as a 'delegate' shuttles between her and the groom; and she abstains from the wedding festivities.

By the end of the 1950s a new form of Indian marriage in Trinidad was observed both among Hindus and Muslims. Instead of the marriage ceremony taking place at the house, sometimes Muslims were married at mosques, and occasionally, Hindus were married in their temples. This shift has been attributed to cases in which the family was too poor to have a wedding at home. It has been suggested that these mosque and temple marriages have been influenced by Christian sects such as the Presbyterian Canadian Mission.

A countervailing force to this new trend was the increasing respect for traditional rituals, following the legalisation of Hindu and Muslim marriages. In this revival, a leading role was played by the Sanatan Dharma (the largest Hindu sect in Trinidad) whose Pundits officiated at most of the Hindu marriages. The smaller and lesser known Hindu sect the Kabir Panth also conducted marriages. Priests from the Arya Samaj also performed marriage ceremonies, but their attempts were dwarfed by the power and influence of the Sanatan Dharma, not only in the realm of marriages, but also in the practice of Hinduism in general.

Although in theory, at least, Hindu and Muslim men could have several wives, a Hindu woman was expected to marry once, while a Muslim woman could do so after divorce. Not surprisingly, there was, by the end of the 1950s and thereafter, a popular feeling among Hindus that a divorce provision was necessary to the marriage act.

Apart from those men who were said to have several wives, some Indian men lived with women as 'keepers'. During their six-month research in Trinidad, the Niehoffs found that

> Hindu women, in particular, resort to the "keeper" relationship if their husband dies, because they are not allowed to go through the wedding rites again. They are simply concubines or "kept" women who also live in separate houses, if the man is legitimately married to another woman. Because of this accepted, though not highly approved relationship, the state of widow-hood in Trinidad lacks the tragic aspect it often has in India. A widow does not spend the remainder of her life in mourning for her husband and in drudgery to his family. Some such relationships prove quite stable, particularly if the man has no legitimate wife.

The Niehoffs, in fact, knew women who had cohabited with men for many years, and though they never got married, they raised a number of children. Such relationships were regarded as being similar to the 'Negro non-legal union'.[195]

As mentioned in the case of Guyana, at the close of the Hindu marriage ceremony, the bride accompanies the groom to his home where she spends several days before returning to her parents' home for a few days. She then goes back to her husband's house, returning at intervals to her mother's house during the first six months of marriage. After this toing and froing, however, the newly married couple remain in the home of the husband's father for about four months before moving to 'one side', more often than not to a house in the immediate vicinity.

On occasions, especially when the bridegroom's father is too old or infirm, the eldest son remains in his father's house.

It is rare to find in Trinidad the extended family household as it has been known in India. Indeed in households where all the married sons and their wives have lived together, the degree of friction and frequency of quarrels, especially between wives often lead to the married sons living in houses built on family property. While the difficulties of married brothers living in the same house and the fact that some mothers-in-law are too overbearing on their daughters-in-law are well known, there are numerous cases in which wives have lived harmoniously with their mothers-in-law. But the fact remains that a married son living with his parents subjects his wife to his mother's authority. This seems an inescapable arrangement, particularly during the early days of marriage for those married couples who are unable to afford their own homes. But in cases where the wife's parents are rich enough to build a house (usually near her father's) for their daughter and her husband, this economic bond had its own drawbacks, as far as the Hindu husband was concerned. For one thing, he feels that his 'rights' over his wife will be prescribed by the physical nearness of her father. 'Husbands like that won't even have the chance to beat their wife' said a Hindu youth.

Another aspect of the extended family life in Trinidad is that the respect shown by younger members of the family to their elders is of a different kind to that which exists in India. For example, there is little adherence to greeting elders by touching their feet. In general, however, at least by the 1950s, it was found that young people tended to conform to certain expectations that older people had of them: for example, that old people should not be cursed, nor should obscene language be used in their presence and that young people should tend to their needs. It was also noted that in the more traditional families, the father received all the earnings of his sons, allocating to them what he considered their appropriate amount of spending money should be. The finanacial affairs are well and truly in the hands of the elders, until such time when they had grown too old to perform this function. In these circumstances, the dutiful eldest son, assumes the mantle of arranging the family's affairs.

In terms of their relative position, Indian men and women in Trinidad were similar to their counterparts in India. As a mark of respect, Indian women were expected to cover their heads. And over the years, most rural Hindu, Muslim and Christian women have done so with the Orhni, a thin shawl-like head covering. This item is powerfully distinctive reflecting 'Indianness', and symbolic of a deeply-rooted tradition. The lesser known Burka, a garment covering almost all the body, which was once worn in Trinidad but has now become redundant. Given that there was little social contact between unmarried Indian girls and unrelated males, even after marriage there were social strictures, as at religious functions such as Ram Lila and Krishna Lila, at Hindu prayer meetings and weddings, during which men and women were separated. And Muslims of both sexes, while at prayers in their mosques were also kept apart. This segregation contrasted sharply with the practice of other ethnic groups on the island.

At home, the dutiful Hindu woman is expected to serve food to her husband before she eats and generally the family's money is controlled by the husband. Should the wife need money, she asks her husband if she wants to go somewhere. On land inheritance, a young female is rarely favoured, precedence almost always being given to the eldest son. This has been the practice among Indians of all faiths, Hindus, Muslims and Christians. However, a girl who has looked after her parents during their infirm years of old age may be given land which could also be inherited by a wife on the death of her husband, who either had no brothers or were not particularly close to them.

Another major consideration affecting the Indian family is the birth rate, which has over many years been much higher than other groups in Trinidad. In 1955 the Indians accounted for 35.1 per cent of the island's total population and more than half of the births. So high had been the increase in births among the Indians that in 1957 the census officer predicted that if this rate of increase was maintained by 1963, Indians would form the majority of the population. It would seem that that prediction was close to fulfilment in 1992. Among the reasons given for this difference between Afro-Trinidadians and Indians were the 'different types of family structure and attitude toward marriage'. More fundamentally, however, was the age of marriage – East Indian mothers tending to marry and reproduce much earlier than women in other groups. Birth control measures are not objected to once the number of children is deemed sufficient. Underlying the Indian extended family in the Caribbean is the importance of children, for 'childbirth is governed almost completely by the traditional beliefs and practices of the different subcultures',[196] wrote one authority. Thus the desire for offsprings, the early age of marriage and stable marriages among the Indians have been accountable for the rising Indian population.

Since its implantation in 1845 the East Indian family has been characterised by its malleability, which ensured its survival in the new and ever-changing environment. By the early 1970s, its evolution had been noted by Nevadomsky:

'The traditional Indian family is supported and sanctified by a caste and religious system of a particular kind. As soon as one of those constraints is removed or transformed the system either collapses or undergoes change and a new pattern of integration develops. In short, Trinidad's East Indians are a long way from India in space, time and social structure'.[197]

Endemic in the upholding of the Indian family structure are customs, beliefs and practices, to which we now turn. But as we approach the year 2000 though the Indian family system in Trinidad has indeed retained much of the essential gravitas that it had midway through this century, inevitable changes will continue to be incorporated as gender relations evolve. Much will depend upon Indian women. Since their entry in the society, there has been a 'tremendous shift' in their status, from being keepers of the culture, 'sacrificial and passive', to becoming 'more inte-grated'. In fact, many contemporary Indian women are unwilling to conform to the 'passive' and 'submissive' stereotype. They are, we are told by one Indo-Trinidadian woman writer, more affirmative, selecting the degree to which they would engage in inter-culturation as they become 'Creolized',[198] a process which in such a small island was inevitable. This was aided by growing industrialization in the post-1950s period, which brought greater social and economic opportunities for young Indian women, especially Hindus. And as they become educated and skilled, as breadwinners, they would achieve greater independence, thus freeing themselves from the matriarchal role of the traditional extended family to increas-ingly become part of the nuclear family.

If the Indian woman is the bedrock upon which the Indian family rests, then the implications for the future of this institution is quite clear as the Indian woman in Trinidad and Tobago (and Indo-Caribbean women, generally) struggle for her iden-tity. And if Indians are a marginalized racial group in Trinidad and the Caribbean, the marginalization of Indian women is even greater. Evidence of disenchantment with their continued oppression is reflected in an uncompromising mood among a new generation of well-educated and articulate Indian women. 'There is a need for Indo-Caribbean women to become an articulated sector of the contemporary Carib-bean', wrote Ramabai Espinet, 'and signs are that this process is finally beginning'. She cites the 'new values' that are integral to the creolization—modernization pro-cess necessitating 'new structures of cultural enlargement' to deal with such prob-lems as the high rate of suicide among young Indian women, which rose alarm-ingly in the mid-1980s. Espinet argues that debate on the 'gramozone' weed-killer (suicide) study, commissioned by the Maha Sabha, addressed the 'immense diffi-culties' confronting Indian women who sought to change their position in Trini-dad and Tobago and in Western society generally. The protection of the Indian male was unnecessary for the 'personal agendas' of Indian women had changed. The challenge for Indo-Caribbean people, in general, as she saw it, was a redefini-tion of 'the parameters of gender relations'. In conclusion she added, 'It is clear that the transition of the Indian woman into the sphere of influence and decison-making is long overdue'. And while she saw the achievement of this as being 'shared by the society as a whole', much of the responsibility in effecting this 'transition', she contends, must be borne by Indian men and women themselves.[199]

## Religious Beliefs and Practices

The Indians brought with them strong beliefs in Hinduism and Islam. From the moment of their arrival there have been insistent pressures to modify and even to eliminate their beliefs and practices. Yet, religious belief among the Indians has remained largely unshaken. Apart from the two main religions, there were few Sikhs (and little or no trace of Sikhism) in Trinidad, and according to the Census of

1931, there were 119 Buddhists and 278 Parsis.[200] (Among the Indians there were also a number of businessmen in Port of Spain and San Fernando, most of whom came from Bombay. In fact, many merchants were Indian nationals).

In 1946, from a total of 195,747 Indians in Trinidad, 126,785 (64.7 per cent) were Hindus and 32,615 (16.7 per cent) were Muslims. The rest, 18.6 per cent, were mainly Christians. A census taken fifteen years earlier, showed that of those who were not adherents of the Hindu, Muslim or Christian faiths, amounted to only 0.4 per cent of the total. Almost 40 years later, an estimated 70 per cent of the Indian population still practised Hinduism, 15 per cent were followers of Islam and 15 per cent Christians. From these figures we can deduce that overall the Indian community was largely a religious one.

In terms of their religious background, among the indentured Hindu Indian population, there was a whole range of 'beliefs, doctrines, rites, experiences, relationships, restrictions, politics, economics and orientations regarding matters supernaturnal and spiritual'. Vertovec identified regions from where thousands of Indian migrants came to Trinidad, such as Bengal, Bihar and Orissa, among others in North India, where Shaktism prevailed over other types of religious orientation, followed by Vaishnavism, including the Krishna-centred Chaitanya sect. Vaishnavism was also dominant in Eastern and Western Uttar Pradesh, but with the strong influence of Bhakti sects, especially the Ramanandi, Kabir, Raidasi and Siva Narayani or Sieunarini panths. Shaivism has also been strongly represented in centres such as Benares. And in addition to the greater deities worshipped in different regions (Ram, Hanuman, Durga, Krishna, Shiva, Kali, Ganesh, Surya and Satynarine) a number of gods, goddesses and godlings, saints and spirits were also popular.[201]

Religious activity was even more diverse, given the heterogenous caste composition of the indentured immigrants. However, once they had arrived in the new context of Trinidad, almost by rote, they turned to their various forms of worship, though it was clear enough that they would have to relate their beliefs and practices to the context of their colonial environment. In the early villages, Hindus engaged in fairly standardized 'ritual functions', which included Samskara (the rites of the life cycle, and the rites of the Pujas and Satsangs. Another important religious activity during these early years was the 'Bhagwat', the reading and explanation of the BHAGAVATA PURANA. Over the years, custom and practice had reached a point by the 1920s and 1930s, when it was evident that Hindusim had become 'routinized', through 'relatively informal means'. Refinements, hard-won with the passage of time, resulted in wide acceptance of a body of rituals.[202]

Since they had set up their first 'rude temple' in the early 1860s, Hindus and their forms and places of worship, in particular, have been of curious interest to outsiders, especially Creoles and Europeans. These early structures known as Kutyias in Trinidad were modelled on Hindi Kutis or small shrines that were to be found as an integral part of village life in Bihar and Uttar Pradesh.[203] Gradually, as the few officiating priests among the immigrants reached a consensus, the differing Hindu rites became more standardized, taking the form of a 'Sanatan Dharm style of Hinduism', as Vertovec put it. 'A smaller pantheon of Sanskrit gods became dominant, while local godlings were for the most part disregarded. Primarily, this pantheon consisted of Vishnu (especially in his incarnated forms of Rama and Krishna), Satnarayan (technically another form of Vishnu, but regarded as a more all-inclusive God), Hanuman, Ganesh, Shiva Suryanarayan, Durga, Lakshmi, Saraswati and Kali. A Vaishnavite Bhakti orientation became pervasive'.[204]

In Trinidad the followers of Hindusim were represented by four main sects: the Sanatan Dharma; the Arya Samaj; the Kabir Path and the Seunerinis. The Sanatan Dharma, an orthodox Hindu sect is an affiliate of the Sanatan Dharma Sabha in India. Most of India's Hindus are followers of the SD leadership. The Arya Samaj, less traditional, is indeed reformist, as mentioned earlier in the case of Guyana. This group stresses the importance of the Vedas and, because it stems from a minority group in India, it is not surprising that in Trinidad its followers are much fewer compared with the Sanatan Dharma. The Kabir Panth, founded by the prophet Kabir in the fifteenth century, taught his followers to worship one God who was neither Hindu nor Muslim. Members of this group in Trinidad regard themselves as Hindus. Also known as the Siva Narayans, the Seunerinis were formed by a Rajput named Siva Narayan in the nineteenth century.[205] Followers of this faith believe in one God and are also anti-Brahminical. In addition to these four sects, there were among the Chamars, devotees of a Chamar saint known as Ravidas, a minor group that lacked the organisation of the other sects.

Of the four sects, the Sanatan Dharma has exerted the strongest influence over the island's Hindus. It has the greatest number of followers and is given added force because of its association with the Maha Sabha Hindu political group. Maha Sabha schools outnumber by an estimated four to one by the end of the 1950s, those of the other sects, and not surprisingly, within the Hindu community, the presence of Sanatanist pundits has been ubiquitous.

The Sanatan Dharma has built Hindu temples in many parts of Trinidad. Wealthy Hindus make large contributions, as a religious act, towards such buildings that are usually looked after by a Sadhu who administer offerings to the images and deities such as Siva, Ganesh, Hanuman, Parvati, Krishna and Radha. Certain trees and plants, (including the Tulsi plant, the Bel and Pipal trees) in the grounds of the temples also receive the attention of the Sadhu. It is not unusual to find other buildings near the temples for the purpose of readings of the BHAGAVAD-GITA and the RAMAYANA. These structures, especially the temples, were however, more symbolic than practical, for most Hindus rarely used them since most Hindu religious rituals took place at Hindu homes. One strong reason posited for this was that because the generally poor indentured Indians could not afford to build temples, they worshipped at home, a practice that persisted even after they had been able to acquire land and money. The construction of temples remained strong symbols of Hinduism, reminders to new generations of Indians of their heritage. This religious transmission was nesessary because of the perceived threats from the Christians who had been making steady inroads among the Indians.

The Hindu ritual known as Puja (the family prayer meeting) is held periodically each year, a thanksgiving for the welfare of an individual or the family as a whole. The construction of a new house is usually accompanied with Puja. These prayer meetings featured rituals such as the Hanuman Rot, the Kattha (or Satya Narain Puja) and the Suraj Puja, among others. The Puja is an occasion of social and religious significance. Socially, it brings together family and friends, who have a communal meal. Women congregate and share experiences, news and views. At the end of the ceremony and the end of the meal, Persad, the 'blessed food', a mixture of flour raisins and coconut, is served. The procedures for the ceremonial part of the Puja is described as follows:

> One or two pundits are engaged to officiate, as well as a pundit's helper who is called the Nau. The Nau prepares an alter-place on the ground and gets all the material ready for the ritual. The pundit, the Nau and the delegate of the sponsor, usually one of the female members of his family are the only persons who take part in the ceremony. The main body of the ritual consists in offerings to the deity and prayers (mantra) recited by the pundit.[206]

If the ceremony is not properly performed and vows made to the deities are not fulfilled, it is believed that bad luck will follow; indeed a necessary pre-condition of the Puja is that no meal should be eaten or sexual intercourse indulged in by the sponsor. At the end of the ceremony, gifts are made to both the pundit and the poor, and the jhandy was placed. This last jhandy symbol was made of bamboo poles upon which were placed prayer flags, consisting of different colours: red, white and yellow, for the different deities – Hanuman Rot, Sat Deo and Suraj Naraya and the female deities, respectively. A black flag is raised after the Kali Puja, and it is customary that prayer flags should, once raised, be left untampered until the elements dispose of them.

Unlike the Sanatanists, prayers, offerings and prayer flags in certain parts of the island, is absent from Kabir Panth rituals. In the Seunerini rituals, prayer flags are also not used. Instead worship, according to one scholar, is centred on the sacred writings of their prophet Kabir. In the rituals of both the Kabir Panthi and Seunerini Mahant (instead of Brahmin pundits being used) it has been observed that individuals from both sects often indulged in 'regular Sanatanist prayer meetings with Sanatanist pundits', and both groups tended to follow the ritual offering of food.

Among Arya Samaj followers, it was observed that their ceremonies were further removed from the other Hindu sects. In the Penal-Debe area, one researcher made this interesting observation:

> They met every Monday night for a service which lasted about an hour or a little more and which, in its outer forms resembled a Christian ceremony as much as a

Hindu one. It required the burning of a sacred fire [hawan], the reading and inter-preting of the Vedas, and singing religious songs [bhajan]. People sat on chairs or benches, and the pundit sat at a table facing the group. The customary altar-place on the ground, found at all other Hindu ceremonies, was completely absent. Many other traditional practices found in other Hindu ceremonies, were absent at the Arya Samaj ritual. No one took off his shoes, a practice which is followed at the prayer meetings of all the other sects. Of course, the fact that everyone sat on chairs probably affected this custom. Also all clothing worn was in the Western style, except for the Gandhi cap and an Indian coat [Shervani] worn by a pundit. The other pundit wore a Western suit and neck-tie. ... The recitation and inter-pretation of the Vedas was partly in Hindi and partly in English.[207]

This was a clear shift in Hindu ritual and practice. A reflection of this process of modernization can be witnessed in the urban areas. Commenting on his mother's approach to worship, Shiva Naipaul wrote that on the whole, it could be fairly said, her worship 'is more detached and formal. She goes to a nearby temple with tiled floors and colourful effigies of the gods and goddesses imported from the facto-ries of Bombay and Benares ... For better or worse, she accepts her "Trinidadianess" '.[208]

The religious pilgrimages to sacred sites, rivers and mountains in India have their counterparts (albeit on a much reduced scale) in Trinidad where Pujas are performed on beaches, particularly during the festival of Khatik-ke-Nahan. At this time, Hindu worshippers travelled up and down the island, those from the North go south and vice-versa. Indeed, two kinds of religious journeys (inspired it has been claimed by the Hindu need for pilgrimages), made by Hindus to Roman Catho-lic churches during the 1950s, have been observed. Hindus worshipped at the church in Mount St. Benedict in the North and at the church of La Divina Pastora in Siparia, paying homage to the Catholic Virgin.

Throughout the year Hindus participate in several well-known festivals, includ-ing Janam Astami (the birth of Krishna); Divali (festival of light); Khatik-ke-Nahan (worship at sea); Holi (known also as Phagwah – the festival of colour); and Shivatri (the festival of Shiva). Among the lesser known festivals are Pitr Phat (worship of ancestors); Gobardhaan Puja; and Ganesh Yug (worship of Ganesh).[209] The fact that most of these festivals have been observed among certain North Indian vil-lagers is further evidence that the Hindu ceremonial observances in Trinidad are derived primarily from Northern India.

In addition to the festivals, during the year, readings of the RAMAYANA (the Ramayana Sathsang) or the BHAGAVAD GITA (Bhagwat) are sponsored. Often these 'readings' of the ancient singing, usually accompanied by sermons given by pundits or well-known Hindus, applaud followers for their faith and call upon them to strive to be better Hindus. Such scriptural readings are also occasions for bringing members of the Hindu community together.

Towards the end of the year, in October and November, Hindus engage in dram-atic performances from the RAMAYANA and the MAHABHARATA in the forms of Ram Lila and Krishna Lila, concerning the Hindu gods Ram and Krishna. Fostering such cultural displays is an expensive venture, the cost of which is borne by wealthy Hindus and from public donations. A great deal of time, energy and talent goes into the making of constumes and in the performances, which are fully justified and encouraged by the large crowds that attend them. Increasingly, Trinidadians from different groups have been drawn to the universal messages transmitted through these pageants, and the unstinting efforts of the Maha Sabha leadership has helped to publicise and make these events less parochial. As it was, the earlier lack of pride among many Hindus had to be overcome, and by the late 1950s, there was a marked resurgence in self-respect due to the general improvement among Indians, in terms of education and economic position. Underscoring this redefinition of their identity as Hindus, was the increase in the number of Hindu schools which has helped to inculcate in Indian students a greater degree of consciousness of their traditional heritage, a counterpoise to negative attitudes from various elements in the wider society towards Indians of this faith.

Low caste Indians have had, over the years, to move closer to orthodox Sanatanist rituals. Some castes in India perform animal sacrifices to Kali as in the yearly Kali Puja, and while the Trinidadian Hindu attitude towards animals is much different from that to be found in India, there is commonality in that in both countries orthodox Hindus tend to abstain from eating beef, and the sacredness of the cow is observed. (With time, however, strict adherence to this would change.)

Sacred rituals also thread the major events in the life of a Hindu. Ceremonies attend birth, christening, marriage and death. At childbirth a nurse or midwife is called in. Usually, midwives are Chamars (a low caste well-known in India as being engaged in this occupation) for birth, like menstruation and severing of the umbilical chord, are regarded as unclean. After caring for the mother for six days, the first ceremony is held, which excludes the midwife from either cooking or assisting in the ceremony. At this stage, the midwife's 'dirty' work of delivery, is considered to be be done and she could therefore be dispensed with until, of course, the demand for her work again arises. The Chatti (or sixth day ceremony) is attended by women only, a time when food is prepared and singing and dancing extends through the night. The father gets the first glimpse of his child after this ceremony, and a few days later (in fact, twelve days after birth) another ceremony, the Baraha follows, when both mother and child are regarded as clean enough, and men are allowed to attend. The child is given a secret name, then a 'calling name' and surname (arising from the child's father's name); the former being used daily and for official purposes.

Among the Brahmins, Gosains and Chattris, the jeuneu, a sacred thread is worn during a special ceremony, the 'confirmation ceremony' of the twice-born Hindu castes. Life in Trinidad is not conducive to the constant wearing of this sacred thread, because, it is said, the person concerned is expected to adhere to certain strictures, such as foregoing the consumption of alcohol, meat and other 'unclean' things, a near impossibility for many in Trinidad. Despite taking the thread off (three weeks after the christening ceremony), it is worn again. Moreover, it is customary to expect that before marriage, Hindu men and women would have been 'christened'.

After birth, the next major stage in the Hindu's life is marriage, an integral part of the Indian family and community. For a female child, it is almost certain that she would enter this institution, sooner rather than later. Marriage differs from rites of birth and death in that it requires the participation of two families and some negotiation. Unlike the contractual Muslim marriage, which allows a man four wives, the Hindu marriage is not only a sacrament, but also the merging of two families.

For both participants in marriage, it means a change of status in their community, a move from the first stage (ashram) of life, Bramacharya, to the second, grihastha or householder. Moreover, Indian marriage evokes Indian culture, through food, ceremony and high profile as a social occasion, depending, of course, on how well-off the families concerned are.

But before an Indian marriage takes place (as mentioned earlier) the choice of a partner for a girl is usually made by her parents, although either of the partners could disagree. Unlike the Hindus, Christian Indians engage in a period of courtship in the hope that the boy and girl will come to know each other better. But even among Hindus, strict marriage arrangements at puberty are no longer adhered to, though, especially in some rural districts, parents are prone to become deply concerned with marriage once their daughters reach the age of fifteen. And for many, any deviation from tradition tends to create tension, even though 'love matches' are said to be catching on.

In the ensuing religious ceremony, there is a jovial atmosphere which includes traditional songs being sung by women. Finally the wedding ceremony takes place at the bride's house, where a 'nuptial tent' and 'nuptial pole' are erected.[210] The construction of a Chulha (hearth) for cooking the large quantity of wedding food and seating arrangements for guests complete the scene for a festive end to the wedding day, and hopefully the beginning of a happy married life.

Since their arrival, ceremonies relating to death among the Indians have changed. For example, cremation was not allowed before 1936 and the custom of the 'wake' reflects Afro-Trinidadian influence.[211]

The Hindu attitude to death is that the soul is immortal. When a Hindu is near death, some water and tulsi (basil) leaves are put into the person's mouth and the body is then placed on the floor. The dead body is covered and a diya (or deeya – an earthen oil lamp) is lit and kept alight for ten days. A wake is held all night during which the Ramayan is sung, cards are played and coffee and rum served. The next afternoon, following death, the body is washed and placed in a coffin, before being taken to the cemetery. Before cemeteries were established, however, according to John Morton, the Indians buried their dead in their gardens.

Prior to the body's arrival at the cemetery, the *artis* ceremony is performed five times, and once more inside the cemetery. At the graveside, the Ramayan is chanted, close relatives throw into the grave the first pieces of earth, after which the coffin is covered and two jhandis are erected at opposite ends of the grave. In the immediate post-burial phase, the following procedures were enacted:

Three days after death, fireside ashes are sifted, put on the ground, and covered with a plate. The tracks left in the ashes will indicate the creature into which the deceased has been reincarnated. When there is a death in the family, the men let their beards and hair grow for ten days. At the end of this time, the maha-patra pundit performs the puja during which five of the closest male relatives theoretically have their heads completely shaved except for a small tuft called choti. In actual practice, only the very devout Hindus get shaved and the others will get haircuts. Sometimes one of the five will get shaved and the others will get haircuts only. Even the maha patra pundit, who is also supposed to get his head shaved, does not always do so.[212]

The Maha-patra is followed, three days later, by the sarad-puja ritual and a year later by the Pinda-puja ceremony. Thereafter, in remembrance of the dead, the pitr phat ceremony is held. In modern times, especially among the better-off Indians, grave stones with inscribed names are placed at the grave site.

In Trinidad, unlike India, most Hindus practice burial instead of cremation. And yet again we see how the local law affected Indian custom and practice in that during the ninety-seven years since they first arrived, they had become accustomed to burying their dead. While in recent years, many Hindus have considered cremation as an unpleasant idea, some have been determined to observe their ancient traditions in death and be consumed by the flames, ignited customarily by the eldest son. To burn the corpse, Hindus have traditionally been known to use wood and ghee (butter fat), but increasingly these have been complemented in Trinidad with gasolene or kerosene.

The rites of passage rituals among the Indians in Trinidad have undergone many changes, having been subjected to secular influences. 'The religious rituals have been shortened', wrote Jha, 'while the social aspects are emphasized more and more ... On the whole, however, it can be said that some aspects of the main sacraments have been retained by the Indians in Trinidad'.[213] How much of Hinduism has survived in Trinidad? Among those who have publicly stated their views, Jha has remained consistently optimistic, commenting on the Hindu's 'new self-confidence' and was critical of V.S. Naipaul's view that the East Indians have become materialistic and spiritually atrophied 'because they have been cut off from their roots'. In spite of some acculturation and the continuing conflict between tradition and modernity among the young, Jha maintained that Hinduism's future in Trinidad was bright![214] At the time, much of this optimism seemed well-founded.

Just when it seemed that the materialism, individualism and fragmentation of the early 1970s 'potentially marked the end of a living Hindu tradition' in Trinidad, there had arisen from the racial tensions 'facilitated' by unexpected economic growth and prosperity, a new ethnic assertiveness among Hindus. Amidst pervasive pessimissim the 'pundits' were proven wrong and Cassandras who were more cautious now spoke of a 'Hindu renaissance'. Indeed, there were 'significant transformations' in the social and ritual activities of Hindus, largely the result of individual initiative and group organisation.[215]

Among the national organisations that had emerged by the early 1990s were the Sanatan Dharma Maha Sabha, the National Council of Hindu Organisations (NCHO, formerly the United Hindu Organisation, including the Arya Pritinidhi Sabha, Inc., Kabir Panth Association, Inc; Divine Life Society, Inc; Seunarine Dharma Sabha, Inc; and Trinidad Sevashram Sangha, Inc.); Vishwa Hindu Parishad, Hindu Seva Sangh, Trinidad Academy of Hinduism, Vedanta Society, Sanatan Vidwad Vidyalaya, Bharatrya Vidya Sanatan, Caribbean Hindu Council, Satya Sai Centre, Raja Yoga Centre, Sidha Yoga Dham, and Academy·of Indian Knowledge. There were also councils engage in the promotion of such national Hindu celebrations as Phagwa and Divali; and while a few organisations have come into existence because of disenchantment with the Maha Sabha, some were founded to promote a particular school of Hindu thought. One researcher informs us that both the NCHO and the Maha Sabha have sufficient resources to fund large-scale events. But as the number of of Hindu organisation increases, there has been much criticism of each other, a fairly predictable and healthy organisational tendency.

In addition to national organisations, there are formal groups (for example, the Southern Hindu Sabha of Penal and the Penal Rock Road Hindu Youths), concerned with socio-religious activities on a regional basis. They interact, promoting Yagnas, bazaars and cultural shows, *inter alia.*

Formed in the 1980s, the Hindu Seva Sangh is particularly concerned with inter-organizational work, as Vertovec found. It also makes possible the annual SANKIRTAN (a chanting procession) in central Trinidad. Of much importance also are the new and widely distributed publications, the newspaper SANDESH and the journals MOKSHA and JAGRITI which, in essence, helps to promote the resurgence of Hinduism in the island. The proliferation of grassroots Hindu organisations since the mid-1970s, has invested Hinduism in the villages with a new vitality. This revitalization of belief and practices was, ironically, not caused by the socio-economic changes in Trinidad in the late 1970s and early 1980s. Instead, it was these very 'changes' that had made the 'renaissance' possible.[216]

An important aspect of this revival in Hinduism in the villages is the committed participation of Hindu youth. They are no longer reticent or shy. They must come 'off the defensive' in their relations with other ethnic or religious groups, and eager children and teenagers are instructed by the Seva Sangh that their main concern should be 'aggressive Hinduism'. No longer would a low self-image among Indian children (actively encouraged by elements in Creole society) be accepted. Self-esteem was joyfully in the ascendant. Hindi classes, films and music are attractive to young Hindus, even though many understood little. This regeneration of the ideas and acceptance of Hinduism, of ethnic identity, among Hindus, is all the more important and remarkable among this section of the Indians in that they (and the rest of the Indian community) have been as an identifiable group, stigmatised and treated by many as inferior 'heathen Hindoos'. And some would argue that given their low position in the social structure of Trinidad, the hostile attitude towards them has changed little, if at all!

On reflection, over their one hundered and fifty-four year presence, the constant with which the Hindus have had to contend in Trinidad society (as elsewhere in the Caribbean) is intolerance of their manifest difference. The model that was held up for the Indians to follow was the Africans' and their descendants adoption of European culture, and subsequently, what became a mixture of African and European elements constituting today's dominant Caribbean Creole culture. The inevitable and intelligent (indeed the only) response to this insistent, heavy-handed State-led, institutionalized bombardment intent on devaluing and eventually nullifying Hinduism in Trinidad is eventually one of individual choice: the taking of pride in oneself, of being at peace with oneself, and ultimately to know and value one's heritage and identity, even as creolization continue to exercise its inexorable.

## Islam

Among the early indentured Indians, there were hundreds who followed the Islamic faith. If during these years of immigration to Trinidad, the ratio of Hindus to Indians of other religious persuasion was about nine to one, it had changed by 1946 to seven Hindus to three Muslims and Christians combined.[217] And by the late 1950s, Muslims and Christians were an estimated 17 per cent and 18 per cent respectively, of the Trinidad Indian population, which indicated the greater 'inner strength' of Islam, as opposed to Hinduism from which the majority of Indians converted to Christianity.

Why were the followers of Islam less easily converted to Christianity than Hindus? Among the contributory factors given for this difference were: first that Hinduism because of its diffuseness, was not dependant upon a central organisation; and second the lack of caste traditions among Muslims and the discrimination against the low caste Hindus by the Hindu hierarchy (though caste divisions were, of course, not as pronounced in Trinidad as in India); and third that Christianity was more strongly opposed by Muslims than Hindus, because of their aversion to idol worship.[218]

Unlike the Hindus, caste divisions among the Muslims in Trinidad, were absent, even though there were religious sects among them, namely the Sunnis and the Shias. The Sunni Muslims were of a more orthodox tendency, while the Shia Muslims came into being through belief in the dogma that Ali, the cousin of Muhammad, and his descendants, alone, were the rightful heirs to Muhammad. In the world community of Muslims, the Shias are in a minority; and it is said that they are more prone to emotional expression in religious practices than are the Sunnis, especially during the Muharram (or Hosay) celebration.

In addition to these Muslim sects, by the 1950s, there was a third group known as the Kadiani, founded by Mirza Ghulam Ahmed of Afghanistan. More liberal than the Sunnis and Shias, the Kadiani have been criticised for its progressive stance concerning the use of lotteries to raise funds for religious activities, the use of music, the freedom of the sexes to mix at public places, and over-indulgence in alcohol, the last being an accusation also levelled against the Seunerini sect by other Hindu groups. In Trinidad not all Muslims refrained from drink, and there have been cases where Muslims have been owners of rum-shops.

Another important difference between Muslims and Hindus is that Muslim ritual is more defined. For example, Muslim prayers (Namaaz) are engaged in five times daily and on Fridays, Namaaz is observed at the mosque. Additionally, Muslims engage in several annual ceremonies.

Given the strictures placed upon them at certain places of employment, many Muslims have found it difficult to participate in the five daily prayers, which required the prostration of the follower while saying the appropriate prayers. While such physical difficulties have been seen as helping to undermine the Namaaz ritual in Trinidad, as a researcher in the late 1950s put it, one never saw members of the faith 'offering the Namaaz in the fields or in any public places away from home' as was (and still is) evident in India.[219]

Many of the mosques located in the rural areas, such as Debe, Penal and Siparia were largely made of wood, unlike the heavy but durable stone and/or concrete structures to be found in the urban areas of Port of Spain and the St. Joseph mosque, of which Mohammed Hakim Khan was not only 'the driving force' behind its erection, but also a devoted organiser and one of the 'pioneers' of the Trinidad Muslim League, founded on 15 August 1947.

But if structures were important, they were even more meaningful because of the believers who assembled within them to practice their religion. In one rural mosque, during the Friday services, the men and women would arrive sometime before 12.30 p.m and perform their 'ceremonial ablutions' at a water tap before entering the mosque. Women tended to precede the men who came later. At about 12.30 p.m the Imam's assistant proceeded to the highest point on the building and called the faithful to prayer in the traditional way. Once this ritual was performed, the men and women took up their different positions, men at the front and the women occupying the 'curtained "purdah" section' at the back of the mosque. The *Koran* was then read in Urdu and English, and although the women could not see the Imam, they could clearly hear him. And after completing several prostrations, at the signal of a woman's voice saying 'Khatam' (finished), the Imam moved on to the next part of the service.[220]

If this was traditional practice, gradually change began to take its toll. Apart from the Imam and his assistant who wore Indian garments, many men attending the services were clothed in Western style and their heads were covered with hand-kerchiefs. Upon entry it was also observed that belts and shoes were removed, as the worshippers entered the mosque; and at the end of the service, some food known as Sherni (similar to the Persad doled out at Hindu services) was shared out. It is significant that the central figure in these services, the Imam was not a full-time priest. In fact, many priests, of necessity, had to do other jobs. Neverthe-less, there was much religious work for them to do.

The prayer meetings called Kitabs are held at the homes of devout Muslims. (Kitab is an Urdu word which means book and refers to the *Holy Koran*). Kitabs are said to serve the same function as the Puja among Hindus. Although both ceremo-nies bear some similarity, unlike the elaborate Hindu ritual, the essence of the Muslim function is the reading of the *Koran*. Kitabs confer blessing on the sponsors' homes, honour to those who have died and generally, it serves the purpose of being a thanksgiving ceremony. Guests hear the Imam read and interpret part of the *Koran*, gifts are offered to the poor and Sherni and a meal are served. In deed helping the poor, is an important aspect of the Islamic faith.

Muslims celebrate several rituals annually, including Id-al Adha, Id-al-Fitr, Ramadan, Muhammad's birthday and Muharram (Hosay) The Id-al-Adha com-memorates Abraham's preparation to sacrifice his son; Id-al-Fitr marks the end of the fasting period; Ramadan is the month of fasting; and Muhammad's birthday is celebrated by a service in the mosque. In Trinidad, these intra-Muslim festivals are largely ignored by the wider society (as is the case with certain intra-Hindu ser-vices).

Of the foregoing celebrations which, in the main, attract little attention from non-Muslims there is one that does quite the opposite. It is known as Hosein, Hosea or Hosay in Trinidad. In India, this event (named after the particular month in the Muslim Calendar) is called Muharram. Those who followed the murdered Husein interpreted his death as martyrdom and his gravesite in Baghdad was marked out as a place of pilgrimage.

Down the centuries Husein was mourned and celebrated mainly by the Shia Muslims in India, where Muslims display unusually intense emotions, often inflict-ing wounds on their bodies with knieves and swords. Endemic in their religious fervour was 'dripping blood'. But in Trinidad, this ongoing celebration of Hosea, though on a much reduced scale, is not only observed mostly by Muslims of the Shia sect, but also by large numbers of non-Muslims who have been attracted, over the years, to Hosea. Among those outside the faith who participated were Hindus and Afro-Trinidadians, who warmed to the pulsating rhythms of the Tassa drums beaten with passion during the festivities. So involved were non-Muslims that they have been known to help in the construction of the Tadjah (Tazia), the 'symbolic wood and paper tomb of Hosein … the central focus of the Hosse rites'.[221]

In the course of the celebration, drinking was identified as an integral part (though seen by other orthodox Muslims as a disturbing development) of the celebration.

In fact in rural areas, the proprietors of rum shops have been known to finance Tadjas and drinking, music (tassa drumming) and, of course, the stick-fighting which has come to characterize the celebration, thus giving to the occasion a carnival atmosphere, more secular than religious. (The creole Carnival was then – and still is – biggest secular celebration, and with the popularity of Hosea, the Colonial authorities feared the mingling of the masses would lead to combined agitation). But the use of alcohol at Muslim religious celebrations, such as Hosea is unique, for although many Muslims in Trinidad drink, as one researcher put it, there was 'no evidence of the use of alcohol' at any other religious function.

No wonder then that orthodox Muslims such as the Sunni group were opposed to Hosea, as indicated by letters written to the *Trinidad Guardian*, as recently as thirty-four years ago, in which the writers described the 'Hosay' festival as an embarrassment and 'an un-Islamic Festival'. Other Muslims lamented the secularization of an otherwise 'sacred and solemn occasion' for Muslims, which had become a 'disgrace to Islam'.[222]

Since then the dichotomy within the Muslim community on this issue has remained more or less the same. But criticism of this festival stretches much further back to the nineteenth century, when 'disturbances' had already erupted in connection with Hosea. J.H. Collens wrote in the 1880s that the Sunnis petitioned the Government 'to put down the Taziya procession on the ground that it was an insult to their religion, having on several occasions led to riot and murder and that at best it was a foolish ceremony'.[223] The celebration on the streets was not a major occasion for venting stifling frustration of labourers on the sugar plantations. It should not surprise us therefore that many Indians felt a sense of solidarity with the Shias and it seemed that they took Hosea with some seriousness. 'Each estate has its Taziya', Collens informs us, 'jealously guarded by the labourers who have helped either by subscription or otherwise, to construct it. All the estates in the same locality join together, and form up in procession, sometimes serious quarrels and fights taking place at this stage of the proceedings. Having paraded for sometime, with dancing, cries of 'Hosein Hassan' etc, they at length repair to the sea, if practicable – if not to the nearest body of water – and throwing their Taziyas into it, the ceremony is ended'.[224]

Although the Government did not accede to the Sunnis' petition, certain restrictions were placed upon the festival. Yet in spite of the controversy surrounding Hosea, there is a serious side to it in that many Muslims who had participated (and still do) see it as a 'religious act' in that it entails a vow which once made is considered 'dangerous' if left unfulfilled or carried out improperly. For participants, the Hosea celebration has always been a serious matter, from the beginning of the Tadja's construction through the procession to the blessing rites before the 'tomb of Husein' is finally dumped into the water. It is clear, however, that the secularization of Hosea has made it more a local public 'fete' than a religious celebration indulged in by Muslims and non-Muslims, contrasting sharply with other intra-Muslim celebrations.

Pilgrimage is also important to the followers of Islam and indeed many Muslims have made the Haj (pilgrimage) to Mecca. But while it remains a desirable goal to many Trinidadian Muslims, only a few have become Hajji, men who had actually made the journey. Nevertheless, the inner strength of Islam has been maintained, over the years, and have been strengthened, in the main through such well administered organisations as the Trinidad Muslim League and the Anjuman Sunnat-ul-Jamaat Association, whose 'missionaries' have traversed the island, time and again, to consolidate the then fragile unity of Islam.

Given these historical developments, many take an optimistic view of the future of Islam in Trinidad. Commenting on the Muslims' survival, M.M. Kemal Hydal has expressed the opinion that guided by his principles the Muslim 'can live in harmony with people of different races and creeds while maintaining much of his ethnic identity as an East Indian'.[225]

The life cycle rituals are, according to one writer, of less significance among Muslims than they are among Hindus, essentially because in the Muslim community such rituals are fewer and simpler following the Islamic code which is not as flexible as Hinduism.[226]

At birth a prayer is said without ceremony by an Imam or other person, several days later a fete for women only is held when the mother prays, giving thanks to Allah; and forty days after birth, a dinner is held at which guests bring gifts for the child, food is served, prayers are said and there is dancing and singing. At this time, the mother is regarded as being 'clean'.

Unlike Hindus, dowries do not constitute part of the wedding arangements, although some money (depending on family wealth) is given to the bride. This money known as the Mahaar is a gift to the bride to be spent as she pleases. In the social sphere, however, Muslim marriages are similar to Hindu marriages, though it is said that Muslims engage in 'less open' alcohol consumption on these occasions. And while the rites are different, there is similarity in the eating arrangements and hospitality offered to wedding guests. As mentioned earlier in the case of Guyana, the bride remains closeted in her room with female company, aloof from the festivities.

For both Muslims and Hindus there had been a trend, certainly by the late 1950s, for some marriage ceremonies to be performed in the mosques and temples. An important factor in resorting to this type of wedding has been the lack of money by the family concerned to fund a home wedding.[227]

Once the wedding arrangements have been made the ceremony become the main focus. Officiating at Muslim marriages are the Maulvis who instructs the bridegroom on what has to be said concerning the 'articles of beliefs' (Kalimas). (In the case of a mixed marriage, for example, where a Muslim marries a Christian, the wedding ceremony tended to be conducted according to the procedures followed in both faiths.) Ultimately if the Muslim marriage contract proves unworkable, the ties can be severed on 'certain grounds'.[228]

In death, Muslims by custom are buried, thus posing no problem to East Indians of this faith since they first arrived from India. Once the body is washed and dressed, it is customary to call in the Imam, who offer prayers, followed by a wake (spent more or less in the same way as Hindus), of which orthodox Muslims have tended to complain of the party-like atmosphere. The next day, the body is taken to the mosque, then to the cemetery for burial. Among the taboos observed, at this time of grief, were the abstention of mentruating women from touching the deceased or joining the formal procession to the place of final rest. In their method of burial, the Muslims are careful not to allow the body to come into contact with earth; and a few days after the funeral, a prayer meeting is held, followed by a 'special Kitab', forty days later. On this occasion, after the Imam's prayers and reading of the *Holy Koran*, food is served to those present,[229] thus ending the period of mourning.[230]

Overall the Indian family (especially among Hindus and Muslims) in the Caribbean remain a closely-knit and strong institutional survival than is the residual elements of the Indian caste system and its residual elements. In India also, and during the years of Indian immigration to the Caribbean, the caste system had been undergoing change. Summarizing his survey of the role which caste has been playing in modern India, Srinivas states that under the Constitution of India the practice of Untouchability, in any form is forbidden, an offence punishable according to law,[231] and aimed 'to help promote the educational and economic interests of the weaker sections of the people, and in particular the Scheduled Castes and Scheduled Tribes'.[232]

Among Indians in Trinidad, at least, the Niehoffs' findings that the caste system was 'less necessary for persistence of cultural identity than the Indian family type and heredity religious beliefs'[233] still seem to be relevant.

Christianity, the dominant religion when the Indians entered Trinidad, and African cult beliefs had already proliferated among the susceptible. But much before the Indians' came, the island's initial colonization by the Spaniards (and later, in the eighteenth century with the French planters) reinforced belief in Roman Catholicism which became the dominant religion. Eighty-six years after they first landed, the number of Indians who had converted to the various Christian faiths were as follows: Presbyterianism – 10,335; Roman Catholic – 8,469; Church of England – 3,946 and Others – 433.[234]

Clearly, Presbyterianism was the most successful in terms of numerical superiority among those Indians converted, but its influence was far greater. For the first twenty-three years, however, there was little personal interest either in their conversion to Christianity or in education. They were seen by those who had brought them across the high seas simply as economic units, cheap disposable plantation labour until the Canadian missionary John Morton arrived in 1868 and launched a well thought through two-pronged attack of conversion and education, each aiding the other. Pressured from all sides, during these early years, the Indians clung to the religious beliefs they had brought with them.

Morton, who believed that the only way to salvation was through the Christian God, was revolted by the Indians' beliefs and particularly heathenism. If he was looking for a mission in life, he found it in the challenge that the work among the Indians presented to him. And as it turned out, he did not return to Trinidad simply for the good of his health. He could hardly bear to see the Indians coming from and going back to India unconverted. For their own good, he felt he should impose his religious beliefs upon them, by preaching the gospel of Christ.

Fired with this God-inspired justification and determination, Morton saw the historic Susamachar Church rise in the southern town of San Fernando, the first of the Canadian Mission churches in the island, where the Christian services were communicated to the Indian congregation in Hindi. This was not so much an inspired move as one that Indians have been used to for centuries, namely that they were as Hindus flexible and thus able to absorb other religions. If this had surprised Morton, it need not have, for the Indians would not ultimately altogether abandon their all-embracing Hindu background. This Indian attitude would remain indelibly etched in their collective memory for generations. In recent years, however, Westernised Indian preachers at Susamachar found it expedient to discontinue services in Hindi, thus doing away with Morton's Bible and hymn books in Hindi.[235] Having used Indian preachers, at the outset, in the process of conversion, ironically long after he was gone, Indians would continue his work with a missionary zeal that even he could not have imagined. So much so that the tenuous links with the Canadian Presbyterians had, over the years, become firm bonds of fellowship.

When the process of conversion of the Indians began at Iere Village (where Canadian Mission work was initiated) Morton was surprised at the ease with which his work moved forward. The Indians' willingness could be better understood when it is considered that they were a socially and economically oppressed minority, much looked down upon; and from this perspective (informed by their survival instinct, and invoking their 'coolie cunning') they soon recognised the advantages of becoming Christians; an approach adopted until about the 1930s, a period when non-Christian Indians found it difficult (if not impossible) to get jobs, especially a Government or Foreman's job. If it paid an Indian to convert to Christianity, this became less of a motive between 1937 and 1957 because they found they could get along without it. But so embedded had the 'conversion' way of thinking become that it was difficult to easily disregard the practical benefits Christianity offered.[236] Once set in train, it was difficult to reverse attitudes quickly. But in spite of this, as early as the turn of the century, to his dismay, Morton tells us that in 1905, no longer strangers, the 'two great non-Christian elements' had become deeply committed to their particular faiths even as the Canadian Mission Church developed and became better organised.[237]

The gradual improvement in the Indians' social position, largely due to economic gains, had indeed brought about improved organisation of their traditional religions. During the period from 1930 to 1960 the Hindus had, through the Sanatan Dharma and the Arya Samaj made great strides, having perceived the threat that Christianity posed to the survival of their religious faiths.

The vigilant Hindu leadership was aggressive in counteracting the Christian influence upon Hindus, notably the leader of the Sanatan Dharma who felt that, at heart, Indian Christians, were either Hindus or Muslims and that if the proper approach towards them was adopted these people were not beyond reconversion back to their original faith. This leader disagreed with those in the Hindu community, who 'ostracized' Indian Christians; an exclusion that had for sometime become a real problem. Fortunately this negative attitude had changed, and Christian Indians and Hindus have been able to mix easily at their various gatherings.

If the rate of conversion to Christianity had not improved markedly in recent years, the impact of Christian teaching upon the Indian community has been great. By about 1960, the vast majority of educated Indians had come from Canadian Mission schools, both at Primary and Secondary levels; and given that an integral part of this education was religious instruction in the Presbyterian faith to which all the Indian students (Hindus and Muslims) were exposed, it was to be expected that long before they completed their education, many of these children who had not converted were well versed in Christian theology. A case in point are many of those Hindus who, having attended the Christian Naparima College, found that their faith had been 'shaken'.

Christianity has also furthered the process of acculturation among the Indian Christians, especially those in the towns and the cities, who were better educated and enjoyed a higher standard of living than their rural counterparts. These urban dwellers imbibed Western customs much more readily than Hindus and Muslims, showing a disregard for Hindi as a spoken language. And whereas many Hindu and Muslim women wore the Orhni, few Christian women did so. Dress styles have indeed changed a great deal: fewer Saris were being worn by Christian Indian women who don swim-suits on beaches, while Hindus and Muslims tended to bathe in their dresses. Hairstyles also present contrasts: the younger Christian Indian women wore their hair short, while most Hindus and Muslims tended to wear theirs long, braided hair, Indian style. Not only are Indian Christians' food tastes largely 'westernized', they also prefer to eat with a knife and fork instead of eating with their fingers, a transition that has become increasingly widespread among East Indians generally.

Many Indian Christians, however, still draw the line by abstaining from pork and beef consumption. Overall, while the Indian Christians gravitate more and more towards a Westernized way of life, culturally they seem reluctant to lose their indentities as Hindus and Muslims.[238] In the process of 'creolization', the Indian community have adapted to a remarkable degree, as they came under the influence of local folk beliefs and practices. In the densely populated Indian community of Siparia, in south Trinidad, there is a well known Catholic Church called La Divina Pastora which, dating from the Spanish period, houses a wooden image of the Virgin. The Indians are said to worship here because they believe in the miraculous power of the Virgin, who returned to the Church each time it had been removed. On homage day to La Divina, officially recognised at Easter time, the Virgin is taken out of the church and a procession follows through the streets, reminiscent of the Virgins taken of churches in Spain, during SEMANA SANTA (Holy Week). While few Indians attend the ceremonies on this occasion, which is regarded as a 'creole' affair, a considerable number of them have been known to congregate at the church from various parts of the island on the night of Holy Thursday, to pray and make offerings, using the medium of their Hindi language. The Indians refer to La Divina as SIPARU MAI, meaning 'mother of Siparia'. So strong was their belief that mothers prayed for the health and strength of their children and barren wives hoped for sons. Apart from the oil, candles and rice offerings, jewellery including earrings, necklaces, bracelets and other valuables were left as offerings by Indian women to SIPARU MAI.[239]

Indians (Hindus and Muslims) have also made pilgrimages, in large numbers, to the Roman Catholic monastery of St.Benedict high up in the hills of northern Trinidad. Furthermore, Indians of all faiths also pay homage to the dead on 'All Hallows Eve' with elaborate preparations just a few days before, cleaning and banking sunken graves, and on the eve of All Saints Night relatives of the deceased light candles and diyas on the mounds marking the graves upon which flowers (and depending on individual taste) oil and/or rum were placed. Indians of all faiths (Hindus, Muslims and Christians) are represented on this night of illumination by candles and oil lamps, and many of them keep vigil until the lights go out. And, while Christmas and New Year's Day have also influenced the Indian community, it is not unusual to find Hindu deities in Christian homes and vice-versa.[240]

Overall, here, as in Guyana, the Canadian Mission Presbyterian Church had through their self-conscious activities encouraged, energetic and enterprising Indians to become educated, and thereby contributed enourmously in the process of the integration of the Indians

Supernatural beliefs had also, over the years, influenced many Indians in Trinidad (mainly in the rual areas), regardless of the faith they professed. Gradually a folk religion emerged among them, involving JUMBIES (spirits) and the practice of OBEAH or sorcery.

From the moment of their arrival, the process of religious incorporation began, and in time, they absorbed a good deal of the beliefs and practices of their Afro-Trinidadian neighbours. Given that Hinduism, as it existed in India, has been able to absorb elements of other religious beliefs, including influences from Buddhism,

Islam and Christianity, 'a peculiarity of all Indian sects is that in matters of belief they are not exclusive nor hostile to novelties', wrote Eliot. 'When an idea wins converts it is the instinct of the older sects to declare that it is compatible with their teaching or that they have something similar or just as good'.[241] Such flexibility, it seems was also present among Trinidadian Indians, who assimilated certain aspects of the religious concepts of their Afro-Trinidadian neighbours.[242]

Generally settled in the quiet countryside, East Indians found themselves amidst the 'mysterious shadowy world of spirits'. A JUMBIE, in the context in which the Indians used the word, referred to supernatural spirits, usually meaning malicious, bad. Among the Indians, the better-known spirits were the LAGAHU (described as a werewolf) and the SUKOIYAA ( vampire), both of whom came from Afro-Trinidadian culture. The LAGAHU which stalks around at night is said to be ridden by the the Devil who pays him; and the appearance of excessive hairiness, bruised hands and knees at day time, were evidence of being a LAGAHU at night.

A SUKOIYAA, on the other hand, is a female spirit which, not unlike the LAGAHU, is transformed from being human into an evil thing at night. In its nocturnal pursuits, this spirit is said to shed its skin, roam the countryside and suck the blood of people while they sleep. While few, if any, SUKOIYAAS have been caught, in theory at least, it is said that a suspected person could be found out if a visit to her house was made just before dawn in search of her skin which is shed and hidden under a mortar. If salt is rubbed into this skin, it will cause irritation to the person in the morning, thus revealing her identity.[243]

In addition to these two spirits, there are the DIABLESSE, a 'clove-footed witch', in the form of an attractive woman, who at night entices men off their path; and the CHURAIL, an Indian spirit in the form of a woman who had failed to survive her pregnancy and/or child birth, and whose evil intentions were directed to the next wife of her former husband, who should replace her. Then there are the feared Spanish spirits who are said to still live in such trees as the silk-cotton, neem, calabash and mango trees. Moreover, evil spirits are believed to take possession of some people who are endowed with the power of 'big-eye', 'mal-de-ojo' or 'najar'. Of course, Indians in certain parts of the island have been more susceptible to such beliefs than in others. The Niehoffs, commenting on their research conducted more than thirty years ago in the Oropouche area, stated that it was their clear belief that the Indians were 'deeply immersed in a welter of spirit beliefs, quite apart from the participation of individuals in their accepted religious faiths. Young children are indoctrinated by informal means ... Even members of the Christian community are affected by this widespread belief in supernatural beings. Undoubtedly, due to the influence of Christian religious teachings, there is less spirit belief among these people than among non-Christians'.[244] Apart from belief in the supernatural world, the Indians also believed, to some extent in OBEAH, the local Trinidadian practice, which can be used for either good or evil. Often the Obeahman was called upon in times of sickness to restore good health and to harmonize marital relations and love-affairs, *inter alia*. Niehoff found that in the realm of magic and spirits much of what the Indians had known in India was similar to what they had found among Afro-Trinidadians, 'a form of adaptation to local conditions' which did not lead to surrendering their traditional beliefs. 'Hinduism has never been known as a religion of exclusive beliefs', Niehoff concludes, 'so it put no strain on these people to accept new forms of dealing with the supernatural'.[245]

Outside the Oropouche area, there has been little evidence, since these findings, as to the extent to which the spirit world and OBEAH had affected the Indian population.

The historical and continuing Hindu religious links between East Indians and Afro-Trinidadians are also evident in the Shango/Orisha cult in Trinidad. While Indians have congregated largely around the sugar estates, they have not confined themselves to these areas. Once they were free from the shackles of the laws of indenture, they began to make their way into the wider society and today they could be found in various villages and towns across the island. Contact between Indians and Afro-Trinidadians (moreso in some areas than others) has made it possible for an East Indian Orisha cult leader to emerge in the 1970s; and elsewhere in the island (at Longdenville, Tacarigua, Tunapuna, Curepe, Enterprise and Moruga), Indians have been involved in Orisha cults. It was found that 'through the Shango/Orisha cult Africans of Yoruba ancestry in Trinidad have not only integrated religion but also the whole community – the outsiders, the non-African groups, the late-comers and the East Indians'.

The Shango/Orisha cult has been described as an amalgam of the Yoruba traditional religion, Catholicism and the Baptist faith. Referring to the view that 'syncretism of the Yoruba/Orisha tradition in Trinidad was not only through the acculturation of Christian practices, but to accommodation of Hinduism and Islam', Mahabir and Maharaj states that the 'integrated complex of drum, chant, dance, liturgy, shaped ritual, spirit possession and animal sacrifice which mark the worship of Gods in the Orisha cult are akin to the Kali-Mai (Black Mother) cult of Hinduism in Trinidad'. They go on to demonstrate the relationship between elements of the Hindu and Muslim religions and the Shango/Orisha cults. 'By incorporating African, Indian and other elements', they conclude, 'the cult members contribute to the perpetuation of a multicultural heritage in Trinidad'.[246]

## Food and Music

In India, we are informed of a structured attitude towards food. Srinivas informs us that 'Brahmins are usually vegetarians, abstaining even from eggs. The Shudra castes eat eggs and meat. Pork is inferior to mutton and pork eaters to mutton eaters. Beef eaters are the lowest of all'.[247] But, as Debysingh argued, there is flexibility in these traditional relationships between caste status and dietary practices, stating that 'the taboo against raising and eating poultry, varies from region to region and between urban and rural areas.[248]

While both Muslims and Hindus avoid eating pork, many Christian Indians indulge in non-vegetarianism.[249] If the lower castes have been identified as the polluted meat eaters (after all they were among the poorest of the poor and simply
could not afford to be too choosy!) the caste organisation itself was subjected to
the 'polluting' effects of both the migration and indentureship experience of Indians in the Caribbean in relation to food preparation, while planters and estate
managers turned a blind eye to caste observances.[250] But according to Lowenthal,
in spite of its dissolution as a functional form, caste has surivived as 'an aspect of
prejudice, a matter of style, an ingredient of personality'.[251] Niehoff has also commented on the food-caste relationship. 'Although food taboos have been greatly
relaxed', he wrote, 'the eating of pork by many but the low castes is still repugnant'.[252] Yet, in some parts of the island, there has been a change in the Indians'
attitude towards chicken and eggs. It was found that 'almost all' rural families in
the Oropouche area kept chickens,[253] even though goat's meat was most popular.

In her study 'Cultural change and Adaptation as Reflected in the Meat Eating
Habits of the Trinidad Indian Population', Debysingh pointed out that while vege-
tarianism 'has all but disappeared' among the island's Hindus, Muslims are more
strict in their observance of the traditional taboo against eating pork. Concluding
her research, she found that 'substantial changes have occurred in dietary habits
reflecting an overall integration into a Trinidad cultural milieu and environment.
At the same time, the persistence of certain meat avoidances, especially with regard to beef and pork, remains a strong indicator of the cultural distinctiveness of
the Indian population'.[254]

Nevertheless, after their long presence in the island, it would be surprising if
there was not some merging of food habits in what has clearly become a multi-
racial, multi-religious society. Indeed Indian eating habits have become nationally
recognised, manifest in the 'barra-man', 'doubles', roti and dhal pourri and curry
dishes, not only in Trinidad, but throughout the Caribbean where Indians have
settled. But if eating habits are integral to the culture which is dynamic, ever-changing, then the purity of East Indian culture becomes questionable. Recent research
done on the 'Transitional Changes and Merging of the Eating Pattern of the Trinidad East Indian' have found that while there are many Indians as well as members
from other ethnic groups, who would wish to 'creolize' the East Indian at a stroke,
such an achievement would be impossible, for it seems that the evolutionary process of a Trinidad and Tobago culture will indeed become reality only 'as the various
races accept and reject those parts of the foreign culture impinging on their own'.

Thus after more than one hundred years of exposure to acculturative influences,
and in the face of the continuing pressure from Creole society, the East Indians
have doggedly persevered and against mighty odds have managed to maintain their
cultural identity. So much so that in recent times, there has been 'an unusual cultural revival', with such large organisations as the Sanatan Dharma Maha Sabha

and the Trinidad Muslim League promoting various aspects of Indian life and heritage. In the melting-pot of Caribbean cultures, one might well ask: Is there a future for Indian culture in Trinidad? J.C. Jha wrote in the early 1970s that Trinidad had formally recognised Indian culture and, as manifestations of this, he argued that Indian history and culture were integral parts of the educational programme at the St. Augustine campus of the University of the West Indies, and that courses in Hindi and Urdu were held elsewhere in the country.[255] Was this view too optimistic?

At that time, others felt that in Trinidad the degree of cultural alienation of the Indian community was pronounced. In an article published in 1974, a Trinidadian economist, having considered the trend which 'within the next five years or so' would rob the Indians of the foundations of their culture, warned that the recent upsurge of East Indian cultural pride was devoid of its spiritual and philosophical foundations and as such, 'the religious value Ahimsa (non-violence) which orientates the individual towards non-aggression will no longer be as persuasive as it has been in past generations'.[256] If this sounded too gloomy, there was more to come. He predicted that 'politicization' of the East Indians would lead to further alienation from the wider society.

Such alienation, as existed, was widespread and deeply felt during 1979. Given that calypso and steelband music are well-known as part of the cultural heritage of Trinidad and Tobago (indeed there were two Indian calypsonians: Rajah and Prince) the winning calypso competition, the 'Caribbean Man', aroused a national controversy as the definition of 'Caribbean Man' which related essentially to people of African descent, thus excluding other ethnic groups. Moreover, calypsoes and calypsonians tended to project African identity and culture exclusively, and when reference is made to Hindus, as in Lord Shorty's 'Om Shanti', objections were raised by the Sanatan Dharma Maha Sabha, which represented an estimated 250,000 Hindus. Others, such as followers of the Baptists and Hindu faiths, protested against the 'desecration' and 'mockery' of their religious beliefs by calypsoes.[257] Hindu priests had no doubt that the calypso was being used as a medium through which fun is poked at them.[258]

Historically between 1946 and 1986, for example, the image of the Indians in calypso have been reflected in the various stages of Afro-Indian relations arising from 'external situations and internal developments'. The calypso, as an artform, has been used to lampoon Trinidad and Tobago's public and political figures; and in these attacks 'race' has always been integral. Indians who were earlier seen as 'pariahs' have been recently viewed with envy and some respect for their material improvements. Yet, in spite of this change from comic figure to admired group, and from laughable and despised race to envied group, today, Indians still remain 'outsiders'. According to Trotman who, echoing a familiar concern, warned that the Indians 'are still seen ... as an outside clan, not fully Trinidadian with a natural right to the national Trinidad inheritance: they are an outside club of usurpers who, overnight, have stolen the patrimony of the real Trinidadians – those of African origins. The Indians are still pictured as a monolith without religious or class differences. The task of complete acceptance and total integration is still in progress and will not be observed in the calypso until it is a reality in the society'.[259]

If according to one estimate, by 1980, the population of Trinidad was likely to show a greater proportion of Indians *vis-à-vis* Afro-Trinidadians, the exclusion of Indians and other groups was a significant omission from the calypso 'Caribbean Man' which called for Caribbean unity. Furthermore, it was argued that if cultural change was to be effected in Trinidad, Indians must be prepared to participate fully in national life to bring about greater socio-economic and political equality, thus avoiding the elevation of Afro-Trinidadian culture and identity at the expense of Indo-Trinidadian culture. 'All in all', wrote Deosaran, 'the culture problems of Indians and Africans here (in Trinidad) must be shared with each group. The calypso, as a popular and effective social stimulus could play a significant role without unduly offending the feelings of certain cultural groups in our midst'.[260] Indeed the earlier history prior to the Muharram massacre in 1884 (at the height of this Muslim festival's popularity) showed clearly that Africans were regular participants in the Muharram celebrations; and that the Tassa drum was instrumental in the development of the innovative steelpan which was central to Carnival as a street festival, and a source of national pride.[261] Though gradual, change is bringing the two social groups closer. Today, some aspects of Indian music in Trinidad (more than anywhere else in the Caribbean) is beginning to reflect its essentially Caribbean orientation in the mixture of musical styles that are integrated in the unprecedented calypsoes of Drupatee, the female Indian singer (significantly a 'coolie woman' singing 'African' music in a male-dominated musical genre) Ricki Jai, Kenny J, Kanchan and the new and popular 'chutney soca'. Nevertheless, Indian films and music continue to enjoy great popularity among Indians, especially the young.

Commenting on the problem of cultural organisation for the Indians, however, Singh has directed attention to the social level of leadership within the Indian community, where a 'leadership vacuum' had developed. He feared this could lead to 'ethnic disintegration' for most of the Indians' problems are deeply rooted in the 'play of power forces in the society'.[262]

While both commentators direct our attention to politics, Dookheran has attempted to explain why: 'An economic system that creates the need for a trade-off between cultural persistence and economic betterment, accepts implicitly a strategy for the absorption of a sub-culture into the dominant culture'.[263] But such an 'absorption' has not been realised. On the contrary, the Indians (in the main Hindus) have transformed their villages into bastions of Indian culture; and remarkably this cultural 'persistence' is being maintained by Hindu youth.

But this is not to say that East Indians, including Hindus, have been immune to the pressures of creolization. For it is clear that 'Indo-Caribbeans make contributions to the dynamic, existing creole culture at the same time as that culture acts on them to reshape their cultural identities'. Allahar and Varadarajan add that on a 'country by country basis, the forces of creolization are forging new cultures within and not necessarily among the different Caribbean countries'. Is it a question of ethnicity taking precedence over nationalism or vice-versa? And do both relate to class? Given the arguments put forward in debating these questions, it becomes quite clear that a common Caribbean culture is untenable.

In comparing East Indians in Trinidad and Guyana, particularly in relation to the absence of Hindi film music in public transport vehicles in Trinidad and its presence in Guyana, the differences between the two countries become clearer. For one thing, the East Indians in Guyana form the majority, over half of the population, and they have had (and now again have) an Indian as Head of the Government, thus bolstering the confidence of the Indo-Guyanese. Through the sheer force of numbers, the Indians have managed to maintain their cultural activities, but this does not mean, as mentioned above, that they were untouched by creolization. Adding to a sense of their 'Indianness' and cultural inclusiveness as the People's National Congress's rule, lasting some three decades, a period which most Indo-Guyanese will never forget. But this regime in itself did not, and has not, deflected or derailed the insistent process of creolization. For, as researchers have has pointed out, the Indo-Guyanese is 'more Guyanese ... than he or she is Indian'. But this statement is much more complex and contentious than it seems. For example, it could not be strictly applied to either Trinidad or Guyana, where during the Black Power period and the racial violence of the 1960s, respectively, East Indians rallied around race,[264] rather than class or nationalism.

By comparison, the position of the East Indians in Trinidad is quite different. Economically, they have achieved a good standing, though they do not constitute half of the population (many now argue, that they are the largest racial group) and they never had an East Indian as Head of State. As one of the former British islands, Trinidad is also more of a part of the English-speaking Caribbean, than is Guyana. The major difference between the two countries, however, is that Trinidad produces oil, a product that had a radical impact on Indo-Trinidadian culture. The oil prosperity had ushered in a demand for, and a marked increase in, North-American consumer goods and values, which brought added pressure upon Indo-Trinidadians to become even more creolized. So much so, that they have been described as being more 'American' than Indian.

By contrast, Guyana's economic base has been less diverse, being largely oriented towards the sugar industry, of which East Indians have long been the mainstay. If concentration on this crop has bred conversatism among Guyana's East Indians, it has also encouraged cultural assertiveness. And if the oil wealth has helped to modernize (to infuse a sense of individual freedom) sections of Indo-Trinidadians, sugar has, in effect, served to maintain the isolation of the Indo-Guyanese, thus preserving their 'Indianness' and emphasizing their belief in community and survival, rather than individual concerns.

Indo-Trinidadians, on the other hand, have increasingly demanded and applied modern methods to production and have, as a consequence, grown accustomed to change. But between them and Afro-Trinidadians there is still a 'sullen separation that masquerades as racial harmony', which is still today clear to any observer. Returning to the public/private attitude of the Indo-Trinidadian taxi-drivers as regards playing Hindi film music in their cars, Allahar and Varadarajan wrote:

> It is perhaps, not so strange after all then, that … He will not play his tape of Lata's (Mangeshkar) Love Songs because 'Blackman' in the back will find 'coolie music' provocative, in isolation of pan-Caribbean cultural norms, an unwelcome intrusion into the public domain of a culture, of a way of life, that he does not want to comprehend.

But 'Blackman' is not the only passenger that might not like 'coolie music', for there is a new generation of Indo-Trinidadians in their early twenties who are 'entirely creolized'.[265] So while sections of Hindu youth strive to maintain their 'Indianness', other sections of Indo-Trinidadian youth embrace a creole culture. The latter of the two tendencies, some experts believe, is the direction which offers the best prospects for racial harmony in Trinidad.[266]

# JAMAICA

## *Awareness of Cultural Heritage*

Among the thousands of Indian indentured immigrants who went to Jamaica, there were many skilled agriculturists and artisans such a jewellers, carpenters, blacksmiths, potters and tailors,[267] from whose ranks the cultural fabric of the Indians were woven into an ever-changing pattern.

Although throughout the period of indentureship, the Indians were motivated by a deep pride in their cultural and religious heritage, the end of indentureship did not lessen or end the Indians' dependence upon the plantations for jobs and housing. From the story of John Parboosingh,[268] (formerly Parboodat) we get a better insight into what it was like, as a free Indian, to settle in Jamaica, raise a family and relate to the community as as a whole.

Through his indentureship position as a Headman, Parboosingh gained invaluable experience that served him well later. Relatively young, single and ambitious (he was seventeen years old when he emigrated to Jamaica from Faizabad in India) his thriftiness enabled him to open a small shop at Hopewell Pen, along the island's hilly north coast. Here the Indians came to buy food: codfish, herring, rice, flour and salt. With limited capital, twenty pounds saved over the ten years of his indentureship, it was difficult to maintain the viability of his shop. Yet he survived that crucial early period.

The transportation of goods bought in the Kingston, posed a 'very big problem', because of mountainous roads. Indeed, Parboosingh, of necessity, regularly visited the capital, part of the way on horseback and the rest of the journey by train. After conducting his business in Kingston, he was relieved to return to the cool and pleasant countryside, and the warmth of the Hopewell community.

In a relatively short time, the hard-working young man had got his shop-keeping business off to a resonably good start, laying a foundation that was sound enough to allow room for expansion. It was about this time that he married a Christian woman, Frances de Rizzio, whose family was well respected. Her father, Richard de Rizzio, who had emigrated from Goa in India, spoke several languages and it seemd natural that he should be employed as an 'Interpreter' in Jamaica's Immigration office. One of Richard's concern, we learn from entries in his diary, was the distress he felt 'at the injustices they (the Indians) suffered', due to the problem of language (their inability to speak English) and the 'callousness of local officials'. Ivan Parboosingh, who had read his grandfather's diary, tells us of one Indian labourer who was insane and instead of being admitted to the Mental Hospital was locked up in prison, because the language he spoke could not be understood by anyone at the Hospital. Another entry records the story of an Indian who was imprisoned for stealing some bananas. He came out from jail, to find that his attractive wife was pregnant for the Overseer. The enraged man killed his wife. 'He killed the wrong person', wrote the Interpreter, Richard de Rizzio.

His regard for common human decency and welfare of the Indians knew no bounds, even though their interests were supposed to be safeguarded by the office of the Protector of Immigrants and legal enactments. The problem of language crops up, time and again. 'Efforts to obtain even a hearing were often in vain and might even lead to imprisonment', wrote Ivan Parboosingh, because the authorities appealed to, had been impatient in their reaction since they 'could not understand the applicant's language and was ignorant of the true situation'. Barrack rooms were still the order of the day, but there was evidence of better accommodation, here and there. At Hopewell estate, the rooms occupied by the Indians were frowned upon by Afro-Jamaicans, a prejudice rooted in slavery. No vestige of their former bondage was acceptable after their long struggle for freedom.

Freed from their own brand of bondage, the Indians were also seeking improvements, by rejecting the houses they lived in. Ivan Parboosingh describes how these new structures were erected by the Indian labourers, stating that they 'built huts with logwood or other hardwood uprights, neatly wattled with narrow strips of bamboo and the whole wall covered with white marl that was softened with water to cover the wood smoothly. The net result resembled a white concrete wall. The roof might be of zinc or dried guinea grass neatly laid on. The floor was made of native lumber. Labour for building was provided by what was called "morning work"', usually performed on Saturdays by friends, who more often than not, were paid in kind, for example, by being provided with food and drink over the three Saturdays of work needed before completion of a small hut. Of course, those who could have afforded it, built more ambitious structures with imported lumber, zinc or shingles and glass windows, provided their workmen with 'regular pay'.

The growing Indian population had important implications on John Parboosingh's life. Fortunately for him, his wife was a serious-minded person, with a strong belief in Christianity. She was also very pragmatic, displaying considerable entreprenurial skill. On the other hand, Parboosingh, committed to his Hindu faith, through which he became deeply involved with the people around him. In this sense, his shop was a blessing, serving as the ideal meeting place where a cross-section of people came and went, on a regular basis. If he was practical, his wife was even more so, a good manager 'adept at planning and ordering their life together'. Their son, Ivan, puts the seal on the success of their marriage, stating that they 'gave to all their children a wonderful start in life and splendid examples of India-born values on which to build their lives as Jamaicans'.

If Parboosingh's shop was a focal point of interest, how did it relate to the community? The expansion of the shop to include a bar and grocery, was underscored by an increased demand. The decision to open a bar was, however, not an easy one for the Parboosingh not least because of the problem of maintaining 'strict discipline'. Law and order were in deed provided by a plain-clothes policeman, whose main task was to deal with unruly customers. The addition of a store which sold shoes, cloths and hats, among other items, made the premises even more attractive.

For a religious man like Parboosingh, the bar posed the problem of encouraging over-indulgence in alcohol and alcoholism. But while this negative aspect was to be discouraged, he recognised the positive value of the bar-room to those who congregated there. It became 'the only place where there were benches and adequate light', as Ivan put it, where not only alcohol, but also bread, bulla biscuits and tinned food were bought. Here the labourers came washed and cleaned, after a hard day's work and at weekends. Many could not afford alcoholic drinks until Friday when they were paid, but there was no doubt about the sense of community, which was reflected, for example, when a stranger entered the village and came to the bar. Such a person, as a matter of course, came under suspicion, because he was not a 'born ya' ( local person) but a 'come ya', a newcomer; and at times of stolen property or civil disturbance the stranger came under immediate suspicion, the onus being placed upon him to prove his innocence.

The bar and grocery store was also an emporium of news from home and abroad, gained from the *Daily Gleaner* and disseminated to the people through Parboosingh's reading from 'the throne' (a part of the shop counter) of the entire newspaper, including the advertisements. Thus the Indian labourers, semi-literate and illiterate, were at least, heard the news which seemed more easily communicated as interpreted and translated by a fellow-Indian. The alcohol, the talk, the gossip, the news, the idea of maintaining comradeship, was all worth it, for the men who walked about two miles or more on difficult tracks to get to and from Parboosingh's bar and grocery store.

For Ivan, then a boy growing up, the bar and its customers was fascinating, especially the transformation that the consumption of alcohol brought about in a few individuals, such as Mass Charley, who tended to challenge others to fist fights. The various states of inebriation of the men, brought out hitherto hidden aspects of their lives, stories handed-down from their forebears and jokes, some lampoons at other individuals and some smutty, which often raised raucous laughter. At other times, there was shouting, foul language and brawls, the very fears of the peace-loving, clean-living and Christian scripture-loving proprietor Parboosingh. Though he remained committed to his Hindu faith, aware of the dominance and relevance of Jamaican life, he encouraged his wife to raise their children as Christians.

The low wages received by the Indians, necessarily, meant that they had to spend all their meagre earnings. Yet they were a hardy and hopeful people; and at times of distress (for example, when they had to pay court fines or doctor's fees and in times of sickness) the communal jahaji bhai spirit came to the rescue. At times of death, the bereaved family received the attention and sympathy of the community. The local carpenter, for instance, would offer his services, free of charge, con-structing the coffin made of wood supplied by Parboosingh's store. Funeral ex-penses were beyond the reach of many Indians and it was just as well that the store-owner wrote off such debts.

Weddings too, were special occasions, at which elements of the creolisation of the Indians were clearly in evidence in the dress style. The Indians would put on formal wear – 'stiff collar, black bow tie, black suit with tails, even spats were worn over the shoes', wrote Ivan Parboosingh. 'The women wore long silk dresses with ribbons all over and a big hat with a veil. There had to be a carriage to take the couple to and from the church. At first a buggy with a coachman, then later a car. At home there was usually a roasted pig etc with a huge wedding cake. There were no invitations – the whole village attended'. And to round off the English flavour of the proceedings, witty and eloquent speeches were made. Alas, not everyone could marry in such grand fashion. The point was made that unmarried couples were no less wedded to each other and devoted to their children than those who were more fortunate to have the full pomp of marriage Jamaican style.

Other important occasions for the Indians were Christmas, the excitement and the prospect of financial gain through gambling, or attendance at cricket matches and horse-racing. Saturday was market day which was of special importance to Indians, who displayed for sale the products of their labour on the land in the form of a wide range of fruits vegetables and ground provisions. Although bare-footed, the Indian sellers wore bright-coloured clothes, especially the women, who bar-gained all day with customers. While their husbands or partners visited the rum-shops, women tended to take care of business.

Unlike Indians in the villages in Trinidad, in Jamaica, the family clothes, as Parboosingh recalled, was washed on Monday by women at the nearby riverside, a place about a mile away from their homes, and to which enough food was taken to sustain them for the time the washing lasted. A special feature of this laundry work which made it less than a chore, was the accompanying songs and hymns, heartily sung by the women. Moreover, Sunday was the day of worship; and as time wore on, most of the Indians became Christians (though many retained their Hindu beliefs) and some of whom were regular and strict church-goers.

By all accounts, the Indians were peaceful and conflict with Afro-Jamaicans was minimal. With time, however, it was observed that the the level of alcohol consumption among the Indians in Hopewell had increased. Some of them were arrested for drunk and disorderly conduct, but surprisingly, we are told, they never took the opportunity of swearing at the police in Hindi. The Indians also enjoyed smoking ganja, which they had brought with them from India. Unlike the consumption of alcohol, the effects of ganja-smoking seemed less harmful.

John Parboosingh was not as fluent in English as he would like to have been. Yet, he symbolised a figure of wisdom and authority, a man who gave practical help and advice to those who needed it in the Hopewell community, when this was necessary. And to add to his business enterprise, having won the trust and confidence of his fellow-Indians, he was encouraged to to keep in an 'iron safe' the savings of those for whom this was possible. Many Indians, after completing their ten-year indentureships still desired to go back to India. Many prayed that this would happen one day. Among those who had been offered a return passage to India, about this time, was Chatterpaul, who having saved ten pounds, and against Parboosingh's advice, spent it all on a puja, before leaving the island. He was never heard of again. For the majority of Indians, however, Jamaica had already become the accepted land where they would spend the rest of their lives.

As in Trinidad and Guyana, the Indians settled near the plantations on lands leased to them. These settlements were the early centres of Indian culture in Jamaica and with time, as the Indians migrated from the plantations to the villages and towns, they were confronted with certain realities. In this stratified society they had to cope with the fact that their religions were discriminated against; Indian marriages were unrecognised; Indian children were bastards and property rights were infringed. This institutional discrimination not only encouraged 'abuse and ridicule' of Hindus and Muslims, but also a dampening of participation in the Indians' cultural activities.[269] Overall, the lack of recognition of Hindu and Muslim marriages, coupled with inadequate medical and educational facilities, provided ideal conditions for the Christian missionaries to intervene. And not surprisingly, the missionary 'services' offered were coercive to the psychologically and physically disadvantaged Indians in Jamaica, who were driven into the process of being culturally Westernized.

The Indians' cultural background was reflected in the fact that an estimated 72 per cent of the 36,412 who had arrived in Jamaica came predominantly from Uttar Pradesh, Bihar and adjacent areas in northern India, more than 90 per cent were Hindus, while approximately 10 per cent were Muslims.

Within this Jamaican Indian society, as it evolved, according to one account, among the characteristic features identified,were 'The Panchayat System; the joint family system; distinctly Indian language, music, dance and food; regular celebrations of Hindus and Muslim festivals; philosophical and transcendental approach to everyday life; ... faith in Hinduism and Islam and various purificatory rites and some practices associated with the religious traditions'.[270] Counteracting insistent pressures to discourage Indian culture in Jamaica, the Indians have managed to maintain a deep sense of their cultural heritage.

Indeed a semblance of the structure of Indian society was replicated in Jamaica. The Panchayats which, during indentureship were concerned primarily with the general welfare of the community were to be found in the post-indentureship period representing several Indian settlements near the plantations. But in Jamaica, they were not as effective as they were in the more populous villages in Guyana and Trinidad. By the 1930s, the Panchayats began to lose credibility and Indians migrated to different parts of the island in search of economic betterment. The Panchayats were further weakened by the Indians' adoption of the Christian religion [271] and although by the 1960s, there was a marked absence of the Panchayat system, older Indians in Jamaica still believed in its merits.

The question of cultural integration is, of course, not only one between the Indians and other groups in the wider society, but also, and perhaps to a lesser extent, an intra-Indian group issue. And although there were attempts to create inter-caste divisions within the Hindu community, by about the 1940s, such attempts were not renewed. Furthermore, Hindu-Muslim relations in Jamaica, unlike those in Guyana and Trinidad, had also been cordial in spite of attempts to arouse ill-feeling.[272]

Prior to the mid-1940s the joint-extended family systems were prevalent among Indians. But socio-economic changes in Jamaican society since the 1940s had forced changes on these systems as younger Indians settled for more freedom by leaving home after marriage.[273] Nevertheless, within the joint and extended families, the bonds of 'ingrained feelings, detachments and responsibilities' remained. In addition, older Indians continued to exercise authority, accepting responsibility for the younger Indians who, in turn, obliged with regular visits to the family and by attending to the needs of the old. In this, the relationships between members of the family remained more or less traditional. Until the 1950s, arranged marriages at an early age was common among the Indians. This general 'Indianness', however (present in India, Trinidad and Guyana) was rare in Jamaica, where 'self-centredness' was observed among the educated Indians. Additionally, personal and family life and purificatory rites[274] among Hindus were also observed. Regarding dress, since 1900 there had been a gradual adoption of Western clothes. Language and food were also subjected to inevitable change; and from about the 1950s, Hindi was less frequently used. Urdu also lapsed into disuse for want of 'devotion and dedication' among youths. Indian food, however, has had a major impact in that 'curry goat' has become one of Jamaica's national dishes.

Indian housing and furniture and kitchen appliances, faced with more modern designs, have also been gradually replaced.[275] But certain traditions in music and dance have persisted in the use of musical instruments which the indentured Indians had taken to Jamaica, such as the Mridangam and Dholak, Nagara and Tassa. And as recently as the 1950s they sang classical songs, music such as Bhairavi, Thumri, Dadra, Todi, Rag Malhar and Rag Basant. Folk music among the Indians has always been popular. These praise-worthy developments were, however, relative, and the much-needed contact with Indians from Guyana and Trinidad had led to the introduction of new influences in Jamaica.[276]

## Cultural Renaissance?

Amidst the 'cultural renaissance' in Jamaica, by the early 1970s, Indian music had achieved new heights with the formation of a few 'professional' musical bands; and by mid-decade there was demand for recordings of Indian folk music.

If Indian folk dance was used to express emotion, this was not well-received by those Indians from northern India with an Islamic cultural background, who attributed 'low status' to dancing and dancers. Not surprisingly, few women performed. Indeed, prior to 1921 there were no professional women performers. But while folk dances were popular, new elements have been integrated in Indian dancing such as a 'carnival type reggae' dance, and 'free style dances mixing Indian hand and feet movements with Western ballroom styles'. During the 1970s there had been renewed efforts to gain official recognition for Indian music and dancing Jamaica.[277]

Apart from the 'decorative patterns' of Indian folk art among Indians in Jamaica, since the 1930s, there has been a decline in art and craft (seen for example in the Taziya at the Hosea festival), pottery, carpentry and jewellery have been some of the Indians' main contributions. In fact, Indian jewellery had made an 'enduring impression' not only in Jamaica, but throughout the Indo-Caribbean diaspora.

Indian festivals have also had a special significance. Although the decline of Hinduism and Islam has led to the observance of fewer religious festivals, as in Guyana and Trinidad, the Hindus celebrate Divali and Phagwah, while the Muslims celebrate Eid and the festival of Hosea (Muharram or Hosein) has evolved into a 'modern secular carnival of Indian culture'.[278]

As a separate cultural group, Indian-Afro-Jamaican relations have been described as being 'fairly cordial' and inter-marriage, it was argued, has helped to bring about greater understanding between the two groups. Nevertheless, one authority offers us this observation: 'The Afro-Jamaicans ... were generally guided by the superficial mask of superiority for being similar to the Europeans in church affiliation, dress and language ... (a situation which existed throughout the Caribbean) the Creole as a rule, looks down on the Indian: he is semi-civilized, he speaks a barbarous language and his manners are barbarian'.[279] At school, however, Hindu children 'paid heavy psychological penalties' for their uncompromising stand as Hindus.

If the Indians in Jamaica were an 'orderly people' (in 1848 only about twelve people were imprisoned),[280] their 'alien' religious and cultural beliefs, in short, their heathenism, were seen as a threat to the host society. The de-culturization process, enforced on the plantations, was speeded-up by the Christian missionaries. In response, by the mid-1970s, the Indians' attempt to halt the trend of accepting anglicized Christian names were made through the adoption of Indian names. Added pressures were put on the Indians to adopt Western cultural values, through the denial of urgent, adequate medical and educational facilities. But foregoing such vital needs was too great a sacrifice. And so the Christian missionaries appeared as a god-send. Thus many oppressed Indians traded-in their 'religious and cultural identity' to the satisfaction of the Presbyterian Church. Two main factors helped to facilitate this change among the Indians: first the 'inherent Hindu characteristic of tolerance and respect for other religions; and secondly, the conversion of a few local sirdars to Christianity', who did their new masters bidding.[281] Further, the teaching of the Bible in Canadian Mission Schools helped to consolidate the emerging Indian Christian group.

In effect, Indian culture was discouraged while the dominant Western and church values offered opportunities for education, jobs and social mobility. Thus it was argued that the process of deculturization was facilitated by separation from India and a lack of strong Indian leadership. Moreover, after the end of Indian indentured immigration in 1917, the Indians in Jamaica were further isolated by the fact that they were physically a long distance away from the larger Caribbean Indian populations in Trinidad and Guyana.[282]

Among the more important factors hampering the establishment of Indian culture in Jamaica, Ehrlich has cited 'poverty, illiteracy and lack of essential privileges; discriminatory laws; emotional and religious exploitation and de-Indianization activities of the Christian missionaries; lack of selfless social and religious leadership among the Indians; school syllabus; severance of umbilical cord; and the general stratification of Jamaican social structure which kept on skimming off the potential Indian leaders from the grassroots'.

And writing on the cultural heritage of the Indians in Jamaica, Laxmi Mansingh observed that in modern Jamaica 'the preoccupation of the majority group with the idealization of ethnicity and the struggle of millions of Blacks around the world has been ignoring the needs of ethnic minorities'. She went on to argue for a 'cultural coalition' of the various groups in Jamaica, emphasizing 'Unity in Diversity'.[283]

If the cultural influences of Jamaican society on the East Indians is evident, what is perhaps less well known is the extent of Hindu influences on Jamaican national life and in particular on Rastafarianism. It has been argued that the Indians by introducing a number of entirely new systems including religious thoughts, philosophy and rituals, social structure and culture and professional skills into Jamaica have had a 'subtle, significant and indelible impact on the life and thoughts' of the mass of people in Jamaica. Though many Jamaicans are either unaware of this contribution (indeed some may take this for granted, while others may be surprised), summarizing their findings Ajai and Laxmi Mansingh found that:

> ... vegetarianism, ceremonial smoking of Ganja for meditation purposes, wearing of locks, hailing Haile Selassie with 'Jah' [Jai] Rastafari; isolating menstruating women from prayers and kitchen, absence of women from the religious hierarchy, measurement of history in cycles [*yuga*], reverence of soul etc, found in Rasta codes and practices have precedents in Hindu tradition in Jamaica .[284]

# SURINAM

## *Ethnic Groups and Languages*

Surinam is one of the most racially segmented societies in the Caribbean, exhibiting a unique variety of ethnic and cultural groups, including Creoles, Indians, Javanese, Chinese, Europeans, Syrians, Lebanese, Amerindians and 'Bush Negroes' of the interior. With the exception of the indigenous Amerindians, all the other groups came from other countries, essentially to work on the plantations.

As a Dutch colony, Surinam society was, at first, comprised of two social and cultural systems: the slaves and the small group of Europeans. While there was a strict division between the two, through the contact they had, each was able to influence the other. Thus, the 'Creole' culture of the slave population came into existence.

Over the years, sexual liaisons, though forbidden between the white masters and their black women slaves, resulted in a growing number of 'coloured' people who were elevated socially above the slaves. Through this privileged group, the process of acculturation of the Afro-Surinamese population moved apace. In effect, this colonised buffer group formed a cultural link between the European upper strata of the society and the Afro-Surinamese, particularly after slavery was abolished in 1863.

Thereafter the labour shortage became acute and the planters introduced various groups of labourers, an accumulation which had, by 1959 evolved into a total population of 264,372 composed of Creoles – 115,382 (43.6 per cent); Indians –

93,537 (35.4 per cent); Javanese – 43,195 (16.3 per cent); Chinese – 4,441 (1.7 per cent); Europeans – 4,473 (1.7 per cent; and Others (Syrians etc) – 3,344 (1.3 per cent).[285]

These groups of people profess various religions. The Creoles were all Christians, half of them adhered to the Roman Catholic faith, while the other half followed one or other of the Protestant denominations. At the same time, about 80 per cent of the Indians were Hindus, 20 per cent followers of Islam and about 4 per cent were Christians, mostly Roman Catholics. The Hindus were divided into two sects, the orthodox Sanatan Dharma and the reformist Arya Samaj. The majority of the Javanese were followers of Islam, a faith which the Christian missionaries (as in Trinidad) had been unable to penetrate and win converts.

By 1959 Dutch was the official language in Surinam and the language of instruction in schools. Other languages include Surinamese or 'Sranan Tongo' (also called 'Negro English') spoken by Creoles; Hindi, spoken by the Indians, particularly in the Districts outside Paramaribo; the Javanese spoke Javanese and the Chinese used their own language. At the time, all groups frequently used Surinamese or Dutch.

Some twenty-five years later, however, the Indians faced a complex language situation in Surinam, arising from the fact that the various ethnic groups altogether speak an estimated eighteen languages, reflecting a truly multilingual society. Among the Indians (Hindus and Muslims), Sanskrit, Arabic, Hindi, Urdu, Sarnani, Dutch and Sranan are spoken. Recent research has shown that compared with Hindi, Urdu and Dutch, Sarnani appears to be a language of 'low social status'. But although Sarnani is being promoted as a high status language, its further enhancement seems in jeopardy.

While the Indians were fluent in the languages they had brought with them from India, in time, they became multi-lingual speaking a number of languages other than their own, thus bringing about the present position in which different languages are used by the Indians in different situations. As Sita Krishna found, they use some languages 'for intra-ethnic contact', and other languages they use for inter-ethnic contact'.[286] Let us now consider Surinam's early religious and cultural organisations.

The teachings of the Arya Samaj had reached the Indians in Surinam by way of Guyana where the sect's missionaries had been engaged in establishing its work. Between 1920 and 1930 much progress was made among the Hindus in Surinam, essentially because of the more germane set of values that were being propounded. Caste status and the old priestly elite could no longer be maintained or justified in the new environment. Thus the Arya Samaj's work in Guyana became relevant in neighbouring Surinam in that it 'provided a vehicle for the expression of the prestige aspirations of those men who made a success of their lives within the limits of the local community, but who resented the implication that on account of their birth they were in some way inferior to the persons claiming higher caste status'.[287]

Under the Arya Samaj, old values were re-assessed and reformed and serious friction developed with the Sanatanist followers of the Sanatan Dharma. The Arya Samaj also attacked Christian education and other Christian denominations for their campaign to convert Indians from their traditional religion and culture, which was contrary to the Samaj's emphasis on the value of Indian heritage.

The emergence of the Arya Samaj had the dual effect of bringing about a 'cultural renaissance' and strengthening of 'ethnic self-assurance' among Surinam's Hindus, who confronted an overpowering Western culture. By 1959 an estimated 16 per cent of the total Indian population were supporters of the Arya Samaj and earlier in 1930, to strengthen its focus, the 'Arya Dewaker' (Aryan Sun) society was founded.[288] Together, these groups have, over the years, worked diligently to promote Hinduism.

Among followers of the Islamic faith, the oldest organisation, the Surinam Islamic Association dates back to 1929. Within this group, there was also a movement of reform, the Ahmadiya, that engendered a religious and cultural renaissance. The Muslims in Surinam first became acquainted with the new ideas about 1930, when the scholar Amir Ali visited Surinam from Trinidad. The Ahmadiya movement was funded by Mirza Ghulam Ahmed, whose interpretation of the *Koran* was in response to the demands of modern life as it related to the strengthening of Islam in India and abroad.

In Surinam, at that time, however, all was not calm among the Muslims. There was debate between the Ahmadiya and the orthodox Sunnis on whether or not Jesus Christ was curcified. The former put forward the argument that Christ had spent his last days in Afghanistan and Kashmir, where he preached and was buried in Srinigar. The Sunnis, on the other hand, could not accept this view or recognise the founder of the movement either as a prophet or the validity of his teachings. So great was the attraction of the Ahmadiya that, in a short time, it came to dominate the Surinam Islamic Association, which finally resulted in the resignation of many Sunnis. Thereafter, a number of splinter Islamic associations were formed, before being consolidated into one body after the Second World War.[289]

The advent of Ahmadiya which had caused Muslims to reappraise their religion and culture, performed a function not unlike the Arya Samaj in the case of the Hindus. The Ahmadiya called upon Muslims to form a tighter bond with the Motherland, India at first, and after 1947 (with the separation of India and Pakistan) the Movement kept in close contact with Muslims in Lahore, Pakistan. The tension and conflict among Muslims generally was paralleled by similar tensions between Hindus and Muslims. This was a phase of the Indians' history in Surinam when a cultural renaissance had become necessary, for as immigrants in the colonial social structure, they were perceived as 'foreigners' and labelled with the epithet 'coolie'.

As it was, the arrival of the Indians and Javanese had reinforced the plural nature of Surinam society.[290] And much concern was expressed among them on marriage and kinship.

As early as 1913, the Surinam Immigrants' Association had submitted a letter to the McNeill and Chimman Lal Commission urging them to recognise Indian marriages as performed according to Muslim and Hindu rites. And on other occasions, the Association repeated its request and predictably the introduction of new regulations were received by the Indian community 'with great satisfaction'.[291]

Generally Indian parents were charged with the responsibility of choosing a spouse for their children. More particularly, it is the duty of the father of a girl of marriageable age to select a suitable partner for her. As Jayawardena noted a girl of marriageable age who remain unmarried is living testimony of her father's 'failure to do his duty', and in fact the way a father performs this task, to some degree, determines his social standing in the Indian community. But in recent times, this responsibilty of choosing for their children is less than it used to be.[292]

In general, the age of marriage for an Indian girl was about fifteen, and boys married between the ages of fifteen and twenty, though there was a tendency among followers of the Arya Samaj and Ahmadiya sects to marry at a later stage. An analysis of the age of marriage showed a tendency to marry earlier in the Districts. For example, by 1960 in Nickerie and Saramacca most girls married when they were fourteen to sixteen years old, while in Paramaribo there was a rising trend to the age of seventeen or upwards. As far as the men were concerned, the preferred age was between eighteen to twenty-one, while in the town it was between nineteen and twenty-three.[293]

One investigation found that Indians prefered to marry outside their neighbourhood, and that in Paramaribo, more men had had homes before they actually got married. Following the trend elsewhere in the Caribbean, in terms of caste and marriage, little of the original Indian caste system has survived in Surinam concerning the selection of a spouse. Be that as it may, the importance of Indian marriage has remained paramount, an act of involvement in Indian culture. One could not, in effect, be an Indian without being closely connected to 'the values and customs relating to marriage and the wedding ceremony, organisation of domestic group, and kinship relations', as Speckmann put it. 'For this reason, these three institutions lie at the heart of the Indian way of life'.[294]

The marriage rite according to Hindus is one of the twelve Samskaras, the religious ceremonies which purify and sanctify Hindus, during the various phases of life. A broad distinction must be made concerning the Hindu marriage rites, as performed by the two main sects, the Sanatan Dharma and the Arya Samaj. Although the ceremony is the same in both groups, certain elements that are integral to the Sanatanists are absent from the Arya Samaj marriage practice.

While there is little difference between Hindus and Muslims, no rite is required to be performed prior to the Muslim marriage. The wedding preparations include sending out invitations, erection of a tent and all the necessary arrangements for cooking a large amount of food. The bridegroom makes his way, with his Best-man in procession to the bride's house, where the wedding ceremony is conducted by a priest. This is followed by a feast, which continues into the night, accompanied by loud music emanating from a loud-speaker. And, as in the case of Hindus, the following morning the bridegroom abstains from eating and customarily he is given money by the bride's father and members of his family. The married couple then go to the bridegroom's house, where the bride remains for three to four days, before returning to her parents for fourteen days. Her next visit to her husband is usually intended to be either a place of permanent abode or after a period of time, a place from which they would move to other independent accommodation.

Research has shown that while family ties are not as important for the younger generation, the rise of individualism and weakening of the family bond are clearly evident in the urban areas. And significantly, there is a tendency towards the 'nuclear family' and more equality between married people.[295]

Historically, the acculturation process that had speeded-up after the Second World War, became increasingly pronounced as urbanization removed the constraints of geographical and social isolation of the East Indians as an ethnic group. As a consequence, this process has been mirrored by the fact that on matters relating to Indian family life and kinship, there has also been an increasing adaptation to Western values.[296]

## GRENADA[297] AND CUBA

The islands of the Caribbean have become well-known to tourists who see in them beauty and physical comfort. And in this respect (particularly before the 'Revolution') Grenada was no exception. Given this 'Kodachrome syndrome', Grenada was described by one visitor as being 'so pretty, so lush, so quaint, so balmy, so easy going – so goddam picturesque – that life had to be sweet there ... In this beautific setting man must find the idyll of his heart, the Eden of his spirit'. The distorting lens of the picturesque long dominated and precludes, either overtly or covertly, the human misery that is so endemic in this fine tropical setting.

In fact, historically, among those who amassed great wealth from the sugar plantations, were the absentee landlords, who had never set foot in the Caribbean. They exploited the labour at their command from afar. In this respect, Grenada was no exception – two-thirds of its sugar estates were owned by absentee planters. It is therefore not surprising that the inefficient administration of the estates following the entry of East Indian indentured labourers (a traffic legalised by the Grenada Ordinance of 1856), continued with devastating consequences. Chronic sickness and ill-treatment of the Indians on the plantations led to them being 'abandoned to their fate', as useless to both their employers and themselves. By the 1870s most of the two thousand Indian immigrants had been 'kicked off' the estates and left to 'die on the roads'. In effect then, instead of getting better, the inhuman treatment meted out to them, during their indentureship experience and after, grew worse for many, who were reduced to physical wrecks, 'grinning skeletons'. Predictably, their numbers dwindled. By 1921 there was an estimated 181 India-born[298] Indians among the rest of the small Indian community. Moreover, their minority status in Grenada was underlined by the fact that they were the victims of the prevailing Creole attitude and prejudices towards them as 'heathen Hindoos' and 'coolies'.

Given that their language and culture, in recent times, reflect the island's Colonial history, the Indians spoke a patois mixed with remnants of Hindi. Yet, they remained outside Creole society. In an effort to bring 'civilization' to them, the Indians were subjected to the evangelism of religious conversion by the Canadian Presbyterians, who took their Mission to Grenada in 1884. Being a smaller community and physically and culturally separated from the larger, more exclusive populations of their fellow-Indians in Trinidad, Guyana and Surinam, they were, in a word, overwhelmed by the norms and values of Creole society; and how mych more remote must India (and the prospect of successfully invoking – never mind enacting – elements of Indian culture) have been, even for the most sensitive among them.

Overall then, the dwindling East Indian population in Grenada had been, since indentureship began, facing the real danger of 'cultural absorption', and it seemed there was little they could do to change the trend. Desperate intermittent cultural contact with Indians in Trinidad could not avert the inevitable process of 'deculturization' attributed by one researcher to the neglect of cultural educators.[299]

Following Cuban independence from Spain in 1902, the boon of American investment, led to growth in sugar production and railroad expansion. The consequent demand for labour on the sugar plantations (a scarcity which came with the abolition of slavery in 1886), saw the influx of East Indian immigrants into Cuba mainly from Jamaica. An estimated two thousand East Indians entered between 1905 and 1916, and most of them were contracted to work for the Guantanamo Sugar Company in Guantanamo sugar mills, located in the South-east of the island.

As was the case in the English-speaking Caribbean islands, here too, the Spanish language, at least in the early years, proved to be a 'barrier' to the Indians, and because of this they were relegated to the back of the queue as non-Spanish speaking. And here too, they were badly housed, many of them inhabited crowded barracks and worked on the land. With time, however, as a new generation became more familiar with the local language and customs, they became more integrated. Yet some vestiges of Indian customs have remained, such as the practice of the Sant religion, the eating of roti and goat meat and the observance of the Kali Puja, among others. The Indians also perform dances and play musical instruments that originated in India. In exotic Cuba, how 'exotic' such Indian practices must seem.

Even though little has been known of the East Indian immigrant presence in Cuba, they have survived as a distinct group, ninety-four years after their arrival.

Jaime Sarusky informs us that their assimilation into Cuban society is 'an indisput-able fact' and their integration has proceeded in a 'slow and progressive manner'. East Indian men and women have married Cubans and their children (unhindered by the strictures of tradition and religious beliefs) are forging a new social reality. Rather than confine themselves to employment in agriculture, members of the new generation have moved into different fields as professionals, teachers, public servants and business employees. But although they have inter-married and are few in number, elements of their cultural past remain a part of their small com-munity, as shown in the respect and pride they have for 'family traditions'.[300]

## MARTINIQUE AND GUADELOUPE

Indian culture is still very much in evidence in the French West Indies. But al-though in the northern part of Martinique the cult of Maldévidan was being prac-tised, by the early 1960s, the vast majority of East Indians (if not all) were said to be Roman Catholics or under the influence of Christianity. To a large extent, the Hindu marriage ceremonies of the early years of indentureship had given way to Christian church marriages. It seemed, however, that the Indians, many of whom were among the poorest people in Martinique, were able to practice both Hinduism and Roman Catholicism without difficulty. The leading God int heir cult is Maldevidan, who is shown as a man riding an animal, a God likened to Christ and known by other names such as Madeyan and Vishnu. The main godess is Marie-eman, who is lik-ened to the Virgin Mary. In Guadeloupe East Indian cult members call her Mali-eman. Apart from these two, there are many other gods and godesses (though not all), who are identified with Roman Catholic saints.[301]

Of the 70,000 or more indentured Indians who went to Martinique, unlike those taken to Guyana, Trinidad and Surinam, most came from South India. It is said that they 'died like flies', but some of those who survived sought refuge in Trini-dad, where they settled in an area west of Port of Spain. But for those who stayed in the French islands, it was necessary for their survival to cling to certain aspects of the culture that they had brought with them from India.

For an Indian from Trinidad, like V.S. Naipaul, discovering Indians in Martinique was something of a surprise which naturally aroused his curiosity. When he went there in the early 1960s, he reported that only four or five thousands had remained on the island, labouring, in the main, on the sugar estates and as sweepers in the city; and so far as he could see, they made 'no mark on the society; no Indian even opened a shop'. He gave a number of reasons as to why this was so, including the fact that their number was too small. He commented 'it might be that the Martinique Indians came from a single depressed Hindu caste. There is evidence for this in their physical similarity and their religious practices', and observed the remarkable similarity between the sweepers' settlement in India and in Fort-de-France, their new place of abode; stating also that those who had emigrated to Port of Spain proved to be the 'most assimilable' of Trinidad Indians. Finally, Naipaul left us this impression of the Indians' predicament:

> It is easy to see how such people, without the traditions, aptitudes and drive of other castes, would be helpless; or how any small, alien impoverished group would remain submerged in Martinique, where society was as rigidly organised as Indian society but where standards were incomprehensible and beyond attainment. The white-mulatto-black presented a common front of unaccommodating Frenchness; the Indian remained an outsider.[302]

In the intervening years since Naipaul wrote, it seems that the status and concerns of the Indians in these islands had changed little. In Guadeloupe, Singaravelou saw the socio-economic emergence of the East Indians (especially in the two generations prior to 1975) as following their socio-cultural integration. And identifying some of the main aspects of that integration, he cited language, conversion to the Roman Catholic religion, adoption of new (European-Creole) dress styles, 'nigger amusements' and inter-marriage. Moreover, among the barriers preventing a more effective integration between Indians and Creoles, seen as the most important, were the prejudices of each group. In other words, the Indians perceive Creoles as 'lazy' and 'thriftless', while Creoles label Indians as 'ambitious'.

Nevertheless, there has been some integration of East Indians, though not enough. In his well-considered view of Indian integration in Guadeloupe, Singaravelou's comments reflect the justifiable fears and experiences of East Indians elsewhere in the Caribbean: 'their integration is real, even if it is not total. Nevertheless, they do not feel at home, and accuse the Creoles of braking their progress. Some of them are afraid of the possible political change which would lead to autonomy or independence; (thus leaving them defenceless against an hostile Creole majority). But they refuse to turn back to the land of their ancestors they know nothing of'.[303]

In spite of these real concerns, there has been a revival of 'Indianness' in the French West Indies. Beyond the bounds of the plantations, especially in Guadeloupe, where most of the Indians still reside, there has been an intimidating, hostile society which Indians felt cared little for them. No wonder that the Indian was viewed in Naipaul's words as 'an outsider'.

The 'sea of anonymity, silence and indifference', which Moutoussamy spoke about while the Indians were still indentured labourers had not changed in the early post-indenture years, so that they were still fighting against those forces that would dispossess them of their identity. Indian culture in Guadeloupe had not lapsed and died. In fact, the industrious and courageous Indian community had thrown up an outstanding son, Henri Sidambarom, who for some twenty years had guided the Indians in an exemplary fashion. As the 'spiritual father' of the East Indians, he fought doggedly not only for Indians to become French citizens, but also for Guadeloupeans of other ethnic groups. His success in Guadeloupe, however, was not repeated in Martinique, where there was a smaller Indian community.

But his achievment was no less real and undiminished, for at last, the Indians who had contributed so much for over one hundred and thirty years were officially allowed to think of Guadeloupe and Martinique as their homeland. Further, in their continuing efforts towards the 'humanization of nature' (replicated by Indians elsewhere in the Caribbean), and given their increased assertiveness in Guadeloupe and Martinique in recent years, these stalwart Indians sought with even more determination to emphasize their cultural identity. There were an estimated 65,000 Indians in both islands, five-sixth in Guadeloupe and one-sixth in Martinique.

Thanks to the vatialous (priests), cultural and religious values have survived. So determined was the effort that even where there were no scriptural texts, Hindu priests employed the oral traditions to keep alive Indian religious beliefs and practices. It is indeed a strange mixture, an adaptation of their associations with Yanaon, Pondicherry, Karikal and Calcutta to their new Caribbean environment, where elements of the Catholic faith (as mentioned earlier) was integrated without a denial of their belief in Hinduism.

Some thirty years ago, a few Indian leaders felt that a Guadeloupean national identity *had* to include the Indian community, and so a campaign to generate a cultural resurgence was set in motion. Consequently, between April 1971 and March 1988 the Guadeloupean Association of Friends of India was formed; the Association of Martinique and India was created; the first gopuram in Guadeloupe was erected; trips to India were organised; Pondicherry became a twin-city with Basse-Terre in Guadeloupe; 1985–86 was commemorated as the year of India; and a mela was organised in Martinique in 1988.[304]

The location of the Indians at the bottom of this French island society was clearly no longer acceptable, especially among the young Indians who speak about a 'pilgrimage' to India, the Motherland. This is not meant to be a 'physical going back to the ancestral land', but rather a rekindling of the concept of 'Indianness' in the Caribbean.

The preservation of elements of Indian culture was therefore seen as a historical necessity. A lack of initiative in maintaining the Indians' cultural contribution in the West Indies had to be resisted because, as Moutoussamy (Deputy for Guadeloupe in the National Assembly in France) argued, recovering the past was necessary for the maintenance of their aesthetic values and would serve the purpose of authenticating their West Indian identity, thus making the society all the stronger. He emphasized that the Indians did not want to go back to India for they belonged to Martinique and Guadeloupe. But this did not mean a devaluation of their religious masts, sanctuaries, chapels, plants, cooking, rites, customs, music, dance, dress, language and traditions, where they exist.

Prior to 1950, the Indian family was still a more or less cohesive unit. After marriage, sons and their spouses lived with their in-laws in and around the sugar plantations' quarters, in a communal, convivial atmosphere. From the 1950s, however, with the strong desire for economic betterment among a new generation, there has been a tendency for the Indian family to 'scatter and disintegrate'. Although women's liberation have, at last, forced many Indian men to make adjustments, the all-important, far from passive Indian women have managed, against great odds, to keep their errant families together.

Among many Indian families in Martinique and Guadeloupe, the cycle of life is observed as follows:

> … each stage in life, from birth to death, is still stamped with the seal of Indianness. Thus after a woman gives birth, the placenta is placed in a pot and buried at night, close to the house. Twelve hours later, the baby is purged of bodily fluids and breast-fed. The first haircut is customarily performed so as to protect the newborn from possible misfortunes; the same operation and principles go for the ear-piercing of a baby girl. Today, Hindu-style marriages have completely disappeared. However, death always requires the performance of certain rites. The death of a person may be announced by beating a drum, and the wake tends not to be grief stricken, since an effect is made to reduce the finality of death. After the funeral, mourning is concluded with the ceremony of milk or pal tellital followed by kalmandlon. Year in year out, at All Saints Day in November, many Indian families commemorate their loved ones who have passed away by performing the ceremony of semblani. Lastly, in the case of serious illness, Indian men and women may invoke the help of their divinities by wearing a kanghannon.[305]

Since their arrival, the assimilation of the East Indians in Martinique and Guadeloupe has been considerable, and threatens the survival of their 'Indianness'. But in spite of the various forms of pressure placed upon the Indians, over the years, many leaders have expressed hope. Having described the existing beliefs and practices of the Indians, Moutoussamy concluded: 'May Indianness be the sap which, through consolidation and mutual acceptance of values, through the abolition of prejudices and complexes, and through reciprocal and fraternal acknowledgement of one another, rises above social taboos, in order to ensure a more complete integration of the Indian in French West Indian society'.[306]

From the years after the abolition of indentureship until well past the second half of the twentieth century, East Indians and their descendants in the Caribbean had, gradually, through sheer persistence, moved from the margins of their colonial societies towards establishing their presence as best they could and in as many areas of colonial and post-colonial life, as possible. And given the circumstances, as they engaged with the wider society, often they had to guard against their 'unfashionable' identity as 'East Indians' being devalued. Thus in the pre- and increasingly in the post-Independence period, they faced the challenge of proving their worth as identifiably Indo-Caribbean people.

# CHAPTER FOUR

# ESTABLISHING AN IDENTITY

To identify all the individuals who have made outstanding contributions towards a better appreciation and understanding of the Indo-Caribbean experience, will be a time-consuming, near impossible and ill-advised task. However, in the field of sport, given the international significance of Test Match Cricket as not merely stimulating 'delight or devotion', but as a 'spectacle that can galvanize a people's spritual resources, stimulate their national self-esteem and remind them of their place in the world,[1] special mention must be made of the famous Indo-Caribbean Test Match cricketers Sonny Ramdhin of Trinidad and Rohan Kanhai, Joe Solomon and Alvin Kallicharan from Guyana, role models for a multititude of Indo-Caribbean youths.

Apart from their cricketing brilliance, these sportsmen have delighted and surprised many people in the outside world, most tellingly by the fact that they are East Indian-West Indians, born and bred. For many poor young men, exceptional ability in sport, offered often the only means towards achieving higher social status and fame, if not a fortune. And in this respect, if Sonny Ramadhin was immortalized in calypso, Rohan Kanhai would later arouse unprecedented interest, both in his artistry and background.

C.L.R. James spoke of him as 'the satyric passion for the expression of a natural man bursting through the acquired restraint of disciplined necessity'. The comparisons and superlatives were many and unanimous. But who was he?

Rohan Baboolal Kanhai, the grandson of indentured labourers from the United Provinces of India, was born on 26 December 1935, at Plantation Port Mourant on the Corentyne Coast in Berbice, Guyana. The statistics show that he played in 79 Test Matches between 1957 and 1974 (the last thirteen of which he Captained), scored 6,227 runs, including 15 centuries and 28 half centuries, notching up a career-best score of 256 runs in 1958–59 in Calcutta. And before he was retired, he was regarded by the pundits (including Sir Gary Sobers and Sunil Gavaskar) who unanimously agree that Kanhai was indeed the greatest batsman they had ever seen! How did he achieve this seemingly unattainable honour and glory?

Along the Corentyne Coast, the 'coolie heart-land', Kanhai appeared, the 'culmination of the long, tortuous Indo-Guyanese journey through indentureship, the obnoxious "logies" or slave ranges, gnawing self-doubts, and the fight to regain their humanity and a redefinition of self', as Clem Seecharan claimed. The economic strides that the Indians had made, bred a spirit of confidence, which was reinforced by their pride in being Indian following Indian Independence in 1947. All around him, as he grew up, Kanhai felt the vibrant mood of rebellion among Indo-Guyanese people, notably the better educated among whom was Cheddi Jagan. Thus, arising from his Indo-Guyanese heritage, he grew in confidence which allowed his unique talents to flower and eventually receive due recognition.

Like no other batsman, he had all the ingredients of greatness and more. He possessed an additional indefinable flair and touch as he made his way to the wicket, a quality that made excitement grow, that made of cricket 'an art and an encounter with the truth and the joy that lies in all supreme human achievement'.[2] And James, the West Indian and world cricket writer *par excellence*, in his article 'Kanhai: A Study in Confidence' wrote:

'West Indian cricket had reached such a stage that a fine cricketer would be adventuresome, and Kanhai was adventuresome; I try to relate that adventuresomeness of his cricket *to the particular type of West Indian he was at that particular time*. People felt that it was more than a mere description of how he batted ... They felt it was not only a cricket question, because was an East Indian and East Indians were *still looked down upon by other people in the Caribbean*'.[3] (Author's emphasis).

Kanhai knew only too well of the 'coolie bully' attitude among Afro-Guyanese, their sense of superiority over East Indians, a feeling that extended beyond Guyana. Indeed, some years ago, before the West Indies Test Cricket Team played England in Guyana, Captain Viv Richards proclaimed loudly the pride he felt in the Team's Africanness. James also made the important point that he found in Kanhai's batting a 'unique pointer of the West Indian quest for identity, for ways of expressing our potential bursting at every seam'. Birbalsingh has noted that other Indo-West Indian cricketers (apart from Kanhai and Solomon, whose careers began in the 1950s) started to emerge from the Guyanese sugar estates and recognised this also as the 'socio-historical context' within which Ramadhin's achievement (forged from the environment of a south Trinidad sugar estate) must be evaluated, and concluded gloomily that in view of their minority status in the English-speaking Caribbean, their cricketing and other abilities are not encouraged. But he saw the Caribbeanness of the Indian players as a positive expression of the shared colonial institutions of oppression (slavery/indenture) 'to express an impulse for freedom that was universal'.[4]

Nevertheless, during a recent panel discussion on Indo-Caribbean cricketers, in which Sonny Ramadhin and Joe Solomon participated, much was said about the absence of Indo-Caribbean cricketers in relation to the West Indian Test Team and the particular difficulties that Rohan Kanhai faced in becoming and maintaining his captaincy of the Team. His brother spoke of how embarassing it was to learn about the manner in which Kanhai was 'kicked out'. Less partisan, as Moderator of the discussion, Birbalsingh took a philosophical view of this vexed question. 'It appears that factors which affect West Indian politics also affect West Indian cricket', he said in conclusion. 'Whether these are imagined or real does not matter. This is the way people feel ande think'.[5] But the wonder of the Indo-Caribbean experience, not only in cricket, is that the Indians have managed to keep their hopes alive, determined to express themselves, their indentity in various ways, and no less so through literature.

In recent post-Independence years, many talented Indo-Caribbean women poets and writers including Mahadai Das, Shana Yardan, Rajkumari Singh, Leela Sukhu, Niala Rambachan and Ramabai Espinet, and a growing number of young Indo-Caribbean men writers, such as Rooplal Monar, David Dabydeen, Cyril Dabydeen, Noor Kumar Mahabir, Sasenarine Persad and Arnold Itwaru, among others, have been making important contributions, evoking traditional and modern images of Indo-Caribbean life, most of it as writers in exile in Europe and North America.

Earlier, however, another generation of Indo-Caribbean writers had to engage in the task of breaking new ground, in a relatively new field, to add their authentic voices to the existing literature penned by non-Indian Caribbean writers. Among them are the lesser known Ismith Khan, and the more prominet V.S. Naipaul, his brother Shiva Naipaul (of Brahmin background) Sam Selvon (a Creolised Indian), and the much-praised young writer, Harold Sonny Ladoo, from a peasant/working class family, three writers offering different perspectives on the Indo-Isimidadian and Caribbean experience. Seepersad Naipaul (father of the brothers previously mentioned) is also important, because during his time (notably the early years) he was clearly an exceptional forerunner of Indo-Caribbean writing, especially short stories (then the popular form of fiction among budding Caribbean writers), rather than novels. 'West Indian novelists tend to base their fictions upon the racial groups they grew up in', wrote the West Indian literary critic, Ken Ramchand, 'not because they are writing to or on behalf of those groups but in the first place because they know those groups best. In general therefore, the Indian character either does not appear, or is peripheral in works by non-Indian writers. Novels by writers of Indian origin, on the other hand, are peopled mainly by Indian characters. Such works yield up to readers who already possess the facts (either from first-hand experience or from documentary sources) impressions and insights into the facts such as the novel form is peculiarly fitted to give'.[6] Thus, Indo-Caribbean writers, seeking an identity were, through their imaginative, creative works, inscribing themselves!

It should be noted that complementing the literary works of the writers identified above, are the invaluable contributions of Indo-Caribbean authors and scholars, not only those in the Caribbean but also those resident abroad, who have in recent years, been providing an interested and growing readership with important scholarly papers and books, in various disciplines, a corpus of work so vital, not only in clarifying our understanding of Indo-Caribbean history and culture, but also in widening and deepening our hitherto impoverished understanding of what has been regarded as 'Caribbean Studies'.

In all then, given this burgeoning literature which reflects various aspects of their life in the Caribbean, the East Indians have, in word and deed, moved from being tolerant labourers to becoming participants, at times, in violent resistance against oppression of those in authority, so that they can press on with the creative process of forging their Caribbean identity, moving inexorably towards creolization without necessarily subsuming their individuality, which has been (and still is), constantly under threat. Nothing can or should be taken for granted, for historically, the political representation of the Indians have been, all too often, linked to race.

Birbalsingh, in his appraisal of novelist H.G. de Lisser's view of Indians in Jamaica, as stated in the novel *The Cup and the Lip*, echoes what has been a familiar attitude towards Indians in the Caribbean. Birbalsingh noted:

> Feelings of suspicion and fear are bred by (de Lisser's) perception of the Indians as an alien or interloper, a new arrival whose very newness confers less legitimacy on his right to a place in the Caribbean. According to this perception, greater legitimacy belongs to Blacks and others who have lived in the region for longer than Indians, and suffered imperialist exploitation for longer.

This 'perception' of Indians in the Caribbean was not, however, confined to de Lisser and other novelists. Its a view which Birbalsingh sees as supplying the rationale for the long hold on power of the Eric Williams and Forbes Burnham regimes in Trinidad and Tobago and Guyana, respectively, 'for it is the essential fear of domination by a group believed to lack true Caribbean legitimacy that inspires black Guyanese, in particular, to suffer undemocratic elections, corrupt government and many other privations for a quarter of a century, mainly for the sake of keeping Indians away from political power'.[7]

But if the Indians in the early days of indenture in the Caribbean were totally marginalised, in modern times (unlike Trinidad, Guyana and Surinam, where Indians have slowly established themselves as vibrant, separate communities) acceptance, as Tinker argued, into a multicultural society never occurred in the smaller Indian communities, where Indians were an 'almost invisible minority' in Jamaica, an assimilationist philosophy in the French West Indies and Grenada has resulted in their survival being 'only numerical'.[8] But whether almost completely assimilated or set apart, as an identifiable presence of some two million people, Indians are not prepared to acquiesce in further marginalization, secure in the knowledge that they have, as the scholar David Lowenthal put it, 'made the most profound impact in the Caribbean'.[9] The demise of Williams and Burham have indeed increased the intensity and urgency of East Indian agitation for social, political and cultural change. For almost three decades – among the very few that has remained at the forefront of this process of change and respect for cultural diversity in the Caribbean (including Jagernath Lachmon of Surinam and Basdeo Panday of Trinidad and Tobago) the committed voice of Cheddi Jagan.

# GUYANA

Long before indentureship had ended, there was an ongoing and deep inner disenchantment among the Indians (especially those who were educated), about the unsatisfactory nature of their lives, still overshadowed by the 'system', a 'condition of mind', as Peter Ruhomon put it, which was 'only awaiting the light of education to dissipate its darkness and create a new vision of the future'. So, there had already been among certain sections of the Indian population an awareness of their lack of political representation, which was reflected in the fact that from a a total East Indian population of 126,517 only 251 were recorded on the Voters' List of 1911, as provided under the Constitution Ordinance.

The Indians' political consciousness, after a long gestation, was manifested in 1916, when a few of the educated among them stood for the first time as candidates for political office. They included J.A. Luckhoo, his brother E.A. Luckhoo, J.A. Verasawmy and Ashrafally. On this historic occasion, only J.A. Luckhoo was successful, being elected to represent South West Essequibo. Though limited, their victory pointed up the shortcomings of the political system. It was left to investigators Pillai and Tivary, two Indian Government officials, to rebut the charge against the Indians (made by the Immigration Agent General who naively believed they had no interest in politics) by pointing out that 'the system of semi-slavery under which they (the Indians) laboured was not conducive to develop their political consciousness'.[10] Pillai and Tivary recommended that in order to effect the full enfranchisement of the East Indians in the Colony, a list of those eligible should be prepared; that the literacy test should be abolished and that ballot papers should be presented in a manner that would facilitate recording the votes of those who were literate, as well as those who were not.

Support for changes to include East Indian voters were also given by Kunwar Maharaj Singh, who visited British Guiana in 1925. It was not, however, until 1928, after the Wilson-Snell Commission of 1926 had reported that the recommended change to the British Guiana Constitution was implemented. The ensuing elections held in 1930, under the new Constitution, saw the entry of E.A. Luckhoo and A.E. Seeram to the Legislature, followed in the elections of 1935 by the success (apart from E.A. Luckhoo), of Jung Bahadur Singh (Demerara-Essequibo); P. Bacchus (Western Berbice) and C.R. Jacob (North Western District).

At last, the political awakening among the East Indians was being translated into political reality, and none too soon: political power in the Colony, which had always been the prerogative of the sugar barons (for example, Booker Bros, the Demerara Sugar Company and Dawson and Company), was still very much in their hands, and at the expense of an increasingly impoverished people. A stark representation of the agricultural workers' income as it related to their generally debased condition in the 1940s (reflecting how little the system had changed since indenture) is pitifully expressed in the evidence presented by a sugar worker to the Venn Commission of Inquiry in the Sugar Industry:

*Chairman:* What do you want to tell us?

*Indian Witness:* We have to walk about five or six miles every day to get to work on the back-dam. We leave home at six o'clock to start work at seven or eight o'clock and work until five or six o'clock.

*Chairman:* Do you work all the year round at that distance from your home, or only now and then?

*Indian Witness:* I walk that distance most of the time.

*Chairman:* Is that your main complaint?

*Indian Witness:* No, I have no rice-field, no cow and no money. I live on the estate in a range (barracks) and do estate work. Since I came to the Colony I have been doing that work.

*Chairman:* How much did you earn last week?

*Indian Witness:* I earn from 5 dollars to 10 dollars a week, but as I am an old man I cannot earn more than 5 dollars to 7 dollars a week, which is insufficient. The week I buy clothes, I cannot buy rations.

Life in 1942 was indeed tough for the wage earner. One cost of living survey showed that the average working class family of 4.6 persons had a total weekly income of $7.41, but had to spend $8.23. On such an income the food consumed lacked nutritional value, which had dire consequences, leading to disease and low life expectancy. Tuberculosis, bad housing, high unemployment and crime constituted a scenario which was unavoidable for the working masses.

Against this background, working class representation, in addition to the afore-mentioned Indian political representatives was urgently needed as trade unions emerged. The formation of the British Guiana Labour Union in 1922 was a water-shed in labour organisation in the Colony. The British Guiana Workers' League followed, and 17 years later, there were at least ten trade unions. But soon enough, the all-powerful employers attempted to divide the growing strength and assertive-ness of workers into racial and industrial categories, with predominantly Afro-Guianese factory workers as members of the Man Power Citizens' Association. Notwithstanding efforts to maintain workers' solidarity, the Guiana Industrial Workers' Union, formed in 1948, failed to counteract the employers' divide and rule strategy. It was clear that the fundamental weakness of workers from both racial groups was the absence of political support.

In fact, working class representation did not come until 1943, when a new Con-stitution for British Guiana was implemented, providing for a Legislative Council, comprising fourteen elected members, seven nominated and three official mem-bers. Expectations of an early election were dashed, for it was not until November 1947 that the elections under a new Constitution were eventually held. This delay-ing tactic was designed to deter militant workers, whose standard of living was steadily declining, from taking action. Unavoidably, the preceding Depression of the 1930s and the effects of the Second World War, brought increasing urgency for economic, social and political redress. While the previously elected members continued in office, insistent workers' demands led to the Governor's nomination of Ayube Edun (President of the MPCA) and H.N. Critchlow (General Secretary of the BGLU), to the Legislative Council. About this time (the decade of the 1940s), which was propitious for the 'people's politics', one political actor in the drama that was about to unfold, would later write:

> Students and ex-servicemen were returning home. Many of the students had been to the United States and worked their way through colleges and universities; the ex-servicemen had been recruited from the working class and the unemployed. These were imbued with the spirit of the Atlantic Charter, with the struggle for freedom and independence which had assumed a world wide character.[11]

That 'political actor', drawn from the ranks of 'students' abroad and ready to make his entry into the nascent politics of British Guiana and guide the proud awakening of the people (not least the Indo-Guyanese) was Dr Cheddi Jagan.

## *The Rise of Cheddi Jagan*

The question of nationalist politics in relation to East Indians in the Caribbean is of particular relevance to Guyana and the historic role of the Indian Cheddi Jagan, the first non-White to assume political leadership of his country in the British Caribbean.

Jagan, the son of Indian indentured emigrants, was born on 22 March 1918. He knew very little about his parents before they arrived in British Guiana, but presumes that they were not unlike millions of Indian peasants who were exploited by Zemindars and in dire want of employment. His mother and father came from Basti in Uttar Pradesh, some sixty miles from Allahabad. They had only been born months before they were recruited to undertake the long voyage: his father's age on arrival in Guyana was two years and his mother's was just eighteen months. These children were, of course, part of a larger family group of five persons including two grandmothers and a paternal uncle. Although this family suffered no deaths during the passage to British Guiana, the cunning Arkatis had managed to separate Jagan's grandmothers from their husbands, who were left in India.

The five emigrants reached British Guiana on the *Elbe* – one of the sailing ships – in 1901, after a journey lasting 82 days, during which they slept on blankets spread on the floor. They were all under five-year terms of indenture, contracted to different sugar estates in Berbice. Jagan's paternal grandmother was bound to Albion and his maternal grandmother to Port Mourant. In theory, the women were required to work for only three years, but in practice, and of economic necessity, they could not avoid working the full five years.

Predictably, plantation life was demanding, and at an early age Jagan's parents began work in the cane fields to help their mothers. Both children worked in creole gangs. Jagan's mother worked between 7.00 a.m to 6.00 p.m manuring sugar cane and three times a week, from midnight to 6.00 a.m, she fetched bagasse (dry cane fibres). She was paid 8 cents (4d.) for the first job and 4 cents (2d) for the second. Her weekly wage was 60 cents (2s.6d). When Jagan's father was about fourteen years old, he began the task of cutting cane and by then, his mother had graduated to moulding the canes. In short, the hours were long and arduous: they had to be up at 4.00 a.m. and had to walk from three to five miles in search of work.

Although Jagan's Hindu parents were married while young – as was customary among Indians then – at about ten years of age, they did not live together until they were sixteen. His mother, who never went to school, worked until he was nine years old. As a boy, he was aware that on the plantation there were two classes: the exploiters and the exploited; and his parents who lived in the 'bound coolie yard' (formerly the 'nigger yard' of slave days) were among the exploited. 'Like most people of the labouring class whose privations began in infancy', he wrote, 'disease began to affect my father's health when he was about fifty. However, because he was a man of fine and indomitable spirit, he died fighting to the very end'.[12]

His father knew he could do nothing to escape from the sugar plantations, but he was sure his son could and would if he provided him with the opportunity to do so, essentially through education. Cheddi Jagan, the eldest of ten children – five brothers and five sisters – spent his early life in Port Mourant, Berbice, and after receiving his Primary school education, at the age of fifteen, he entered Queen's College in Georgetown, an experience which he said was, in many ways, both a challenge and a disappointment.[13] His local education was followed by a white-collar job in Georgetown, before leaving in 1936 for the United States, where he stayed for seven years to further his studies at Howard and North-Western universities. Hard work had brought its own reward in the form of his Doctor of Dental Surgery degree. In deed the young Jagan had embraced the opportunity of study abroad, working his way through college at various jobs, and the overall experience gained served him well, not only with an understanding of the strong traditions of the American people's struggle for independence, freedom and democracy, but also the practical predicament and concerns of their lives. His contact with working people left a marked impression upon him, and he was drawn towards the struggle of the American Labour movement and political representation.

Soon after his return from the United States in 1943, Jagan almost at once became involved in Georgetown political groups. In fact, it has been argued that the origin of the People's Progressive Party, British Guiana's first political party, can be dated to the year of Jagan's return. Although this grouping was not geared to fight elections for the next decade, much of the groundwork of a mass-based political party was in the process of being laid. Essentially, these gatherings constituted a coterie of Guianese intellectuals of various political ideologies who, in anticipation of national independence, focused their attention on the Colony's social and economic problems.

Two years later, Jagan emerged as Treasurer of the Man Power Citizens Association (MPCA), the largest trade union in the sugar industry, and through his involvement with the trade union movement, he was able to establish contact with other trade unionists such as Ashton Chase, who succeeded Hubert Critchlow as Secretary of the British Guiana Labour Union and Jocelyn Hubbard (one of the 'most ideologically committed' Communists in British Guiana), who was Secretary of the British Guiana Trades Council. Hubbard was instrumental in affording Jagan a 'direct line of communication' to the Caribbean Labour Congress (CLC), formed in 1945. The Congress contained Communists and had links with the British Communist Party which was interested in Jagan's ambitions.[14]

At the time, Communists and their groups were not the suspect people and organisations they were to become. In fact, the CLC and the British and Communist-oriented unions were important organisations forming the World Federation of Trade Unions. But given the global embrace of the WFTU, with the advent of the Cold War in the post-war years, the attitude towards Communists and Communism hardened when the Western powers formed the International Confederation of Free Trade Unions, as a counterpoise to the WFTU. This split in international labour organisation was reflected locally. In opposition to the British Guiana TUC's membership of the WFTU was the MPCA, BGLU and Mineworkers Union, who were members of the International Confederation of Free Trade Unions. Further pressure from the anti-Communist British and American labour movements pressed the BGTUC to also accept membership of the ICFTU. Thereafter, the American labour movement exerted increasing control over the local labour movement.

Faced with the profound effects of these shifts on the nationalist movement, Jagan and his fellow ideologues had to choose between the conservatism of the British Guiana Trade Union movement and the socialist ideas of the British Communist Party. The principled Jagan resigned from his post as Treasurer of the MPCA because of his objection to the way Union funds were used and the Union's collaboration with the sugar barons.

And so in 1946, recognising the need for a working class organisation and a political newspaper, Dr. Jagan initiated the formation of the Political Affairs Committee and the *Pac Bulletin* for the purpose of winning constitutional change. Marxist-Leninism was the political ideology of the PAC, the strategy through which it was hoped British Guiana's independence would eventually be won.[15] As it was, these ideologues were still without a real political constituency in the Colony. In 1947, however, Jagan took the struggle forward by contesting and winning a seat in the Legislative Council. He used this colonial Government platform to air the PAC's views, venting criticism of the sugar barons, the MPCA, voting qualifications and the depredations of Colonialism. This unprecedented entry of working class leadership arising from a working clas background in the person of Jagan, made the goals of the nationalist movement seem less remote. 'We the people have won', he told a public meeting. 'Now the struggle will begin'.[16] While the black intelligentsia rallied round, predictably he was rebuffed by the vigilant and divisive Colonial establishment.

Even though his communism was criticised and a Marxist–Leninist approach was not strictly adhered to by all the PAC members, at the time, according to one account, the PAC's free and open policy on political issues made it British Guiana's 'major forum of political debate', bringing unity among the members through a 'common commitment to national independence and politico-cultural integration'. This commitment reflected Jagan's growing anguish and desire to improve the lot of his people. After the shooting of the Enmore martyrs in 1948, at the graveside on the day of the burial, he made a silent pledge to which he remained true. 'The Enmore tragedy affected me greatly', he wrote later, 'there was no turning back ... I would dedicate my entire life to the cause of the struggle of the Guyanese people against bondage and exploitation'.[17] With this commitment, he faced the crucial years ahead in the struggle for independence.

Within the nationalist movement, however, 'ideological factionalism' did not emerge until the announcement in 1949 that a Constitutional Commission was to be set up to look into the question of 'constitutional advancement'.[18] The PAC's discussion of Whitehall's announcement revealed that a number of individuals (including Cheddi and Janet Jagan, his American-born wife), Martin Carter, Brindley Benn, Sidney King and Rory Westmaas, were uncompromising Marxists, advocating constitutional advancement and unqualified independence. This 'hard core' saw Guianese independence as linked to an international anti-imperialist struggle among colonial peoples, and therefore felt that British Guiana should establish friendly relations with the Socialist countries, primarily the Soviet Union. Of course, not all the PAC nationalists held these convictions. In fact, between 1949 and 1951 those nationalists who were 'militantly anti-Communist' and 'anti-Socialist', were natural opponents of Jagan who they saw as a 'threat to capitalist investment and private enterprise'. Consequently, this element sought a new strategy outside the PAC.

The split which occurred during this period between those of the left and those of the right of the PAC was not a 'serious problem' for the nationalist movement, because firstly it was 'almost purely ideological'; and secondly those involved had little or no following among the masses. The factionalisation of the PAC, did not hamper the PAC's success in bringing about 'a comprehensive nationalist movement'. However, with the East Indian Jagan, as a leading figure, none of the many Afro-Guyanese nationalists in the PAC were able to effectively oppose him, if only on the basis of race. This gap was filled in 1950 when Forbes Burnham joined Jagan politically. Burnham's representation of the Afro-Guianese cultural section was important in aggregating the British Guiana nationalist movement.

Although Burnham's educational background and progressive student political activity in London seemed unquestionable, Jagan, among others in the PAC leadership, were unsure of the part Burnham could play in the nationalist movement. Burnham's 'independent and forceful personality', his 'middle class' background and ideological position and politics were all questionable as far as Jagan and his supporters were concerned. In effect, then, although Burnham had a role to play, he never became fully integrated in the dominant PAC political orientation.[19]

Apart from this problem of sharp differences among the members at the top of the leadership, the PAC as a political organisation was too far removed from the masses, which could not be mobilized unless the PAC was re-organised as a political party. This was particularly important, given the prospect of general elections that was likely to follow Constitutional change.

In 1950 the leadership, recognising its limitations, dissolved the PAC and the People's Progressive Party (named, as the author was told by Jagan, after the American Progressive Party) came into being. The following year, at its first Congress, the PPP Constitution was adopted.[20] Three years later, Constitutional change was effected and after an election campaign, the PPP won eighteen of the twenty-four seats, an historic victory for the East Indian Jagan who from April to October 1953, headed the elected Government of the PPP in British Guiana and was Minister of Agriculture. But the appearance of unity within the Party was only a facade.

It seemed, even at this time of post-election victory, that the PPP leadership had misjudged the strength of their internal and external opposition. The Party was, however, fully aware of the sugar workers' preference for the Guiana Industrial Workers' Union rather than the Man-Power Citizens Association, so that when the sugar workers struck for improved wages and working conditions, it was an unusually entrenched confrontation between the PPP-backed GIWU and the Company-backed MPCA. As the strike began to bite, conservative Guianese groups were critical of Dr. Lachmansingh's role as Minister of Health and Housing, while he was still leader of the GIWU whose members were on strike.

Although Lachmansingh was able to announce on 24 September 1953 that the sugar strike was over, a Labour Relations Bill was produced by Ashton Chase who, as Minister of Labour, announced that the strike had ended because of a Government promise to consider choosing a new union bargaining agent. In accordance with this, Chase felt that legislation should be passed in one day through the suspension of standing orders. Needless to say, this demand met strong opposition from members of the Legislative Assembly.

Interestingly, only three days before, Archbishop Knight not only expressed his deep concern in the State Council over the violence on the sugar estates, but also moved that the Government Ministers who were involved in 'promoting and sustaining' the strike, posed a 'grave danger to the Constitution' and was a 'direct threat to the peace and security' of the citizens of British Guiana. Morever, Knight pressed his case by requesting that the Colonial Secretary should, after due enquiry, 'take such action as he may see fit to ensure confidence in the government'. Ominously the Archbishop's motion was passed by six votes to two.

'The heart of the matter was not a theoretical dispute about trade unionism', it has been argued, 'but whether the MPCA could be ejected by the GIWU'. Predictably the MPCA was against the Bill and by now, both local and international pressure had become intense. Governor Alfred Savage, alarmed by the strikes, demonstrations and a perceived threat to Parliamentary proceedings, saw no alternative but to call upon Winston Churchill, as British Prime Minister, and Colonial Secretary, Oliver Lyttleton for help. Savage was in favour of swift action (and at a time when British forces were in combat against Communists in Malaya) gunboat diplomacy seemed the only way forward. And so during a Legislative Assembly meeting on 7 October Jagan, aware of the impending arrival of British troops in British Guiana, declared that the PPP hoped for peaceful Constitutional change. There were no further meetings of the Assembly and on 9 October, Chief Secretary John Gutch announced suspension of the Constitution in order 'to prevent Communist subversion of the government and a dangerous crisis both in public order and in economic affairs'.[21] The idea was to forestall any further moves by Jagan and the PPP to turn British Guiana into a Communist state. That day became known as 'Black Friday'.

As it was, this became the political irony of ironies, as a democratically elected Legislative Assembly was forced out by a Government which claimed to represent the 'Mother of Parliaments'. 'Britain claimed to be a part of the "free" world', it was argued, 'locked in a titanic conflict with the "undemocratic" Soviet Union. But now Britain had arbitrarily over-ruled the wishes of the people of British Guiana. Were two different standards being applied, or could the Conservative Government prove both the wisdom and morality of the action it had taken?'[22]

Consequently, the Robertson Commission of Inquiry investigated the suspension and made recommendations;[23] and between 1953 and 1957, an 'interim government' was installed. At the end of the period, a new constitution was introduced, a time during which the tensions within the Party had become evident, as two opposing factions emerged: one led by Jagan, the other by Burnham. At this stage, although the trend was clear to many, the argument was nevertheless that the factionalism was not based on race.[24]

It is interesting that at this time, the Jagan-Burnham split did not reflect a similar rift between the Afro-Guianese and East Indian electorate across the country. And in spite of the political cleavage, Jagan still led 'a relatively integrated nationalist movement'. But it was not long before the political mood changed dramatically.

The loss of two important East Indian supporters of Burnham was followed by the departure of one of Jagan's Afro-Guianese supporters namely, Sidney King, who joined Burnham's newly-formed Peoples National Congress. Moreover, the PNC received a further boost in 1959 when Afro-Guianese members of the United Democratic Party rallied behind Burnham.[25] In effect then, by 1960 what many had feared happened. The two major political parties, the PPP and the PNC (in spite of their leadership pronouncements) represented essentially Indian and Afro-Guianese memberships, respectively. Thus, the seeds of 'racial politics' were sown.

A further disintegrating influence on the idea of a comprehensive nationalist movement was the formation of the United Force Party, led by the Portuguese businessman, Peter D'Aguiar. If Burnham was favoured by the British Government the entry of the UF in Guianese politics offered the possibility of further strengthening his position. In effect, the UF, apart from the hollow rhetoric on race relations in British Guiana, served to widen the cleavage between the PPP and the PNC.

In this setting of political disunity, the electorate went to the polls in 1961. The elections, enacted under a new Constitution providing for a Legislative Assembly of 35 members, resulted in the PPP winning 20 seats (significantly all these were in rural areas with dense Indian populations) the PNC won 11 seats (confirming the Party's Afro-Guianese support in the urban areas) and the UF won 4 seats. From this election, one clear and chilling conclusion was drawn: 'that very few voters crossed racial lines'.[26]

At this time, while racial conflict was not pronounced, it would have been foolish, however, to devalue or ignore the deep, brooding underlying tensions that existed between the two major political groups. Yet another win for Jagan (despite local and international pressures to dislodge him from power) aroused both real and imagined fears among Afro-Guyanese and UF supporters of political domination of the East Indians led by a red-hot Communist. Not surprisingly, therefore, a few months after the elections, racial conflict took a new, unprecedented turn when the Jagan Government's budget and tax proposals were used as flashpoints for demonstrations of protest by the PNC and UF, and three important Public Service unions. As the protest gathered momentum, leading to racial violence between Indians and Afro-Guianese, British troops were employed to bring order. The years 1957 to 1961 were indeed trying for Jagan, who shouldered enormous responsibilities. He not only headed the Government (the first native British Caribbean leader to do so), but was also the Minister of Industry and Trade.

On reflection, by 1961, Jagan's PPP could at least claim credibility as a viable Government, which was able to bring together elements of the East Indian and Afro-Guyanese communities. Burnham, on the other hand, with little support from working class East Indians, strove to undermine the PPP's power-base by first wooing support from the new PNC, especially from the black middle class and the Portuguese. The split between Jagan and Burnham was seen by many not only in

British Guiana, but also among Third World leaders, as an unfortunate development.

The emergence of a Communist Cuba was seen by many as an unfortunate event in the Caribbean, especially because it was so close to the United States. Communism in the Caribbean therefore had to be kept out of the area at all costs, even if this meant deposing pro-Communist leaders. In British Guiana, anti-Communists from the United States were already at work during the election campaign, and both the Washington and British Governments had been monitoring developments in the Colony. As Premier of British Guiana, Jagan sought economic aid from the United States Government, but was confronted with scepticism from the Kennedy Administration because of his uncritical pro-Soviet Union position. Even so the State Department (in line with the British Government's view at the time, that there was no alternative to Jagan), was willing to consider the real prospect of working with the PPP, until United States foreign relations expert Dean Rusk, as Arthur Schlesinger put it, 'personally reversed this policy' in a letter to the British authorities early in 1962. And incredible as it may seem, the United States Government had committed themselves to undermining the Government democratically elected by the people of British Guiana.[27]

Little did the PPP Government know what fate awaited it as Jagan pressed on with his Prime Ministerial duties. His two main political rivals, Burnham and Peter D'Aguiar, undaunted by their election defeat called on the British Government to name a date for Independence. Prior to such an event, however, D'Aguiar demanded that new elections be held on the basis of proportional representation. President John F. Kennedy felt it was important to get British endorsement of his decision to remove the Jagan Government, and towards this end, anti-Communist United States trade unionists pursued their disruptive work of discrediting Jagan and the PPP. It could be said that the beginning of the end for the Jagan administration had begun with the introduction of the Government's Budget in January 1962.[28] Although Jagan took the hard decision of imposing tax increases on the poor, he felt it was incumbent upon the Guianese to share in the necessary process of modernization. While this 'most sensible budget' in the history of Guyana received praise from both *The New York Times* and *The Times* in London, Burnham and D'Aguiar saw it as a fine opportunity to discredit the Government. If Jagan had overestimated his popularity among Afro-Guianese in Georgetown, he was soon to find out just how serious it was. Apart from the fact that the city's trade unions, the Civil Service and the police were mainly Afro-Guianese, the fact that Georgetown's newspapers unanimously opposed the Budget, arguing 'inconsistently' that it was both Marxist and anti-working class, was of little help to the PPP Government.

The many demonstrations which followed Burnham with a long-awaited, marvellous opportunity to create the maximum disturbance by working up his followers into a 'state of frenzy'. By the early months of 1963, so tense had Georgetown become that Jagan turned to his most loyal supporters, the sugar workers. He may not have liked this racial cleavage between the city and the provinces, but that is how it was. Thereafter, race relations deteriorated, and during the escalating violence, many people lost their lives or were injured. Amidst this unprecedented and ugly strife, Jagan was informed that 7 December was the date set for the proportional representation elections.

In this state of chaos, Burnham spoke with optimism of the PNC winning the election with a clear majority. As it was, the PPP failed to win a majority of the total votes and a bitterly disappointed Jagan, envisaging a government by coalition, offered the Premiership to Burnham. With the United Force's support, Burnham was in a commanding position and on 13 December, Governor Luyt, invited him to form the British Guiana Government. Six days later, as Prime Minister, Burnham made clear his commitment to racial harmony.

The following year 1965 was a dismal one for the PPP, which had shown little interest in the prospect of Independence set for 26 May 1966. By then, the terms 'Apan jaht' and 'racial voting' had become common parlance in Guyanese politics.[29] It is interesting that while Burnham was overjoyed, D'Aguiar, even at that stage, was apprehensive. For his part, Jagan felt there was little to celebrate and with good reason. Independence brought with it a higher profile for Burnham who assumed the former Governor's role, as Chief of the Security Forces: both the Guyanese Defence Force and the Guyana Police were under his command. Anthony Verrier, the defence correspondent of *The Observer* who had spent several weeks in Guyana in 1966 noted that

> … the biggest question hanging over Guyana is what will happen in 1968. General elections are due then, and from Mr. Burnham downwards few expect his party, the African People's National Congress, to retain power through the ballot box. Guyana's Constitution provides for proportional representation, and it is no secret that this was devised by the British Government in 1964 in the hope of permanently excluding Mr. Burnham's opponent, the allegedly Communist Dr.Cheddi Jagan who leads the Indian PPP. Unfortunately for these calculations, it now appears that the past, let alone present, fertility of the Indian population is such that its voters in 1968 are likely to outnumber the PNC and its coalition partners put together.[30]

Unlike the Jagan Premiership, Burnham was no mere office-holder, he had real power, and he knew it, even though members of the Opposition and some of his supporters, at the time, seemed unaware. He already had plans for securing his hold on power, announcing that if he won the 1968 elections, he would establish a Republic. There was a good turnout on Election day 16 December 1968; and although it was peaceful, the main complaint arising from the Election was the question of proxy votes. Did an individual have the right to cast three? The 'overseas vote' was particularly questionable. Of the 68,000 'overseas' citizens who had been registered some 36,000 had participated in the election, resulting in the PPP and the UF receiving an estimated 1,000 votes each. Incredibly, the other remaining 34,000 votes went to the PNC, ensuring it a decisive victory. According to one account, the Guyana Government's 'claim that 68,000 Guyanese were living overseas was absolutely false. At the most there were about 30,000, yet 36,000 overseas votes had been recorded. Also between 1964 and 1968 the total electoral list had strangely increased by 21 per cent, while in the eleven-year period from 1953 to 1964, it had gone up by only 19 per cent'.[31]

If D'Aguiar had earlier doubts, at this point, even he was alarmed. 'I feel that I should have acted quicker', he said, 'that I shouldn't have been so naive, that I should have seen what was going to happen'. He felt that Burnham's Premiership marked the end of elections in Guyana, and commenting on the 1968 PNC victory, he said 'it was a seizure of power by fraud, not an election'.[32]

Predictably, Burnham's opponents seized the opportunity to accuse him of rigged elections, and while he may have been embarrassed, he felt secure in the knowledge that the forces of law and order were on his side, and that Jagan's continued pro-Soviet declarations could only serve to strengthen his power base *vis-a-vis* relations with the United States.

In victory then, Burnham was magnanimous and he could have afforded to be so. Ignoring the fraudulent manner in which he had come to power, he was still convinced that many East Indians had voted for him, in spite of the fact that his administration had done much to alienate them. And for those in the opposition who might have been pushed too far, he issued a warning. 'We do not deny the right of the opposition to oppose' he told a mass meeting, a few days after the election, but 'We will not permit the disruption of our national life in any manner. we are equipped materially and psychologically to deal firmly, impartially and swiftly with all who by any means or in any guise may be so ill-advised as to seek to spoil our record of peace and tranquility to gratify their puerile ambitions'.[33]

As he prepared for the Commonwealth Prime Ministers meeting in London, the much neglected Amerindian people revolted in the Rupununi in January 1969, reminding the rest of the Guyanese population that they too existed, though only barely so. Subsequently, at a meeting with 150 Amerindian Chiefs and their advisers on 28 February 1969, Burnham assured them of full integration as Guyanese citizens, and one of them was chosen to serve on the Lands Commission. Alas the political promises made were not enough for the Indians.[34]

Unhampered, Burnham forged ahead with his political ambitions, still seeking 'socialist' solutions for the country's deepening social and economic difficulties. His mind was set on making a Republic, a 'Cooperative Republic', which would, of course, incorporate all the people. This grand concept, he felt, would effectively counter Jagan's Communism and D'Aguiar's Capitalism. And so with Burnham's careful political timing, on 23 February 1970 (the 207th Anniversary of the slave leader Cuffy's Berbice slave rebellion of 1763) Guyana became a Co-operative Republic, but remained a member of the Commonwealth.

Burnham saw Co-operatives neither as a 'mere appendage to the economic life' of Guyana nor as just another exercise in social welfare. He elaborated, 'Our basic proposition is: ... the organisation of our human and material resources through the cooperative movement with Government providing financial assistance, management, training and administrative direction'. He urged the Guyanese people to grasp the value of coming together as a group, of pooling their physical, material and human resources, 'so that as *small men we can become real men*'.[35]

If the Co-operative Republic day celebrations were 'frantic' in Georgetown, for Guyanese in the countryside, it was a moment for serious thought, for 'with the exception of a very few East Indians', wrote one historian, 'he (Burnham) had thoroughly alienated the East Indian majority'. The seriousness of Burnham's predicament in ensuring racial harmony was underlined by the fact that providing opportunities for East Indian advancement only antagonised his Afro-Guyanese supporters, who dominated the Guyana Defence Force and the Police.

The polarization of Guyana's two main racial groups and the rise in crime and violence prompted Rickey Singh to write that

> Public morality is not what it should be, and it is eroding all our institutions and the very quality of our life. Our predicament is *not* eased by the fact of having political parties which are bent on destroying each other at all cost, irrespective of the consequence to the national life.
>
> Hence while the present ruling party did its very best to encourage indiscipline among school children, policemen, civil servants, church and trade unions to embarass and bring about the downfall of the PPP, the latter is now doing nothing to help the PNC in creating an atmosphere of stability.[36]

Not surprisingly then, an estimated 5,000 to 7,000 Guyanese (in the main Indo-Guyanese people) were emigrating to the United Kingdom, the United States and Canada. Thousands had already 'voted with their feet' before Burnham announced that elections would be held on 16 July 1973. The fear, suspicion and harrrassment endemic in this election did little to instill confidence among the people. Reported irregularities once again brought into question the entire electoral process in Guyana.[37]

Notwithstanding the means, the end was achieved. The PNC won a two-thirds majority in the Legislative Assembly and despite talk of collaboration between Burnham and Jagan in a coalition Government, the die had already been cast back in 1968 when Burnham's power became entrenched, though this was not as evident then.

If Burnham had no intention of sharing power, this became increasingly clear in the ensuing years for those who yearned for a new path for Guyana. By 1977 prospects for the Caribbean Common Market (CARICOM) were not as bright as was hoped, and, in particular, the Guyanese economy, as far as the majority of people were concerned, was in the doldrums. It was against this background of economic depression at the end of 1977 that the Rev. Jim Jones, an American, established his

People's Temple at Jonestown. He was not short of money and had a multiracial following. As cooperatives go, on the face of it, this commune augured well for the Government which endorsed the Jonestown experiment.

In California, as criticism against the People's Temple mounted, there was the demand for an inquiry. Subsequently, American Congressman Leo Ryan's investigation into conditions at Jonestown in 1978 ended in his murder. Rather than submit to exposure, Jones called upon his followers to commit mass suicide. On Saturday 18 November 1978 more than 900 of them were found dead, an incredible incident that attracted international attention to Guyana and its problems.

Frantic efforts to find alternatives to the PNC did not lessen. By 1979 there was growing support for the Working People's Alliance which included Walter Rodney, Moses Bhagwan, Eusi Kwayama and Clive Thomas, who advocated free elections, national unity and social justice. This was a disturbing development for the all-powerful PNC Government, which was determined to tolerate only as much opposition as it thought necessary. Following a fire at the Ministry of National Development and the Office of the General Secretary of the PNC building, Walter Rodney, Rupert Roopnarine and Dr. Omawale were charged and released on bail. The trial of these men was cause for deep concern among many people in Guyana. Basic freedoms, it was felt, were denied the defendants, whose appeal was rejected and who were denied a trial by jury. After a hearing in June 1980, the trial was adjourned to August. But on Friday evening 13 June, Walter Rodney was murdered. Most people in Guyana were outraged, and Heads of States from Jamaica, Grenada and Cuba, condemned this heinous act. Rodney's funeral on 23 June, drew over 25,000 people of various races and creeds, and speaking at Merriman's Mall, Rupert Roopnarine spoke of the 'stain of disgrace and degeneracy' linked with the murder of a 'good and just man'. Just a few days before his death, Rodney had emphasized the WPA's determination 'to work for a government of national unity and reconstruction; for the inter-racial unity of all working people'.[38]

Before the end of the year, on 6 October 1980, a new Constitution which came into effect, installing Burnham as the first Executive President of Guyana, cause further concern. Rickey Singh editor of *Caribbean Contact*, wrote that the Constitution had placed Burnham 'above the law', making him 'immune from persecution for any offence whatsoever either in his official or personal capacity'.[39] And commenting on the PNC victory at the elections on 15 December 1980, a team of international observers concluded that the elections were 'massively and flagrantly rigged'.[40]

By the turn of the new year, human rights practices in Guyana were cited in the United States State Department's Annual Report (1980) to the Congress, which stated that the 'general economic situation has deteriorated in recent years'.[41] Between 1981 and 1983, as harassment of the Opposition continued, the economy's continuing decline brought hardship in many spheres of life for the Guyanese people and again the violation of 'human rights' became an issue. In the depth of their depressed state many courageous Guyanese people were asking how long would it take for their country to start anew, to become a full vibrant nation. Ironically, the PNC's continuing oppressive tactics, had the unforseen effect, of forging co-operation between Afro-Guyanese and East Indians for it had become abundantly clear that unless these two sections got together, there was little chance of bringing about the a new beginning.

## Jagan's Re-emergence

Since 1964 Guyana had not had free and fair elections, a fact which has led to a socio-political, economic and moral crisis. Twenty-seven years since he led the Government, Dr. Jagan, as Leader of the Opposition and General Secretary of the PPP had waged a relentless campaign to restore democratic rule and to re-orient Guyana on the path to economic recovery. Following Burnham's death in 1985, little had changed economically. If anything the downward slide had continued; so much so, that by June 1991 it was reported that the wages of a Security Guard was 80 cents for a twelve-hour day 'not quite enough to buy a pound of chicken.'[42]

In recent years, there has been lively public debate in Guyana and while free elections in Europe meant new faces in government, this was not the case in Guyana which was ruled from the top by President Desmond Hoyte, Burnham's successor. Over the years, however, Jagan has continued to press the PNC and to seek international support for free and fair elections to save Guyana from further ruin. Consequently, by September 1990, it was disclosed that several United States Congressmen had sent a letter to the Secretary of State, James Baker, urging him to with-hold United States aid if the Hoyte Government failed to implement electoral reforms. Among the Senate signatories was Senator Edward Kennedy. As it was, this support was a break-through for Jagan who had been lobbying politicians in the United States so that free and fair elections could be effected. To this end he visited Washington, where he sought the assistance of an American law firm, whose representative Jeff Dunoff was sent to Jamaica during the July 1990 Summit of the Caribbean Common Market. Dunoff shared a press conference with Jagan. Earlier both men were engaged in talks at the Carter Centre in Atlanta, and now in Jamaica contents of the letters to James Baker were disclosed. It was reported that the letters contained an appeal to the American Government not to subsidize fraudulent regimes and to insist upon a number of conditions; international observance of the Guyanese electoral process; appointment of an independent and impartial elections commission; preparations for a new voter registration list; and guarantees against ballot tampering and fraudulent counting.[43]

Jagan received another filip in his campaign for free and fair elections, when that same year 1990, Arthur Schlesinger Jr, former aide to President Kennedy publicly apologised for his role, and that of the United States Administration, in helping to remove the PPP Government headed by Dr. Jagan in the early 1960s. This apology was given during a symposium sponsored by the American weekly magazine *The Nation*. Schlesinger admitted that Jagan was right in his claims of United States intervention in Guyanese politics. 'I felt badly about my role thirty years ago', he said, 'I think I did a great injustice to Cheddi Jagan'.[44] Schlesinger is reported to have advised Kennedy that Jagan's opponents, at the time 'would cause us fewer problems' and recommended the establishment in Guyana of a system of proportional representation. This was done with the collusion of the British Government and the CIA, which rallied support for the opposition led by Burnham. The civil and racial strife that followed eventually brought down the Jagan Government in 1964. In retrospect, *The Nation* in an Editorial of 4 June 1990 stated that if Jagan had been allowed to rule, Guyana 'would have avoided some of the bloodshed, racial conflict, misery and chaos that came in the wake of his party's defeat'.

So towards the end of 1990, it seemed Jagan no longer appeared as a threat to the United States Government. In fact Congressman Weiss indicated that the United States was no longer worried by a government led by Jagan, and said that the current mood in Congress was pro-democracy; that Congress was concerned about free and fair elections and not whether Jagan was Marxist.[45]

Morever, Americas Watch representative Jeremy Slade who went to Guyana to look into electoral laws and procedures said that there should be 1,800 observers, two for each polling station on election day in Guyana. He detected a marked reluctance by the PNC Government to undertake free registration and to count the ballots at the place of poll. In addition, moves were being made in Britain, through the British Government and MPs to exert pressure on the Guyanese authorities with the objective of creating free and fair conditions for General Elections. The Canadian Government was also willing to monitor the poll; and following a memorandum sent to British Prime Minister Margaret Thatcher by the Chairman of the UK Branch of the PPP on electoral practices under the PNC regime, Tim Sainsbury replied on behalf of the Prime Minister:

> We are aware of the allegations that have been made regarding the conduct of elections in Guyana. Both Mr. Major, the Secretary of State for Foreign and Commonwealth Affairs and Mrs.Chalker, Minister of Overseas Development, reminded President Hoyte of the importance which this Government attaches to the principle of free and fair elections when they met in October and December 1989. I also emphasized the need for elections to be free and fair when the Foreign Minister of Guyana called me on 21 May 1990.

By the end of 1990 then, the local and international pressure which Jagan had been working assiduously for, had begun to gain momentum. Earlier in the year, referring to the Caribbean leaders who were reluctant to support his campaign for free and fair elections in Guyana, he stated that they 'must have received a jolt when in February 1990 President George Bush, in a Republic Day Message to President Hoyte said he hoped that the upcoming elections would be held according to the norms of democracy, cherished by the people of the United States and Guyana'. He added that the jolt must have been stronger, two months later, in April for soon after his visit to Washington, Assistant Secretary of State for Caribbean Affairs, Sally Cowal, was asked by a Washington correspondent, Wesley Kirton 'How would the United States administration view a Jagan victory in Guyana?' She replied that the United States Government would recognise a Government which emerged from a certified free and fair election. Cowal repeated this view a year later in Georgetown at a press conference after the opening of the new United States Chancery Building. She said 'Whoever is elected in an election that was certified (as free and fair) by international observers', that elected official who represented the will of the people of Guyana 'will find us ready to discuss an aid programme'. Jagan was, at last, beginning to see light at the end of a long and dark tunnel in his patient campaign for political and economic improvements to Guyana.

Free and fair election and much-needed foreign aid were so inextricably linked that the PNC regime was forced to reconsider what had become an indefensible position. Faced with growing local and international pressure the PNC had agreed to hold elections in 1991. According to one report the election had 'already been running late. The opposition members of Parliament resigned their seats on April 2nd, protesting that the House should have been dissolved by February. The Government has been extending its life, two months at a time, ever since, pleading that time is needed to prepare a new electoral register. The register will be ready by early August and the election date should, barring accidents, be announced soon afterwards'.[46]

Over the years in opposition, to his great credit, Jagan had maintained a dialogue with other political leaders and parties. Not surprisingly, many of these leaders have opposed him. 'Their politics of disfavour', as Festus Brotherson Jr, (a former political aide of President Burnham and former editor of *The New Nation*, the offical organ of the PNC) put it, 'have strengthened rather than weakened the PPP leader's chances of electoral victory'. One of the charges laid against Jagan was that he should step down and make way for new and younger politicians. Among those who hold this view is Eusi Kwayama (formerly Sidney King) of the Working People's Alliance, who in removing himself from the contention for the top political office, urged others 'too old' to follow him.

But whatever lingering doubts Opposition leaders may have had of Jagan's approach to Guyanese politics had been dispelled in recent years. Brotherson wrote: 'First is the decline of communism as an important factor in politics both locally and abroad. This means that the former premier is less likely to be opposed by the Americans (indeed has proven to be so) and be less able to form and sustain foreign communist alliances of any important consequence where he to become President. Besides, like all other individuals and parties on the left in Guyana, he has reshaped his views to reflect more pragmatism'.

Apart from these changes, Brotherson paid tribute to the man who had spent almost three decades in the political wilderness. 'Dr. Jagan's most commendable qualities', he wrote, 'are his undisputed sincerity of purpose and personal integrity. Although many people might disagree with his ideas, none can impugn his character. He is genuinely committed to the development of Guyana and he cannot be accused of being corrupt. These traits stand out in a society bereft of developmental direction and drifting in a sea of corruption ... It is quite conceivable that Dr. Jagan could be the next President of Guyana once the general elections are fairly conducted'.[47]

It is with the prospect of the elections in mind that Jagan prepared to deliver his address to the Twenty-fourth PPP Congress in June-July 1991. How tenacious he had been in opposition. He opened by saying that the Congress was being held at a 'very crucial juncture in mankind's historical development', and quoted the words of Tom Paine, the famous British freedom fighter at the time of the American Revolution, who inspired American revolutionaries: 'We are living in times that try men's souls'. And he pointed out that the Party had been in existence for 40 years and was the leading force in the politics of Guyana.

He spoke about the Cold War which had divided mankind into two hostile worlds, one West and one East, one Capitalist and one Socialist, and the divided worlds of 'the powerful super-rich conspicuous consumers' and that of the powerless, 'the marginalised dependent poor'. The gap between them is widening he declared. He spoke of the skewed distribution of income in Latin America and the Caribbean. In 1980, five per cent of the population at the top enjoying 40 per cent of the national income, while 40 per cent at the bottom were scrounging on 8 per cent of the national income and warned that the future will be worse.

The PNC must be responsible for the mess created in Guyana, where life had become one of mere existence and survival. 'Sixty per cent of our people are below the poverty line', he said. 'Inflation is running between 80–100 per cent. The minimum wage ... is $65 per day', which fell short of earning him the much-desired 'pound of chicken'. Then there were the problems of water, electricity, fuel and transportation and the exodus of the country's best sons and daughters completed the picture of Guyana 'bleeding to death'. He appealed for a stop to this flow of manpower and spoke of the psychology of hopelessness, dependency and disintegration and if in reality Guyana was a 'dying state', it was urgently necessary to restore its health.

He told Congress delegates they should be proud that in the interest of achieving national, racial and working class unity there was 'always a methodology ... Ours is not the politics of rabble-rousing and name calling. Our methodology from the very beginning was to identify the root causes of the problems and to prescribe a scientific cure. And that is what we are always doing. For us economics interact with politics, ideology, institutions and culture'. He then went on to outline a comprehensive programme of which the PPP Manifesto will be a part. Jagan did not see development as just economic, development of GDP growth. He was careful to emphasize 'a human development strategy, a wider all-embracing concept for the creation of a caring society with humanitarian values, ethical and moral standards. Economic growth and development will be linked with social justice and basic needs – jobs and job satisfaction, safety at work places, education, medical care, housing, security in old age, human rights' guarantees and last but not least environmental protection'.

He also spoke about the creation of a 'model' Third World country, incorporating the United Nations, the Organisation of American States and the European Economic Community conventions on human rights that will set up a CARICOM Human Rights Convention which leaders have been 'avoiding for a long time';[48] and once in Government the party intended to restore the right of the Guyanese people to free and fair elections periodically, thus necessitating the setting up of an independent Elections commission.

Jagan assured the Congress that the Constitution would be revised, and made it clear that there would be no imperial President and no Dictator. The President's powers will be decreased, the Prime minister's powers will be increased and there will be more cooperation, consultation and collective leadership between the two Executives. And significantly, the phrase 'transition from capitalism to socialism' which was wrongly inserted in the Constitution will be removed.

Furthermore Parliamentary democracy, with specialised committees along the lines of parliaments in England, Canada and the United States, would be implemented and there would, of course, be free and open debate at the University of Guyana. On the sensitive, but central question of race, he declared that the Congress cannot tolerate racial or political discrimination in any form. 'We will ensure that the State institutions, the Ombudsman, police complaint authority, service commissions and employment agencies are independent', he said, and a Commission for Racial Equality will be set up. And he spelt out guidelines for the rule of law, financial accountability, eliminating corruption nationally, international loans and international goodwill with those Guyanese abroad with capital and skills.

Jagan then spotlighted the good fortune of the PPP in that most of its supporters were engaged as land-farmers and businessmen. 'We will continue to develop the gold, diamond, bauxite and sugar industries', he said. 'But it is the agro-industrial sector which is going to play the key role in turning around the economy, which we badly need to feed the people, meet the high cost of living and bring in foreign exchange. This sector will also help to feed the Caribbean which has a high import bill'.

He assured businessmen about taxation and spoke of state enterprises in the Soviet Union and Eastern Europe (and this would have heartened even some of his staunchest critics), where the state sector failed 'because of over-capitalization, corruption, lack of accountability and bureaucratic command type of government and management'. He recognised these imperfections as someone who believes in Socialism and said he would do everything to avoid such methods which led to failure in these countries. He declared that working people must have a say and that the state must help to protect the poor. He also gave the assurance that private business would be protected. He pointed out that a harmonious relationship with the trade union movement was priority and believed that a partnership between labour and capital would be mutually beneficial. On the social services, it was imperative to provide free education, free medical care and housing, he said. He then outlined Congress's ambitious plans for the Amerindians in Guyana, going further than any political party had ever gone before, stating that a PPP Government would introduce Amerindian involvement and development. 'These brothers and sisters of ours', he said, 'have been reduced to third class citizens and we intend to bring them up to the status like everyone else'. The urgency of their problems demanded the immediate setting up of an American task force to consult all the Amerindian people so that community projects will suit their needs will be embarked upon. 'We will set up a special Amerindian Fund and, if possible, have a minister in charge of Amerindian Affairs', he added.

Given that in 1977, the PNC refused his Party's call for a National Patriotic Front 'We came out with a policy that the winner-will-not take all in recognition of the need for unity for economic, ethnic, cultural and security reasons', he said. And after making approaches to other political parties, the PPP got together with the Guyanese Action for Reform and Democracy and won the support of Sam Hinds.

On the question of Marxism, Jagan said that the positive sides of the market economy should be chosen as well as the socialist utopia in which people are at the centre of development. 'We must be careful that in throwing out the bath water we do no throw out the baby'. And for those who still saw him as an avowed, hard-line Marxist, he went further assuring them that because of the complexity and rapidity of changes in the Soviet Union and Eastern Europe, new assessments had become necessary. 'Our embrace of Marxist-Leninism lies in the commitment to build a society free from exploitation and governed by those who produce the wealth', he said, adding that it was 'necessary to review some deeply entrenched, previously unquestioned tenets of scientific socialist theory'. On reflection, in the context of the Cold War, Jagan recognised that the tendency to follow Soviet foreign policy, remaining silent even when his Party disagreed on some questions, was the wrong approach. Now the main item on the agenda, in the interest of the Guyanese people was, as he put it, the task of building a national and revolutionary democracy.

In closing his important Congress address Jagan spoke of forging genuine partnership with the Party's friends at home and abroad, recognising the need for inter-dependence. Co-operation was a key word and he reiterated the PPP strategy of 'winner will not take all'. In conclusion, he invited all sections of the Guyanese people to join the PPP in his efforts to restore national independence, democratic freedom and the pursuit of happiness. He was confident that having won three times in a row, in the forthcoming elections 'We will win!'

A few weeks later, at a meeting in London's Conway Hall, on Sunday 18 August 1991, Jagan said that a PPP victory at the elections will mean not a socialist or communist Government, but will be one that is multi-party, multi-racial and multi-class. Marxism and other isms, he said, were 'red-herrings' not relevant to today's political situation in Guyana. According to Howard French of the *New York Times*, Jagan proclaims his rebirth, calling himself a 'Gorbachev before Gorbachev'.[49] Jagan told his London audience that what the people of Guyana wanted was 'food in their bellies and brains in their heads'.

Greyer, older and wiser, he spoke passionately for two hours, all eyes and ears in the packed Hall, homing-in, picking up every gesture of his hands and nuance of his voice. His endurance and polished performance was astonishing. Many in the audience were clearly too young to remember those exciting and trying days when he became the first Prime Minister of Guyana, though they would have heard about him. Not surprisingly, one of these young people asked him how old he was and what was the state of his health. 'I am 73 years old and I'm in good health', he said calmly and he assured the young man who had put the question to him that he intended to live long enough to fulfill his pledges. Having finished his speech, he left the rostrum (above which was emblazoned in large letters 'To Thine Own Self Be True') and made his way, perhaps for the last time before the long-awaited elections, out of that familiar Hall (where he had addressed many audiences over the years) with his clear vision of a free Guyana, and intent on providing the Guyanese people not with isms, but with 'food in their bellies' and in helping them to develop the 'brains in their heads'.

A few years earlier, confronted with the question of Indo-Caribbean political leadership, he commented on the evolution of Blacks and Indians in the region, and concluded, 'they are not exactly the same as the roots from which they sprang; indeed they have many things in common, more that unites than divides them. They must find the means of cooperation, including political power-sharing'.[50]

As ever, Jagan the politician remained patient and optimistic, a beacon in the Caribbean darkness, as he and and the vast majority of his countrymen of all races and classes, at home and abroad, await the reality and outcome of a return to democracy in Guyana. At last, in October 1992 Elections were held, and after twenty-eight years, he was again at the forefront of leadership (a position which many had for a long time thought was impossible) as the President of the Co-operative Republic of Guyana. As Leader of his country, he addressed the opening ceremony of the Special Session of the CARICOM Heads of Government Conference in Port of Spain on 28 October 1992. 'Our primary aim', he said, 'must be the eradication of poverty'. He spoke of the hard challenges of the 21st century and referred to his predecessor, Desmond Hoyte, who was charged with 'certain mandates' which he assured the Conference he would pursue in a manner which is expected of him. He extended greetings from the people of a Free Guyana and concluded: 'We have a common destiny! It is time for action'. Few denied Jagan's commitment to the land of his birth. For the rest of his Presidency, with characteristic integrity, he steadfastly maintained the solemn 'pledge' had had made some forty-seven years earlier. And more than four decades after he had written *Forbidden Freedom*, he was still optimistic about the Guyanese people's will and determination to survive, their desire and capability (given the required assistance) og building a new Guyana. In the process of doing so, he had no doubt that the people of all races in Guyana would make their contribution 'to the goals of world peace and a new Global Humanitarian Order'.

Dr. Cheddi Jagan was a rare phenomenon, without peer in world politics. In the troubled times before he died (characterised by ethnic divisions), it was widely acknowledged that he deserved support not only from the Guyanese people, but also from the friends of Guyana in the international community. But even though he had again become Head of State, the decades of oppression, violence and emigration had reinforced an Indo-Caribbean identity which, if anything, was strengthened after his death.

# TRINIDAD

## *Early Representations*

Bearing in mind that the Indians in Trinidad were, and are, not a homogenous group, the question of their integration into the larger society has historically and predictably brought their early and later, political parties and leaders, into contention over various issues. And contrary to their employers' attitude, unanimity among them was therefore, not to be taken for granted.

One of the earliest examples of discordance was to be found between the East Indian National Association and the East Indian National Congress, the pre-eminent Indian organisations in Trinidad, and on the crucial question of social interaction with members of other groups in the society at large, two leading Indians expressed their strong views in public. While Seepersad Naipaul, the Indo-Trinidadian journalist was against Indians inter-marrying and assimilating the Western style of dress, Adrian Cola Rienzi, of a younger generation of Indians and more radical, felt that by marrying a European, Afro-Trinidadian or Chinese, an Indian person was not compromising his sense of morality. On the contrary, Rienzi pointed out that each party to such a union, necessarily brought with them their own history and culture, which must be respected. Hitherto, few Indians of his standing had gone as far. In fact, he went further, encouraging young Indians to look to their future in Trinidad, rather than dwell on the glory that was India; and he showed his disenchantment with Indians by expressing his disgust over India's lack of 'self-determination', a land where women were 'unfree' and where 'millions were suppressed in the name of religion, ancient custom and "their excessive religiousity"'[51]

Having been through the severe tests of survival in a period during which living conditions had deteriorated considerably (for they no longer had even the binding entrapment of the minimal protective cover of the 'social security' of the indenture system after 1917), Indian engagement in the important 1919 Strikes (before trade unions were legalized), the hunger marches, strikes and riots of the 1930s, had resulted in an evident degree of Afro-Indian solidarity. But given the racial tensions that followed in the years before Independence and after, that kept Indians and other groups (particularly Afro-Trinidadians) at logger-heads, the debate as to the extent of the Indians' integration into the mainstream of society has persisted.

Some fifty years after they had first arrived in Trinidad, J.C. Jha wrote 'the Indians (both indentured and free) saw themselves as transients', aliens with only a minimal interest in the affairs of the island. India and Indian affairs provided them with 'inspiration and guidance'. Soon, however, as their rights were being eroded, and their numbers increased, they began to organise and agitate peacefully.[52] But such organisations as there were had to surmount many difficulties. As one historian put it:

> If during working hours an indentured labourer was not in the field or factory one could confidently expect to find him either sick in hospital or locked away in jail. The plantation itself was a prison of sorts which kept its victims confined to a system of interlocking incarceration. Walls erected at different but connected levels. First of all the legal restrictions on movement outside the estates. Secondly, the weight of inertia upon the individual bred by poor living conditions and wasting diseases. Next, the knowledge that the formidable apparatus of the state including police and magistrates, and not excluding for these purposes the makers of public opinion was marshalled to ensure that labour played only its expected role. On top of this many indentured workers were encouraged into heavy debt to the company store for rations provided at inflated prices. Often too one week's wages would be held as a guarantee of good performance at the workplace. Most inhibiting of all, however, was the daily revelation that the leaders whom one could expect to speak up on behalf of the workers were often suborned to the purposes of the employers.[53]

It comes as no surprise therefore, that in their attempts to redress outstanding grievances of the East Indian community, the early pressure groups in Trinidad between 1897 and 1921 achieved few successes. But the fact that they existed at all in such an hostile environment was in itself a worthy achievement.

For both the indentured and free Indians in Trinidad, because of their religious dress, manners and customs, they were subjected to ridicule, taunts and the wanton assaults of members of other groups in the wider society, as they sought urgent change to their unsatisfactory position and status.[54] They had no alternative but to remain aloof, come to terms with their position and consolidate their communal position *vis-à-vis* their oppressors.

Understandably, their frustration and desperation, at times, led to periodic violent protests which, in turn, encouraged Government officials to adopt more hostile and repressive attitudes towards Indians, to the extent that demands for necessary wage increases were regarded as seditious. Violence was, however, not an element of protest which undertook lightly. Demonstrations such as the Hosea (Hussay) processions were public displays of unity and, not infrequently iinsubordination against oppressive British rule. Indians in Trinidad were well-informed of events in India and of the ill-treatment of Indians elsewhere in the Caribbean, in Guyana and Surinam, for example, where workers clashed with plantation managers. Thus recurrent violent protest in Trinidad in 1872, 1883 and in the 1884 Hosea Riots, served notice to the Government that 'Coolie disturbances' were not the strivings of 'ring leaders' but a hardened rank and file resistance against the dehumanising nature of the system of indenture.

Although in the 1890s, the foremost Hindu institutions were Panchayats (a fact recognised by planters) it was not until 1897 that favourable conditions made possible the organisation of an East Indian pressure group.[55] It is significant that at this time a few educated Christian Indians, such as James Namsoo, recognised the political and constitutional value of the Indian population in the southern part of the island, which had grown. Of the 88,501 Indians who went to Trinidad, many had returned to India or had died between 1845 and 1891. By April 1891 there were 45,577 Indians, composed of natives of India and 24,641 born in Trinidad – a total of 70,218 (42,903 males and 27,313 females), among whom there was a sense of community encouraged by deepening alienation from the wider society.

This emergent political consciousness among the Trinidad Indians was linked to events in India. As Jha put it, 'If the Ilbert Bill controversy and the reduction of the age of entry to the Indian Civil Service provided the immediate reason for organising the National Congress of India in 1885, the Immigration Ordinance of 1897 united the Indians in Trinidad as never before'. So a 'pan-Indian' political consciousness came into being, providing opportunities for the isolated community to organise themselves in relation to parallel developments in India, such as English education, and ideas of equality and nationality which also had an impact on the Trinidad Indians. It should not surprise us therefore that the Indian National Congress was the model for the Trinidad East Indian National Association, an indigenous organisation which not only promoted Indian nationality, but also local constitutional changes and the 'rights and privileges' of British citizenship. And like the Congress in India, at least during its early phases, the Trinidad EINA, a 'debating society', was a moderate pressure group which 'passed resolutions, urged redress of grievances and avoided bitter attacks'.[56]

The Indians had begun to respond publicly to their oppressed status. One Indian complained to the editor of the *Port of Spain Gazette* that it was 'unjust and unfair' to call the Indians 'immigrants' years after expiration of their 'industrial' service, when many Irishmen and other whites were not so called; and contended that they were denied the same freedom as their fellow-labourers such as Barbados.

The EINA, with a membership of 200 in 1897, objected to the new Immigration Ordinance, particularly the provision requiring them to carry 'free' papers. As it was, they had to be content with an amendment to one of the clauses of the main Ordinance, a minimal success that nevertheless had the effect of promoting the EINA, at least in the eyes of the authorities, as a viable organisation. Impressed by the Association's 'orderliness and respectful demeanor', the Governor used his powers to repeal the 'obnoxious clauses' of the Ordinance and significantly, the EINA received official recognition as being representative of the Indians in Trinidad. Between 1898 (when the Association was formally organised) until 1909, the EINA remained the unrivalled representative of the Indians. That same year, the East Indian National Congress, formed in Couva, with a middle-class, moderate leadership, was also confined to 'peaceful protest'.

About this time, another Indian pressure group, the National Panchayat (a Council of 12 persons, unlike the village Panchayats) emerged to consider the Presbyterian missionary John Morton's proposal to abolish the Indians' right a free return passage to India. The Indians were astounded by this 'cruel motion' passed at a meeting of the Agricultural Society in Port of Spain. This issue, a matter of central concern within the Indian population, aroused much indignation. Appearing before the National Panchayat, it seemed Morton had satisfied them of his main concern that future Indian immigrants should be recruited under a new contract which would ensure their permanent settlement in the Colony. This was precisely what the planters wanted, a timely outcome, given that the Guyana Government was also considering the question of a revision of the return passage question.

There is evidence that towards the end of the nineteenth century, Brahmin priests and Muslim maulvis provided a 'marginal form of leadership' among the Indians. They were particularly concerned with the preservation of their Indian heritage, which was threatened by the host society.

Into the first decade of the twentieth century, adopting a 'peaceful protest' approach, the leaders of Indian pressure groups were faced with one of their greatest challenges: contesting the illegality of non-Christian marriages. In 1904 a major protest against this was made to the Governor by the EINA, and a year later, the Association also opposed the rise in price of Crown Lands from £2 to £4 per acre. Four years later, both the EINA and EINC focused attention on the Sanderson Committee Inquiry.

Politically, developments among the Indians in Trinidad, to some extent, helped by the Sanderson Committee recommendations, moved apace. Unlike the situation in Guyana, where in E.A. Luckhoo's opinion, the Indians were 'not quite alive yet' to their political rights and interest, in 1909, the Indian Barrister George Fitzpatrick, on behalf of the Trinidad Indians, said in London that the Indian community should be represented by an Indian in the Legislative Council. At this time, there seemed to have been a considerable degree of unity among Indians who adhered to the major religious faiths within the EINA and EINC. At a well-attended meeting of the Indian community in Trinidad (advertised in *Port of Spain Gazette* and *The Mirror*) held at Princes Town, George Fitzpatrick was elected to represent them before the Sanderson Committee. Before him, few Indians in the Caribbean (notably Bechu, the indentured labourer from British Guiana) had the opportunity of giving evidence to a Royal Commission. Overall, Fitzpatrick argued that the Indians' grievances were not 'properly redressed'[57] and such representations as he had made, engendered its own momentum.

By 1912, the Trinidad Democratic League was founded, arousing further Indian interest in local politics. About this time, there were also a number of new developments impinging on the growing political awareness of Indians in Trinidad. Political agitation in India and the gradual spread of education among Indians in Trinidad, heightened political awareness and brought forward new leaders. Economically too, the island enjoyed an expansion in the number of rubber trees planted, in the acreage under rice cultivation, and in the production and export of coconuts and bananas. And of major importance, the discovery of oil in 1907–8 initiated oil production which, in turn, led to better roads, an increase in the number of motor vehicles, and improvements in communications generally. Taken together, this economic buoyancy came at a time of unity within the Indian community, largely due to the unfavourable Eurocentric attitudes and perceptions of other groups in the wider society, preejudices based essentially on race.

At last in 1912, the EINA was rewarded with the nomination of George Fitzpatrick to the Legislative Council. He had been faithful to his people's cause and his example was symbolic of other possibilities. A year later, he was joined in the Indian leadership by the young English-educated Indian F.E.M. Hosein who, projecting a more radical approach to the political development of the Indians, pointed out that for so long as their interest remained unaffected and at one with the entire colony, they would remain 'passive and their present development will not go beyond the holding of annual and general meetings'. Hosein also referred to the Indians' 'industry and thrift' and their hard-won status, which now included Fitzpatrick's representations on the Legislative Council.

Fortuitously, Gandhi's agitation in South Africa in 1913 was at a time when the McNeill and Lal Commission visited Trinidad. Both the EINA and EINC made representations. The Commission, *inter alia*, recommended the continuation of Indian immigration (an issue on which the EINA and the EINC differed) and the recognition of marriages performed by Hindu priests and Muslim Kazis.

By 1914, the EINA and EINC, still 'peaceful' pressure groups, were joined by a number of similar groups, including Friendly Societies, debating and literary clubs and sports organisations. Together, these groups aroused a greater awareness of the Indians'position in Trinidad society and the political consequences of this was reflected in the fact that in the 1916 Municipal elections large numbers of Indians voted. Jha has maintained that while in many cases these pressure groups were effective to the extent that 'their voice was heard', they were also subjected to strong criticism from some Indians.

The second decade of the twentieth century had far-reaching consequences for Trinidad Indians. Leaders such as C.H. Gopaul, C.D. Lalla and Jules Mahabir, joined the 'reform movement', which coincided with the advent of Gandhi's leadership in Indian nationalist politics from 1920, a leadership that was influential among Indians in Trinidad.[58] Overall, in spite of religious and caste differences, by the turn of the century, East Indian pressure groups were remarkably united displaying solidarity among Hindus, Muslims and Christians, thus engendering a new level of consciousness, as they confronted deep-seated problems.

Given that the roots of 'ethnic stereotyping' in Trinidad can be traced back to the slave and indentureship systems, it has been argued that from the very beginning the importation of Indians into the Caribbean had been the cause of a 'relentless campaign' launched by Coloured-Black spokesmen in Trinidad. This 'Coloured-Black bitterness', it was felt, could only be adequately explained through an understanding of the power struggle between the 'middle class intelligentsia' and the 'coloured-White elite'.

While Indian immigration was used initially to keep intact the colonial economic and social structure, it was also used to perpetuate White colonial rule. Thus White political control was effected through the system of Indian immigration in which the 'roots of Afro-Indian conflict' in the colony was to be found.[59] In order to understand this, Singh directs our attention to the emergence of a middle class in the nineteenth century, when in 1802 the island became a British colony. 'Trinidad was rather exceptional in that it possessed a free coloured population', he argued, 'a composite social category consisting of persons of mixed White-African ancestry that out-numbered the White population. Many free Coloureds were wealthy and educated but subject to humiliating legal and social sanctions imposed by the dominant Whites'.[60] Demographically, the influx of Indians into Trinidad worried [61] the Coloured and Black spokesmen, who saw Indian immigration as a 'projected political question'. As Singh saw it, 'Behind the campaign against Indians loomed the spectre of the empty land space of an as yet underdeveloped ... colony being filled by Indians rather than Africans'.[62]

Joining the chorus of opposition against this immigration (which grew in 'intensity and vehemence') were the Afro-Trinidadian working class leaders. As far as the Coloured-Black intelligentsia were concerned, the targeted goal was abolition of

Indian immigration which, it was hoped, would remove the 'Indian spectre'.[63] Predictably, this 'negative view' of the Indians resulted in 'political bifurcation', precisely what any divide-and-rule strategy demands.[64]

The political cleavage between Afro-Trinidadians and Indians was clearly evident[65] to visitors from abroad, including the British Labour M.P, Joseph Pointer, as mentioned earlier. Singh concludes that conciliation between the two groups was ill-timed. 'Too much bitterness had been generated by the campaign against Indian immigration', he contended, 'and too many derogatory remarks made about Indians',[66] and for too long a period of time. Middle class Indian leaders and spokesmen, aware of these prejudices, nonetheless took the struggle for political representation forward.

To some extent, the Sanderson Committee's recommendation played a 'catalytic role' in the appointment of George Fitzpatrick to the Legislative Council, political encouragement which gathered momentum and was enjoined by other forces during widespread discontent in 1919, as Afro-Trinidadians and sections of Indian workers took strike action.[67]

The behaviour of the Indian community with respect to the agitation for representation, seemingly confusing and ambivalent, was characterised by much acrimony, ridicule and personality clashes. Apparently both the EINA and EINC were given to understand by Major Wood (of the visiting Wood Commission) that their representation on the Legislative Council would be maintained, at the very least, and that this would be accomplished either through nomination or election, or both. So when Sarran Teelucksingh was elected to the Council in 1925, and no Indian was nominated, Indians felt that a promise had been broken. Thereafter, towards the end of the 1920s, the Indians, still anxious and insecure as to their position in society, faced an uncertain future. [68] As Singh concluded, Indians have been for 'most of the indentureship period the "objects" of Trinidad's history, [they] are now among the "subjects" and as "subjects" they are no longer leaving the definition of their status and role in the society' to the descendants of the masters or to the descendants of the slaves'.[69]

## East Indians and the TWA

If the Indians were constrained by the restrictions of indentureship, by the time the system was abolished, in the wake of the First World War, their earlier representations for 'rights and privileges' took on added meaning. As 'free' workers, they were, at least potentially, less easily controlled and 'more assertive' in demanding social and economic reforms. Between 1919 and the Second World War, the Indians were significant participants in labour politics. During the 1919 strikes, for example, Indian workers joined Afro-Trinidadian workers who had stopped work in Port of Spain; and in the rural districts, labourers on the sugar estates went on strike from Cunupia to Chaguanas, with reported violence. Labourers at the

Golconda and Tamana estates were charged with inciting a strike,[70] and in the ensuing violence, a man was bludgeoned to death while trying to go on strike. Consequently, a white overseer was arrested and charged with murder.[71] Further south, at
Tabaquite, labourers employed by the Central Oilfields refused an offer of 20 per
cent and went on strike for a 25 per cent wage increase.

This series of strikes was indeed cause for official concern. Armed marines (ironically from *HMS Calcutta*) and policemen from the local Constabulary were sent to
the sugar-belt to deal with the recalcitrant Indians. The Trinidad labouring class
for so long shackled by the bondage of slavery and the demanding and restrictive
work practices of the indentured labour system, had begun to make its presence
felt as the effects of the strikes spread to Tobago. This spontaneous collaboration
between Indian and Afro-Trinidadian workers for higher wages and better working conditions, prepared the way for future political co-operation.

By 1920, the TWA having sought to eliminate economic and political inequality
brought into being a working class consciousness, a development of central importance to Trinidad and Tobago in that for the first time, the two major groups
were drawn together in agitation for a common objective. (Hitherto 1919, Pointer's observation of the counter-productive racial division of the Trinidad working
people, and his attempt at initiating a process of co-operation, came to nothing.
Solidarity between the two groups simply did not exist, and the possibility of this
seemed remote.) It was only when the relentless ravages of malnutrition, bad housing and disease, a direct result of low wages and poverty, was forced upon the
masses that the idea of co-operation became reality. To get that elusive higher wage,
workers of both races went on strike and in the process received fines and jail
sentences. Two strikers, one of African descent, the other of Indian descent, were
killed. The overall effect was that the strikes brought about an awareness of class
feelings which, to some extent, transcended racial feelings. The potency of such
collaboration could only have increased the perceived growing threat to white domination, since the Indians could no longer be looked upon as a substantial safeguard
against troublesome Afro-Trinidadians, and vice-versa.

Also by the end of 1920, the strong influence of developments in Europe, affected the nature of agitation in Trinidad and Tobago and the Caribbean. Improvement in communications had brought in its train a wide range of literature from
abroad and the development of European workers' organisations encouraged local agitators to adopt similar attitudes and approaches. The frequent rebuffs of the
Colonial Government had tested to the limit, reliance on the use of agitation by
peaceful means. Petitions, memorials and meetings as methods of seeking reforms
were unacceptable. Consequently, the more militant and effective means of agitation, through demonstrations, strikes and incendiarism, as practised in Britain and
France, were eventually adopted by the TWA in Trinidad, which rejected the use-
lessness of constitutional methods. In time, changing circumstances and disen-

chantment brought a new perspective. Inevitably, the 'radical' ideas of Alfred Richards in 1906 were interpreted as reactionary by the TWA militants in 1917; and the Bolshevik Revolution and the 'Socialist' views of workers in Europe had, on the whole, a telling effect in the West Indies, and particularly on those who were at the forefront of the labour movements.

Among workers' organisations in the other West Indian colonies, apart from established links with the British Guiana Labour Union, the TWA's activities were also directly influential in the formation of trade unions in Barbados. Clearly then, the cumulative effect of pressure groups like the TWA and the BGLU, and other militant West Indian workers' movements that resorted, of necessity, to strikes after the First World War, had some impact on the Colonial Office's decision to send Major Wood to report on conditions in the West Indies and to recommend any necessary changes.[72]

The fact that very little of the TWA's activities was reported in the press between 1920 and 1924 suggests that it may have suffered a considerable decline. From its involvement as the vanguard of the workers' struggle, it was reduced once again to petitions relating to a number of labour issues. The TWA's other agitations, at the political level, included petitions for withdrawal of the Seditious Publications Ordinance, institution of competitive examinations for entry to the Civil Service, establishment of representative government and a West Indian Federation.

With this new approach, the organisational structure of the TWA was based on occupational sections.[73] The shift in emphasis from active organisation and agitation among the rank and file for a living wage and better working conditions, to a policy committed to political and social reforms due to Government pressures, contributed significantly to the fall in its membership. And once again, the TWA's political strategy seemed too far removed from the workplace to arouse the necessary interest among men and women who were desperately labouring to earn enough simply to survive each day. About this time, it seems the TWA was unable to perform any trade union function, and it was at this low point in 1924 that Captain Arthur Andrew Cipriani intervened in the affairs of the TWA. He was a French-Corsican Creole, a man of wealth who was fond of horse-racing and one might well speculate as to whether he was one of the 'capitalists' who became an 'honorary member' of the TWA, which David Headley (a former President of the Association) had spoken about in January 1920.[74]

Also in the 1920s, the TWA with a predominantly Afro-Trinidadian membership, was essentially working class oriented. And although the EINA and EINC and the Young East Indian Party made representations on behalf of the Indian community, they were essentially middle class pressure groups.[75] The TWA was therefore more relevant and indeed proved to be attractive to working class Indians who were deeply concerned with immediate industrial concerns.

By 1925 when elected members were introduced into the Legislative Council,

Cipriani had emerged as the undisputed 'champion' of the working class in the politics of Trinidad and Tobago. That year Teelucksingh was elected as representative of the sugar-belt Constituency of Caroni,[76] and apart from being consecutively elected to the Legislative Council from 1925 to 1946, he became a member of the TWA. His involvement with the Association, however, was brief. Another Indian representative on the Council, Timothy Roodal, joined the TWA and later became its Vice-President. This Indian 'labour-based' representation on the Council held much promise, but unfortunately, things turned out differently.

It was clear that between 1925 and 1933 the architect of all the TWA's plans was Cipriani, who took firm control as President and Treasurer for the duration of that period. In effect, the TWA was very much a one-man band. The Constitution of Trinidad was so limited in scope that despite Cipriani's consistent agitation, essentially in the form of debating the problems of the working class, he must have been acutely aware that without the mandate of the 'bare-footed' masses his more or less self-appointed representations were little more than an admirable gesture. (He was hampered from making progress by the fact that the overwhelming majority of the Legislative Council members were either official or nominated).[77]

The quality of the Association's involvement with workers leaves no doubt as to Cipriani's attitude towards the use of industrial action. The TWA, under Cipriani's leadership, was opposed to strikes, though it intervened on behalf of those workers who had gone on strike. In this way, it offered its limited services to all grades of workers, members as well as non-members.

But already by the mid-1920s, the TWA had become less 'industrial' and increasingly more political, to the extent that Cipriani stood as the official TWA candidate for the Legislative Council elections on an 'out and out Socialist programme'. His platform constituted a Workmen's Compensation Ordinance, trade union legislation, an eight-hour working day, the abolition of child labour, compulsory education, competitive examinations for entry into the Civil Service, poor law relief, abolition of the Seditious Publications Ordinance and a Commission of Inquiry into the Cane Farming industry. Interestingly, during his election campaign, the slogans 'Trinidad for Trinidadians' and 'Votes for Sons of the Soil'[78] were used. Such slogans may have alienated many Indians who were campaigning for political and social reform and who knew intimately that they were still not regarded as being an integral part of the mainstream of Trinidad society.

Regardless of his failings, through his long Presidency of the TWA from 1924 to 1933, Cipriani, given the circumstances, was the foremost 'labour' leader in the Colony; and during his leadership, the TWA consisted of 16 branches with a total membership of 16,526.[79] A number of Cane-Farmer societies had affiliated to the TWA, contributing 7,280 members, almost half of the total TWA membership.

In the face of economic depression in the 1930s there was little that the Cipriani-led TWA could do to restrain workers turning against the Association and its grand programme of political action, and take the law into their hands by resorting in desperation to direct industrial action. Despite the imposition of strict censorship on the influx of foreign ideas (contained in newsprint) and work practices, the labour situation had deteriorated considerably by the early 1930s, thus triggering immediate and widespread disturbances.

Since the abolition of the system of indentured labour in 1917, many thousands of Indian labourers hitherto able to obtain some degree of redress for grievances through an appeal procedure to the Protector of Immigrants in any matter of in-justice or neglect arising out of their conditions of service, were suddenly disad-vantaged following removal of this employer responsibility. As free labourers they were now responsible only to themselves for the extent of any bargain struck with an employer. The employer, on the other hand, with the removal of legal obliga-tions to which he was subjected under the system of indenture was able to hire and fire at will. Under these circumstances, the labourer, deprived of the medium (for what it was worth!) through which his day-to-day grievances found expression, was forced to rely heavily on the goodwill of the employer. As the Forster Com-mission noted, in the 'absence of any means of collective bargaining the measure of the labourer's well-being and contentment depended upon the manner in which that good-will was exercised'.[80]

Indian workers were therefore extremely vulnerable to exploitation by the em-ployers. This fundamental lack of machinery for dealing with workers' grievances brought about a rapid deterioration of the labourer–employer relationship nation-ally, and an almost equally rapid increase in anger and frustration. Against this background, the events of the years of depression from 1930 to 1937 were to prove decisive in bringing about much needed trade union-industrial relations legislation.

Although Cipriani and the TWA received the support of Indian leaders such as Timothy Roodal and C.B. Mathura (President of the Young Indian Party) in the 1930s there was growing disenchantment among the Indian working class. So much so that by 1934, rather than channel their grievances through the TWA, Indian workers resorted to public demonstration. That year, low wages and high prices forced sugar workers to take action, resulting in strikes and riots. These acts of desperation (involving approximately 15,000 workers) were the precursor of more general and far-reaching labour disturbances in the 1930s.[81] So, just short of two decades after the structures of indentureship were dismantled, the Indian working people were able to demonstrate its own heightened sense of the industrial-politi-cal problems they faced. And significantly, they began to recognise that theirs (like other groups of workers) was, in essence, a class struggle against their employers which, if only temporarily, transcended racial divisions. This fostered 'the remark-able emergence of working class consciousness which succeeded in throwing a bridge across the ethnic divide'.[82]

Cipriani's position on the issue of labour and trade unionism was rather vague, since his attitude had been one of by-passing or relating the issue to other matters. In 1929, however, he stated that Self-Government was a clear labour issue, which he said was the answer to the economic crisis. During one of his mass meetings on Self-Government, he justified his rejection of trade union activity by saying he was not prepared to advise workers to go on strike, for strikes were likely to lead to disturbances, 'slaughter' and the loss of lives.[83]

Although the writing, as it were, had been for a long time on the wall, Cipriani was prepared to indulge in the politics of Self-Government at the expense of fore-going the urgently necessary adoption of trade unionism. His 'revolutionary' weapon was Constitutional Reform, through which he expected to 'overthrow' the Government. But his aversion to trade unionism did not affect his persistent demands on behalf of the working class for trade union legislation. In March 1930, he wrote to Walter Citrine, General Secretary of the British Trades Union Congress, asking for his help towards the introduction of trade union legislation for Trinidad and Tobago. A few months later, in September 1930,[84] Lord Passfield (Sidney Webb), as Secretary of State for the Colonies, issued a Circular Despatch, instructing the Government to introduce a Trade Union Bill.

On 25 April 1930, just five months before the Bill was introduced, it was found that it contained no provision for peaceful picketing or immunity for actions in tort. The decision to exclude these provisions from the colony's laws meant that the Government would have full control over the trade unions. It was Citrine who, pointed out that the Bill contained no provision for safeguarding the right of pick-eting or giving unions immunity against actions in tort similar to the British Trade Union Disputes Act of 1906.[85] Accordingly, Cipriani opposed the two omissions from the Bill, which was passed in 1932. But after agitating for so long to get a 'permissive law' as part of his trade union legislation campaign, Cipriani ignored the newly acquired legality for the formation of trade unions and chose instead to transform the TWA into the Trinidad Labour Party. This decision not to register the TWA under the Trade Union Ordinance was an unsubtle move, for it was difficult to imagine Cipriani dabbling in the unsavoury business of trade union-ism.[86]

So between 1934 and 1939 the existing machinery through which workers' griev-ances could be channelled was both inadequate and inefficient, and in many areas, non-existent. And not surprisngly, Cipriani's representations in the Legislative Council on behalf of the working class proved how ineffective his individualistic, reformist approach was in attaining better wages and working conditions. The rise of a vigorous oil industry* caused the kind of industrial development which led to the demands for a better quality of labour requiring higher wages and improved working conditions.

Hampering improvements in the workers' industrial problems prior to 1937 was the general malaise of working class leadership in Trinidad. The strategy of suc-cessful colonisation demanded the creation of a class of ideologically colonised persons (a cadre) in order to enforce external domination. This class consisted of the colonised elite; a class whose members educated in colonial attitudes, were imbued with an elitist concept of society and its organisation. Their future collaboration was, more often than not, ensured by the grant of a colonial title or job in the colonial service. The colonisers recruited only those who were likely to conform to specific standards laid down by colonial society, including Black and Coloured professionals, clergymen and businessmen, who formed the petty bourgeoisie.

The 'national leaders' came predominantly from this class which facilitated the continuation and domination of Empire. The appointment of E.M. Lazare to the Legislative Council was a case in point. In these circumstances, the working class activities of Uriah Butler were interpreted as subversive. Butler's essential industrial agitation was perceived as posing a real threat to Colonial authority and with good reason, as it turned out. And so too, were the activities and politics of the young, radical Indo-Trinidadian, Adrian Cola Rienzi.

Within the Indian community, at the leadership level, younger, educated Indians challenged their elders. While in England, Mitra Sinanan criticised the 'inadequate' leadership of the Indian working class provided by such wealthy Indians as Teelucksingh and Roodal.[87] Of greater importance, however, was the challenge posed by Adrian Cola Rienzi, who had returned from England. His approach to labour politics (especially his role in the formation of trade unions), based on class rather than on race, was appropriate and timely in bringing the major groups of workers in Trinidad together. On labour matters, his views were predictably at variance with Cipriani's. He was also closely and crucially associated with Tubal Uriah 'Buzz' Butler and the formation of the Oilfield Workers' Trade Union.[88]

Rienzi, whose grandfather came to Trinidad as an indentured labourer, was born in 1906 in San Fernando, where he attended Naparima College, which he left at the age of fourteen to work as a Clerk in a solicitor's office for a wage of 2s. 6d per week. By 1925 he had become President of the San Fernando branch and Chief Organiser of the TWA in south Trinidad. He was a serious-minded and ambitious young man, who corresponded with Shapurji Saklatvala (the Indian-born Communist British Member of Parliament; and his commitment to radical ideas and an awareness of labour militancy, brought him into conflict with Cirpiani's brand of working class leadership.

By the end of 1927, the divide between Rienzi's left-wing views and Cipriani's parochialism was clear, and as one of his last acts of defiance against the Governor and Cipriani, Rienzi converted a group of boy scouts into the Young Socialist League. Subsequently, he withdrew from the activities of the TWA and renewed his interest in matters affecting the Indians in Trinidad and the nationalist struggle in India. He also became active in a new Indian organisation in Trinidad, the Indian National Party (which was intended to replace the EINA and the EINC) and was elected as its General Secretary. One of the Party's successes was the acquisition for a night shelter for destitute Indian pavement-dwellers. From the organisational experience he had gained, Rienzi tried to build a united organisation of Indians in

* See George E. Higgins: *A History of Trinidad Oil* (Trinidad: Trinidad Express Newspapers Ltd, 1996).

every district. But whereas the traditonal leaders had tried in a conservative way to mobilise the Indians, Rienzi's views were regarded as being 'notoriously seditious' and soon he left the island to study law in Britain, where he became associated with a number of socialist groups.

On his return to Trinidad, he was still regarded with grave misgivings and was refused admission to the Bar. He was eventually admitted after promising he would not indulge in 'agitation'. But, a year later, he was again active in politics. In December 1935, he showed he was ahead of his contemporaries as economic conditions deteriorated, provoking hunger marches and mass protest. He saw this as an opportunity to co-ordinate the economic, social and political discontent of the working class and indicated how far ahead of his fellow-politicians he really was by putting forward the concept of Afro-Indian political unity. This was the first time that any local activist had projected this concept in order to broaden the narrow ethnic outlook of the Afro-Trinidadian and Indian petit bourgeoisie. The struggle for independence in Africa and India, he argued, must be seen in the context of a larger struggle against Imperialism, which required the efforts of the two main local groups.

At about this time, Rienzi had founded the Trinidad Citizen's League, whose members included Butler, whose 'hymn-singing and oath-taking' were not enough to win Indian working class support or to influence the petit bourgeoisie generally. More importantly, he lacked the strategy for dealing with the crisis likely to arise in the event of a popular confrontation with the government. As it happened, Butler had provoked just such a crisis when the Oilfield Workers he led went on strike. Butler fled the scene, leaving the workers leaderless, and Rienzi was approached by a deputation of workers to fill the leadership vacuum. Thus, he was instrumental in the formation of the oilfield and sugar workers' unions and in the establishment of the Trinidad and Tobago Trades Union Congress.

If indentureship had restricted combinations of Indian workers, his role in organising the sugar workers must be seen as a declaration of intent by the working class that they would continue to resist oppression. His leadership was also important because it marked a period of Afro-Indian relations, which was particularly encouraging.[89] Significantly in 1938, he was elected to the Legislative Council. What in fact was the extent of Afro-Indian cooperation in the 1930s and 1940? One measure of this was that when Rienzi was elected to the Council,[90] he received considerable support from Afro-Trinidadians. Interestingly, his opponent was of African descent, and it seemed, at this stage, that he had managed to bridge the gap between the 'two great races'.

From a soundly based trade union platform, Rienzi agitated, among other things, for greater worker involvement, through Constitutional reform in the forums of the Legislature and later in the Executive Council, until his political career ended in 1944 to the disappointment of his rank and file supporters in the trade union movement. When he subsequently became a Second Crown Counsel, the 'radicals' felt he had sold out.

But why did Rienzi bring his political career to this sudden end, which terminated 'the only movement that had so far succeeded in binding Africans and Indians together?' For one thing, despite his efforts on behalf of the workers, forces in the larger society were working against him. And since the First World War there was a resurgence of African consciousness, namely the growth of Pan Africanism and Garveyism, which won committed following. Indeed in the the 1930s African consciousness was encouraged and the alleged inferiority of the African was challenged.[91] But this black upsurge also had the effect of reinforcing the fears among Afro-Trinidadians of Indian dominance, and from the late 1930s, according to Rienzi, it was increasingly difficult to oppose a growing separatist black consciousness in the trade union movement.[92] Nevertheless by the time that Rienzi had decided to leave the labour struggle to others, he had already made his mark in Trinidad and Tobago's labour and political history[93] at an important juncture, which signalled the end of a notable and successful attempt at Afro-Indian working class solidarity.

Voting qualifications was a matter of serious concern to Rienzi, who maintained that this should not be based only on the English language test, a position which was opposed by both the European and Afro-Trinidadian interests represented on the Franchise Committee. Rienzi warned that this form of discrimination against the Indian community could seriously undermine Afro-Indian solidarity. It was only after an island-wide campaign that this 'test' was abandoned.[94] Rienzi's devoted work, based on class rather than on race, now seemed in jeopardy and may have contributed significantly to his departure from politics. As one writer noted, 'with his departure the backbone of the movement towards solidarity was broken. From this time the traditional, separatist group of older East Indians began once again to assert themselves and this led to even further withdrawal on the part of the East Indians'.[95] Thereafter, Indian leadership shifted sharply from its working class orientation towards isolationist tendencies under the domination and control of the elite among the Indian people.

## Indian Elites, the PNM and Black Power

After this phase of Afro-Indian solidarity in the 1930s, the involvement of Indians in politics was dominated and controlled by the Indian elites, who were primarily concerned with protecting their particular interests.[96] Overall, however, it was clear that by 1946, given the various ethnic groups in existence, some sort of a 'racially mixed social system' had to be achieved. But how could this be realised when in fact, Trinidad could not be said to have a 'national identity' and there were no political parties.[97] Also one could not ignore endemic tensions. The real prospect of Afro-Trinidadian political domination and the discouragement by Nehru, who said that Indians overseas should no longer regard India as their homeland, engendered further racial exclusiveness among Indians as a minority group.

So bearing in mind that the political system in Trinidad lacked consensus, before Independence, the existing political groups did not cut 'across the ethnic-cultural lines'. And although religious and cultural diversities are significant in the 'political socialization and recruitment' of the East Indians, they were not a tightly organised unit. Instead, the community is made up of different religious groups. The Hindus, for example, belonged to various sub-groups, including the Sanatan Dharma, the Kabir Panth and the Seunarine. The Arya Samaj was also formed and gained a following. But there was no doubt that in Trinidad, the majority of Hindus supported the Sanatan Dharam and that both in social and political life the Sanatanist Hindus have been influential. Prior to 1952, two Sanatanist organisations were in existence: the Sanatan Dharam Association and the Sanatan Dharam Board of Control. That year both organisations merged to form the Sanatan Dharam Maha Sabha, with Bhadase Maraj as President. Under his leadership the SDMS (or MS) became one of the most powerful religious and political organisations among Hindus in Trinidad.

By building schools throughout the island, the MS provided education for thousands of Indian children and jobs for Indian teachers. The religious and cultural reinforcement of this development did not go unnoticed by leaders of other ethnic groups. In 1956 Dr. Eric Williams, who had emerged as undisputed leader of the People's National Movement, described these schools as 'political cells'.[98]

Clearly, among the Indians as a whole, there was sub-group rivalry between the Hindu-Muslim and Christian religious groups. Commenting on the effect of inter-group differences as they relate to ethnic solidarity, one study found that both Hindu and Christian elites believed that the 'majority of Muslims do not stand committed to the party supported by other Indian groups. Most of the Hindu and Christian elites believe that Muslims have joined hands with the PNM and have betrayed the cause of the East Indian community'.[99] Therefore, in order to establish a strong and effective Indian political party, it was necessary that the leadership should transcend 'narrow in-group loyalties' and widen its constituency beyond religion and caste to include the masses. But, it was claimed that threats from outside to the identity of the Indians as an ethnic group were (and are) met with solidarity (in varying proportions, informed by class) within the Indian groups.[100]

Ethnicity, it was argued, had not at this point, achieved dominance in Trinidadian politics. Indian leadership, prior to the 1956 elections, was headed by two main groups: one consisting of S. Teelucksingh, T. Roodal and Rienzi; the other, was organised by the EINC and the EINA. Both organisations acted independently on several issues and neither contested the elections. On this occasion, Butler's British Empire Workers and Citizens Home Rule Party did not have the support of the Sinanan brothers, Ashford and Mitra. Also contesting the elections was the People's Democratic Party led by its founder, Bhadase Maraj, a wealthy businessman.

At this time, it was argued that political parties in Trinidad were based on per-sonalities, rather than on grass-roots organisation with well thought through elec-tion strategies, and that they were lacking in 'ideological orientation'.[101] With full internal Self-Government as the political goal, the 1956 Constitution nevertheless encouraged the birth of party politics in Trinidad and Tobago, instead of the exist-ing 'personality oriented' political groups and parties. But already, it seemed these parties were ethnically based.

The formation of the People's National Movement, led by Eric Williams, the 'most significant event' in the political development of Trinidad and Tobago, in-troduced a 'new style' of political leadership, presenting the electorate with a 'clear policy and programme'. Responding to this development, the People's Democratic Party emphasized a more multi-racial approach by forming an alliance with the Party of Political Progress Group.[102]

The PNM, it seemed, was determined not to make any political alliances for the elections, although Williams was concerned that the Indians formed the dominant group in the PDP. The elections brought not only victory for the PNM, but also evidence of clear racial divisions [103] and bitterness between the Afro-Trinidadian and Indian groups represented, in the main, by the two leading parties.

It was clear at the time, that a two-party system had come into operation, re-flecting an essentially ethnic orientation. As one study showed: 'polarization was taking place on racial lines', as manifested in the fact that Stephen Maharaj left the Butler Party to join the Democratic Labour Party, while Butler became a supporter of the PNM.[104] The first test of the party political strength came with the 1958 West Indian Federal Election, a contest (fought on local rather than Federal issues) which intensified racial feelings, thus causing further polarization of the parties. Thereafter, the PNM no longer took the Indian threat lightly, and race became a central issue in the party politics of Trinidad and Tobago.[105]

In its attempt to form a viable opposition to the PNM, the DLP lacking an ideology and programme, could not be described as a rank and file organisation. And given that the leadership of Maraj and S.N. Capildeo was focused on the 'Hindu cause', many Christian and Muslim Indians expressed their disenchantment with the party by supporting the PNM. As the DLP prepared for the 1961 General Election, after 'bitter factional fights', Dr. Rudranath Capildeo emerged as Leader of the Party.

Even though Williams showed contempt for the DLP during the election cam-paign, the PNM put forward eight Indian candidates, who contested seats in the heavily populated Indian areas. Of these eight, three were Muslims. The DLP also adopted a multiracial slate, twenty non-Indians and nine Indian candidates. Of the Indian candidates, two were Muslims. But in spite of the multi-racial mix of the candidates presented, both parties failed to transcend ethnicity as the basis of their support.[106]

The racial violence during the 1961 elections had the effect of Indians closing ranks behind the DLP, especially because the PNM leadership and Government had indicated its determination to return to power. As it turned out, racial pride of the two largest ethnic groups was the main political issue. Although issues relating to electoral districts or unfair election practices were highly probable reasons for the DLP's defeat, it was argued that the Party failed primarily because of the 'narrow sectarian base of its top leadership, its lack of internal cohesion, and the absence of an efficient party organisation'.[107]

Following the 1961 General Election, the DLP had to contend with two important problems: first the question of the Independence of Trinidad and Tobago; and second, the future institutional structure of the island. On both issues, the Party and delegations from leading Indian organisations lodged their protests. And in spite of the seeming decrease in racial tension following Independence in August 1962, there was a deep sense of unease among Indian social and political leaders, of which Williams was fully aware and exploited; an outcome that had resulted in black neo-colonial nationalist domination, which H.P. Singh had warned against as early as 1955. Thereafter, what unity there was within the DLP declined with Capildeo's departure from the political scene in Trinidad to accept a teaching post in London early in 1963.[108] And while the PNM enjoyed its hold on political power, many among the Indian elites continued to be restive.

Apart from some Muslim support, there was a strong sense of alienation from the political system, felt by all the representative groups within the Indian population. Even Indian office-holders in the PNM Government, such as Dr. Winston Mahabir, feared implementation of 'apartheid in reverse', which would result in denying political representation of the Indians.[109]

In fact, there was concern among Indian elites of the dual thinking on racial policy in the PNM: one approach, led by Eric Williams was 'comparatively liberal' while another, led by P.V. Solomon, included 'hard core racialists'. Not surprisingly, Indian religious leaders urged political and social leaders to face the fact that there was a 'race problem' in Trinidad. Subsequently, the Indian elites (reflecting similar views held by Indians in Guyana) were primarily concerned with the fact that discrimination towards Indians should be eliminated. Significantly, Hindus were the main advocates, followed by Indian Christians and Muslims. The elites also favoured more social and cultural contact between Indians and Afro-Trinidadians, a suggestion which received most support from Muslims, followed by Indian Christians and Hindus. Another solution to the race problem, proposed by a minority, was 'separate homelands' in the Caribbean for the Indians.[110] (This call for separation would be echoed in future years).

Clearly, the conservative and sectarian Indian elites, seeking limited political objectives did not tackle their problems in terms of class struggle. Neither was gender of any relevance. The idea that Indian women might graduate to leadership positions did not enter the deliberations. However, commenting on the Indian elites, one writer observed 'The whole of their socio-economic background and their value orientation tend to make them defensive. As a rising property-owning class, they seek peace rather than political stability; they seek maintenance of the *status quo* rather than any radical change in the economic and political structure of the country'.[111]

In 1965 the opportunity to transform the DLP into a 'genuine multi-racial party based on secular-rational political ideology' presented itself, as relations between the PNM Government and Afro-Trinidadian industrial workers steadily deteriorated since the 1961 General Election. Moreover, the leadership of the major trade unions criticised the PNM Government's industrial policies, as the number of strikes increased, involving oil and sugar workers, among others.

And while Capildeo denounced the Industrial Stabilisation Act on his return to Trinidad in July 1965, and welcomed the fact that Trinidadians were discussing issues not personalities, he would not admit C.L.R James into the DLP. The introduction of Afro-Trinidadians in the Party would have led the Indian masses to perceive the DLP as a 'Negro Party'. The DLP leadership was therefore relieved when Stephen Maharaj left the Party and with James, and pro-labour leaders, formed the Workers and Farmers Party.

The 1966 and 1971 elections showed how ineffective the DLP's leadership was, and how much discrimination there was against the Party. In November 1966, the first election in post-Independence Trinidad and Tobago was held, and significantly, all four parties contesting the elections (the PNM, the DLP, the Liberals and the WFP) presented 'multi-racial slates', indicating the real need to bridge the gap between the main ethnic groups. And yet again, the election results underlined the relevance of ethnicity in the voting behaviour of the electorate.[112]

The DLP next contested the 1968 County Council elections but won less than a quarter of the number of seats, which showed once again, not only that the DLP's support was restricted to heavily populated Indian constituencies, but also that it could not win wider support from the electorate. So, it was argued that because of 'its lack of internal cohesion, ideological confusion, inexperienced leadership and narrow ethnic orientation', the DLP could offer no viable alternative to the PNM.[113] While the DLP was preoccupied with its narrow concerns, general opposition to the ruling PNM had increased, and before 1970 (as was the case in the 1930s), particular Indian working class issues overlapped with more common general working class concerns. By the end of 1969, despite the establishment that year of the Caribbean Free Trade Association, and the increase in exports between 1968 and 1969 to the Commonwealth Caribbean by an estimated 41 per cent, the job crisis had deteriorated.

The politics of sugar, traditionally and still a very sensitive issue, needed to be tackled. The Indian population which had, in the main, resided since indentureship on the sugar estates and in the surrounding rural areas, was still in effect, tied to the land. They were (and are) the rural people who have yet to be fully integrated into the 'mainstream of the larger society'. For too long the trouble had been that while sugar continued to be shamelessly neglected, there was little hope of agricultural reconstruction being effected.

Growing disenchantment among working people generally, led to a call by George Weekes (then General Secretary of the OWTU) for Black Power and revolution' which received increasing attention and support. The idea of Black Power manifested in the daring confrontation between Black Panthers (and other militants) and the American establishment, caught the imagination of local radicals, and by the end of 1969 it had assumed a definite form in Trinidad. The decision by the Government to ban the Trinidad-born American Black Power advocate, Stokely Carmichael, gave added conviction to the movement.

The series of historic events[114] during the months from February to April 1970, broadly based on race and revolutionary consciousness, shook the people of Trinidad and Tobago into a new, heightened awareness, particularly the Government and employers. On 4 March, a massive Black Power demonstration with an estimated 10,000 people led by Geddes Granger, the National Joint Action Committee's major spokesman, moved through Port of Spain from Woodford Square to Shanty Town. The large crowd was addressed by many speakers who were greeted by enthusiastic shouts of 'Power!' Significantly, the demonstrations and their consequential activities, during that unique week, were centred in Port of Spain and its immediate environs. At that stage, it seemed the protests were essentially an urban uprising. The term Black Power and its connotations, and the destruction of Indian shops and business-premises were indeed cause for concern among Indians, many of whom having resided mainly in the rural areas, were increasingly becoming settlers in the towns. Did Black Power include them? And if so, how could it be reconciled with the destruction of Indian property? Was this movement class-based or not? Much had to be explained to the Indian community generally in order to allay the rivalry and fear that existed between Afro-Trinidadians and Indians.[115]

In this connection, Black Power rhetoric was turned into action. Granger announced that a 'Long March' from Port of Spain to the sugar-belt areas would take place. In response, Bhadase Maraj, said he intended to be present to see that Indian workers would do their jobs unmolested. Granger's approach was that 'demonstrators are instructed to subject themselves to the authority of the sugar workers and let (them) determine the time and place of entry to the fields and the nature of the tasks to be performed'.[116] Before the 'Long March' began Granger told the large crowd in Woodford Square that they were leaving on a very 'historic mission' and asked them to repeat the words: 'I pledge to create brotherhood and unity between brother and brother, between the two black races of Trinidad and Tobago'. In this, he was echoing the thoughts, actions and hopes of Rienzi. After walking some 28 miles, the marchers 'tired and solemn', eventually entered Couva carrying the banner 'Indians and Africans Unite'.

Following the demonstrations, the attempted mutiny by a section of the Trinidad Defence Force and the possibility of a General Strike, created a climate in which many political prisoners were taken. In the aftermath, many questions were asked by Indians, among whom there were lingering doubts as to the Indians' role in this mass movement of black protest. In this connection, Stokely Carmichael's concept of Black Power helped little. Cheddi Jagan, the former Premier of Guyana, referring to a speech made by Carmichael, condemned the Indian racialist elements, who were trying to stir up divisions because of Carmichael's call for separate organisation of the non-White groups. 'Whatever may be the merits for separate organisation for Blacks and Whites in the United States', Jagan said, 'there is no justification for it in a concretely different situation in Guyana and the Caribbean. And if the struggle is economic, political and ideological and is against imperialism, there is no necessity for expressing it in racial terminology. This is emotional and unscientific and causes confusion'.[117]

As far as Trinidad and Tobago was concerned, it would seem that Granger's brand of Black Power was not based on racial, but on class lines. The banner proclaiming urgent Afro-Indian unity borne during the Long March, carried real conviction. But although it may not have received the desired Indian support, it was argued that the Indians were willing to allow the urban black leaders to use whatever leverage they had to help with their industrial grievances. However, the coming together of the militants and sugar workers was a source of sensitive concern to both the Brahmin, caste-orientated Maraj and the Government as James Millette noted.[118]

Whatever the implications of Black Power in Trinidad and Tobago, on balance, and for what it was worth at the time, one had to accept the example of Granger, who had publicly apologised for the destruction of the business premises owned by Indians. Participation by Indian drummers, dancers and singers was also indicative of the need and possibility of working class solidarity, based on economic and social activity, rather than on emotive, racial division, which had hitherto repeatedly, split the labour movement. Yet, the insistent suspicion and crass racism of some Black Power supporters, at rank and file level, were uncompromising. A banner calling for 'Power to the black man', held aloft by an Indian, was unceremoniously snatched away by a Black youth, who said 'Give me that, you mamaguy yourself'.[119]

It was therefore not surprising that the divide and rule principle, as implemented by the black-dominated, independent Trinidad and Tobago Government, was still very much a major cause of conflict among workers. There was little evidence of that grand and stirring motto of nationhood: 'Together We Aspire, Together We Achieve'. The split in the trade union movement and more particularly the gap (which was gradually being closed) between the sugar and oil workers, had to be maintained, if not widened, for unity between these groups of workers was seen as a serious threat to Williams and his Government. Williams had learned much from the Colonial rulers, whose misdeeds he had documented with great skill, passion and eloquence! And so long as these workers remained apart, there was little to worry about. In other words, given the strictures of existing labour laws, isolated groups could be easily and creditably contained. In effect then, 'Massa Day' in this former slave Colony was far from being 'done'.

## New Alliances, 'New' Politics

As the 1971 General Election approached, the DLP continued to face leadership difficulties. Under Vernon Jamadar's guidance, the Party made another attempt to attract Indian and Afro-Trinidadian professionals, by forming an 'electoral merger' with the Action Committee of Democratic Citizens led by A.N.R. Robinson (a former leading PNM member), once regarded as the 'logical successor' of Williams.[120] Many saw this alliance as a new departure in Trinidad and Tobago, the 'most serious electoral threat' to the PNM. In Jamadar's view racial unity was a fundamental objective of the merger. Indeed, he recognised the need for the 'brothers of slavery and indenture' to come together.[121] But while the merger had its advantages, there were serious difficulties to face. The sceptics were proven right: the merger collapsed just before the election. As it was, the 1971 General election results were dramatic. In a poll that was the lowest in the country's history, the PNM won all 36 seats.[122]

Following this victory, there were many critical comments as to the 'legitimacy' of the Government. The PNM's 'mandate to govern' and its 'moral authority' were challenged. A.N.R. Robinson (formerly a Minister of the PNM Government) took the view that acceptance of a Senatorship in the regime would be tantamount to selling the country for a mess of pottage. 'Let us see how the privileged section of the community will behave', he said.[123]

Whatever the opposition, Williams' main fear was the trade union movement which (as some trade union leaders were agreed) he was determined to crush. In 1971, he introduced a draft of the Industrial Relations Act (a rehash of the Industrial Stabilsation Act) for public comment, and a few months later in 1972 the IRA became law. Predictably, implementation of the Act had by 1975 provoked widespread opposition from trade union leaders: a series strikes and a March during which Afro-and Indo-Trinidadian trade union leaders, Weekes, Panday, Shah, Young, Lennard, and a politician, Winston Jamadar, among others, were arrested.

Undaunted, the oil and sugar workers and their supporters eventually made their way into Woodford Square the following day, to hear some of their leaders who were on bail. Thereafter, in 1976 when the first General Elections of the country as a Republic were held, the labour-oriented political leadership of the United Labour Front party had joined forces with its political allies. This was the only way that evident and growing mass discontent could be effectively channelled politically. In these circumstances, one is reminded of Prime Miniser Williams's stirring words on the eve of Independence in 1962: 'Their history was in the past made for the people of Trinidad and Tobago ... with independence, the people of Trinidad and Tobago will make their own history', being no longer passive, but active for there 'are many injustices to correct and many indignities to remove'.[124]

After independence was won, however, the question remained: would that elusive resurgence of Afro-Indian solidarity become effective? Many progressive-minded people remained hopeful. And significantly, by 1986, after thirty years in Government, the pioneering PNM was defeated at the General Elections by a coalition of parties, the National Alliance for Reconstruction. At the top level of this Party, there were several Indians (many of them academics), a few of whom were placed in Ministerial and other influential positions. How far they would be able to use their political potential to advance the cause of the majority of impoverished Indians was a matter of much speculation, though not entirely devoid of some hope. Interestingly, it was during this period of Government, when the 'Muslimeen Uprising' erupted (making world headlines for almost a week) that an Indian member of the NAR Government, Winston Dookheran, deputised for the Prime Minister, A.N.R. Robinson who was held in the Red House with a number of other political hostages. This episode in the country's history had shaken those in power out of their complacency, and there followed repeated calls for the stricter enforcement of law and order, as though this was the antidote to pervasive poverty and unemployment, and much-needed action to narrow the gap between the haves and the have-nots. But even the fleeting appearance of an Indian, Winston Dookheran, as emergency national leader at that moment of crisis, was enough to arouse old, racial fears of Indian dominance. And so in the wake of the 'Uprising', the NAR coalition which promised so much, and delivered so little, came to grief. The Party's dismal failure at the polls in 1991, saw the return of a PNM Government, whose attitude hitherto towards the Indians is well-known, and the return of Basdeo Panday (who had left the NAR) as Leader of a new Party – the United National Congress, which won thirteen seats – and Leader of the Opposition, a position he has long held with distinction, and for which he was widely admired. He had been, and is, indeed, a staunch defender and upholder of the rights and dignity of the Indians in Trinidad; and not surprisingly he is perceived by many of his Indo-Trinidadian supporters, especially the ordinary working men and women in the villages and rural areas, as a politician of principle, one of the very few whom they could trust, and clearly their front-runner as a future Prime Minister. Partisan though this may be, one would be hard put to attribute such an accolade to many others, whose political opportunism has bred deep distrust among Indians. Yet, Panday's position as 'moral and political leader of his constituency (in the widest sense, that section of the Indo-Trinidadian community which he had long represented) had become during his years in Opposition, increasingly under some suspicion.

For the first time since he became the sugar workers' Trade Union representative, political leader of the ULF, a Deputy Leader of the NAR and later Leader of the UNC, his political leadership had been closely scrutinized by many people within and outside his UNC Party, but most vehemently and with striking stubbornness by a hitherto relatively unknown Indo-Trinidadian woman politician, Hulsee Bhaggan, a very rare and unique occurrence in the history of politics in Trinidad and Tobago. She had taken people of various racial backgrounds by surprise, and many (perhaps because of gender and her originality) were suspicious of her motives, and hasty in their judgement. So what, in terms of politics, did she represent?

For most of her time as a politician, she made headline news, through dramatic representations of Indians generally and, in particular, by championing the cause of women. She was the first of a new generation of Indo-Trinidadian women from Hindu backgrounds (the daughters of generations of hard-working, unrecognised and unrewarded Indian women), who are educated, independent, full of conviction and assertive. She demonstrated that she could neither be fobbed-off with easy answers, nor would she patiently await her turn to come at some unspecified time in the future, while she languished in the faint glow of being a self-satisfied Indian woman MP overshadowed by her male colleagues. Her demands were, of necessity, more urgent, reflective of the dire economic circumstances of the poor and vulnerable masses, who cry out for direct action. Thus, she entered the political foreground.

She was unsparing in her criticism of Panday for alleged acts of misconduct and for what she saw as his deficiencies as political leader of the UNC, of which she was a member. She called into question, the male-dominated bastions of Indo-Trinidadian political parties, and more generally, the workings of the political process. Hitherto, gender relations and sexual politics seemed to have conveniently escaped the notice of the leading politicians. Her voice reverberated far and wide (campaigning for international solidarity, not only in the Caribbean, but also in the Americas), and perhaps loudest locally. In her view, such wide-ranging development was likely to encourage other Indo-Trinidadian women to become more active and rally support for their well-known committed sister.

Bhaggan's dramatic entry onto centre stage of Trinidad and Tobago politics had caught the imagination. Whatever disagreement she may have had with Panday was, it seems, no mere quarrel, but a difference of approach so fundamental that she proceeded to form her own, and at the time, the country's newest political party, the Movement for Unity and Progress,[125] thus becoming the first woman founder of a political party in Trinidad and Tobago. The Party was launched at the Centre Point Mall in Chaguanas with the purpose, as Bhaggan said, of filling a vacuum in Trinidad and Tobago politics. She saw the MUP as a viable alternative to the ethnic impasse in the country's politics. At a political meeting, a few days before the formation of the Party, Bhaggan was heckled and booed, but she was undeterred, proclaiming the 'dawn of a new political culture away from ethnic cleavages', reminiscent of the time and the mood of many people when the Alliance for Reconstruction took power in 1986. Nevertheless, Bhaggan's detractors were equally persistent, some shouting 'We want Panday and UNC', a slogan which she used as the cue for making reference to the problem of Panday's leadership, and at the same time, of taking the opportunity to set out her position. 'This is what is taking place in the UNC', she told the crowd gathered at El Socorro Park, 'when the leader speaks, not a dog barks. We want to move away from the politics of backwardness and decadence. We want to restore morality and decency in politics'. She then hit at the heart of politics in Trinidad and Tobago, and appealed to her hecklers to 'get away from the PNM and the UNC and their appeal to ethnicity. Be part of the new political culture and the new dawn in Trinidad and Tobago'.[126]

Not surprisngly, some of her opponents called for her resignation as a Member of Parliament, while others pressed for evidence to justify her claim that Afro-Trinidadians were raping Indian women, for it was she who publicly and best represented the plight of the rape victims, while other politicians remained diplomatically silent.

Her tenacity and courage as a politician had been tested, and she had gained much respect and support for her fearless conviction. She had championed many causes that would have been lost had it not been for her leadership, though as the nation's 'chief protester', she was not always successful. In 1993, she was imprisoned for seven days, a harsh penalty, but no deterrent. If anything, such an action by the State underlined her commitment towards realizing her full potential. So it was not surprising that she became the first woman 'to officially and publicly aspire' to the Prime Ministership of Trinidad and Tobago. Someone with such high aspirations could not therefore be confined to the male-dominated political culture, and because of this, she was seen by many in power as a threat, a loose cannon, and with some justification, for she had the great gift of attracting the press to her unorthodox advocacy of many grassroot problems. Her entry into public life cannot be ignored for she had in deed filled a political gap, which was slowly being recognised, especially by those closest, as it were, to her constituency. Appropriately, she had been honored with the Jansi Ki Rani Award, named after the Indian Princess who fought against the British Raj; and she had been ennobled in song (an endorsement and significant vote of confidence in her work) by the pre-eminent Trinidadian and Caribbean artist David Rudder, who composed and sang 'Hulsi X'. Such appreciation of her efforts should not surprise us, for in her impassioned person, was a reflection of a non-acquiescent generation of Indo-Trinidadian women, proud and determined to proclaim their individuality, their identity, the manifestation of a new politics that will have a significant impact on the political re-alignments that are likely to occur as gender relations stake its steadily growing legitimate claims on the political agenda of the future. And there are signs that this could well happen sooner rather than later. According to one report, the NAR (which had once promoted the centre-ground of Afro-Indian politics), was likely to be disbanded with the possibility of some of its senior leaders joining the MUP, for there seemed to be nowhere else to go in local Parliamentary politics. If such a shift does take place, then it was felt that the long-desired change in bridging the ethnic divide in Trinidad and Tobago's politics, volatile and unpredictable though it was, could well be initiated.

But as speculation about the future continued, Basdeo Panday remained at the forefront of Indo-Trinidadian leadership, and despite the alleged sexual harassment charges brought against him as leader of the UNC, speaking in Princes Town, he told a large crowd of the Party faithful that (in the event of him going to jail or if he dies before the next Election, they must elect a new leader) the Party must be prepared to replace him. 'No matter what happens to me me', he is reported to have said, 'whether I am in jail, whether I am dead, dying – if anything happens to me, I want you to select another leader, and I want you to carry on (this victory), so come next elections we shall have a UNC Government'. Giving no hint as to who his successor might be (and as the Elections of 1996 approached), he underlined his position in relation to the Party. This Party is not Basdeo Panday, and Panday is not this Party: this Party is the UNC which we have created in order to bring a better life for our people'.[127]

Projecting his Party rather than himself is to be welcomed and commendable, but the reality of politics in Trinidad and Tobago was that personalities (as he well knew, given the recent defection of Hulsee Bhaggan) could not be ignored. There were many leaders who sought domination and control of the people, who would do all in their power to widen schisms, to divide rather than unite, to invoke race and ethnicity to maintain their power bases. Changing the society had been perhaps the central platform in Panday's political life as Opposition Leader, yet he had remained rooted to his particular 'constituency' for it seemed abundantly clear that the Indians' real fears and anxieties about black (Afro-Trinidadian) racism and domination (this was no chimera when H.P. Singh wrote his perceptive articles in *The Observer* and pamphlets in the 1950s and 1960s) had first be allayed, if they were to participate more fully in the political life of the country.

If 'race' has played an important part, especially from 1956 to 1962 when Indian nationalism in Trinidad was expressed in opposition to the black nationalism and racism of Eric Williams and his PNM colleagues, in the immediate post-Independence politics of Trinidad and Tobago, it has been no less so in recent years. At the 1976 elections, although union leaders of Indian and African descent came together under the leadership of the United Labour Front, the PNM saw the Front as an 'Indian party', and during the 1981 elections the ULF was again dubbed an Indian party because it was led by an Indian Basdeo Panday, who was deeply concerned, in fact, disturbed by the logic that only an 'African party' could replace the PNM, thus minimising the importance of the ULF. Politically, Indians were expected to follow African leadership. But going down the road of Burnham's Guyana was clearly not the way forward. Historically, the clear trend has been that more Indians had voted for an 'African party' than Afro-Trinidadians had for an 'Indian party', which begs the question: Is this an indication of a greater degree of Indo-Caribbean voting flexibility as opposed to Afro-Trinidadian voting flexibility?

Commenting on the difficulties facing Indian politicians in plural societies such as Trinidad and Tobago, Guyana and Fiji, Panday (with his experience as a former high-ranking official of the NAR) stated that a point is reached when the Indian electorate itself 'succumbs to the propaganda of hopelessness. It then not only accepts its inferiority, but also actually participates in its own denigration. It is this excruciating desire to participate meaningfully in the political life of the country that motivated the Indians to support the National Alliance for Reconstruction in such vast numbers in 1986, but it is also the same tendency of self-denigration that produced the political window-dressing and tokenism ... of the present National Alliance for Reconstruction Government'.[128]

The multi-ethnic, coalition structure of NAR was indeed a major achievement in Trinidad and Tobago's political history, one that augured well for the future of the country's segmented society. NAR's victory inspired great hopes that some formula would be found to accommodate the various groups represented within the party. One such formula, 'Consociationalism' (a sharing of political power among the different ethnic groups) seemed the best option, and it was hoped, one that would prevent a collapse of the coalition. As it was, the loss of NAR's legitimacy left a 'power vacuum', as one writer described it, and ushered in 'acts of non-compliance and rebellion'. It was in these circumstances that on 27 July 1990, the Jamaat-al-Muslimeen, under the leadership of Imam Yasin Abu Bakr, attempted to oust Robinson's NAR Government, an act of insurrection which was reflective of 'popular discontent' and the 'resurgence of racism', the very things that many people thought that NAR had come together to avoid.

So why did this Uprising happen? Although the Jamaat-al-Muslimeen is essentially a religious organisation, it would be a mistake to offer an explanation to its acts of violence as the means through which it attempted to overthrow the Government of Trinidad and Tobago. There can be no doubt regarding their militancy as an Islamic group. But for the Jamaat-al-Muslimeen, replacing the Government was not their primary concern, even though this became a commitment because of certain developments that occurred during the 'critical' five-year period from the assassination of Abdul Kareem in july 1985 to the insurrection of 27 July 1990. This was a time when the Jamaat, 'seriously at odds' with the PNM and NAR administrations on matters concerning its members' well-being and its continued existence, 'became increasingly despairing of any prospect of resolving the problems by peaceful means'.

But why was the State so insistent on its opposition to the Jamaat-al-Muslimeen? Ethnically and ideologically, the Jamaat differed from the mainstream of Trinidad and Tobago's Muslim community, and while Muslims form a majority within the East Indian population, the majority of the country's Muslims are Indian. The 'Africans' are viewed by the majority of Indian Muslims with 'indifference, if not with suspicion'. According to Millette;

> The leadership figures of mainline Muslims are rich, comfortable folk whose main political strategy has been for years to attach themselves to the political fortunes of the PNM in its struggles with an opposition in which the Hindu majority of the Indian population always formed an important part. They had little time for conviviality and fellow feeling with a Black Muslim community largely made up of the poor, dispossessed, drop out elements of urban Port of Spain.
>
> Added to this, the Muslimeen were ideologically radical, while mainstream Muslims were largely conservative, particularly at leadership levels ... Both [the State and the established Muslim community] feared the consequences of institutionalizing a radical Islamic community in the country.

If the Jamaat was discriminated against on religious grounds, were there other factors involved in the State's attitude towards them? Historically, Millette saw the Muslimeen revolt as part of a radical challenge to the post-Independence Parliamentary politics of Trinidad and Tobago and noted:

> discounting the failure of the WFP [Workers and Farmers Party] in 1966 and the NAR election victory in 1986 which brought 'change but no change' – at least not for the better – there have been six specific challenges to the post-independence State since 1965, five against the PNM, one against the NAR ... On average, therefore, over the 25 years elapsing between 1965 and 1970 there has been a serious challenge to the state at least once every four years. It is in the context of this pattern of radical political challenge to the post-independence State that the Muslimeen revolt must also be placed ... The young people in particular were markedly restive ... Some of these youths [in Port of Spain] in their early teens, were to make their appearance in the ranks of the Muslimeen militants in the period that the media have aptly described as 'the days of wrath'.[129]

Alas, the idea that there was power in the streets ready to be mobilized for a takeover, was misconceived. The people, though dissatisfied and demoralized, were unprepared and refused to be led in the direction to which the Jamaat-al-Muslimeen was pointing its fire power.

In the aftermath of the bloodshed of those trying days in 1990, with the benefit of hindsight, one political analyst drew attention to the fact that Panday's United National Congress did not condemn the Muslimeen insurrection. They were more concerned with the guarantee of an 'amnesty' to the Muslimeen. 'The critical point', Premdas argues, 'relates to the sorts of challenges that are likely to follow when consociational consensus breaks down'. The problem then was the loss of legitimacy and an ongoing 'crisis of confidence ... [which] erodes the national will, destroying the very basis of long term development'.[130]

Eight years earlier, in 1982 (and almost two decades after H.P. Singh's critical review of C.L.R. James's 'West Indians of "East Indian" Descent', a study in 'Coolietude') James publicly stated that 'there has been a division between the Blacks in ... industry and the East Indians in the sugar plantation ... Dr. Williams has written in public that one important thing that he has done is to keep the Indian and the African people apart. In reality, it is my belief, and I say it very plainly, that there is no salvation for the people of Trinidad unless those two sections of the population get together and work together'.[131]

Beyond the jarring, familiar rhetoric, how does one bring about the real change that Panday and others talked about. Few, prior to the 1996 Elections, any longer doubts the ability of Indians to hold high office. The presence of Indians at the highest levels of political life was, to say the least, encouraging, but the growing ranks of the poor and unemployed were unimpressed, because the fact that some Indians were in positions of power had not changed the deplorable condition of the needy. Political opportunism and self-aggrandizement continue to take precedence over the urgent demand not only to address, but also to act upon a new approach to bring about the expected 'change' that would harness the vast reservoir of capabilities of women and the ever-growing numbers of youth and the unemployed. The politicians, it was argued, should be, in practice, the servants of the people who elected them, and to the nation, at large. Politicians should be 'clean and noble' and be transformed from its 'corrupt, dishonest and manipulative' practices, according to Hulsi Bhaggan. Predictably, most politicians broadly agreed with this long hoped-for political change.

On reflection, when the Indians in Trinidad commemorated the 100th Anniversary of the first Indians' arrival in Trinidad in 1945, they looked back over that period and assessed the progress and contribution they had made to the Colony. It was to their credit that all their sacrifice, determination, inventiveness and skill were directed at building a firm economic and cultural base and through their own communal efforts (for none, as they well knew, would be forthcoming from the Colonial Government) a number of organisations that were clearly not political. But just over fifty years later (and after years of increasing involvement in politics which had helped in transforming the Colony into a Republic) Indo-Trinidadians celebrated the 150th Anniversary of the Indians' arrival, a day which was, for the first time, declared a national holiday. But since this was declared, the argument has not abated as to whether this day should be called 'Indian' Arrival Day or Arrival Day, as it is officially titled. What was perhaps not surprising during this debate in Parliament and amongst the people was evidence of vitriol and spleen that had hitherto been submerged, the dark side of racial animosity and tension rearing its ugly head, which was reminiscent of a less threatening atmosphere in 1945, but with an equally strident charge of the Indians' 'disloyalty' to Trinidad, of their alleged greater loyalty to their 'culture' and to the building of a 'Little India' in

Trinidad. Regardless of the acrimony, the statutory public holidays Emancipation Day and Arrival Day have established a basis for the development of a sense of parity and belonging among Afro- and Indo-Trinidadians, which hopefully, they will in time, come to embrace more readily.

On the positive side, however (and after much political manoeuvering) this special Anniversary was marked by a three-day State visit by the President of India. Dr. Shankar Dyal Sharma, who was met on arrival in Trinidad by his counterpart. President Noor Hassanali, an Indo-Trinidadian, whose wife's direct family lineage could be traced back to a passenger among the terrified indentured Indians aboard the *Salsette* in 1858. After addressing a special joint sitting of the Trinidad and Tobago Parliament on the morning of the 150th Arrival Day, Dr. Sharma travelled to the Divali Nagar site in central Trinidad, where a function organised by the National Council of Indian Culture, attended by a massive crowd of several thousands heard him speak, a speech during which he gave historical perspective to that moment. 'Today you are a new generation reaping the fruits of your ancestors', he said. 'Tomorrow our successors will reap what they sow'. He told the attentive Indians (young and old, resplendent in colourful Indian dress and costumes, including Saris and Shalwars, whose faces, as never before, reflected Indo-Trinidadian pride writ large) that their forefathers had left the Motherland, friends and relations, with hopes and ambitions, ready for the adventure of a better life, and that having toiled long and hard in deplorable inhuman conditions, and having come through the hardship of indentured laboured which was 'only paralleled by the bondage of their brethren from the African continent', they have eventually taken their rightful place in Trinidad and Tobago society. 'Today we salute the triumph of the human spirit which made that possible', he added.

Dr. Sharma was able to see the genius of Indo-Trinidadian creativity, expressed in the representations of one hundred and fifty Trinidad Indian villages, depicting various aspects of Indo-Trinidadian history and culture (preceded by the first float, a replica of the *Fatel Rozack*) which was paraded before him. The President spoke of the 'beauty and variety' of the spectacle and, given his political astuteness, he made the point that the celebrations of Phagwah, Divali, Eid and Hosay were celebrated with the same 'enthusiasm for Carnival and Emancipation'; and aware of the political problems of race and ethnicity in Trinidad and Tobago, he quoted Jawaharlal Nehru: 'No nation can be great whose people are narrow in thought and action'.

Earlier that day in Parliament, President Sharma told Parliamentarians, members of the Judiciary, diplomats and other dignitaries that 'the essential element in democracy is the spirit of pluralism and synthesis, of diversity and harmony, of sharing and composite growth'. But, in essence, the message the wily seventy-seven year old Indian statesman came to deliver in multi-racial Trinidad and Tobago on that historic Arrival Day, was to emphasize the 'importance of unity in diversity and of freedom and equality to the building of a democratic world order'.[132]

Much earlier, in answer to the question: what is the point of elections in the Caribbean if voting was racially motivated? Panday, as Leader of the Opposition, stressed that the struggle was a moral one, cutting across class lines 'because you cannot try to change a society such as Trinidad and Tobago without lifting the struggle to moral dimensions, to fill the people with that evangelical zeal for change'.[133] When electoral change came with the General Elections of 1996, Panday was among the main beneficiaries of the defeat of the NAR. He now presides over his country as the first elected Indo-Trinidadian Prime Minister (which says much for Panday personally and reflects the degree of politial maturity of Trinidad and Tobago) thus joining the other Indo-Caribbean Prime Ministers, Cheddi Jagan of Guyana and Jaggernath Lachmon of Surinam. While Panday's Prime Ministership continues, to many people, he is symbolic of Indo-Trinidadian identity. But the reality is that in ever-changing circumstances, while some Indo-Trinidadians, especially the young, are determined to maintain their 'Indianness', others more exposed to creole culture and recognising its merits, readily embrace aspects of this culture which seems to offer the best prospects for racial harmony. In turn, this raises the fear that such acculturation means further encroachment into what many Hindus, in particular, regard as their 'Indianness'. Whatever choices individuals make in a multicultural society such as Trinidad and Tobago, their identity will crucially depend on safeguards for essential individual and group freedoms, indeed a recognition and accommodation of difference, of sharing in society's benefits and obligations through which a position of 'equality' would hopefully be achieved.

# SURINAM

## *Post-colonial Cultural Pluralism*

Dutch and British Colonial policies and practices provide us with interesting contrasts that had important implications on how these colonial and post-Colonial societies have largely developed. Fischer found that there was widespread love for the Indies among Netherlanders who had lived there, though he was careful to distinguish between the British and the Dutch:

> The British went to India for centuries and performed their duty as they saw it, but they never or rarely loved India ... But the Dutch grew deeply attached to Indonesia. Many married Indonesians. Many would have been happy to have lived out their lives on a mountain or a plantation in Java or Bali or Sumatra ... When India won her freedom the British left with regrets, perhaps, but with no personal heart pangs. The chapter had ended. The tie was cut.[134]

Thakur has argued that the qualitative differences between the British and Dutch arose from differences in approach to the people who inhabited their colonies, the outcome of which was 'relatively harmonious relationships between the Dutch colonizers and their colonized subjects, as opposed to the antagonism and bitter racial tension in Britain nowadays'.

Given the available evidence, Thakur added that 'these contemporary practices against non-Whites in Britian have their roots in the attitudes and value systems of the British, and partly in their Colonial policies. The Dutch, on the other hand, had deliberately set out, both in policies and practices, to develop culturally plural societies'.[135]

Historically the moves made in the nineteenth century to widen the existing political representation to include the multi-ethnic communities had, by the turn of the twentieth century, evolved into growing political awareness among the new middle class, including urban Creoles and East Indians. Thus, the plural structure of society in Surinam is reflected in its political organisation, through ethnically based political parties.[136]

## *'Consocialism'*

Before Surinam became fully self-governing in 1948, there was for some years, an advisory Legislative Council. Indeed universal suffrage was introduced following a multi-ethnic campaign led by the young Indian lawyer, Jagernath Lachmon. Having achieved Independence, Surinam had to face other political realities, such as 'apan jaht' which became pronounced. As this practice is understood in the Caribbean, it means voting for candidates belonging to one's own race or group. But this has tended to foster in-group identifications that can be counter-productive to national identity. Yet it can also have positive foundations which can be justified, serving 'not only as a means of political mobilization, but also as a source of social liberation' by asserting 'an identity that usually had been scorned or abused by earlier elites that now were being displaced. It is hardly a dysfunctional phenomenon to see the downtrodden finding new ways to make a fist, even if the end result was social division and a new kind of elitism'.[137] Overall, however, 'apan jaht' had a positive effect among Surinamers who formed ethnic political parties. And to avoid the negative aspects of 'apan jaht', Surinamers also adopted 'Consociationalism' or 'Consociational democracy'. Edward Dew gives us this definition:

> When a multi-ethnic population in which no group constitutes anything near a majority practices 'apan jaht' in an open and fair electoral system, the result should be an electoral outcome in which no party has a majority. Thus multi-ethnic coalitions become essential. That, in short, is what consociational democracy is – a form of government, for culturally plural societies in which the ethnic issue is addressed by means of proportionality and power-sharing.[138]

'Relative affluence' in Surinam, it was pointed out, has created the opportunity for Lachmon and Johan Pengel to adopt 'apan jaht' Consociationalism for some twenty years, until ethnic tensions reappeared in all its ferocity in the mid-1970s. It is significant that among those most opposed were young people.

But although no one ethnic group dominated Government proceedings, the population increase among East Indians was significant. According to Hira, the East Indian population increased from 29 per cent to 37 per cent from 1939 to 1971. As the largest ethnic group, the Indians were seen as a threat by other groups who feared an Indian take-over, a fear that had hitherto the early 1990s, not materialised for since 1958 the political viability of 'power sharing' has been largely accepted, especially by the United Hindustani Party (VHP) led by Dr. Jagernath Lachmon and the Progressive National Party (PNP) led by Dr. Sedney. When the VHP won the 1969 elections with 49 per cent of the seats, Dr. Lachmon said he could have become Prime Minister, but declined because in so doing there would have been trouble with the Creoles. Given the delicate situation, he explained his strategy:

> So I put in as Prime Minister Dr. Jules Sedney, leader of the Progressive National Party, the second largest of the Creole parties, and I became speaker and President of the House ... It is a narrow path to walk here in Surinam ... When the population is racially divided, peace depends on how the big group behaves ... My people understood this, and I think the Creoles understood it too. I've tried to get away from racial politics[139]

The adoption of this 'adaptive strategy' is an integral part of Lachmon's Dutch cultural inheritance, but his class politics remained a contentious issue. While Hira identified the two main Creole parties and the VHP as representing the 'comprador bourgeoisie', it was this class politics which led to the *coup d'etat* in February 1980. Despite the fact that this was turbulence of the highest political order, it did not produce ethnic tensions. 'Political differences were not expressed with references to ethnic interests', Hira has maintained, 'but with reference to national and social interests'.[140]

By the time of the Coup, Consociationalism had degenerated into two groups of squabbling power-sharers, and it was left to be seen what would follow Desi Bouterse's leadership of Government. Old style 'apan jaht' politics was still adhered to by the lower and middle classes, but the call for democracy was not long in coming. In 1982 this call was underlined by rallies and marches organised by respected newspapers, unions, religious and civic groups. Bouterse, angered by anti-Government demonstrations, decided to act against those who opposed him. One account informs us that some sixteen prominent leaders of the 're-democratization movement' were arrested, fifteen of whom were killed.[141]

Politically this act of violence had prompted a re-evaluation of Bouterse's Cabinet and 'Supreme Council' characterised by a tripartite military-business-labour structure. Had he gone too far in the 'progressive' direction he chose? It became clear that foreign aid from the Dutch Government would not be forthcoming until the 'apan jaht' political parties were again involved in a legitimate power-sharing democracy. And so in January 1986 Bouterse invited Lachmon and Henk Arron to join his supreme Council, Pertab Radhakrishan of the VHP was named as Prime

Minister, and several posts were allocated to members of the three parties. But even though the reversion to Consociationalism had helped to minimise ethnic fears and conflicts, it could not avert the Bush Negroes 'declared war' on the Government.

Earlier, Bouterse had announced that there would be a referendum on the Constitution on 30 September 1987 and if accepted, national elections would follow on 25 November 1987. In the referendum the public gave its overwhelming support for the Constitution and in the consequent national elections (the first in ten years) the Front won 40 of the 51 seats. The elder statesman Lachmon, after holding office during the years 1958 to 1966 and 1969 to 1973, continued as Speaker of the National Assembly; Arron took office as Prime Minister, as he was in 1973–1980; and Ramsewak Shankar was President, thus undermining Bouterse's former authority. The new Government was immediately concerned with economic and political recovery, but in their deliberations they had to face the nagging question: Could 'apan jaht' Consociationalism bring more stable government? The questions posed in 1988 were that when Jaggernath Lachmon passes from the scene, how would this affect the identity of the East Indians? and would his successor be able to secure the desired equality for this ethnic group?[142]

# GUADELOUPE

## *East Indian Integration and the 'Creole Movement'*

Unlike Guyana, Trinidad and Surinam where the East Indian populations are large, in Jamaica, Grenada, St. Lucia, Martinique, Guadeloupe and other islands, where their numbers are much less, they form an ethnic minority. But as such, they have been (and are) especially important in Guadeloupe, where an estimated 50,000 from a total population of 330,000 are of Indian origin.[143] Though smaller than Martinique, the Guadeloupean Indian population is larger and spread over a wider geographical area, with a higher socio-economic status, but it is not a homogenous population.

Relative neglect of the social organization of the East Indian community in the French West Indies has prompted further inquiry into relations between the Indians and Creole society and the growing interest in an Indian identity, especially in the 1980s in Guadeloupe. Historically, assimilation, Nationalism and the Creole language have all contributed to the problem. Guadeloupe, Martinique, Guyane and Rèunion became overseas Departments of the Government of France in 1946. By the mid-1950s, there were clear signs of disenchantment from those who had earlier supported assimilation, for instead of bringing about the expected social and economic equality, assimilation had indeed increased the French Government's control over the colonies, thereby imposing French culture and language, at the cost of the indigenous peoples' culture. Also, during the 1950s, the Left-wing parties in both Martinique and Guadeloupe campaigned for political independence. By the 1960s, the movement for independence had gained momentum, was checked and then re-emerged in the 1970s with a 'cultural message'. The Creole langauge and the Gwo-ka music, it was claimed, symbolised the local cultural imperative *vis-à-vis* the imposed French culture. Championed by the Creole middle class, Creole became synonymous with identity and change.

In the acculturation and socialization process of East Indians in Martinique and Guadeloupe, Creole has been crucial, gradually replacing the Tamil and other Indian languages as the *lingu franca* of the plantations. Many Indians, especially of the lower classes are bilingual. So why did the East Indian community become hostile to the pre-eminence of Creole? Although Creole has acted as both 'an agent of domination and a means of integration within Guadeloupean society as the group has become progressively Creolized – culturally, linguistically and biologically', it has been regarded as 'one of the unique repositories of African slave culture'. For militant nationalists, Creole was synonymous with both liberation and Guadeloupean independence, a connection which has been the cause of uneasiness among many in the East Indian community, who viewed the nationalist ideology as being controlled by the Creole petit bourgeoisie and intelligentsia, so that for the Indian Creole, apart from being a language common to everyone in the island, it also referred specifically to black, brown and white Guadeloupeans of Afro-European lineage. The separation was clear, as far as the Indians were concerned. The 'one people, one path' ideal of Creole was far from the truth. Indeed the reaction of the Indian community has been one of ambivalence, distrust and hostility. To understand this it is necessary to review the Indians' struggle, their desire to be treated as equals and to be integrated in Guadeloupean society.

The Indians' relations with Creoles has its roots in the nineteenth century, a time when, as indentured labourers, they answered the call of the crisis on the plantations. The French Antilles received 70,000 Indian immigrants during the years from 1854 to 1885, the majority of them, 45,000 settled in Guadeloupe. This population was reduced towards the end of the nineteenth century by a combination of factors, including high mortality, low female fertility and the end of immigration. Later, however, the Indian population had increased.[144]

Like Trinidad and Guyana, Indian immigration was maintained by the planters who faced strong opposition from the local black/mulatto middle class. Physically and culturally, the Coloureds and Blacks were different from the other non-White groups on the island. Adding to the Indians' distinctiveness and further separation were, as Schnepel argued, 'economic tensions' and 'status differentials' and the fact that they were the last group of immigrants to arrive, relegated them to the bottom of the social hierarchy. The white planters helped little to bridge the gap between the Indians and non-White Creoles. In fact, they did the opposite, adopting the divide and rule approach, which deepened tensions between Indians and non-Whites.

By 1900, fifteen years after Indian immigration to the French Antilles had ended, the Indians sought improvement of their status, requesting French nationality and a more integrative attitude towards them. Outstanding Indians, such as Sidambarom, who was born in 1863 and rose from being a plantation worker to the responsible and prestigious positions of Municipal Councillor and Justice of the Peace, spoke out on behalf of his fellow-Indians, arguing that French citizenship should be applied to them as well. This recognition came in the 1920s, but, as the years passed, the circumstances of being a rural-based community hampered them 'from exercising their full and legitimate civil rights'.[145] It was claimed, for example, that inadequate roads made schools inacessible, and that the encouragement of parents to press their children to labour on the plantations, at the expense of their education, caused increasing backwardness, especiallyly among Indian girls and women, thus placing them at a further disadvantage when compared with Creoles.

But since Departmentalization and the institution of a national education system in 1946, Indians have made significant progress in education; and through characteristic industriousness and thrift (born out of necessity) they had acquired land on which they cultivated various crops and engaged in animal husbandry to the extent that they managed to attain some economic independence. The increase in the number of educated Indians has also led to their entry into hitherto closed occupations, such as the professions, teaching, the Civil Service and as owners of business and retailers, mainly where the Indian population is large, as in St. Francois and Capesterre. Arising from this economic foundation was an ever-expanding Indian middle class.

In Guadeloupe, as in Trinidad and Guyana, the epithet 'coolie' used by Creoles, has been symbolic of the continuing discriminatory pressure to devalue the Indians' and their culture. The passage of time has left deep scars among Indians and many of them have yielded to Creole pressure by seeking 'acceptance' through the adoption of the Creole culture. As a consequence, the pace at which Indian religion, language, dress, intra-group marriage and caste were being eroded, quickened dramatically. This process of creolization has been manifest, not only culturally, but also linguistically and racially.

But this movement away from the Indians' traditions and cultural activities had courted a countervailing response from about the early 1970s, as some Indians became acutely aware of a loss of cultural heritage and its central role in defining the Indians' identity. So it was that the promotion of 'Indianness' came to the fore and was followed by the formation of a number of associations for the promotion of knowledge of Indian arts and culture.[146] But while most Indians were agreed with the end (for example, the promotion of an Indian identity in the face of Creole domination) not all sections of their community concurred with the means.

Common to both the elites of the Creole Movement and the Indian elite, was the claiming of their cultural identity. There were (and are), however, differences which arise from the ethnicity of both movements, as Schnepel contends. By promoting Indian cultural activities in the Antilles, the French Government has effectively shifted interest away from the socio-historical and political-economic aspects of the Indian indentured immigrant experience, resulting in the movement becoming apoliticized; a movement not only controlled by the Government, but also by the Indian elites, thus keeping it effectively out of reach of the vast majority of Indo-Guadeloupeans.

By contrast, the Creole Movement had appropriated cultural symbols (such as the Creole languages, slavery and Gwo-ka music) for political gain, with its goal of national independence. This cultural emphasis, adopted by Creoles had, however, brought race into politics. Moreover, both the Creole and Indian elites had strategically kept their particular movements apart; and while the idea of a Pan-Indian movement in the Caribbean had been raised (in fact, such close relations as existed involved only the islands of Martinique and Guadeloupe, with marginal interest in extending ties with the Anglophone Caribbean), the Creole Movement was less international in its approach, preferring to take a narrower, concentrated nationalist line. For the nationalists from Guadeloupe, Martinique did not figure in their independence plans; and any links with the English-speaking Caribbean were perceived as being the wrong models for French Creoles.

So how do Indians relate to the national struggle for political independence in Guadeloupe? According to one observer, Indians are unhappy with the introduction of race in local politics and they feel insecure about their Indian cultural identity. Not surprisingly, their support of the nationalist movement (though committed, as in the unions) is only marginal. In the past, political representations of Indians' interest have not been effective. In this sphere of activity, they have been slow, as slow as they had been in claiming their cultural identity. Today, they have indeed come a long way after their failure in 1947 to form a party to defend their particular interests. They are now members of the various political parties, pressing their many concerns, notably through the efforts of Ernest Moutousammy, who has achieved political prominence.

Of much concern to members of the Indian community are the 'racial attacks' to which Indians standing for political office have been subjected. The Creole opposition disapprove of Indian candidates' concentration on matters relating to Indians' interests. But, Indian voters, like the Indian community, do not form a homogenous block. Yet, on the whole, there has been a tendency among Creoles to accuse Indian politicians of racial bias.[147]

Given the racial tensions that had existed generally between Creoles and Indians in the past, in more recent times, the cultural differences between both groups as manifested through their approaches to the Nationalist movement have been manipulated by both elites. But the matter of the incorporation of Indian identity within the Nationalist movement remains problematic. The evolutionary nature of the problem, which must be recognised, makes it hard to predict. 'Changes within East Indian social organisation and patterns of behaviour in Guadeloupe', wrote

Schnepel, 'raise new issues for consideration. Serious research is needed which locates the structure of cultural differences in the larger Guadeloupean society and analyses how it inhibits, or conversely encourages, collective ethnic action and political participation'.[148]

In addition to the foregoing discussion and the views of Indo-Caribbean authors and commentators, analysts have put in weighty claims, arguing from their different standpoints, but few have tried to juxtapose, never mind correlate their private thoughts and beliefs with objectivity. The diverse views put forward, however, need some orchestration, some greater will of externalization on the part of the participants that would guide them towards a more representative social system, that *must*, of necessity, recognise difference. While some Indians (either as ordinary working men, professionals or as writers) are cautious, others are bolder, and undeterred they endeavour to transcend the barriers and enter society, as 'full participants' in a national culture. Therein lies their predicament.

Commenting on the Caribbean region as a whole, researchers have recognised that 'if there are clear forces in the contemporary Caribbean which move inexorably in the direction of creolization, there are those that resist it, and in their resistance, almost dialectically, serve to shape and define it'. With each generation, shifts, though not always clearly discernible, takes place so that in the contemporary Caribbean Indo-Caribbean people, by definition part of their environment, can readily assert that they 'are of it, by it and for it'.

Arising from decolonization and emergent nationalism, the contemporary Caribbean mirrors a unique ethnic and cultural mosaic. Each of the constituent countries in the region observe and maintain its own incomparable 'socio-cultural and sub-cultural' characteristics that questions a 'Caribbean culture'. The idea of a Caribbean 'cultural monolith' is inapplicable to the populations of the various countries for 'if their structural similarities are undeniable', wrote Allahar and Varadarajan, 'there is no reason why their cultural dis-similarities cannot be acknowledged; for structural similarities are not sufficient to produce an integrated community at the level of culture'.

Several writers have contributed to the debate on 'differential creolization' in the Caribbean which deals with 'conflict and consensus between and among identifiable ethnic communities'. In essence, Smith sees the Caribbean as a plural society lacking a common will, while Braithwaite and Hall regard creolization 'as a regional unifier' that transcends nationalism.

Recognising some value in each of these arguments, others were dissatisfied that such viewpoints did not address differences within the region. And bearing in mind that the 'starting point of the process of creolization is the racial and ethnic make-up of a given country, the proportions in which the various groups exist, the country's level of industrial development, its degree of urbanization, its linguistic and religious roots' *inter alia*, the idea of a single unifying process of creolization in the whole Caribbean is untenable. Marked differences among Caribbean countries contradicts the idea of a 'common West Indian Culture'. Therefore, it should be made clear, as Allahar and Varadarajan have done that:

> When a culture is seen to comprise such things as a given type of family structure, a broadly defined set of physical (phenotypical) and ethnic attributes, a common range of religious beliefs and practices, a broad degree of consensus regarding the form and content of political institutions and processes, and perhaps even a shared commitment to patriotism, the Caribbean is anything but united. In other words, since culture is a lived process that binds the members of a community together ... the existence of a discrete Trinidadian, Guyanese, Jamaican ... culture, takes precedence over an agreed upon, all-encompassing West Indian or Caribbean culture.[149]

So, as the process of creolization in the Caribbean continues, Indo-Caribbean people and their descendants, especially those who know little or nothing about their past which has gone into making who they are, should consider the culture from which they have come. 'We forget' V. S. Naipaul has noted, 'it is part of the trouble'. Indeed, as the foregoing narrative shows, the history of the Indo-Caribbean people is essentially one of struggle for their identity, for their survival.

# CONCLUSION

While disparities between the rich and poor in Caribbean societies (including those that had received small numbers of Indians) brings sharply into focus the class distance that has long separated the privileged elites from the impoverished masses in Guyana (especially during the Burnham and Hoyte regimes) Trinidad and Surinam (larger countries with larger Indian populations), ethnic group interest still, though relative, remain a lingering problem as the Indians continue their struggle for cultural, economic, social and political recognition. Given that they are no longer 'immigrants', their history reflects an implacable engagement against oppressive forces that have done all in their power to keep them at the bottom rungs, largely separated from the rest of society. They have been used as a buffer between the European elites and Afro-Caribbean masses. At this time, following Indo-Caribbean PEOPLE s 150th Anniversary celebrations and reflection, especially during the last decade when serious attempts had been made at reappraising Caribbean historiography, we are reminded of generations who have been subjected to strict legal control affecting all aspects of their lives, an experience evoked through ancestral voices like Mohammed Sheriff, Bechu, Fazal, Moolian, Maharani, Bharath, Sankar, the lists of immigrants' names that fill mouldy volumes of official colonial registers and records (long hidden and dusty) and the nameless, unfortunate thousands, including those of more recent times, which echo the deplorable working and living conditions, social and cultural exclusion, violent physical attacks and abuse from Europeans and Creoles; and of the plight of unlettered, but intelligent and dignified men, women and children whose deeply ingrained scars (lacerations of both the body and the sensibilities) were marked as in any ritual of sacrifice, by an outpouring (over a prolonged period) of blood, sweat and bitter tears that have ironically nurtured tender succulent canes which in turn, were finally converted into the sweetest of comsumer goods, the source of fabulous wealth for complaining sugar barons. Alas, this was a daily grind, a repetitive process which represented in all its starkness a demoralising system founded upon the sexual brutalisation of Indo-Caribbean women, as well as the unsparing exploitation of their menfolk. In all, the Indians have remained positive, making as they have always done, invaluable contributions to national and regional development, notwithstanding the current state of ferment in the Caribbean.

Though many are proud of their Indian heritage, with few exceptions, contemporary Indians (unlike many of their predecessors, the early disoriented, ill-informed batches of indentured labourers, who were unknowingly part of a British-led 'triangular trade* are deeply attached to their New World environment, having continuously adjusted in varying degrees, to changes imposed upon them and to the changing contexts and by adopting new concepts, they have helped to shape the cicumstances of their children's lives and, in turn, the succeeding generation have influenced their descendants, who became increasingly integrated in their particular societies.

But even though they have for generations embraced their Caribbean homelands, they are nevertheless still stereotyped and their history and culture are largely misunderstood by other Caribbean ethnic groups, in the main, because of an educational system that was Eurocentric and tended to perceive and treat the 'Indians' more as aliens, exotic groups (on the periphery of society), rather than as an integral part of 'Caribbean Studies', which should include in its curriculum aspects of African and Indian/South Asian history and culture. Race relations can benefit a great deal from the introduction of such an educational programme for schools, where, for too long, prejudices based on ignorance have been given legitimation. More surprising perhaps is the fact that far too many Indo-Caribbean people (notably non-Hindus) are themselves lacking in knowledge of their own history and culture and are therefore confused about their identity. This is all the sadder because many of them either think they already know enough of their past or that knowing more is irrelevant. Of course, there are others, the few, who are well versed in where they have come from, but for them and Indians generally (given the heterogenous nature of the different communities) the question is: in which direction should they now turn? For one thing, the hard-won lessons of the past, present in their collective memory will be invoked in their autonomous struggles which reflect an integral part of the history of racism in the Caribbean: a story of restriction, rejection and political oppression with violent and tragic results in Guyana. So disenchanted had Indo-Caribbean people become that many have called for the creation of 'bharatiyadesh', an 'Indian' homeland in the Caribbean through the political unification of Guyana, Surinam and Trinidad. But for thousands, the degree of alienation was so urgent and profound that the only alternative was exile (no easy option, and yet another heart-searching uprooting of strong ties with the lands of their birth, socialization and settlement) in the United States, Canada, Britain, France, Holland and elsewhere in Europe, where they now constitute part of an ever-widening Indian diaspora; and where many of them, living as commuter-immigrants give voice to their double identity, their double oppression (particularly in the case of Indo-Caribbean women) and in these colder climes their haunting Caribbean pre-occupations. For many others, matters relating to the Caribbean are anachronistic and therefore of little value. Those of this persuasion, identify strongly with their adopted country where a new generation has now come of age, ready to proclaim their Indo-Canadian, Indo-American and Indo-British presence.

But while local descendants of the indentured immigrants in the various Caribbean communities cope with the sharp end of the continuing crossing from their 'Indianness' to their distinctive identities, they are likely to face the future perhaps with a greater sense of urgency than their forebears, against all forms of oppression to counteract the imperialist social and cultural stigma of indentureship, negative images of the despised 'coolie' who has been so calculatingly used by the inheritors of post-Independence power; political actions often taken in the name of the people by the descendants of enslaved Africans, which has in recent years inhibited the Indians' progress. For while some Indians have undoubtedly 'made it' and are respected for their wealth and overall success, the stark fact remains that the vast of majority Indo-Caribbean people are (or in the process of being) dispossessed and displaced, ekeing out a living here and there, and far too many of them are still very poor and in need.

Diversity, so characteristic of this part of the world, must be cherished and until the elites can recognise 'difference' and act in response to the popular appeal of the masses to bring about social change through genuine respect for the fundamental human rights of others, the contradictions endemic in the Caribbean societies cited above, underscored by domination and control, will continue to be over-emphasized at the expense of a more integrative approach to future policy-making. Politicians, who so readily exploit human differences of one sort or another, do so often knowing well the essential similarities that bind people socially. But whether or not the elites recognise and respect difference for what, in essence, it represents, the Indians' massive contributions to their societies are incalculable. And historically (like the enslaved Africans before them) they have been resilient in adversity, and after more than a century and a half of resistance and revolt endemic in the process of arising from their bonded status and its residual prejudices, both individually and collectively, their lives movingly evoke an epic and exemplary story of human resourcefulness, dignity and self-determination, sustained by a deep spirituality invoked through their imaginative interpretation of songs, dance, artforms, elaborate rituals and colourful, symbolic festivals of ancient tradition.

British (and later other European) ships took manufactured goods to India, then embarked from the ports of Calcutta and Madras with indentured 'Coolies' for the Caribbean plantations and on the return voyage to Britain, carried cargoes of agricultural products from the Caribbean and the United States.

But as we approach the end of the century, new identities, new world views are being forged from tensions arising from ever-changing and depressing economic and environmental circumstances in the Third World, generally and particularly in the Caribbean in response to the new technologies and possibilities of the richer world that are likely to test the human spirit in disturbing ways. But for some time now, the peoples of this region have been creating a multi-hued, multi-faithed admixture of enriching cultures and indeed if this is to continue into the millenium, pondering (more than five centuries after the intrepid Genoese sailor mistakenly believed he had reached the East – and lest we forget the concern of one writer that the 'struggle of man against power is the struggle of memory against forgetting')[150] the history of the Indo-Caribbean people could well surprise us by yielding some invaluable lessons and some warnings, a legacy and compass melding elements of East and West which informs us of the Indo-Caribbean people and their descendents' odyssey towards new horizons.

# NOTES

## CHAPTER ONE

1. Davis, David Brion: THE PROBLEM OF SLAVERY IN WESTERN CULTURE (New York: Cornell University Press, 1966).
2. Williams, Eric: FROM COLUMBUS TO CASTRO: THE HISTORY OF THE CARIBBEAN 1492–1969 (London: Andre Deutsch, 1970), p. 14.
3. Ibid., p. 16.
4. Ibid., pp. 36–7.
5. Davidson, Basil: BLACK MOTHER (Penguin Books 1980), p. 65.
6. Curtin, Philip D: THE ATLANTIC SLAVE TRADE: A CENSUS (University of Wisconsin Press 1969).
7. Williams, Eric: CAPITALISM AND SLAVERY (London, Andre Deutsch 1964).
8. Davidson, op. cit., pp. 81–2.
9. Mannix, Daniel P and Cowley, M: BLACK CARGOES: A HISTORY OF THE ATLANTIC SLAVE TRADE 1518–1865 (New York: Penguin Books 1962), p. 171.
10. See Benezet, Anthony: SOME HISTORICAL ACCOUNT OF GUINEA … (Philadelphia, Joseph Cruikshank 1771; THE CASE OF OUR FELLOW CREATURES, THE OPPRESSED AFRICANS … (Society of Friends, 1783; OBSERVATIONS ON THE INSLAVING, IMPORTING AND PURCHASING OF NEGROES 1760; A CAUTION AND WARNING TO GREAT BRITAIN AND HER COLONIES (Philadelphia, Henry Miller 1766); A SHORT ACCOUNT OF THAT PART OF AFRICA INHABITED BY NEGROES … (1762).
11. Rodney, Walter: HOW EUROPE UNDERDEVELOPED AFRICA (Washington, Howard University Press, 1974), pp. 81–2.
12. Mannix, D.P and Cowley, M: op. cit., pp. 185,190.
13. Letter to Horace Greeley, 22 August 1862 in R.P. Basler (ed) COLLECTED WORKS … Rutgers University Press (1953), Vol. 5, p. 388.
14. Mathieson, W.L: BRITISH SLAVERY AND IT'S ABOLITION 1823–1838 (London, Longman Green & Co. 1926), p. 21.
15. PARLIAMENTARY PAPERS, 19, 121, 123; HANSARD (124), XI, 732.
16. Williams (1970), op. cit., pp. 69–94.
17. Mathieson, op. cit., p. 127.
18. Buxton, Thomas Fowell: MEMOIRS OF SIR THOMAS FOWELL BUXTON, ed. Charles Buxton (London, John M. Murray 1872), pp. 72–3.
19. Mathieson, op. cit., pp. 181–2.
20. Knaplund, P: 'Mr Over-Secretary Stephen', JOURNAL OF MODERN HISTORY, Vol. 1, No. 1, March 1929.
21. Knaplund, op. cit.
22. Hitchins, F.H: THE COLONIAL LAND AND EMIGRATION COMMISSION (Philadelphia, University of Philadelphia, 1931), Appendix 6, Summary, p. 319.
23. Campbell, Persia: CHINESE COOLIE EMIGRATION TO COUNTRIES WITHIN THE BRITISH EMPIRE (London, P.S. King & Son 1923), pp. 89–90.
24. PARLIAMENTARY PAPERS, 1852–3, Vol. 263, Encl.3, No. 8.
25. Clementi, Cecil: THE CHINESE IN GUYANA (Georgetown, The Argosy Co, 1915).
26. PARLIAMENTARY PAPERS, 1852–3, Vol. 262, Encl. No. 2.
27. Campbell, op. cit., p. 97.
28. Ibid., p. 135.

29. The African connection with India str etches into the ancient past. See B.B. Lal: 'The Only Asian Expedition in Threatened Nubia: Work by an Indian Mission at Atfyeh and Tumas', THE ILLUSTRATED LONDON NEWS, 20 April 1963, pp. 579–81; C.A. Winters: 'Lectures in Africana: Kushite Diaspora', JOURNAL OF BLACK STUDIES, Fall 1985, San Francisco State University, USA; V.T. Rajshekar: 'The Black Untouchables of India: Reclaiming Our African Identity and Cultural Heritage' in INTRODUCTION TO THE STUDY OF AFRICAN CLASSICAL CIVILIZATION, London: Karnak House, 1992. See also Herodotus: HISTORIES, (Harmondsworth: Penguin 1972).

30. H.B.E. Frere: FORTNIGHTLY REVIEW, 1883, p. 355; D.R. Banaji: SLAVERY IN BRITISH INDIA (Bombay: Toporavela Sons & Co, 1933) pp. 36, 202–3.

31. Anon: A FEW WORDS PROMOTING AND ENCOURAGING OF FREE EMIGRATION TO THE WEST INDIAN COLONIES (Liverpool, T. Carter 1842).

32. Thorner, Daniel: THE TRANSFORMATION OF THE RURAL ECONOMY: THE BRITISH IN INDIA, IMPERIALISM AND TRUSTEESHIP (Ed). Martin D. Lewis, Boston, D.C. Heath & Co, 1962), p. 53.

33. Dutt, Ramesh: THE ECONOMIC HISTORY OF INDIA UNDER BRITISH RULE, Vol. 1 (New York: Augustus M.Kelly 1969), pp. 85, 450.

34. Thorner, op. cit., p. 55.

35. Dutt, op. cit., pp. 256–7.

36. Nehru, J: THE DISCOVERY OF INDIA (New York: John Day and Co.1945), p. 298.

37. Williams, op. cit., p. 347.

38. Cumpston, I.M: INDIANS OVERSEAS IN BRITISH TERRITORIES 1834–1854 (London, Oxford University Press, 1953), pp. 51–2; Laurence, K.O: IMMIGRATION INTO THE WEST INDIES IN THE NINETEENTH CENTURY (Barbados, Caribbean Universities Press 1971), pp. 19–20.

39. PARLIAMENTARY PAPERS, 1840, Vol. XXXVII, 'East India and Mauritius'.

40. Ibid.

41. Tinker, Hugh: A NEW SYSTEM OF SLAVERY: THE EXPORT OF INDIAN LABOUR OVERSEAS, 1830–1920 (Oxford University Press, 1974) p. 19.

42. Cumpston, op. cit., pp. 44–8.

43. Nath, Dwarka: A HISTORY OF THE INDIANS IN BRITISH GUIANA (London, Nelson 1950), pp. 8–9.

44. Cumpston, op. cit., p. 18.

45. Scoble, J: BRITISH EMANCIPATOR, 9 January 1839; Nath, op. cit., pp. 14–18; Cumpston, op. cit., pp. 28–9.

46. Nath, op. cit., p. 29; Tinker, op. cit., p. 81.

47. Cumpston, op. cit., pp. 85–6.

48. Nath, op. cit., pp. 28–9.

49. Ibid., p. 32.

50. Cumpston, op. cit., pp. 97, 99, 102.

51. Laurence, K.O (1971), op. cit.,pp. 19–20.

52. Ibid., p. 21.

53. PARLIAMENTARY PAPERS, 1847, Vol. XXXIX (325), Grey to Gomm, 29 September 1846.

54. Laurence, op. cit., p. 20.

55. Cumpston, op. cit., p. 115.

56. CO.318/165: Colonial Land and Emigration Commissioners to Merivale, 26 March 1850.

57. Laurence, op. cit., p. 21.

58. Ibid.

59. Ibid., pp. 23, 27.

60. Laurence, op. cit., p. 26.

61. Roberts, C and Byrne, J: 'Summary Statistics on Indenture and Associated Migration Affecting the West Indies', POPULATION STUDIES, Vol. 20, No. 1, p. 127.

62. Laurence, op. cit., p. 40.

63. Ibid., pp. 40–2.

64.  De Waal Malefijt, A: THE JAVANESE IN SURINAM (Assen 1963), pp. 22–7.

65.  In 1862 a ship landed at the Danish island of St. Croix with 321 Indians. But high mortality among these migrants due, in part, to malpractices on the plantations, led to a ban on further Indian immigration to the island. See Tinker, H: op. cit., p. 104.

66.  Laurence, op. cit., p. 45.

67.  Saha, Panchanan: IMMIGRATION OF INDIAN LABOUR 1834–1900 (Delhi, People's Publishing House, 1970), pp. 78–94.

68.  Tinker, H: (1974) op. cit., p. 86.

69.  Vatuk, Prakash: 'Protest Songs of East Indians in Guyana', JOURNAL OF AMERICAN FOLKLORE, July-September 1964, p. 224.

70.  BENGAL HURKARU, 21 December 1838.

71.  Saha, op. cit., p. 80.

72.  Ibid., p. 83.

73.  BENGAL HURKARU, 12 July 1838.

74.  HANSARD, Vol. LX, House of Commons, 1 March 1842, pp. 1321–2.

75.  Brougham's Speech in House of Lords, 16 July 1838.    Quoted in Geoghegan's Report on Coolie Emigration, Calcutta 1873.

76.  Saha, op. cit., pp. 81–2.

77.  BENGAL HURKARU, 20 October 1843.

78.  Saha, op. cit., pp. 91–2.

79.  PARLIAMENTARY PAPERS, Vol. XX, 1871, Report of the Commission of Enquiry, pp. 545–6.

80.  Saha, op. cit., p. 85.

81.  Emmer, P.C: 'The Meek Hindu: The Recruitment of Indian Indentured Labourers for Service Overseas, 1874–1916' in COLONIALISM AND MIGRATION: INDENTURED LABOURERS BEFORE AND AFTER SLAVERY (ed) P.C. Emmer (Dordrecht, The Netherlands: Martinus Nijhoff, 1986) pp. 187–207.

82.  Tinker, op. cit., p. 39.

83.  Lockyer, Charles: AN ACCOUNT OF THE TRADE IN INDIA (London 1711), pp. 26–7.

84.  Banaji, D.R: SLAVERY IN BRITISH INDIA (Bombay, D.B. Toraporavala Sons and Co., 1933).

85.  Tinker, op. cit., p. 44.

86.  Ibid., p. 46.

87.  Ibid., p. 48.

88.  Ibid., pp. 51–2.

89.  Saha, op. cit., p. 74.

90.  Tinker, op. cit., p. 53.

91.  Ibid., p. 54.

92.  Ibid., pp. 54–5.

93.  Ibid., p. 56.

94.  Mahabir, Noor Kumar: THE STILL CRY: PERSONAL ACCOUNTS OF EAST INDIANS IN TRINIDAD AND TOBAGO DURING INDENTURESHIP (1845–1917), pp. 49–51. (I am grateful to Selwyn Cudjoe of Calaloux Press for permission to use this material).

95.  Ibid., pp. 63–67.

96.  Ibid., pp. 79–81.

97.  Ibid., pp. 91–97.

98.  Ibid., pp. 141–154.

99.  Ibid., pp. 58–60.

100.  Ibid., p. 120.

101.  Ibid., p. 118.

102.  Ibid., p. 134.

103.  For more information on Emigration depots and sub-depots, including their regulation and amalgamation and the emigrants' stay there, see 'Seasoning the Emigration: Depot Accommodation at Calcutta Under the Indenture System' in Mangru, B: INDENTURE AND ABOLITION (Toronto: Tsar 1994) pp. 1–16.

104. Ibid., pp. 137–8.

105. Ibid., pp. 138–140.

106. Reddock, Rhoda: 'Indian Women and Indentureship in Trinidad 1845–1917: Freedom Denied'. CARIBBEAN QUARTERLY, Vol. 32, September–December 1986.

107. Mangru, Basdeo: BENEVOLENT NEUTRALITY: INDIAN GOVERNMENT POLICY AND LABOUR MIGRATION TO BRITISH GUIANA 1854–1884 (London, Hansib Publications 1987), p. 96.

108. Ibid., p. 97.

109. Vatuk, op. cit., p. 224.

110. Ibid., p. 225.

111. Tinker, op. cit., pp. 153–4.

112. Ibid., pp. 142–143.

113. Mangru, op. cit., p. 116.

114. PARLIAMENTARY PAPERS, 1840, Vol. XXXVII, 'East India and Mauritius'.

115. Tinker, op. cit., pp. 145–6.

116. Ibid., p. 149.

117. Ibid., p. 157.

118. For a full account of the *Salsette*'s voyage and its context see Ron Ramdin's 'Introduction' to THE OTHER MIDDLE PASSAGE (London: Hansib 1994).

119. Carlile, James (ed.): JOURNAL OF A VOYAGE WITH COOLIE EMIGRANTS FROM CALCUTTA TO TRINIDAD BY CAPTAIN AND MRS. SWINTON (Alfred Bennett 1859).

120. Ibid., p. 6.

121. Ibid., p. 10.

122. Ibid., p. 15.

123. Ibid., p. 4.

124. Tinker, H., op. cit., pp. 158, 161, 167.

125. Mangru, B: op. cit., pp. 110–111.

126. Ibid., pp. 120–4.

127. Tinker, H., op. cit., pp. 158, 161, 165.

128. Mahabir, N.K: op. cit., pp. 51–55.

129. Ibid., op. cit., pp. 67–69.

130. Ibid., pp. 80–82.

131. Ibid., pp. 98–100.

132. Ibid., pp. 153–58.

133. Davidson, B: op. cit., pp. 111–20.

134. Ibid., pp. 116–19.

135. Iyer, Raghavan: 'Utilitarianism and All That', ST. ANTHONY'S PAPERS, No. 8, (London, Chatto & Windus, 1960), p. 10.

136. Ibid., p. 11.

137. Ibid., p. 13.

138. Ibid., pp. 23–4.

139. Ibid., pp. 42, 66, 69.

140. Ibid., p. 13.

141. Jagan, Cheddi: THE WEST ON TRIAL: MY FIGHT FOR GUYANA'S FREEDOM (London, Michael Joseph 1966), pp. 30–1, 160.

# CHAPTER TWO

1. Rodney, Walter: A HISTORY OF THE GUYANESE WORKING PEOPLE 1881–1905 (Kingston, Jamaica, Heinemann Educational Books, 1981), p. 3.

2. Ibid., p. 2; Dalton, Henry: HISTORY OF BRITISH GUIANA (London 1855), Vol. 1, p. 484.

3. Ehrlich, Allen S: 'History, Ecology and Demography in the British Caribbean: An Analysis of East Indian Ethnicity'. SOUTHWESTERN JOURNAL OF ANTHROPOLOGY, Vol. 27, 1971.

4. Williams, Eric: 'The Historical Background of British Guiana's Problems', THE JOURNAL OF NEGRO HISTORY, Vol. 30, 1954, p. 377.

5. Despres, Leo: 'Differential Adaptations and Micro-cultural Evolution in Guyana'. SOUTHWESTERN JOURNAL OF ANTHROPOLOGY, Vol. 25, 1969, p. 21.

6. Farley, Rawle: 'Rise of a Peasantry in British Guiana'. SOCIAL AND ECONOMIC STUDIES, Vol. 2, 1954, p. 91.

7. Cumpston, I.M.: op. cit., pp. 18–19.

8. Tinker, H: op. cit., p. 43.

9. Nath, D: op. cit., pp. 11–12.

10. Ibid., p. 10

11. Mangru, Basdeo: 'The Sex-ratio Disparity and Its Consequences Under Indenture in British Guiana'. INDIA IN THE CARIBBEAN (eds) Dabydeen, D and Samaroo, B. (London, Hansib/University of Warwick 1987), pp. 211–228.

12. Tinker, H: op. cit., p. 65.

13. Nath, D: op. cit., p. 14.

14. Jenkins, Edward: THE COOLIE: HIS RIGHTS AND WRONGS (London, Strachan & Co. 1871), p. 95.

15. Nath, op. cit., pp. 15–16.

16. Vatuk, Prakash, op. cit., p. 227.

17. Nath, op. cit., p. 30.

18. Ibid., p. 27.

19. Mangru, Basdeo: BENEVOLENT NEUTRALITY (1988), op, cit.

20. Nath, op. cit., pp. 30–1.

21. Tinker, op. cit., p. 82.

22. PARLIAMENTARY PAPERS, 1847–8, XLVI: Harris to Grey, 19 June 1848.

23. DES VOUEX COMMISSION REPORT, 1871, p. 47.

24. Nath, op. cit., p. 64.

25. Ibid., p. 63.

26. DES VOEUX COMMISSION REPORT, 1871.

27. Ibid., p. 48.

28. Nath, op. cit., p. 64.

29. Ibid., p. 66.

30. Ibid., p. 67.

31. For more on Crosby see 'James "Papa" Crosby: Protector of Indentured Indians, 1858–1880', in Mangru, B: INDENTURE AND ABOLITION (Toronto: Tsar, 1993) pp. 17–42.

32. Ibid., p. 60.

33. Des Voeux, George William: MY COLONIAL SERVICE IN BRITISH GUIANA, ST. LUCIA, TRINIDAD, FIJI, AUSTRALIA, NEW ZEALAND AND HONG KONG (London, John Murray, 1903), Vol. 1, p. 116.

34. DES VOEUX COMMISSION REPORT (1871) op. cit.

35. Ibid., p. 2.

36. Nath, op. cit., pp. 72–3.

37. Ibid., p. 68.

38. Ibid., pp. 69–70.

39. Des Voeux, op. cit., Vol. 1, p. 130.

40. Ibid.

41. Ibid., p. 138.

42. Nath, op. cit., pp. 78, 89–93.

43. REPORT OF THE COMMITTEE ON EMIGRATION FROM INDIA TO THE CROWN COLONIES AND PROTECTORATES (Hereafter referred to as the SANDERSON COMMITTEE REPORT), Cd.5193, Cd.5194, June 1910, p. 55.

44. Ibid.

45. Ruhomon, Peter: CENTENARY HISTORY OF THE EAST INDIANS IN BRITISH GUIANA 1838–1938 (The Daily Chronicle, Guyana), p. 261.

46. Ibid., p. 263.

47.    Ibid., pp. 263–65.
48.    Ibid., pp. 265–7.
49.    Ibid., p. 270.
50.    Ibid., p. 271.
51.    Nath, op. cit., p. 79.
52.    IMMIGRATION AGENT GENERAL REPORTS, 1910–1917.
53.    Vatuk, op. cit., p. 227.
54.    Nath, op. cit., p. 90.
55.    Ramnarine, Tyran: 'The Growth of the East Indian Community in British Guiana,
1880–1920'. Ph.D Thesis, University of Sussex, 1977, p. 78.
56.    Ibid.
57.    PARLIAMENTARY PAPERS, 1898, L (C.8657), p. 93.
58.    CO. 111/439, Bruce to Holland, No. 147, 10 June 1887; Ramnarine, op. cit., pp. 80–95;
THE ARGOSY, 12 March 1895; J.E.Hewick, 'Our People', TIMEHRI, No. 18 (December 1911).
59.    Ramnarine, op. cit., p. 95.
60.    D.W.D. Comins: NOTE ON EMIGRATION FROM INDIA TO BRITISH GUIANA
(Calcutta: Bengal Secretariat Press, 1893), p. 25.
61.    CO.114/103: Excise Report of the Comptroller of Customs, 1903– 4.
62.    Ramnarine, op. cit., pp. 103–4.
63.    Comins, op. cit., p. 24.
64.    PARLIAMENTARY PAPERS, 1898, C.8657, App. C, Pt.11, Sec.73.
65.    CO.114/143: Report of the Immigration Agent General, 1912–13.
66.    Ramnarine, op. cit., pp. 107–8.
67.    PARLIAMENTARY PAPERS, 1898, L. C.8657, p. 63.
68.    THE ARGOSY, 14 February 1906.
69.    Kirke, Henry: TWENTY-FIVE YEARS IN BRITISH GUIANA 1872–1897 (Georgetown,
The Daily Chronicle,1848), pp. 250–1.
70.    Bronkhurst, H.V.P: AMONG THE HINDUS AND CREOLES OF BRITISH GUIANA
(London, 1888), p. 72.
71.    Ramnarine, op. cit., see 'The social Impact of East Indians and Their Adjustment to Creole
Society'.
72.    Dodd, David: 'The Wellsprings of Violence: Some Historical Notes on East Indian
Criminality in Guyana', CARIBBEAN ISSUES, Vol. 11, No. 3, Dec. 1976; Ramnarine, T: 'Indian
Women and the Struggle to Create Stable Mental Relations on the Sugar Estates of Guiana During
the Period of Indenture, 1839–1917'. Paper presented to the 12th Conference of Caribbean Historians, U.W.I, St. Augustine, 1980.
73.    CO. 114/68: Report of the Immigration Agent General, 1895–6.
74.    Comins, op. cit., p. 63.
75.    Ramnarine, (1977), op. cit.
76.    THE ARGOSY, 6 October, 1906.
77.    REPORT OF THE GOVERNMENT OF INDIA ON THE CONDITIONS OF IN-
DIAN IMMIGRANTS IN FOUR BRITISH COLONIES AND SURINAM by James McNeill and
Chimman Lal (hereafter referred to as the 'McNeill and Lal Report'), 1914–16, Cd.7744, p. 73.
78.    CO.114/37: Report of the Immigration Agent General 1883; CO. 114/177: Report of the
IAG, 1920.
79.    Bronkhurst, op. cit.; Ramnarine (1977), op. cit., p. 87.
80.    PARLIAMENTARY PAPERS (1945), Cmd.6609, p. 416.
81.    J.E. Hewick, 'Our People', TIMEHRI (December 1971), op. cit.
82.    Comins, op. cit., p. 59; CO.114/30: Report of the Immigration Agent General, 1880.
83.    Ramnarine, op. cit.
84.    McNeill and Lal Report, op. cit.,  p. 79.
85.    See 'Tadjah in British Guiana: Manipulation or Protest?' in Mangru, B: INDENTURE
AND ABOLITION (Toronto: Tsar 1994) pp. 43–58.
86.    PARLIAMENTARY PAPERS, 1870, 751,  p. 158, para. 330.
87.    Bronkhurst, op. cit., p. 22.

88. THE ARGOSY, 21 July 1888; Bronkhurst, op. cit., p. 17.

89. Jenkins, op. cit., p. 93.

90. De Verteuil, L.A.A: TRINIDAD: ITS GEOGRAPHY, NATURAL RESOURCES, ADMINISTRATIONS, PRESENT CONDITION AND PROSPECTS, 2nd ed. (London, Cassell 1884), pp. 80–1.

91. Williams, Eric: HISTORY OF THE PEOPLE OF TRINIDAD AND TOBAGO (London, Andre Deutsch, 1962).

92. Niehoff, Arthur and Juanita: EAST INDIANS IN THE WEST INDIES (Milwaukee Museum Publications in Anthropology, 1960), pp. 14–15.

93. Deerr, Noel: THE HISTORY OF SUGAR, Vol. 2 (London 1950), p. 263.

94. For literature on Portuguese immigrants see Laurence, K.O: IMMIGRATION INTO TRINIDAD AND BRITITSH GUIANA 1834–1871. Unpublished PhD Thesis, University of Cambridge 1958); 'The Establishment of the Portuguese Community', JAMAICAN HISTORICAL REVIEW, Vol. 5, November 1965; IMMIGRATION INTO THE WEST INDIES IN THE NINETEENTH CENTURY (Caribbean Universities Press, 1971).

95. Williams, E: (1962), op. cit., p. 99.

96. IMMIGRATION ORDINANCES PRESENTED TO BOTH HOUSES OF PARLIAMENT IN APRIL 1904. Cd.1989, Pt.1.

97. Yelvington, Kevin A (ed): TRINIDAD ETHNICITY (London: Macmillan 1993) pp. 3–8.

98. Weller, Judith: EAST INDIAN INDENTURE IN TRINIDAD. (Institute of Caribbean Studies, Puerto Rico,1968). See Appendix of this work for yearly arrivals.

99. PARLIAMENTARY PAPERS, 1846, Vol. XXVIII, Pt. II, No. I, pp. 88–9.

100. Weller, op. cit., p. 27.

101. PARLIAMENTARY PAPERS, 1846, Vol. XXXVIII, Pt. II, pp. 89–90.

102. Ibid., McLeod to Stanley, 15 July 1845, p. 88.

103. Gladstone to McLeod, 25 March 1846, p. 91.

104. PARLIAMENTARY PAPERS, 1847, Vol. XXXIX: Harris to Grey, 12 June 1847, p. 131.

105. Weller, op. cit., pp. 28–9.

106. Ibid., p. 29.

107. De Verteuil, op. cit., p. 346.

108. PARLIAMENTARY PAPERS, 1847–8, XLV, Lord Harris to Earl Grey, 8 March 1848, p. 192.

109. Weller, op. cit., p. 29.

110. PARLIAMENTARY PAPERS, 1847–8, XLVI, Lord Harris to Earl Grey, 1 July 1848, pp. 327–8.

111. Weller, op. cit., pp. 30–32.

112. Ibid., p. 32.

113. PARLIAMENTARY PAPERS, 1852–3, LXVII, Pt. III, Appendix No. 6, pp. 249–53.

114. Weller, op. cit., p. 36.

115. Ibid., pp. 36–7.

116. Ibid., p. 58.

117. Ibid.

118. WEST INDIA ROYAL COMMISSION, 1858, pp. 28–9.

119. TRINIDAD ROYAL GAZETTE, Vol. XXXIX, No. 14, 6 April 1870.

120. Comins, D.W.D: NOTE ON EMIGRATION FROM INDIA TO TRINIDAD (Calcutta: Bengal Secretariat Press 1893), p. 41.

121. PARLIAMENTARY PAPERS, 1859, Vol. XX, No. 31, Pt.1, Encl. no.19, p. 330.

122. Tikasingh, Gerard: 'The Establishment of Indians in Trinidad, 1870–1900', PhD Thesis, U.W.I, St. Augustine, 1973, pp. 96–7.

123. TRINIDAD ROYAL GAZETTE, Vol. 42, No. 12, March 1873.

124. Tikasingh, op. cit., p. 98.

125. TRINIDAD ROYAL GAZETTE, March 1873; PORT OF SPAIN GAZETTE, September 1897.

126. TRINIDAD ROYAL GAZETTE (1873), op. cit.

127. TRINIDAD SENTINEL, 23 May 1861.

128. Johnson, Howard: 'Immigration and the Sugar Industry in Trinidad During the Last Quarter of the Nineteenth Century', JOURNAL OF CARIBBEAN HISTORY, Vol. 3, November 1971, pp. 28–72.

129. Tikasingh, op. cit., pp. 107–8.

130. PORT OF SPAIN GAZETTE, 28 May 1897.

131. Comins, 'Diary', 1893.

132. Tikasingh, op. cit., p. 151.

133. PORT OF SPAIN GAZETTE, 19 September 1897.

134. Tikasingh, op. cit., pp. 152–155.

135. TRINIDAD ROYAL GAZETTE, Vol. 39, No. 20, 18 May 1870, p. 9.

136. Tikasingh, op. cit., pp. 156–7.

137. TRINIDAD ROYAL GAZETTE, Vol. 39, no.20, 18 May 1870.

138. Tikasingh, op. cit., pp. 159–61.

139. Ibid., pp. 164–6.

140. Council Paper 13/1906; Tikasingh, op. cit., p. 175.

141. Council Paper, 1894.

142. Comins 'Diary', op. cit.

143. TRINIDAD CHRONICLE, 18 June 1875.

144. Tikasingh, op. cit., pp. 177–80.

145. Ibid.

146. Ramdin, Ron: FROM CHATTEL SLAVE TO WAGE EARNER (London, Martin, Brian & O'Keeffe 1982), p. 38.

147. Tikasingh, op. cit., p. 186.

148. Ibid., pp. 190–1.

149. TRINIDAD CHRONICLE, 1 May 1877; SAN FERNANDO GAZETTE, 22 July 1882.

150. Tikasingh, op. cit., pp. 194–6.

151. De Verteuil, L.A.A: TRINIDAD: ITS GEOGRAPHY, NATURAL RESOURCES, ADMINISTRATION, PRESENT CONDITION AND PROSPECTS (London 1884).

152. Ibid., p. 228.

153. TRINIDAD CHRONICLE, 20 April, 15 June 1874; Morton, John: JOHN MORTON OF TRINIDAD, PIONEER MISSIONARY OF THE PRESBYTERIAN CHURCH TO THE EAST INDIANS IN THE BRITISH WEST INDIES, JOURNALS, LETTERS AND PAPERS. Edited by Sarah Morton (Toronto, Westminster 1916), p. 325.

154. Tikasingh, op. cit., pp. 199–202.

155. Ibid., p. 205.

156. Ibid., pp. 207–8.

157. According to Gerard Tikasingh 'the proportion of 'natives of Trinidad', excluding Trinidad-born Indians declined from 51.7 per cent of the island's total population in 1871 to 43.7 per cent in 1901. Indeed 'Natives of Trinidad' was simply a general term covering people of different national parentage, a group whose absolute growth was reportedly due to the birth of children of immigrants as distinguished from the children of old settlers'. See Tikasingh, G: 'The Establishment of Indians in Trinidad, 1870–1900', PhD Thesis, UWI, St. Augustine 1973.

158. Wood, Donald: TRINIDAD IN TRANSITION: THE YEARS AFTER SLAVERY (Oxford University Press 1968), Chs.IX, X and XI; Maingot, Anthony P: 'Nineteenth Century Trinidad'. PhD Thesis, University of Puerto Rico 1962.

159. Tikasingh, op. cit., pp. 213–4.

160. SAN FERNANDO GAZETTE, 17 October 1874.

161. PORT OF SPAIN GAZETTE, 19 March 1878; McNeill and Lal Report, Pt.1 (1915), p. 21.

162. Tikasingh, op. cit., p. 219.

163. Comins, 'Diary'; SAN FERNANDO GAZETTE, 23 April 1887; Morton, op. cit., p. 216.

164. Tikasingh, op. cit., p. 222.

165. See Comins, 'Diary' and 'Note'.

166. Tikasingh, op. cit., p. 224.

167. Morton, op. cit., pp. 315–316.

168. TRINIDAD ROYAL GAZETTE, Vol. 41, No. 8, 21 February 1872.

169. Tikasingh, op. cit., p. 226.

170. SAN FERNANDO GAZETTE, 3 February 1877; PORT OF SPAIN GAZETTE, 14 February 1885; TRINIDAD ROYAL GAZETTE, Vol. 42, March 1873.

171. Morton, op. cit., p. 200.

172. Tikasingh, op. cit., pp. 232–3.

173. Ibid., pp. 237–40.

174. Ibid., pp. 242–3.

175. PARLIAMENTARY PAPERS, 1882–5, X11: Correspondence Respecting the Recent Coolie Disturbances in Trinidad at the Muharram Festival with the Report Thereon by Sir H.W.Norman, 1885, p. 45.

176. Tikasingh, op. cit., pp. 252–4.

177. Ibid., p. 258.

178. Mandelbaum, D: SOCIETY IN INDIA (Berkeley and Los Angeles 1970), Vol. 1, pp. 97–8, 104–5.

179. Tikasingh, op. cit., p. 261.

180. Mandelbaum, D; 'Family, Jati, Village' in STRUCTURE AND CHANGE IN INDIAN SOCIETY (eds) Milton Singer and Bernard Cohn (Chicago 1970), p. 29.

181. THE NEW ERA, 12 April 1869.

182. McNeill and Lal Report, Pt.11, p. 314; Tikasingh, pp. 269–70.

183. Weller, op. cit., p. 69.

184. PARLIAMENTARY PAPERS, 1882, Cmd.3388, XLIV, p. 411.

185. Comins, op. cit., pp. 30–5.

186. Weller, op. cit., p. 71.

187. TRINIDAD CHRONICLE, 11 August 1871.

188. Ibid., 10 January 1885.

189. Tikasingh, op. cit., pp. 282–3.

190. Morton, op. cit., pp. 282–3.

191. Tikasingh, op. cit., pp. 286–7.

192. Ibid., p. 290.

193. Ibid., pp. 293–5.

194. NEW ERA, 3 May 1889; Tikasingh, op. cit., p. 296.

195. Tikasingh, op. cit., pp. 307–8.

196. TRINIDAD ROYAL GAZETTE, Vol. 42, no.12, 19 March 1873.

197. Comins 'Diary'; Tikasingh, op. cit., pp. 311–12.

198. Ibid.

199. Tikasingh, op. cit., p. 319.

200. Morton, op. cit., pp. 41–2.

201. Tikasingh, op. cit., p. 325.

202. SAN FERNANDO GAZETTE, 23 June 1883.

203. Tikasingh, op. cit., pp. 363–70.

204. TRINIDAD CHRONICLE, 28 October 1882; PORT OF SPAIN GAZETTE, 7 July 1897.

205. Tikasingh, op. cit., pp. 381–2.

206. Ibid., p. 391.

207. Ibid., pp. 402–3.

208. Weller, op. cit., p. 77.

209. Ibid., pp. 72–4.

210. Comins, op, cit, See 'Diary', pp. 19–23.

211. PARLIAMENTARY PAPERS, 1910, Cmd.5193, XXVII, p. 272.

212. Des Voeux, George W: MY COLONIAL SERVICE … ,Vol. I, pp. 304–5.

213. TRINIDAD ROYAL GAZETTE, Vol. LXI, No. 53, 26 October 1892; Weller, op. cit., p. 83.

214. Comins, op. cit., p. 49.

215. PARLIAMENTARY PAPERS, 1910, Cmd. 5193, XXV11, Sanderson Committee Report, p. 3.

216. McNeill and Lal Report, op. cit., p. 15.

217. Ibid.

218. PARLIAMENTARY PAPERS, 1910, Cmd.5193, XXVII, Sanderson Committee Report, p. 29.

219. McNeill and Lal Report, op. cit., p. 15.

220. Weller, op. cit., p. 93.

221. PARLIAMENTARY PAPERS, 1902, LXVI, p. 337.

222. Weller, op. cit., p. 93.

223. TRINIDAD ROYAL GAZETTE, LIII, No. 33, 1 August, 1884.

224. Weller, op. cit., p. 97.

225. Comins, D.W.D: NOTE ON EMIGRATION FROM INDIA TO TRINIDAD, op. cit., p. 12.

226. McNeill and Lal Report, p. 17.

227. IMMIGRATION ORDINANCES OF TRINIDAD AND BRITISH GUIANA PRESENTED TO BOTH HOUSES OF PARLIAMENT in April 1904, Col.1989, Pt.VIII.

228. McNeill and Lal Report, op. cit., p. 15.

229. Ibid., p. 16.

230. Ibid., p. 17.

231. Ibid., pp. 19–20

232. Ibid., p. 19.

233. Ibid. (see section on 'Leave and Desertion').

234. Williams, Eric: HISTORY OF THE PEOPLE OF TRINIDAD AND TOBAGO, op. cit., p. 107.

235. McNeill and Lal Report, op. cit., p. 40.

236. Ibid., p. 32.

237. Ibid., p. 33.

238. Ibid., p. 35.

239. Ibid., pp. 36–7.

240. Ibid., p. 37.

241. TRINIDAD ROYAL GAZETTE, LiX, no.18, 22 April 1885.

242. Comins 'Diary', pp. 5,26; Tikasingh, op. cit., p. 147.

243. Tikasingh, op. cit., pp. 149–50.

244. TRINIDAD ROYAL GAZETTE, 9 July 1890.

245. Comins, op. cit., p. 33.

246. Weller, op. cit., p. 30.

247. PARLIAMENTARY PAPERS, 1910, Cmd.5193, XXVII, p. 297.

248. Weller, op. cit., p. 50.

249. Ibid., p. 51.

250. Haraksingh, Kusha: 'Control and Resistance Among Indian Workers: A Study of Labour on the Sugar Plantations of Trinidad 1875–1917' in INDIA IN THE CARIBBEAN, op. cit., pp. 61–76.

251. Mahabir, N.K, op. cit., pp. 55–60.

252. Ibid., pp. 69–76.

253. Ibid., pp. 82–88.

254. Ibid., pp. 100–137.

255. Ibid., pp. 158–183.

256. Hall, D: FREE JAMAICA 1838–1865: AN ECONOMIC HISTORY(New Haven: 1959) op. cit., p. 274.

257. Eisner, Giesela: JAMAICA, 1830–1930: A STUDY IN ECONOMIC GROWTH (Manchester University Press 1961), pp. 146.

258. McPherson, J: CARIBBEAN LANDS: GEOGRAPHY OF THE WEST INDIES (London, Longmans Green & Co. 1965), pp. 167–8.

259. Ehrlich, A: (1971) op. cit.

260. See Shepherd, V: 'Emancipation Through Servitude: Aspects of the Condition of Indian

Women in Jamaica, 1845–1945' in Beckles, H and Shepherd, V: CARIBBEAN FREEDOM, ECONOMY AND SOCIETY FROM EMANCIPATION TO THE PRESENT (Kingston; Ian Randle Publishers, 1993).

261. McNeill and Lal Report, op. cit., p. 201.

262. Ibid., pp. 202–3.

263. Ibid., pp. 204–5.

264. Ibid., p. 206.

265. Shepherd, V: (1993) op. cit.

266. McNeill and Lal, op. cit, pp. 207–8.

267. Ibid., p. 210.

268. Ibid., p. 212.

269. Ibid., pp. 215–6.

270. Malefijt, A de Waal: THE JAVANESE IN SURINAM (Assen 1963), pp. 22, 26.

271. Klass, Morton: EAST INDIANS IN TRINIDAD: A STUDY OF CULTURAL PERSIST-ENCE (New York, Columbia University Press 1961), p. 9.

272. Malefijt, op. cit., p. 31.

273. Ibid., p. 22.

274. Speckmann, J.D: MARRIAGE AND KINSHIP AMONG THE INDIANS IN SURINAM (Assen 1965), p. 27.

275. Ibid., p. 28.

276. Ibid., p. 29.

277. McNeill and Lal Report, op. cit., p. 171.

278. Ibid., p. 174.

279. Ibid., p. 171.

280. Ibid., pp. 169–170.

281. Ibid., p. 156.

282. Ibid., p. 167.

283. Bronkhurst, H.V.P: THE COLONY OF BRITISH GUIANA AND ITS LABOURING POPULATION (London 1883), p. 257.

284. Comins, D.W.D: NOTES ON EMIGRATION FROM THE EAST INDIES TO SURINAM OR DUTCH GUIANA (Calcutta 1892).

285. Ibid., p. 17.

286. Speckmann, op. cit., p. 32.

287. Ibid., pp. 32–3.

288. Tinker, op. cit., pp. 236–7.

289. FRIEND OF INDIA, 3 August 1839.

290. Tinker, op. cit., p. 237.

291. Ackroyd, Peter: DICKENS: A BIOGRAPHY (London; Minerva, 1991) p. 844.

292. Bhattacharya, S: A DICTIONARY OF INDIAN HISTORY (University of Calcutta 1967), pp. 761–4.

293. PARLIAMENTARY DEBATES, CLIII, 3 March 1859, Vol. CLIV, 11 July 1859.

294. Tinker, op. cit., p. 239.

295. DAILY TELEGRAPH, 24 October 1865.

296. Bolt, Christine: VICTORIAN ATTITUDES TO RACE (London 1971). See Chap. 111.

297. Tinker, op. cit., p. 240.

298. Ibid., p. 244.

299. Ibid., p. 245.

300. Ibid., p. 250.

301. Harris, John: A CENTURY OF EMANCIPATION (London, Dent & Sons Ltd, 1933), p. 98.

302. Tinker, op. cit., pp. 259–60.

303. Ibid., p. 262.

304. Ibid., p. 264.

305. Ibid., p. 109.

306. Ibid., p. 265.

307. PARLIAMENTARY PAPERS, 1878–9, Cmd.2437, Vol. 51, 'Correspondence Relative to the Formal Arrangements for Indian Coolie Emigration to Jamaica'.

308. Tinker, op. cit., p. 266.

309. Ibid., pp. 276–7.

310. Ibid., p. 278.

311. Ibid., p. 287.

312. CURZON PAPERS: Minute, 27 January 1903.

313. Tinker, op. cit., p. 300.

314. Neame, L.E: THE ASIATIC DANGER IN THE COLONIES (London, Routledge 1907), p. 17

315. Ibid., p. 81.

316. Ibid., p. 107.

317. RAND AND DAILY MAIL, 1 February 1908.

318. Tinker, op. cit., pp. 302–3.

319. Ibid., pp. 306–7.

320. Ibid., p. 308.

321. Ibid., pp. 308–9; See also SANDERSON COMMITTEE REPORT.

322. Ibid., p. 313.

323. Ibid., p. 322.

324. Hardinge, Lord (Viceroy): MY INDIAN YEARS 1910–1916: THE REMINISCENCES OF LORD HARDINGE OF PENHURST (London: John Murray 1948) p. 140.

325. Tinker, op. cit., p. 330; See also HARDINGE PAPERS.

326. Gandhi, M.K: COLLECTED WORKS, Vol. X11; Also Huttenback, R.H: GANDHI IN SOUTH AFRICA: BRITISH IMPERIALISM AND THE INDIAN QUESTION, 1860–1914 (Ithaca, New York, 1971).

327. Tinker, op. cit., p. 332; Telegram, Viceroy to Secretary of State, 24 October 1914; India Office File J & P.3779 (1914): 'Indian Labour in the Colonies'; Tinker, op. cit., p. 338.

328. HARDINGE PAPERS, Vols 1 and 11, January–June; July–December 1915.

329. Tinker, op. cit., p. 338.

330. Ibid., p. 348.

331. Samaroo, B: 'Two Abolitions: African Slavery and East Indian Indentureship', in INDIA IN THE CARIBBEAN, op. cit., pp. 25–38.

332. Ramnarine, Tyran; 'One hundred Years of East Indian Disturbances on the Sugar Estates of Guyana 1869–1978: An Historical Overview' in INDIA IN THE CARIBBEAN, op. cit., pp. 119–141; Haracksingh, K, op. cit., pp. 61–76.

333. McNeill and Lal Report, op. cit., p. 169.

334. PARLIAMENTARY PAPERS, 1852–3, LXVII, Pt. III, p. 177.

335. Ibid., No,31, Grey to Harris, 25 February 1851, p. 181.

336. Ibid., Appendix No. 18, p. 271.

337. TRINIDAD ROYAL GAZETTE, XXVII, no. 19, 8 May 1861.

338. PARLIAMENTARY PAPERS, 1864, Cmd.3304, Pt.I, XL, p. 33.

339. PARLIAMENTARY PAPERS, 1847, XXXIX, p. 116.

340. PARLIAMENTARY PAPERS, 1859, XX, p. 317.

341. PARLIAMENTARY PAPERS, 1859, Cmd.2452, p. 268.

342. Ibid., No. 5, p. 267.

343. PARLIAMENTARY PAPERS, 1910, Cmd.5193, XXVII, SANDERSON COMMITTEE REPORT, p. 105.

344. Weller, op. cit., p. 104.

345. PARLIAMENTARY PAPERS, 1851, Cmd.5183, XXII, 11th Report of the Colonial Land and Emigration Commissioners, p. 22.

346. PARLIAMENTARY PAPERS, 1852–3, LXVII, Pt.III, Harris to grey, 28 May, 1851, p. 106.

347. Ibid., p. 107.

348. Ibid., Grey to Harris, 29 November, 1849, p. 163.

349. Ibid., Harris to Grey, 6 September, 1849, p. 12.
350. PARLIAMENTARY PAPERS, 1859, Pt. I, p. 317
351. PARLIAMENTARY PAPERS, 1866, Cmd.3679, Report of the Colonial Land and Emigration Commissioners, p. 30.
352. Ibid.
353. Weller, op. cit., pp. 109–10.
354. Tinker, op. cit., p. 366.
355. Ramdin, Ron: FROM CHATTEL SLAVE TO WAGE EARNER (London: Martin, Brian & O'Keeffe, 1982) pp. 42–63.
356. Campbell, Carl: 'Immigration into a Divided Society: A Note on Social Relationships in Trinidad, 1845–1870'. Paper presented at Fourth Conference of Caribbean Historians, Mona, Jamaica, 1972; Look Lai, Walton: CARIBBEAN LABOUR, CARIBBEAN SUGAR: CHINESE AND INDIAN MIGRANTS TO THE BRITISH WEST INDIES, 1838–1918 (Baltimore: Johns Hopkins University Press, 1993) pp. 263–4, 269–70.

# CHAPTER THREE

1. Singh, Kelvin: BLOODSTAINED TOMBS: THE MUHARRAM MASSACRE 1884 (Warwick University Caribbean Studies 1988), p. 33.
2. Macmillan, W.M: WARNING FROM THE WEST INDIES (London, Faber and Faber 1935), p. 4.
3. Augier, R: THE MAKING OF THE WEST INDIES (London 1960), p. 20.
4. Thompson, E.P: THE MAKING OF THE ENGLISH WORKING CLASS (Harmondsworth, Penguin 1968).
5. Singh, op. cit., p. 35.
6. Ibid., p. 4.
7. Tinker, op. cit., pp. 371–2.
8. Nath, op. cit., p. 144.
9. REPORT OF KUNWAR MAHARAJ SINGH ON HIS DEPUTATION TO BRITISH GUIANA 1925 (Delhi 1926).
10. Tinker, op. cit., p. 383.
11. Singh, op. cit., p. 3.
12. Laurence, K.O: IMMIGRATION TO THE WEST INDIES IN THE NINETEENTH CENTURY, op. cit., p. 79.
13. Ibid., p. 76; Cumpston, op. cit., p. 179.
14. Tinker, op. cit., pp. 371–2.
15. Laurence, op. cit., p. 45.
16. PARLIAMENTARY PAPERS, 1874, XLVII, Report by Geoghegan on Coolie Emigration from India.
17. Tinker, Hugh: 'Indians Abroad: Emigration, Restriction and Rejection' in EXPULSION OF A MINORITY, (ed). Michael Twaddle (London, Athlone, University of London, 1975), pp. 15–29. Quoted by Vertovec, S. in HINDU TRINIDAD, op. cit., p. 21.
18. Sukdeo, F: 'The Contribution of East Indians to Economic Development in Guyana'. Paper presented at Symposium on East Indians in the Caribbean, 1975; Ramnarine, T: 'One Hundred Years of East Indian Disturbances on the Sugar Estates of Guyana, 1869–1978: An Historical Overview' in INDIA IN THE CARIBBEAN, op. cit., pp. 119–40.
19. Venn, J.A: THE SUGAR INDUSTRY IN BRITISH GUIANA. REPORT OF A COMMISSION OF INQUIRY (1949).
20. Ibid.
21. Sukdeo, F: (1979), op. cit.
22. Ramgopaul, L: OUR RICE INDUSTRY (Georgetown 1964).
23. Sukdeo, op. cit.
24. Ibid.
25. Debiprashad, S and Budhram, D.R: 'Participation of East Indians in the Transformation of Guyanese Society'. Paper presented at Symposium on East Indians in the Caribbean, September 1979; See also the published article in INDIA IN THE CARIBBEAN, op. cit., pp. 145–70.

26.   Sukdeo, F, op. cit.
27.   Ibid.
28.   Ibid.
29.   Ibid.
30.   BRITISH GUIANA POPULATION CENSUS 1931 (Georgetown 1937), p. 38.
31.   BRITISH GUIANA POPULATION CENSUS, 1960, Vol. III (Georgetown 1969).
32.   Ibid.
33.   Sukdeo, F, op. cit.
34.   Debiprashad, S and Budhram, D.R, op. cit.
35.   Sukdeo, F, op. cit.
36.   Hubbard, H.J.M: 'Race and Guyana' in THE DAILY CHRONICLE, November 1969, p. 23; Sukdeo, I.D: 'The concept of Racial Integration with Reference to the East Indians in Guyana'. Paper presented at Symposium on East Indians in the Carib bean, June 1975, p. 9.
37.   Sukdeo, I.D, op. cit.
38.   Debiprashad and Budhram (1979), op. cit.
39.   CARIBBEAN TIMES, 1 October 1994.
40.   Tikasingh, Gerard: 'The Representation of Indian Opinion in ·Trinidad 1900–1921'. Paper presented at Symposium on East Indians in the Carib bean, June 1975, p. 9.
41.   Ramesar, Marianne: 'The Impact of the Indian Immig rants on Colonial Trinidad Society', CARIBBEAN QUARTERLY, Vol. 22, No. 1, March 1976.
42.   Ibid., p. 11.
43.   Ibid., pp.·12–13.
44.   Ibid., p. 15.
45.   Ibid., p. 16.
46.   Vertovec, Steven: HINDU TRINIDAD: RELIGION, ETHNICITY AND ECONOMIC CHANGE (London, Macmillan Carib bean 1992), p. 132.
47.   Hintzen, Percy C: 'Capitalism, Socialism and Socio-P olitical Confrontation in Multi-Racial Developing States: A Comparison of Guyana and Trinidad'. PhD. Dissertation, Yale University, 1981.
48.   Dookheran, Winston: 'East Indians and the Econom y of Trinidad and Tobago' in CAL-CUTTA TO CARONI, ed, La Guerre, John (Longman Carib bean 1974), pp. 72–3.
49.   Ibid., pp. 73–8.
50.   Henry, Ralph: 'Notes on the Evolution of Inequality in Trinidad and Tobago' in TRINI-DAD ETHNICITY (ed) Yelvington, K (London: Macmillan Press 1993) pp. 56–80.
51.   Ramsaran, D: BREAKING THE BONDS OF INDENTURESHIP: INDO-TRINIDADIANS IN BUSINESS (St. Augustine, ISER, 1993) pp. 15–48, 147–51.
52.   Ching, Annette, M.T: 'Ethnicity Reconsidered with Reference to Sugar and Society in Trinidad', D.Phil Thesis, University of Sussex, 1985; Vertovec, S, op. cit., pp. 139–41.
53.   Vertovec, S: op. cit., pp. 131–43.
54.   Singh, Kelvin: 'East Indians and the Lar ger Society' in CALCUTTA TO CARONI, op. cit., p. 66.
55.   Tikasingh,(1975) op. cit.
56.   Ehrlich, Allen S: 'East Indian Cane Workers in Jamaica'. PhD Thesis, University of Michigan 1969; see also 'The Interplay of Rice and Cane: East Indians in Rural Jamaica', U.W.I 1973.
57.   Ibid.
58.   Ibid.
59.   Shepherd, Verene: 'Depression in the Tin Roof Towns: Economic Problems of Urban Indians in Jamaica 1930–1950' in INDIA IN THE CARIBBEAN, op. cit., p. 174.
60.   Ibid., p. 175.
61.   Thakur, Gopal J and Mansingh, Laxmi: 'The East Indians and the J ewellery Industry in Jamaica'. Paper presented at Symposium on East Indians in the Carib bean, September 1979.
62.   Shepherd, op. cit., p. 177.
63.   Ibid., p. 184.
64.   Ibid., p. 188.
65.   Hira, Sandew: 'The Evolution of the Social, Economic and Political Position of the East Indians in Surinam, 1873–1980' in INDIA IN THE CARIBBEAN, op. cit., pp. 194–96.

66.   Singaravelou: 'Some Aspects of contemporary Economic and Social Integration of East Indians in Guadeloupe'. Paper presented at Symposium on East Indians in the Caribbean, June 1975.

67.   See de Verteuil, Anthony: EIGHT INDIAN IMMIGRANTS (Port of Spain: Paria Publishing Co, 1989).

68.   See Nanan, Sharon: 'Voices From the Boundary: The Indo-Caribbean Experience in Britain', MA Thesis, University of Warwick, 1990; Gosine, Mahin: 'Assimilation, Class and Social Mobility Among Caribbean East Indians in the United States'; 'The Coolie Connection: From the Orient to the Occident'. For Indians in Britain, see Visram, Rozina: AYAHS, LASCARS AND PRINCES (London: Pluto Press 1986) among others; Israel, Milton: IN THE FURTHER SOIL: A SOCIAL HISTORY OF INDO-CANADIANS IN ONTARIO (Toronto: M.G. Vassanji, 1994); Johnston, H.J.M: THE EAST INDIANS IN CAN ADA (Ottawa: Canadian Historical Association, 1984). For more on Indo-Caribbeans in Canada see Bibliography, especially Birbalsingh, F; Itwaru, A; Dabydeen, C and Espinet, R, among others.

69.   Furnivall, J.S: COLONIAL POLICY AND PRACTICE (London, Cambridge University Press 1948), p. 307.

70.   Smith, M.G: THE PLURAL SOCIETY IN THE BRITISH WEST INDIES (University of California Press, Berkeley and Los Angeles 1965), p. xi.

71.   Mayer, Alfred G: 'Historical Notes on Ideological Aspects of the Concept of Culture in Germany and Russia' in A.L. Kroeber and Clyde Kluckhohn CULTURE:A CRITICAL REVIEW OF CONCEPTS AND DEFINITIONS (Cambridge, Mass. Peabody Museum Papers) Vol. 47, No. 1, 1952.

72.   Kluckhohn, op. cit.

73.   Smith, M.G: op. cit., p. 3.

74.   Ibid., pp. 10,13.

75.   Allahar, A and Varadarajan, T: 'Differential Creolization: East Indians in Trinidad and Guyana', INDO-CARIBBEAN REVIEW, Vol. 1, No. 2, 1994, p. 126.

76.   Ehrlich, op. cit.

77.   Smith, op. cit., pp. 13–15.

78.   Ibid., pp. 16–17.

79.   Samaroo, B: 'Missionary Methods and Local Responses: The Canadian Presbyterians and the East Indians in the Caribbean'. Paper presented at a Symposium on East Indians in the Caribbean, U.W.I, 1975.

80.   Grant, K.J: MY MISSIONARY YEARS (Halifax 1923) pp. 161–166.

81.   Leonard, D.L: MISSIONARY ANNALS OF THE NINETEENTH CENTURY (Cleveland 1899), pp. 65, 227–8.

82.   Samaroo (1975), op. cit., p. 4.

83.   Ibid., p. 5.

84.   Ibid., pp. 6–7.

85.   Ibid., p. 9.

86.   Ibid., p. 10.

87.   TRINIDAD GUARDIAN, 9, 21 August, 1929.

88.   Morton, Sarah (ed): JOHN MORTON OF TRINIDAD, op. cit., pp. 187, 237.

89.   Samaroo, op. cit., p. 15.

90.   Ibid.

91.   Ibid., pp. 20–1.

92.   Ibid., pp. 31–2.

93.   Ibid., p. 33.

94.   Samaroo, op. cit., pp. 33–4.

95.   Ibid., p. 35.

96.   Ibid., pp. 36–7.

97.   Ibid., p. 38.

98.   Ruhomon, op. cit., p. 100.

99.   Weatherly, U.G: 'The West Indies as a Sociological Laboratory' in AMERICAN JOURNAL OF SOCIOLOGY, Vol. 29, No. 3, 1923, pp. 292–3.

100.   Ruhomon, op. cit., p. 206.

101. Ibid., p. 225.
102. Ibid., p. 228.
103. Ibid., p. 230.
104. Ibid., p. 231.
105. Ibid., pp. 231–44.
106. Ibid., p. 282.
107. Ibid., p. 242.
108. Ibid., p. 245.
109. Ibid., pp. 245–7.
110. Ibid., p. 248.
111. Ibid., p. 280–1.
112. Ibid., p. 249.
113. Ibid., p. 251.
114. Vertovec, S: op. cit., pp. 50–7.
115. Ibid., p. 55.
116. Bhattacharya, S: A DICTIONARY OF INDIAN HISTORY (University of Calcutta 1969), pp. 432–423; See also Vertovec, S: HINDU TRINIDAD: RELIGION, ETHNICITY AND SOCIO-ECONOMIC CHANGE (London: Macmillan Caribbean 1992).
117. Mueller, Max: WHAT CAN INDIA TEACH US? A COURSE OF FOUR LECTURES (London: John Murray & Co. 1892).
118. Ibid.
119. Ibid., pp. 253–4.
120. Williams, Monier, quoted by Ruhomon. See BRAHMANISM AND HINDUISM (London, John Murray 1887).
121. Ibid., p. 255.
122. Ibid., p. 256.
123. Ibid., p. 257.
124. Ibid., p. 258.
125. Schacht, J and Bosworth, C.E: THE LEGACY OF ISLAM, 2nd ed. (Clarendon Press, Oxford 1974), pp. 2–3.
126. Ruhomon, op. cit., pp. 259–60.
127. See the 'Trinidad' section of the text on Islam.
128. See Mangru, B: 'Tadjah in British Guiana: Manipulation and Protest' in INDENTURE AND ABOLITION, pp. 43–58.
129. Ibid., pp. 110–11.
130. Ibid.
131. Ibid., p. 114.
132. Ibid., p. 115.
133. Jayawardena, C and Smith, R.T: 'Marriage and the Family Amongst East Indians in British Guiana', SOCIAL AND ECONOMIC STUDIES, Vol. 8, no. 4, December 1959, pp. 374–5.
134. Ruhomon, op. cit., pp. 115–16.
135. Dunn, Z: 'The Canadian Mission in British Guiana: The Pioneer Years 1885–1927', MA Thesis, Queen's University, Kingston, Ontario 1971.
136. 'The Canadian Mission to the Guyana Presbyterian Church' in INDENTURE AND EXILE (Toronto, Tsar,1989), pp. 218–19.
137. Ibid., pp. 219–20.
138. Bisnauth, Rev. D.A: A SHORT HISTORY OF THE GUYANA PRESBYTERIAN CHURCH (Georgetown, Guyana: Labour Advocate Printery, 1979) pp. 46–9.
139. Ibid., p. 223–4.
140. Jha, J.C: 'The Hindu Festival of Divali in the Caribbean' CARIBBEAN QUARTERLY, Vol. 22, No. 1, March 1976, p. 55.
141. Ibid., pp. 54–60.
142. Vatuk, op. cit., p. 228.
143. Debiprashad and Budhram, op. cit.; Sukdeo, I.D, op. cit.

144. Allahar, A and Varadarajan, T: 'Differential Creolization: East Indians in Trinidad and Guyana', INDO-CARIBBEAN REVIEW, Vol. 1, No. 2 (University of Windsor, Canada, 1994) pp. 123–38.

145. Ramesar, Marianne: 'The Position of East Indians in Trinidad 1890–1917', Sixth Conference of Caribbean Historians, Puerto Rico, April 1974.

146. De Verteuil, L.A.A: TRINIDAD, ITS GEOGRAPHY, NATURAL RESOURCES, ADMINISTRATION, PRESENT CONDITION AND PROSPECTS, 2nd ed. (London, Ward & Lock, 1884), p. 350.

147. Sampath, Hugh: 'An Outline of the Social History of East Indians in Trinidad', PhD Diss. Columbia University 1951.

148. Ibid.

149. For a breakdown of the various Provinces and Districts from which the Indian migrants came to Trinidad during the period 1881–1917, see Vertovec, S: HINBDU TRINIDAD, Appendix (London: Macmillan 1992) pp. 232–43.

150. Hutton, J.H: CASTE IN INDIA (Oxford University Press, 1951), p. 9.

151. Rivers, W.H: THE TODAS (London 1906); See Sampath, H: op. cit.

152. Chandrasekhar, S: 'The Emigration and Status of Indians in the British Empire', SOCIAL ISSUES, Vol. 24, no. 2, 1945, pp. 152–60.

153. Sampath, op. cit., p. 20.

154. Vertovec, S, op. cit., pp. 87–92.

155. Ibid., p. 40.

156. Sapir, Edward: SELECTED WRITINGS OF EDWARD SAPIR IN LANGUAGE, CULTURE AND PERSONALITY (ed). D.G.Mandelbaum (London, Cambridge University Press 1949).

157. Mahabir, op. cit., p. 183.

158. Ibid., p. 167.

159. Ibid., p. 43.

160. Cudjoe, Selwyn: 'Foreword', THE STILL CRY: PERSONAL ACCOUNTS OF EAST INDIANS IN TRINIDAD AND TOBAGO DURING INDENTURESHIP (1845–1917), op. cit., p. 12. (Special thanks to Selwyn Cudjoe for permission to use material from this book).

161. Tinker, (1974), op. cit., pp. 208, 211.

162. Vertovec, S; op. cit., p. 94.

163. Niehoff, A and J, (1960), op. cit., p. 85.

164. Ibid., p. 86.

165. Kirpalani, et al: INDIAN CENTENARY REVIEW: ONE HUNDRED YEARS OF PROGRESS (Guardian Commercial Printery, Port of Spain, Trinidad 1945), p. 55.

166. Niehoff, op. cit., p. 78.

167. Ibid., p. 79.

168. Ibid., p. 81.

169. Ibid., p. 82.

170. Ibid., p. 83.

171. Ibid., p. 84.

172. Hamel-Smith, Angela: 'Primary Education and East Indian Women in Trinidad 1900–1956'. Paper presented to the Third Conference of East Indians in the Caribbean, August-September, 1984, pp. 3–4.

173. Ibid., p. 12.

174. Kellner, George: EDUCATIONAL ANTHROPOLOGY: AN INTRODUCTION (New York 1975).

175. Gajraj, Sandra: 'The Indian Cultural Presence in the Secondary School System in Trinidad and Tobago: Images and Perceptions'. Third Conference of East Indians in the Caribbean 1984, p. 4.

176. Anand, J.B: EDUCATION AND SELF-DISCOVERY (London, Hodder and Stoughton 1977), p. 82. Quoted by Gajraj, pp. 4–5.

177. Gajraj, op. cit., p. 8.

178. Ibid., p. 11.

179. Ibid., p. 13.

180. Ibid., p. 16.

181. Ramdin, Ron: WORLD IN VIEW: WEST INDIES (Heinemann Educa tional Books, Oxford 1991).

182. Klass, Morton, EAST INDIANS IN TRINIDAD, op. cit., p. 93.

183. Mandelbaum, David: 'Family in India' in SOUTHWESTERN JOURN AL OF ANTHROPOLOGY, Vol. 4, No. 2 (University of Mexico) p. 123.

184. Matthews, Dom Basil: CRISIS IN THE WEST INDIAN FAMILY (Government Printing Works, Port of Spain, Trinidad 1953), p. 2. Quoted by Niehoff.

185. Reddock, (1986) op cit, pp. 27–49; Mangru, B: op. cit., in INDIA IN THE CARIBBEAN, op. cit., pp. 211–30.

186. Kondapi, C: INDIANS OVERSEAS 1838–1949 (Oxford University Press, London 1951), p. 90; REPORT ON THE EMIGRATION FROM THE PORT OF CALCUTTA TO BRITISH AND FOREIGN COLONIES by C. Banks, 1905–1907 (Bengal Secretariat Book Depot).

187. Hart, Daniel: HISTORICAL AND STATISTICAL VIEW OF THE ISLAND OF TRINIDAD (London, Judd and Glass 1865), p. 101.

188. Niehoff, op. cit., p. 100.

189. Morton, Sarah, op. cit., p. 342.

190. Froude, J.A: THE ENGLISH IN THE WEST INDIES (New York, Longmans Green and Co. 1909), p. 67; Stark, James H: GUIDEBOOK AND HISTORY OF TRINIDAD 1892 (Boston, Mass., J.H. Stark 1897).

191. Collens, J.H: GUIDE TO TRINIDAD (Port of Spain, 1886), p. 197.

192. LAWS OF TRINIDAD AND TOBAGO (1950) by Eliot Francis, C.T. Roworth, London), pp. 56, 69.

193. Klass, op. cit., pp. 110–11.

194. Niehoff, op. cit., p. 105.

195. Ibid., p. 107.

196. Ibid., pp. 110–11.

197. See Kirian, G and Sri vastava, R.P: OVERSEAS INDIANS: A STUDY IN ADAPTATION (New Delhi: Vikas Publishing House, 1993) pp. 180–214

198. Mohammed, Patricia: 'The "Creolization" of Indian Women in Trinidad', THE INDEPENDENCE EXPERIENCE 1962–1987 (ISER, UWI 1987), pp. 381–397.

199. Espinet, Ramabai: 'Representation of the Indo-Caribbean Woman in Trinidad and Tobago' in INDO-CARIBBEAN RESIST ANCE (ed) Frank Birbalsingh (Toronto, Tsar 1993), pp. 42–61.

200. Kirpalani (1945), op. cit., p. 61.

201. Vertovec, S: op. cit., pp. 106–7.

202. Ibid., pp. 108–16.

203. See Grierson, George A: BIHAR PEASANT LIFE, (London: Truebner & Co, 1985), p. 331; Planalp, Jack M: 'Religious Life and Values in a North Indian Village', PhD. Diss., Cornell University, 1956, p. 237; Vertovec, S, op. cit., p. 110.

204. Vertovec, op. cit., pp. 111–12.

205. Wilson, H.H: RELIGION OF THE HINDUS (London, Trubner and Co.1862), p: 359.

206. Niehoff, op. cit., p. 117.

207. Ibid., p. 118.

208. Naipaul, Shiva: BEYOND THE DRAGON'S MOUTH (London, Abacus 1984), p. 28.

209. Marriott, McKim: 'Little Communities in an Indigenous Civilization' in VILLAGE INDIA, ed. McKim Marriott, American Anthropological Association, Memoir 83, p. 192.

210. Jha, J.C: 'The Hindu Sacraments (Rites de Passage) in Trinidad and Tobago', CARIBBEAN QUARTERLY, Vol. 22, No. 1, March 1976, pp. 46–7.

211. Niehoff, op. cit., p. 132.

212. Ibid., p. 133.

213. Jha, op. cit., pp. 50–1.

214. Jha, J.C: 'Hinduism in Trinidad' in INDENTURE AND EXILE (ed) F. Birbalsingh (Toronto, Tsar 1989), p. 232.

215. Vertovec, S; op. cit., pp. 162–4.

216. Ibid., p. 191.

217. Kirpalani, op. cit., p. 61.
218. Niehoff, op. cit., p. 136.
219. Ibid., pp. 138–9.
220. Ibid.
221. Ibid., pp. 141, 143.
222. Ibid.
223. Collens, J.H: A GUIDE TO TRINIDAD: HANDBOOK FOR THE USE OF TOUR-ISTS AND VISITORS, 2nd edn, (London, Elliot Stock, 1888), p. 237.
224. Ibid.
225. Hydal, M.M. Kemal: 'The Religious Experience of the Indians in Trinidad: The Muslim Experience'. Paper presented at Conference on East Indians, U.W.I 1984.
226. Niehoff, op. cit., p. 146.
227. Ibid.
228. Jha, (1976), op. cit., pp. 49–50).
229. Niehoff, op. cit., p. 147.
230. Jha (1976), op. cit., p. 50.
231. See CONSTITUTION OF INDIA – Articles 17,15, 29(2), 38 and 46.
232. Srinivas, M.N: CASTE IN MODERN INDIA AND OTHER ESSAYS (Bombay, Asia Publishing House, 1962).
233. Niehoff, op, cit, p. 188.
234. Ibid., p. 148.
235. Morton, J: JOHN MORTON OF TRINIDAD, op. cit., pp. 110–11.
236. Niehoff, op. cit., p. 150.
237. Morton, op. cit., p. 456.
238. Niehoff, op. cit., pp. 152–3.
239. Ibid., pp. 155–6.
240. Ibid., pp. 156–7.
241 Eliot, Sir Charles: HINDUISM AND BUDDHISM: AN HISTORICAL SKETCH, 3 Vols, Vol. II (London, E. Arnold & Co. 1921), pp. XXXIX–XL.
242. Niehoff, op. cit., p. 159.
243. Ibid., p. 160.
244. Ibid., pp. 167–8.
245. Ibid., p. 188.
246. Mahabir, N.K and Maharaj, A: 'Hindu Elements in the Shango/Orisha Cult in Trinidad' in INDENTURE AND EXILE, op. cit., pp. 1989.
247. Srinivas, M.N: RELIGION AND SOCIETY AMONG THE COORGS (Asia Publishing House, Bombay 1965), pp. 27–8.
248. Debysingh, Dolly: 'Cultural Change and Adaptation as Reflected in the Meat-Eating Habits of the Trinidad Indian Population'. CARIBBEAN QUARTERLY, Vol. 32, Nos.3–4, September–December 1986
249. Ibid., p. 67.
250. Lowenthal, D: WEST INDIAN SOCIETIES (Oxford University Press 1972); p. 148.
251. Ibid., p. 150.
252 Niehoff, op. cit., p. 93.
253. Ibid., p. 94.
254. Debysingh, op. cit., pp. 74–5.
255. Jha, J.C: 'The Indian Heritage in Trinidad' in CALCUTTA TO CARONI: THE EAST INDIANS IN TRINIDAD, ed. J. La Guerre (Longman Caribbean 1974).
256. Dookheran, W, op. cit., p. 82.
257. Deosaran, Ramesh: 'The "Caribbean Man": A Study of the Psychology of Perception and the Media' in INDIA IN THE CARIBBEAN, op. cit., p. 82.
258. TRINIDAD EXPRESS, 9 March 1979.
259. Trotman, D.V: 'The Image of Indians in Calypsoes in Trinidad 1946–1986' in INDENTURE AND EXILE, op. cit., pp. 176–90.
260. Deosaran, op. cit., pp. 106–7.

261. Singh, K, (1988) op. cit.

262. Singh, K: 'The Roots of Afro-Indian Conflict in the Trinidad Indentureship Period'. Paper presented at Symposium on East Indians in the Carib bean, September 1979.

263. Dookheran, op. cit., p. 80.

264. See Gosine, Mahin: 'Ethnic Heterogeneity and the Black Power Movement in Trinidad: An Historical and Socio-Structural Analysis'. (Ann Arbor: MI, University Microfilm, 1982).

265. Allahar, A and Varadarajan, T: (1994) op. cit., pp. 131–5.

266. Ramcharan, S: 'The Social Cultural and Economic Adaptation of Indians in Trinidad: An Analysis of a Multicultural Society' in INDO-CARIBBEAN REVIEW, Vol. 1, No. 1, 1994, pp. 3–13.

267. Mansingh, Laxmi: 'Cultural Heritage Among the East Indians in Jamaica'. Paper presented at Symposium on East Indians in the Carib bean, U.W.I, 1979.

268. Birbalsingh, F: JAHAJI BHAI: AN ANTHOLOGY OF INDO-CARIBBEAN LITERATURE (Toronto: Tsar, 1988) pp. 104–19.

269. Ehrlich, (1969) op. cit., p. 123.

270. Mansingh, op. cit., p. 10.

271. Ibid.

272. Mansingh, op. cit., pp. 11–12.

273. Ibid., p. 13.

274. Ibid., pp. 15–19.

275. Ibid., pp. 21–3.

276. Mansingh, L and A: 'The Cultural Survivals Among the East Indians in Jamaica'. Paper presented at Conference on Carib bean Historians at Curacao, 5–10 April 1979; Mansingh, L: 'Cultural Heritage Among the East Indians in Jamaica', op. cit., pp. 24–5.

277. Mansingh, op. cit., pp. 25–7.

278. Ibid., p. 31.

279. Rubin, Vera and Zavalloni, M: WE WISHED TO BE LOOKED UPON: A STUDY OF THE ASPIRATIONS OF YOUTH IN A DEVELOPING SOCIETY (New York 1969), p. 312; Mansingh, op. cit.

280. DAILY GLEANER, 'Back to India March in the City', 25 October 1948.

281. Mansingh, op. cit., p. 35.

282. Ibid., pp. 36–7.

283. Quoted from Mansingh, op. cit., p. 37.

284. Mansingh, A and L: 'Hindu Influences on Rastafarianism', CARIBBEAN QUARTERLY, Monograoh – Rastafari, U.W.I, 1985. For more on Hinduism and Rastafarianism see Mansigh, A and L: 'Hindu Influences on Rastafarianism' in CARIBBEAN QUARTERLY Monograph – Rastafari, UWI 1985.

285. Speckmann, J.D: MARRIAGE AND KINSHIP AMONG THE EAST INDIANS IN SURINAM (Assen 1965).

286. Kishna, S: 'Language and Language Use of the Hindustani in Surinam'. Conference on East Indians in the Carib bean, August-September 1984.

287. Smith, R.T and Jayawardena, C: 'Marriage and the Family Amongst the East Indians in British Guiana', SOCIAL AND ECONOMIC STUDIES, Vol. 8, 1959, p. 331.

288. Speckmann, op. cit., pp. 48–9.

289. Ibid., p. 49.

290. Ibid., pp. 52–3.

291. Ibid., p. 265.

292. Ibid., pp. 64–6.

293. Ibid., pp. 76–89.

294. Ibid., pp. 130–6.

295. Ibid., pp. 261–2.

296. Ibid., p. 270.

297. For more on the East Indians in Grenada, see Mahabir, N.K: 'East Indians in Grenada: A Study in absorption'. Paper presented at Symposium on East Indians in the Carib bean, September 1984.

298.  Lowenthal, David: WEST INDIAN SOCIETIES (London: Oxford University Press, 1972) pp. 2, 4, 14, 34.

299.  Mahabir, N.K: 'East indians in Grenada: A Study in Absorption' 1984.

300.  Sarusky, Jaime: 'The East Indian Community in Cuba' in INDENTURE AND EXILE, op. cit., pp. 73–78.

301.  Horowitz, M and Klass, M: 'The Martiniquan East Indian Cult of Maldevidan', SOCIAL AND ECONOMIC STUDIES, Vol. 1, March 1961, pp. 93–100.

302.  Naipaul, V.S: THE MIDDLE PASSAGE (London, Andre Deutsch 1962), p. 205.

303.  Singaravelou, (1975) op. cit.

304.  Moutousammy, E: 'Indianness in the French West Indies' in INDENTURE AND EXILE, op. cit., p. 29.

305.  Ibid., p. 34.

306.  Ibid., p. 35.

# CHAPTER FOUR

1.      Birbalsingh, F: 'Indo-Caribbean Test Cricketers' in INDENTURE AND EXILE (Toronto: Tsar 1989) p. 265.

2.      Seecharan, Clem; 'The Tiger of Port Mourant – R.B. Kanhai: Fact and Fantasy in the Making of an Indo-Guyanese Legend' in INDO-WEST INDIAN CRICKET (London: Hansib 1988) pp. 41–77.

3.      James, C.L.R: AT THE RENDEZVOUS OF VICTORY: SELECTED WRITINGS (London: Allison and Busby, 1984) p. 166.

4.      Birbalsingh, F: op. cit., p. 276.

5.      Birbalsingh, et al: 'Indo-Caribbean Cricketers: A Panel Discussion' in INDENTURE AND EXILE, pp. 248–9.

6.      Ramchand, Ken: 'An Approach to Earl Lovelace's Novel Through an Examination in the Dragon Can't Dance', CARIBBEAN QUARTERLY, Vol. 32, March–June 1986, UWI, p. 2.

7.      Birbalsingh, F: 'Jamaican Indians: A Novelist's View', INDENTURE AND EXILE, op. cit., p. 99.

8.      Tinker, Hugh: 'The Origins of Indian Migration to the West Indies', INDENTURE AND EXILE, OP. CIT, pp. 63–71.

9.      Lowenthal, D: WEST INDIAN SOCIETIES, op. cit., p. 145.

10.     Ruhomon, Peter: CENTENARY HISTORY OF THE EAST INDIANS IN BRITISH GUIANA, 1838–1938 (Georgetown: The Daily Chronicle 1946) pp. 190–94.

11.     Jagan, Cheddi: FORBIDDEN FREEDOM: THE STORY OF BRITISH GUIANA. Third Edition (London: Hansib, 1994) pp. 32–41.

12.     ——: THE WEST ON TRIAL: MY FIGHT FOR GUYANA'S FREEDOM (London: Michael Joseph 1966) p. 20.

13.     Ibid., p. 22.

14.     Despres, Leo: CULTURAL PLURALISM AND NATIONALIST POLITICS IN BRITISH GUIANA (Chicago, Rand McNally and Co. 1967), pp. 181–2.

15.     Ibid., pp. 183–4.

16.     DR CHEDDI JAGAN: A BIOGRAPHICAL NOTE (PPP Guyana, U.K Branch 1991).

17.     Ibid.

18.     Despres, op. cit., pp. 184–5.

19.     Ibid., pp. 187–8.

20.     Ibid., pp. 189–90.

21.     Spinner, Thomas J: A POLITICAL AND SOCIAL HISTORY OF GUYANA 1945–1983 (Boulder, Westview 1984), pp. 41–43.

22.     Ibid., p. 46.

23.     REPORT OF THE BRITISH GUIANA COMMISSION, Sir James Robertson (Chairman), Cmd.9274, 1954.

24.     Despres, op. cit., pp. 5–6.

25.     Ibid., pp. 6–7; Jha (1973) op. cit.

26. Ibid., p. 8.
27. Cohen, W.I: DEAN RUSK (Totown, New Jersey 1980); Walton, Richard J: COLD WAR AND OTHER COUNTER-REVOLUTION (New York 1972), pp. 210–13.
28. Spinner, op. cit., p. 94.
29. Despres, op. cit., pp. 228–67.
30. Verrier, A: 'Guyana and Cyprus: Techniques of Peace-Keeping', JOURNAL OF THE ROYAL UNITED SERVICE INSTITUTION, 111, Nov. 1966, p. 299; Spinner, op. cit., p. 121.
31. Greene, J.E: RACE VS. POLITICS IN GUYANA: POLITICAL CLEAVAGES AND POLITICAL MOBILIZATION IN THE 1968 GENERAL ELECTION (Kingston, Jamaica), p. 29; Spinner, op. cit., p. 127.
32. Spinner, op. cit., pp. 127–8.
33. Nascimento, C.A and Burrowes, R.A (eds): FORBES BURNHAM: A DESTINY TO MOULD (Longman Caribbean, 1970), p. 61.
34. Ibid., pp. 136–145.
35. Ibid., pp. 152–160.
36. SUNDAY GRAPHIC, 12 November 1970, p. 5.
37. Mentus, Ric: SUNDAY GRAPHIC, 22–9 July 1973.
38. Spinner, op. cit., pp. 186–7.
39. CARIBBEAN CONTACT, November 1980, pp. 7–10.
40. SOMETHING TO REMEMBER: REPORT OF THE INTERNATIONAL TEAM OF OBSERVERS AT THE ELECTIONS IN GUYANA, December 1980, p. 28; Spinner, op, cit, p. 192.
41. Spinner, op. cit., pp. 194–5.
42. THE ECONOMIST, 22 June 1991.
43. ELECTIONS UPDATE, September 1990 (UK PPP Branch).
44. Editorial; THE NATION (U.S Weekly), 4 June 1990.
45. ELECTION UPDATE (1990).
46. THE ECONOMIST, 22 June 1991.
47. 'Jagan: The Phoenix', CARIBBEN CONTACT, November-December 1990.
48. THE MIRROR (Guyana), 14 July 1991.
49. French, Howard: 'Guyana Marxist Mellowed, Makes A Comeback', NEW YORK TIMES (International), 5 July 1991.
50. Jagan, Cheddi: 'Indo-Caribbean Political Leadership' in INDENTURE AND EXILE, op. cit., p. 25.
51. Ramesar, D: SURVIVORS OF ANOTHER CROSSING: A HISTORY OF EAST INDIANS IN TRINIDAD, 1880–1946 (St. Augustine, Trinidad: UWI 1994) pp. 146–7.
52. Jha, J.C: 'East Indian Pressure Groups in Trinidad, 1897–1921'. Paper presented at Conference of Caribbean Historians, U.W.I, Trinidad 1973.
53. Panday, Basdeo: 'Trade Unionism, Politics and Indo-Caribbean Leadership' in INDENTURE AND EXILE, op. cit., pp. 55–6.
54. Day, Charles: FIVE YEARS RESIDENCE IN THE WEST INDIES (London, Colburn and Co. 1852), pp. 181–2.
55. Jha, J.C, op. cit.
56. Ibid.
57. Ibid.
58. Jha, op. cit.
59. Singh, Kelvin: 'The Roots of Afro-Indian Conflict in the Indentureship Period'. Paper presented at Symposium on East indians in the Caribbean, UWI, 1979.
60. Ibid., p. 5.
61. Carmichael, Gertrude: THE HISTORY OF THE WEST INDIAN ISLANDS OF TRINIDAD AND TOBAGO 1498–1900 (London, Alvin Redman 1961), pp. 213–16.
62. Singh, Kelvin: 'The Roots of Afro-Indian Conflict in the Indentureship Period', op. cit.; Ramesar, M: 'The Impact of the Indian Immigrants on Colonial Trinidad'. Paper presented at Symposium on East Indians in the Caribbean, U.W.I, June 1975.
63. PORT OF SPAIN GAZETTE, 5 December 1890.
64. Ramdin, Ron: FROM CHATTEL SLAVE TO WAGE EARNER, op. cit., pp. 56, 68.

65.   THE MIRROR, 14 October 1912.
66.   Singh, (1979), op. cit.
67.   Ramdin, op, cit, pp. 54–63.
68.   Tikasingh, op. cit.
69.   Singh, op. cit.
70.   TRINIDAD GUARDIAN, 11 December 1919.
71.   Ibid., 31 December 1919; 7 February 1920.
72.   Ramdin, op. cit., pp. 68–9.
73.   FORSTER COMMISSION REPORT (Cmd. 5641), 1938, p. 48.
74.   DAILY CHRONICLE (Georgetown, British Guiana), 13 January 1920.
75.   Jha (1973), op. cit., pp. 13–14; TRINIDAD GUARDIAN, 28 July 1922.
76.   Craig, Hewan: THE LEGISLATIVE COUNCIL OF TRINIDAD AND TOBAGO (London, Faber and Faber), 1952, p. 86.
77.   Ibid., p. 61.
78.   PORT OF SPAIN GAZETTE, 16 September 1924.
79.   Trinidad Working Men's Association Report, 1926.
80.   FORSTER COMMISSION REPORT, op. cit., p. 75.
81.   CO/585: Report of the Labour Disturbances Commission 1934; PORT OF SPAIN GAZETTE, 21 July 1934; Basdeo, S: 'Indian Participation in Labour Politics in Trinidad 1919–1939'. Paper presented at Symposium on East Indians in the Caribbean, St. Augustine, 1979.
82.   Basdeo, op. cit.
83.   PORT OF SPAIN GAZETTE, 23 April 1929.
84.   FORSTER COMMISSION REPORT, op. cit., p. 48
85.   Citrine to Cipriani, Cable 1932. Private and Confidential Files, British Trades Union Congress, Congress House, London.
86.   Ramdin, op. cit., pp. 75–6.
87.   Basdeo, op. cit.
88.   Ramdin, op. cit., Chaps. 3–7.
89.   Samaroo, B: 'Politics and Afro-Indian Relations in Trinidad' in CALCUTTA TO CARONI, pp. 84–97.
90.   THE PEOPLE, 8 January 1938.
91.   Samaroo, B.(1974), op. cit., p. 93.
92.   Ibid., p. 94.
93.   Basdeo, op. cit., p. 22; Samaroo, B. (1974), op. cit., p. 93.
94.   Malik, Yogendra: EAST INDIANS AND POLITICS IN TRINIDAD: A STUDY IN MINORITY POLITICS (Oxford University Press, 1971), p. 75.
95.   Samaroo, (1974), op. cit., p. 96.
96.   Ibid.
97.   Malik, op. cit., pp. 22–25.
98.   TRINIDAD GUARDIAN, 30 August 1956.
99.   Malik, op. cit., pp. 37–9.
100.  Niehoff, op. cit., p. 69.
101.  Malik, op. cit., pp. 84–5; Ibid., p. 88.
102.  Ibid., pp. 92–3.
103.  Ibid., pp. 120–127.
104.  Malik, op. cit., p. 100.
105.  Ibid., pp. 104–5.
106.  Ibid., pp. 109, 115, 116.
107.  Ibid., p. 126.
108.  Malik, op. cit., p. 141.
109.  TRINIDAD GUARDIAN, 1 January 1961.
110.  Singh, H.P: HOUR OF DECISION (Trinidad 1962).
111.  Malik, op. cit., pp. 67–8.
112.  Ibid., p. 157.
113.  Ibid., p. 159.

114. Oxaal, I: RACE AND REVOLUTIONARY CONSCIOUSNESS (Cambridg e, Mass. 1971); Ryan, S: REVOLUTION AND REACTION: PARTIES AND POLITICS IN TRINIDAD AND TOBAGO, 1970–1981 (St. Augustine, Institute of Social and Economic R esearch 1989)

115. See Gosine, M: 'Ethnic Heterogeneity and the Black Power Movement in Trinidad: An Historical and Socio-Str uctural Analysis'. (Ann Arbor, MI University Microfilms 1982)

116. Oxaal, I: RACE AND REVOLUTIONARY CONSCIOUSNESS (1971), op. cit., p. 34.

117. Ibid., p. 41.

118. Ibid., p. 37.

119. Nicholls, David: 'East Indians and Black Power in Trinidad', RACE, XI (1971), p. 454.

120. Ryan, S: RACE AND NATIONALISM IN TRINIDAD AND TOBAGO (University of Toronto Press, 1972) p. 446.

121. TRINIDAD GUARDIAN, 12 February 1971.

122. Ryan, op. cit., p. 475.

123. TRINIDAD GUARDIAN, 6 June 1971.

124. Williams, Eric: HISTORY OF THE PEOPLE OF TRINIDAD AND TOBAGO, 1964, p. 282.

125. A Draft Constitution w as prepared and published to concide with the launc h of the MUP on 11 December 1994.

126. See THE NEW POLITICAL CULTURE (Toronto: Caribbean Press Inc, 1995). In this published speech, Bhaggan advocated a programme of reform, a moving away from the old to a new political cultur e.

127. INDO-CARIBBEAN WORLD (Toronto) Vol. 12, No. 8, December 1994.

128. Panday, op. cit., p. 202.

129. Millette, James: POWER IN THE STREETS: THE MUSLIMEEN UPRISING IN TRINI-DAD AND TOBAGO (Trinidad: February 18 Movement 1992) pp. 15–16.

130. Premdas, Ralph: 'Ethnic Conflict in Trinidad and Tobago' in TRINIDAD ETHNICITY (London: Macmillan 1993) pp. 156–159.

131. James, C.L.R: 'Introduction' – FROM CHATTEL SLAVE TO WAGE EARNER, op. cit., p. ix.

132. THE TRINIDAD GUARDIAN, 31 May 1995.

133. Panday, op. cit.

134. Fischer, L: THE HISTORY OF INDONESIA (New York, Husker 1959), p. 79.

135. Thakur, Andhra P: 'British and Dutch Colonial Policies in Guyana and Surinam' in INDENTURE AND EXILE, pp. 115–20.

136. Hira, Sandew: 'The Evolution of the Social, Economic and Political Position of the East Indians in Surinam, 1873–1980' in INDIA IN THE CARIBBEAN, p. 202.

137. Dew, Edward: 'Surinam: Transcending Ethnic Politics the Hard Way' in INDENTURE AND EXILE, p. 126.

138. Ibid., p. 127.

139. Thakur, op. cit, p. 120.

140. Hira, S, op. cit., p. 206.

141. Dew, E: op. cit., p. 130.

142. Ibid., pp. 136–7.

143. Schnepel, Ellen M: 'The Creole Movement and Its Significance f or the Socio-political Inte-gration of East Indians on the Island of Guadeloupe, French West Indies' in THE ENIGMA OF ETHNICITY: AN ANALYSIS OF RACE IN THE CARIBBEAN AND THE WORLD. (St. Aug-ustine, U.W.I 1993), p. 197.

144. Ibid., pp. 204–5.

145. Ibid., p. 207.

146. Ibid., pp. 208–9.

147. Ibid., pp. 214–215.

148. Ibid., p. 216.

149. Allahar, A and Varadarajan, T: INDO-CARIBBEAN REVIEW, Vol. 1, No. 2, 1994, pp. 123–139.

150. Milan Kundera quoted by Salman Rushdie in IMAGINARY HOMELANDS (London: Granta Books 1991) p. 14.

# BIBLIOGRAPHY

## COLONIAL OFFICE FILES

CO. 111/439, 488, 501–2, 504–5, 508, 513, 528, 536–7, 540, 552, 558, 579–80, 586.
CO. 114/68, 113.
CO. 295/374, 376, 397, 400, 403, 413, 428, 437–8, 441, 445, 461, 471, 478.
CO. 318/165, 296, 299.
CO. 323/554, 597, 614, 717, 753.
CO. 384/103, 104, 106, 114, 116, 118–120, 139, 166–7, 173, 179, 180–1, 185, 187, 190–2.
CO. 571/1, 2, 4–5.

## INDIA OFFICE RECORDS

A good deal of material has been consulted from the following general categories of the India Office Library Records (IOLR):

L/P & J: PUBLIC AND JUDICIAL DEPARTMENT RECORDS, 1795–1858.
L/P & J/3: CORRESPONDENCE WITH INDIA, 1795–1947.
L/P & J/6: DEPARTMENTAL PAPERS: ANNUAL FILES, 1880–1930.
L/P & J/7: DEPARTMENTAL PAPERS: ANNUAL FILES, 1931–1947.
L/E: ECONOMIC DEPARTMENT RECORDS, 1786–1947.

For a more detailed listing of source materials in the India Office Library Records relating to Indian emigration during 1830–1950, see Timothy Thomas's 'GUIDE' to INDIANS OVERSEAS.

## PARLIAMENTARY PAPERS

P.P. 1837–8, LII.
P.P. 1839, XXXIX.
P.P. 1840, XXXIV.
P.P. 1841, XVI.
P.P. 1842, XIII.
P.P. 1843, XXXV.
P.P. 1845, XXXV.
P.P. 1846, XXX.
P.P. 1846, XXVIII.
P.P. 1847, XXXIX.
P.P. 1847, XXXIII.
P.P. 1847, XXVI.
P.P. 1861, LXV.
P.P. 1870, (751).
P.P. 1874, XLVII.
P.P. 1875.LLV.
P.P. 1875, LLX.
P.P. 1882, Cmd.3388, XLIV.
P.P. 1898, L, (C.8657).
P.P. 1910, Cd.5193.
P.P. 1914–16, Cd.7744.
P.P. 1922, XVI, Cmd.1679.
P.P. 1945, Cmd. 6609.

# OTHER OFFICAL DOCUMENTS

## REGISTERS IN THE NATIONAL ARCHIVES

## OF TRINIDAD AND TOBAGO

## CONCERNING EAST INDIANS

Birth (Registers) 1850 onwards.
Bounty Certificates – 1882–1907.
Bounty Immigrants – 1861–1863.
Bounty (Register) – 1868–74, 1882.
Crown Lands and Monies granted to Indian Immigrants in lieu of Return Passage to India 1871–1890.
Deceased Immigrant Property 1896–1918.
Death (Registers) 1865–1950.
Distribution of Immigrants from Ships – 1884–96, 1877, 1907–9, 1910–11.
Estate Registers of Bounty Immigrants 1882–1886.
Free Certificates Destroyed in Office 1907.
General Letters of 1929.
General Registers – 1845–1917. Registers exist for all these years except 1906–1909.
House Rates for San Fernando 1860–1923.
Indian Immigrants' Remittances to Relatives and Friends in India 1885–1891.
Indian Marriage and Divorce 1893–1901.
Letters from India 1914–16, 1916, 1922, 1926–27, 1928–32.
Money Order on India 1911–1921.
Passengers 1906–1932.
Passports 1899–1938.
Paupers and Lepers 1929
Protector of Indian Immigrants 1928
Redemption Fees – 1898–1913.
Returning Immigrants 1851–1939.
Ship Registers (with Emigration Passes) 1851–1917.
Tax Assessment Rolls – 1880–1923.

Colonial Report, British Guiana, 1953.(London 1953).
Debates of the British Guiana House of Assembly.
Debates of the British Guiana State Council.
Debates of the Legislative Council of British Guiana.
Guyana: Parliamentary Debates.
The Historical Society of Trinidad and Tobago Publications 999 Documents.
Correspondence Respecting the Recent Coolie Disturbances in Trinidad at the Muharram Festival, with the Report Thereon by Sir H.W. Norman, 1885.
Report of the West India Royal commission, London 1897.
Immigration Ordinance of Trinidad (1899) and British Guiana, Cd.1989, Presented to Parliament in April 1904.
Report of the Commission of Enquiry into the Recent Disturbances at Port of Spain, Trinidad, 1903, Cd.1662.
Further Papers Relating to the Disturbances at Port of Spain, Trinidad in March 1903, Cd.1988, 1904.
Report of the Government of India on the Conditions of Indian Immigrants in Four British Colonies and Surinam by James McNeill and Chimman Lal, 1914–16, Cd.7744.
Report of the Hon. E.F.L Wood, M.P (Parliamentary Under-Secretary of State for the Colonies) on his visit to the West Indies and British Guiana, Cmd.1679, London 1922.
Report of the West India Sugar Commission, Cmd.3517, 1930.
Labour Conditions in the West Indies: Report by Major G. St. Orde Brown, Cmd.6070, London 1939.
Recommendations of the West India Royal commission, 1938–1939, Cmd.6174.
Report of the Commission on the Trinidad and Tobago Disturbances, Cmd.5641, 1938.
Wages Committee Report, 1920.
Labour Policies in the West Indies, ILO 1952.

Labour Administration in the Colonial Territories, 1944–1950.
Labour Supervision in the Colonial territories, 1944–1950.
Labour Supervision in the Colonial Empire, London 1951.
Labour in the United Kingdom Dependencies, London 1957.
Administration Reports of the Commissioner of Labour, Trinidad and Tobago, 1947–1951.
Administration Report of the Industrial Adviser, Trinidad and Tobago, 1945–1946.
Report of the Board of Inquiry into a Trade Dispute in the Sugar Industry of Trinidad, December 1960.
Report of a Board of Inquiry into the Dispute Between the All Trinidad Sugar Estates and Factories Workers'
Trade Union and the Sugar Industry Labour Union nu F.C. Catchpole, November 1955.
Trinidad and Tobago Blue Book, 1925.
Parliamentary Debates of the House of Representatives, Trinidad and Tobago, 1963.
The Industrial Stabilisation Act, Trinidad and Tobago, 1965.
The Mbanefo Commission of Inquiry into Subversive Activities, Trinidad and Tobago 1965.
The Industrial Relations Act, Trinidad and Tobago, 1972.
Mission Report, Jamaica and Trinidad, Birmingham Chamber of Commerce, 1976.
Budget Speech, Trinidad, 1970.
Private and Confidential Files, British TUC. Congress House, London.
Report of the first British Guiana and West Indies Labour Conference, Georgetown, British Guiana, 1926.
Report of the First British Commonwealth Labour Conference, London, 1925.

# BOOKS, THESES, ARTICLES AND PAMPHLETS

Acheen, Rene: 'Problem of Indian Immigration at the Bar of Public Opinion in Martinique in the Years 1882 and 1886'. Conference on Caribbean Historians, Mona, Jamaica, U.W.I, 1972.

Adams, Harriet, Chalmers: 'The East Imdians in the New World'. NATIONAL GEOGRAPHIC MAGAZINE, 18, 1907.

Adamson, Alan H: SUGAR WITHOUT SLAVES: THE POLITICAL ECONOMY OF BRITISH GUIANA 1838–1904.(New Haven, Yale University Press 1972).

Afolabi, Ojo, G.J: YORUBA CULTURE (London, Oxford University Press 1966).

Agrosino. Michael V: 'Sexual Politics in the East Indian Family in Trinidad', CARIBBEAN STUDIES, 16, 1976.

Ahe, Molly: 'Orisha Tradition and Culture', TRINIDAD GUARDIAN, 30 October 1983.

Ahshan, Syed Reza: 'East Indian Agricultural Settlements in
Trinidad: A Study in Cultural Geography'. PhD. Diss. University of Florida 1963.

Aiyappan, A: SOCIAL AND PHYSICAL ANTHROPOLOGY OF THE NYADIS OF MALABAR (Madras 1037).

Aldus, Don: COOLIE TRAFFIC AND KIDNAPPING (London, McCorquodale & Co.,1876).

Allahar, A and Varadarajan, T: 'Differential Creolization: East Indians in Trinidad and Guyana', INDO-CARIBBEAN REVIEW, Vol. 1, No. 2, 1994, pp. 123–29.

Alleyne, J.M: 'The Creolization of Africans and Indians'. Symposium on East Indians in the Caribbean, U.W.I, Trinidad, September 1979.

Ambimala, Wanda: 'The Orisha Tradition: A World View', THE RELIGION OF THE ORISHAS (Trinidad, Orisha Movement, n.d.)

Amos, S: THE EXISTING LAWS OF DEMERARA FOR THE REGULATION OF COOLIE EMIGRATION (London 1871).

Anand, J.B: EDUCATION AND SELF DISCOVERY (London, Hodder & Stoughton 1977).

Andrews, Charles Freer: 'An Interim Statement Concerning East Indian Conditions in British Guiana', WEST INDIES PAMPHLET 3, 1929.

——: 'The Indian Emigration Problem', FOREIGN AFFAIRS, Vol. 8.

Ankum-Houwink, J: 'Chinese Contract Migrants in Surinam between 1853 and 1870'. BOLETIN DE ESTUDIOS LATIN AMERICANOS Y DEL CARIBE 17, December 1974.

Apple, Arnold: SON OF GUYANA, London: Oxford University Press, 1973

Arasaratnam, Sinnappah: INDIANS IN MALAYSIA AND SINGAPORE, London: 1970.

Araxa, U: RITUAL SONGS AND FOLKSONGS OF THE HINDUS OF SURINAM (Leiden, E.J. Brill, 1968).

Arnold, Thomas: 'Remnants of the Great Coolie Scramble: East Indian Immigration to the Windward Islands with Special Reference to St. Vincent, 1860–1880'. Paper given at the Institute of Commwealth Studies, University of London, 24 November 1993.

Arya, Satya Prakesh: 'The Folk-Religion of Western Uttar Pradesh', FOLKLORE (Calcutta, 1973).

Aspinall, Algernon: A WAYFARER IN THE WEST INDIES (London 1928).

Astor, Lord: THE COLONIAL PROBLEM (1957).

Auguelli, John and Harry W. Taylor: 'Race and Population Patterns in Trinidad', ANNALS OF THE ASSOCIATION OF AMERICAN GEOGRAPHERS, 50, 1960.

Augier, F.R, Gordon, S, et. al: THE MAKING OF THE WEST INDIES (London 1960).

Augier, F.R: 'Crown Colony Government in Jamaica 1865–1885'. PhD. Thesis, University of St. Andrews 1954.

Azimullah, Evert: JAGERNATH LACHMON: EEN POLITIEKE BIOGRAPHIE (Paramaribo, Vaco Press 1986).

Bacchus, Mohammed Kazim: EDUCATION AND SOCIO-CULTURAL INTEGRATION IN A PLURAL SOCIETY. Centre for developing Area Studies. Occasional Paper Series, No. 6, Montreal, McGill University 1970.

Baden-Powell, B.H: THE INDIAN VILLAGE COMMUNITY. (London, Longmans, Green and Co.)

Bagley, C: THE DUTCH PLURAL SOCIETY: A COMPARATIVE STUDY IN RACE RELATIONS (Oxford University Press 1973).

Bahadoorsingh, Krishna: TRINIDAD ELECTORAL POLITICS: THE PERSISTENCE OF THE RACE FACTOR, (London: Institute of Race Relations 1968).

Bahadur Singh, I.J. (ed): THE OTHER INDIA. (New Delhi: Arnold Heinemann, 1979).

Bahadur Singh, I.J (ed): INDIANS IN THE CARIBBEAN (New Delhi: Sterling Publishers, 1987).

Baksh, Ahamad: 'The Educational and Occupational Mobility Patterns of East Indians in Guyana'. Symposium on East Indians in the Caribbean, U.W.I, Trinidad, September 1979.

———: THE MOBILITY OF DEGREE-LEVEL GRADUATES OF THE UNIVERSITY OF GUYANA (University of Guyana, n.d.)

Baksh, Ishmael: 'Some Factors Related to Educational Expectation Among East Indian and Negro Students Attending Public Secondary Schools in Trinidad'. PhD. Diss, University of Alberta 1974.

Baksh, Ishmael: 'Stereotypes of Negroes and East Indians in Trinidad: A Re-examination'. CARIBBEAN QUARTERLY 25, 1979, pp. 52–71.

Bali, Bhagwan: ENKLE OORZAKEN VAN DE SUBORDINATIE DE BRITS – INDISCHE IMMIGRATION IN SURINAME 1873–1902 (Manuscript 1984).

Banaji, D.R: SLAVERY IN BRITISH INDIA (Bombay, D.B. Toraporavala Sons & Co. 1933).

Banks, C: REPORT ON EMIGRATION FROM THE PORT OF CALCUTTA TO BRITISH AND FOREIGN COLONIES 1908.(Calcutta, Bengal Secretariat Book Depot 1909).

Barrett, Rev. William G: IMMIGRATION IN THE BRITISH WEST INDIES: IS IT THE SLAVE TRADE REVIVED OR NOT? (London, A.W. Bennett, 1859).

Barry, B: 'The Consociational Model and its Danger', EUROPEAN JOURNAL OF POLITICAL RESEARCH, Vol. 3, No. 4, 1975.

Bartels, C.A: 'Class Conflict and Ideology in the Formation of Modern Guyanese Politics'. PhD. Diss., University of Alberta, Alberta 1976.

Basdeo, Sahadeo; 'The 1934 Indian Labour Disturbances in Trinidad: A Case Study in Colonial Relations'. Symposium on East Indians in the Caribbean, St. Augustine, Trinidad, 1975.

———: 'The Development of East Indian Immigration to the West Indies 1839–1860'. PhD. Diss., University of Calgary 1972.

———: 'Indian Participation in Labour Politics in Trinidad 1919–1939', CARIBBEAN QUARTERLY 32, 1986, pp. 50–62.

Bashan, A.L. (ed): A CULTURAL HISTORY OF INDIA (Oxford: Clarendon Press 1978).

———: STUDIES IN INDIAN HISTORY AND CULTURE, (Calcutta: Sambodhi, 1964).

Bassier, W.M.Z: 'Kali Mai Worship in Guyana: A Quest for a new Identity' in INDIANS IN THE CARIBBEAN, I.J. Bahadur Singh (ed). (London, Oriental University Press, 1987), pp. 269–93.

Beachey, R.W: THE WEST INDIAN SUGAR INDUSTRY IN THE LATE NINETEENTH CENTURY (Oxford 1957).

Beall, Jo: 'Women Under Indenture in Colonial Natal, 1860–1911' in SOUTH ASIANS OVERSEAS, C.Clarke, C. Peach and S.Vertovec (eds), (Cambridge: Cambridge University Press, 1990), pp. 57–74.

Beaubrun, Michael H: 'Socio-cultural Factors Affecting the Incidence and Treatment of Alcoholism in the Caribbean'. Proceedings of the First Aruban and Antillean Congress on Alcoholism (Aruba 1970).

Beaumont, Joseph: THE NEW SLAVERY: AN ACCOUNT OF THE INDIAN AND CHINESE IMMIGRANTS IN BRITISH GUIANA (London: W. Ridgway, 1871).

Beckwith, Martha W: THE HUSSAY FESTIVAL IN JAMAICA: WITH MUSIC RECORDED BY PHONOGRAPH. (Poughkeepsie, New York, Vassar College 1924).

Bedassie, Sukiya: 'The Chamar Pujas in Trinidad'. Caribbean Studies Thesis, U.W.I, 1975.

Belcher, E.A and Williamson, J.A: MIGRATION WITHIN THE BRITISH EMPIRE (London, W.Collins, Sons & Co. 1924.)

Bell, K.N. and Morrell, W.P. (eds): SELECT DOCUMENTS ON BRITISH COLONIAL POLICY, 1830–1860.(Oxford, Clarendon Press, 1928).

Bell, Robert R: 'Marriage and Family Differences Among Lower Class Negro and East Indian Women in Trinidad', RACE 12, 1970.

Benezet, Anthony: SOME HISTORICAL ACCOUNT OF GUINEA ... (Philadelphia, Joseph Cruikshank 1771).

——: THE CASE OF OUR FELLOW CREATURES, THE OPPRESSED AFRICANS ... (Society of Friends 1783)

——: OBSERVATIONS OF INSLAVING, IMPORTING AND PURCHASING OF NEGROES (1760).

——: A CAUTION AND WARNING TO GREAT BRITAIN AND HER COLONIES (Philadelphia, Henry Miller 1766).

——: A SHORT ACCOUNT OF THAT PART OF AFRICA INHABITED BY NEGROES (1762).

Bentley, Gerald and Henry, Frances: 'Some Preliminary Observations on the Chinese in Trinidad'. In Frances Henry, ed., MCGILL UNIVERSITY STUDIES IN CARIBBEAN ANTHROPOLOGY, McGill University Centre for Developing Area Studies, Montreal, Occasional Paper Series 5, 1969.

Berreman, Gerald D: 'Caste as a Social Process', SOUTHWESTERN JOURNAL OF ANTHROPOLOGY 23, 1967, pp. 351–70.

——: 'Social Categories and Social Interaction in Urban India', AMERICAN ANTHROPOLOGIST 74, 1972, pp. 567– 86.

Berrill, K: THE BRITISH GUIANA DEVELOPMENT PLAN, 1960–4 (Cambridge 1950).

Bertram, G.C.L: 'The Indians of British Guiana'. POPULATION REVIEW, Vol. 6, 1962.

Besson, Gerard and Brereton, Bridget: THE BOOK OF TRINIDAD, Port of Spain: Paria Publishing, 1991.

Bharati, Agehananda: 'A Social survey' in PORTRAIT OF A MINORITY: ASIANS IN EAST AFRICA, Dharam P. Ghai and Yash P.Ghai (eds), Nairobi: Oxford University Press, 1970, pp. 15–67.

Bhattacharya, S: A DICTIONARY OF INDIAN HISTORY (University of Calcutta Press 1967).

Bigelow, John: JAMAICA IN 1850 (New York, George Putnam, 1851, reprinted in 1970).

Birbalsingh, Frank: 'Indo-Caribbean Test Cricketers' in INDIA IN THE CARIBBEAN, (Hansib/University of Warwick 1987).

——: 'Indians in the Novels of Edgar Mittelholzer'. Symposium on East Indians in the Caribbean, U.W.I, Trinidad, September 1979.

——(ed.): INDENTURE AND EXILE: THE INDO-CARIBBEAN EXPERIENCE (Toronto, Tsar, 1989).

——(ed): INDO-CARIBBEAN RESISTANCE (Toronto, Tsar 1993).

——: 'Cheddi Jagan: The Writing of a Visionary Politician' – Forthcoming publication.

Bisnauth, Dale A: 'The East Indian Immigrant Society in British Guiana, 1891–1930'. PhD. Diss., U.W.I., 1977.

——: A HISTORY OF THE PRESBYTERIAN CHURCH IN GUYANA (Georgetown, Labour Advocate Printery, 1979).

——: HISTORY OF RELIGIONS IN THE CARIBBEAN (Kingston, Kingston Publishers Ltd, 1989).

Bissondoyal, B: THE TRUTH ABOUT MAURITIUS, Bombay: 1968.

Blanshard, Paul: DEMOCRACY AND EMPIRE IN THE CARIBBEAN ( New York 1947).

Blunt, E.A.H: THE CASTE SYSTEM OF NORTHERN INDIA (London, Oxford University Press 1931).

Bolt, Christine; VICTORIAN ATTITUDES TO RACE (London 1971).

Boodhoo, Ken: 'Sugar and East Indian Indentureship in Trinidad', CARIBBEAN REVIEW 5, 1973.

——: 'East Indian Labourers', in READINGS IN CARIBBEAN HISTORY AND ECONOMICS, Roberta M. Delson (ed) (New York: Gordon & Breach, 1981, pp. 143–52.

Bose, N.K: 'The Spring Festival of India'. CULTURE AND SOCIETY IN INDIA (London 1967).

Bourne, Compton: 'Banking in Boom and Bust Economies: Lessons from Trinidad and Tobago and Jamaica', SOCIAL AND ECONOMIC STUDIES 34,(4), 1985, pp. 139–63.

Boxhill, C: 'From East Indian to Indo-Trinidadian'. Symposium on East Indians in the Caribbean, U.W.I 1975.

Braithwaite, Edward: THE DEVELOPMENT OF CREOLE SOCIETY IN JAMAICA: 1770–1820 (Oxford: Clarendon Press, 1971).

Braithwaite, Farley S and Aho, W: 'Race, Occupational Mobility and Career Aspirations Among Secondary School Teachers in Trinidad and Tobago'. Symposium on East Indians in the Caribbean, Trinidad 1975.

Brawer, M.J: 'Fertility Differences, Family Structure and Modernization in Two Populations in Trinidad'. PhD. Diss., Columbia University 1965.

Brereton, Bridget: 'The Experience of Indentureship: 1845–1917' in CALCUTTA TO CARONI: THE EAST INDIANS OF TRINIDAD (ed) John La Guerre (London, Longman Caribbean 1974).

——: 'The Foundations of Prejudice: Indians and Africans in Nineteenth Century Trinidad'. CARIBBEAN ISSUES, 1974.

——: A HISTORY OF MODERN TRINIDAD, 1783–1962 (Heinemann 1981).

——: 'Social Organisation and Class, Racial and Cultural Conflict in Nineteenth Century Trinidad' in TRINIDAD ETHNICITY (ed) Kevin Yelvington, (Warwick University Caribbean Studies, London, Macmillan Press

1993).

———: RACE RELATIONS IN COLONIAL TRINIDAD, 1870–1900. (Cambridge, Cambrdige University Press 1979).

Brereton, B and Dookhera, W (eds): EAST INDIANS IN THE CARIBBEAN: COLONIALISM AND THE STRUGGLE FOR IDENTITY. (New York, Kraus International Publications, 1982).

Brierly, J.N: TRINIDAD: THEN AND NOW. (Port of Spain: Franklin's Electric Printery 1912).

Briggs, George W: THE CHAMARS (Calcutta 1920).

Brizan, George: 'The Colonial Land and Emigration Commission and Emigration to Jamaica 1840–60'. CARIBBEAN QUARTERLY 20,1974.

Bronkhurst, H.V.P: THE COLONY OF BRITISH GUIANA AND ITS LABOURING POPULATION (London, T. Woolmer 1883).

———: AMONG THE HINDUS AND CREOLES OF BRITISH GUIANA (London 1888).

———: A DESCRIPTIVE AND HISTORICAL GEOGRAPHY OF BRITISH GUIANA AND THE WEST INDIAN ISLANDS (London 1886).

Brown, Brian: 'Interface in Trinidad: A Study of the Hundred Year Relationship Between Hindu and Presbyterian Elements of the East Indian Community in Trinidad'. PhD. Diss. San Francisco Theological Seminary, 1972.

Brown, John W: WORLD MIGRATION AND LABOUR (Amsterdam 1926 ).

Brown, Wenzell; ANGRY MEN, LAUGHING MEN: THE CARIBBEAN CAULDRON (New York, Greenberg 1947).

Brummell, J: DEMERARA AFTER FIFTEEN YEARS OF FREEDOM (London, T. Bosworth,1853).

Budhram, D.R and Debiprashad, S: 'Participation of East Indians in the Transformation of Guyanese Society'. Paper presented at Symposium on East Indians in the Carib bean, September 1979.

Buhler, Georg: THE SACRED LAWS OF THE ARYAS. (Oxford, Clarendon Press 1882).

———: THE LAWS OF MANU (Oxford University Press, 1886).

Buiskool, J.A.E: SURINAME NU EN STRAKS, EEN SOCIAAL – ECONOMISCHE EN STAATKUNDIJGE BESCHOUWING (Amsterdam 1946).

Burghart, Richard: 'Conclusion: The Perpetuation of Hinduism in an Alien Cultural Milieu' in HINDUISM IN GREAT BRITAIN, Richard Burghart (ed), London: Tavistock, 1987, pp. 224–51.

Burn, W.L: EMANCIPATION AND APPRENTICESHIP IN THE BRITISH WEST INDIES (London 1937).

Burnley, William (ed): OBSERVATIONS ON THE PRESENT CONDITION OF THE ISLAND OF TRINIDAD AND THE ACTUAL STATE OF THE EXPERIMENT OF NEGRO EMANCIPATION. (London, Longman's 1842).

Burton, Benedict: INDIANS IN A PLURAL SOCIETY: A REPORT ON MAURITIUS, London: 1961.

Burton, Richard F: SINDH AND THE RACES THAT INHABIT THE VALLEY OF THE INDUS. (London, W.H. Allen 1851).

Butterworth, A.R: THE IMMIGRATION OF COLOURED RACES INTO THE BRITISH COLONIES. (London, 1898).

Buxton, Thomas Fowell: THE AFRICAN SLAVE TRADE (London 1840).

Cahia, J: 'A Propos de l'Immigration Tarmoule en Guyane Francaise'. BULLETIN DE L'ECOLE FRANCAISE D'EXTREME – ORIENT, 60, 1973.

Calder-Marshall, Arthur: GLORY DEAD (London, Michael Joseph 1939).

Campbell, Carl: 'Immigration into a Divided Society: A Note on Social Relationships in Trinidad, 1845–1870'. Paper presented at the Fourth Conference of Caribbean Historians, Mona, Jamaica, 1972.

———: 'The East Indian Revolt Against Missionary Education, 1928–1939' in CALCUTTA TO CARONI, 2nd edn, John La Guerre (ed), St. Augustine, Trinidad: Extra Mural Studies Unit, University of the West Indies, 1985.

Campbell, Persia: CHINESE COOLIE EMIGRATION TO THE COUNTRIES WITHIN THE BRITISH EMPIRE. (London, P.S.King and Son 1923).

Canadian Missionary Council: THE CANADIAN PRESBYTERIAN MISSION TO EAST INDIANS IN THE BRITISH WEST INDIES (Toronto 1911).

———: EAST MEETS WEST IN TRINIDAD. (Toronto, Young Peoples Missionary Education 1934).

Carleton, Robert O: 'The Economic, Geographic and Sociological Condition of the East Indians in British Guiana'. (Masters Essay, New School Research, New York 1949).

Carlile, James (ed): JOURNAL OF A VOYAGE WITH COOLIE EMIGRANTS FROM CALCUTTA TO TRINIDAD by Captain and Mrs. Swinton. (Alfred Bennett 1859).

Carmichael, Gertrude: A HISTORY OF THE WEST INDIAN ISLANDS OF TRINIDAD AND TOBAGO. (London 1961).

Carnoy, M: EDUCATION AS CULTURAL IMPERIALISM. (New York, David McKay Co. Inc, 1974).

Carter, Marina: 'Indian Labour Migration to Mauritius and the Indenture Experience'. D.Phil, Thesis, University of Oxford, 1987.

Case, F.I: THE CRISIS OF IDENTITY: STUDIES IN THE GUADELOUPEAN AND MARTINIQUAN NOVEL. (Sherbrooke, Naaman 1985).

Central Statistical Office, Government of Trinidad & Tobago 1973.POPULATION ABSTRACTS, Port of Spain: Government Printery.

————: 1983.POPULATION AND HOUSING CENSUS 1980.Port of Spain, Government Printery.

————" : 1984.AGRICULTURAL CENSUS 1982 (Preliminary Report No. 1), Port of Spain Government Printery.

Chakravarti, N.R: THE INDIAN MINORITY IN BURMA: THE RISE AND DECLINE OF AN IMMIGRANT COMMUNITY, London: 1971.

Chanana, Dev Raj: SLAVERY IN ANCIENT INDIA. (New Delhi, People's Publishing House 1960).

Chandrasekhar, S: 'The Migration and Status of Indians in the British Empire', SOCIAL ISSUES, Vol. 24, No. 2, 1945.

Chase, Ashton: A HISTORY OF TRADE UNIUONISM IN GUYANA 1900–1961.(New Guyana Co. Ltd, Guyana 1964).

Checkland, S.G: THE GLADSTONES: A FAMILY BIOGRAPHY 1764–1851.(London, Cambridge University Press 1971).

Chen, Jack: THE CHINESE OF AMERICA. (San Francisco, Harper & Row; 1980).

Chen, Willi: KING OF THE CARNIVAL AND OTHER STORIES, London: Hansib, 1988.

Chin, Henk E & Buddingh, Hans: SURINAM: POLITICS, ECONOMICS AND SOCIETY. (London, Frances Pinter 1987).

Ching, Annette M.T: 'Ethnicity Reconsidered with Reference to Sugar and Society in Trinidad'. D.Phil, Thesis, University of Sussex,1985.

Chitmukulu, M: 'The Origins of Afro-Indian Unity'. MOKO, 24, 1970.

Clark, H.J: IERE: THE LAND OF THE HUMMING BIRD. (Port of Spain, Government Printing Office,1893).

Clarke, Colin: 'Residential Segregation and Inter-Marriage in San Fernando, Trinidad', GEOGRAPHICAL REVIEW, 61, 1971.

————: 'Caste Among Hindus in a Town in Trinidad – San Fernando'. In CASTE IN OVERSEAS INDIAN COMMUNITIES (ed) Barton M. Schwartz, San Francisco, Chandler Publishing Co. 1967.

————: 'Spatial Pattern and Social Interaction Among Creoles and Indians in Trinidad and Tobago' in TRINIDAD ETHNICITY. (London, Macmillan Press, 1993).

————: EAST INDIANS IN A WEST INDIAN TOWN. (London: Allen & Unwin, 1968).

————: 'Pluralism and Stratification in San Fernando, Trinidad', in SOCIAL PATTERNS IN THE CITY, B.D. Clarke and B. Gleare (eds), Institute of British Geographers, special publication, No. 5, pp. 53–70.

Clasp. Bertram: EAST INDIAN IMMIGRATION TO TRINIDAD: IT'S ECONOMIC AND SOCIAL PROBLEMS. St. Augustine, U.W.I, Trinidad 1969.

Clementi, Cecil: A CONSTITUTIONAL HISTORY OF BRITISH GUIANA. (London 1937).

————: THE CHINESE IN BRITISH GUIANA. (Georgetown 1915).

Cohen, W.I: DEAN RUSK. (Totowa, New Jersey: Cooper Square Publishers 1980).

Cohn, Bernard S: 'Chamar Family in a North Indian village', THE ECONOMIC WEEKLY 13, 1961, pp. 613–28.

Collens, J.H: GUIDE TO TRINIDAD. (Port of Spain 1886).

Comins, D.W.D: NOTE ON EMIGRATION FROM THE EAST INDIES TO SURINAM OR DUTCH GUYANA. (Calcutta 1892).

————: NOTE ON EMIGRATION FROM THE EAST INDIES TO JAMAICA. (Calcutta 1893).

————: NOTE ON EMIGRATION FROM THE EAST INDIES TO ST. LUCIA. (Calcutta 1893).

————: NOTE ON EMIGRATION FROM INDIA TO BRITISH GUIANA. Calcutta 1893).

————: NOTE ON EMIGRATION – INDIA TO TRINIDAD. (Calcutta, Bengal Secretariat Press 1893).

————: NOTE ON THE ABOLITION OF RETURN PASSAGES TO EAST INDIAN IMMIGRANTS FROM THE COLONIES OF TRINIDAD AND BRITISH GUIANA (1892).

Conybeare, H.C: STATISTICAL, DESCRIPTIVE AND HISTORICAL ACCOUNT OF THE BASTI DISTRICT, Allahabad: N.W. Provinces & Oudh Government Press (Vol. VI of the Gazetteers,1981).

Coopsammy, M: 'The Boy From Petitville' in OTHER VOICES: WRITINGS BY BLACKS IN CANADA. Ed. Lorris Elliot. (Toronto, Williams-Wallace 1985).

Cothonay, R.P.M. Bertrand: TRINIDAD. JOURNAL D'UN MISSIONAIRE DOMINICAIN DES ANTILLES ANGLAISES. (Paris: Victor Retaux et fils,1893).

Cox, Oliver C: CASTE, CLASS AND RACE. (New York 1948).

Craig, Hewan: A HISTORY OF THE LEGISLATIVE COUNCIL OF TRINIDAD AND TOBAGO. (London, Faber and Faber 1952).

Craton, Michael: TESTING THE CHAINS: RESISTANCE TO SLAVERY IN THE BRITISH WEST INDIES. (Cornell University, Ithaca and London 1982).

Critchell, L: 'Crossroads of the Caribbean'. NATIONAL GEOGRAPHIC MAGAZINE, Vol. 72, 1937.

Crookall, L: BRITISH GUIANA; OR WORK AND WANDERING AMONG THE CREOLES AND COOLIES, THE AFRICANS AND INDIANS OF THE WILD COUNTRY. (London 1898).

Crooke, W: NATIVES OF NORTHWESTERN INDIA. (London 1907).

——: RELIGION AND FOLKLORE IN NORTHERN INDIA. (New Delhi, S. Chand & Co. 1925).

——: THE TRIBES AND CASTES OF THE NORTH-WESTERN PROVINCES AND OUDH, Calcutta: Central Printing Office, 1896.

Cross, Malcolm: THE EAST INDIANS OF GUYANA AND TRINIDAD. (London Minority Rights Group 1972).

——: 'East Indian/African Relations in Trinidad and Guyana in the Late Nineteenth Century' – Forthcoming publication.

——: 'The Political Representation of Organised Labour in Trinidad and Guyana: A Comparative Puzzle', in LABOUR IN THE CARIBBEAN, M.Cross and G.Heuman (eds), London: Macmillan, 1988, pp. 285–308.

——: 'Colonialism and Ethnicity: A Theory and Comparative Study', ETHNIC AND RACIAL STUDIES 18, 1978, pp. 189–207.

Cross, M and Schwartzbaum, Allen M:'Social Mobility and Secondary School Selection in Trinidad and Tobago', SOCIAL AND ECONOMIC STUDIES 18, 1969, pp. 189–207.

Crowley, Daniel J: 'East Indian Festivals in Trinidad Life'. CARIBBEAN COMMISSION MONTHLY INFORMATION BULLETIN, 7, 1954.

——: 'Plural and Differential Acculturation in Trinidad'. AMERICAN ANTHROPOLOGIST 59, 1957.

——: 'A Trinidad Hindi Riddle Tale'. CARIBBEANA, 1955.

Cudjoe, Selwyn: 'Foreword' – THE STILL CRY: PERSONAL ACCOUNTS OF EAST INDIANS IN TRINIDAD AND TOBAGO DURING INDENTURESHIP (1845 –1917). (Trinidad, Calaloux Publishers,1988).

Cumpston, I.M: INDIANS OVERSEAS IN BRITISH TERRITORIES 1834–54.(London, Oxford University Press 1953).

——: 'A Survey of Indian Immigration to British Tropical Colonies to 1910', POPULATION STUDIES 10,1956, pp. 158–65.

Cundall, Frank: POLITICAL AND SOCIAL DISTURBANCES IN THE WEST INDIES. (Kingston 1906).

Curtin, Philip D: THE ATLANTIC SLAVE TRADE: A CENSUS. (University of Wisconsin Press 1969).

Dabydeen, Cyril: A SHAPELY FIRE: CHANGING THE LITERARY LANDSCAPE. (Oakville, Mosaic 1987).

——; 'The Country'; 'Atlantic Song'; 'Offsprings'; 'We are the Country'; 'Village' in INDIA IN THE CARIBBEAN (Hansib/University of Warwick 1987).

Dabydeen David: COOLIE ODYSSEY. (Hansib/Dangaroo Publication 1988).

——: 'Indo-Guyanese Resistance' in INDO-CARIBBEAN RESISTANCE. (Toronto, Tsar 1993).

Dabydeen, D and Samaroo, B (eds): INDIA IN THE CARIBBEAN. (Hansib/University of Warwick 1987).

——(eds): ACROSS THE DARK WATERS. Forthcoming Warwick University Caribbean Studies publication.

Daalder, H: 'The Consociational Theme', WORLD POLITICS, Vol. 26, No. 4, 1977, pp. 607–9.

Dalley, Fred: TRADE UNION ORGANISATION AND INDUSTRIAL RELATIONS IN TRINIDAD. (London, HMSO 1947).

Dalton, Henry: HISTORY OF BRITISH GUIANA. (London 1855).

Daly, Stephanie: 'The Development of the Law Affecting East Indians in Trinidad and Tobago'. Conference on East Indians in the Caribbean, U.W.I, Trinidad 1984.

Daniel, Edward W: WEST INDIAN HISTORIANS, Book 3.(London 1938).

Das, Mahadai: 'Bleeding Hands'; 'They Came in Ships'; 'Beast'; in INDIA IN THE CARIBBEAN. (London 1987).

Davy, John: THE WEST INDIES BEFORE AND SINCE SLAVE EMANCIPATION. (London: W. & F.G. Cash, 1854).

Davids, Leo A: 'The East Indian Family Overseas'. SOCIAL AND ECONOMIC STUDIES, 1964.

Davis, David Brion: THE PROBLEM OF SLAVERY IN WESTERN CULTURE. (New York, Cornell University Press, 1966).

Davis, J Merle: THE EAST INDIAN CHURCH IN TRINIDAD. (New York 1942).

Day, Charles: FIVE YEARS OF RESIDENCE IN THE WEST INDIES. (London, Colburn and Co.1852).

Debiprashad, S and Budhram, D.R: 'Participation of East Indians in the Transformation of Guyanese Society'. Paper presented at Symposium on East Indians in the Caribbean, September 1979.

Debysingh, Molly: 'Cultural Change and Adaptation as Reflected in the Meat-Eating Habits of the Trinidad Indian Population'. CARIBBEAN QUARTERLY, Vol. 32, Nos. 3–4, September-December 1986.

Deen, Shamsu: SOLVING EAST INDIAN ROOTS IN TRINIDAD (Freeport, Trinidad: H.E.M. Enterprises Ltd, 1994).

Deer, Noel; HISTORY OF SUGAR, 2 Vols. (London 1950).

——: `Indian Labour in the Sugar Industry', INTERNATIONAL SUGAR JOURNAL 40, 1938, pp. 94–8.

De Lisser, H.G: THE CUP AND LIP. (London 1956).

Deosaran, Ramesh: 'The Schools and Multiculturalism: Some Psychological and Political Implications'. CARIBBEAN ISSUES, 2, 1976.

——: `The "Caribbean Man"': A Study of the Psychology of Perception and the Media' in INDIA IN THE CARIBBEAN.

——: `Multiculturalism for Democratic Living', CARIBBEAN ISSUES 4, 1978, pp. 3–21.

Depoo, T, Misir, P and Mangru, B. (eds): THE EAST INDIAN DIASPORA. (New York: Asian-American Center, 1993).

Despres, Leo A: CULTURAL PLURALISM AND NATIONALIST POLITICS IN BRITISH GUIANA. (Chicago, Rand McNally 1967).

——: `Anthropological Theory, Cultural Pluralism and the Study of Complex Societies', CURRENT ANTHROPOLOGY 9, pp. 3–26.

Des Voeux, G.W: 'Experiences of a Demerara Magistrate 1863–69'. (Georgetown, DAILY CHRONICLE 1948).

—— MY COLONIAL SERVICE IN BRITISH GUIANA, ST. LUCIA, TRINIDAD, FIJI, AUSTRALIA, NEW FOUNDLAND AND HONG KONG. (London, John Murray 1903).

Devas, R.P: THE HISTORY OF THE ISLAND OF GRENADA, 1650–1956.(St. Georges 1964).

De Verteuil, Anthony: EIGHT EAST INDIAN IMMIGRANTS. (Port of Spain, Paria, 1989).

——: THE YEARS OF REVOLT: TRINIDAD, 1881–1888.(Port of Spain, Paria, 1984).

——: `Madrasi Emigration to Trinidad, 1846–1916'. Paper presented to the Twenty-Second Conference of the Association of Caribbean Historians, St. Augustine, Trinidad, 1990.

De Verteuil, L.A.A: TRINIDAD: ITS GEOGRAPHY, NATURAL RESOURCES, ADMINISTRATION, PRESENT CONDITION AND PROSPECTS. Second Edition. (London, Cass & Company 1884).

Dew, Edward: THE DIFFICULT FLOWERING OF SURINAM: ETHNICITY AND POLITICS IN A PLURAL SOCIETY. (The Hague, Martinus Nijhoff 1978).

——: `Surinam: The Test of Consociational Democracy'. PLURAL SOCIETIES, Autumn 1972.

——: `Testing Elite Perceptions of Deprivation and Satisfaction in a Culturally Plural Society'. COMPARATIVE POLITICS, January 1974.

——: `The Year of the Sergeants'. CARIBBEAN REVIEW, (Spring 1980).

——: `Suriname: Transcending Ethnic Politics the Hard Way' in THE ENIGMA OF ETHNICITY: AN ANALYSIS OF RACE IN THE CARIBBEAN AND THE WORLD. (St. Augustine, U.W.I, 1993).

Dey, Mukdal K: 'The Indian Population of Trinidad and Tobago'. INTERNATIONAL JOURNAL OF COMPARATIVE SOCIOLOGY, 3, 1962.

Dodd, David J: 'The Wellsprings of Violence: Some Historical Notes on East Indian Criminality in Guyana'. CARIBBEAN ISSUES, 1976.

Dookhan, Isaac: 'The Gladstone Experiment: The Experience of the First East Indians in British Guiana'. Symposium on East Indians in the Caribbean, Trinidad, U.W.I, 1975.

——: A PRE-EMANCIPATION HISTORY OF THE WEST INDIES, London: Collins, 1971.

——: A POST-EMANCIPATION HISTORY OF THE WEST INDIES, London: Collins, 1971.

Dookheran, Winston: 'East Indians and the Economy of Trinidad and Tobago' in CALCUTTA TO CARONI (Longman Caribbean 1974).

Dookheran, Winston and Brereton, B. (eds): EAST INDIANS IN THE CARIBBEAN: COLONIALISM AND THE STRUGGLE FOR IDENTITY, New York: Kraus 1982.

Dotson, Floyd and Lillian O: THE INDIAN MINORITY OF ZAMBIA, RHODESIA AND MALAWI, New Haven: Yale University Press, 1968.

Dowson, John: A CLASSICAL DICTIONARY OF HINDU MYTHOLOGY AND RELIGION, GEOGRAPHY, HISTORY AND LITERATURE. (London, Routledge & Kegan Paul 1972).

Drummond, Lee: 'The Cultural Continuum: A Theory of Inter-systems', MAN (N.S.) 15, 1980, pp. 352–74.

DuBois, Abbe J.A: DESCRIPTION OF THE CHARACTER, MANNERS AND CUSTOMS OF THE PEOPLE OF INDIA AND OF THEIR INSTITUTIONS, RELIGIOUS AND CIVIL. (Calcutta 1905).

Duggal, Ved P: 'Relations Between Indians and Africans in Guyana'. REVISTA INTERAMERICANA, 1973.

Dumont, Louis: 'World Renunciation in Indian Religions', CONTRIBUTIONS TO INDIAN SOCIOLOGY 4, 1960, pp. 33–62.

Durbin, M.A: 'Formal Changes in Trinidad Hindi as a Result of Language Adaptation'. AMERICAN ANTHROPOLOGIST 1973.

Dutt, Ramesh: THE ECONOMIC HISTORY OF INDIA UNDER BRITISH RULE. (New York, Augustus M.Kelly 1969).

Dwarka Nath: (See Nath, Dwarka).

EAST INDIANS IN THE WEST INDIES: A REPORT COMMISSIONED BY THE CONSERVATIVE PARTY OF THE UNITED KINGDOM, 1955.

THE ECONOMIST, 'Ominous Footprints on the Oil Sands', Vol. 276, no. 7150, 13 September 1980.

Edwards, Bryan: HISTORY, CIVIL AND COMMERCIAL, OF THE BRITISH COLONIES IN THE WEST INDIES, 5 vols. (London, T.Miller, 1819).

Ehrlich, Allen S: 'Race and Ethnic Identity in Rural Jamaica'. Paper presented at the American Anthropological Association Meeting, New York 1971.

——: 'Race and Ethnic Identity in Rural Jamaica: The East Indian Case'. CARIBBEAN QUARTERLY 1976.

——: 'History, Ecology and Demography in the British Caribbean: An Analysis of East Indian Ethnicity'. SOUTHWESTERN JOURNAL OF ANTHROPOLOGY, 1971.

——: 'East Indian Cane Workers in Jamaica'. PhD.Thesis, University of Michigan 1969.

——: 'Ecology, Perception and Economic Adaptation in Jamaica'. HUMAN ORGANISATION 1974.

——: 'The Interplay of Rice and Cane: East Indians in Rural Jamaica'. Symposium on East Indians in the Caribbean, U.W.I, 1975.

Eisner, Giesela: JAMAICA 1830–1930: A STUDY IN ECONOMIC GROWTH. (Manchester University Press 1961).

Elder, J.D: THE YORUBA ANCESTOR CULT IN GASPARILLO. Mimeographed, 1969.

——: AFRICAN SURVIVALS OF TRINIDAD AND TOBAGO. (United Kingdom, Paria Press 1980).

Eliot, Sir Charles: HINDUISM AND BUDDHISM: AN HISTORICAL SKETCH, 3 Vols. (London, E. Arnold & Co. 1921).

Emmer, P.C.(ed): COLONIALISM AND MIGRATION: INDENTURED LABOUR BEFORE AND AFTER SLAVERY. (Dordrecht, The Netherlands: Martinus Nijhoff, 1986).

——: 'The Importation of British Indians into Surinam (Dutch Guiana) 1873–1916', INTERNATIONAL LABOUR MIGRATION, Shula Marks and Peter D. Richardson (eds), London: University of London, Temple Smith, pp. 90–111.

——: 'The Great Escape: The Migration of Female Indentured Servants From British India to Surinam 1973–1916' in ABOLITION AND ITS AFTERMATH, P.D. Richardson (ed), London: Frank Cass, 1986, pp. 245–66.

Enthoven, R.E: THE TRIBES AND CASTES OF BOMBAY. (Bombay 1920).

Erickson, Edgar L: 'The Introduction of East Indian Coolies into the West Indies', JOURNAL OF MODERN HISTORY, 1934.

——: 'East Indian Coolies in the West Indies', PhD. Diss, University of Indiana, 1930.

Espinet, Charles and Pitts, Harry: LAND OF CALYPSO. (Port of Spain, Trinidad 1944).

Espinet, Ramabai: 'Representation of the Indo-Caribbean Woman in Trinidad and Tobago' in INDO-CARIBBEAN RESISTANCE (ed). Birbalsingh, F, (Toronto, Tsar, 1993).

——: 'The Invisible Woman in Trinidad and Tobago' – Forthcoming publication.

——(ed): CREATION FIRE, (Toronto, Sister Vision Press, 1990).

Falconbridge, A: AN ACCOUNT OF THE SLAVE TRADE ON THE COAST OF AFRICA. (London 1788).

Farrar, Thomas: NOTES ON THE HISTORY OF THE CHURCH IN GUYANA. (Georgetown 1892).

Farley, R.E.G: 'Aspects of the Economic history of British Guiana, 1781–1852: A Study of Economic and Social Change in the Southern Caribbean Frontier'. PhD. Thesis, University of London 1956).

——: 'The Rise of the Peasantry in British Guiana'. SOCIAL AND ECONOMIC STUDIES, Vol. 2, No. 1 1954.

——: 'The Rise of Village Settlements in British Guiana'. CARIBBEAN QUARTERLY, No. 1, 1964.

Farquhar, J.N: MODERN RELIGIOUS MOVEMENTS IN INDIA. (London, Macmillan 1929).

Felix, Lynette: 'A Comparison Between the Shango Cult and the Spiritual Baptist Community in Port of Spain'. CARIBBEAN STUDIES PROJECT, University of the West Indies,1971.

Ferreira, Jo-Anne S: 'The Portuguese of Trinidad'. In Gerard Besson and Bridget Brereton (eds), THE BOOK OF TRINIDAD. (Port of Spain, Paria 1991).

Firth, Raymond, David Pocock, H.S. Morris, Adrian Mayer, Burton Benedict: 'Factions in Indian and Overseas Indian Societies', BRITISH JOURNAL OF SOCIOLOGY 8, 1957, pp. 291–342.

Fischer, L: THE STORY OF INDONESIA. (New York, Harker 1959).

Forbes, Richard H: 'Hindu Organisational Process in Acculturative Conditions: Significance of the Arya Samaj Experience in Trinidad'. Conference on East Indians in the Caribbean, 1984.

——: 'Arya Samaj in Trinidad: An Historical Study of Hindu Organisational Process in Acculturative Conditions', PhD. Diss, University of Miami, 1984.

Fox, Richard G: 'VARNA Schemes and Ideological Integration in Indian Society', COMPARATIVE STUDIES IN SOCIETY AND HISTORY, 11, 1969, pp. 27–45.

———: FROM ZAMINDAR TO BALLOT BOX. (Ithaca, New York; Cornell University Press, 1969).

Fraser, L: HISTORY OF TRINIDAD, 2 Vols. (Port of Spain, Trinidad 1891–96).

Fraser, Peter: 'The Immigration Issue in British Guiana, 1903–1913: The Economic and Constitutional Origins of Racist Politics in Guyana'. JOURNAL OF CARIBBEAN HISTORY 14, 1981.

Freilich, Morris: 'Cultural Diversity Among Trinidadian Peasants'. PhD. Diss. Columbia University 1960.

Freitag, Sandria B: 'Sacred Symbol as Mobilizing Ideology: The North Indian Search for a "Hindu" community', COMPARATIVE STUDIES IN SOCIETY AND HISTORY 22, 1980, pp. 597–625.

French, Howard: 'Guyana Marxist, Mellowed, Makes A Comeback'. NEW YORK TIMES (International), 5 July 1991.

Fried, Morton: 'Some Observations on the Chinese in British Guiana'. SOCIAL AND ECONOMIC STUDIES 5, No. 1, 1956.

Froude, J.A: THE ENGLISH IN THE WEST INDIES. (London 1888).

Fuller, C.J: 'Gods, Priests and Purity: On the Relation Between Hinduism and the Caste System', MAN ( N.S) 14, 1979, pp. 459–476.

Furnivall, J.S: PROGRESS AND WEALFARE IN SOUTH EAST ASIA. (New York 1941).

———: NETHERLANDS INDIA. (Cambridge University Press 1939).

———: COLONIAL POLICY AND PRACTICE. (Cambridge 1948).


Gajraj, Sandra: 'The Indian cultural Presence in the Secondary School System of Trinidad and Tobago: Images and Perceptions'. Conference on East Indians in the Caribbean, U.W.I, Trinidad, August-September 1984.

Gambhir, Surendra K: 'Diglossia in Dying Languages: A Case Study of Guyanese Bhojpuri and Standard Hindi', ANTHROPOLOGICAL LINGUISTICS 25 (1), 1993, pp. 28–38.

Gamble, W.H: TRINIDAD, HISOTRICAL AND DESCRIPTIVE: BEING A NARRATIVE OF NINE YEARS' RESIDENCE IN THE ISLAND. (London, Yates & Alexander 1866).

Gandhi, M.K: COLLECTED WORKS. (Delhi 1958).

Gangulee, N: INDIANS IN THE EMPIRE OVERSEAS: A SURVEY. (London, New India Publishing House, 1947).

Garg, D.K and Mansingh, A: 'East Indian Leadership and Social Organisations in Jamaica'. Paper presented at Symposium on East Indians in the Caribbean, September 1979.

Gates, Brian: AFRO-CARIBBEAN RELATIONS. (London, Ward Lock International 1980).

Geoghegan: NOTE ON EMIGRATION FROM INDIA. (Calcutta 1893).

Gilbert, William H: PEOPLES OF INDIA. Smithsonian Institution War Background Studies, No. 18, Washington D.C, 1944).

Gillion, K.L: FIJI'S INDIAN MIGRANTS. (London, Oxford University Press 1973).

———: 'The Sources of Indian Emigration to Fiji', POPULATION STUDIES 10, 1956, pp. 139–57.

Gilzean, A.R: 'Contracts with Cane Cutters'. TIMEHRI, New Series 4, 1890.

———: 'Rice Cultivation in British Guiana'. TIMEHRI, New Series 1, 1887.

Girvan, Norman: ASPECTS OF THE POLITICAL ECONOMY OF RACE IN THE CARIBBEAN AND THE AMERICAS. Mimeographed paper prepared for the GLASCO-UNAM Conference in Mexico 1980.

———: Foreword: TRIBUTE TO A SCHOLAR: APPRECIATING C.L.R JAMES, (ed). B. Ragoonath. (Consortium Graduate School of Sciences, University of the West Indies, Trinidad 1990.

Glazier, Stephen D: 'African Cults and Christian Churches in Trinidad'. Presented at the 23rd Annual Meeting of the African Studies Association, Pennsylvania 1980.

Gleason, Judith: ORISHA: GODS OF YORUBA. (New York, Athenaeum 1971).

Goklieri, V: 'Indian Films in Trinidad'. PEOPLE, October/November 1977.

Gopie, Kamala-Jean: 'The Next Indo-Caribbean Generation in Canada' in INDO-CARIBBEAN RESISTANCE. (Toronto, Tsar, 1993).

Gosine, Mohendra: 'Culture and Economic Participation in a Social Movement: The Case of the East Indians and the Black Power Movement in Trinidad'. Conference on East Indians in the Caribbean, U.W.I., Trinidad, August-September 1984.

——— (ed); DOT-HEAD AMERICANS: THE SILENT MINORITY IN THE UNITED STATES. (New York, Windsor Press, 1990).

——— (ed) : THE COOLIE CONNECTION: FROM THE ORIENT TO THE OCCIDENT. (New York, Windsor Press, 1992).

Grant, K.J: MY MISSIONARY YEARS. (Halifax, 1923).

Grant, R.W: 'The Contribution of the Presbyterian Church to the Education of East Indians in Guyana 1894–1964' in FOCUS ON BRITISH GUIANA (ed) E.H.Johnson. (Toronto, Presbyterian Publications, n.d.)

Greaves, I.C: MODERN PRODUCTION AMONG BACKWARD PEOPLES. (London 1935).

Green, Helen: 'Values of Negro and Indian School Children in Trinidad'. ECONOMIC STUDIES, 1965.

———: 'Socialization Values in the Negro and East Indian Subcultures in Trinidad'. JOURNAL OF SOCIAL PSYCHOLOGY, 1964.

Green, William: BRITISH SLAVE EMANCIPATION: THE SUGAR COLONIES AND THE GREAT EXPERIMENT, 1830–1865.(Oxford, Claredon Press, 1976).

Greene, John Edward: RACE VS. POLITICS IN GUYANA: POLITICAL CLEAVAGES AND POLITICAL MOBILIZATION IN THE 1968 GENERAL ELECTION, Mona, Jamaica ISER, 1974.

Greenwood, Thomas: 'East Indian Emigration: The Indian Government's Policy'. WEST INDIA COMMITTEE CIRCULAR, April 1921.

Gregory, Robert C: INDIANS AND EAST AFRICA: A HISTORY OF RACE RELATIONS WITHIN THE BRITISH EMPIRE, 1890–1939, Oxford: 1971.

————: AN ECONOMIC AND SOCIAL HISTORY, 1890–1980 (Westview Press, Boulder, 1993).

Grierson, George A: REPORT ON COLONIAL EMIGRATION FROM THE BENGAL PRESIDENCY, Calcutta: Bengal Secretariat, 1883.

————: BIHAR PEASANT LIFE, (London: Truebner & Co, 1885).

Guiral, P: L'IMMIGRATION REGLEMENTEE AUX ANTILLES FRANCAISES ET A LA REUNION. (Paris, 1911).

Gumperz, John J: 'Dialect Difference and Social Stratification in a North Indian Village', AMERICAN ANTHROPOLOGIST 60, 1958, pp. 668–82.

Hale, C.M: 'An Indian Colony'. IMPERIAL ASIATIC QUARTERLY, 1911.

Hall, D.G: FREE JAMAICA, 1838–1865: AN ECONOMIC HISTORY. (New Haven 1959).

————: 'The Flight from the Estates Reconsidered: The British West Indies, 1838–1942'. JOURNAL OF CARIBBEAN HISTORY 10, 1978.

Hall, Stuart: 'Pluralism, Race and Class in Caribbean Society' in RACE AND CLASS IN POST-COLONIAL SOCIETY (Paris, UNESCO 1977).

Hamel-Smith, Angela: 'Primary Education and East Indian Women in Trinidad 1900–1956'. Conference on East Indians in the Caribbean, U.W.I, Trinidad, August-September 1984.

Hamid, Idris: A HISTORY OF THE PRESBYTERIAN CHURCH IN TRINIDAD, 1868–1968: THE STRUGGLES OF A CHURCH IN COLONIAL CAPTIVITY. (Port of Spain: St. Andrew's Theological College, 1980).

Hanley, Eric R: 'All Ah We Hustlin: Economic Opportunities in an East Indian Village in Guyana'. Symposium on East Indians in the Caribbean, Trinidad, U.W.I 1975.

Haraksingh, Kusha; 'Indian Indentureship in the Indenture Period'. CARIBBEAN ISSUES, 1976.

————: 'Control and Resistance Among Indian Workers: A Study of Labour on the Sugar Plantations of Trinidad 1875–1917', in INDIA IN THE CARIBBEAN, pp. 61–77.

————: 'Estates, Labour and Population in Trinidad, 1870–1900'. Paper presented at the Tenth Conference of Caribbean Historians, St Thomas, U.S. Virgin Islands, 1978.

————: 'The Hindu Experience in Trinidad'. Paper presented at the Third Conference of East Indians in the Caribbean, St. Augustine, Trinidad, 1984.

————: 'Aspects of the Indian Experience in the Caribbean'. In CALCUTTA TO CARONI: THE EAST INDIANS IN TRINIDAD, 1985.

Hardinge, Lord: MY INDIAN YEARS 1910–1916. (London, John Murray 1948).

Harewood, Jack: 'Racial Discrimination in Employment in Trinidad and Tobago', SOCIAL AND ECONOMIC STUDIES 20, (3), 1971, pp. 267–93.

Harnarine, Harold: 'Business Enterprise and Asiatic Groups in the West Indies'. SOCIAL SCIENTIST, 1963–4.

Harper, Edward B: 'Ritual Pollution as an Integrator of Caste and Religion' in RELIGION IN SOUTH ASIA, Edward B. Harper (ed), Seattle: University of Washington Press, 1964, pp. 150–96.

Harricharan, J.T: THE WORK OF THE CHRISTIAN CHURCHES AMONG THE EAST INDIANS IN TRINIDAD, 1845–1917.(Port of Spain, 1976).

Harris, Alan: 'The Indian Heritage: The Ancestral Homeland, Religious Legacy'. TAPIA, September 1972.

Harris, J.H: COOLIE LABOUR IN THE BRITISH CROWN COLONIES AND PROTECTORATES. (London 1910).

Hart, Daniel: TRINIDAD AND THE OTHER WEST INDIAN COLONIES. (Port of Spain 1866).

————: HISTORICAL AND STATISTICAL VIEW OF THE ISLAND OF TRINIDAD. (London, Judd & Glass 1865).

Hazareesingh, K: A HISTORY OF INDIANS IN MAURITIUS, Mauritius: 1950.

Henry, Edward O: 'The Mother Goddess Cult and Interaction Between Little and Great Religious Traditions' in RELIGION IN MODERN INDIA, Giri Raj Gupta (ed), New Delhi: Vikas, 1983, pp. 150–96.

Henry, Frances: 'Religion and Ideology in Trinidad: The Resurgence of the Shango Religion'. CARIBBEAN QUARTERLY, 9, Nos.3–4, 1983.

Henry, Ralph, M: 'Notes on the Evolution of Inequality in Trinidad and Tobago' in TRINIDAD ETHNICITY. (London, Macmillan Press 1993).

Herskovits, Melville J: THE MYTH OF THE NEGRO PAST. (Boston, Beacon Press 1958).

——: TRINIDAD VILLAGE. (New York, Alfred Knopf 1947).

Hewick, J.E: 'Our People', TIMEHRI, 1911.

Hibbert, Christopher: THE GREAT MUTINY: INDIA 1857.(New York, Penguin, 1980).

Higman, Barry: 'The Chinese in Trinidad, 1806–1838'. CARIBBEAN STUDIES 12, No. 3, 1972.

Higgins, ????

Hill, A.C and Kilson, M: APPROPOS AFRICA. (London, Cass 1969).

Hill, Arthur H: 'Emigration From India', TIMEHRI, No. 23, Vol. 43– 52, 1919.

Hill, Jack Johnson: 'A Prolegma to a Journey in Cultural Continuity: Toward an India Social Ethic'. Conference on East Indians in the Carib bean, U.W.I, Trinidad, August-September 1984.

Hintzen, Percy C and Ralph R. Premdas: 'Race, Class and Development Toward an Explanation of Poverty and Repression in less Developed Countries', PLURAL SOCIETIES 15, 1984, pp. 193–219.

Hira, Sandew; 'The Evolution of the Social, Economic and Political Position of the East Indians in Surinam, 1873–1980' in INDIA IN THE CARIBBEAN (Hansib/Uni versity of Warwick 1987).

Hitchens, F.H: THE COLONIAL LAND AND EMIGRATION COMMISSIONERS. (Philadelphia, University of Pennsylvania Press, 1931)

Hodge, Merle: CRICK CRACK MONKEY. (London 1970).

Hoefte, Rosemarijn: 'Control and Resistance: Indentured Labour in Suriname', NIEUWE WEST-INDISCHE GIDS 61, 1989, pp. 1–22.

——: `Female Indentured Labour in Suriname: For Better or Worse?' BOLETIN DE ESTUDIOS LATINAMERICANOS Y DEL CARIBE (June 1987).

Hopkins, Thomas J: 'The Social Teaching of the Bhagavata Purana', in KRISHNA: MYTHS, RITES AND ATTITUDES, Milton Singer (ed), Honolulu: East-West Center Press, 1966, pp. 3–22.

Horowitz, Michael: 'The Worship of South Indian Deities in Mar tinique'. ETHNOLOGY, 1963.

Horowitz, M and Klass, Morton: 'The Martiniquan Cult of Malde vidan'. SOCIAL AND ECONOMIC STUDIES, 1961.

Horton, V.P. Oswald (ed): CHINESE IN THE CARIBBEAN. Souvenir, Thirteenth Anniversary of the Chinese Republic, 1911– 41.(Kingston, Jamaica: Gleaner Co. 1941).

Hosein, F.E.M: 'East Indians in Trinidad', PORT OF SPAIN GAZETTE, 5 May 1913.

Houk, James: 'Afro-Trinidadian Identity and the Africanisation of the Orisha Religion' in TRINIDAD ETHNICITY. (London, Macmillan Press 1993.)

Hubbard, H.J.M: RACE AND GUYANA: THE ANATOMY OF A CULTURAL ENTERPRISE. (GEorgetown, Daily chronilce, 1969).

Huttenback, R.H: GANDHI IN SOUTH AFRICA: BRITISH IMPERIALISM AND THE INDIAN QUESTION, 1860–1914.(Ithaca, New York 1971).

Hutton, J: CASTE IN INDIA. (Oxford University Press 1951).

Hydal, Maulana M.K: 'The Religious Experience of the Indian in Trinidad: The Muslim Experience'. Conference on East Indians in the Carib bean, U.W.I, Trinidad, August-September 1984.

Hypes, James L: SPOTLIGHT ON THE CULTURES OF INDIA. (Washington, D.C, 1937).

Ibbetson, D: PUNJAB CASTES, 1916.

Ibbotson, Peter; 'Indians in Fiji, Trinidad and Mauritius'. ASIAN AND AFRICAN REVIEW 1962.

Ince, Basil: 'Race and Ideology in the Foreign Relations of Independent Guyana: The Case of East Indians'. Conference on East Indians in the Carib bean, U.W.I, Trinidad, June 1975.

Innis, L.O: TRINIDAD AND TRINIDADIANS: A COLLECTION OF PAPERS, HISTORICAL, SOCIAL AND DESCRIPTIVE, ABOUT TRINIDAD AND ITS PEOPLE. (Port of Spain, Mirror Publishing Works, 1910).

Ireland, W. Alleyne: DEMERARIANA: ESSAYS HISTORICAL, TECHNICAL AND DESCRIPTIVE. (Georgetown, Baldwin & Co, 1897).

Irick, Robert Lee: CH'ING POLICY TOWARDS THE COOLIE TRADE, 1847– 1878.(Taipei, China: Chinese Materials Centre, 1982).

Irwati, K: KINSHIP ORGANISATION IN INDIA. (Poona, Deccan University Press 1953).

Ishwaran, K (ed): CHANGE AND CONTINUITY IN INDIA'S VILLAGES. (New York: Columbia University Press, 1970).

——: `Bhakti Tradition and Modernization: The Case of Lingayatism', JOURNAL OF ASIAN AND AFRICAN STUDIES 15, 1980, pp. 72–82.

Itwaru, Arnold: 'Exile and Commemoration' in INDENTURE AND EXILE, (Toronto, Tsar 1989).

Iyer, Raghavan: 'Utilitarianism and All That', ST. ANTHONY'S PAPERS, No. 8, (London, Chatto & Windus, 1960).

Jagan, Cheddi: FORBIDDEN FREEDOM. (London, Lawrence & Wishart, 1954).

——: THE WEST ON TRIAL. (London, Michael Joseph 1966).

Jagan, Cheddi: BRITISH GUIANA'S FUTURE, PEACEFUL OR VIOLENT. (Georgetown 1963).

——: `Indo-Caribbean Political Leadership' in INDENTURE AND EXILE, pp. 15–25.

Jagan, Cheddi and Karran, Ram: RACE AND POLITICS IN GUYANA (Georgetown, PPP).

Jain, Ravindra K: 'Religion and Morality: A Preliminary Framework for Comparison of Beliefs and Practices Among the Hindu Tamils of India and Malaysia'. Paper presented at the VIIIth Congress of Anthropological and Ethnological Sciences, 1968.

——: `South Indian Labour in Malaya, 1840–1920', in INDENTURED LABOUR IN THE BRITISH EMPIRE 1834–1920, Kay Saunders (ed), London: Croom Helm, 1984, pp. 158– 82.

——: `Freedom Denied? Indian Women and Indentureship', ECONOMIC AND POLITICAL WEEKLY 21, 1986, p. 316.

——: `Overseas Indians in Malaysia and the Caribbean: Comparative Notes', in IMMIGRANTS AND MINORITIES 7, 1988, pp. 123–43.

——: SOUTH INDIANS ON THE PLANTATION FRONTIER IN MALAYA, New Haven: 1970.

James, C.L.R: WEST INDIANS OF EAST INDIAN DESCENT. (Port of Spain, 1965).

——: `Kanhai: A Study in Confidence' in AT THE RENDEZVOUS OF VICTORY (London, Allison & Busby 1984).

Jayawardena, Chandra: CONFLICT AND SOLIDARITY IN A GUYANESE PLANTATION. (London, Athlone Press, 1963).

——: `Family Organisation in Plantations in British Guiana' in INTERNATIONAL JOURNAL OF COMPARATIVE SOCIOLOGY, 1962.

——: `Marital Stability in Two Guyanese Sugar Estate Communities'. SOCIAL AND ECONOMIC STUDIES, 1960.

——: `Religious Belief and Social change: Aspects of the Development of Hinduism in British Guiana', COMPARATIVE STUDIES IN SOCIETY AND HISTORY 8, 1966, pp. 211–40.

——: `Migration and Social Change: A Survey of Indian Communities Overseas', GEOGRAPHICAL REVIEW 58, 1968, pp. 426–29.

——: `Ideology and Conflict in Lower-Class Communities', COMPARATIVE STUDIES IN SOCIETY AND HISTORY 10, 1968, pp. 413–46.

——: `The Disintegration of Caste in Fiji Indian Rural Society', in ANTHROPOLOGY IN OCEANIA, L.R. Hiatt and Chandra Jayawardena (eds), Sydney: Angus and Robertson, 1971, pp. 89–119.

——: `Social Contours of an Indian Labour Force During the Indenture Period', in RAMA'S BANISHMENT, Vijay Mishra (ed), Auckland: Heinemann, 1979, pp. 40–65.

——: `Culture and Ethnicity in Guyana and Fiji', MAN (N.S) 15, 1980, pp. 430–50.

——: `Farm, Household and Family in Fiji Indian Rural Society' in OVERSEAS INDIANS, George Kurian and Ram P. Srivastava (eds), New Delhi: Vikas, 1983, pp. 141–79.

Jayawardena, C and Smith, R.T: 'Caste and Social Status Among the Indians of Guyana' in CASTE IN OVERSEAS INDIAN COMMUNITIES. Ed, by B.M.Schwartz. (San Francisco, Chandler Publishing Co.1967).

Jenkins, John; THE COOLIE: HIS RIGHTS AND WRONGS. (London, Strahan & Co. 1871).

Jha, Jagdish Chandra: INDENTURED INDIAN MIGRATION, 1835–1917.(St. Augustine, Trinidad, 1973).

——: `Hindusim in Trinidad' in INDENTURE AND EXILE, op. cit., pp. 25–33.

——: `Aspects of East Indian Family in Trinidad and Tobago'. (St.Augustine, Trinidad, 1973).

——: `The Hindu Sacraments (rites de passage) in Trinidad and Tobago'. CARIBBEAN QUARTERLY, 1976.

——: `The Background of Legislation of Non-Christian Marriages in Trinidad and Tobago'. Symposium on East Indians in the Caribbean, St. Augustine, Trinidad.

——: `The Indian Mutiny-cum-Revolt of 1857 and Trinidad', Mimeographed, U.W.I, 1972.

——: `East Indian Pressure Groups in Trinidad 1897–1921'. Conference on Caribbean Historians, St Augustine, Trinidad, 1973.

——: `East Indian Heritage in Trinidad (West Indies)'. St Augustine, Trinidad, U.W.I, 1973.

——: `The Hindu Festival of Divali in the Caribbean'. CARIBBEAN QUARTERLY, 1976.

Johnson, Howard: 'Immigration and the Sugar Industry in Trinidad During the Last quarter of the Nineteenth Century', JOURNAL OF CARIBBEAN HISTORY, Vol. 3, November 1971.

——: `The Origins and Early Development of Cane Farming in Trinidad, 1882–1906'. JOURNAL OF CARIBBEAN HISTORY 5, 1972.

——: `The Anti-Chinese Riots of 1918 in Jamaica'. IMMIGRANTS AND MINORITIES 2, No. 1, 1983.

——: `The Chinese in Trinidad in the Late Nineteenth Century'. ETHNIC AND RACIAL STUDIES 10, No. 1, 1987.

Johnson, Kim Nicholas: 'Considerations on Indian Sexuality'. Paper presented to the Third Conference on East Indians, 29 August-4 September, 1984, U.W.I, St. Augustine, Trinidad.

Johnson, Samuel: THE HISTORY OF THE YORUBAS (London, Routledge & Kegan Paul 1969).

Johnston, Judith: 'The Changing Cultural Context of the Neo-Natal Period in an East Indian Rural Community of South Trinidad'. Symposium on East Indians in the Caribbean, U.W.I, Trinidad, September 1979.

Jolly, A.L: 'Peasant Farming in Two Districts of the Oropouche Lagoon, June 1944–45', TROPICAL AGRICULTURE 25, 1948, pp. 22–32.

Jolly, J: INSTITUTES OF VISHNU, (Oxford, Clarendon Press 1880).

Josa, F.P.L: 'The Hindus in the West Indies', TIMEHRI, December 1912.

Joseph, E.L: HISTORY OF TRINIDAD (Port of Spain 1840).

Karve, Irawati: KINSHIP ORGANIZATION IN INDIA, Bombay: Asia Publishing House, 1965.

Kelly, John D: 'From Holi to Diwali in Fiji: An Essay on Ritual and History', MAN (N.S.) 23, 1988, pp. 40–55.

Key, Lesley: 'East Indian Immigration and the Afro-Guyanese, 1871–1921'. Conference on Caribbean Historians 1972.

Khan, Abrahim: 'Kali-mai Puja in Guyana', RELIGION 7, 1977, pp. 35–45.

Kingsley, Charles: AT LAST: A CHRISTMAS IN THE WEST INDIES, (New York 1871).

Kirke, Henry: TWENTY-FIVE YEARS IN BRITISH GUIANA, 1872–1877.(Georgetown, The Daily Chronicle 1948).

Kirpalani, et al: INDIAN CENTENARY REVIEW:ONE HUNDRED YEARS OF PROGRESS (Guardian Commercial Printery, Trinidad 1945.

Kishna, Sita: 'Language and Language Use of the Hindustani in Suriname'. Conference on East Indians in the Caribbean, U.W.I, Trinidad, August-September 1984.

Klass, Morton: 'East and West Indians: Cultural Complexity in Trinidad'. SOCIAL AND CULTURAL PLURALISM IN THE CARIBBEAN (ed) Vera Rubin, (New York Academy of Sciences, 1960).

———: EAST INDIANS IN TRINIDAD: A STUDY IN CULTURAL PERSISTENCE. (New York, Columbia University Press,1961).

———: `Life Cycle in an East Indian Village in Trinidad'. PEOPLES AND CULTURES OF THE CARIBBEAN: AN ANTHROPOLOGICAL READER (ed) Michael Horowitz (Garden City, 1971).

Knaplund, P: 'Mr. Over-Secretary Stephen'. JOURNAL OF MODERN HISTORY, Vol. 1, No. 1, March 1929.

Knowles, L: THE ECONOMIC DEVELOPMENT OF THE OVERSEAS BRITISH EMPIRE, 3 Vols. (London, Routledge 1928–36).

Kolenda, Pauline M: 'Region, Caste and Family Structure: A Comparative Study of the Indian "Joint" Family' in STRUCTURE AND CHANGE IN INDIAN SOCIETY, Milton Singer and B.S. Cohn (eds), Chicago: Aldine, 1968, pp. 335–96.

Kondapi, C: INDIANS OVERSEAS, 1838–1949.(Bombay, Oxford University Press 1951).

———: `Indians Overseas: The Position in Trinidad', INDIA QUARTERLY, 4, 1948.

Kuczynski, R.R: DEMOGRAPHIC SURVEY IN THE BRITISH COLONIAL EMPIRE, Vol. 3: WEST INDIAN AND AMERICAN TERRITORIES. (London: Oxford University Press, 1953).

Kulkarni, Jaishree: 'The Effect of Indian Nationalism on East Indians in Trinidad', Caribbean Studies Thesis, University of The West Indies, 1974.

Kuper, Hilda: 'An Interpretation of Hindu Marriage in Durban', AFRICAN STUDIES 16, 1957, pp. 221–235.

———: INDIAN PEOPLE IN NATAL, Durban: Natal University Press, 1960.

———: '"Strangers" in Plural Societies: Asians in South Africa and Uganda', PLURALISM IN AFRICA, Leo Kuper and M.G. Smith (eds), Berkeley: University of California Press, 1969, pp. 247–82.

Kurian, George and Ram P. Srivastava, (eds): OVERSEAS INDIANS, Delhi: Vikas, 1983.

Ladoo, Harold Sonny: NO PAIN LIKE THIS BODY (London: Heinemann 1972).

La Guerre, John G (ed): CALCUTTA TO CARONI: THE EAST INDIANS IN TRINIDAD. (Longman Caribbean, 1974).

———: `Africans and East Indians in Trinidad', TAPIA, October 1972.

———: `Afro-Indian Relations in Trinidad and Tobago', CARIBBEAN ISSUES, 1974.

———: `Afro-Indian Relations in Trinidad and Tobago: An Assessment'. St. Augustine, Trinidad, U.W.I, 1975.

———: `The Indian Middle Class Today' in CALCUTTA TO CARONI.

Lal, Brij V: 'Fiji Girmitiyas: The Background to Banishment', in RAMA'S BANISHMENT, Vijay Mishra, (ed.), Auckland: Heinemann, 1979, pp. 12–39.

———: GRIMITIYAS: THE ORIGINS OF THE FIJI INDIANS, Canberra: Journal of Pacific History, 1983.

———: `Kunti's cry: Indentured Women on Fiji Plantations', in INDIAN ECONOMIC AND SOCIAL HISTORY REVIEW 42, 1985, pp. 55–71.

Lal, Victor: FIJI: COUPS IN PARADISE (London, Zed Books, 1990).

Lamine, M: 'The Place of the Indian Community in NJAC's Philosophy of Black Power'. Symposium on East Indians in the Caribbean, 1975.

Lamming, George: 'Foreword' in Walter Rodney's A HISTORY OF THE GUYANESE WORKING PEOPLE, 1881–1905, (Heinemann 1981).

———: `The West Indian People', NEW WORLD QUARTERLY, 2, (1), 1966.

Landis, Joseph B: 'Race Relations and Politics in Guyana'. PhD. Thesis, Yale University 1971.

——: `Racial Attitudes of Africans and Indians in Guyana', SOCIAL AND ECONOMIC STUDIES, 1973.

Lannoy, Richard: THE SPEAKING TREE. (London: Oxford University Press, 1971).

Larbie, Kaye and Quamina, Lynda: EAST INDIANS IN THE CARIBBEAN: A SELECT BIBLIOGRAPHY, (University of the West Indies 1979).

Lassere, G: LA GUADELOUPE ETUDE GEOGRAPHIQUE (Bordeaux 1961).

Laurence, K.O: IMMIGRATION INTO THE WEST INDIES IN THE NINETEENTH CENTURY (Barbados, Caribbean Universities Press 1971).

——: `Immigration into Trinidad and British Guiana 1834– 1871'. PhD. Thesis, University of Cambridge, 1958.

——: `The East Indian Indenture in Trinidad'. CARIBBEAN QUARTERLY, 1971.

——: `The Evolution of Long Term Labour Contracts in Trinidad and British Guiana' in CARIBBEAN IN TRANSITION: PAPERS ON SOCIAL, POLITICAL AND ECONOMIC DEVELOPMENT. (eds) F.M. Andic and T.G. Matthews, Rio Piedras, Institute of Caribbean Studies, 1965.

——: `Indians As Permanent Settlers in Trinidad Before 1900', in CALCUTTA TO CARONI, John La guerre (ed), St. Augustine: University of the West Indies (2nd edition), 1985, pp. 95–114.

——: `Review of Weller, The East Indian Indenture in Trinidad', in CARIBBEAN QUARTERLY 17, pp. 34–47.

LAWS OF TRINIDAD AND TOBAGO 1950: Eliot Frances (C.T.Roworth, London).

Lee Tom Yin: THE CHINESE IN JAMAICA. (Kingston: Chung San News, 1963).

Lemon, Anthony: 'The Indian Communities of East Africa and the Caribbean', in STUDIES IN OVERSEAS SETTLEMENT AND POPULATION, A. Lemon and N.Pollock (eds), London: Longman, 1980.

Leonard, D.L: MISSIONARY ANNALS IN THE NINETEENTH CENTURY (Cleveland,1899).

Levy, Jacqueline: 'Chinese Indentured Immigration to Jamaica During the Latter Part of the Nineteenth Century'. Paper presented at the Fourth Conference of Caribbean Historians, Mona, Jamaica, 1972.

Lewis, Oscar: VILLAGE LIFE IN NORTHERN INDIA. (Urbana: University of Illinois Press, 1958).

Lobscheid, Rev. William: CHINESE EMIGRATION TO THE WEST INDIES: A TRIP THROUGH BRITISH GUIANA UNDERTAKEN FOR THE PURPOSE OF ASCERTAINING THE CONDITION OF THE CHINESE WHO HAVE EMIGRATED UNDER GOVERNMENT CONTRACT, WITH SUPPLEMENTARY PAPERS RELATING TO CONTRACT LABOUR AND THE SLAVE TRADE. (Demerara, Royal Gazette, 1866).

Lockyer, Charles: AN ACCOUNT OF TRADE IN INDIA, (London 1711).

Long, Edward E: 'British Guiana and Indian Immigra tion'. WEST INDIA COMMITTEE CIRCULAR, January/February 1925.

Look Lai, Walton: INDENTURED LABOUR, CARIBBEAN SUGAR: CHINESE AND INDIAN MIGRANTS TO THE BRITISH WEST INDIES, 1838–1918, (Baltimore/London: Johns Hopkins University Press, 1993).

——: `Chinese Indentured Labour: Migrants to the British West Indies in the Nineteenth Century'. AMERASIA JOURNAL 15, No. 2 (1989).

Lowenthal, David: WEST INDIAN SOCIETIES (London, Oxford University Press, 1972).

——: RACE AND COLOUR IN THE WEST INDIES (Middletown, Connecticut, Wesleyan University Press, 1967).

Luckhoo, J.A: 'East Indians in British Guiana', TIMEHRI, Vol. 2 (Georgetown 1912).

——: `The East Indians in British Guiana: From Their Advent to this Colony to the Present time; A Survey of the Economic, Educational and Political Aspects', TIMEHRI, 6, 1919.

Lustick, I: 'Stability in Deeply Divided Societies', WORLD POLITICS, Vol. 31, No. 3, 1979, pp. 325–42.

Lunning, H and Sital, P: 'The Economic Transformation of Small Holder Rice Farming in Surinam' in M.Cross and A. Marks, PEASANT PLANTATIONS AND RURAL COMMUNITIES IN THE CARIBBEAN (Leiden 1979).

Lutchman, Harold A: 'Race and the Public Service in Guyana'. University of Guyana, 197–?

——: `Middle Class Colonial Politics: A Study of Guyana With Special Reference to the Period 1920–1931'. PhD. Diss. Manchester University 1970.

Lyphart, Arend; 'Consociational Democracy', WORLD POLITICS, January 1969.

MacDonald, John S and MacDonald, L.D: 'Transformation of African and Indian Family Traditions in the Southern Caribbean'. COMPARATIVE STUDIES IN SOCIETY AND HISTORY, 15, 1973.

MacDonnell, A.A: INDIA'S PAST (Oxford, Clarendon Press 1927).

MacKay, J.D: 'Under the Southern Cross: A Story of East Indian Indenture in British Guiana'. Conference on Caribbean Historians, Jamaica 1972.

McLewin, P: 'Power and Economic Change: The Response to Emancipation in Jamaica and British Guiana'. PhD. Diss, Cornell University 1971. Ann Arbor, Michigan, University Microfilms 1977.

Macmillan, W.M: WARNING FROM THE WEST INDIES, (London 1936).

McNeill, James and Lal, Chimman: (See McNeill and Lal Report).

McPherson, J: CARIBBEAN LANDS: A GEOGRAPHY OF THE WEST INDIES, (London, Longman 1965).

Madan, T.N: 'Is the Brahmanic GOTRA a grouping of kin?', SOUTHWESTERN JOURNAL OF ANTHRO-POLOGY 18, 1962, pp. 59–77.

Mahabir, N.K: 'Hosay as Theatre'. THE TORONTO SOUTH ASIAN REVIEW, 5 (1), 1986.

——: `East Indians in Grenada: A Study in Absorption'.
Paper presented at Symposium on East Indians in the Carib bean, September 1984.

——: THE STILL CRY: PERSONAL ACCOUNTS OF EAST INDIANS IN TRINIDAD AND TOBAGO DURING INDENTURESHIP, (Trinidad, Calaloux Publishers, 1988).

——: `The Hindu View of Christ', MOKSHA (Indian Review Publications, Trinidad 1986).

——: `Hindu Festivals, Ceremonies and Rituals in Trinidad'. Mimeographed 1986.

——: `The Fire-Walking Ceremony in Trinidad' in DIVALI NAGAR, (Trinidad: National Council of Indian Culture 1987).

Mahabir, N.K and Maharaj, A: "Kali Mai: The Cult of the Black Mother in Trinidad'. Mimeographed 1985.

Mahajani, Usha: THE ROLE OF INDIAN MINORITIES IN BURMA AND MALAYA. Bombay: Vora, 1960.

Mahar, Pauline: 'Changing Religious Practices of an Untouchable caste', ECONOMIC DEVELOPMENT AND CULTURE CHANGE 8, 1960, pp. 279–287.

Maharaj, D: 'Cane-farming in the Trinidad Sugar Industry'. PhD. Diss. University of Edinburgh, 1969.

Maharaj Mohandaye, Adita: 'The Changing Pattern of the East Indian Family in Trinidad', Caribbean Studies Thesis, University of the West Indies, St.Augustine, n.d.

Maharaj, Ramesh: 'Challenges to East Indians in Trinidad and Tobago' in INDO-CARIBBEAN RESIST-ANCE, (Toronto, Tsar, 1993).

Maharaj-Rambachan, Niala: 'Some Aspects of Hindu Folk Songs in Trinidad', 1974.

Mahase, Anna: MY MOTHER'S DAUGHTER: THE AUTOBIOGRAPHY OF ANNA MAHASE Snr. (Trinidad: Royards Publishing Company, 1992).

Mair, L: WELFARE IN THE BRITISH COLONIES (London 1943).

Malefijt, De Waal: THE JAVANESE IN SURINAM (Assen 1963).

Malik, Yogendra: EAST INDIANS AND POLITICS IN TRINIDAD: A STUDY IN MINORITY POLI-TICS (Oxford University Press 1971).

——: `The Democratic Labour Party of Trinidad: An Attempt at the Formation of a Mass Party in a Multi-racial Society'. PhD. Diss, University of Florida 1966.

——: `Socio-politcal Perceptions and Attributes of East Indian Elites in Trinidad', WESTERN POLITICAL QUARTERLY, 1970.

——: `Agencies of Political Socialization and East Indian Ethnic Identification in Trinidad'. SOCIOLOGI-CAL BULLETIN, 1969.

Mandelbaum, David: 'Family in India' in SOUTHWESTERN JOURNAL OF ANTHROPOLOGY, University of Mexico.

——: SOCIETY IN INDIA, Vol. 1, (Berkeley & Los Angeles 1970),

——: `Family, Jati, Village' in STRUCTURE AND CHANGE IN INDIAN SOCIETY, (eds). Milton Singer and Bernard Cohn, ((Chicago 1970).

Mandle, Jay: THE PLANTATION ECONOMY: POPULATION AND ECONOMIC CHANGE IN GUY-ANA, 1838–1960.(Philadelphia: Temple University Press, 1973).

Mangat, J.S: A HISTORY OF THE ASIANS IN EAST AFRICA, 1886 TO 1945, Oxford,1969.

Mangru, Basdeo: 'The East Indian Indenture in Guyana: A New Form of Labour Manipulation 1838–1870'. Symposium on East Indians in the Carib bean, U.W.I, Trinidad, September 1979.

——: `The Sex Ratio Disparity and Its Consequences Under Indenture in British Guiana' in INDIA IN THE CARIBBEAN.

——: BENEVOLENT NEUTRALITY: INDIAN GOVERNMENT POLICY AND LABOUR MIGRATION TO BRITISH GUIANA 1854–1884, (Hansib Publishing Ltd, 1988).

——: `Tadjah in British Guiana' in INDO-CARIBBEAN RESIST ANCE, (Toronto, Tsar, 1993).

——: `Disparity in Bengal and Madras Emigration to British Guiana in the Nineteenth Century', REVISTA INTERAMERICANA 13, 1983, pp. 99–107.

——: INDENTURE AND ABOLITION: SACRIFICE AND SURVIVAL ON THE GUYANESE SUGAR PLANTATIONS. (Toronto: Tsar, 1993).

Mannix, Daniel and Cowley, M: BLACK CARGOES: A HISTORY OF THE ATLANTIC SLAVE TRADE 1518–1865, (New York, Penguin Books, 1962).

Mansingh, Laxmi: 'Cultural Heritage Among the East Indians in Jamaica'. Paper presented at Symposium on East Indians in the Carib bean, U.W.I, 1979.

Mansingh, L and A: 'The Cultural Survivals Among the East Indians in Jamaica'. Conference on Caribbean Historians at Curacao, April 1979.

———: `Hindu Influences on Rastafarianism'. CARIBBEAN QUARTERLY Monograph – Rastafari, University of the West Indies, 1985.

Marcus, George: 'Incomplete Transformation: Social Change in a Guyanese Rural Community', JOURNAL OF GEOGRAPHY, 1960.

Marriott, McKim: 'Little Communities in an Indigenous Civilization' in VILLAGE INDIA (ed). McKim Marriott, American Anthropological Association, Memoir 83.

———: `Interactional and Attributional Theories of Caste Ranking', MAN IN INDIA, 1959, pp. 39, 92–107.

———: `Cultural Policy in the New States', in OLD SOCIETIES AND NEW STATES, Clifford Geertz (ed.), New York: Free Press, 1963, pp. 27–56.

———: `Caste Ranking and Community Structure in Five Regions of India and Pakistan', Poona: Deccan College Building Centennary and Silver Jubilee Series, 30.

———: `Multiple Reference in Indian Caste Systems', in SOCIAL MOBILITY IN THE CASTE SYSTEM IN INDIA, James Silverberry (Ed), The Hague: Mouton, 1968, pp. 103–14.

Masson, George H: 'Indentured Labour and Preventable Diseases'. PROCEEDINGS OF THE AGRICULTURAL SOCIETY OF TRINIDAD, 1910.

Mateer, Rev. S: NATIVE LIFE IN TRAVANCORE (London, W.H.Allen & Co, 1883).

Matthews, Dom Basil: CRISIS IN THE WEST INDIAN FAMILY (Government Printing Works, Trinidad 1953).

Mathieson, W.L: BRITISH SLAVERY AND ITS ABOLITION 1823–1838 (London, Longman Green & Co. 1926).

Menezes, Mary Noel: SCENES FROM THE HISTORY OF THE PORTUGUESE IN GUYANA. (London, 1986).

Mentus, Ric: SUNDAY GRAPHIC, 22–29 July 1973.

Mayer, Adrian: 'The Holi Festival Among the Indians of Fiji', EASTERN ANTHROPOLOGIST 6, 1952, pp. 3–17.

———: `The Organization of Indian Settlement in Fiji', MAN 53,(284), 1953, pp. 182–5.

———: `Fiji Indian Kin-groups: An Aspect of Change in an Immigrant Society', OCEANIA 24, 1954, pp. 161–71.

———: `CASTE AND KINSHIP IN CENTRAL INDIA, London: Routledge and Keegan Paul, 1960.

Metcalf, Thomas R: THE AFTERMATH OF REVOLT: INDIA 1857–1870, Princeton, NJ: Princeton University Press, 1964.

Michaelson, Maureen: 'Caste, Kinship and Marriage: A study of Two Gujarati Trading Castes in England', PhD. Thesis, University of London (SOAS), 1983.

Milliroux, F: DEMERARA: TRANSITION FROM SLAVERY TO LIBERTY. (London 1877).

Milne, R.S: POLITICS IN ETHNICALLY BIPOLAR STATES, Vancouver: University of British Columbia Press, 1981.

Mintz, Sidney: CARIBBEAN TRANSFORMATION. (Chicago, Aldine, 1974).

———: SWEETNESS AND POWER: THE PLACE OF SUGAR IN MODERN HISTORY. (New York, Viking, 1985).

Misir, Premnarine: 'Aspirations of East Indian Teachers in Guyana: A Comparative Analysis'. Symposium on East Indians in the Caribbean, Trinidad 1979.

Mitra, Sarat Chandra: 'Notes on the Godlings and Goddesses of South Bihar', JOURNAL OF THE ANTHROPOLOGICAL SOCIETY OF BOMBAY 15, 1934, pp. 489–95.

Mittelholzer, Edgar: CORENTYNE THUNDER, (London 1941).

Mohammed, Patricia: 'The "Creolization" of Indian Women in Trinidad' in Selwyn Ryan (ed.), TRINIDAD AND TOBAGO: THE INDEPENDENCE EXPERIENCE 1962–1987, ISER, St. Augustine, 1988.

———: `Structures of Experience: Gender, Ethnicity and Class in the Lives of Two East Indian Women' in TRINIDAD ETHNICITY (ed.) Kevin Yelvington (London, Macmillan Press, 1993).

———: `Women and Education in Trinidad and Tobago, 1938–1980', M.Sc, Thesis, Department of Sociology, U.W.I., St Augustine, 1987.

Mohammed, Shamoon: 'Background of Indian Culture in Trinidad and Tobago', WEST INDIAN DIGEST 13, (127), 1958, pp. 29–30.

Mohan, Peggy: 'Trinidad Bhojpuri: A Morphological Study', PhD. Thesis, University of Michigan, 1978,

Molony, J.C: A BOOK OF SOUTH INDIA (London, Metheun & Co, 1926).

Moohr, Michael: 'The Economic Impact of Slave Emancipation in British Guiana, 1932–1852'. ECONOMIC HISTORY REVIEW 25, No. 4 (1972).

Moore, B.L: 'Retention of Caste Notions Among the Indian Immigrants in British Guiana in the Nineteenth Century'. COMPARATIVE STUDIES IN SOCIETY AND HISTORY, 1979.

Moore, Brian: RACE, POWER AND SOCIAL SEGMENTATION IN COLONIAL SOCIETY: GUYANA AFTER SLAVERY, 1838–1891.(New York, Gordon & Breach, 1987).

Moore, Robert J: 'East Indians and Negroes in British Guiana 1838– 1880'. PhD. Diss, University of Sussex, 1970.

Moreno Fraginals, Manuel, ET AL, (eds): THE SPANISH-SPEAKING CARIBBEAN IN THE NINETEENTH CENTURY. (Baltimore, John Hopkins University Press, 1985).

Morris, H.S: 'The Indian Family in Uganda', AMERICAN ANTHROPOLOGIST 61, 1959, pp. 779–89.

——: `Caste Among the Indians of Uganda', in CASTE IN OVERSEAS INDIAN COMMUNITIES, Barton M.Schwartz (ed), San Francisco: Chandler, 1967, pp. 267–82.

——: THE INDIANS OF UGANDA (London: Wiedenfield and Nicolson, 1968).

Morton, Sarah, (ed): JOHN MORTON OF TRINIDAD, PIONEER MISSIONARY OF THE PRESBYTERIAN CHURCH IN CANADA TO THE EAST INDIANS IN THE BRITISH WEST INDIES, JOURNALS, LETTERS AND PAPERS. Ed. by Sarah Morton (Toronto, Westminster 1916).

Moutousammy, E: 'Indianness in the French West Indies' in INDENTURE AND EXILE, 1989.

Mukherjee, B.B: AN ECONOMIC AND COMMERCIAL GEOGRAPHY OF INDIA (Calcutta 1938).

Mukherjee, Radhakamal: 'Economic Issues in Asiatic Emigration'. TWENTIETH CENTURY, April 1935.

Mulchansingh, Vernon C: 'The Oil Industry in the Economy of Trinidad', CARIBBEAN STUDIES 11, 1971, pp. 73–100.

Murray, G: NOTES ON NATIVE AND COLOURED RACES OF THE BRITISH WEST INDIES, BRITISH GUIANA, BRITISH HONDURAS, THE BAHAMAS AND BERMUDA (London 1924).

Naidoo, M.B: 'The East Indians in Trinidad – A Study of an Immigrant Community'. JOURNAL OF GEOGRAPHY, 1960.

Naidu, V.S: 'Ancient Hindu Theory of the State'. Symposium on East Indians in the Caribbean, U.W.I, Trinidad, 1979.

Naipaul, Seepersad: THE ADVENTURES OF GURUDEVA AND OTHER STORIES. (London, Andre Deutsch, 1976)

Naipaul, Shiva: FIREFLIES (London, Andre Deutsch, 1970).

——: THE CHIP CHIP GATHERERS (London, Andre Deutsch, 1973).

——: BEYOND THE DRAGON'S MOUTH (London, Abacus 1984).

Naipaul, V.S: A HOUSE FOR MR. BISWAS (London, Andre Deutsch, 1961).

——: AN AREA OF DARKNESS (London, Andre Deutsch, 1964).

——: THE MIDDLE PASSAGE (London, Andre Deutsch, 1962).

——: MIGUEL STREET (London, Andre Deutsch, 1959).

——: THE SUFFRAGE OF ELVIRA (Andre Deutsch, 1958).

——: IN A FREE STATE (London, Andre Deutsch, 1971).

——: THE ENIGMA OF ARRIVAL (London, Viking 1987).

——: INDIA: A WOUNDED CIVILIZATION (London, Andre Deutsch 1977).

——: INDIA: A MILLION MUTINIES NOW (London, Heinemann 1990).

——: `Introduction', EAST INDIANS IN THE CARIBBEAN: COLONIALISM AND THE STRUGGLE FOR IDENTITY, Bridget Brereton and Winston Dookeran (eds), New York: Kraus, 1982.Papers presented at First Conference of East Indians in the Caribbean, St. Augustine, Trinidad, 1975.

Nair, K: Sankaran-Kutty: 'Indians in British Guiana'. INDO-ASIAN CULTURE 1958.

Nanan, Sharon: 'Voices from the Boundary: The Indo-Caribbean Experience in Britain'. MA Thesis, University of Warwick, 1990.

Nandi, S and Tyagi, D.S: 'Forms of Villages', in PEASANT LIFE IN INDIA, N.K. Bose (ed), Calcutta: Anthropological Survey of India Memoir No. 8, 1961, pp. 1–7.

Napal, D: MANILAL MANGANLALL DOCTOR: PIONEER OF INDO-MAURITIAN EMANCIPATION, Mauritius: 1963.

Narain, Iqbal: THE POLITICS OF RACIALISM: A STUDY OF THE INDIAN MINORITY IN SOUTH AFRICA, Agra, 1962.

Nascimento, C.A and Burrowes, R.A (eds): FORBES BURNHAM: A DESTINY TO MOULD (Longman Caribbean 1970).

Nath, Dwarka: A HISTORY OF INDIANS IN BRITISH GUIANA (London, Nelson 1950).

Nayagam, Xavier S Thani: 'Tamil Emigration to Martinique'. JOURNAL OF TAMIL STUDIES, 1969.

Neale, Walter: ECONOMIC CHANGE IN RURAL INDIA, New Haven: Yale University Press, 1962.

Neame, L.E: THE ASIATIC DANGER IN THE COLONIES. (London, Routledge 1907).

Neehall, Roy: 'The Creolization of Caribbean History' in INDO-CARIBBEAN RESISTANCE (Toronto, Tsar, 1993).

Nehaul, B.B.G: 'The Influence of Indian Immigration', TIMEHRI 1955.

Nehru, Jahwaharlal: THE DISCOVERY OF INDIA (London, Meridian Books 1946).

Nelson, Donna: 'Caste Hierarchy and Competition in an Overseas Indian Community', CONTRIBUTIONS TO INDIAN SOCIOLOGY (NS) 7, 1973, pp. 1–15.

Nelson, Emmanuel: REWORLDING: THE LITERATURE OF THE INDIAN DIASPORA, New York: Greenwood, 1992.

Nevadomsky, Joseph: 'Changes in Hindu Institutions in an Alien Environment', EASTERN ANTHRO-POLOGIST 33, 1980, pp. 39–53.

——: 'Cultural and Structural Dimensions of Occupational Prestige in an East Indian Community in Trinidad', JOURNAL OF ANTHROPOLOGICAL RESEARCH 37, 1981, pp. 343–59.

——: 'Changing Conceptions of Family Regulation Among the Hindu East Indians in Rural Trinidad', ANTHROPOLOGICAL QUARTERLY 55(4), 1982, pp. 189–98.

——: 'Social Change and the East Indian in Rural Trinidad: A Critique of Methodologies', SOCIAL AND ECONOMIC STUDIES 31, 1982, pp. 90–126.

——: 'Economic Organization, Social Mobility and Changing Social Status Among East Indians in Rural Trinidad', ETHNOLOGY 22 (1), 1983, pp. 63–79.

——: 'Changes Over Time and Space in the East Indian Family in Trinidad', in OVERSEAS INDIANS, George Kurian and Ram P. Srivastava (eds), New Delhi: Vikas, 1983, pp. 180–214.

——: 'Developmental Sequences of Domestic Groups in an East Indian Community in Rural Trinidad', ETHNOLOGY 24, 1985, pp. 1–11.

Newman, P.K: 'Racial Tension in British Guiana'. RACE, 1962.

Newton, Arthur P: THE EUROPEAN NATIONS IN THE WEST INDIES (London 1933).

Nicholls, David: 'East Indians and Black Power in Trinidad'. RACE 1971.

Niehoff, Arthur: 'The Survival of Hindu Institutions in an Alien Environment'. EASTERN ANTHRO-POLOGY 1959,

——: 'The function of Caste Among the Indians in the Oropouche Lagoon, Trinidad', in CASTE IN OVER-SEAS COMMUNITIES, (ed.) Barton M.Schwartz, San Francisco 1967.

Niehoff, A and J: EAST INDIANS IN THE WEST INDIES (Milwaukee 1960).

Olivier, Lord: WHITE CAPITAL AND COLOURED LABOUR (London 1929).

——: SUGAR COMMISSION REPORT (London 1930).

——: 'Scandal of West Indian Labour Conditions'. CONTEMPORARY REVIEW, Vol. 153, 1938.

O'Malley, L.S.S: INDIAN CASTE CUSTOMS (Cambridge 1932).

——: POPULAR HINDUSIM (Cambridge, Cambridge University Press, 1935).

Omosade, Awolalu J: YORUBA BELIEFS AND SACRIFICIAL RITES (London, Longman 1979).

Opler, Morris: 'The Place of Religion in a North Indian Village', SOUTHWESTERN JOURNAL OF AN-THROPOLOGY 15, 1959, pp. 219–26.

Ortner, Sherry B: 'Theory in Anthropology Since the Sixties', in COMPARATIVE STUIDES IN SOCIETY AND HISTORY 26, 1984, pp. 126–66.

Ostor, Akos: 'PUJA in Society: A Methodological and Analytical Essay on an Ethnographic Category', EAST-ERN ANTHROPOLGIST 31, 1978, pp. 119–76.

Ottley, C.R: EAST AND WEST INDIANS RESCUE TRINIDAD (Diego Martin, Trinidad 1975).

Ottley, Rudolph: WOMEN IN CALYPSO, Part 1 (Arima: Trinidad, 1992).

Oxaal, I: RACE AND REVOLUTIONARY CONSCIOUSNESS (Cambridge, Mass, Shenkman Publishing Co, 1971).

Panday, Basdeo: 'Trade Unionism, Politics and Indo-Caribbean Leadership' in INDENTURE AND EXILE (Toronto, Tsar, 1989).

Parasram, Rampersad: 'A Comparison Between Two Ethnic Groups in Chaguanas, Caroni.' Conference on East Indians in the Caribbean, U.W.I, Trinidad, August–September 1984.

Pares, Richard: WAR AND TRADE IN THE WEST INDIES (Oxford 1936).

——: A WEST INDIA FORTUNE (London, Longman 1950).

Parmasad, K.V: 'Kheesas and Kaharis: A Collection of Indian Folk- Stories and Sayings in Trinidad'. BA Thesis, U.W.I, St. Augustine, 1973.

——: 'By the Light of the Deya' in THE AFTERMATH OF SOVEREIGNTY: WEST INDIAN PER-SPECTIVES (eds) D. Lowenthal and L. Comitas, New York 1973.

——: SALT AND ROTI: INDIAN FOLK TALES OF THE CARIBBEAN, Chaguanas, Trinidad: Sankh, 1984.

Parrinder, Geoffrey: WEST AFRICAN RELIGION (London, Epworth Press 1961).

Parry, J.H and Sherlock, P.M: A SHORT HISTORY OF THE WEST INDIES. 3rd edition. (London/Basingstoke, Macmillan 1981).

Peck, Nathaniel and Price, Thomas: REPORT OF MESSRS PECK AND PRICE WHO WERE AP-POINTED AT A MEETING OF THE FREE COLOURED PEOPLE OF BALTIMORE, HELD ON THE 25TH NOVEMBER 1839, DELEGATES TO VISIT BRITISH GUIANA AND THE ISLAND OF TRINI-

DAD FOR THE PURPOSE OF ASCERTAINING THE ADVANTAGES TO BE DERIVED BY COLOURED PEOPLE MIGRATING TO THESE PLACES. (Baltimore, 1840).

Penders, L.M: INDONESIA: SELECTED DOCUMENTS ON COLONIALISM AND NATIONALISM 1830–1942 (Queensland; University of Queensland Press 1977).

Penson, L: THE COLONIAL AGENTS IN THE BRITISH WEST INDIES (London 1924).

Peoples Progressive Party: Education and Research Committee, 'The Racialists in Guyana'. (Georgetown, New Guiana, 1964).

Perry, J.A: 'A History of the East Indian Indentured Worker in Trinidad 1845–1917'. PhD. Diss, Louisiana State University 1969.

Persaud, Harry: 'Appendix: Introduction to Dr. Cheddi Jagan' in INDENTURE AND EXILE (Toronto: Tsar, 1989).

Persaud, Kamal: RACISM AGAINST THE INDIANS IN THE EASTERN CARIBBEAN (Trinidad, Battlefront Press 1988).

Persad, K and Maharaj, A.B: 'Introduction' in H.P. SINGH: THE INDIAN STRUGGLE FOR JUSTICE AND EQUALITY AGAINST BLACK RACISM IN TRINIDAD AND TOBAGO 1956–1962.(Couva: Indian Review Press, 1993).

Phillipo, James M: JAMAICA: ITS PAST AND PRESENT STATE (London, Dawsons 1969). First Edition 1843.

Phillips, Leslie H.C: 'Kali-Mai Puja', TIMEHRI XXXIX, 1960, pp. 37–46.

Pim, Sir Allan: COLONIAL AGRICULTURAL PRODUCTION (London 1946).

Pitman, Frank W: THE DEVELOPMENT OF THE BRITISH WEST INDIES (New Haven 1917).

Planalp, Jack M: 'Religious Life and Values in a North Indian Village', PhD. Diss, Cornell University, 1956.

Pocock, David F: 'Indians in East Africa', PhD. Thesis, University of Oxford, 1955.

———: 'Inclusion and Exclusion: A Process in the Caste System of Gujerat', SOUTHWESTERN JOURNAL OF ANTHROPOLOGY 13, 1957, pp. 19–31.

———: ' "Difference" in East Africa: A Study of Caste and Religion in Modern Indian Society', SOUTHWESTERN JOURNAL OF ANTHROPOLOGY 13, 1957, pp. 285–300.

Polak, H.S.L: 'Indian Labour Migration Within the British Empire'. ASIATIC REVIEW, Vol. 14, 1918.

———: THE INDIANS OF SOUTH AFRICA: HELOTS WITHIN THE EMPIRE, AND HOW THEY ARE TREATED, Madras: 1909.

Pollard, H.J: 'The Erosion of Agriculture in an Oil Economy: The Case of Export Crop Production in Trinidad', WORLD DEVELOPMENT 13 (7), 1985, pp. 819–835.

Potter, Lesley Key: 'The Post-Indenture Experience of East Indians in Guyana 1873–1921'. Symposium on East Indians in the Caribbean 1975.

———: 'The "Paddy Proletariat" and the Dependent Peasantry: East Indian Rice-Growers in British Guiana 1895–1920'. Conference on Caribbean Historians, Barbados 1977.

———: 'East Indians Without Sugar – Essequibo, Guyana 1923–39'. Symposium on East Indians in the Caribbean, U.W.I, Trinidad, September 1979.

Poynting, Jeremy: 'East Indian Women in the Caribbean: Experience and Voice' in INDIA IN THE CARIBBEAN (Hansib/University of Warwick 1987).

———: ' "You Want to be a Coolie Woman? ": Gender and Ethnic Identity in Indo-Caribbean Women's Writing' in CARIBBEAN WOMEN WRITERS (ed) S. Cudjoe (Massachussetts, Calaloux Publishers, 1990).

———: 'Literature and Cultural Pluralism: The East Indian in the Caribbean'. PhD. Thesis, University of Leeds, 1985.

Prasad, B: INDIA'S HINDU-MUSLIM QUESTIONS (London 1946).

Premdas, Ralph: VOLUNTARY ASSOCIATIONS AND POLITICAL PARTIES IN A RACIALLY FRAGMENTED STATE: THE CASE OF GUYANA. The University of Guyana, Occasional Paper No. 2, 1972.

———(ed): THE ENIGMA OF ETHNICITY: AN ANALYSIS OF RACE IN THE CARIBBEAN AND THE WORLD. (St. Augustine, U.W.I, 1993).

———: 'The Anatomy of Ethnic Conflict: Domination Versus Reconciliation' in THE ENIGMA OF ETHNICITY, St. Augustine, 1993.

———: 'Ethnic conflict in the Caribbean: The Case of Guyana' in THE ENIGMA OF ETHNICITY.

———: 'Guyana: The Critical Elections of 1992 and a Regime Change', CARIBBEAN AFFAIRS, Jan-March 1993, Vol. 6, No. 1.

———: 'Ethnic Conflict in Trinidad and Tobago: Domination and Reconciliation' in TRINIDAD ETHNICITY (London, Macmillan Press 1993).

Premdas, R and Hintzen, P: 'Guyana: Coercion and Control in Political Change' in THE ENIGMA OF ETHNICITY: AN ANALYSIS OF RACE IN THE CARIBBEAN AND THE WORLD (St. Augustine, U.W.I, 1993).

Premium, Barton: EIGHT YEARS IN BRITISH GUIANA, 1840–1848. (London, Longmans, 1850).

Proctor, J.H. Jr: 'East Indians and the Federation of the British West Indies'. INDIA QUARTERLY, 1961.

Quamina, L and Larbie, K: EAST INDIANS IN THE CARIBBEAN: A SELECT BIBLIOGRAPHY ( U.W.I, 1979).

Ragatz, Lowell: THE FALL OF THE PLANTER CLASS IN THE BRITISH CARIBBEAN (New York 1928).

Raheja, Gloria G: 'India: Caste, Kingship and Dominance Reconsidered', ANNUAL REVIEW OF AN-THROPOLOGY 17, 1988, pp. 497–522.

Rambiritch, Birbal and Pierre L. van den Berghe: 'Caste in a Natal Hindu Community', AFRICAN STUDIES 20, 1961, pp. 217–25.

Ramchand, Kenneth: 'An Approach to Earl Lovelance's Novel Through an Examination of Indian-African Relations in THE BRAGON CAN'T DANCE'. CARIBBEAN QUARTERLY, Vol. 32, March-June 1986.

Ramdin, Ron: FROM CHATTEL SLAVE TO WAGE EARNER: A HISTORY OF TRADE UNIONISM IN TRINIDAD AND TOBAGO (London, Martin, Brian and O'Keeffe 1982).

——: THE MAKING OF THE BLACK WORKING CLASS IN BRITAIN (Aldershot, Gower Publishing Co, 1987)

——: WORLD IN VIEW: THE WEST INDIES (Oxford, Heinemann Educational Books, 1990).

——INTRODUCTORY TEXT – THE BLACK TRIANGLE (London, Seed Publications 1984).

——: INTRODUCTION – THE OTHER MIDDLE PASSAGE: JOURNAL OF A VOYAGE FROM CALCUTTA TO TRINIDAD, 1858.(London, Hansib Publishing Co. 1994).

——: 'Black Workers and the British Trade Union Movement' in INDO-BRITISH REVIEW, University of Kent.

——: 'Letter to a Close Relative on the 150th Anniversary of the Arrival of the East Indians in Trinidad' in INDO-CARIBBEAN REVIEW, Vol. 2 (1), Toronto 1995, pp. 67–72.

Ramesar, Marianne: 'Factors on the Settlement of the Indians in Trinidad: 1921–1946'. Paper presented at the XLII International Congress of Americanists Symposium on Descendants of Asian Immigrants in Plantation America. Paris 1976.

——: 'The Integration of Indian Settlers in Trinidad After Indenture 1921–1946.CARIBBEAN ISSUES, No. 2(3), 1976, pp. 54–70.

——: 'Indian Immigration into Trinidad, 1897–1917', MA, (U.W.I, Mona, 1973).

——: SURVIVORS OF ANOTHER CROSSING: A HISTORY OF EAST INDIANS IN TRINIDAD 1880–1946 (St. Augustine, U.W.I, 1994).

——: 'The Position of the East Indian in Trinidad, 1890– 1917'. Conference of Caribbean Historians, Puerto Rico 1974.

——: 'The Repatriates' – Forthcoming publication.

——; 'The Role of the British West Indian Immigrants in Trinidad 1870–1921'. St. Augustine, ISER, 1977).

——: 'The Impact of the Indian Immigrants on Colonial Trinidad Society'. CARIBBEAN QUARTERLY, 1976.

——: 'The Impact of the Indian Immigrants on Colonial Trinidad – An Assessment at the End of Indenture System'. Symposium on East Indians in the Caribbean, Trinidad, U.W.I, 1975.

Ramgopaul, L: OUR RICE INDUSTRY (Georgetown, 1964).

Ramnarine, Tyran: 'One Hundred Years of East Indian Disturbances on the Sugar Estates of Guyana 1869–1978: An Historical Overview' in INDIA IN THE CARIBBEAN.

——: 'The Growth of the East Indian Community in British Guiana, 1880–1920', PhD. Thesis, University of Sussex, 1977).

Ramnath, Harry: INDIA CAME WEST (Marabella, Trinidad, n.d).

Ramraj, Victor J: 'Trapdoors Into a Bottomless Past: V.S. Naipaul's Ambivalent Vision of the Indian Experience'. Symposium on East Indians in the Caribbean, U.W.I, Trinidad, September 1979.

——: 'Needs and Directions of Indo-Caribbean Studies' in INDO-CARIBBEAN RESISTANCE (Toronto, Tsar,1993).

Ramsaran, D: BREAKING THE BONDS OF INDENTURESHIP: INDO-TRINIDADIANS IN BUSI-NESS (St. Augustine: ISER, 1993).

Ratiram, Seeta: 'Folk Songs of the Hindus of Trinidad' (Trinidad 1973).

Rauf, Mohammed A: 'Crabwood Creek: A Study of Cultural Continuity and Ethnic Identity on different Generational Levels Among East Indians in Guyana'. PhD. Diss, Ohio State University, 1969.

——: INDIAN VILLAGE IN GUYANA: A STUDY OF CULTURAL CHANGE AND ETHNIC IDEN-TITY. Monographs and Theoretical Studies in Sociology and Anthropolgy in Honour of Nels Anderson. Publication No. 6.(Leiden, Brill 1974.

Ray, Michael: 'Bamboo Marriage', CANADA-WEST INDIES MAGAZINE, No. 24.

Reddock, Rhoda: 'Indian Women and Indentureship in Trinidad 1845– 1917: Freedom Denied'. CARIB-BEAN QUARTERLY, Vol. 32, September-December 1986.

Reddock, Rhoda: `Women, Labour and Struggle in 20th Century Trinidad and Tobago, 1898–1960'. PhD. Thesis, ISS, The Hague, 1984.

———: WOMEN, LABOUR AND POLITICS IN TRINIDAD AND TOBAGO, London: Zed Books, 1994).

Reis, Charles: THE GOVERNMENT OF TRINIDAD (Port of Spain, 1947).

Revert, E: LA MARTINIQUE, ETUDE GEOGRAPHIQUE ET HUMAINE (Paris 1949).

Richardson, Bonham C: 'Livelihood in rural Trinidad in 1900'. ANNALS OF THE ASSOCIATION OF AMERICAN GEOGRAPHERS, 1975.

———: `The Rice Culture of Coastal Guyana: A Study in Location and Livelihood'. PhD. Diss, University of Wisconsin, 1970.

Richardson, F.L.W, Jr: 'Indian Peasants: Thirty Years of Rural Reconstruction'. APPLIED ANTHROPOLOGY, Vol. 2, 1943.

Risley, H.H: THE PEOPLE OF INDIA (London, Thacker & Co, 1908).

———: TRIBES AND CASTES OF BENGAL (Calcutta, 1892).

———: TRIBES AND CASTES OF BENGAL: ANTHROPOMETRIC DATA (Calcutta 1891).

———: TRIBES AND CASTES OF BENGAL: ETHNOGRAPHIC GLOSSARY (Calcutta 1891).

Rivers, W.H.R: THE TODAS (London, 1906).

Riviere, William Emanuel: 'Labour Shortage in the British West Indies after Emancipation'. JOURNAL OF CARIBBEAN HISTORY 4, (1972).

Roberts, B.C: LABOUR IN THE TROPICAL TERRITORIES OF THE COMMONWEALTH (London, 1964).

Roberts, G.W and Byrne, J: 'Summary Statistics on Indenture and Associated Migration Affecting the West Indies, 1934–1918'. POPULATION STUDIES, 1966–7.

Roberts, G.W and Johnson, M.A: 'Factors Involved in Immigration and Movement in the Working Force of British Guiana in the Nineteenth Century'. SOCIAL AND ECONOMIC STUDIES, 1974.

Roberts, G.W and Braithwaite, L.E: 'Mating Among East Indian and Non-East Indian Women in Trinidad', SOCIAL AND ECONOMIC STUDIES, 11, 1962.

Robinson, A.N.R: THE MECHANICS OF INDEPENDENCE, Cambridge: MIT Press, 1971.

Rodney, Walter: A HISTORY OF THE GUYANESE WORKING PEOPLE 1881–1905 (Kingston, Jamaica, Heinemann Educational Books, 1981).

———(ed): GUYANESE SUGAR PLANTATIONS IN THE LATE NINETEENTH CENTURY: A CONTEMPORARY DESCRIPTION FROM THE ARGOSY. (Georgetown: Bovell, 1979).

Rodway, James: HISTORY OF BRITISH GUIANA, FROM THE YEAR 1688 TO THE PRESENT TIME, 3 Vols. (Georgetown 1891, 1893, 189?).

Rohlehr, Gordon: 'Images of Men and Women in the Calypsoes of the 1930s on the Sociology of Food Acquisition in the Context of Survivalism', GENDER IN CARIBBEAN DEVELOPMENT, (ed), Patricia Mohammed and Cathy Shepherd, Trinidad and Tobago: Women and Development Studies, (Forthcoming).

Roopchand, T: 'The Hindu Temple Service: A Functionalist Approach'. GUYANA JOURNAL OF SOCIOLOGY, 1976.

Rose, H.A: A GLOSSARY OF TRIBES AND CASTES OF THE PUNJAB AND NORTHWEST FRONTIER PROVINCE (Lahore 1919).

Rothermund, Dietmar: 'Government, Landlord and Tenant in India, 1875–1900', INDIAN ECONOMIC AND SOCIAL HISTORY REVIEW 6, 1969, pp. 351–67.

———: GOVERNMENT, LANDLORD AND PEASANT IN INDIA, Wiesbaden: Franz Steiner Verlag, 1978.

Roy, Jay Narain: MAURITIUS IN TRANSITION, Allahabad, 1960.

Rubin, Vera: 'Culture, Politics and Race Relations'. SOCIAL AND ECONOMIC STUDIES 1962.

———: `Social and Cultural Pluralism in the Caribbean'. ANNALS OF THE NEW YORK ACADEMY OF SCIENCES, 1960.

Rubin, V and Zavalloni, Marisa: WE WISH TO BE LOOKED UPON, New York: Teachers College, Columbia University, 1969.

Ruhomon, Joseph: 'The Creole East Indian', TIMEHRI, August 1921.

Ruhomon, Peter: CENTENARY HISTORY OF THE EAST INDIANS IN BRITISH GUIANA 1838–1938 (Georgetown 1947).

Russell, R.V: THE TRIBES AND CASTES OF THE CENTRAL PROVINCES OF INDIA (London, Macmillan 1916).

Ryan, Selwyn: 'The Struggle for Afro-Indian Solidarity in Trinidad and Tobago'. TRINIDAD AND TOBAGO INDEX, 1966.

———: RACE AND NATIONALISM IN TRINIDAD AND TOBAGO (University of Toronto Press, 1972).

———: TRINIDAD AND TOBAGO: THE INDEPENDENCE EXPERIENCE 1962–1987, Institute of Social and Economic Research, U.W.I, St. Augustine, 1988.

Ryan, Selwyn: `Political Change and Economic Reconstruction in Trinidad and Tobago', CARIBBEAN AF-FAIRS 1, 1988, pp. 127–60.

———: THE MUSLIMEEN GRAB FOR POWER: RACE, RELIGION AND REVOLUTION IN TRINIDAD AND TOBAGO, (Port of Spain, Inprint 1991).

Sadler, Geoff: CONTEMPORARY NOVELISTS, Fourth Edition, (London, St. James Press 1986).

Samaroo, Brinsley: 'The East Indian Response to Constitutional Change in Trinidad and Tobago'. St. Augustine, U.W.I, 1971.

———: `Indians in Politics', TAPIA, December 1970.

———: `Politics and Afro-Indian Relations in Trinidad' in CALCUTTA TO CARONI (Longman Caribbean 1974).

———: `The Vanguard of Indian Nationalism in Trinidad: The "East Indian Weekly" 1928–1932'. Conference on Caribbean Historians, Cave Hill, Barbados 1977.

———: `Missionary Methods and Local Responses: The Canadian Presbyterians and the East Indians in the Caribbean'. Symposium on East Indians in the Caribbean, St. Augustine, U.W.I, 1975.

———: `The Presbyterian Canadian Mission as an Agent of Integration in Trinidad During the Nineteenth and Early Twentieth Century. St. Augustine, 1972.

———: `Two Abolitions: African Slavery and East Indian Indentureship' in INDIA IN THE CARIBBEAN.

Samaroo, B and Dabydeen, D (eds): INDIA IN THE CARIBBEAN (Hansib/University of Warwick, 1987).

———(eds): ACROSS THE DARK WATERS – forthcoming publication.

Sammy, G.M: 'Transitional Pattern Changes and Merging of Eating Patterns of the Trinidad East Indian'. Conference on East Indians in the Caribbean, U.W.I, Trinidad, August-September 1984.

Sampath, Hugh: 'An Outline of the Social History of the Indians in Trinidad'. PhD. Diss, Columbia University 1951.

Sampath, Niels: 'An Evaluation of the "Creolization" of Trinidad East Indian Adolescent Masculinity' in TRINIDAD ETHNICITY. (London, Macmillan Press, 1993).

Sanders, Ron: 'Indian Indenture: The Legacy in Guyana and Trinidad'. STABROEK NEWS, Guyana, 9 April 1988.

Sanderson, Lord: REPORT OF THE COMMITTEE ON EMIGRATION FROM INDIA TO THE CROWN COLONIES AND PROTECTORATES (London 1910).

Sandhu, Kernial Singh: INDIANS IN MALAYA, London: Cambridge University Press, 1965.

Sandoval, Jose Miguel: 'State Capitalism in a Petroleum-based Economy: The Case of Trinidad and Tobago', in CRISIS IN THE CARIBBEAN, Fitzroy Ambersley and Robin Cohen (eds), London: Heinemann, 1983, pp. 247–68.

Sankar, Dilip; 'Hindu Wedding Songs and Rituals in Trinidad'. (Trinidad 1973).

Sankar, Y: 'Social Class and Linguistic Development in the East Indian Community in Guyana'. Symposium on East Indians in the Caribbean, U.W.I, Trinidad, September 1979.

Sapir, Edward: SELECTED WRITINGS OF EDWARD SAPIR IN LANGUAGE, CULTURE AND PERSONALITY (ed) D.G. Mandelbaum. (London, Cambridge University Press, 1949).

Sarusky, Jaime: 'The East Indian Community in Cuba' in INDENTURE AND EXILE.

Saunders, Kay (ed): INDENTURED LABOUR IN THE BRITISH EMPIRE, 1834– 1920.(London, Croom Helm, 1984).

Sastri, A Mahadev: 'The Hindu Sea-Voyage Problem: A Shastric Solution', Mysore: Theosophical Society, 1910.

Saunders, Kay (ed): INDENTURED LABOUR IN THE BRITISH EMPIRE 1834– 1920, London: Croom Helm, 1984.

Schacht, J and Bosworth, C.E: THE LEGACY OF ISLAM, 2nd Edition. (Oxford, Clarendon Press 1974).

Schlesinger, Arthur: A THOUSAND DAYS (Boston, Houghton-Mifflin 1965).

Schlote, Werner: BRITISH OVERSEAS TRADE FROM THE 1700's TO THE 1930's. (London, Oxford University Press, 1952).

Schnepel, Ellen M: 'The Creole Movement and Its Significance for the Socio-Political Integration of East Indians on the Island of Guadeloupe , French West Indies' in THE ENIGMA OF ETHNICITY: AN ANALYSIS OF RACE IN THE CARIBBEAN AND THE WORLD. (St. Augustine, U.W.I, 1993).

Schomburgh, R.H: A DESCRIPTION OF BRITISH GUIANA (London, Frank Cass 1870).

Schwartz, Barton M: 'Patterns of East Indian Family Organisation in Trinidad'. CARIBBEAN STUDIES, 1965.

———: `Differential Socio-religious Adaptation'. SOCIAL AND ECONOMIC STUDIES, 1967.

———: `Extra-Legal Activities of the Village Pundit in Trinidad'. ANTHROPOLOGICAL QUARTERLY, 1965.

———: `Ritual Aspects of Caste in Trinidad', ANTHROPOLOGICAL QUARTERLY, 1964.

———: `Caste and Endogamy in Trinidad'. SOUTHWESTERN JOURNAL OF ANTHROPOLGY, 1964.

———: CASTE IN OVERSEAS INDIAN COMMUNITIES (San Francisco, Chandler Publishing Co, 1967).

Schwartz, Barton M: 'The Dissolution of Caste in Trinidad'. PhD. Diss, University of California 1966.
——: 'The Failure of Caste in Trinidad' in CASTE IN OVERSEAS INDIAN COMMUNITIES.
Schwartzberg, Joseph: 'The Distribution of Selected Castes in the North Indian Plain', THE GEO-GRAPHICAL REVIEW 55, 1965, pp. 477–95.
Schwartzberg, Joseph: 'Caste Regions of the North India Plain', in STRUCTURE AND CHANGE IN INDIAN SOCIETY, Milton Singer and B.S.Cohn (eds), Chicago: Aldine, 1968, pp. 81–113.
Scoble, John: HILL COOLIES: A BRIEF EXPOSURE OF THE DEPLORABLE CONDITIONS OF THE HILL COOLIES IN BRITISH GUIANA AND MAURITIUS. (London, Harvey and Danton 1840).
Scoles, Ignatius: SKETCHES OF AFRICAN AND INDIAN LIFE IN BRITISH GUIANA. (Georgetown 1885).
Seaforth, C.E: 'The East Indian Influence on Caribbean Usage of Medicinal Plants'. Conference on East Indians in the Caribbean, U.W.I, Trinidad, August-September 1984.
Sebastien, Rafael: 'A Typology of the Caribbean Peasantry – The Development of the Peasantry in Trinidad, 1845– 1917'. SOCIAL AND ECONOMIC STUDIES 29, No. 2 (1980).
Seecharan (Shiwcharan) Clem and Birbalsingh, Frank: INDO-WEST INDIAN CRICKET (London: Hansib Publishing Co, 1988).
Segal, Daniel A: ' "Race" and "Colour" in Pre-Independence Trinidad and Tobago' in TRINIDAD ETHNICITY.
Selvon, Samuel: A BRIGHTER SUN (London, Wingate 1971).
——: TURN AGAIN TIGER (London, MacGibbon & Kee 1958).
——: WAYS OF SUNLIGHT (London, MacGibbon & Kee 1957).
——: THE PLAINS OF CARONI (London, MacGibbon & Kee 1970).
——: THE LONELY LONDONERS (London, Wingate 1956).
——: 'Three Into One Can't Go – East Indian, Trinidadian, West Indian' in INDIA IN THE CARIBBEAN.
——: Biographical Sketch in CONTEMPORARY AUTHORS and WORLD AUTHORS.
Sewell, William G: THE ORDEAL OF FREE LABOUR IN THE WEST INDIES (New York 1861).
Shahabuddeen, M: FROM PLANTOCRACY TO NATIONALISATION: A PROFILE OF SUGAR IN GUYANA. (Demerara: University of guyana, 1983).
Shamaz, S: 'Workers in Trinidad', CANADIAN FORUM, Vol. 27, 1947.
Sharma, Ursula: 'The Problem of Village Hinduism: "Fragmentation' and Integration', CONTRIBUTIONS TO INDIAN SOCIOLOGY (NS) 4, 1970, pp. 1–21.
——: 'Status Striving to Abolish Status: The Arya Samaj and the Low Castes', SOCIAL ACTION 26, 1976, pp. 215–36.
Shepherd, Verene: 'The Education of East Indian Children in Jamaica 1879–1950'. Post-Graduate Seminar Paper, U.W.I, Mona, Jamaica, December 1983.
——: 'Depression in the Tin Roof Towns: Economic Problems of Urban Indians in Jamaica 1830–1950', in INDIA IN THE CARIBBEAN.
——: 'Control, Resistance, Accommodation and Race Relations: Aspects of the Indentureship Experience of East Indian Emigrants in Jamaica, 1845–1921' – Forthcoming publication.
——: 'Emancipation Through Servitude: Aspects of the Condition of Indian Women in Jamaica, 1845–1945' in Beckles, Hilary & Shepherd, Verene: CARIBBEAN FREEDOM: ECONOMY AND SOCIETY FROM EMANCIPATION TO THE PRESENT (Kingston: Ian Randle Publishers, 1993).
——: 'Indians and Blacks in Jamaica in the Nineteenth and Early Twentieth Centuries: A Micro-Study of the Foundations of Race Antagonisms'. IMMIGRANTS AND MINORITIES 7, No. 1 (1988).
Sherring, Rev. M.A: HINDU TRIBES AND CASTES (Calcutta: Thacker, Spink & Co. 1881).
Shiels, Ross: 'Indentured Immigration into Trinidad 1891–1916'. B.Litt, Thesis, University of Oxford, 1967.
Shigematsu, Shinji: 'Overseas Indians – Bibliography of Books and Articles', 1873–1971', ASIAN STUDIES 21, 1975, pp. 25–49.
Shiwcharan, Clem: INDO-WEST INDIAN CRICKET (London: Hansib, 1988).
——: 'Indians in British Guiana 1919–1929: A Study in Effort and Achievement'. PhD Thesis, University of Warwick 1990).
——: BECHU: 'Bound Coolie' Radical in British Guiana (London: Hansib – forthcoming).
——: JOSEPH RUHOMON'S INDIA: THE PROGRESS OF HER PEOPLE AT HOME AND ABROAD AND HOW THOSE IN BRITISH GUIANA MAY IMPROVE THEMSELVES (The Centenary Edition). Introduced with notes and appendices by Clem Shiwcharan (Seecharan) (London: Hansib, 1994).
Sieunarine, Sharmate: 'The Social and Cultural Change in the East Indian Community of El Dorado in 1960–1980'. Caribbean Studies Thesis, U.W.I, St. Augustine, n.d.
——: 'Indians in British Guiana 1919–1929: A Study in Effort and Achievement'. PhD. Thesis, University of Warwick 1990.
Simey, T.S: WELFARE AND PLANNING IN THE WEST INDIES (London 1946).
Simpson, George E: RELIGIOUS CULTS OF THE CARIBBEAN: TRINIDAD, JAMAICA AND HAITI

(Puerto Rico, Institute of Caribbean Studies 1970, First ed. 1965).

Singaravelou, Prof: 'Some Aspects of Contemporary Economic and Social Integration of East Indians in Guadeloupe – French West Indies'. Symposium on East Indians in the Caribbean, U.W.I, 1975.

——: 'Indian Religion in Guadeloupe'. CARIBBEAN ISSUES, 1976.

Singaravelou, Prof: LES INDIENS DE LES GUADELOUPE: ETUDE DE GEOGRAPHIE HUMAINE (Bordeaux, 1975).

——: LES INDIENS DE LA CARAIBE, 3 Vols. (Paris: L'Harmattan 1987).

——: 'La Creolisation des Indiens et L'Indianisation des Creoles: Example de la Caraibe'. Paper presented at the Ve Colloque International des Etudes Creoles, St.-Devis, la Reunion, April 1986.

Singaravelou (cont): 'East Indian Immigration and the Plantation System in the French Caribbean' in PLAN-TATIONS AROUND THE WORLD: PROCEEDINGS OF THE FIRST WORLD PLANTATION CON-FERENCE, Baton Rouge, Lousiana, 2–5 October, 1984, Sue Eakin and John Tarver eds, (Alexandria, Louisiana State University Agricultural Center, 1986).

Singer, Milton B: 'The Great Tradition of Hinduism in the City of Madras', in ANTHROPOLOGY OF FOLK RELIGION, Charles Leslie (ed), New York: Vintage, 1960, pp. 105–66.

Singer, Philip A.E: 'Hinduization and Creolization in Guyana: The Plural Society and Basic Personality'. SOC-IAL AND ECONOMIC STUDIES, 1967.

——: 'Caste and Identity in Guyana', in CASTE IN OVERSEAS INDIAN COMMUNITIES, Barton M.Schwartz (ed), San Francisco: Chandler, 1967, pp. 93–116.

Singh, H.P: HOUR OF DECISION (San Juana, Vedic Enterprises 1962).

——: THE INDIAN ENIGMA: A REVIEW OF MR. C.L.R JAMES' 'WEST INDIANS OF EAST IN-DIAN DESCENT' OR A STUDY OF COOLIETUDE (San Juan, Vedic Enterprises 1965).

Singh, Kelvin: 'East Indians and the Larger Society' in CALCUTTA TO CARONI.

——: 'The Roots of Afro-Indian Conflict in Trinidad in the Indentureship Period'. Paper presented at Sym-posium on East Indians in the Caribbean, September 1979.

——: THE BLOODSTAINED TOMBS (Macmillan/University of Warwick, 1988).

Singh, Kunwar Maharaj: REPORT BY KUNWAR MAHARAJ SINGH ON HIS DEPUTATION TO BRIT-ISH GUIANA IN 1925 (London, India Office 1925).

Singh, Rajkumari: DAYS OF THE SAHIB ARE OVER (Georgetown: R. Singh 1971).

Singh, Tara: 'Suicide and Homicide: A Cross-Cultural Case Study With Emphasis on East Indians in Guyana'. Symposium on East Indians in the Caribbean, U.W.I, Trinidad, September 1979.

Sitahal, Harold: 'The Mission of the Church in Trinidad'. Masters Thesis, McGill University 1967.

Skinner, Elliot P: 'Social Stratification and Ethnic Identification' in PEOPLE AND CULTURES OF THE CARIBBEAN. Compiled by M.Horowitz (New York 1971).

Smillie, E.E: 'An Historical Survey of Indian Migration Throughout the Empire'. CANADIAN HISTORICAL REVIEW, Vol. 4, 1923.

Smith, M.G: DARK PURITAN (1963).

——: STRATIFICATION IN GRENADA (University of California Press, Berkeley & Los Angeles, 1965).

——: A FRAMEWORK OF CARIBBEAN STUDIES (Extra-Mural Department, U.W.I, Mona, 1955).

——: THE PLURAL SOCIETY IN THE BRITISH WEST INDIES (University of California Press, 1965).

——: 'Race and Ethnicity' in THE ENIGMA OF ETHNICITY: AN ANALYSIS OF RACE IN THE CARIB-BEAN AND THE WORLD. (St. Augustine, U.W.I, 1993).

——: WEST INDIAN FAMILY STRUCTURE (University of Washington Press, Seattle 1962).

Smith, Robert, Jack: 'Muslim East Indians in Trinidad: Retention of Ethnic Identity Under Acculturative Conditions'. PhD. Diss, University of Pennsylvania, 1963.

Smith, R.T: 'Some Social Characteristics of Indian Immigrants to British Guiana', POPULATION STUD-IES, 1959.

——: 'Race and Political Conflict in Guyana', RACE, Vol. 12, 1971.

——: BRITISH GUIANA, London: Oxford University Press, 1962.

Smith, R.T and Jayawardena, C: 'Caste and Social Status Among the Indians of Guyana' in CASTE IN OVER-SEAS INDIAN COMMUNITIES. Edited by B.M. Schwartz. (San Francisco, Chandler Publishing Co, 1967).

——: 'Hindu Marriage Customs in British Guiana'. SOCIAL AND ECONOMIC STUDIES, 1958.

——: 'Marriage and Family Among East Indians in British Guiana'. SOCIAL AND ECONOMIC STUD-IES, 1959.

Sohal, Harrinder Singh: 'The East Indian Indentureship System in Jamaica 1845–1917'. PhD. Thesis, Univer-sity of Waterloo, Canada 1979.

Solein, N.L: 'Household and Family in the Caribbean', SOCIAL AND ECONOMIC STUDIES 9, 1963, pp. 101–6.

Sookdeo, Sandra: INDIAN DANCE FOR THE CARIBBEAN (Trinidad: Chakra Publishing House, 1994).

Speckmann, J.D: MARRIAGE AND KINSHIP AMONG THE INDIANS IN SURINAM (Assen 1965).

——: 'The Indian Group in the Segmented Society of Surinam'. CARIBBEAN STUDIES 1963.

———: 'The Caste System and the Hindustani Group in Surinam', inCASTE IN OVERSEAS INDIAN COMMUNITIES, Barton M. Schwartz (ed), San Francisco: Chandler, 1967, pp. 201–12.

Sperl, Savitri Rambissoon: 'From Indians to Trinidadians: A Study of the Relationship Between Language, Behaviour, Socio-Economic and Cultural Factors in a Trinidad Village'. M.Phil, Thesis, University of York, 1980.

Spinner, Thomas J: A POLITICAL AND SOCIAL HISTORY OF GUYANA 1945–1983.(Boulder, Westview 1984).

Srinivas, Mysore N: RELIGION AND SOCIETY AMONG THE COORGS. (Bombay, Asia Publishing House, 1965).

———: CASTE IN MODERN INDIA AND OTHER ESSAYS (Bombay, Asia Publishing House, 1962).

Srinivas, M.N and A.M. Shah: 'Hinduism', INTERNATIONAL ENCYCLOPEDIA OF THE SOCIAL SCIENCES, Vol. 6, 1968, pp. 358–66.

Srivastava, A: 'Images of Women in Indo-Caribbean Literature' in INDENTURE AND EXILE.

Steele, Beverley: 'East Indian Indenture and the Work of the Presbyterian Church Among the Indians in Grenada'. CARIBBEAN QUARTERLY, 1976.

Stephanides, Stephanos: 'The Kali Puja and Wilson Harris's THE FAR JOURNEY OF OUDIN' in INDENTURE AND EXILE (Toronto, Tsar, 1989).

Stewart, John D: 'Coolie and Creole: Differential Adaptations in a Neo-Plantation Village – Trinidad, West Indies'. PhD. Thesis, UCLA, 1973.

Sukdeo, Frank: 'The Contribution of East Indians to Economic Development in Guyana'. Paper presented at Symposium on East Indians in the Caribbean 1975.

Sukdeo, I.D: 'The Concept of Racial Integration with Reference to the East Indians in Guyana'. Paper presented at Symposium on East Indians in the Caribbean 1975.

———: 'Racial Integration with Special Reference to Guyana'. PhD. Diss, University of Sussex 1969.

Sutton, Paul: 'Black Power in Trinidad and Tobago: The Crisis of 1970', JOURNAL OF COMMONWEALTH AND COMPARATIVE POLITICS 21, 1983, pp. 115–32.

———: 'Trinidad and Tobago: Oil Capitalism and the "Presidential Power" of Eric Williams', in DEPENDENCY UNDER CHALLENGE, Anthony Payne and Paul Sutton (eds), Manchester: Manchester University Press, 1984, pp. 43–76.

Swinton, Captain Edolphus and Mrs: JOURNAL OF A VOYAGE WITH COOLIE EMIGRANTS FROM CALCUTTA TO TRINIDAD. (London: Alfred Bennett, 1859).

Tambiah, S.J: 'Dowry, Bridewealth, and the Property Rights of Women in South East Asia', in BRIDEWEALTH AND DOWRY, Jack Goody and S.J.Tambiah (eds), Cambridge: University Papers in Social Anthropology No. 7, 1973, pp. 50–169.

Tandon, Yash and Arnold Raphael: THE NEW POSITION OF EAST AFRICA'S ASIANS (2nd edition), London Minority Rights Group, 1984.

Taylor, Jeremy: 'Drowning in Petrodollars', NEW INTERNATIONALIST 94, 1980, pp. 13–14.

Taylor, Patrick: 'Ethnicity and Social Change in Trinidadian Literature' in TRINIDAD ETHNICITY. (London, Macmillan Press 1993).

Tewarie, B: 'The Work of Harold Sonny Ladoo – The Drama of the Low Caste Hindu Pesantry: The Last Terrible Victims of the Colonial Experience in the New World'. Symposium on East Indians in the Caribbean, U.W.I, Trinidad, September 1979.

———: 'Hinduism, Nation-building and the State' in TRINIDAD AND TOBAGO: THE INDEPENDENCE EXPERIENCE 1962–1987.(St. Augustine, ISER, U.W.I, 1988).

Thakur, Andra: 'British and Dutch Colonial Policies in Guyana and Surinam' in INDENTURE AND EXILE 1989.

———: 'Social Changes in a Rice Growing Village in Guyana'. Symposium on East Indians in the Caribbean, U.W.I, Trinidad, September 1979.

———: 'The Politics of Race and Class 1953–1964'. MA Thesis, University of Alberta, Edmonton, Alberta 1973.

Thakur, Gopal J and Mansingh, Laxmi; 'The East Indians and the Jewellery Industry in Jamaica'. Paper presented at Symposium on East Indians in the Caribbean, U.W.I. September 1979.

Thakur, Parasram Sri: 'A Study of Rural Guyanese Children: An Exploration in Projective Technique'. Symposium on East Indians in the Caribbean, September 1979.

Thakur, Rishee: 'East Indians in Caribbean Historiography' in INDENTURE AND EXILE.

Thakur, R: 'Imperialism and Nationalism in the Caribbean: The Political Economy of Dependent Under-Development in Guyana'. MA. Thesis, University of British Columbia, Vancouver, B.C, 1978.

Thomas, Clive: THE POOR AND THE POWERLESS, London: Latin American Bureau, 1988.

Thomas, Timothy: INDIANS OVERSEAS: A GUIDE TO SOURCE MATERIALS IN THE INDIA OFFICE RECORDS FOR THE STUDY OF INDIAN EMIGRATION 1830–1950. (London, The British Library, 1985).

Thompson, E.P: THE MAKING OF THE ENGLISH WORKING CLASS (Harmondsworth, Penguin Books 1968).

Thompson, E.T: 'Population Expansion and the Planta tion System', AMERICAN JOURNAL OF SOCIOLOGY, Vol. XLi, November 1935.

Thompson, E.W: DON'T FORGET THE WEST INDIES (London 1942).

Thorne, John Thomas: SOME HAPHAZARD NOTES OF A FORTY-TWO YEARS' RESIDENCE IN BRITISH GUIANA. (Demerara: Argosy 1899).

Thorner, D.C: THE TRANSFORMATION OF THE RURAL ECONOMY: THE BRITISH IN INDIA, IMPERIALISM AND TRUSTEESHIP. (ed) Martin D.Lewis, (Boston 1962).

Thurston, E: CASTES AND TRIBES IN SOUTHERN INDIA (Madras 1909).

Tikasingh, Gerard: 'The Emerging Political Consciousness Among Trinidad Indians in the Late Nineteenth Century'. Conference on Caribbean Historians, U.W.I, Trinidad, 1973.

——: 'The Representation of Indian Opinion in Trinidad 1900–1921', Symposium on East Indians in the Caribbean, Trinidad, U.W.I, 1975.

——: 'The Establishment of the Indians in Trinidad, 1870–1900', PhD. Thesis, University of the West Indies, St. Augustine, Trinidad, 1976,

——: 'Social Change in the Emerging East Indian Community in the Late 19th Century', JOURNAL OF CARIBBEAN STUDIES 1, 1980, pp. 120–38.

——: 'Toward a Formulation of the Indian View of History: The Representation of Indian Opinion in Trinidad, 1900–1921, in EAST INDIANS IN THE CARIBBEAN, Bridget Brereton and Winston Dookheran (eds), London: Kraus, 1982, pp. 11–32.

THE TIMES (London): Supplement on Trinidad and Tobago, 25 January, 1966.

Tinker, Hugh: 'Indians Abroad: Emigration, Restriction and Rejection' in Michael Twaddle (ed.), EXPULSIONS OF A MINORITY: ESSAYS ON UGANDAN ASIANS (London, Athlone Press 1975).

——; 'The Origin of Indian Emigration to the West Indies' in INDENTURE AND EXILE.

——: A NEW SYSTEM OF SLAVERY: THE EXPORT OF INDIAN LABOUR OVERSEAS 1830–1920.(London, Oxford University Press 1974).

——: SEPARATE AND UNEQUAL: INDIA AND THE INDIANS IN THE BRITISH COMMONWEALTH 1920–1950 (London, C. Hurst & Co, 1976)

——: 'British Policy Towards a Separate Indian Identity in the Caribbean 1920–1950'. Symposium on East Indians in the Caribbean, Trinidad, U.W.I, 1975.

——: THE BANYAN TREE (Oxford, Oxford University Press, 1977).

——: 'Into Servitude: Indian Labour in the Sugar Industry, 1833–1970' in INTERNATIONAL LABOUR MIGRATION, Shula Marks and Peter Richardson (eds), London (University of London) Temple Smith, 1984, pp. 76–89.

——: 'Colour and Colonisation: A Study in Rival Commonwealth Ideals of Settlement', THE ROUND TABLE, October 1970.

——: 'Odd Man Out: The Loneliness of the Colonial Politician, The Career of Manilal Doctor', THE JOURNAL OF IMPERIAL AND COMMONWEALTH HISTORY, October 1973.

Tracey, Kenneth A: 'Race Relations in Anthropological Perspective'. Conference on East Indians in the Caribbean, U.W.I, Trinidad, June 1975.

Trollope, Anthony: THE WEST INDIES AND THE SPANISH MAIN. (London: Chapman & Hall, 1860).

Trotman, D.V: 'The Image of Indians in Calypso: Trinidad 1946–1986' in INDENTURE AND EXILE.

——: CRIME IN TRINIDAD: CONFLICT AND CONTROL IN A PLANTATION SOCIETY, 1838–1900.(Knoxville: University of Tennessee Press).

——: 'Women and Crime in the Late Nineteenth Century Trinidad', CARIBBEAN QUARTERLY, Vol. 30, No. 3 & 4, September–December 1984.

Tyson, J.D: REPORT ON THE CONDITION OF INDIANS IN JAMAICA, BRITISH GUIANA AND TRINIDAD. (Simla, Government of India Press 1939).

——: MEMORANDUM OF EVIDENCE FOR THE ROYAL COMMISSION TO THE WEST INDIES, New Delhi: Government of India Press, 1939.

Uchida, Naosaku: THE OVERSEAS CHINESE: A BIBLIOGRAPHICAL ESSAY. (Stanford: Stanford University Press, 1959).

Underhill, Edward B; THE WEST INDIES: THEIR SOCIAL AND RELIGIOUS CONDITION (London:Jackson, Walford & Hodder, 1862).

United Nations: THE ECONOMY OF LATIN AMERICA AND THE CARIBBEAN IN 1983, Santiago, Chile: Cuadernos de la CEPAL, 1985.

Van der Berghe, Pierre: 'Asians in East and South Africa: A Comparison', in PORTRAIT OF A MINORITY, Dharam P. Ghai and Yash P. Ghai (eds), Nairobi: Oxford University Press, 1970, pp. 151–75.

Van der Burg, Corstain and Peter Van der Veer: 'Pundits, Power and Profit: Religious Organization and the

Construction of Identity Among the Surinamese Hindus', ETHNIC AND RACIAL STUDIES 9, 1986, pp. 514–29.

Van der Veer, Peter: 'Authenticity and Authority in Surinamese Hindu Ritual' – Forthcoming publication.

Van der Veer, Peter and Steven Vertovec: 'Religious Therapies and Their Valuation Among Surinamese Hindustani in the Netherlands', in ASPECTS OF THE SOUHT ASIAN DIASPORA, Steven Vertovec (ed.), New Delhi: Oxford University Press, n.d. (Forthcoming publication).

Van der Veer, Peter and Steven Vertovec: 'Brahmanism Abroad: On Caribbean Hinduism as an Ethnic religion', ETHNOLOGY, n.d. (Forthcoming).

Vatuk, Ved Prakash: 'Protest Songs of East Indians in British Guiana', JOURNAL OF AMERICAN FOLK-LORE 77, 1964.

Vedalankar, Pandit N, and M.Somera: ARYA SAMAJ AND INDIANS ABROAD, New Delhi: Sarvadeshik Arya Pratinidhi Sabha, 1975.

Verrier, Anthony: 'Guyana and Cyprus: Techniques of Peace-Keeping'. JOURNAL OF ROYLA UNITED SERVICE INSTITUTION, 111, November 1966.

Vertovec, Steven: ' "Official" and "Popular" Hinduism in the Caribbean: Historical and Contemporary Trends in Surinam, Trinidad and Tobago' – Forthcoming publication.

———: HINDU TRINIDAD: RELIGION, ETHNICITY AND SOCIO- ECONOMIC CHANGE. (London, Macmillan/Warwick University Caribbean Studies, 1992).

———: 'Hinduism and Social Change in Village Trinidad', D.Phil, Thesis, University of Oxford, 1987.

———: 'Hinduism in Diaspora: The Transformation of Tradition in Trinidad', in HINDUISM RECONSIDERED, G.D. Sontheimer and H.Kulke (eds), New Delhi: Manohar, 1988, pp. 157–86.

" ": 'Oil Boom and Recession in Trinidad Villages', in SOUTH ASIANS OVERSEAS, C. Clarke, C. Peach and S. Vertovec (eds), Cambridge: Cambridge University Press, 1990, pp. 89–111.

———: 'Religion and Ethnic Ideology: The Hindu Youth Movement in Trinidad', in ETHNIC AND RACIAL STUDIES 13, 1990, pp. 225–49.

———: 'Inventing Religious Tradition: YAGNAS and Hindu Renewal in Trinidad', in RELIGION, TRADITION AND RENEWAL, A. Geertz and J.S Jensen (eds), Aarhus, Denmark: Universitas Forlag, 1991, pp. 77–95.

" ": 'East Indians and Anthropologists: A Critical Review', SOCIAL AND ECONOMIC STUDIES 40, 1991, pp. 133–69.

———: ASPECTS OF THE SOUTH ASIAN DIASPORA, New Delhi: Oxford University Press (forthcoming).

———: '"Official" and "Popular" Hinduism in the Caribbean: Historical and Contemporary Trends' (Forthcoming).

Visram, Rozina: AYAHS, LASCARS AND PRINCES (London: Pluto Press, 1986).

Von Grunebaum, G.E: MOHAMMEDAN FESTIVALS (New York, Henry Schuman 1951).

Wagner, Michael J: 'Structural Pluralism and the Portuguese in Nineteenth Century British Guiana: A Study in Historical Geogrpahy'. Phd. Diss, McGill University 1975.

Walker, H. de R: THE WEST INDIES AND THE EMPIRE, London: T. Fisher Unwin, 1901.

Wallace, A.F.C: 'Revitalization Movements', AMERICAN ANTHROPOLOGIST 58, 1956, pp. 264–81.

Wallbridge, E.A: THE DEMERARA MARTYR: MEMOIRS OF THE REV. JOHN SMITH, MISSIONARY TO DEMERARA. (Georgetown Daily Chronicle, reprint of London 1848 edition).

Walne, Peter: A GUIDE TO MANUSCRIPT SOURCES FOR THE HISTORY OF LATIN AMERICA AND THE CARIBBEAN IN THE BRITISH ISLES (London 1973).

Walpole, K.A: 'The Humanitarian Movement of the Early Nineteenth Century to Remedy Abuses on Emigrant Vessels to America', TRANSACTIONS OF THE ROYAL HISTORICAL SOCIETY, Vol. XIV, 1931.

Warner, Keith: 'Ethnicity and the Contemporary Calypso' in TRINIDAD ETHNICITY (London, Macmillan Press, 1993).

Watts, David: THE WEST INDIES: PATTERNS OF DEVELOPMENT, CULTURE AND ENVIRONMENTAL CHANGE SINCE 1492.(Cambridge: Cambridge University Press, 1987).

Weatherly, U.G: 'The West Indies as a Sociological Laboratory'. AMERICAN JOURNAL OF SOCIOLOGY, Vol. 29, 1923.

Webber, A.R.F: CENTENARY HISTORY AND HANDBOOK OF BRITISH GUIANA. (Georgetown: Daily Chronicle, 1931).

———: THOSE THAT BE IN BONDAGE. Wellesley, Mass, Calaloux Publications, 1988.

Weller, Judith Ann: THE EAST INDIAN INDENTURE IN TRINIDAD. Rio Piedras, Institute of Caribbean Studies, 1968.

'What East Indians Have Given To West Indian Society', TAPIA, 1972.

White, L.G.W: SHIPS, COOLIES AND RICE (London 1936).

Whittington, Viola-Gopaul: HISTORY OF THE SPIRITUAL BAPTIST WRITINGS (Trinidad, Privately printed 1983).

Wight, Martin: THE DEVELOPMENT OF THE LEGISLATIVE COUNCIL, 1606– 1945 (London 1946).

Wilkins, W.J: MODERN HINDUISM, BEING AN ACCOUNT OF THE RELIGION AND LIFE OF THE HINDUS IN NORTHERN INDIA, London: T. Fisher Unwin, 1887.

Williams, Eric: 'The British West Indian Slave Trade After Its Abolition in 1807'. JOURNAL OF NEGRO HISTORY, Vol. 28, 1942.

———: 'The Historical Background of Guiana's Problems' THE JOURNAL OF NEGRO HISTORY, Vol. 30, 1945.

Williams, Eric: CAPITALISM AND SLAVERY (Chapel Hill 1945).

———: A HISTORY OF THE PEOPLE OF TRINIDAD AND TOBAGO (London, Andre Deutsch, 1970).

———: FROM COLUMBUS TO CASTRO: THE HISTORY OF THE CARIBBEAN 1492–1969.(London, Andre Deutsch, 1970).

Wilson, John: INDIAN CASTE (Bombay, William Blackwood & Sons 1877).

Wood, Donald: TRINIDAD IN TRANSITION: THE YEARS AFTER SLAVERY. (London, Oxford University Press 1968).

WRITERS OF THE INDIAN DIASPORA: A BIO-BIBLIOGRAPHICAL CRITICAL SOURCEBOOK, New York, Greenwood, 1993.

Yardan, Shana: NEW WRITING IN THE CARIBBEAN, (ed). A.J.Seymour (Georgetown, Guyana Litho Co, 1972).

Yelvington, Kevin A: 'Introduction – Trinidad Ethnicity' in TRINIDAD ETHNICITY (London, Macmillan Press, 1993).

———: 'Ethnicity At Work in Trinidad' in THE ENIGMA OF ETHNICITY (St. Augustine, U.W.I,1993).

Young, Arthur: 'Chinese in the West Indies', CHINA WEEKLY REVIEW, 48, No. 11 (11 May 1929).

Young Sing, Gloria E: 'The Evolution of the Present Pattern of Agricultural Land Use in the Island of Trinidad in the West Indies', PhD. Thesis, Queens University Belfast, 1964.

Yule, H and Burnell, A: HOBSON-JOBSON (London, Routledge & Kegan Paul 1903).

Zunnier, Heinrich R: MYTHS AND SYMBOLS IN INDIAN ART AND CIVILIZATION (Princeton, Princeton University Press 1974).

# NEWSPAPERS, JOURNALS AND LEAFLETS

THE ARGOSY
BENGAL HURKARU
BRITISH EMANCIPATOR
BRITISH GUIANA MISSION JOURNAL
CARIBBEAN CONTACT
CARIBBEAN QUARTERLY
THE COLONIST
THE DAILY CHRONICLE
THE DAILY GLEANER
THE DAILY TELEGRAPH
THE ECONOMIST
FRIEND OF INDIA
INDIA QUARTERLY
INDIAN OPINION
INDO-CARIBBEAN REVIEW (Toronto)
INDO-CARIBBEAN WORLD
JAMAICAN TIMES
JOURNAL OF MODERN HISTORY
JOURNAL OF NEGRO HISTORY
KAIRI
THE MIRROR (TRINIDAD)
THE MIRROR (GUYANA)
MOKO
THE NATION
NEW ERA
THE NEW NATION
THE NEW YORK TIMES
NEWS BULLETIN
THE OBSERVER
THE PEOPLE
PORT OF SPAIN GAZETTE
SAN FERNANDO GAZETTE

SOCIOLOGICAL BULLETIN
SOCIAL AND ECONOMIC STUDIES
SOUTHWESTERN JOURNAL OF ANTHROPOLOGY
THE SPECTATOR
STABROEK NEWS
SUNDAY EXPRESS
SUNDAY GRAPHIC
TAPIA
THE TIMES
TIMEHRI
TRINIDAD CHRONICLE
TRINIDAD EXPRESS
TRINIDAD GUARDIAN
TRINIDAD ROYAL GAZETTE
TRINIDAD SENTINEL
TWENTIETH CENTURY
WESTERN POLITICAL QUARTERLY
WEST INDIAN DIGEST

Also: IN TRIBUTE TO OUR ANCESTORS: AN ANTHOLOGY OF POEMS BY INDO-GUYANESE PORTS, 1986; SOUVENIR CATALOGUE: An Exhibition of Historical Photographs on Early Life of East Indians in Guyana by Laxmi Kallicharan for Caribbean Focus, United Kingdom, 1986.